CB
351
.B239
2004

Barber, Malcolm.

Two cities.

$128.00

The Two Cities

First published to wide critical acclaim in 1992, *The Two Cities* has become an essential text for students of medieval history. For the second edition, the author has thoroughly revised each chapter, bringing the material up to date and taking the historiography of the 1990s into account.

The Two Cities covers a colourful period from the schism between the eastern and western churches to the death of Dante. It encompasses the crusades, the expansionist force of the Normans, major developments in the way in which kings, emperors and popes exercised their powers, a great flourishing of art and architecture and the foundation of the very first universities. Running through it is the defining characteristic of the high middle ages – the delicate relationship between the spiritual and secular worlds, the two 'cities' of the title.

This survey provides all the facts and background information that students need, and is defined in straightforward thematic chapters. It makes extensive use of primary sources, and makes new trends in research accessible to students. Its fresh approach gives students the most rounded, lively and integrated view of the high middle ages available.

Malcolm Barber is Professor of Medieval History at the University of Reading. His many books include *The Templars* (2002) (with Keith Bate), *The Cathars* (2000), *The New Knighthood, A History of the Order of the Temple* (1994) and *The Trial of the Templars* (1978).

The Two Cities

Medieval Europe, 1050–1320

SECOND EDITION

Malcolm Barber

Routledge
Taylor & Francis Group

LONDON AND NEW YORK

First published in 1992
First published in paperback in 1993
Reprinted 1994, 1995, 1997, 1999, 2000, 2001, 2003
Second edition published 2004 by Routledge
2 Park Square, Milton Park, Abingdon, Oxon, OX14 4RN

Simultaneously published in the USA and Canada
by Routledge
270 Madison Ave, New York NY 10016

Routledge is an imprint of the Taylor & Francis Group

Transferred to Digital Printing 2006

© 1992, 1993, 2004 Malcolm Barber

Typeset in Stempel Garamond by M Rules

British Library Cataloguing in Publication Data
A catalogue record for this book is available from the British Library

Library of Congress Cataloging in Publication Data

Barber, Malcolm
Two cities : medieval Europe, 1050–1320 / Malcolm Barber. – 2nd ed. p. cm.
Includes bibliographical references and index.
1. Civilization, Medieval. 2. Europe – History – 476–1492. I. Title.
CB351.B239 2004
940.1'7 – dc22   2003019889

ISBN 0-415-17414-7 (hbk)
ISBN 0-415-17415-5 (pbk)

Printed and bound by CPI Antony Rowe, Eastbourne

To Elizabeth, Ruth and David

Contents

Part IV Perceptions of the world

Illustrations

Plates

Maps

Tables

Figures

Preface to the first edition

My aim in this book is to introduce the fascinating world of the European middle ages to those who have not previously encountered it. It is based upon nearly twenty-five years of teaching this period, and although this won't save it from error, of course, it may have induced a certain wariness. I alone am responsible for the book's contents, but many friends read parts of the typescript and tried hard to improve it. I am very grateful for their corrections of mistakes of fact and interpretation, often accompanied by colourful marginal comments. I owe particular thanks to Ben Arnold, Grenville Astill, Peggy Brown, Nicola Coldstream, Eddie Coleman, Anne Curry, Barbara Dodwell, Bernard Hamilton, Brian Kemp, Graham Loud, Angus MacKay, Paddy McNulty, Bob Moore and Judi Upton-Ward. The inter-library loan staff at Reading University, as always, have obtained a wide variety of materials very efficiently, and this has greatly eased the pressures of trying to write a long book while working in a busy university history department. I am grateful too for a grant received from the Wolfson Foundation in 1976, part of which was spent on travel in France. Although I had not then planned to write on this theme, what I learned at that time has made an important contribution to the book.

Preface to the second edition

In addition to those who so generously helped me on the first edition, I should like to thank Alison Beach, Brenda Bolton, Eric Christiansen, Sue Edgington, Gill Evans, Christine Firth, Sandy Heslop, Christopher Holdsworth, Zsolt Hunyadi, Colin Morris, Rita Tyler and Rafal Witkowski.

Acknowledgements

The author and publishers would like to thank the following copyright holders for permission to reproduce material:

Columbia University Press for extracts from: Helmold of Bosau, *The Chronicle of the Slavs*, tr. F.J. Tschan, 1935 (reprint 1966), pp. 43, 72, 131, 168–9, 172, 264–5, 273; Otto of Freising, *The Deeds of Frederick Barbarossa*, tr. C.C. Mierow, 1955, pp. 17–20, 27, 63, 65–6, 67, 82, 88, 115, 116, 127–8, 163–4, 167, 169, 175–7, 183–4, 189, 199; Otto of Freising, *The Two Cities*, tr. C.C. Mierow, 1928 (reprint 1966), pp. 27, 93, 95–6, 299, 357–8, 370, 402, 411–12, 432, 443, 456, 486, 491–2, 500, 508; William of Tyre, *A History of Deeds done beyond the Sea*, 2 vols, tr. E.A. Babcock and A.C. Krey, 1941 (reprint 1976), vol. 1, pp. 53–4, 146, 296, 298, 338, 507–8, 552–6, vol. 2, pp. 132–4, 139–40, 170, 236, 357–8, 405, 431, 464–5.

Oxford University Press for extracts from: *The Ecclesiastical History of Orderic Vitalis*, tr. M. Chibnall, 6 vols, 1969–80, vol. 2, pp. 31, 269, vol. 3, pp. 121–3, 205–7, 299, vol. 4, 175–6, 237–51, 319, vol. 5, 205, 289, vol. 6, 100–1, 401, 535, 551–7; *The Historia Pontificalis of John of Salisbury*, tr. M. Chibnall, 1956, pp. 3, 49, 51, 55, 61–2, 65–7; Jocelin of Brakelond, *The Chronicle of Bury St Edmunds*, tr. D. Greenway and J. Sayers, 1989, pp. 26, 33–4, 36, 61, 76–7, 113–15.

University of Tennessee Press for extracts from: Fulcher of Chartres, *A History of the Expedition to Jerusalem 1095–1127*, tr. F.R. Ryan, intr. S. Fink, 1969, pp. 66, 80, 123, 149, 174, 189–90, 217–19, 251–2, 278.

Syracuse University Press for extracts from: *The Liber Augusta or Constitutions of Melfi*, tr. J.M. Powell, 1971, pp. 3–5, 7–9, 11, 12–13, 21, 32–3, 46, 48–9, 129–30.

Harper and Row for extracts from: Guibert of Nogent, *Self and Society in Medieval France*, tr. J.F. Benton, 1970, pp. 60–2, 63–4, 70–1, 115.

Princeton University Press for extracts from: *Abbot Suger on the Abbey Church of St Denis and its Art Treasures*, tr. E. Panofsky, 1946, 2nd edn, 1979, pp. 40–1, 43–5, 49–51, 58–9, 64–5, 75–7, 87–9, 93–7, 113, 117, 121.

Ashgate Publishing for extracts from *The Book of the Deeds of James I of Aragon*, tr. D. Smith and H. Buffery, 2003, pp. 79, 210–11, 221, 334–5, 366, 379–80.

The Pontifical Institute of Medieval Studies for extracts from: *The Play of AntiChrist*, tr. J. Wright, 1967, from 'The writings of historians tell us' to 'That you come quickly under his command'.

Burns and Oates for extracts from: *The Summa Theologica of Thomas Aquinas*, tr. The Fathers of the English Dominican Province, 1917, part II (ii), Q.32, art. 5, pp. 416–17.

Cistercian Publications for extracts from: 'Cistercians and Cluniacs: St Bernard's Apologia to Abbot William', in *The Works of St Bernard, vol. 1*, tr. M. Casey, 1970, pp. 52, 63–6.

The University of Pennsylvania Press for extracts from: *Las Siete Partidas*, tr. S.P. Scott, ed. R.I. Burns, 2001, vol. 1, pp. 14, 112, vol. 5, p. 1443.

Introduction

Accordingly, since things are changeable and can never be at rest, what
man in his right mind will deny that the wise man ought, as I have said,
to depart from them to that city which stays at rest and abides to all
eternity? This is the City of God, the heavenly Jerusalem, for which the
children of God sigh while they are set in this land of sojourn, oppressed
by the turmoil of the things of time as if they were oppressed by the
Babylonian captivity. For, inasmuch as there are two cities – the one of
time, the other of eternity; the one of the earth, earthy, the other of
heaven, heavenly; the one of the devil, the other of Christ – ecclesiastical
writers have declared that the former is Babylon, the latter Jerusalem.

(Mierow 1966:93)

Fernand Braudel said that a general history 'always requires an overall model, good or
bad, against which events can be interpreted' (1973:xi) The quotation above, which is
taken from the prologue of Otto of Freising's universal history, *The Two Cities*,
provides the model for this book.

Otto was born into the high German nobility between the years 1111 and 1115; his
father was Leopold, Margrave of Austria, and his mother was Agnes, daughter of the
Emperor Henry IV. He was therefore closely related to subsequent imperial rulers, for
he was half-brother to Conrad III (1137–52) and uncle of Frederick Barbarossa
(1152–90). In his youth he studied arts and theology at Paris. This, together with his
social connections, set him on the road to a successful ecclesiastical career. He did not,
however, see his entry into the Church simply in career terms; in *c.*1133 he stayed at the
Cistercian monastery of Morimond in Burgundy and was so deeply impressed by the
ascetic lifestyle of the monks that he joined the Order. In 1136 he was elected Abbot
of Morimond and, the next year, Bishop of Freising in Bavaria. Thereafter, like many
of the great churchmen of the twelfth century, he played a dual role as monk-bishop
and active politician, in particular acting as close adviser to his nephew, the
Hohenstaufen, Frederick I. He wrote *The Two Cities* in the mid-1140s, completed it
in 1147, and then revised it in the following years. In 1156 he began to record the *Deeds*

of Frederick Barbarossa, but he died in September 1158, and the work was eventually completed by his secretary, Rahewin.

The Two Cities contains eight books, the first seven of which extend from the time of Adam to the year 1146, while the eighth brings history to a culmination in the Last Judgement. As Otto himself explains:

> I have undertaken therefore to bring down as far as our own time, according to the ability God has given me, the record of the conflicts and miseries of the one city, Babylon; and furthermore, not to be silent concerning our hopes regarding that other city, so far as I can gather hints from the Scriptures, but to make mention also of its citizens who are now sojourning in the worldly city. In this work I follow most of all those illustrious lights of the church, Augustine and Orosius, and have planned to draw from their fountains what is pertinent to my theme and purpose.
>
> (Mierow 1966:95)

St Augustine's *City of God*, written between 413 and 427, provided him with the basis of his theology and the overall historical structure, while *The Seven Books against the Pagans*, written in 417 by Augustine's pupil, Paulus Orosius, was the source of much historical and geographical information. In addition, he drew on a wide range of other authorities, as well as using his own experience and contemporary informants for the seventh book covering recent times between 1085 and 1146.

Explicitly or implicitly, the activities and thoughts of human beings in the centuries between *c.*1050 and *c.*1320 were moulded by two powerful forces: on the one hand, the pressures and the temptations of the material world, made all the more manifest by economic development, and on the other, the deeply held belief in the need to aspire towards a higher, spiritual life, itself displayed with increasing clarity by contemporary social changes. From the rarefied intellectual heights of Gilbert de la Porrée, Bishop of Poitiers, whose speech was so difficult according to Otto, that 'what he meant was never clear to childlike minds, scarcely even to me of education and learning' (Mierow 1955:88) to the *rustici*, who, it was hoped, would be seduced from base appetites to more spiritual food by being shown the sacred stories in paint, mosaic and stone (Camille 1985:32), this inherent tension between the 'two cities' provided the creative conflict which was fundamental to the culture of the high middle ages (see Morrison 1980), and which forms the connecting theme of this book.

Part I

The social and economic structure

1

The physical environment

1236

About this same time, for more than two months in January, February, and part of March, the deluges of rain were so great that nobody could remember anything comparable. For about the Feast of Saint Scholastica [10 February], at the time of the new moon, the sea was so swollen by the torrents of the rivers rushing into it, that all the rivers, especially those falling into the sea, made the fords impassable, having overflowed their usual banks. Bridges were hidden, mills and their ponds were destroyed, cultivated lands and reed meadows were overrun. Among other unusual things, the River Thames overflowed its usual bounds, and entered the great palace at Westminster, spreading out and covering the area, so that some people were able to sail in small vessels even in the middle of the hall, and some went to their chambers mounted on horses....

In the summer of the same year, after the winter had already been rainy without measure, as has been said, it continued dry with an almost intolerable heat for more than four months in succession. The result was that marshes and ponds were completely empty, the water-mills stood dried up and useless, and cracks opened up in the earth. In many places the ears of corn scarcely reached two feet.

(Luard 1880:3:339, 369–70)

Matthew Paris, the St Albans chronicler, lived a relatively comfortable life as a member of a large and prosperous monastic community, yet he was acutely sensitive to changes in the natural environment around him. In his most important work, the *Chronica Majora*, which covers the period from 1236 to his death in 1259 – and from which the above two quotations are taken – he reports on events year by year, frequently summarising the most notable features of the past twelvemonth at the close of the year (see Tables 1 and 2). His apparent aim was to record English affairs, but his range is much wider than this, encompassing news and documents from all over the British Isles, from the immediate continent of France, Germany, Italy and Iberia, from the

Table I The medieval year

The structure of the religious festivals affected not only the clergy and the pattern of worship, but also all activities from agriculture to law. However, these in turn in many cases had been adapted to pagan festivals and folkloric customs, so that there was a consequent close correlation with the rhythm of cultivation. Even so there might be considerable local variation, for a saint unheard of in one region might be highly venerated in another, while there are evident constraints imposed by environmental differences.

	CHURCH	AGRICULTURE	
	29 September	Feast of St Michael	
	18 October	Feast of St Luke	
	1 November	ALL SAINTS. Hallowmas	
	2 November	All Souls' Day	
	11 November	Feast of St Martin	
	30 November	Feast of St Andrew	
Advent	Fourth Sunday before Christmas Day	Beginning of Advent	**Winter**
	6 December	Feast of St Nicholas	
	8 December	Conception of the Virgin	
	21 December	Feast of St Thomas the Apostle	
Christmas	25 December	CHRISTMAS DAY. Used as the beginning of the year in many regions until *c.*1250. Midwinter day	
	26 December	Feast of St Stephen	
	27 December	Feast of St John the Evangelist	
	28 December	Feast of Holy Innocents	
	1 January	CIRCUMCISION OF THE LORD	
	6 January	EPIPHANY	
	2 February	Purification of the Virgin. Candlemas	**Spring**
	24 or 25 February	Feast of St Mathias	
	Shrove Tuesday	Day before beginning of Lent	
Lent	Ash Wednesday	Beginning of Lent. Forty days before Easter	
	Palm Sunday	Sunday before Easter	
		Holy Week	
	Good Friday	Friday before Easter Sunday	
Easter	Between 22 March and 25 April inclusive	EASTER SUNDAY	**Summer**
	Second Monday and Tuesday after Easter	Hocktide	
	25 March	ANNUNCIATION OF THE VIRGIN Widely used as the beginning of the year following Christmas	
	25 April	Feast of St Mark	
	1 May	Feast of Saints Philip and James. Mayday.	

Easter	Fifth Sunday after Easter Day	Rogation Sunday. The rogation days until the Ascension were a period of supplication for the harvest.
	Thursday following Rogation Sunday	ASCENSION OF THE LORD Forty days after Easter
	Seventh Sunday after Easter	PENTECOST (Whit Sunday) Ten days after Ascension
	Sunday after Pentecost	Trinity Sunday
	Thursday after Trinity Sunday	CORPUS CHRISTI. From 1264.
	24 June	Feast of St John the Baptist. Summer Solstice. Midsummer Day
	29 June	Feast of Saints Peter and Paul
	22 July	Feast of St Mary Magdelene
	25 July	Feast of St James
	1 August	Feast of St Peter's Chains Lammas
	10 August	Feast of St Lawrence
	15 August	ASSUMPTION OF THE VIRGIN
	24 August	Feast of St Bartholomew
	8 September	Nativity of the Virgin
	14 September	Exaltation of the Cross
	21 September	Feast of St Matthew
	29 September	Feast of St Michael

(Right-hand bracket labels: Summer for the period up to 25 July; Autumn (harvest) for the period from 1 August to 29 September.)

Scandinavian countries of Norway and Denmark, and from the Latin settlements in the Middle East which the French called Outremer, from which he avidly gathered news of the crusaders and the peoples they met. By no stretch of the imagination can Matthew be seen as a systematic or scientific writer, for his approach is gossipy and impressionistic, but his consistent interest in the weather and natural phenomena, together with attempts at interpreting these events, is striking. No year passes without some comment on rain and floods, on drought, on wind and storms, on frost, hail and snow, on the state of the air and atmospheric disturbances, on the tides, on earthquakes, on comets, stars and eclipses, on diseases among humans and animals (see Plate 1). In each of the eighteen years in which he provides a summary he always includes a passage commenting on the predominant weather conditions and the effects upon crops and animals.

The extent of Matthew's interest in these matters and the space that he devotes to them is a reflection of the fundamental importance of these purely physical influences. Their effects can be seen on everything from the details of daily life to the existence of whole communities. Orderic Vitalis, whose chronicle of the Norman monastery of St Evroult is one of the most important records of life in north-west Europe in the first half of the twelfth century, was sometimes unable to write because his fingers were too cold to grip his pen (Chibnall 1972:3:119). At the other end of the scale natural disaster

Plate 1 Drowned in the Flood. According to Genesis 6:5–22, God regretted the creation of humankind, which had become sunk in wickedness. Except for Noah and his family and representatives of each species of animals, he therefore brought about a great Flood 'to destroy all flesh'. These events are among those illustrated in mosaic at the Basilica of St Mark in Venice in the first decade of the thirteenth century. They are a striking representation of human powerlessness in the face of supernatural and natural disaster. (Photograph reproduced by permission of Scala.)

could strike thousands of people with devastating force. Walter, chancellor of the crusader principality of Antioch in northern Syria between *c.*1114 and *c.*1122, left a graphic account of an earthquake on 29 November 1114:

> in the silence at the dead of night, when human frailty was accustomed more suitably and more sweetly to sleep, there was an immense and terrible earthquake in Antioch and its region. And as a matter of fact, in that same unexpected earthquake men were horribly knocked around, and they felt, saw, heard the collapse of walls, towers and different buildings deeply threatening themselves and others; some thought to escape the collapse by running away, some to slide down from the walls, certain men gave themselves up and threw themselves down from high houses. More, indeed, were caught piecemeal in their sleep by the collapse, in such a way that even if a part of the wall remained intact, they were nowhere to be seen. Others, indeed, were terrified; they abandoned their homes, scorned their wealth, left everything, and behaved as if demented in the streets and squares of the town. They stretched their hands towards the heavens because of their manifold fear and powerlessness, and cried tearfully without ceasing in different languages: 'Spare us, Lord, spare your people!'
>
> (Asbridge and Edgington 1999:80–1)

In 1169 Etna erupted, burning Catania. Peter of Blois, later Archdeacon of London, but resident in Sicily at the time, described it as a land which 'devours its inhabitants' (Migne 1855c:133). The hazards of the physical world were ignored at one's peril. Nobody could be indifferent to them even if, unlike many of his fellows, he had a full belly and an armed following. In October 1216 King John, while crossing the Wellstream near Wisbech,

> lost his chapel with its relics, and some of his sumpter animals with various pieces of bedding, and many members of his household were drowned in the sea and swallowed up in the quicksand there, because they had rushed off incautiously and precipitately before the tide had gone out.
>
> (Stevenson 1875:183–4)

Matthew Paris appears to have left England only once – when he was sent to Norway in 1248 – but the preoccupations which he exposes were, with regional variations, common to all his contemporaries. The area under consideration, that of western Christendom, encompassed in essence the large peninsula which is now called Europe together with its associated islands and, in addition, important far beyond their size, the crusader settlements in Palestine and Syria (see Map 1). This peninsula is so deeply indented that in western Christendom nowhere was more than 500 miles from the sea. Three major mountain zones of widely differing age cut across it, running mainly west–east. The most northerly range consists of the Charnian system, thrown up approximately 600 million years ago, but now largely planed down, and the Caledonian mountains, approximately 400 million years old, retaining a height of between 3,000 and 7,000 feet. The Charnian system (or Baltic Shield) covers most of eastern Scandinavia and Finland, while the Caledonian range extends from northern Ireland through Scotland to Scandinavia and north-west Russia. South of the north European

Table 2 The medieval day

Although mechanical clocks were in use in some towns by the end of the thirteenth century, they were not influential in measuring time for most of this period. The sundial, the water clock and candles were all used, but it is probable that bells were far more important for most of the population. It seems likely too that, for many peasants, judgement derived from the experience of constantly working outside was sufficient in itself. The day was divided into twenty-four hours. Each hour was a twelfth of the period from sunrise to sunset and from sunset to sunrise, so its length depended on the season and the region. The monastic day was divided according to the canonical hours, but they too were equally affected by the amount of daylight. The canonical hours were also used as meeting times for other purposes, such as the assembly of an ecclesiastical council.

Monastic Horarium
Example of the Benedictines in the twelfth century (after D. Knowles (1963), *The Monastic Order in England*, 943–1216 (Cambridge University Press), pp. 714–15)

	Summer	Winter (mid-November)
Matins (Lauds)	3.30 or 4.00 a.m.	6.00 a.m. (daybreak)
Prime	6.00 a.m.	6.45 a.m. (full daylight)
Terce	8.00 a.m.	8.00 a.m.
Sext	11.30 a.m.	12.00 p.m.
None	2.30 p.m.	1.30 p.m.
Vespers	6.00 p.m.	4.15 p.m.
Compline	8.00 p.m.	6.15 p.m.

plain are the remains of the American fold, approximately 200 million years old and consisting mainly of scattered mountain blocks up to 6,000 feet in height. The remnants of this formerly great mountain range appear in isolated blocks in Ireland, Cornwall, Brittany, the Central Massif of France, the Spanish Meseta, the Ardennes, the Vosges, the Black Forest and the Bohemian Massif. Some of these have been smoothed down, but others, of more resistant rock, like the Spanish Meseta, remain prominent. Far younger than these is the Alpine system, which was created by pressure exerted against the Amorican remnants approximately 20 million years ago and retains many peaks above 12,000 feet. This begins in north Africa with the Atlas Mountains and continues through southern Europe, including the Pyrenees, the Apennines and the Alps. One spur then extends east through the Carpathians, while another pushes south into the Balkans. Between the north-western highlands and the mountains of the Amorican and Alpine ranges lies the north European plain, stretching from southern England and the Atlantic seaboard of continental Europe, where it is at its narrowest, into the wide expanse of the Asian continent. Finally, the Mediterranean coast lands, separated by the Alps from many of the influences which shape the north, form the most distinctive physical region of Europe.

The soil of these regions varies enormously (see, for example, Figure 1). In some

Map 1 Physical map of Europe, western Asia and northern Africa

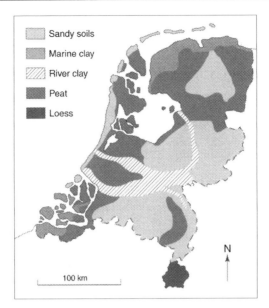

Source: P. Hoppenbrouwers (1997), 'Agricultural Production and Technology in the Netherlands, *c.* 1000–1500', in *Medieval Farming and Technology. The Impact of Agricultural Change in Northwest Europe,* ed. G. Astill and J. Langdon (Leiden: Brill), p. 92.

Figure 1 Dominant soil types in the Netherlands

cases it derives from the parent rock, having developed *in situ*: sandy soils are associated with granite, while clay soils derive from limestone or basaltic lava. However, much soil has been transported from one place to another by the powerful agents of water, ice and wind; rivers deposit alluvial loam on their flood plains; glaciation has left heavy boulder clay in some parts of the north European plain and in others, where the ice-sheet had temporarily halted its retreat, terminal moraines; the wind has laid down deposits of fine *loess*. Latitude and relief produce further modifications. In the far north, for instance, low temperatures and poor vegetation hamper the rapid formation of soil, and on mountain sides all over Europe, the soil is often thin, following the damaging effects of erosion.

Climate is affected by three major influences: distance from the sea, latitude and relief. With the exception of central Spain, the region north of the Alps covered by western Christendom is strongly influenced by the predominant westerly winds blowing off the Atlantic. These winds bring a reasonably even distribution of rainfall, except in hilly western regions like Ireland and Brittany, where it tends to be heavy, and because the land heats up more rapidly in summer and cools more rapidly in winter than the sea, they modify the extremes of temperature which characterise the climates of the continental type found further inland. In contrast, the lands surrounding the Mediterranean do not feel this Atlantic influence, for the summer high pressure of the Sahara deflects the westerlies northwards, creating summer drought and producing high temperatures. The limited rainfall of the Mediterranean area therefore comes mainly during the winter. The sun heats the surface of the earth most thoroughly when its rays are vertical, and it is from this surface that the atmosphere receives most of its heat. Relief causes further variation, for temperature drops with altitude as a direct consequence of distance from the earth's surface. The basic division of temperature by latitude is therefore often changed out of all recognition by the proximity of the sea and the configuration of the land.

Vegetation originally reflected these variations in relief, soil and climate. In mountainous regions, coniferous forest predominated until altitude forced it to give way to the mosses, lichens or shrubs known as tundra and eventually to the bare rock of the higher peaks. Deciduous forest, sometimes mixed with conifers, prevailed in the north European plain, although this forest lacked continuity, often being broken by grass or scrub-land, and in places of extensive glaciation, by marshes and lakes. The major forests consisted of oak and ash accompanied by extensive undergrowth, but these were replaced on calcareous soils by beech with its much thinner undergrowth. South of the Alps there was a gradual transition from the coniferous and deciduous forests characteristic of northern and central Europe to a much sparser distribution of evergreen trees and plants, like the evergreen oak, olive and laurel, whose long roots enable them to survive the summer drought. Open country was more common here, often consisting of brushwood, known locally as *maquis*.

The great majority of people spent their entire lives in an unceasing effort to produce food from this environment. The vegetation cover was the element most susceptible to the activity of people with only a limited technology and, as a consequence, the Mediterranean region, which could be cleared easily and provided a rapid growing season, initially became the area of the most precocious development. North of the Alps the grasslands and the beech woods were most easily settled. The thickly forested areas of oak and conifers were less promising and only thinly populated. Human life sustained itself chiefly from cereal cultivation, but some areas, high in the mountains or in very northerly latitudes, were simply too inhospitable to support large settlements, for the soil was too thin and the growing season too short. Even in southerly latitudes the infertility of, for instance, the gravel and sand of the terminal moraines was an insuperable barrier, while a very wet area, like Brittany, was forced into a predominantly pastoral agriculture. Sometimes quite fertile soils could not be fully exploited for they were too heavy and it was not until the heavy plough became widespread in the twelfth and thirteenth centuries that appreciable progress was made in these regions. Even the most favourable areas, where lighter and fertile soils had been deposited by river and wind action and where vegetation could be cleared, were very vulnerable. Cereals are annual plants with a distinct growing season and their yield was vitally affected by annual variations within the cycle of the seasons. An average or good year could produce enough to support these communities through the winter, but the margins were narrow and slight seasonal variations could cause starvation. Moreover, these cereals drew the fertility from the soil, and this had to be replaced not only by fallowing, but also by ploughing and manuring, a process which could not be accomplished without the help of domestic animals which themselves needed feeding. A balance was difficult to achieve. In some parts of the Mediterranean, for instance, the light rainfall and the high evaporation rate produced some very fertile soils, unaffected by the leaching which occurs in the wetter regions, and irrigation enabled these soils to be exploited. However, these lands were also badly affected by soil erosion which occurred rapidly after the clearance of the vegetation cover, and in the long term limited the proportion of the land which could be cultivated for any length of time.

Nor could the cultivators of the soil afford to relax their efforts. In his *Chronicle of the Slavs*, completed in 1172, Helmold, a priest from Bosau on the Plöner-See in the diocese of Oldenburg, who was himself probably the son of a peasant coloniser, describes how nature had reclaimed farm settlements at Wagrin in the see of Oldenburg, originally destroyed in the Slav uprising of 983.

> There remain to this day numerous indications of that old occupation, especially in the forest which extends in a wide sweep from the city of Lütjenburg into Schleswig. In its vast and scarcely penetrable solitude traces of the furrows which had separated the plowlands of former times may be descried among the stoutest trees of the woods. Wall structures indicate the plans of towns and also of cities. In many streams ancient embankments, once thrown up to collect the tributary waters for the mills, show that all that woodland had once been inhabited by the Saxons.
>
> (Tschan 1935:72)

The whole of life, and with it social custom and organisation, was therefore forced to conform to the limitations of the physical environment. There was real pleasure in achieving modifications. William, Archbishop of Tyre between 1175 and *c.*1186, whose history of the Crusader States is one of the most important chronicles of the twelfth century, describes with pride the irrigation of the fertile soils around the city which was the seat of his province.

> All the country round about derives immense benefits from these waters. Not only do they supply gardens and delightful orchards planted with fruit trees, but they irrigate the sugar cane also. From this latter crop sugar is made, a most precious product, very necessary for the use and health of mankind, which is carried from here by merchants to the most remote countries of the world.
>
> (Babcock and Krey 1941:2:6)

Matthew Paris too was not simply a recorder of woe. Under the year 1248 he wrote: 'This year passed away, the air temperate and calm, the granaries full of produce, and the wine-presses overflowing. A measure of grain fell to a price of two shillings and a cask of good-quality wine was voluntarily sold for two marks' (Luard 1880:5:46).

Irrigation schemes such as that described by William gave a measure of environmental control, but it could easily be lost, even during prosperous periods when productivity was high enough to support a growing population, for progress could be halted and even reversed by natural disasters over which humans had little or no control. Fulcher of Chartres, a chaplain of Baldwin I, first King of Jerusalem, describes what could happen to the beautiful plantations William so admired. In May 1117,

> an infinite number of locusts swarmed into the land of Jerusalem, devouring more completely than usual the vines, field crops, and trees of all kinds. You could see them advance like an army of men in good order as if they had previously arranged it in a council. When they had made their day's journey, some on foot and some flying, they mutually chose a resting place for themselves. And so when they had eaten up everything green, and had gnawed the bark of the trees, the wingless locusts as well as the others departed in companies.
>
> (Ryan 1969:218)

Contemporaries leave no doubt that such disasters were frequent. Famine was an ever-present fear. During Matthew Paris's lifetime, 1258 was an appalling year:

> In this year the north wind continued to blow for several months and although April, May, and the better part of June had already passed, scarcely any small and rare flowers had appeared and few seeds had germinated, so that there was little hope of fruitful crops. Because of the scarcity of grain, an innumerable multitude of the poor died. And as a consequence of hunger, swollen and livid bodies were to be found everywhere, their carcasses rotting miserably, in fives or sixes in pigsties and dung-pits and on muddy highways. Nor did those who had their own houses dare, in their own hunger, to look after the dying, because of the disease and contagion of the ill. And when several dead bodies were found, large and capacious ditches were dug in the cemeteries in which were placed many bodies.

Worse was to come:

> at the end of July and August, since the harvest had been deficient both this year and the last, the misery of hunger and want attacked to such an extent, that those who usually helped others, themselves died from want. And what alarmed the people more than the nobles was that the continuous downpours of rain threatened to choke the abundant harvest, which God had previously presaged.

The consequence was that the corn failed to ripen and was still standing in the fields on All Saints' Day (1 November). By this time a measure of corn was selling for sixteen shillings, a sharp contrast to the good year of 1248, when it had stood at two shillings (Luard 1880:5:690, 710–11, 728).

In the twelfth and thirteenth centuries major improvements were made in transport and communications which had a profound effect upon the economy, but this should not conceal the fact that very often local shortages could not be alleviated quickly enough to prevent loss of life. Even when help did arrive it was sometimes too late to be fully effective. Matthew Paris believed that, in 1258, 'England would have perished in herself', had not corn ships arrived from Holland and Germany and even then it was too late for many. Bulky goods could indeed be moved more easily by water, but overland only small groups or individuals with urgent business could expect to achieve more than about 30 miles per day (Boyer 1951). The crusaders of the twelfth century, most of whom travelled to the east overland, found the logistical problems of moving a large company horrendous, but the movement of a court following an itinerant ruler could be just as difficult, for the courtiers if not for the ruler. For Peter of Blois, during his time in the service of Henry II, it was positively traumatic. Because of the temporary nature of the stops, those forced to be present in the king's train were never comfortable. Peter complains of awful food: leaden bread, sour and mouldy wine which could be drunk only through clenched teeth, and fish that had not seen water for four days. Moreover, the king's constant last-minute changes of direction often left his entourage stranded without a bed for the night so that, blundering about in the surrounding countryside in the dark, they often fought for the shelter of some wretched hovel (Migne 1855c:47–50). Even water could sometimes be a barrier rather than a lifeline. Inhabitants of small islands, such as the several hundred which lay in the Aegean Sea, often led very isolated lives, cut off by storms and currents, and existing on a limited and inadequate diet (Luttrell 1989). Any means which helped the traveller therefore were seen as charitable acts, deserving of merit. Bridges were especially valued. Nivelon of Chérisy, Bishop of Soissons, returning from the Fourth Crusade which had been diverted against Constantinople in 1203–4, was among the many western recipients of the relics of that city. Among his prizes was an elbow of St Stephen which he donated to the cathedral at Châlons-sur-Marne, which was dedicated to that saint, with the proviso that from the increase in donations which this would bring from visiting pilgrims, half the income should go to the church and half to the building of a bridge. The bridge was, in fact, completed in 1217 (Mortet and Deschamps 1995:2:199–210). The relics here served the double purpose of helping to finance the bridge and providing saintly protection against destruction by flooding.

Indeed, the interpenetration of the supernatural with the natural world was never far from the minds of the commentators. Just as the pious motives behind the contribution to the bridge at Châlons might help to ensure its survival, so too men's sins might bring the wrath of God upon the community. Fulcher of Chartres knew why they had been struck by the plague of locusts.

> Oh the wickedness of men who persist in their wicked perversity! How often and how much our Creator touches us with His reproaches and admonishes us, terrifies us by His portents, stirs us by His threats, instructs us by His lessons, and represses us by His punishment. But we always persist in our iniquities, despise His admonitions, and contemptuously violate His precepts. ... What wonder is it that God permitting, the mice destroy our crops while they are sprouting from the roots in the ground or the locusts devour them ripened in the ear, or that they are damaged in the granaries by worms of every kind or by rotting, when we dishonestly sell the tithes owed to God or sacrilegiously retain them entirely?
>
> (Ryan 1969:218–19)

Sometimes there were signs portending the behaviour of the elements. On 24 July 1239 Matthew Paris observed a large star tracking across the sky, leaving in its wake a trail of smoke and sparks. He did not know what this meant, but he was nevertheless struck by the sudden improvement in the weather and with it the gathering of a wonderful harvest (Luard 1880:3:566). These signs were not accepted uncritically, nor were people always confident about their interpretation, but they were seen as an integral part of the environment.

However, the frequent references to the weather are not easily transformed into a convincing overall interpretation of history based on climate. The observations of contemporaries were by their very nature short term, for the short term was crucial to their lives. Nevertheless, study of long-term climatic variations shows that, within human history, these are so slight that an oscillation of the average temperature of more than plus or minus one degree Centigrade is very unusual. Climatologists recording the advance and retreat of glaciers, dendrologists measuring the thickness of the tree rings, and historians tabulating the varying dates of the wine harvest have concluded that, with one possible exception, conditions which could have had a long-term impact on the forest cover have not recurred for three millennia. Interestingly for the study of the middle ages, the one exception appears to be the generally milder period between the ninth and the twelfth centuries, particularly marked between c.1080 and c.1180, and it is tempting to correlate this with the economic expansion so evident during this period. However, the temptation should be resisted, for there are other, non-climatic reasons for this expansion, and the data simply do not exist which could make any such link convincing. Moreover, in some places this expansion continued into the thirteenth and even the fourteenth centuries, a period which has been found to be one of glacial thrust and advance (Le Roy Ladurie 1972:127, 236, 255).

Illness and disease were no more susceptible to control than famine and, indeed, sometimes there is an evident interconnection. Although the period between the mid-eleventh and the early fourteenth centuries saw no great outbreak of bubonic plague such as had struck Justinian's empire in the sixth century and which was to devastate the population in 1348 and the decades which followed, nevertheless outbreaks of disease were common and endemic. Rome was notoriously unhealthy, partly because the drainage system of the imperial era had fallen into disuse by the beginning of the sixth century, leaving many of the former agricultural estates in the vicinity to revert to marshlands (Krautheimer 1980:64). Only dire political necessity resulting from the French successes in the Albigensian Crusade persuaded Raymond VI, Count of Toulouse, to go to the city to negotiate with the pope in the winter of 1209–10. This done, according to the poet William of Tudela, he set off at once, 'travelling fast out of Lombardy by long stages for fear of contracting disease there' (Shirley 1996:31). He had good reason for his haste. In 1137 the German Emperor Lothar began to sicken at Trent on his way back from Rome and, although he insisted on continuing his journey, died on 4 December while crossing the Alps (Celli-Fraentzel 1932:102). When Frederick Barbarossa took his troops to Rome for his coronation in the summer of 1155, he was forced to move his army away from the swampy lands around the city because so many soldiers had become ill, probably with malaria. Finally, he had no alternative but to abandon his plans to invade Apulia and to return north (Mierow 1955:151–5). Otto of Freising's observation that unhealthy climate caused more damage to the army than the weapons of their enemies underlines how the best planned political and military operations could be wrecked by a hostile environment.

Even when disease did not kill, it could have severe long-term effects. Peter of Blois, who himself contracted malaria when he was in Sicily in 1167, brilliantly diagnosed a knight named Geldewin at Ambroise on the Loire River as suffering from 'medium tertian ague' (that is, malaria of a bilious remittent type), but despite his careful and accurate analysis of the symptoms, he could do nothing to alleviate them (Holmes and Weedon 1962:252–6). Crusading also left its mark. Richard of the Temple, Prior of the Augustinian house of the Holy Trinity in London, described how some of those who had returned from the Third Crusade in 1192 had been infected by 'incurable disease' from which they never recovered 'even in their homeland' (Nicholson 1997:379). One of the most evident scourges was leprosy. Previously little known in western Europe, it is mentioned frequently in the high middle ages, and the number of special colonies created for lepers multiplied rapidly during this time. It is difficult to discern if it was on the increase, for the fashion for endowing hospitals, many of which were specifically for lepers, reached its height in the thirteenth century. Nevertheless, the increased attention paid to it seems unlikely to have been solely the consequence of fashion, and it may be that the increase in contact with the Middle East helped establish leprosy in more western European families than had previously been the case. The foundation of the Order of St Lazarus in the Kingdom of Jerusalem in the 1130s, specifically for lepers of all classes, suggests the scale of the problem in the east. In the west the growth of squalid and crowded slums associated with some of the swollen towns of the twelfth and thirteenth centuries encouraged conditions in which diseases of all kinds thrived, including leprosy. The apparent decline in the disease during the fourteenth century may have been due to the rise of pulmonary tuberculosis among Europeans, the bacilli of which spread much more easily than leprosy, thus driving it out through competition (McNeill 1977:164–7).

These environmental forces were constant, but so too was the struggle to overcome and offset them and, from about the mid-eleventh century, two powerful pressures began to release hitherto latent expansionist forces. These two pressures were religion and population growth. Between them the papacy and the monastic orders infused Christians with an enthusiasm for pilgrimage and crusade which increased the desire for travel and conquest and which pushed the boundaries of western Christendom far beyond those of preceding centuries. At the same time – and not always distinguished very clearly from the religious impetus – the continuously growing number of mouths stimulated a search for a means to increase the production of food by the incorporation of previously uncultivated land or by the conquest of the territories of neighbouring, non-Christian peoples.

The major population movements which had affected western Christendom in the early middle ages had found their origin outside its borders: the Germanic tribes and then Islam, the Vikings and the Magyars had pressed in from the north, south and east. But during the eleventh century western Christendom, perhaps partly because of the infusion of these restless peoples, itself began to expand. Men whom the Caliph at Córdoba or the Byzantine emperor at Constantinople regarded as little more than barbarians began to take the initiative. In the north-east the Saxons started to make inroads against the Slav tribes settled beyond the River Elbe, previously, despite temporary changes, the eastern frontier of Latin Christendom. In the Iberian peninsula, the Castilians and the Leonese, who had largely been confined to the lands north of the rivers Ebro and Duero, began the slower process of forcing the Muslim masters of the peninsula further and further south. In the central Mediterranean the maritime cities of Italy showed signs of their later commercial dominance. Venice, which had throughout the early middle ages kept contact with Constantinople, now established an increasingly strong grip on Byzantine trade. On the west coast of Italy, Pisa and Genoa, although less powerful, nevertheless were, in the early eleventh century, strong enough to retake the large island of Sardinia from the Muslims. During the twelfth century these three cities were to become the leading carriers in a greatly enlarged Middle Eastern trade, especially in the new Latin Christian colonies established in Syria and Palestine by the crusaders. In southern Italy, where control had been divided between Byzantium and Islam, the Normans erupted onto the scene in the early decades of the eleventh century, coming first as brigands and pilgrims. However, by the early twelfth century they had established political control of the area and half a century later the Kingdom of Sicily, consisting of Apulia, Calabria and the island of Sicily, was a state of European importance. But perhaps the clearest expression of this expansionism was the crusade. In 1099 a Latin army captured Jerusalem and four states were established in the Levant. Although Jerusalem was the centrepiece, so powerful was the idea that between c.1080 and c.1150 men began to fight under the crusading banner along both the other great frontiers which faced pagan or infidel peoples, in Germany and in Spain.

This movement was that of a whole society, led by warriors and militant clergy and backed by colonising peasants. The warriors were attracted by the prospect of fighting, of booty and, possibly, permanent extensions to their existing lands; the clergy ostensibly by their desire to increase the territory of Christ, but in some cases at least perhaps equally inspired by the motives that impelled the warriors; and the peasantry because their social leaders offered them favourable conditions of settlement, including personal freedom, fixed money rents in place of seigneurial labour burdens, a degree of self-government in judicial affairs and even an amnesty for crimes committed. All classes hoped that they could gain some spiritual credit by attacking and conquering non-Christian peoples.

The result was the taming of more and more previously wild land. Beyond the Elbe settlers were drawn from the west, in particular from Holstein, Frisia, Holland and Westphalia. In 1106 Frederick, Archbishop of Hamburg, concluded an agreement with

> those living beyond the Rhine, who are called Hollanders. ... Therefore the aforesaid men met our majesty and made a strong request, and we conceded to them for cultivation, land which was sited in our bishopric, hitherto uncultivated and swampy, and superfluous to the needs of our people.

The charter stipulated that they paid one *denarius* per annum for each manse, the size of which was laid out (720 royal rods × 30), that they paid the tithe, that they complied with synodal justice, but that they could settle internal disputes among themselves, and that they should have the right to build churches to which the bishop granted a tithe of the tithes. The charter neatly encapsulates the double strand: new land, new churches. More than half a century later, in 1164, Wichmann, Archbishop of Magdeburg, was following the same policy although he actually bought out any persons having rights on the land in question, which lay near the walls of the city beyond the Elbe. By this date the process was sufficiently common for it to be possible to employ agents or locators to carry out the project.

> I have given by this agreement, this particular place, with everything dependent upon it, to a certain Werner, whom they call 'de Paderborn', and a certain Godfrey, in order that they may settle new inhabitants there, who may drain, plough and make fruitful by sowing, the adjoining land, which is marshy and grassy and fit for nothing except grass and hay, and that from this same cultivation they may pay an annual *cens* at fixed times towards the revenues of the archbishop.

Fixed rents in kind and money and tithes of corn and fruit were to be paid, but no outside jurisdictional authorities could intervene, nor could the inhabitants be forced to do service of any kind with the significant exception of the obligation 'to protect them and their fields from inundation and when water bursts out of the ditches and embankments'. Werner received one-third of the profits of the administration of justice and the revenues from two manses for his work (Kötzschke 1912:1–2, 36–7).

The technical expertise of these 'Hollanders' was crucial in areas prone to flooding. Between *c.*1000 and *c.*1300 they brought into production a considerable proportion of the great areas of peat which covered large parts of the northern and western parts of the Netherlands (see Figure 1), as well as developing extensive systems of dyking to defend against flood and to drain new land. However, as Wichmann's charter recognises, risks still existed. The effect of dyking and damming of rivers was sometimes to cause sudden changes in water levels when an unexpected surge could not be contained within an embanked and narrowed river (Hoppenbrouwers 1997: 91–111).

By 1164 the chief threat to the settlers was environmental disaster such as flooding, for the Slavs had largely been subdued. It had not always been so, for there had been dangerous uprisings in the past, notably in 983, 1018 and 1066, which had destroyed much of the conquest and superficial conversion accomplished until then. But in the long term the Slavs did not prove such formidable enemies as the Muslims of Iberia, the equivalent great frontier in the south, where from the 1080s to the 1140s the Almoravides, and from 1170 the Almohades, reversed many Christian successes and added a further hazard to life on the frontier. In central Spain the new farmer faced long, dry summers and freezing winters, but even if he survived the problems posed by nature, frontier warfare, often of the hit-and-run variety, could destroy what had been won. If a fort fell the inhabitants might be slaughtered or sold as slaves, permanent installations were often crippled, wells poisoned, orchards burnt, woods cut down. It was not until the decisive Christian victory of Las Navas de Tolosa, south of Toledo, in 1212, that the settlers could feel secure from a Muslim revival. The following extract from a charter made in January 1133, during the siege of Fraga in Aragon, gives some sense of these problems:

> I, Alfonso, by the grace of God, king, willingly and of my own account as a remission of mine and my parents' sins, am pleased to give, concede and confirm to God and to the church of Jesus of Nazareth of Mount Aragon and to the abbot Fortun and his successors and all the chapter, half the town and castle that is called Curb, with all of its lands in their entirety, deserted and peopled, and with all its pasture and water, woods and scrub, as their own heritage for ever. And I order you to people it as quickly as you can and make there a good castle for the honour of all Christianity.
>
> (Lacarra 1947–8:563–4)

The more obvious manifestations of expansion can be drawn from these frontier examples, but equally important was colonisation within the existing area of western Christendom. In the early middle ages many regions had been sparsely populated. As the need for food and space became more acute in those areas which were well peopled, a drive began to occupy areas of previously uncultivated land. In *c*.800 when Charlemagne issued his famous capitulary, *De Villis*, it had been necessary to warn the stewards not to allow fields to become overgrown with woods (Loyn and Percival 1975:69), but in the twelfth century these woods were being cleared and new settlements created. One of the many lords who encouraged large-scale assarting was Suger, Abbot of St Denis, who issued a charter in 1145 for just such a purpose.

> I, Suger,... have conceded that whoever will wish to settle in a certain *ville neuve* which we have built, which is called Vaucresson, will have, for a *cens* of twelve *deniers*, a manse of land, that is to say, a piece of one arpent and a quarter, and they will be exempt from all *tailles* and customary exactions. In the same way, no one from this village will go out or depart on military service as a result of a summons from the king or a baron or a *sergent* of St Denis, except on the

abbot's own order, and with the abbot personally, or with the prior if the abbot is away, nor will they perform suit of court in any place whatsoever outside their village except for the abbot. And they will pay four *deniers* in *cens* and the tithe to us for each arpent of the land of St Denis, wherever they possess it: nor may any outsider receive land adjacent to the same village for the purpose of cultivation, unless he has a manse there. Moreover, common fines, the pleas concerning which they hold among themselves, we have fixed at ten *deniers*.

(Lecoy de la Marche 1867:360–1)

All this activity stemmed initially from an increase in population. Overall, it seems reasonable to conjecture that conditions favouring a decline in the death-rate prevailed in the twelfth and thirteenth centuries, although in addition the disappearance of slave gangs and the widespread establishment of family units must have had a limited impact on the birth-rate as well (Duby 1974:194). During the twelfth century the impetus generated by expansion was consolidated by improvements in material conditions, especially in diet and housing. The attitudes which this engendered are encapsulated in the decrees issued by Charles the Good, Count of Flanders, in the aftermath of a local famine in 1124–5. According to Galbert, a notary of Bruges, he laid down that

whoever sowed two measures of land in the sowing time should sow another measure in peas and beans, because these legumes yield more quickly and seasonably and therefore could nourish the poor more quickly if the misery of famine and want should not end in that year.

(Ross 1982:87)

While such developments benefit both sexes, there is evidence to suggest that the improvements in diet, which resulted in increased intake of proteins and iron, had particular effects upon the longevity of women. Women need about twice as much iron as men; during pregnancy and lactation this increases to three times. In earlier centuries many women may have been severely anaemic as a result of inadequate diet, making them especially vulnerable to illness and disease and causing a diminution in fertility. Evidence that this had changed in the high middle ages can be seen in the reversal of the previous preponderance of males over females in the adult population (Bullough and Campbell 1980; Herlihy 1975). The effects on death-rates are evident, but a further consequence may have been a slight increase in the birth-rate as well.

This is not to claim a higher degree of contemporary consciousness of these population changes than actually existed. Few people were in a position to take an overall view and those that did – such as the popes – saw the world not in relation to economic growth or population pressure, but in moral and religious terms. Helmold does clearly refer to those 'in straits from lack of fields' (Tschan 1935:168–9), and in the 1190s the Cistercian, Geoffrey of Auxerre, even claimed that it was becoming difficult for hermits to find isolated places (Constable 1996:46), but equally Fulcher of Chartres complained about the need for more permanent immigrants in Outremer. 'Following that [i.e. a pilgrimage],' he says,

some remained in the Holy Land, and others went back to their native countries. For this reason the land of Jerusalem remained depopulated. There were not enough people to defend it from the Saracens if only the latter dared attack us.

(Ryan 1969:149)

Although the Latin states in the east did attract more settlers than was once thought, as the substantial immigrant population in certain rural parts of the Kingdom of Jerusalem shows (Ellenblum 1998:73–85), Fulcher's complaint serves as a warning against too sweeping a view. If small states like those of Outremer with their constant stream of western visitors found it difficult to retain sufficient settlers, then it is not to be expected that the vast interior of Spain, for instance, would be fully populated. The crowded towns and countryside of Flanders and Tuscany contrast with the shortage of colonists in the lands of the Duero and the Tagus. To assess the fundamental impetus as population growth is therefore to look at the problem historically rather than to generalise about contemporary motivation.

Nobody knows the numbers involved and some historians believe that there is no value in attempting to estimate them (see Figure 2). Nevertheless, the following round figures broadly accord with the fragmentary data and may be useful at least in indicating relative changes. European population (defined in the modern sense to include European Russia) in *c.*AD 200 may have been about 67 million, but with the economic and political crises of the late Roman Empire, together with the onslaught of plague, it is unlikely to have been above 27 million in 700. Thereafter, there seems to have been a slow recovery to about 42 million in 1000, although this was fitful and may have suffered setbacks, especially in the turbulent years of the ninth century. The medieval peak of about 73 million was reached in *c.*1300. This suggests that the centuries between 1000 and 1300 were crucial, for the 15 million rise of the previous three centuries more than doubled during this period. Thus, in the specific case of England, for example, it has been calculated that the population grew from between 1.5

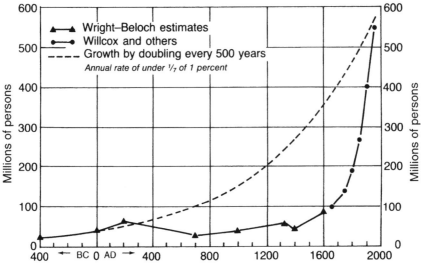

Source: M.K.Bennett (1954), *The World's Food* (New York: Harper), p. 5. (Reproduced by permission.)

Figure 2 European population

million and 2.5 million at the time of Domesday in 1086 to between 3.8 million and 7.2 million in *c.*1300. The wide margins show how difficult it is to be precise, but it is likely that the population doubled and may perhaps have tripled over the period (Campbell 1997:225). While this is very unspectacular in a modern context, in that between 1900 and 1947 alone the European population grew by 147 million, it was nevertheless very significant in the medieval environment. As Figure 2 shows, a very small annual increase, if unchecked, has far-reaching consequences. The immense changes of the high middle ages therefore stemmed from only a slight upward turn. Even so, the rise could not continue indefinitely, given limited technology and finite resources of land. There appears to have been a slowing down after *c.*1250, for the rise from then until 1300 was only about 4 million in comparison with the 19 million of the previous hundred years. The evidence used to show signs of growth can equally be tested for symptoms of stagnation or decline and, indeed, the migrations were slowing or stopping altogether. In those parts of Italy which were the most economically advanced of their time and therefore most sensitive to change, there was even a reverse, with a shrinkage of the cultivated area. During the fourteenth century there was a dramatic fall in population; the 73 million of 1300 had shrunk to 51 million by 1350 (M.K. Bennett 1954:3–22). Prolonged famines became more common and, most devastating, bubonic plague returned to the west for the first time since the sixth century.

Between 1315 and 1322 the whole of northern Europe – an area estimated to cover 400,000 square miles – was afflicted by a massive famine and widespread murrains among cattle and sheep on a scale nobody then alive could recall either in reality or myth. The immediate causes were several years of unrelenting cold winters and wet summers, exacerbated in areas like Flanders by the continuation of a war with the French Crown which had already been fought intermittently for over twenty years, helping to deepen recession in the once buoyant economy of the region. The result was an unprecedented rise in prices, estimated at 800 per cent in France between 1315 and 1318, which could not be sustained by a population whose living standards had already declined as a result of previous demographic pressure. Although the peasantry and the urban poor were the worst affected, nobody was immune, except perhaps for the few individuals and institutions which could exploit the acute shortage of salt, itself caused by the lack of sunshine during the extremely wet summers (W.C. Jordan 1996).

Fulcher of Chartres would have fully understood:

> It is quite clear that nothing in this world is certain, nothing stable and nothing agreeable for long. Consequently it is not good to sigh for terrestrial goods, but it is better to keep the heart always turned toward God. Let us not put our trust in worldly goods lest we lose eternal life.
>
> (Ryan 1969:251–2)

2

Social structure

Meanwhile, the body of King Henry was still unburied in Normandy. He had died on the first day of December [1135]. His body was brought to Rouen, and there his entrails, brain, and eyes were buried together. The remainder of the corpse was cut all around with knives, sprinkled with a great deal of salt, and wrapped in oxhides, to stop the strong, pervasive stench, which was already causing the deaths of those who watched over it. It even killed the man who had been hired for a great sum of money to cut off the head with an axe and extract the stinking brain, although he had wrapped himself in linen cloths around his head: so he got no benefit from his fee. He was the last of many whom King Henry put to death.

They took the royal corpse to Caen, and it lay there for a time in the church in which his father had been buried. Although it had been filled with much salt and wrapped in many hides, a fearful black fluid ran down continuously, leaking through the hides, and was collected in vessels beneath the bier and cast away by attendants who grew faint with dread. See, then, whoever you are reading this, how the corpse of a most mighty king, whose crowned head had sparkled with gold and the finest jewels, like the splendour of God, whose hands had shone with sceptres, while the rest of his body had been dressed in gorgeous cloth of gold, and his mouth had always fed on the most delicious and choice foods, for whom everyone would rise to their feet, whom everyone feared, with whom everyone rejoiced, and whom everyone admired: see what the body became, how fearfully it melted away, how wretchedly cast down it was! See, I say, the outcome of events, upon which final judgement always depends. And learn to hold in contempt whatever comes to such an end, whatever is reduced to nothing in this way.

At last the remains of the royal corpse were brought to England, and buried within twelve days of Christmas at the abbey of Reading, which King Henry had founded and endowed with many possessions.

(Greenway 2002:66–7)

This vivid description of the death of Henry I by Henry, Archdeacon of Huntingdon, conveys two fundamental medieval social ideas. Decay afflicts all material things and therefore ultimately only the spiritual and the eternal are important, but that nevertheless, during life, society was hierarchical, presided over by great rulers like King Henry himself.

Many clerical writers in fact strove to convey the necessity for faithfully performing a preordained functional role within the hierarchy as a means both of seeking salvation after death and of ensuring the smooth ordering of human activity in life, for Heaven itself was hierarchical and human society should reflect this. The most common image used for the human version was that of the body, whose individual parts, important in themselves, nevertheless could function only in relation to the whole. The Cardinal Peter Damian, writing in the mid-eleventh century, put it succinctly:

> Moreover the eyes, tongue, feet and hands each have their own particular function in the human body; yet the hands do not touch, the feet do not work, the tongue does not speak nor the eyes see of themselves and for their own sake; the special function of each part of the body can be attributed to the whole.
>
> (McNulty 1959:62–3)

Just over a century later, John of Salisbury, at that time a member of the household of the archbishop of Canterbury, used this as the central theme of his *Policraticus*, for he believed that unless each part performed its allotted role, then the body itself would become diseased. 'For inferiors must serve superiors, who on the other hand ought to provide all necessary protection to their inferiors' (Nederman 1990:126). Although not all models exactly conformed – there was in the eleventh century, for instance, considerable competition between that of the episcopate and that of the monks (Duby 1980:126–45) – the basic idea of interdependence was common to all.

The cement which held this together was Christian belief. The Castilian law code, *Siete Partidas*, assembled by King Alfonso X in the 1260s, after describing the nature of law and custom, set out the fundamentals of the faith (Scott 2001:1:14).

> The origin of laws, temporal as well as spiritual, is this, that every Christian should believe firmly that there is one true God who has neither beginning nor end, who is neither subject to limitation nor change, and has power over all things, and that the brain of man cannot understand or describe Him perfectly; and that Father, Son, and Holy Spirit are three persons and one thing, simple, without division, which is God the Father, neither created nor begotten by another, the Son begotten by the Father only, and the Holy Spirit proceeding from the both of them, all three of one substance and equal and of a power enduring together forever; and that although each one of these three persons is God, they are not three Gods, but only one, and moreover, although God is one, this does not prevent there being three persons. This is the beginning of all spiritual as well as corporeal matters, not only those which are apparent but those which are not so.

God sent his Son into the world in order to open the way to salvation,

> in order to save the race of men, he underwent death and passion upon the cross; and in spirit he descended into Hell, and arose on the third day, and

ascended to Heaven in body and in soul, and will come at the end of time, to judge the quick and the dead, to give to each one what he deserves: at whose coming all will be resurrected in body and soul as they formerly were, and be judged for good or evil, according to their works: and the good will have glory without end, and the bad eternal punishment.

It was within the Church that all Christians would be saved,

in which is made the sacrifice of the body and blood of Jesus Christ, Our Redeemer, by the symbols of bread and wine, and we believe that no other can perform this sacrifice but one who has been ordained for that purpose by the Holy Church.

Those who received baptism could be saved and could atone for sins after baptism by penance, but any Christian who acted in a manner contrary to these beliefs, or any person who, for one reason or another, did not adhere to them, was damned. Otto of Freising conceded that God's power could not actually be restrained by ecclesiastical rulers or sacraments, but that for him it was impossible to believe that an unbaptised person could be saved. 'And so in such matters the divine power is limited, not for Him but for me' (Mierow 1966:299). For medieval Christians therefore the precondition for the membership of society was adherence to this set of beliefs. Those who did not conform were to be converted, excluded or overcome. In this sense medieval European society was synonymous with Christendom for, although these beliefs were sometimes distorted by superstition or by pagan survivals, all Christians, from the humblest serf to the greatest monarch, believed that they had a soul to save and, as the death of Henry I shows, that their bodies were merely transitory vehicles, and consequently were greatly terrified by the prospect of eternal damnation. To be deprived of the society of Christians and the services of the clergy as a result of excommunication was not a matter to be taken lightly.

The clergy, as the propagators of the hierarchical model, and as intercessors between the heavenly and earthly realms, saw themselves as first in status. They were the exclusive guardians and interpreters of the truth. Pope Gregory VII, writing to the Duke of Bohemia in 1080, left no doubt on the matter.

In reply to the request of Your Excellency that we would sanction the celebration of the sacred offices in your country in the Slavonic tongue, let it be known that we cannot in any way grant this petition. It is evident to those who consider the matter carefully that it has pleased God to make Holy Scripture obscure in certain places lest, if it were perfectly clear to all, it might be vulgarised and subject to disrespect or be misunderstood by people of limited intelligence as to lead them into error.

(Emerton 1966:148)

Indeed, the major feature of this period is that the clergy, under the impetus of the papal attempts at reform which began in the 1050s and intensified under Gregory VII, increasingly emphasised that it was separate from other classes of society in that it lived under its own legal code and was governed by its own courts.

At the apex of this clerical society was the pope, supported by his cardinals who, from 1059, acted not only as counsellors and administrators but also as an electoral college. Below were the two chains of the secular and the regular clergy. The life of the secular clergy focused upon the bishopric which, for diverse historical reasons, varied in size and importance with the region. The bishop was the central figure at the local level because to him were reserved the sacraments of ordination and confirmation, a power transmitted from Christ and the Apostles through the agency of the pope. The bishop administered the diocese through his consistory court, which headed a whole hierarchy of courts in which sat the archdeacon and the rural deans. In the chief towns of the diocese the bishop had his own group of advisers, including the archdeacon and the canons of the local cathedral or collegiate church. The lives of the canons were often governed by a rule bearing many similarities to that of the regular clergy for it imposed upon them a vow of chastity and corporate life. However, in the early middle ages, canons were not always easy to define. Therefore, in the eleventh and twelfth centuries distinctions began to be drawn between regular canons, whose way of life made them difficult to distinguish from the monks, and secular canons, more concerned with wider clerical duties in the diocese, including episcopal business, work in the parishes or the provision of the educational facilities of the Church (Constable 1996:11–13, 54–9). They were usually provided for by a prebend, assigned from the estates of the Church. These diocesan clergy formed the chapter which, theoretically, possessed the right to elect the bishop, although it was generally subject to varied degrees of outside pressure, both lay and ecclesiastical.

However, the line between clergy and laity was not always clear cut, for the Church could, at times, be very broad indeed, incorporating considerable numbers of men who claimed to be 'clerks' (a status which could be obtained as early as 7 years of age), but who had not taken holy orders. In the eleventh and twelfth centuries there remained some ambiguity about their position for, holding positions such as presbyter, subdeacon or deacon, they might enjoy the privileges of clerics, while following a most inappropriate lifestyle. Innocent III, with his usual logic, forced the issue: a man could not both hold a benefice and be married. He could, however, choose to remain a simple clerk, below the level of subdeacon, a status which would allow him to leave the ecclesiastical structure if he wished. Even so, for a very small minority of men from the ranks of the upper nobility it remained possible to manipulate the situation. Drawing on the material benefits of high ecclesiastical office, they nevertheless avoided taking major orders, leaving open the possibility of returning to secular life should the family be struck by a succession crisis. When that happened they took care to be knighted in a conspicuous manner (preferably by the king), thus underlining their secular status and anticipating any future problems over the legitimacy of their children. This device was also used in a different context by William of Nogaret, one of the chief advisers of the French king, Philip IV. Until 1298, like many university-trained lawyers, he held clerical status, but when relations between the king and Pope Boniface VIII became fraught, this became untenable. Within a year the change had been made; thereafter he always referred to himself as a knight (Dunbabin 1988:26–39).

By *c.*1160 the Church had accepted the teaching of the theologian Peter Lombard that there were seven sacraments, rites which, as the means of grace, were separated from the others of the Church. Although ordination and confirmation remained exclusive to the bishop, an ordinary priest could administer the other five sacraments of baptism, penance, the eucharist, marriage and extreme unction, although many in fact found the duties of their office confusing and functioned only fitfully. In theory to be ordained, a man needed to be personally free, legitimate, unmarried and literate, but in practice one or more of these provisions was often ignored. The social position and economic condition of the parish priests varied widely. Some rectors, who held their own tithes and drew income from the glebeland assigned to their church, maintained a position in society perhaps comparable to lesser members of the knightly class, a position which could be improved by the acquisition of a plurality of livings. However, many vicars were paid by the lay or monastic patron of their church and often received only a small proportion of their tithes, the remainder being appropriated. In the worst position of all were the substitutes of absentee rectors or vicars who, forced to exist on a tiny stipend, endured a poverty-stricken existence comparable to many of the peasantry among whom they lived. In this period no church reform even really reached this level, despite many attempts.

In the tenth and eleventh centuries this structure was closely enmeshed in secular society, for many appointments at all levels were under secular control and, most offensive to the eleventh-century reformers, religious offices were bought and sold like commodities at a market (see Plate 2). From the late eleventh century the efforts of the papacy and its supporters did partially free the clergy from lay control, an action regarded as a prelude to a more general reform of society as a whole, but they failed to break the web of lay patronage decisively, for the Church was too wealthy and its members too important for lay powers to allow it to escape completely. According to Orderic Vitalis, despite the reformers, William Rufus, the English king, 'for the sake of profit … delayed appointing prelates to churches, and the leaderless people or shepherdless flock fell victim to the teeth of wolves'. For this reason he kept the see of Canterbury vacant for three years. Nevertheless the reformers did make the clergy more aware of themselves as a separate order, and in this context Orderic's comment on the above matter is significant.

> It is manifestly unjust and contrary to all reason that the things given to God by the generosity of Christian princes, or honourably increased by the care of stewards of the Church's goods, should revert to lay hands and be applied to unholy secular uses.
>
> (Chibnall 1973:4:175–7)

Ecclesiastical offices may have continued to provide incomes for secular-minded political appointees, but among the higher clergy at least they were no longer blatantly bought and sold or filled by persons so patently ill equipped to tackle the duties involved. During the twelfth and thirteenth centuries, the papacy further emphasised the clergy's role by its systematic development of ecclesiastical administration, jurisdiction and finance and, through an extensive system of appellate jurisdiction, greatly increased its control over ordinations, benefices and ecclesiastical property.

Naturally, before the reform, the lifestyle of clerics bore considerable resemblance to that of the seculars with whom they were so closely connected. It was even more difficult for the papacy to effect permanent changes here than it was for it to tackle the evils of lay control and simony. Archbishops and bishops were not only spiritual leaders, but also great lords who held power over extensive lands and rights and many men. The reform movement had only limited impact here and, indeed, it is difficult to see what could have been done short of adopting a proposal as far-reaching as that put forward by Pope Paschal II in 1111, when he suggested that the Church free itself of

Plate 2 Simon Magus is described in Acts 8:9–24 as a sorcerer who convinced the people of Samaria that he possessed great powers. After conversion to Christianity he offered money to the Apostles Peter and John in order to receive the Holy Ghost, from which derives the term 'simony', the elimination of which was so central to church reform in the second half of the eleventh century. This twelfth-century capital from the church of Neuilly-en-Donjon (Allier) shows his confrontation with Peter in Rome during which he claimed that his magical powers enabled him to fly, but Peter's prayers to God resulted in a dramatic fall to his death.

all taint of materialism by giving up its regalia and concentrating solely on its spiritual duties. The following description by Robert of Graystanes, sub-prior of Durham, of Antony Bek, Bishop of Durham between 1283 and 1311 and titular Patriarch of Jerusalem from 1306, gives some idea of the mightiest of this breed. According to this account,

> after the king, he was second to none in appearance, deeds, and military power. He was occupied more by the affairs of the kingdom than by those of his see, providing the king with powerful support in war and far-sighted advice in council. Sometimes in the Scottish war he had twenty-six standard-bearers in his household, and commonly 140 knights in his following, so that he was seen as a lay prince rather than as a priest or a bishop. And, although he enjoyed being closely attended by crowds of knights in this way, he nevertheless conducted himself as if he did not care about them, the great counts and barons of the kingdom genuflecting before him, and, he, being seated, making light of the knights who, like servants, were kept standing for a very long time in his presence. Nothing which could magnify his glory was expensive for him. He once spent forty *solidi* in London for forty fresh herrings; the other magnates, then assembled in Parliament there, did not care to buy because of the excessive price. He bought the costliest cloth and, from it, made covers for his palfreys (which he called by name), because a certain person said that he did not believe that Bishop Antony would dare to buy it. Impatient of rest, scarcely ever staying in bed for more than one sleep, he said that whoever turned aside for bed was not a man. Never remaining in one place, he continuously travelled from manor to manor, from south to north and vice-versa.

It is not surprising to find such a great man in almost constant rivalry with the Archbishop of York, so that even the king had difficulty mediating between them (Raine 1839:64). Bek, it should be emphasised, was not 'corrupt' in the reform sense, for he was celibate and was not a simonist; he simply lived in a style he thought appropriate to his position in society (see Fraser 1957).

Nor was it necessary to be imbued with a powerful sense of vocation to be an effective bishop. Orderic Vitalis was well aware that undifferentiated condemnation of the exercise of patronage could sometimes be misplaced. Reviewing the reign of William Rufus, he comments how

> very often shallow, unlearned men are chosen for high ecclesiastical office, not because of any holiness of life or knowledge of church doctrine or learning in the liberal arts, but by the influence of noble kinsfolk and the help of powerful friends. Yet after their promotion God in his mercy pities and spares them, in time filling them with the riches of divine grace, so that through them the house of God is lit with the brightness of heavenly wisdom and many find a way to salvation through useful activities.
>
> (Chibnall 1975:5:205)

Indeed, many bishops strove to fulfil their duties conscientiously and to live austere lives. The detailed records of episcopal visitations, which are available from the mid-thirteenth century, give solid evidence of their attempts to improve clerical standards.

The visitations of Odo Rigaud, the Franciscan Archbishop of Rouen, are the first of this kind. Odo became archbishop in 1247 and remained so until his death in 1276. From the 1250s he was a close associate of King Louis IX, a position which involved him in great affairs of state like the negotiations which resulted in the Treaty of Paris of 1259 with Henry III, yet the records show that throughout he maintained close attention to the detail of a province which encompassed six suffragan bishops in a manner which would neither have been expected nor indeed administratively possible in the eleventh century.

What men like Odo Rigaud discovered, however, does underline the difficulty of reforming clerical lives at the lower levels of the hierarchy. An inspection of the Chapter at Rouen in March 1248, for instance, found that

> they violated their ordinances by talking in the choir. Clerics wander about the church and gossip with women while the service is being celebrated. The statute concerning the processional into the choir is not observed. The Psalms are too briskly run through and sung without pauses. The regulation concerning the Recessional at the Office of the Dead is not observed. When they ask permission to go out they give no reason for their going.

Individuals are accused of incontinence, theft, manslaughter, haunting taverns, drunkenness, dicing and trading (S. Brown 1964:39–40). Odo ordered that the archdeacons correct these abuses before the next Feast of the Assumption of the Virgin (15 August) and that if they did not he would intervene personally.

It was even more difficult to enforce corrections upon parish priests scattered about the province. The authorities had been trying to do so since the time of Pope Leo IX. Orderic Vitalis describes how Leo held a council at Reims in 1049 where he forbade clerks to bear arms or to take wives. 'From that time the fatal custom began to wither away little by little. The priests were ready enough to give up bearing arms but even now they are loath to part with their mistresses or to live chaste lives' (Chibnall 1972:3:121–3). Orderic was optimistic if he thought that the fighting clerk was about to disappear for, not only were such individuals conspicuous during the First Crusade and in contemporary entertainments like *The Song of Roland*, but also they were still to be found, apparently quite commonly, a century later in 1204 during the Fourth Crusade. The Picard knight, Robert of Clari, who describes the crusade very much from the point of view of the ordinary soldier, tells how his brother, Aleaumes of Clari, a clerk, wanted to be involved in the attack on Constantinople.

> And some said that it was not right that he should share as a knight, and he said that it was, because he had had a horse and a hauberk like any knight and had done as many feats of arms as any knight that was there, and more too. And finally the count of St. Pol gave judgment that he should share as a knight, because he had done more deeds of arms and of prowess, as the count of St. Pol himself bore witness, than any one of three hundred knights had done, and for that he ought to share as a knight.
>
> (McNeal 1936:117–18)

It seems that his fighting record was more important in the decision than the prohibition upon clerics shedding blood.

For many, however, clergy and layman alike, the highest expression of the Christian life was to be found not among the secular clergy but among the regulars, the monks. The *Siete Partidas* provides a definition:

> Some persons choose to live a life which is austere and secluded from other men, because they believe that in this way they serve God better without hindrance. And, since the riches of this world are an impediment to this, they think it better to renounce them all, and to conform to what our Lord Jesus Christ said in the Gospel, that to all those who abandon father, mother, wife, children, or other relatives, and all temporal goods for him, he will give in return an hundred fold and, besides, life which will endure for ever. Such persons as these are called the regular clergy, because they all have certain rules by which they are compelled to live, according to the regulations which they have received from the Holy Church at the origin of its religion, and, for this reason, they are included in the Order of the Clergy.
>
> (Scott 2001:1:112)

Here too there was a hierarchy from the pope, who in some cases was himself drawn from the monastic life, to the abbots, priors and choir monks and, after the establishment of the new orders of the twelfth century, to the lay brothers.

In the west, the life which was 'austere and secluded from other men' had largely been moulded by the Rule of St Benedict (*c*.535). Its balance between prayer, reading and manual labour under the guidance of an abbot who was not expected to enforce superhuman standards of asceticism, had provided the means by which men could form organised and largely self-sufficient communities adapted to many different environments, an essential prerequisite in the unsettled centuries following the decline of the Roman Empire. The durability of these Benedictine houses is shown by their survival and indeed expansion for, with the exception of a brief period under Charlemagne and Louis the Pious, both of whom showed great interest in the development of the monastic life, political conditions were seldom favourable and, often, as in the late ninth century when the Viking attacks were at their height, in some regions quite disastrous. Yet, throughout these centuries, they continued to attract recruits and landed endowments. By the late eleventh century there was a vast spread of houses varying from small hermitages to great communities like Cluny in Burgundy, which had as many as 300 monks, themselves forming the core of a much larger settlement of ancillary persons. Particularly noticeable were those groups of houses, like Cluny itself, founded *c*.910, and Gorze (in Lorraine), reformed *c*.933, which had been brought into being by the desire to free monasticism from the direct lay control which had become common during the early middle ages when political power was largely localised. Cluny had been immensely successful, influencing somewhere in the region of 1,500 other houses, and maintaining its independence through a system of vertical links not dissimilar to the lay feudal world from which it sought to extricate itself.

By the late eleventh century the monastic community itself, although covering almost the entire spectrum of the ages of man, was largely drawn from the propertied classes, a characteristic which, despite the reforming orders of the twelfth century which rested on a wider social base, could still be seen in the thirteenth century. Indeed, it seems that the offering of a gift was more important than the age, education or state of health of the entrant, although from the mid-twelfth century the papacy did lay down certain minimum conditions, while the climate of opinion created by reform led to greater care in the way that the donation was expressed in case it should be seen as simony. Life within the house often reflected the status of the entrants. Taking the evidence of diet as an index, it can be seen that apart from some attempts at the enforcement of more stringent rules in the aftermath of the eleventh-century reforms, there was a general tendency to relax or evade dietary regulations. Red meat, for instance, although forbidden by the Cluniac Rule, nevertheless was commonly part of the diet by the late twelfth century, while the overladen tables of houses like that of Christ Church, Canterbury, on feast days became quite notorious (Knowles 1934:275–88). The variety and quantity of food consumed itself contributed to social definition, as it did with their upper-class equivalents in secular life (B. Harvey 1993:34–6). Nor did the monks engage in much manual work as prescribed by the Rule of St Benedict; indeed, few of them came from a class of people accustomed to such activity. On the other hand, liturgical duties tended to grow to fill the time available, so that they became the major constituent of the monastic round.

Not everybody who lived in the monastery abandoned the secular world entirely on their own initiative, however. Entry while still a child to become an oblate was common. Indeed, Dom Jean Leclercq sees this fact as the reflection of a fundamental psychological difference between the black monks and the new orders of the twelfth century, in that most of the latter were recruited as adults who could bring to bear their own experiences of secular society, experiences largely missing from the lives of the 'monastic children' (Leclercq 1979:9–14). Suger of St Denis had been sent to the monastery by his parents, and Guibert, Abbot of Nogent in the early twelfth century, who wrote a kind of Augustinian 'Confessio' recounting his life and times, was vowed to the religious life while still a baby by his mother in gratitude for his survival following his premature birth. Most typical, perhaps, is Orderic Vitalis, brought up in the Severn Valley, but at the age of 10 sent to the monastery of St Evroult in Normandy where he spent the rest of his life. In a moving passage at the close of the eighth and last book of his *Ecclesiastical History*, written in 1141, when he was an elderly monk in his middle sixties, he recounts the circumstances. God, he says, inspired his father to vow him to the monastic life.

> So, weeping, he gave me, a weeping child, into the care of the monk Reginald, and sent me away into exile for love of thee and never saw me again. And I, a mere boy, did not presume to oppose my father's wishes, but obeyed him willingly in all things, for he promised me in thy name that if I became a monk I should taste the joys of Paradise with the Innocents after my death. So with this pact freely made between me and thee, for whom my father spoke, I abandoned my country and my kinsfolk, my friends and all with whom I was acquainted.... And so, a boy of ten, I crossed the English Channel and came into Normandy as an exile, unknown to all, knowing no one. Like Joseph in Egypt, I heard a language which I did not understand.

In fact, like Suger, Orderic adapted successfully. As he puts it, 'But thou [God] didst suffer me through thy grace to find nothing but kindness and friendship among strangers' (Chibnall 1978:6:551–7). When he was 16 he was ordained subdeacon, two years later deacon and, eventually, aged 33, priest, a pattern which shows that although the monastic orders were becoming increasingly clericalised, not all monks were necessarily priests.

The types of monasteries with which Orderic had become familiar remained important centres, but during the twelfth and thirteenth centuries a new climate began to offer more varied outlets for those seeking the religious life. From the early twelfth century new orders were being founded, notably the Cistercians and the Carthusians, which claimed to be more faithful to the Rule of St Benedict, adopting a life of greater isolation from the rest of society, governing their daily customs by more stringent rules of asceticism, and rejecting what they saw as the distraction of oblates. The development of 'orders' helped to create a type of monasticism which, at least externally, was more institutionalised than in the past, parallelling the aristocracy's emphasis on its own identity during this same period (Constable 1996:19–20). Even the new orders, in their turn, by the later twelfth and early thirteenth centuries, were suffering competition for recruits, first from the proliferation of smaller-scale charitable foundations, establishments like hospitals, leper-houses, or refuges for various classes of unfortunates, and second from the creation of the orders of friars, the Franciscans and Dominicans.

Mobility within these hierarchies of secular and regular clergy was not achieved easily, but men could and did rise within the Church. Suger is an outstanding example. Born into a family of minor knights he became abbot of the most influential community in Francia and was the key adviser to two kings, Louis VI and Louis VII (Grant 1998:75–7, 310–12). His rebuilding of the abbey-church was both lavish and innovatory and was destined to have a lasting influence upon European architecture. Maurice of Sully, Bishop of Paris between 1160 and 1196, provides a similar example among the secular clergy. Like Suger, he mobilised resources to pay for the huge building project of the cathedral of Notre-Dame, together with a whole complex of associated buildings, including a bishop's palace. His ambition does not seem to have been constrained by his modest background. In a less spectacular way there are hints of others achieving the same kind of rise. A document of Peterborough Abbey recording the manumission of a serf called William of Wythington in 1278 concludes with the phrase, 'Given at Peterborough for the love of a certain abbot, the lord Robert of good memory, our predecessor and uncle of the said William'. On a more modest scale, in 1297, since an unfree man could not become a priest, a later abbot of Peterborough manumitted William of Walecot, 'who derives his origin from our serfs', for this purpose, 'not wishing that he, for whose beauty of character there is praiseworthy testament, declare that he be impeded from his plan by reason of servitude' (Dugdale 1846:1:394, 395).

Naturally, this ecclesiastical order believed that it had the right and duty to direct and influence Christian society. Its courts had jurisdiction not only over clerics, but also over the laity, for they dealt with matters like wills and matrimonial cases and they upheld their claim to act in issues which they considered to be of a moral nature. Indeed, through the courts, through the refinement of canon law, and through the writings and preaching of its leading opinion makers the Church sought to mould social relations in ways which accorded with its view of Christian morality.

The most obvious and perennial problem was that of establishing durable peace and social order. This meant particular concern with the behaviour and values of the nobility which, in the eleventh and early twelfth centuries, was often subject to little superior control, for overlords lacked the military and administrative resources for the purpose, especially in the territories between the Rhine and the Mediterranean. The situation was exacerbated by feuds and vendettas, sometimes carried on for several generations, and by violence generated by a mobile noble 'youth', identified by Georges Duby as young adults not yet in possession of a patrimony who sought action and spoils whenever the opportunity presented itself (Duby 1968b). Orderic Vitalis makes frequent allusions to the evils which resulted from noble lawlessness, a condition which he saw as particularly likely to arise under a feeble or corrupt ruler, among whom he placed Robert, Duke of Normandy, eldest son of William the Conqueror (Chibnall 1973:4:147).

The Church responded by attempting to impose restrictions in which vulnerable social groups were placed under its protection and warfare was banned at certain times, such as feast days. Individual bishops held councils, in which such decrees were issued, reinforced by powerful visual symbolism. These efforts culminated in the attempt by Pope Urban II to divert warlike energies against an external enemy in the calling of the First Crusade in 1095. Under Popes Gregory VII and Urban was formed the concept of the *miles Christi*, 'the soldier of Christ', whose vocation was as valid as that of the monks and whose combat with material evil paralleled that of the religious in their fight with the invisible forces of the Devil. John of Salisbury's distinction between those who were selected and those who usurped the functional role of defender of Christian society grew out of these ideas. This image was useful to the nobility, providing a focus for the growing sense of aristocratic exclusivity which began to manifest itself during the twelfth century. During the 1130s and 1140s these attitudes began to centre upon the ceremony in which a man was dubbed a knight, dedicating his sword to the altar and making a profession of vows to the service of the Church. A further step was taken by the influential Cistercian abbot, Bernard of Clairvaux, who promoted an institutionalised form of religious knighthood by encouraging men to join the new military order of the Templars, whose members swore not only the usual monastic vows, but also to defend the land of Jerusalem from the infidel. Nevertheless, despite the importance of this cult to the noble self-image, there were still frequent laments that in practice aristocratic behaviour did not match up to these clerical standards. Research into the *chansons de geste*, for example, a genre of epic poetry which reflected so many of the aristocratic mores, has shown that the ethical ideas of the Church hardly impinged upon this literary form at all before about 1180 and the tales themselves show little interest in the way that the rest of society was affected by noble actions (Flori 1975; Noble 1973). Nor did the new literary genre of courtly love, which had originated in Provence in the late eleventh century and was by this time well established in certain court circles in northern Europe, have much effect on the realities of noble life. The essence of this fashion was the worship of a lady, both in word and deed, and the true knight was he who had the necessary virtues and accomplishments to please his lady, for whom he was ostensibly prepared to undergo any hardship. However, like religious chivalry, while it added an extra dimension to the ethos of knighthood, it did not impose much practical restriction upon noble activities.

Perhaps the most subtle critic of these double standards was the German poet, Gottfried of Strassburg. In *Tristan*, written in the early thirteenth century, Gottfried vividly portrays the courtly ideals (Hatto 1960). Although orphaned, Tristan is carefully brought up and, at the age of 7, is sent away to be educated, an education which encompassed literary, linguistic and musical skills and the physical attributes of 'the chivalric art', riding with the shield and lance. For recreation he fenced, wrestled, ran, jumped and threw the javelin, and no one could hunt or track as well as he, so that he 'excelled at all manner of courtly pastimes'. At 14 he was sent to travel to learn about

the land and its people 'so successfully that at this time no youth in the whole kingdom
led so noble a life as he'. Later, after many adventures, he arrived at the court of King
Mark and, when his true identity as the king's nephew is revealed, is made a knight in
a splendid investiture ceremony.

> And so the gay lord of Parmenie and all his following had gone to the minster,
> heard mass, and received the blessing that it was proper for them to receive.
> Mark took charge of Tristan and bound on his sword and spurs. 'Listen,
> nephew Tristan,' he said, 'now that your sword has been consecrated and you
> have become a knight, give thought to the glory of knighthood, and to yourself
> and who you are. Let your birth and nobility be ever present in your mind. Be
> modest and straightforward: be truthful and well-bred. Always be kind to the
> lowly: to the mighty always be proud. Cultivate your appearance. Honour and
> love all women. Be generous and loyal, and never tire of it. For I stake my
> honour that gold and sable never sat better on shield and spur than loyalty and
> generosity.'

Here then is the ideal knight, a paragon of virtue. But Gottfried has carefully
constructed this picture only to show that the reality cannot match the ideology and,
with the help of the device of the love potion, the façade begins to crumble. The court
is revealed as a hotbed of treachery and gossip, the king as a fool and a weakling,
Tristan's knightly exploits as subordinate to his infatuation and lust for Mark's future
wife, Isolde. Indeed, in the relationship between Tristan and Isolde the ethic of love for
a lady is transformed from a mannered courtly form into a pernicious world of double-
dealing and crime, necessary to cover up the sins of the lovers. Isolde's friend, Brangane,
is persuaded to substitute for Isolde on her wedding night with King Mark in order to
conceal the fact that Isolde is no longer a virgin. But, although King Mark is fooled, the
moral corruption now spreads like a stain.

> And now Isolde surveyed her whole situation. Since none but Brangane knew
> the secret of her subterfuge, she need have little fear for her honour in the
> future, once Brangane were gone. But now she lived in great fear and she
> dreaded keenly lest Brangane, perhaps loving Mark, might divulge her shameful
> deed to him and the whole story of what had taken place. In this the fearful
> Queen showed that people dread scandal and derision more than they fear the
> Lord.

Thus Isolde moves from cheating to attempted murder. However, perhaps
symptomatic of the whole dichotomy is Tristan's combat with the Irish champion,
Morold, revealed not as a chivalric and honourable contest but as a sordid and sickening
struggle, full of spurting blood and splintered bone, in which no mercy is shown by
either side. As Tristan stands over his helpless and mortally wounded opponent, he
sneers at him, 'You will need all the physic Isolde your sister ever read of, if you intend
to recover', and then, appropriating for himself the role of instrument of God, he
grasped his sword in both hands and struck off Morold's head (Hatto 1960:68–9, 110,
208, 133–6).

A more solid foundation for the noble class than this porous chivalric code was the
consolidation of family lines, both through the preservation of the integrity of lands

through primogeniture (aided by the entry of some younger sons into monasteries) and an increased emphasis on genealogies, many of which were being laid down and formalised or even invented. Such a family was the great German dynasty of the Welfs, who asserted their status through genealogies first written out in the mid-1120s, but made more explicit in the *Historia Welforum* of *c*.1170 in which their real eighth-century Frankish origins were embellished with the familiar motif of a Trojan past. Under Henry the Proud, Duke of Bavaria between 1126 and 1139, as well as ruler of Saxony in his later years, the family adopted the symbol of the lion on their coins and seals, an association made famous by his son, Henry, who, in 1166, erected an impressive cast sculpture of a lion in front of his new castle at Brunswick (K. Jordan 1986:1–2, 21, 114–15, 121, 156–9, 204). Interest in genealogies and family symbols soon began to spread down the noble hierarchy. The development of heraldry is a good reflection of this. Largely confined to the very greatest until *c*.1160, by the late twelfth century ordinary knights were using such devices (Ailes 1982:32–41). William of Tyre, criticising the actions of Hugh of Vermandois, the brother of the King of France, during the First Crusade, but writing at a period contemporary with these developments, draws a moral which, although decorated with classical allusion and in some senses drawing on traditional Germanic concepts of wergild too, very much reflects the trends of this time.

> While on this mission, however, he besmirched his fair name; for, after completing that affair, he did not carry back the answer to those who had sent him, nor did he trouble himself to return. His dereliction in this matter was all the more conspicuous because of his exalted rank; for, as our Juvenal says, 'Every fault of character has in itself more conspicuous guilt according as he who sins is esteemed the greater.'
>
> (Babcock and Krey 1941:1:298)

Such class distinction was reflected in the portrayal of the upper classes in sculpture and painting, where their refined physical appearance and opulent dress contrasts with a coarse and ugly peasantry (Heslop 1990) (see Plate 3).

In the twelfth and thirteenth centuries, therefore, religious and courtly ethics, tighter inheritance customs, genealogies and heraldry, and a conspicuous lifestyle, all played their part in transforming the relatively low status of the vassal of the Carolingian era into the defined and superior upper class of the high middle ages. But perhaps most important of all in the stabilisation of the aristocratic class was the patrimonialisation of the fief. In most regions men of military rank gave homage and fealty to their lord in the form of a mutual contract which usually meant allegiance and military service in exchange for material support, often in the form of a landed estate. However, as families consolidated their hereditary lines they came to see the fief as the holder's patrimony rather than simply a means of endowing an individual warrior, a development which, on certain conditions, most kings and magnates came to accept. Economic growth and the accompanying increase in monetary circulation made it convenient for both lord and vassal to commute military service for a cash payment at certain times, for the hosting seldom provided the lord with an effective army, while the vassals were increasingly interested in developing their landed property. Moreover, for rulers anxious to develop their financial resources, the regularisation of rights of relief, escheat and wardship, together with the usual feudal aids, became a guaranteed source of

Plate 3 Antipas ('Herod the tetrarch') (4 BC–AD 39), ruler of Galilee, was one of the sons of Herod the Great, King of the Jews. This capital from the Cathedral of Saint-Etienne, Toulouse (*c.*1120–40), tells the story of the beheading of John the Baptist at the behest of Salome, herself acting at the instigation of her mother, Herodias, whom John had denounced for her incestuous marriage to Herod (Matthew 14:1–12; Mark 6:14–29). The transformation of the courtly lifestyle in the twelfth century is reflected in the way these figures are portrayed. Herod is elegantly dressed as befits a ruler, his authority and maturity emphasised by his beard and long hair. Salome's wantonness is indicated not only by her body language and facial expression, but also by her unbraided hair.

revenue. During the twelfth century it became possible to grant fiefs in money as well as land, a trend particularly noticeable in the highly commercialised world of the crusader Kingdom of Jerusalem. Further advantages for rulers accrued, for greater incomes and more established procedures enabled them to impose a much higher degree of legal control over vassals who, in the eleventh century, had experienced relatively little judicial restraint. Recalcitrant vassals were now faced with the threat of effective military force, while rear-vassals could be brought into direct contact with their ultimate overlord by allowing them to appeal to his higher court.

These changes did not take identical form in every region. The *servientes regis* of Hungary and the *ministeriales* of Germany illustrate two of these variants. *Servientes* are first recorded in the reign of Béla III (1172–96). They performed military service for the king, but at the same time enjoyed the advantages of direct access to the royal courts as well as exemption from certain taxes. Increasingly assertive during the thirteenth century, they gained considerable privileges from Andrew II in the Golden Bull of 1222, and by the 1260s had evidently been absorbed into the nobility as a whole (Fügedi 1998:35–7). Although the Hungarian nobility included some who held lands conditionally (mostly on the frontiers), its situation differed from that of the French in that their charters are not imbued with 'the vocabulary of fief-holding'; nevertheless, they too absorbed the concepts of Christian knighthood and adopted names drawn from a common chivalric literature (Rady 2000:77, 128–9, 181–2). In Germany the most common type of knight was the *ministerialis* who, unlike his equivalents in France and England, retained unfree status. His situation, however, was 'not institutionally borrowed from serfdom', for his functions, status and lifestyle differed little from those of free vassals elsewhere. Although the origins of the position are unclear, it seems likely that German lords had, in the early middle ages, kept a closer control over their vassals than their contemporaries in France, leaving some of the Carolingian elements of vassal status intact. The growth in agrarian income and the expansion of German territory from the second half of the eleventh century then enabled lords to endow many more *ministeriales*, creating for themselves formidable retinues. The role was seen as neither menial nor degrading, for the advantages of the position were such that even free knights sometimes sought such service, while examples of manumission are relatively unusual. In theory, the relationship with lords was proprietorial, but in practice many of the customs and laws governing *ministeriales* have the appearance of a contract. *Ministeriales* held multiple allegiances, as well as allods, and often exercised great authority over many men, including high administrative office in imperial service. The case of the *ministeriales* emphasises the variety of knighthood.

> They made up one of the forms which differed from the northern French knightly paradigm: for Castile had a knighthood without fiefs, England a knighthood without allods, southern France a knighthood without service-obligations, Italy a knighthood which was urban, Outremer, Prussia and elsewhere a knighthood which was monastic, and Germany a knighthood which was unfree.
>
> (Arnold 1985:55)

It is clear then that, despite the evident flaws in the picture, by the thirteenth century the whole class regarded itself as an exclusive caste, governed by its own courts and legal codes, and asserting the right to be judged only by their peers. The *Liber Augustalis* of 1231, the compilation of laws put together by the Emperor Frederick II for the Kingdom of Sicily, shows clearly how rank and class were founded in law, for this was not simply a class society, but one of 'estates', that is legally defined groupings. For example, a townsman or rustic who struck a knight was punished by amputation of the hand, whereas if the reverse had been the case the knight was to lose the privileges of his class. 'For it is equitable to deprive him of knightly honour if, unmindful of shame and unaware of decency, he tries to dishonour knighthood, the foundation of his dignity' (Powell 1971:129–30). The costs of such a derogation could be severe, not only socially but also financially, for by the late thirteenth century there are signs that the nobility of some regions, notably France and Spain, regarded themselves as exempt from the direct personal taxation with which the rest of society was burdened in time of war. The origins of this development are not clear, but it seems likely that in countries where a regular system of taxation had been derived from servile payments like the French *taille* and *gabelle*, the exemption remained and hardened into a noble privilege.

The English nobility, however, although similarly affected by the code of behaviour which the class had developed, failed to secure the legal privileges of the continental aristocracy. Above the line which divided freeman from serf, all were equally entitled to access to the royal courts. Moreover, the administrative efficiency of the English kings which had created this situation, also led them to employ the knights of the shire (roughly equivalent to the *petite noblesse* on the continent) in an ever-widening range of local governmental duties, particularly the obligation to serve on juries providing information for judicial inquiries. As their military role waned, the knights found their time consumed by local government business, and to many, the obligations of knighthood in England seemed to outweigh the social advantages. In the thirteenth century therefore the number of knights in England began to diminish. From 1234 the monarchy made efforts to reverse this trend, at first by ordering all freemen holding knights' fees directly of the king to be knighted, and later by including all those who owned land of a certain monetary value in this order. In fact, this latter measure, known as 'distraint of knighthood', soon degenerated into a fiscal device, the crown profiting from selling exemptions. In these circumstances the noble class could not crystallise around the concept of a privileged knighthood as on the continent.

It was not, of course, possible to create an entirely closed society. The poorer nobility were sometimes forced to give up the struggle to maintain themselves in noble style, and the economically successful from other sectors of society replaced them. Seigneurial administrators, prosperous peasants, merchants and lawyers, married into the nobility or acquired a fief and slowly gained tacit (if not legal) acceptance. By the later thirteenth century rulers like the French monarch were bringing new blood into the noble class by means of the *lettre d'anoblissement*, which could be sold to those prepared to pay, or granted to royal servants as a reward to service. Such concessions could act as a considerable stimulus to social mobility, as the case of John of Taillefontaine, a clerk ennobled by Philip IV in 1295, demonstrates. He is described as having once carried 'the burden of servitude' from which he had been freed by Philip III. He now had 'the right to acquire noble fiefs... to assume for himself the belt of knighthood... [and to] enjoy in perpetuity the privileges and honour of nobility' (J.R. Bloch 1934:132).

Further fluidity resulted from the extinction of noble lines. Orderic Vitalis gives an account of the fate of a family in the eleventh century, the descendants of a minor noble, Giroie of Montreuil, one of the founders of St Evroult. Giroie had seven sons and four daughters, more than enough, it might be thought, to secure the succession. However, despite this plenty, only the second son survived long enough to continue the male line: two others died from accidents, one from wrestling, the other from a misdirected lance; two died from illness, one from leprosy, the other from insanity; another one was killed riding as a body-guard; and another, apparently, from eating a poisoned apple. 'So in different ways, all the sons of Giroie were carried away by death, and not one of them survived to old age' (Chibnall 1969:2:24–31). It is not surprising that some noble families were reluctant to allow younger sons to take major orders, even though they may have been clerks for many years, for fear that a series of dynastic mishaps like those of this house might necessitate their re-emergence into secular life. Orderic's example can be confirmed by more broadly based modern research. Benjamin Arnold found that of approximately seventy families of *ministeriales* enfeoffed by Bishop Gebhard of Eichstätt and his brother Count Hartwig of Grögling in the second quarter of the twelfth century, thirty had died out by *c.*1220 (Arnold 1985:180), while Edouard Perroy concluded from his researches into the noble lines of the region of Forez that they seldom lasted beyond six generations and often not beyond three in the direct line (Perroy 1962).

Aristocratic society remained one dominated by men. A noble woman entered matrimony because she had a dowry to offer and retained that state if she produced a male heir. Guibert of Nogent provides an account of his mother's life which, although emotionally coloured by his ambiguous attitude towards her, gives a good sense of the position of a woman from the minor aristocracy of northern France at the turn of the twelfth century. 'When hardly of marriageable age, she was given to my father, a mere youth, by the provision of my grandfather, since she was of the nobility, had a very pretty face, and was naturally and most becomingly of sober mien' (Benton 1970: 63–4). When Guibert's father died, she once again became a pawn on the feudal chessboard, about which she could do little except exercise an ability for passive resistance.

> When my father's kinsmen, eager for his fiefs and possessions, strove to take them all by excluding my mother, they fixed a day in court for advancing their claims. The day came and the barons were assembled to deliver justice. My mother withdrew into the church, away from the avaricious plotters, and was standing before the image of the crucified Lord, mindful of the prayers she owed.
>
> (Benton 1970:70–1)

Almost nothing is heard of unmarried noble women, although it is likely that more remained in noble households than the sources indicate. Those who did not might become nuns, which sometimes offered a career of some importance if a woman rose to be abbess, or of some satisfaction if she had a vocation. Even Guibert's strong-willed mother, who appears to have resisted all pressure to remarry for more than a decade, eventually entered a nunnery where she was safe from the designs of her late husband's kinsmen.

Neither the cult of courtly love, nor that of the Virgin Mary, which became an increasingly popular form of mass piety during the same period, made much practical difference. In so far as aristocratic women gained any degree of influence during the high middle ages the impact of economic change was far greater. The patrimonialisation of the fief, for instance, meant that there was less emphasis on its holder providing military service personally. Women therefore held, inherited, sold and alienated land, and pleaded in the law courts (although in this case their role was more restricted than men). Indeed, given the high death-rate among adult noble men, they were quite likely to inherit fiefs. In certain circumstances women did assume a directive role: husbands or sons were often away, at war, on crusade or pilgrimage. Most notable is the case of Blanche of Castile, mother of St Louis, and regent of France during his minority in the 1220s and early 1230s, and again while he was on crusade between 1248 and 1254. But, even when they became queens and independent rulers there remained a caveat, for both clerical and aristocratic opinion saw them as inherently weaker than men, not only physically but morally as well. Any achievements, therefore, were seen as being against the usual nature of things. Writing to Queen Melisende of Jerusalem on the death of her husband, Fulk, in 1143, Bernard of Clairvaux offered his advice on the conduct of her responsibilities in the following terms:

> The king, your husband, being dead, and the young king still unfit to discharge the affairs of a kingdom and fulfil the duty of a king, the eyes of all will be upon you, and on you alone the whole burden of the kingdom will rest. You must set your hand to great things and, although a woman, you must act as a man by doing all you have to do 'in a spirit prudent and strong'. You must arrange all things prudently and discreetly, so that all may judge you from your actions to be a king rather than a queen and so that the Gentiles may have no occasion for saying: Where is the king of Jerusalem? But you will say: Such things are beyond my power; they are great matters which far exceed my strength and my knowledge; they are the duties of a man and I am only a woman, weak in body, changeable of heart, not far-seeing in counsel nor accustomed to business. I know, my daughter, I know these are great matters, but I also know that although the raging of the sea is great, the Lord is great in heaven.
>
> (B.S. James 1998:346)

Most men, however, saw women much more in terms of Matthew Paris's description of Beatrice of Provence, whose real virtue was seen as her ability to produce high-class offspring. She was mother to the queens of France, England and Germany, and grandmother to the queens of Scotland and Navarre, by means of which 'she illuminated the extent of Christendom' (Luard 1880:5:654).

The social elites of the clergy and aristocracy could not exist in a vacuum, as John of Salisbury makes clear.

> Furthermore, the feet coincide with peasants perpetually bound to the soil, for whom it is all the more necessary that the head take precautions, in that they more often meet with accidents while they walk on the earth in bodily subservience; and those who erect, sustain and move forward the mass of the whole body are justly owed shelter and support. Remove from the fittest body the aid of the feet; it does not proceed under its own power, but either crawls shamefully, uselessly and offensively on its hands or else is moved with the assistance of brute animals.
>
> (Nederman 1990:67)

It was the great increase in productivity achieved by these 'feet' which sustained a whole new lifestyle and culture for the rest of society in the twelfth and thirteenth centuries and, for a significant proportion of them, brought about far-reaching changes in their own mode of existence as well.

Although in the late eleventh century small, independent proprietors still existed, most peasants were dependants, owing servile obligations stemming both from their personal bond to their lord and from the nature of their tenure. There was some economic differentiation between those who possessed a holding and perhaps a plough-team or a share in a plough-team, and the landless proletariat, who squatted on the waste or worked as servants for the other peasants, but apart from such differences, elaborate classifications among the peasantry had largely disappeared. Only the *maires* or reeves stood out, for these men performed administrative functions on behalf of the lord and, during this period, many of them benefited from the opportunities which this position gave to improve their social and economic status. While there was a variety of means of exploiting the land, ranging from the manor divided between the lord's demesne and the peasant holdings to a rent-paying tenantry working land on which the lord held no demesne at all, the village community was the social unit most fundamental to the peasantry. In these communities the parish church acted not only as a centre of worship, but also as a courtroom, a place of refuge and an assembly hall. Through village assemblies matters of general interest were discussed and agreements made which were essential for the operation of the communal system of cultivation. In some parts of Europe, notably in the French Alps and the Rhône valley, confraternities of a charitable and religious nature had existed for centuries, based upon the village community or upon groups of villages, and forming a social organism unrelated to the manor. The rhythm of life was the rhythm of cultivation. Communal restraints often hindered individual action which would alter this rhythm, although many peasants, with or without their lord's knowledge, did make 'assarts' or encroachments upon the waste and the woods, and these were cultivated as small enclosures. Peasants living in an area designated as forest land faced additional restraints. Forest land was preserved for hunting and in England, for instance, the monarchy maintained huge tracts in which the beasts of the chase were protected and assarts were forbidden. The mass of cases recorded in the English Forest Eyre Rolls provides abundant evidence of the tensions that such restraints created among rural communities.

A glimpse of peasant life can sometimes be obtained through the documents which record seigneurial exploitation, such as surveys of various kinds and manorial court records, but since these were intended primarily as economic instruments their value as evidence for social history is indirect and uneven. Manorial court records such as those which were enrolled by the steward for the Abbot of Ramsey in 1278 give some flavour of this world, although they are often frustrating in that the outcome of potentially interesting incidents cannot always be traced. The abbey held extensive lands in Huntingdonshire for which there was a half-yearly court; the rolls are mainly a financial record of fines extracted for minor offences. Evidence was gathered from jurors, who were sworn to establish the facts. In the manor of Hemingford, for instance, men and women were fined for, among other things, petty theft, failing to turn up for jury service, for breaking the assize of beer by illegal brewing, for failing to ensure that they were a member of a tithing (by which in theory unfree men were associated in groups of ten or twelve so that they would be mutually responsible for each other's behaviour), wrongful planting of willows on boundaries, ploughing up a road, and negligently allowing cattle to trample the peas of a local vicar. In a neighbouring manor, that of Elton, fines for the evasion of compulsory boon work on the abbey's land were common, and there were disputes as to whether or not certain individuals had tried to avoid their share of such work by feigning illness. Some, who although unfree, were nevertheless living and working outside the abbey's jurisdiction and were able to pay for this concession, while others tried to avoid payments which their servile condition obliged them to make. Other references to fines for beating up a man, for children born out of wedlock, and for rape and attempted rape, show that the life of the villages was not exclusively concerned with disputes over labour services or land boundaries (Maitland 1889:88–95).

Just occasionally these rolls take the reader a little deeper into the lives of the peasants as the following self-explanatory entry for Elton shows.

> Michael Reeve complains of Richer Jocelin's son and Richard Reeve and his wife for that when he was in the churchyard of Elton on the Sunday next before the feast of All Saints in this year, there came the said Richer, Richard and Richard's wife and insulted him before the whole parish with vile words charging him with collecting his own hay by means of the labour services due to the Abbot, and with reaping his own crop in autumn by means of boon-works done by the Abbot's customers (*de custumariis Abbatis*), and with ploughing his own land in Eversholmfield by means of ploughs 'booned' from the vill, and with releasing the customers from their labours and carrying services on condition of their letting and handing over their land to him at a cheap rate, and of taking gifts from the richer tenants as a consideration for not turning them into tenants at money rents and with obliging the poorer tenants to become payers of money rent. And the said Richard and Richer are present and defend etc., and crave that [the truth] be inquired by [the?] twelve jurors. Who come and say that of none of the charges is he [Michael] guilty. Therefore let the said Richard and Richer make satisfaction to the said Michael, and be in mercy for trespass.
>
> (Maitland 1889:95)

The Ramsey court rolls reflect the life of sedentary communities in lowland England, but the rhythm of life was not the same for all the peasants of western Christendom. In mountainous or hilly regions, like the Pyrenees, mobility might be much greater, especially among the shepherds who moved every season seeking pasture for their flocks. When James Fournier, Bishop of Pamiers, made a series of inquiries into these Pyrenean communities between 1318 and 1324, he was seeking evidence of heretical belief, but the depositions which resulted are the nearest that the peasants of this era ever came to speaking for themselves (Le Roy Ladurie 1978). Some sense of the picture evoked can be gained by taking one of these witnesses, a shepherd, John Maury, born in Montaillou, where his family had a house and sheep (Duvernoy 1965:2:469–519). In 1324 he recalled his life over the previous two decades, at first in the village, where at the age of 12 he was looking after his father's flocks, out in all weathers and up before dawn. When he was old enough he took to a much more mobile existence, seldom spending long in any one place, but crossing and recrossing the mountains with his flocks, sometimes lodging in houses or inns, sometimes staying in his brother's cabin in the mountains, sometimes hiring himself out to an employer. Often his wanderings took him far into Aragon, where he was told at one village, that of Casteldans, near Lérida, to move on unless he could find a wife there, since his sheep would 'consume all the pasture of that place'. This seems to have set him thinking of marriage, but he failed to find anyone suitable at Casteldans. Soon afterwards, however, having taken a lodging at Juncosa, he arranged a marriage with a girl called Mathena, the daughter of the house, who was from the same region as he, since she had 'pleased him'. He knew nothing else about her and was apparently shocked when he learned of her interest in the Cathar heresy and nearly put her aside after his betrothal. Throughout this time John met many other shepherds with whom he sometimes joined up, including his brother, Peter, and friends from Montaillou, but the partnerships were impermanent and often he would not see Peter for weeks or months, having no idea where he had gone. At the same time he met heretics, whom he heard preach and with whom he had discussions, often ranging widely over issues of the faith and the nature of the world, even though he himself was never a committed 'believer' in Catharism, nor apparently had received any formal education. Like the Ramsey peasants, he did not always live in harmony with his neighbours, on one occasion being involved in a brawl so serious he was obliged to remove himself from Montaillou for fear of retaliation, an option perhaps not so readily available in Huntingdonshire. Although the lives of the Ramsey peasants are probably more typical, the Fournier depositions are an important reminder of the variety of peasant life within the differing topography and climates of the west.

For many, the manor, the village and the family continued to fill the social horizon throughout the period, but equally many others began to feel the effects of the slow disintegration of the traditional bonds of agrarian society under the impact of economic and demographic change. Lords began to employ their powers of jurisdiction as a means of monetary income. A growing population meant rising seigneurial revenues from monopolies like the watermill or the winepress and increased customary dues and profits from justice. Tithes, usurped by many lords during the ninth and tenth centuries, and tallage, previously only imposed sporadically, were gradually converted into regular cash payments. On the other hand, a larger population also often meant that the lord was over-provided with labour which, being forced, was generally only grudgingly and inefficiently provided. As a result, in the twelfth century, the commutation of *corvées* for a cash payment became common and, in their place, hired labour was used as and when it was needed. Instead of heavy labour services, serfs now provided their lord with the series of payments – *formariage*, *mainmorte* and *chevage* – which marked their servile status. These developments encouraged a further step. During the late twelfth century and thirteenth century, it became common for serfs, either individually or in groups, to buy their freedom for a lump sum, changing their status to that of rent-paying tenants (M. Bloch 1964). Increased profit could be made here too, not only from payment for manumission, but also from rents and entry fines.

These trends were closely related to the intensity of regional economic development, for the greatest stimulus was received by those estates within the proximity of an expanding and prosperous town. In northern Italy, the old manors were breaking up, and leases replaced peasant services. Often the landlord was not a noble living on his estates, but a merchant whose milieu was urban rather than rural. In contrast, in the less urbanised south of Italy, the great *latifundia* endured and the mass of peasantry remained serfs. In the Low Countries the same pattern can be discerned. In Flanders, where commercial and industrial centres had grown up only a short time after those of northern Italy, peasants were being enfranchised in the twelfth century, while in Namur and Luxembourg, the areas of the Low Countries least affected by economic growth in this period, many peasants remained serfs until the fourteenth and fifteenth centuries (Lyon 1963).

The effect on the peasantry was to separate personal from tenurial obligation for, with the decline of labour services and the conversion of jurisdictional rights into monetary profits, the lord had less and less interest in preserving the old seigneurial structure. Some free peasants began to acquire holdings which carried with them servile obligations, while serfs were sometimes settled on lands for which their tenure demanded only rent, even though they owed services because of their personal status. Similarly, some peasants, through either selling produce to nearby towns or exploiting authority delegated to them by their lord, acquired several holdings and prospered, while others, living on holdings fragmented by excessive population and burdened with heavy monetary payments, began to find survival increasingly difficult. Some became indebted because they had borrowed to buy their freedom or to pay their dues. By the second half of the thirteenth century many found that they were left with only their labour to sell during a period when, because of rising food prices and abundant labour, real wages were falling. Economic distress drove many to the towns in an effort to find employment, where they joined the growing pool of unskilled labour which the towns attracted, but for which they could not always provide. These economic circumstances therefore produced a form of rural poverty in a sense that it had not been previously understood for, in the past, 'poor' meant those, like monks and hermits, who had adopted poverty as a vocation (Duby 1966:25–32). The commercial world of the high middle ages, however, created a distinct rural proletariat, whose presence, as in the rising of the Pastoureaux in northern France in 1251, could sometimes spark off latent tensions.

Not all estate owners reacted to the economic situation in the same way. Local variations such as the market price of corn, wage rates, the supply of labour and the supply of and demand for food all helped to determine attitudes. In addition, the administrative and political costs of enforcing labour services had to be taken into account. On some of the larger ecclesiastical estates of south and east England, for instance, which were the areas most sensitive to economic growth, the peasantry were faced with something of a 'seigneurial reaction' in the thirteenth century. At this time many of these ecclesiastical lords began to retrieve their lands from the 'farmers' who had been left in charge of their estates, and take them back into direct cultivation. These lords then made every effort to exploit the labour services owed to them, primarily in order to make the maximum profit from the sale of cereals. The fullest exploitation of services may well have seemed to them the most effective way of benefiting from the economic situation. Moreover, on ecclesiastical estates in general the need for labour remained higher than on their lay counterparts, for the monks required a considerable demesne for their own sustenance. The papal injunction that ecclesiastical estates should be protected in their physical integrity, rather literally interpreted, served to reinforce this attitude, for it led some ecclesiastical lords to consider the best method of profiting from the economic situation without breaking this prohibition. English legal development also favoured this method. The Normans and the Angevins had succeeded in extending and defining the common law to a far greater extent than either the Capetians or the Staufen. All free men were allowed access to the royal courts, a situation which inevitably stimulated legal theorists to attempt a definition of the unfree. In theory, men whom the lawyers identified as servile were unable to plead in the royal courts in matters relating to their tenure. However, the effects of this regional variation should not be exaggerated. It is evident that even on large ecclesiastical estates peasants were being manumitted during this period, a fact which demonstrates the strength of this trend. It does seem though that the movement towards emancipation may have been less rapid and more uneven than that on the continent.

The social group most evidently affected by the economic and demographic changes of the period, however, was the townsmen. For the ecclesiastical social theorist of the eleventh century they had no proper place in the functional hierarchy, while a conservative cleric like Guibert of Nogent in the early twelfth century could see in the aspirations of the urban classes only an attempt by serfs to break out of their customary obligations and bonds. Nevertheless, sophisticated observers like John of Salisbury recognised very well that a simple threefold functional division was a quite inadequate way of defining society in the twelfth century. 'And there are so many of these occupations that the number of feet in the republic surpasses not only the eight-footed crab, but even the centipede; one cannot enumerate them on account of their large quantity' (Nederman 1990:126). By the mid-thirteenth century synodal statutes, aimed at regulating the spiritual life of the province, the administration of the dioceses and parishes and the conduct of the clergy, reflect this variety very clearly. The statutes of Guiard of Laon, Bishop of Cambrai between 1238 and 1248, set down a list of activities regarded as proper and improper for clerics which, incidentally, also suggest a moral hierarchy of secular occupations in the episcopal mind. The clergy were allowed to engage in the following occupations: gardener, tree-cutter, feeder of cattle, farmer, painter, scribe, repairer and seller of books, preparer of parchments and inks, apothecary, fisherman, cabinet-maker, joiner, blacksmith, lime-burner, stonemason, goldsmith, barber, phlebotomist and cutter of woollen garments. They were prohibited from exercising 'shameful and dishonest business and offices', which meant money-changer, shopkeeper, butcher, broker, and advocate in the secular courts. If 'they should seek to be businessmen and are involved with usury, they should know themselves to be under interdict'. Moreover, it was 'not seemly' for them to be fullers, shoemakers, weavers, actors, jugglers, secular *baillis*, goliards, toll-gatherers, suppliers of ointment, tripe-sellers and rope-makers (Avril 1995:51–2).

It was in the towns that the greatest variety of these occupations was to be found. During the twelfth and thirteenth centuries most existing cities and towns experienced large increases in population, while many smaller settlements expanded into sizeable communities. In some cases completely new towns were created. Commercial and industrial enterprise was the most powerful driving force, most evidently in Tuscany and Lombardy where the maritime cities of Venice, Genoa and Pisa stimulated inland centres like Milan, Florence and Siena, and in north-west Europe, where in towns like Tournai, Lille, Ypres, Bruges and Ghent, local cloth manufacture developed into an international trade. The Mediterranean cities of Aragon and Provence benefited from the same conditions which had encouraged Italian development; Barcelona and Marseille grew on the profits of sea-borne trade. The inland towns of the Midi never grew to the size of their Italian counterparts, but centres like Toulouse, Carcassonne, Montpellier, Narbonne and Nîmes prospered through the woollen textile industry and the wine trade. At the other end of the commercial chain in the Levant Italian, Provençal and Spanish mercantile colonies grafted themselves onto the populous cities of the coast in the Crusader States, while a distinct class of non-noble Franks, governed in the thirteenth century by its own law code, established itself in local trade and manufacture. Lesser cities and towns serviced the urban giants: the fair towns of Champagne, the banking specialists of Piedmont, Savoy, Franche-Comté and Burgundy. Settlements also developed around the chief European mining centres, in Saxony, the Tyrol, Bohemia and Sweden. Completely new towns were created along the expanding frontiers of Europe. In eastern Germany and Poland, many towns were founded in the basins of the Oder and the Vistula, frequently on the model of the most famous foundation, that of Lübeck on the Baltic coast. Often, initially, these towns were used as military outposts, but as they became more secure, settlers were attracted from the west and commercial colonies were encouraged. In Castile and León, the Moorish enemy proved less tractable than the Baltic Slavs, and the character of the towns of the region was more exclusively military. As a consequence some, like Mérida, declined as rapidly as they had grown when the frontier moved south, while others, like Madrid, more favourably placed, expanded into major cities. In the same way, new towns were 'planted' within the old frontiers of western Europe, often by lords hopeful of extra profit from economic expansion.

This commercial revival was socially significant in that it produced a new class of urban dwellers whose wealth and power was based primarily on trade, industry and banking, rather than on land and military force. In origin, many of these men were landed proprietors, sometimes of aristocratic background, and almost always legally free. Few of the migrants to the growing towns were fugitive serfs. In Italy many of the new town dwellers came from the *castelli* or fortified villages of the region, where they had been free proprietors of some standing. In this region too, a high proportion of rural lords invested at least a portion of their landed profits in trade and, in the course of time, many took up residence in the towns, even though for some the basis of their power remained in the countryside. In Flanders and in Germany the aristocratic element was less in evidence, but here a proportion of the inhabitants derived from a third group, that of the ministerial class.

The needs of these new commercial classes did not fit neatly into the existing framework, and in some regions, as the inhabitants of the embryonic towns began to feel their economic strength, social and political conflict was the consequence. The early history of urban life in medieval Europe is marked by the formation of merchant groups concerned to gain for themselves certain basic privileges which would give them the opportunity to develop their trading activities beyond a rudimentary stage. They achieved a high degree of independence in Italy and Flanders. In Italy, political control of the towns had originally been delegated to local bishops who acted as the emperor's representatives. In most towns economic self-interest and political ambition gave the merchants and the aristocracy a social coherence lacking in other parts of Europe and they were able to eject the bishops, although sometimes only after a fierce struggle. The governments then created in the successful towns reflected the economic aims of the mercantile element, unfettered by restrictions from above. In the frontier towns of Christendom the burgher class also carved out for itself a favourable position. East of the Elbe the episcopal authorities were still struggling to establish themselves rather than representing a vested interest, while the lords colonising the region were anxious to encourage trade. The towns of Castile and León, if they proved to be of more than temporary importance, received extensive rights from the monarchy. Many were allowed a municipal council with considerable freedom of action in the hope that they would act as centres of defence, drawing on the urban militia. Indeed, Spain produced a unique social group, that of the *caballeros villanos*, who had contributed to the fighting in the same way as the knights (MacKay 1977:3–4, 37–9, 50).

In other regions the new classes were less successful. They aimed to secure for themselves chartered privileges, the chief theme of which was the assurance that the burgesses would be free of the usual apparatus of seigneurial jurisdiction and dues. The charter established the town as an entity, legally, if not always physically, separate from the countryside. In northern France, the most common form of mercantile alliance was the commune, which claimed to enter into a free agreement with the lord, making its loyalty dependent on the lord's acknowledgement both of the validity of the communal oath and the liberties that were being claimed. In some cases, like that of Laon, these aspirations provoked violent conflict. However, the communal movement was fairly localised, being largely confined to northern France and Italy, and many charters show no evidence that they were gained by the action of a commune. It seems unlikely that, in practice, there was any striking difference, for instance, between the communes and the *villes libres* which are often mentioned at this time, except perhaps that the communes are more usual in northern France, while the *villes libres* are typically found in the south. In both cases it is probable that some form of association had existed among the merchants of the town and that they had gained a privileged position *de facto* some time before the grant of a charter. Indeed, some large towns of obvious economic importance did not receive a charter at all, although it is evident that their merchants enjoyed privileges similar to those enshrined in written form elsewhere.

However, although the conditions for the development of trade had been created within the Frankish lands, the social pre-eminence and political freedom of the burgesses could not compare with their Italian contemporaries. The monarch or the lord still retained a degree of control over the town, and in many cases, military obligations and feudal aids were owed. The charter of the town of Dreux, on the border of Normandy, for instance, granted to the burgesses in 1180 by Count Robert, brother of King Louis VII, binds the town tightly to his lordship. The count grants a commune and swears not to take the servile payments of *tolte* or *taille* or to force the burgesses to use the former seigneurial monopoly of the mills. The lord's ban of wine is restricted to certain periods of the year. Otherwise the burgesses are dependent upon the count's overlordship: they swear fealty to him, to defend his castle against all, to prepare three carts for his military expeditions, and to submit to the seigneurial monopoly of the winepresses (Duchesne 1631:237–8). In fact, in the Capetian lands, high justice was seldom granted and there was almost always a royal *prévôt* attentive to the affairs of the town, while in those parts of France controlled by the Angevins, royal grants were closer to a definition of obligations than a charter of emancipation. In some towns the local seigneur retained a considerable interest. In Senlis, for instance, there were *hommes de corps*, who had to pay *cens* (annual rent) and perform labour services, as well as a privileged bourgeoisie. Many English towns possessed charters granting them burgess tenure and the status of a borough, but the royal or seigneurial castle remained to overlook them, and indeed, any sign of social disruption soon led to the intervention of the castellan. The wealthy merchants of London alone could expect their social superiority and economic strength to weigh very heavily with the English monarch.

Only in Lombardy and Tuscany, and to a lesser extent in Flanders, can the great majority of this new bourgeoisie be seen as more than a middling element within the structure of society as a whole, but all over Europe, within their own towns, there emerged groups of people, wealthy on the profits of mercantile and industrial enterprise who, from an early date, gained a degree of social dominance and political control which reflected their economic success. Often these were the descendants of people whose early enterprise had led them to form alliances to gain for themselves the basic privileges necessary for trading and, as time went on, they became even more clearly differentiated from the mass of the urban population, the small-scale retail traders, the craftworkers and the labourers, which the towns attracted. The result was the development of this ruling group into an oligarchy which concentrated mercantile wealth and political power in its own hands, manipulating the crafts by means of guild regulations and the surrounding countryside by means of market controls. Government was usually through a council, which had often developed from the judicial body which had emerged when the town gained its basic privileges. In these councils the ancient offices of *consul* and *échevin*, which dated from the Roman and Merovingian periods respectively, took on new meaning. Election to the consulate or the *échevinage* was confined to the limited group of families whose economic power ensured for them a share in the government of the town. For more than two centuries a small number of families in each town dominated urban life, reaching the height of their power between the later twelfth century and the middle of the thirteenth century, when the first signs of deep-seated social unrest began to shake their position.

At no time therefore can the towns be seen as centres of freedom and equality. Town charters record the privileges of people of property, not of the mass of the urban population, for burgess rights were generally available only to those who possessed a house and a certain minimum amount of movable property. This distinction between the 'emancipated' property-holders and the remainder of the urban population was reflected in the urban guild structure. In most towns the burgess class belonged to the guild merchant which had often originated in the early merchant associations. This guild merchant emphasised the superiority of the ruling class. In Flanders, for instance, an entrance fee of one gold mark excluded all but the very rich. These guilds regulated the trading conditions within the town, often creating monopolies for their members which gave them marked economic advantages over outsiders. However, their role as religious or benevolent associations, whose regular meetings provided an excuse for a convivial assembly, was as important as their economic activity. Guild members entertained visiting dignitaries or celebrated feast days at increasingly elaborate banquets, which although costly, nevertheless served to underline the exclusive nature of their membership.

The chief concerns of this urban elite lay in trade, industry and banking, and the leading exponents of these skills were to be found in the cities of Tuscany and Lombardy. In the eleventh and twelfth centuries they had been first and foremost travellers, but by the later thirteenth century the characteristic figure had become the sedentary businessman who, making use of the increasingly sophisticated business techniques pioneered in Italy, conducted his business by correspondence with his agents residing at the company's branches in foreign cities. An index of this change was the use of insurance, previously largely unnecessary, but in regular use in Italy from the early fourteenth century onwards. Despite the development of the guild system, the vast majority of these enterprises were based upon the family under its patriarchal head. Often important families dominated their own 'quarter' in the town, their *casa*, in which their properties were grouped together and where their employees, servants and sometimes their slaves, all lived, making up the 'family' in its widest sense. Here too merchandise was stored and accounts and records kept. Urban schools, teaching skills like writing, calculation, geography and vernacular languages, were far more common in Italian towns than elsewhere and provided a foundation for sons who would, one day, take over the family business. A common pattern was that, as they approached adulthood, many of them gained practical experience in the foreign branches of the company and then, after some years abroad, returned to their native city where they entered into an active political role.

It should not, however, be assumed that the lifestyle of these ruling classes was unaffected by more traditional social forces. The Tuscan towns were centres of Franciscan and Marian devotion, while in Lombardy religious debate was traditionally vigorous, producing religious activists ranging from mild reformers through the whole variety of heretical sects. Most of all, the piety of the urban classes was shown by the thirteenth-century fashion for endowing small-scale charitable institutions of direct value to the town, such as hospitals and leper houses. Mercantile account books show funds set aside for pious institutions and wills demonstrate deep concern that the mercantile profession should not be the gateway to eternal damnation. Like most men, the merchant could not bring himself to consider the afterlife in all his dealings, but he was not blind to the dangers that he ran in the pursuit of monetary gain. Chivalric ideas too remained a potent force, for a strong consciousness of aristocratic mores remained; indeed, John Larner has suggested that such values were themselves an integral part of the commercial daring which made the Italian cities the economic pacemakers of western Christendom (Larner 1980:95–102).

In Italy this plutocracy dominated social life and held wide political power within the city-state, but for many members of the upper bourgeoisie in other parts of Europe, the attainment of the urban consulate was not the only object of their social ambition. In many cases the founder of the family had been of rural background and modest means. His migration into the town had presented him with the opportunity to make a moderate fortune, perhaps from shopkeeping or local trade, and provided the basis upon which his sons and grandsons might be able to build a position of international commercial importance. As a family with a share in international trade it became vitally necessary to protect their interests by taking an active role in the government of the town, for passivity might mean financial ruin as a consequence of the frequently oppressive taxation policies of the ruling oligarchy. With a place as a member of the oligarchy, urban property in the form of shops, houses, warehouses and considerable liquid capital, the next important step was to renew or enlarge links with the countryside by the acquisition of rural property. Prestige and security were inseparable from landed wealth, while the land could be used as security for loans, and it was an insurance against financial disaster or early death which could otherwise leave the merchant's family without means of support.

With these achievements behind them, many then strove to gain entrance to the nobility. Some achieved their aim by marriage, while in other cases, princely generosity in return for the rendering of financial services was a means of acquiring a coveted title. Employment as a royal or princely officer had its attractions too, for as their administrations became more sophisticated, rulers found it of value to develop an administrative nobility, a *noblesse de robe*. A small number of the upper bourgeoisie even managed to receive the final accolade and rise into the prestigious military aristocracy. With the acquisition of nobility the new man of rank often found trade to be an embarrassment, and instead began to turn his attention to the princely courts, seeking favours in the form of pensions and offices. He was no longer an aggressive and enterprising merchant, but now aspired to become a polished courtier whose life and culture were orientated towards aristocratic society.

Most towns were therefore dominated by a small oligarchy of the wealthy and the prestigious, but in areas of strong monarchical control, like northern France, power was often shared with royal officials whose number and influence varied but who, in general terms, were gaining ground as the sophistication of royal administration developed in the thirteenth century. Indeed, towns were not simply enclosures within feudal society, for most of the operations essential to the working of government were to be found there. Sheriffs and viscounts lived in them and mints were always placed in towns. If the town had developed into a capital city like Paris or a great international centre like Rome, the array of officials and support staff might be huge. All towns therefore had a certain number of professional men, lawyers, notaries, doctors, many of whom sought service at the royal and princely courts, while the great university towns, such as Paris or Bologna, housed considerable numbers of students and their teachers, many of whom also operated with an eye to a place should it become available.

The world of the urban upper classes was clearly differentiated from that of the small-scale merchants, who sold their goods retail from a stall or shop, and from that of the craftworkers or artisans, whose horizons were filled by the small workshop and the operation of the master and apprenticeship system. The artisans worked for a restricted market, the conduct of which was closely governed by the detailed regulations of the guilds or corporations. In places, they belonged to a guild of their own, but its officers were nominated by the patricians and its activities closely circumscribed. The degree of independence maintained by the artisans varied widely throughout Europe, but, for all, the guild regulations were legal obligations which decisively affected their lives. Conditions of sale and set standards of production were enforced, and so too were the standards of entry into the craft, the terms of apprenticeship, the hours and wages of journeymen, and the number of employees allowed to each master. Generally apprentices were provided with their training on a domestic basis in the house of their master and after a suitable period could expect to attain the position of master themselves. At least in its early phases the apprenticeship system ensured that the craftworkers received a proper training and that dishonesty was kept to a minimum, but increasingly in the later middle ages the guild regulations were abused, for the number of masters was restricted and apprentices were exploited as cheap labour. In most cases the guild regulations did ensure a degree of security and a minimum return for the small producer, but their overall effect was to stifle initiative and accentuate the contrasts between the ruling urban class and the craftworkers. In the last resort the corporative regulations were operated by the oligarchy and were therefore no barrier to their enterprise, but to the artisans they were the means by which their freedom of action was controlled.

The life of the skilled craftsman, confined and narrow as it appears, was tolerably secure in comparison with that of the mass of workers. In Italy and Flanders especially, the textile industry was organised on a capitalist basis and engendered a large urban proletariat. The chief employers held over their workers an economic control as close as any servitude sanctioned by law. In Florence, the Seven Greater Guilds of the city had their own courts and law-enforcement agents. They adjusted rates of pay and hours of work to suit the employers; they regulated the flow of immigrant labour into the city to meet their needs. Associations and assemblies were forbidden, and to strike was, to the employers, a violation of both the human and divine order. Workers who disobeyed these laws were punished by fines, corporal means or blacklisting, and in the case of those who fomented strikes, by hanging. Some worked in their own homes, which seldom consisted of anything beyond a single room in an alley tenement, while others were grouped together in a primitive factory organisation, especially in the fulling and dyeing branches of the industry. This urban proletariat formed a large unprivileged sector of the town, living in poverty and misery, often reduced to begging when thrown out of work by the economic fluctuations to which international trade is prone.

The development of large urban agglomerations therefore not only created a new ruling class, but also produced, in far larger numbers, a new urban poor. This underclass does not have a voice of its own, but on this subject the contributions of the charitable institutions set up to aid the poor are revealing, not so much for information on their avowed function, but rather for the clauses showing groups which were excluded. The late-twelfth-century statutes of the hospital at Angers, for instance, tell the brothers and sisters that they must send out into the city, twice a week, to seek the sick, and that they must not turn away poor pregnant women. However, they must not receive lepers, violent persons, cripples, bereaved persons, thieves newly mutilated or branded, or children left exposed. The statutes of the hospital at Troyes, dated 1263, are more explicit: foundling children are not to be taken in 'because if they were received, there would flow such a large number of boys that the goods of the house would not be sufficient; and because it does not appertain to us, but to the parish churches' (Le Grand 1901:25, 115). Indeed, in the cites and towns at least, charitable agencies could not cope with the social problems created by rapid growth. Particularly vulnerable were single women, dependent upon their own, usually poorly rewarded labour; if they became ill, there was seldom any sustained instititutional support. In Paris, which was the largest city in western Christendom by the end of the thirteenth century, Sharon Farmer estimates that about half the population 'hovered somewhere in the vicinity of poverty'. For some, crises could be mitigated with the help of friends and relatives or by begging, but not everybody was able to find relief in this way (Farmer 1998). Monastic charity could sometimes help, but it was often uneven: hand-outs of food, for instance, were closely tied to the dietary patterns of local Benedictine houses, which could not be relied upon to relate to actual needs at any given time, nor to keep pace with the growing numbers of poor (B. Harvey 1993:9–16). As Ludo Milis has pointed out, such houses had no interest in or perhaps even understanding of what he calls the 'the structural relief of poverty', for the primary aim of their members was the achievement of salvation (Milis 1992:54–61). Close by the great Gothic cathedrals there lived some of the most wretched in society, their existence as much a consequence of the profound social and economic changes of the period as were the cathedrals themselves.

Urban growth similarly encouraged the spread of prostitution. Although prostitution was not confined to towns – armies, fairs, trade routes and passenger ships were among many other places where it was common – the urban environment nevertheless provided both sufficient numbers of clients and the rapid monetary circulation needed for a viable living to be made. Research on this subject is limited, but Leah Otis's study of Languedocian towns suggests that no specific provision was made for prostitutes until the late thirteenth century, when the first signs of municipal regulation can be seen, usually involving designated districts where prostitutes could live under a certain degree of legal protection. Before this time the authorities had generally acted only in response to public protest, expelling from the town prostitutes, who, it had been claimed, were a nuisance. The municipal authorities seem therefore to have regarded the matter as one of public order, their approach perhaps reinforced by contemporary theological opinion which defined prostitution as a necessary evil and thus better for being regulated. The problem was not negligible: there appears to have been at least one prostitute for every thousand inhabitants in most medieval towns (Otis 1985:1–39, 100, 210–11; Rossiaud 1988:72–85).

The degree of social stability achieved in the towns in the first half of the thirteenth century did not endure. After this time many regimes seem ill-at-ease, pumping out propaganda emphasising their commitment to the 'common good'. But their actions often belied their words and increasingly the oligarchies faced not only opposition from groups within the town seeking to break their monopoly of power, but also deep rifts within their own ranks, producing inter-family rivalry and the rise of dissidents among the ruling classes who exploited urban grievances in an effort to seize power for themselves. Trouble occurred in Arras as early as 1253 and in Siena in 1257. The pent-up discontent of the Flemish craftworkers exploded in 1280 when revolt spread rapidly through Bruges, Ypres, Douai and Tournai. The most frequent bone of contention was the distribution of taxation. The town governments levied taxes on basic products like grain or wine, a method which affected everyone according to their needs and not their fortune, or they favoured the *capage*, which was an equal contribution per head. Agitation against this reached a high pitch of intensity in the fourteenth century, particularly when collection coincided with a bad harvest or the spread of disease. The Flemish revolt which culminated in the battle of Courtrai in 1302 had originally been provoked by heavy royal taxation, a disproportionate amount of which had been passed on to the mass of the town population. The object of these rebellions, however, was not to overturn the order of society, but rather to gain a share of power. Often, for instance, when the craft guilds succeeded in gaining power, their rule was as exclusive and self-interested as that of the preceding regime.

Life in the towns of the high middle ages was therefore often quite divorced from clerical social models. One group however – the Jews – had never been part of any such model, for to be a member of the body politic, adherence to one faith only was permissible, that of Catholic Christianity. By the eleventh century, nevertheless, Jewish communities could be found all over Christendom, having spread throughout the Mediterranean during the Roman period and, to a lesser extent, into the relatively tolerant barbarian kingdoms in the centuries that followed. During the twelfth and thirteenth centuries their social position become increasingly distinct as a result both of ecclesiastical legislation and the financial needs of secular rulers.

The Church began with the fundamental tenet that the Jews should be preserved and protected, for their presence and contemporary condition served as testament to the Christian belief that God had rejected them as a chosen people in favour of the Christians, who now saw themselves as the new Israelites. At the same time their existence might encourage contact with Christian society or even the spread of Judaism, so that a concomitant of this attitude was that, as far as possible, Christian and Jew should remain quite separate. This was reflected in the work of the canon lawyers, in particular that of the monk, Gratian, whose *Decretum* appeared in *c.*1140, and, in the thirteenth century, in the great collections of decretals or papal decisions issued in consistory, which Gregory IX and Innocent IV ordered to be gathered together and systematically set out. The practical effects of this intellectual effort appeared most evidently in the decrees issued by the great Church Councils, especially the assemblies held at the Lateran in 1179 and 1215. The Jews should be allowed to follow their own religion and no attempt should be made to convert them forcibly. But they should not be allowed to hold positions which gave them authority over any Christian, even over a slave, nor should Jews and Christians marry or even share the same table. In 1215 the council ordered that Jews should wear distinctive clothing and that they should restrict what were regarded as their usurious activities, although the impracticality of both decrees soon became evident. Then, during the decades that followed, the Church reinforced its prohibitions with a positive drive to convert, in particular employing the technique of formal debate, often forcing unwilling opponents to take part.

Nevertheless, despite the amount of ecclesiastical legislation, it was the much more piecemeal actions of secular rulers which had most practical effect, for they regarded the Jews as their own property to be taxed and fined at will and were therefore jealous of attempts at interference whether by high-minded clerical pronouncements or by the violence of the mob. Here, evidence comes from charters and law codes. Rulers saw the position of the Jews very much in terms of respect for their own authority and reprisals often followed against those who attacked 'their' Jews. The reasons for this are made quite clear in a clause of the *Liber Augustalis* of 1231. Here, Frederick condemns usury and sets confiscation as punishment, but he exempts the Jews from this law, for, 'It cannot be maintained that usury is illicit for them. The divine law does not prohibit it.' Restrictions were imposed on the rates of interest, permitting them 'to charge only one ounce for every ten ounces for a whole year', but the law goes on to say that

> whatever they take additionally, they will pay one-ninth to our court. They will not obtain any further legal advantage from abuse of this permission, which we have granted them because we were forced to on account of the needs of men.
>
> (Powell 1971:12–13)

The actions of the ecclesiastical and secular rulers left the Jews in a clearly defined and, in theory, protected position, but the theory seldom matched the practice of their day-to-day existence. On the one hand, it is quite clear that many Christians ignored the strict rules governing separation, especially in the Mediterranean lands of Spain, southern France and Italy. Here Jews, long established, could be found holding positions in administration, buying, selling and leasing land, and following a variety of crafts and trades – none of which would have been possible without daily involvement with Christians – as well as gaining a living from money-lending. On the other hand, the emphasis upon their distinctiveness made them very vulnerable in times of high religious tension, such as when preparations for a crusade were under way and, when this occurred, no amount of clerical censure or princely fulmination could protect them. The Jews of the Rhineland, northern France and England in particular, pushed into an urban ghetto existence, largely as a consequence of Christian restrictions, and dependent more on money-lending than their southern counterparts, had to face a wave of religious prejudice unprecedented in their history.

Ultimately the Jews of northern Europe could not withstand the dual pressure of these continual financial exactions and, during the thirteenth century, increased competition from Christian money-lenders. As they became less useful to rulers there was less reason to protect them. During the thirteenth century, expulsions, a way of both satisfying popular prejudice and of having a last bite at Jewish property, followed. Philip II had tried this, almost as soon as he came to the throne in 1180. According to the pro-Capetian chronicler, Rigord of St Denis,

> influenced by zeal for God, on his orders... the Jews throughout all France were captured in their synagogues and then despoiled of gold and silver and vestments, just as the Jews themselves had despoiled the Egyptians on their departure from Egypt.
>
> (Delaborde 1882:15–16)

Most dramatic of all were the wholesale expulsions by Edward I of England in 1290 and Philip IV of France in 1306, although in the latter case 'the needs of man' led to their return in 1315, just as they had done under Philip II, only for them to be expelled again in 1322 (W.C. Jordan 1989:200–48)

It is perhaps ironic that the Jews, whose position had been so violently undermined by departing crusaders, faced no pogroms in the crusader lands in the east throughout the two centuries of their existence, although they were never allowed to settle in Jerusalem while the city was under Christian control. Indeed, in the thirteenth century there was a large increase in Jewish immigration to the east, for the great scholar Nahmanides believed that Providence had shown that neither Christianity nor Islam was destined to hold the land and that it was for his generation to fulfil the Providential will by resettling the area. It was this positive religious faith which promoted this period of emigration rather than any reaction to the persecutions to which it bears little chronological relationship (Prawer 1988:153–9). Perhaps more than any other theme, the history of the Jews emphasises the extent to which the concept of the unity of the baptised underlies the social structure of this period.

3

Economic development

In his *Historia Pontificalis* John of Salisbury describes in detail the conflict between King Stephen of England and Theobald, Archbishop of Canterbury. By 1148 the dispute had drawn the participants into what John saw as the sink of the papal court at Rome.

> The king meanwhile held to his evil purpose, supported by the advice of certain bishops, and hoping for the partisanship of certain cardinals, who as he knew could be drawn through the mire of any disgrace at the mere gleam of a rusty purse.
>
> (Chibnall 1956:49)

For John this matter was fundamental. In the *Policraticus*, a more reflective and abstract work, he lays down that among the acts of one who could be defined as a good ruler was the abolition of 'the use of gold, silver and all other wicked materials' (Nederman 1990:34). John of Salisbury was not alone in this view, for he reflects a widespread feeling in the twelfth century that the handling and use of money was corrupting and that those who ignored the strong possibility of being ruined by its contagion were almost inevitably going to be polluted by it (Little 1978:34).

These attitudes were inbuilt and traditional, and medieval Christians never freed themselves from an ambiguous attitude towards the creation and use of wealth, from a feeling both of revulsion at the sight of the stain of money and greed spreading through society and of attraction towards the material comforts and lifestyle that it could bring. Indeed, for all the force of his condemnation, John's accusation demonstrates just how the tide was running against him, how relentlessly money and the values that went with it were infiltrating all aspects of society, transforming social relationships and governmental capabilities. This does not mean that in the past money had vanished from circulation or that the economy of the early middle ages had been exclusively based on barter, but rather that the scale and spread of monetary circulation and the availability of credit were so much greater than they had been in the Carolingian era that they effected a qualitative change in society.

The fact was that the artistic, intellectual and governmental achievements of the twelfth and thirteenth centuries were based upon a remarkable economic expansion in the west, an expansion which originated in some regions as far back as the tenth century and sustained itself until the first decades of the fourteenth century and which, even during the immense setbacks of the fourteenth century, was sufficiently solid to prevent a reversion to the primitive economic conditions of the early middle ages. The growth of trade was both a reflection and a cause of these changes, making such spectacular progress in variety, quantity and quality of goods and in techniques and organisation as fully to justify the name of 'Commercial Revolution' (Lopez 1971). It was a revolution in the sense that the links with the Rome of the first and second centuries had long since been snapped by the northern invasions and settlements, and it was a revolution too in that the network of trade which emerged bore little resemblance to that of the more geographically restricted Roman world.

The causes of this revival cannot be pinpointed with statistical exactitude, but undoubtedly at its base lay the slow growth in population which led to taking in of new land, the increase in food production, and the improvement of communications and mobility. These changes, together with small but significant steps towards greater social and political stability following the end of external threats like the Vikings and the Magyars, offered conditions in which merchants with contacts in the east, a breed which had never entirely disappeared in the early middle ages, could achieve a high rate of success in bringing Levantine products such as spices and silks to the north and the west, and fill their return cargoes with more basic and bulky goods like timber, iron and cloth. The eastern Mediterranean was initially largely the preserve of the Italian maritime cities, first Venice and Amalfi and, in the eleventh century, Pisa and Genoa. All four had dealings, both peaceful and warlike, with one or both of the great powers of the early middle ages, Byzantium and Islam and, although some towns, like Amalfi, slowly faded from the front rank, the Italian cities never lost their early advantages in long-distance trade. When the crusaders captured Jerusalem in 1099 and set up a series of Christian settlements on the Palestinian mainland, the Italians were on hand to provide needed sea power in return for trading privileges.

By the early fourteenth century, the Mediterranean trading cities, including not only the Italians but also growing ports like Marseille and Barcelona, were capable of handling almost any commodity: spices (a generic term which included dyestuffs), staple foodstuffs, fur, silks, woollen cloth, alum, arms, glassware, even works of art like paintings and ivories. They took, too, human cargoes, pilgrims and crusaders as fare-paying passengers and, despite the disapproval of many, slaves as well, a trade which increased rather than diminished throughout this period. The expansion of the Mongol Empire during the thirteenth century even provided an opportunity to penetrate Far Eastern markets, a trade link which became progressively more important as the Crusader States declined and eventually fell in 1291. Among the pioneers in this trade were Niccolò and Maffeo Polo, Venetian merchants who began to travel through the Mongol Empire from 1261, when they set out from Sudak in the Crimea. Marco Polo was Niccolò's son and his famous book describes their travels between 1271 and 1292. Even bolder than the Polos were the Genoese Vivaldi brothers who, in 1291, attempted to find the Indies by a westerly route from the Mediterranean and then by sailing along the African coast, but they never returned (Lopez 1943:169–70; J.R.S. Phillips 1998:147–9).

The great leader of this change was the Republic of Venice, set on the lagoons at the head of the Adriatic. Venice was not a former Roman city like so many others, but had developed from scattered communities of fishermen and bargees, reinforced after 568 by refugees fleeing from the Lombards. Its earliest sources of wealth were salt, a commodity needed by all but available only in limited areas and therefore a fundamental item in medieval trade, and fish. In the sixth century the revival of Byzantine power in Italy brought it under the control of a new official, the Exarch of Ravenna, but the widespread revolt against Byzantine rule in eighth-century Italy, enabled the Venetians to achieve enough independence to elect their own *duces* or *doges*, although theoretically they remained part of the Byzantine Empire. The continued link with Byzantium proved advantageous, however, since the Venetians were able to exploit this to gain a privileged position in Constantinople, privileges set down in agreements of 992 and 1082. In the second instance they gained the basis of their own quarter in the city with quays and warehouses, strung out along the Golden Horn, together with freedom from customs dues throughout the Empire, thus giving them an immense competitive advantage in relation to native Greek merchants. These concessions largely arose from Byzantine naval weakness in the late eleventh century and proved to be a cause of deep resentment as Byzantine power revived under the Comnenian emperors in the following decades. The friction caused by these trade privileges contributed considerably to the attack on Constantinople in 1204, which resulted in the fall of the city, and the entrenchment of the Venetians with a trade monopoly.

The establishment of the Crusader States opened a second front for Venice, while at the same time expanding the scope of the operations of Genoa and Pisa, hitherto largely confined to the western Mediterranean and ports of the north African coast. The crusaders needed the fleets of these cities to blockade the coastal towns of Syria and Palestine, without which the Latin settlements would have withered and died or been wiped out by the Muslim enemy. In return the Italians received extensive trading concessions comparable to the privileges enjoyed by the Venetians at Constantinople. The results of these arrangements were impressive. In *c.*1172 Theoderich, one of many pilgrims able to visit the Holy Places because of the regular shipping, counted seventy ships in the harbour at Acre alone, besides the 'buza', the large ships in which he and other pilgrims had sailed (J. Wilkinson 1988:310).

The success of Venice in these centuries reveals a mode of thought very different from that of contemporary nobles and ecclesiastics. The Venetians did not seek land so much as financial power. 'The Venetians, indeed, because of the siting of the city, were using ships instead of horses,' said the anonymous 'Monk of Lido' at the time of the capture of Jerusalem in 1099 (1895:255). This approach is shown most clearly in their agreement of 1123 with the Kingdom of Jerusalem made after their fleet had annihilated the Egyptians off Ascalon in southern Palestine. The Latins in the east were understandably keen that the Venetians should follow this up, in particular by helping in their planned attack on Tyre. They were promised a base in every city of the kingdom: a church, a street, a square, a bath and an oven (the last two being valuable monopolies), 'to be held forever by hereditary right, free from all taxation as is the king's property'. They were to be permitted to use their own measures for trading except when purchasing goods, when the royal measure was to be employed.

> For these privileges the Venetians need pay no tax whatever, whether according to custom or for any reason whatsoever, either on entering, staying, buying, selling, either while remaining there or on departing. For no reason whatever need they pay any tax excepting only when they come or go, carrying pilgrims with their own vessels. Then indeed, according to the king's custom, they must give a third part to the king himself.

In addition the doge would receive an annual revenue of 300 Saracen *besants* from Tyre and was promised that taxation on those with whom Venice traded would not exceed customary levels. In Tyre itself, a generous quarter was marked out with immunities which in effect created 'a little Venice in the east', for not only was the settlement clearly defined physically, but also it was delineated juridically as well, for all litigation involving Venetians, with the exception of Venetian complaints against outsiders, was reserved for Venetian courts. Moreover, their property could be freely bequeathed and no losses should result from shipwreck, while over the inhabitants of their quarter they were granted the same rights of jurisdiction as the king had over his dependants. Then, finally, came the nub of these grants, for after the victory over the Egyptian fleet the way was now open to attack other coastal cities vital to the crusaders.

> The Venetians shall have a third part of the two cities of Tyre and Ascalon, with their appurtenances, and a third part of all the lands belonging to them.... This applies only to lands which are now subject to the Saracens and are not as yet in the hands of the Franks.
>
> (Babcock and Krey 1941:1:552–6)

Tyre was indeed taken in July 1124. It has usually been argued that these sweeping concessions deprived the rulers of the kingdom of so much potential revenue that they ultimately became too impoverished to provide proper defences, that the Italian cities, by their very success, sucked the life-blood from the Crusader States. However, this view has been greatly modified, for the parties with whom the Italians traded were taxed and the massive increase in trade which their presence engendered must have at least compensated for the financial immunities which they were granted (Riley-Smith 1973a).

A taste for eastern goods quickly developed in the west. Nobles, conscious that their lifestyle defined them socially, were eager to be able to offer exotic food at their tables and to dress their wives in silk, while the developing textile industries of the twelfth century benefited from the much greater range of dyestuffs now made available. The rapid expansion of sugar production in the Crusader States is a good indicator of the changing pattern of consumption. Previously unknown in the west, news of its discovery by the crusaders spread very rapidly. Albert, canon of the collegiate church at Aachen, writing not long after 1102, said that once people 'had tasted it they could scarcely get enough of it' (Edgington 2004), and it soon became a major export, initially from the Kingdom of Jerusalem and then, in the thirteenth century, from Cyprus as well (Boas 1999:81). A pattern therefore developed in which the purchase of goods of intrinsically high value from the east began to create an unfavourable trade balance for the west, tending to drain away its stocks of precious metals. This was partly compensated by an increase in production from silver mines, evident from 1168 when silver was discovered at Meissen (Freiberg from 1185), soon followed by Friesach in the eastern Alps and Montieri in central Italy. Production was sustained in the second half of the thirteenth century, when these mines began to falter, by new centres at Jihlava (Iglau) in Bohemia and Iglesias in south-western Sardinia (Spufford 2002:15, 60–7, 352–72). Very little gold was produced but the triangular trade of the Mediterranean, in which the Italians operated not only in the Levant, but through the north African ports as well, helped to offset this. Here they sold western goods to Arab merchants who in turn resold some of them to the caravans which came from the Sahara and the Sudan and which, significantly, paid in gold, ultimately derived from panning the upper reaches of the rivers of central Africa like the Niger (Renouard 1949: 41). Small wonder that by the thirteenth century there was an increasing drive to reach further afield in trading ventures.

Although the Italians became and remained leaders in trade, they were not of course the sole merchants of medieval Europe. In particular the Germans around the Baltic and the North Sea, although less sophisticated in technique, were very active: Bremen and Hamburg at the mouths of the Rivers Weser and Elbe, flowing into the North Sea, Magdeburg higher up the Elbe, and Lübeck on the Baltic, were the northern counterparts of Venice, Genoa and Pisa. Associations of merchants known as *hansas* handled the valuable raw materials of northern Europe, including grain, honey, wax, furs, fish, timber, salt, tar, metals and hides. Their structure connected north Germany to England and the Low Countries to the west, Poland, Russia and Hungary to the east, and Scandinavia to the north. Swedish copper mining provides an example of the stimulus of this growing trade network. In 1288 Peter, Bishop of Västerås, granted his cousin, Nicolai Kristinesson 'an eighth share in the copper mountain, called Tiskasjöberg, in the parish of Torsång, which as is known, had been acquired through our care', in return for a loan to help him cover the expenses of his first year as bishop, a transaction which suggests a considerable degree of mobility of capital in the region. Copper, like salt, occurred only in certain specific areas, and its exploitation on any scale is a good index of the development of commerce (H.M. Larson 1929–30:554–5).

Nevertheless, the economy of the north remained relatively underdeveloped compared with that of the Italian city-states. Despite the damage to Roman commerce brought about by the Franks, Goths and Vandals, long-distance trade between the eastern Mediterranean and western Europe never really dried up in the early middle ages, for it had been sustained by Syrian and Jewish merchants in particular. Moreover, it had by no means been as disrupted by the rise of Islam in the seventh and eighth centuries as the great Belgian historian, Henri Pirenne, had once thought. The Italians therefore had a base to build on, an advantage clearly reflected in the technical expertise which came to characterise their activities in the thirteenth century. The transaction between Peter of Västerås and Nicolai Kristinesson shows that, by the late thirteenth century, the northern economy was no longer as relatively unsophisticated as had once been the case. Nevertheless, in parts of the north, especially in the Slav lands during the twelfth century, the sources leave the reader with a strong sense of pioneering in virgin territory, while even in the following centuries the northern merchants never managed to match the Italians in wealth and variety of commercial interests. The priest, Helmold, for instance, when describing the expedition of the Emperor Henry V against the Slav tribe of the Rugiani in 1124, says that the Rugiani were forced to buy peace, but they had no coins with which to do it.

> Now among the Rugiani there is no coined money, nor is it customary to use coins in reckoning things, but you will get whatever you wish to buy in their market for bands of linen. The gold and silver which they chance to get by their pillaging and their kidnapping of men or in any other way they either devote to ornaments for their wives or put into the treasury of their god.
>
> (Tschan 1935:131)

This is a very different economic environment from that of the Levant, where only the year before the Venetians had made their contract with the Latin settlers. The difference in urban development is equally striking. Constantinople was the most populous city in the world, while Tyre and Acre were established emporia in classical times. As Helmold shows, however, on the Baltic it was not until 1143 that Count Adolf of Holstein began to construct the settlement which was to grow into the great trading city of Lübeck.

> Count Adolf came later to a place called Bucu and found there the wall of an abandoned fortress which Cruto, the tyrant of God, had built, and a very large island, encircled by two rivers. The Trave flows by on one side, the Wakenitz on the other. Each of these streams has swampy and pathless banks. On the side, however, on which the land road runs there is a little hill surmounted by the wall of the fort. When, therefore, the circumspect man saw the advantages of the site and beheld the noble harbor, he began to build there a city. He called it Lübeck, because it was not far from the old fort and city which Prince Henry had at one time constructed. He sent messages to Niclot, prince of the Abodrites, to make friends with him, and by means of gifts drew to himself all men of consequence, to the end that they would all strive to accommodate themselves to him and bring peace upon his land. Thus the deserted places of the land of Wagria began to be occupied and the number of its inhabitants was multiplied.
>
> (Tschan 1935:169)

The quickening tempo of economic life was equally strongly reflected in the regions between these two great inland seas of the Baltic and the Mediterranean. The key area was the Low Countries and its fulcrum was the city of Bruges. The French historian, William the Breton, writing in the early thirteenth century, claimed that Damme, the port of Bruges, was so large and sheltered that it could contain the entire French fleet. Through it passed, he said, 'riches from all parts of the world', including silver ingots, mined metals of all kinds, linen and wool fabrics from the Cyclades, Phoenicia (meaning Palestine and Syria) and China, skins from Hungary, seeds from which scarlet dye could be produced, Gascon wine sent from La Rochelle, and cloths from England and Flanders (Delaborde 1885:2:264). Although the variety of goods is impressive, Bruges owed its importance above all to the cloth trade. Apart from agriculture, textile manufacture was the greatest single industry of the medieval world and, in one form or another, was to be found in almost every medieval town. However, in the north-west, the Flemings became the leading specialist producers, and Bruges was the great collecting centre for Flemish cloth.

Since they tended to concentrate upon manufacture, the organisation of which was complex and time-consuming, the Flemish entrepreneurs were less ubiquitous traders than the Italians, instead consolidating their grip upon an urban workforce dependent upon them both for the provision of raw materials and for the marketing of the finished products. Nevertheless, they were not a negligible force in international commerce, for Flemish commercial links with England and west Germany were established as early as the ninth century, while by the 1180s cloths brought by Artesian merchant-entrepreneurs had become one of the staples of Genoese trade. Many of these merchants sold on credit to the Genoese, thus both increasing the market for their products and providing capital for the more varied ventures of the Genoese (Reynolds 1930). Flemish cloth-making continued to expand in the thirteenth century, reaching its height around 1270. This early predominance clearly owed much to the availability of indigenous raw materials: wool, flax and hemp, dyes like woad and madder, and products needed for the manufacturing processes, like teasels and fullers' earth, which was used as a detergent. However, as the scale and scope of the industry expanded, increasing quantities of wool were imported, especially from England and Spain, as was a huge variety of dyestuffs from almost every known region. Alum, the name given to mineral salts used both for cleansing the cloth and for fixing the dye, was also brought in, largely from the Aegean coast of Anatolia. By the 1280s the Genoese were actually carrying this entirely by sea, having opened up the Atlantic route. However, by this time the stability of this structure and the complacency of some of its beneficiaries first began to be rocked by urban revolts which, complicated by the intervention of outside political interests like the French monarchy, set in train a slow decline, a decline which, by *c.*1320, English, Aragonese and Italian rivals had begun to exploit.

English cloth-making had been important throughout the twelfth and thirteenth centuries, especially in towns in the eastern part of England like Lincoln, Stamford, York, Beverley, Leicester and Northampton. However, the increasing use of the fulling mill in the thirteenth century, which needed flowing water, changed its location from town to country, moving it into the hills of the West Riding, the Lakes and the West Country. This gave the industry a new competitive edge, largely freeing it from the restrictions of the guilds in the old chartered towns, and enabling it to take advantage of the unsuitability of low-lying Flanders for the utilisation of the fulling mill (Carus-Wilson 1954). Aragonese cloth also began to appear on international markets in the thirteenth century, a reflection of the country's transformation from its eleventh-century obscurity. King James I of Aragon noted, for instance, that the income from the so-called 'Caldera de Lérida', the cauldron tax paid by the dyers of the town, increased from 200 *sols* per annum to 3,000 *sols* in a relatively few years between *c.*1225 and *c.*1238 (D. Smith and Buffery 2003:56). In Italy, too, a native cloth industry had developed, producing incomes that, by the late thirteenth century, made the capitalist cloth producers of the *Arti Maggiori* of Florence among the wealthiest manufacturers and traders in Europe. Flanders, squeezed by this new competition and plagued by political pressure and social fissures, began slowly to fade from prominence.

The spread of the fulling mill is in fact only one example of the increased use of machinery in this period; by the late twelfth century mills had become ubiquitous, utilising river, sea and wind power, for activities ranging from grinding corn to tanning leather (Gimpel 1976:1–28; Comet 1997:30–3). One significant side-effect of the combination of mechanisation and the growth of textile manufacture was the appearance of paper manufacturers, who used linen rags as their basic material. They are first seen at Fabriano in the Marches between 1260 and 1276, and soon after at Bologna, Padua, Genoa and Treviso, among other places. Paper had been produced in the twelfth century at Játiva and Alcoy in Valencia by the Arabs, but at Fabriano superior techniques were developed, including the mechanisation of the process by which the paste was brought into workable condition by driving metal hammers with water power. In the mercantile society of central and northern Italy, coming increasingly to rely on written documents to conduct business, this development was immensely important, although the spread in the use of paper to northern Europe was in fact relatively slow. At the University of Paris, for example, parchment continued to be of prime importance.

Although it never employed as many people nor generated as much wealth as textiles, the spectacular growth of the building industry was an even more evident manifestation of industrial expansion. At its most mundane level there was a huge increase in demand for urban housing of all quantities and types, from Florentine town houses such as the Palazzo Davanzati, elegant, stone-built, and equipped with facilities that included en suite toilets in some of the bedrooms, to the crowded and insanitary wooden structures in which most town-dwellers lived. Some indication of the importance of building can be grasped from the walls which Philip II ordered to be built around Paris in 1189–90, prior to his departure on crusade, for these probably enclosed an area some twenty-five times larger than that of the modest settlement around the Ile-de-la-Cité of a hundred years earlier (Boussard 1976:314). The effects were also evident in rural areas. Grain storage facilities, for example, were improved by the use of stone walls or at least the provision of saddle stones to raise the floor (Dyer 1997:297–8). Better storage helped reduce the possibility of local food shortages, while the decline in references to the gangrenous form of ergotism known to contemporaries as *ignis sacer*, which resulted in death, mutilation of limbs and mental instability, may be connected to this, since it was caused by a mould which grew on damp corn. Wood was the most common material used and carpenters probably the largest single group of skilled workers employed in the building industry, for even the great stone edifices like the cathedrals and castles contained huge quantities of timber. Brick, too, slowly became more common where supplies of clay and fuel for the kilns were readily available and where stone was difficult to obtain locally as in the Netherlands and eastern England. Supply industries, which provided the raw materials, like quarrying and forestry, expanded commensurately. Although there were relatively few skilled masons, these industries employed large numbers of unskilled workers, and the building labourer was as characteristic a figure of the twelfth- and thirteenth-century scene as the mailed knight or the cowled monk.

From the early decades of the eleventh century men began, for the first time since the late Roman Empire, to build on a large scale. The monastery, cathedral and castle were their most famous creations but, in response to changing needs they were equally successful at building hospitals, town halls, tithe barns, houses, mills, bridges and roads. The great monastic church of Cluny, rebuilt twice by 1130, provides an early and influential example. Cluny had to cope with a growth in the numbers of choir monks from seventy in the 1040s to two hundred in the 1080s, and needed a whole complex of buildings to fulfil functions as varied as the recitation of the liturgy, the making of manuscripts, the care of the sick and the cooking of food. Other monasteries, anxious to promote pilgrimage as a penitential exercise among the laity, ensured that the routes to such famous centres as Santiago de Compostela in Galicia and Monte Gargano in Italy were well provided with churches and hostels. Tiny villages like that of Conques in the Auvergne are still today overwhelmed by great Romanesque edifices, lavishly decorated with sculpture proclaiming the fate of the saved and the damned in the Last Judgement.

The Romanesque style lasted well into the high middle ages in Italy, but from the mid-twelfth century, emerging from the Ile-de-France, an area of no previous architectural eminence, Gothic began to spread across Christendom. Abbot Suger's promotion of St Denis through an extensive programme of rebuilding and decoration helped to set in motion a movement which between *c.*1150 and *c.*1250 saw the building or rebuilding of great churches in the Gothic style in all the important sees of northern France and England and, to a lesser extent, in Germany and Spain as well. It has been estimated that around 1200 at least twelve cathedrals and about four hundred churches were being built simultaneously in this region (J. James 1982:1). The boom was not confined to northern France. A good proportion of the wealth generated by the Lombard and Tuscan towns, for instance, was absorbed into building projects, symbolised by the construction of elaborately decorated town halls like the Palazzo Pubblico in Siena, begun in 1293. Impelled both by ruling oligarchies' concepts of 'good government' and by endemic rivalry, the cities of northern and central Italy promoted not only the development of this new secular architecture, but also a spate of cathedral building and decoration as well. Siena's efforts to outdo Orvieto and Florence led first to the decision in 1285 to attempt the technically complicated feat of extending its cathedral over the falling ground to the east, but later to a massive new rebuilding project to the south. But the plan was too ambitious and had to be abandoned in the 1340s; the skeletal remains of this memorial to civic pride can still be seen today, testimony to the expectations that the achievements of the medieval building industry could generate.

Abbot Suger's description of the steps taken to rebuild St Denis, completed probably 1148–9, although both melodramatic and self-congratulatory, nevertheless conveys a realistic sense of this developing economic environment. 'Bronze casters having been summoned and sculptors chosen, we set up the main doors on which are represented the Passion of the Saviour and His Resurrection.' Characteristically, he adds that it was 'with great cost and much expenditure for their gilding as was fitting for the noble porch'. The same care was lavished on the choir. 'We caused to be painted, by the exquisite hands of many masters from different regions, a splendid variety of new windows, both below and above.' An official master craftsman and a goldsmith were appointed for their care, repair and decoration to be paid for by 'coins from the altar and flour from the common storehouse of the brethren' (Panofsky 1979:46–7, 72–7). Although many masons and carpenters were sedentary, the great churches and castles would not have been possible without this availability of labour. Mobility of labour was not new in principle, but the scale, organisation and mental attitudes involved certainly were. In the past a nucleus of building workers had tended to grow up in and around the great monasteries, which often had their own workshops. It was a monk, Theophilus, who probably lived in the early twelfth century, who wrote a manual on painting, the decoration of glass and metalwork (C.R. Dodwell 1961). Documents of the eleventh century concerned with skilled labour tend therefore to be monastic. A series of letters, written between 1097 and 1125, and sent, apparently in vain, by Geoffrey, Abbot of La Trinité at Vendôme, to Hildebert of Lavardin, Bishop of Le Mans, asking for the return of John, his monk-architect, demonstrate these points. John had apparently been allowed to go and work on the nave of Le Mans, but was in no hurry to return to the monastery. Indeed, he even seems to have gone to Jerusalem to improve his architectural knowledge. In another, almost contemporary document, between 1082 and 1106, Girard, Abbot of St Aubin of Angers, enfranchised a serf named Fulk, making him a free dependant of the abbey with a house and an arpent of vineyard, a concession granted because of Fulk's skill as a painter. He was engaged to paint the entire abbey, but his property, however, would revert to the abbey, unless he had a son who could succeed him as a painter in the same way (Mortet and Deschamps 1995:1:292–4, 264–5).

Suger's programme was part of this same monastic tradition, but partly because of his special needs, he was forced to call in outsiders, probably from among the sculptors who worked on the pilgrimage churches of Languedoc. Once a project of this size was underway it evidently generated more work and for all his emphasis on the role of voluntary, pious helpers Suger shows clearly that at the quarry of Pontoise from which he derived most of his stone, for instance, he employed a considerable number of carters, ox-drivers and labourers (Panofsky 1979:93). Castle-building made similar demands on labour; indeed, if the situation was urgent, greater pressures were created, possibly even dictating the labour market for short periods. The seven Welsh castles of Edward I, largely built during the 1280s, mostly took between five and seven seasons to build (a season being between April and November) and sometimes involved thousands of men. Beaumaris often absorbed a labour force of approximately 3,000, about one-seventh of whom would have been masons and two-thirds *minuti* or labourers, some of whom had been forcibly mustered. The enrolled accounts confirm the narratives of Suger, for these projects needed, as well, carpenters, smiths, quarriers, carters and boatmen (Edwards 1946).

Less obvious, but of fundamental importance, was the expansion of iron-working. One grant, dated 1158 in the Champagne region, can illustrate the point.

> I, Henry, Count Palatine of Troyes, wish to make known to all in the present and in the future that I have conceded to the brothers of the church of Holy Mary of Igny, in my wood next to the lands of the monastery of Delven and to the village which is called Vassy, one place necessary for iron-workers and land which must be dug for the purpose of making iron and for working a forge from the same wood, to have without opposition and to possess in perpetuity.
>
> (Arbois de Jubainville 1961:3:448)

Workings like this made possible the manufacture of metal parts for edging wooden spades, for ploughs and for mill machinery, which were the key to the more effective use of such equipment. As the document suggests, the extraction and smelting of metals was largely a rural operation, usually small-scale, but the manufacture of many of the finished products tended to be urban based, especially when specialist items like swords or reliquaries were required. The Meuse valley had a long tradition of such work. Many family firms, their skills handed down from father to son, were established here (see Plate 4).

In most industries and trades guild and corporate regulations governed the conduct of economic activity, for people following the same or related occupations and living in close proximity to each other tended to organise themselves into groups for mutual protection, especially in a world where privilege stemmed from membership of the group. Often finding their origin in religious confraternities, bound together by a Christian oath, the earliest guilds were usually general merchant organisations. As the economy expanded they frequently divided into more specialised occupations, in which those dealing with cloth, the supply of victuals, and precious metals like the goldsmiths, were usually prominent. The power and functions of the guilds reflect the variety of circumstances in which they developed. Although craft guilds were sometimes formed to protect the interests of the 'small men', it is striking that in the larger cities and towns, notably in Tuscany and Flanders, an inner group of greater guilds dominated the life of the town and closely regulated the activities of the lesser corporations.

The most common examples can be found in the cloth industry, but regulations covered most urban occupations. The statutes of the fishmongers of the city of London

Plate 4 The cult of St Adalbert was revived at the end of the eleventh century. Seven of the eighteen scenes on the south doors at Gniezno are devoted to his mission to Prussia, which is a considerably higher proportion than is to be found in his two *Vitae*. The doors were cast in the Meuse region, at that time famous for its workshops. (Reproduced by permission of Piotr Namiota.)

of 1280 provide a good illustration of guild operation. The fishmongers were bound to buy and sell in certain specific places within particular boundaries and at the same time conform to certain detailed regulations. These regulations were read out twice a year at *hallmotes* or meetings of all those involved, attended by the Sheriff of London. No fresh fish could be sold or bought for resale before sunrise or salt fish before the hour of prime, and all transactions had to be conducted within a specified area bounded by the Chapel on the Bridge, Castle Baynard and Jordan's Quay. Attempts to meet outside the area and times, called forestalling, were regarded as unfair competition, and punishable by forfeiture of the fish. Outsiders or 'strangers' were allowed to trade, although they had to do the best they could without the benefit of the guild privileges, or partnership with a guild member. Produce had to be fresh and of consistent quality, so that, for instance, oysters, whelks and mussels were not allowed to remain on sale for longer than two ebbs and a flood, and fish that arrived in baskets 'must be as good below as it is above, or better'. The fishmongers had their own court, held by the sheriff, 'in regard to such matters as touch their trade'. Entrance was by apprenticeship, but no master was allowed to take more than two or three apprentices, or for a shorter term than seven years. To ensure that this was maintained both master and apprentice were required to enrol the relevant documents before four reputable men of the trade at the Guildhall, both at the beginning and end of every term. Here, therefore, can be seen that combination of occupational self-interest and consumer protection which characterised the medieval guilds. Needless to say, the regulations were often evaded, both by members and outsiders. A telling phrase inserted towards the end of the fishmongers' regulations refers to what evidently must have been a notorious case. 'As concerning the Abbot of St. Albans, good care must be taken that his buyers buy nothing to be taken out of the City, except for the use of the Abbot and Convent of that house only' (Riley 1861:327–31).

This growth in trade and manufacture was intimately linked to two striking developments of the high middle ages: improvements in transport and communications, and progress in commercial technique and organisation. The impetus of trade, administration, pilgrimage and warfare pushed more people onto the roads than ever before, particularly along the routes linking north-west Europe and south and west Germany to the Mediterranean. The valley of the Rhône provided the obvious connection and extensive use was made of the major Alpine passes which connected Piedmont and Provence. Most commonly used were the passes of Mont Cenis and the Grand-Saint-Bernard, which joined Milan and the Po valley to Arles and Lyon, but during the 1230s the growing importance of south German trade led to the opening of two new, more easterly routes, those of the Simplon and the Saint-Gothard (Renouard 1963). Roman roads continued to be used wherever possible, although they had sometimes deteriorated or, as at Arles, where the bridge over the Rhône had been destroyed, had been interrupted. Even so, key routes, such as the Via Domitia, which linked the cities of Lower Languedoc between Narbonne and Nîmes, as well as other major routes from Toulouse, Carcassonne and Cahors, which joined it, continued to perform important functions, despite competition from newer pilgrimage roads created by the attraction of the shrine of St James at Compostela. The Via Domitia had been refurbished in 118 BC because of Rome's vital need for good communications with Spain, which had been conquered fifteen years before and, although it remained prone to flooding in places, still possessed some excellent bridges, such as those over the Vidourle and the Hérault, carefully constructed with triangular breakwaters and rectangular outlets between the arches to cope with seasonal fluctuations in river levels

(Clément 1984:89–118). Although no revolutionary changes were effected in methods of land transport, the actual movement along these routes was greatly helped by the more widespread diffusion of better methods of harnessing, especially the use of rigid horse-collars in tandem, and the fitting of horseshoes. The more frequent use of horseshoes may, in turn, have been the consequence of the greater incidence of roads with hard surfaces (Raepsaet 1997:56–7).

Even so, land transport remained hazardous and expensive; for bulky goods the original price could often be doubled or more if any great distance had to be covered. Tolls were sometimes very heavy. In the thirteenth century, for example, the village of Saint-Croix-de-Quinlillargues, situated in the Hérault, north of Montpellier, became the focus of bitter contention between the officials of the bishop of Maguelonne, who held the rights, and the muleteers travelling between Nîmes and Toulouse. When the muleteers attempted to avoid the place by taking a detour via Sommières, the bishop set up a series of observation posts so that he could send out armed men to force them back along the route (Clément 1984:331–2). Wherever possible, therefore, use was made of rivers. The River Po and its tributaries connected the Alpine passes with the Adriatic coast and the key city of Venice. The main north–south route utilised the Moselle, Meuse, Saône and Rhône, while southern Germany was opened up by the Rhine and the Danube. In some regions, like Flanders, nature was supplemented by a man-made system of canals and barrages. Not surprisingly, certain areas became focal points of this network, the most important of which was the County of Champagne. Here, during the twelfth century, the counts took advantage of their unique geographical position to encourage a series of international fairs which, at their height, were running at six per annum, at Lagny, Bar-sur-Aube, Provins and Troyes. Each fair was for six weeks and together they covered most of the year. By the late twelfth century they were attracting merchants from all over Christendom, reaching a peak by the 1230s.

The sea, however, remained the cheapest and quickest means of transport. Despite the dangers arising from the right of wreck, from piracy and from natural disasters, as well as the restrictions on their range imposed by the frequent need to take on water, merchants appreciated that the advantages outweighed all other considerations. Merchants therefore aimed to move their goods to the nearest harbour by the shortest route available. The consequence was that ships tended to remain relatively small in size so that they could gain access to the many local harbours which this attitude encouraged. Although larger vessels did exist, ships of about 500 tons remained the most economic. Shipbuilding developed rapidly to meet the demand; the yards at Venice, for instance, were highly efficient, for they were organised for mass production. Using the rib and plank method rather than the mortice and tenon joints which had characterized Roman shipbuilding, within two years of signing the contract with the crusaders, the Venetians were able to put together the magnificent fleet which so impressed the Picard knight Robert of Clari, when it set out in the autumn of 1202.

> And each of the high men had his own ship for himself and his people, and his transport to carry his horses, and the doge had with him fifty galleys all at his own cost.... When they were on that sea and had spread their sails and had their banners set high on the poops of the ships and their ensigns, it seemed indeed as if the sea were all a-tremble and all on fire with the ships they were sailing and the great joy they were making.
>
> (McNeal 1936:42–3)

During the thirteenth century in particular the use of the stern-post rudder, lateen sails and the magnetic compass, together with more sophisticated cartography, including the development of sea-charts and portolan maps, greatly increased the speed of ships previously forced to keep close to the coasts and to anchor at night. Many more ports now had quays, which made loading and unloading easier and quicker, especially for larger ships, although much local shipping still tended to use the beach or shore (Unger 1980:146–7). The direct sea route set up between Genoa and the Low Countries in the 1280s was one of the results of these improvements. Although long sea journeys never became routine and for many landsmen they remained a source of fear and superstition, nevertheless changes such as these gave both shipbuilders and sailors a far higher degree of confidence than in the past. Moreover, the development of shipping was inevitably applied as much to warfare as to trade, increasing the scale and importance of sea battles in both the Mediterranean and along the western and northern coasts (see Plate 5). By this time passenger traffic too had become common and made a sizeable contribution to the economy of the maritime cities of the Mediterranean. The first known passenger list, that of the French ship, the *Saint-Victor*, in 1250, shows that over 75 per cent of its 453 passengers were commoners travelling on their own, including burgesses, barbers and shoemakers. A third-class passenger fare to the Holy Land was within the reach of many people by this time. In 1248 the cost was 56 *sous*, equal to 112 daily earnings of a tailor in Paris, and by 1268 it had dropped to only 35 *sous* (Kedar 1972). This was reflected in the ability to make and sail ships that could transport horses and people in large numbers, especially crucial for the Crusader States. In the early twelfth century it was not possible to take horses to the Holy Land or for large numbers of crusaders to travel by sea, yet by Robert of Clari's time some ships had special landing doors for horses from which, he claimed, a knight could emerge fully mounted. For long sea voyages, horses were kept in the belly of the ships supported by straps and, according to John of Joinville, St Louis's friend and biographer, writing of the mid-thirteenth century, were brought out none the worse except for a certain degree of stiffness.

The expansion of trade and industry not only impelled improvements in communications, however, but also revolutionised commercial techniques and organisation. Although the most precocious developments can be found in Italy, it is important to realise that there were receptive ears in the very furthest corners of Christendom. The following extracts are taken from a thirteenth-century manual called *The King's Mirror*, written in the form of a dialogue between father and son, and emanating not from Florence or Siena, but from Norway. 'If your wealth takes on rapid growth, divide it and invest it in a partnership trade in fields where you do not yourself travel; but be cautious in selecting partners.' This prudence extended to the need for celestial insurance as well. 'Always let Almighty God, the holy Virgin Mary, and the saint whom you have most frequently called upon to intercede for you be counted among your partners.' Capital invested in trade should be divided into three parts so that the risk was spread and any losses compensated. Two-thirds of the profits should be withdrawn and invested 'in good farm lands, for such property is generally thought the most secure'. The remaining third he left to his son's choice, but advised that if he wished to reinvest in trade, 'discontinue your own journeys at sea or as a trader in foreign fields, as soon as your means have attained sufficient growth and you have studied foreign customs as much as you like' (L.M. Larson 1917:85–6).

To an Italian the advice might seem over-cautious, for the author is concerned that his son should have capital in the secure form of landed property. So too were the

Plate 5 Economic growth and political consolidation enabled armies to employ increasing numbers of specialists as well as expand in size. This ferocious sea-battle illustrates a text of Vegetius' *De Re Militari*, written in the late fourth century, *c.*1270. Although uninfluential in his own day, Vegetius' military manual was much admired in the high middle ages. (Reproduced by permission of the Syndics of the Fitzwilliam Museum, Cambridge.)

Italians, but their techniques were particularly framed to enable capital tied up in land to be drawn into risk-taking ventures. Partnerships such as those recommended by the author were effected in Italy from an early date by means of the *commenda* contract, a method which remained popular even as more complex techniques were developed. In partnerships of this type one party was the active member who actually undertook the trade, accompanying the cargo on the ship and investing the capital, while the other, who provided most, if not all, of the capital, was sedentary, usually receiving three-quarters of any profit. Agreements like this encouraged social mobility, for people of relatively small capital were able to engage in international trade, while the flow of necessary capital into that trade, often from landed interests, was facilitated. During the thirteenth century the Italians devised commercial methods to cope with most contingencies. *Compagnia* contracts, for example, were partnerships in which all members were full participants and accepted equal liability, although sometimes outsiders could also invest in the venture (Lopez and Raymond 1998:156–235). Many of the greatest Italian merchants became sedentary, conducting their business through correspondence with their agents in foreign cities, often using courier services to speed up the system. They controlled their affairs through a series of partnerships and kept track of their financial position by careful record-keeping, facilitated by double-entry book-keeping and the adoption of Hindu-Arabic numerals, by using written contracts drawn up by trained notaries who numbered the folios and indexed all the principals, and by insuring goods in transit (Reynolds 1952).

Moreover, the sheer scale of their operations persuaded the Italians that the system of coinage inherited from the Carolingian world was inadequate. Charlemagne had minted silver pennies which, for accounting purposes, were reckoned in *librae* (pounds) and *solidi* (shillings). A *libra* was equivalent to 20 *solidi* or 240 *denarii* (pennies), but the only actual coins were the *denarii* and the *oboli* (half-pennies). Gold coinage was largely confined to those lands, like southern Italy, within the orbit of the Byzantine Empire. Uniformity was quickly lost, for the coins began to suffer both from wear and tear and from debasement by lords who had usurped minting rights during the break-up of the Carolingian Empire in the ninth and tenth centuries. Although the gradual re-establishment of strong monarchical rule, particularly in England, reduced the extent of this interference, nevertheless during the twelfth century it was evident that the coinage system could not carry the weight placed upon it by an expanding economy. The discovery of new sources of silver in the later twelfth century helped to relieve this problem. The Italians began to strike heavier pieces, first in silver, in the form of the Venetian groat or *gros* of 1192, with a value set at a *solidus*, and then in gold when, in 1252, Florence and Genoa both struck gold florins, corresponding to the value of a silver pound *gros*. Other governments followed. Louis IX of France established the silver *gros tournois* in 1266, followed soon after by the *gros parisis*, worth about a quarter more (Cipolla 1967).

These changes certainly eased the path of international trade, but they also created new problems. Silver monometallism was now replaced by a bimetallic system, but it was never easy to impose what the authorities saw as a satisfactory relationship between the two metals, for the governmental desire to set a high value on silver, in which most payments to officials and soldiers were made, conflicted with the tendency of gold, for which stocks were relatively low, to rise in value. Moreover, as the costs of warfare and administration rose in the later thirteenth century, the temptation to debase the coinage, both by interfering with the coins themselves and by adjusting the relationship between money of account and actual coined money, was often too strong to be resisted. John of Salisbury would not have been surprised. In his organic view of society set out in the *Policraticus*, he compares financial officers to the stomach and the intestines, 'these, if they accumulate with great avidity and tenaciously preserve their accumulation, engender innumerable and incurable diseases so that their infection threatens to ruin the whole body' (Nederman 1990:67). One way of offsetting a shortage of high-value specie was through the provision of credit, for more than anything else the commercial changes were concerned with expediting the means by which money could be used and manipulated. Here again the Italians were leaders in the field. In the past, because of Christian censures on the provision of loans with interest, the Jews had been the major money-lenders of western Christendom, but during the thirteenth century they lost most of their market to the Italian banking houses. Bills of exchange, for example, were used not only for their original function of converting one currency into another, but also for making loans, the interest being derived from setting an artificially low valuation on the foreign currency concerned. In a procedure known as dry exchange, no actual change of currency took place at all, for the object was to obtain a loan which the creditor paid back with interest in the original currency. Indeed, despite the restrictive theories of the scholastics on the subject of usury, the papacy itself provided a major stimulus to the development of Italian banking, for the need to finance its crusades against the Staufen, the Aragonese and the Ghibellines, consumed vast sums. Potentially, the papacy had access to large resources, but credit was needed to cope with urgent military and political needs which would not wait for the collection of taxation.

This, in turn, meant heavy dependence upon houses like the Buonsignori of Siena which, on more than one occasion, saved the papacy from disaster (Housley 1982:221–2). The growth of this sector of the economy can be measured in the fall in interest rates in Italy in the thirteenth century. Peter Spufford calculates that rates in the key cities of Genoa, Venice and Florence fell from a level of 20–22 per cent at the beginning of the century to 7–10 per cent by the early fourteenth century, at least where lenders thought that they were dealing with low-risk clients. This meant that new capital projects could be much more readily financed than in the past (Spufford 2002:44–6). Meanwhile, the typical Jewish money-lender of the late thirteenth century began to accord much more closely to those recorded in the notarial records of Perpignan between 1261 and 1286, where most are concerned only with very small-scale loans and with pawnbroking, while their clients are largely local villagers and less prosperous townsmen, rather than leading clerics or nobles (Emery 1959:40, 62, 98, 106–7).

By the thirteenth century the provision of credit was ubiquitous. As the example of the papacy shows it was needed not only for commerce, but for waging wars as well. During the Albigensian Crusades against heresy in Languedoc, Simon of Montfort, its military leader, would not have been able to sustain his attritional campaigns over a nine-year period between 1209 and 1218 without credit provided by the Cahorsins. According to William of Tudela,

> All this enormous booty the count of Montfort owed to a rich merchant called Raymond of Salvanhac, a wealthy native and citizen of Cahors. It was he who financed the crusade, lending money to the count. Then in payment he received cloth, wine and corn; all the booty from Lavaur was handed over to him.
>
> (Shirley 1996:43)

As in other occupations, the professionalisation of those employed to fight was inevitably costly. The Cistercian chronicler of the crusade, Peter of Les Vaux-de-Cernay, recorded how, during the siege of Minerve in 1210, even those refilling the large petrary with which Montfort was battering the eastern walls of the town were costing 21 *livres* per day (Sibly and Sibly 1998:83).

The ultimate basis for this commercial revolution lay in the agrarian world, in which by far the greatest part of the population continued to live. Here too money seeped into every corner. A comparison between the most advanced methods of estate management in the ninth century as shown in the polyptique or inventory of a great French monastery and an extent or survey of manors held in secular hands in the late thirteenth century illustrates the point. Between 806 and 829 Irminon, Abbot of St Germain-des-Prés in Paris, had drawn up the most detailed examination of the abbey's estates. Arable fields, meadows and forest lands were listed, fixed assets in the form of buildings ranging from churches to mills were described, serfs were individually identified and their obligations carefully set out. It is clearly not a world without cash; the peasants, for instance, paid a head tax, the *chevage*, in pennies. Nevertheless, cash was not the customary way of expressing matters. Services ranging from cloth-making to carting manure and payments in animals or eggs are far more prominent than any clear awareness of the monetary profit that these lands might bring to the monastery (Duby 1968a:368–9). But compare the extent of the manor of Willingdon on the Sussex Downs drawn up in 1292, which was a demesne manor in the queen's hands. Some features are the same: the lands and the windmill are described, the free and servile tenants and their services are listed. However, here every item is given a monetary equivalent. Whereas on the estates of St Germain-des-Prés the three flour mills are described as bringing in a rent of 450 *muids* of grain, the windmill at Willingdon is said to be worth 13s. 4d. annually, and while the serfs of St Germain deliver 'for pannage' wine, mustard, withies, hens and eggs, and do service where they are ordered, the customary tenants of Willingdon have each obligation assessed to a fraction of a penny, including the value of any free meals to which they are entitled when involved in obligatory services (A.E. Wilson 1961:23–8). By the late thirteenth century agriculture had become commercialised and lords, lay and ecclesiastical, wanted to know just what they were worth in money terms.

In many cases, however, the motives behind this commercialisation were by no means the same as those which drove the merchant (Hilton 1962). It is clear that there was a wish to convert powers of lordship into monetary profit, as well as gain income from the sale of produce in the market, but it was profit which a good proportion of the nobility and the higher clergy wanted to spend on their main interests, crusading, warfare, building or material comforts. Research has shown that the widespread interest in manumission of serfs in thirteenth-century France stemmed less from an accountant's desire for 'management rationalisation', than from the need to convert fixed rents into larger and more flexible sums for expenditure on these concerns (W.C. Jordan 1986:28–30). Not surprisingly, therefore, although the surrender of certain rights over the peasantry, in particular those associated with serfdom, became common in the thirteenth century, lords still clung to those judicial powers which seemed profitable, such as the exploitation of monopolies and their right to hold on to tithes. The growth in the power of the state in some regions had the same effect, for the countryside bore an increasing burden of taxation, now easier to draw off than in previous centuries. It is no coincidence that Capetian power was based upon the Paris Basin, one of the richest cereal producing areas in western Europe, but the incomes thus gained were utilised by a king like Philip II for his political concerns, which centred above all on his conflict with the Angevins. It is true that not all lords felt impelled to emphasise their status by showy extravagance. Some seem to have wanted their lands run in the manner suggested by the famous treatise on estate management composed by Walter of Henley, probably in the 1280s. Although there is much detailed discussion of the best farming techniques, the financial advice is fundamentally conservative: find out what the lands are worth, do not spend up to that limit but hold something in reserve, and keep a sharp eye out for fraud and laziness among employees and dependants. Above all, do not borrow, for the borrower robs himself (Oschinsky 1971:308–43). Neither the spendthrift nor the careful therefore seem to possess an entrepreneurial spirit, exploiting new technology, raising capital for development, or reinvesting profits in new plant. The West Midlands stewards for whom Walter of Henley seems to have written are a world apart from the risk-taking mercantile nobility of the Italian city-states.

Nevertheless, the effects of this seigneurial activity were more far-reaching than most of them could have conceived. For example, freer movement of capital and goods, together with growth in demand, meant that greater regional specialisation was possible. Concentration on viticulture, stock-rearing or the growth of plants for dyestuffs, began to characterise certain regions, while new crops, such as the rice and citrus fruits of Italy, began to appear. Viticulture dominated favourable areas like the

Rhine, Moselle, Loire, Gironde and Rhône-Saône regions. Large-scale wine production in Aquitaine made the trade one of the key links between south-west France and England, promoting the importance of Bordeaux and helping to create the new port of La Rochelle in the twelfth century. Sheep-farming came particularly to be associated with the newer monastic orders which had sought out uninhabited and uncultivated places in their desire for isolation, only to find themselves drawn back into the commercial orbit when these lands proved ideal for sheep. Cistercian abbeys, for instance, traded in wool from their settlements all over Europe, but particularly in Yorkshire, Wales, Flanders, southern France and Spain. However, their market share was relatively small compared to the production of Castile, where by the early fourteenth century the whole economy was connected to this activity, with over one and a half million sheep. Moreover, these were merino sheep, a superior breed from north Africa, which gave longer wool of better quality than was found elsewhere. Here, transhumance created three great north–south sheep-walks, the *cañadas*, while between 1230 and 1265 there appeared a national organisation, the *Mesta*, which became a powerful association of sheep-owners. Some flocks, controlled by corporations like the military orders, were immense, perhaps as many as 1,000 animals, but there were many small-scale operators as well. Cattle-rearing similarly developed as a specialist activity, especially in Andalusia, catering for the demand for beef and hides. Data from the Kingdom of Sicily show too that there was an extensive trade in horses, especially in the later thirteenth century when they were exported both to Latin Greece and the Crusader States in the east in large numbers. Some of these appear to originate in Sicily itself, while others are en route from Aragon (Pryor 1982:110). The demand for horses of all types was huge, since, apart from their uses in warfare and transport, many more were used for ploughing, harrowing and hauling than had been the case in earlier centuries. Although they were more expensive to feed than oxen, they were more versatile and much faster, so that it was economic for both small peasant proprietors and specialist breeders to produce horses for the market. The trade was particularly important in Denmark, where the export of horses was second only to that of herring (Poulsen 1997:124).

As in other aspects of the economy, regionalism was most marked in Italy where, by the thirteenth century, the contrast between the city-states of the north and centre and the monarchy in the south was very evident. The city-states held the surrounding agricultural lands in a strong grip, bending their production towards the food supply of the towns, while at the same time investing in farming improvements. In contrast, in the south, the economy was geared towards the political and military aims of the kingdom's rulers who, like Frederick II, identified communes with treason and heresy. Given the climatic problems of farming in the south – in particular the prevalent aridity – it is not surprising to find the region remaining largely a food producer for northern cities. The trade between Florence and the Kingdom of Sicily shows this regional relationship most starkly. Florentine population grew from between 15,000 and 20,000 in *c.*1200 to about 96,000 a century later, making it by far the largest city in Tuscany (J.C. Russell 1972:43–4). This would not have been possible without the extensive import of foodstuffs, for it has been calculated that in a normal year the city could provision itself from its *contado* for only five months. When, on behalf of the papacy, Charles of Anjou, the younger brother of Louis IX of France, gained control of the kingdom between 1266 and 1268, powerful Florentine firms like the Bardi and the Acciaiuoli were able to negotiate favourable terms for the purchase of Apulian and

Sicilian grain and other raw materials, for Charles needed cash and access to credit in order to finance his ambitious military plans. At the same time lack of industrial development in the south meant that there was a market there for Florentine finished cloth (Abulafia 1981). The grants themselves were very favourable, but this dependence on outside sources of food did leave the city very exposed during periods of shortage. According to the Florentine chronicler, Giovanni Villani, the shortages of 1303 were so acute that only the import of 26,000 bushels of grain brought from Sicily and Apulia by the Genoese saved the city from famine. Even so, prices were still very high and there was strong suspicion of profiteering among those with access to this trade (Villani 1969:1:85).

Cereal production, however, remained the basis of farming; indeed, between 75 and 80 per cent of calories were derived from cereals (Comet 1997:15). It had been, and continued to be, common practice to sow wheat and rye in the autumn and barley and oats in the spring, especially on demesne lands, but it may be that the relative space given to these crops became more variable and attuned to particular needs than it had been in the past. Productivity certainly increased, helped by better ploughing using effective shoulder collars for horses and asymmetrical metal shares. A three rather than two-field rotational system was more widely used (although by no means universally adopted), and more leguminous plants, especially peas, beans and lentils, were incorporated into the system, a practice beneficial both to the balance of the soil and the nutrition of the general population. The example of Flanders shows how farming could be affected by contemporary economic and social changes. In the eleventh century there was already an extensive commercial agriculture, based mainly on the three predominant soil types, the clay of the coast, where stock-breeding and its products was most common, the loam of the south, which was mostly used for wheat, and the sandy soil of the centre on which barley was grown, chiefly for making ale. This structure reflected both the provisioning needs of the great lords and precocious urban development, but by the second half of the twelfth century the impact of population growth and even greater urbanisation had transformed this regionally specialised agriculture into a more varied and more intensive system. Sophisticated crop rotation systems were introduced in which legumes were the fundamental element and fallowing was greatly reduced, while careful integration of cereal-growing with stock-rearing made more effective use of manure. More industrial crops, mainly geared to the textile industry, were produced. Additional land was brought into cultivation through reclamation, creating large farms, although at the same time increasing numbers of lease-holders (some of whom were urban based) ensured that the proportion of smaller units remained high. In these circumstances the traditional relationships between lords and peasants did not survive, as cash replaced payments in kind and farmers of all types and status attuned themselves to the market (Thoen 1997) (see Figure 3).

However, not everybody was willing or able to respond in the same way, even though Flemish methods could produce yields up to four or five times those of other regions. In northern Italy, for instance, much of the manure was lost, since transhumance was practised among sheep-farmers, who utilised alpine pastures and wet meadows for their grazing, in an economy apparently separate from the arable lands. Some land grants do contain clauses requiring tenants to marl the land, which would have replaced phosphate and lime deficiencies (Duby 1974:189), but there is little sign of any concerted effort to improve soil fertility. In other areas farmers pursued what they evidently believed to be the art of the possible. The Flemish model might have

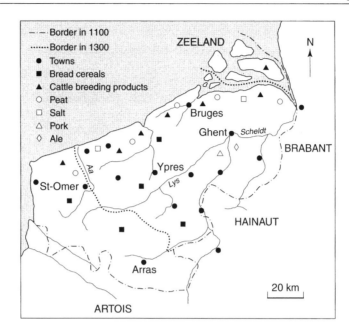

Source: E. Thoen (1997), 'The Birth of "The Flemish Husbandry": Agricultural Technology in Medieval Flanders', in *Medieval Farming and Technology. The Impact of Agricultural Change in Northwest Europe*, ed. G. Astill and J. Langdon (Leiden: Brill), p. 72.

Figure 3 Principal rural products exported to towns in Flanders between the eleventh and the thirteenth centuries

been quite inappropriate in much more thinly populated and less fertile regions, where, as has been pointed out, an attempt to farm as intensively might well have provoked 'ecological disaster' (Dyer 1997:309). The Gâtine of Poitou, some thirty miles west of Poitiers, makes an interesting comparison. This bleak, upland area, with its thin soils and heavy rainfall, had been sparsely populated in the tenth century, for its natural disadvantages had been compounded by its proximity to the sea and therefore the possibility of Viking attack. Yet, in the eleventh and twelfth centuries new peasant settlements were organised and encouraged by the upper nobility who established *burgs* in which the inhabitants enjoyed personal freedom and emancipation from a whole range of seigneurial burdens, while the new monastic orders of Fontevrault and Cîteaux were attracted by the very harshness of the region. Rye was the chief product, but flax, hemp and vegetables were grown and, for a time, even viticulture was apparently viable. Woodlands and fishponds provided additional income. The fact that this was attempted at all in such an unpromising region is a significant indication of twelfth-century growth, but population never became dense and it is noticeable that after *c.*1200 these developments were no longer conspicuous (Beech 1964).

Had John of Salisbury been alive to see the horrors of the famine years between 1315 and 1322 and to observe the impotence of the medieval economy in the face of them, he might well have reflected that a society so reliant on such corrupt and transitory commodities as gold and silver must inevitably come to a bad end (see Plate 6). And, indeed, the fourteenth century did see a drastic undermining of the economic system which had been erected with such confidence in the previous three centuries, not the

Plate 6 During the 1120s the sculptor Gislebertus and his workshop were employed to create a great programme for the cathedral of Autun in Burgundy. His outstanding achievement was the Last Judgement of the west front, but at the same time he produced a series of historiated capitals for the nave. His version of the death of Judas Iscariot, shown as suicide, makes explicit the possibility that he betrayed Christ for money (Matthew 27:3–5), drawing an appropriate moral for contemporary society. (By permission of Europart.)

least in the heartland of that expansion, the Italian peninsula, where a series of banking crashes during the 1340s reverberated through mercantile houses from Milan to Siena. But these crises did not alter the fundamental shift which had taken place in attitudes and which was to continue to prevail after the setbacks of the fourteenth century had passed. Most tenth-century people had seen their world in very literal terms: God was a great and vengeful lord who needed to be propitiated with concrete gifts, human social ties needed to be consolidated in strongly visual ceremonies, trade deals were conducted with palpable goods and obligations worked off in measurable labour. For many, such literal ties still existed in the early fourteenth century, but the economy of the high middle ages could not have expanded as it did if that had been true everywhere. For the economic leaders the acceptance of more abstract concepts had revolutionised relationships with both God and Mammon (Becker 1981:4–9). Belief in the spiritual rewards which would ultimately be derived from the crusading indulgence was matched by the confidence that the bearer of a bill of exchange would get the money.

Part II

The Church

4

The papacy

The Lateran synod of April 1059, presided over by Pope Nicholas II, passed a decree of central importance to the medieval Church: it laid down new rules for the election of the pope. Under its terms the cardinal-bishops, of whom there were seven at this time, should deliberate about the matter, then they should call in the other cardinal-clerics, the priests and deacons, and finally the rest of the Roman clergy and the people should give their assent to the chosen candidate. The significance of this decree was that the Bishop of Rome should be chosen by what contemporary clerical reformers saw as 'canonical election' and not, as had so often happened in the tenth and early eleventh centuries, either by imperial or royal designation or by pressure exerted by one or other of the factions of Rome. For these reformers the decree on papal elections was a major step in the implementation of a wider programme of reform within the Church and indeed within Christian society as a whole. Their intention was to free the clergy from lay control by wresting the appointment of bishops from the hands of lay rulers, by preventing the purchase of ecclesiastical offices and thus eliminating simony from the Church (see Plate 2), and by ending the system of proprietary churches by which laymen established both churches and clergy on their own lands, thus ensuring overwhelming secular influence at local level. A concomitant of such changes would be the transformation of the lives of the clergy themselves, for an inevitable consequence of such powerful lay influence was that many clerics undertook important roles in administration, government and military affairs, and their lifestyle reflected this.

Such a programme had immediate practical implications for lay rulers in that they had been accustomed to rely on the clergy to fulfil the wide range of tasks which enabled their governments to function; to deprive them of control over ecclesiastical benefices would be to remove one of the most important foundations of their authority. But beyond even these important practical matters, the reformers' claims resurrected a fundamental issue which had existed since the era of Constantine in the early fourth century, which was that of the rightful relationship between the spiritual and temporal powers. An attempt to reform the Church by purifying it from what was seen as the taint of lay corruption necessarily suggested the superiority of the spiritual power over the lay and, indeed, it implied the right of that spiritual power to take action of some kind against recalcitrant lay rulers who would not co-operate with that programme. In the middle and late eleventh century this was to come to mean above all struggle with the German emperor on whom, during the tenth century under the Ottonians, had fallen the mantle of Charlemagne.

Fully to appreciate the significance of the reformers' goals, it is necessary to describe the political and religious environment within which they tried to assert their views. The reformers frequently underpinned their arguments by reference to the past: to the canons of the Church (in particular a collection of eighth- and ninth-century forgeries known as the Pseudo-Isidorian decretals), to the writings of the Church Fathers, to the pronouncements of early medieval popes such as Gelasius I and Gregory the Great. But their selective quotation failed to make clear that, in reality, they had been forced to adopt a defensive position in the face of both Roman and Germanic rulers. In 800, Pope Leo III had not been able to return to Rome without Charlemagne's military help against the Roman factions; in 963 Otto I had actually deposed Pope John XII, while in the previous year, in a document known as the *Ottonianum*, the emperor had apparently extracted a promise from the Romans that they would not elect a pope without first notifying the imperial legates and ensuring that the candidate had sworn an oath to the emperor's son or to his legates. The early medieval popes had occasionally won symbolic victories, such as Leo III's actual crowning of Charlemagne in 800, but these had few practical applications in the tenth and early eleventh centuries.

Nevertheless, although these rulers gained evident political advantages from their intervention in the affairs of the Church, equally they took seriously the Church's teaching that they were responsible to God for their actions. It was this sense of duty which, in 1046, led the Salian emperor, Henry III, offended by the spectacle of three men simultaneously claiming to be pope, to march to Rome and depose them all. Instead, he placed his own candidate on the throne as Clement II, thus inaugurating a series of German popes of high moral calibre and reforming instincts, perhaps most evidently epitomised by Leo IX, who became pope in 1048 (see Table 3). Leo IX was invested with his ring and staff by the king and he swore a feudal oath to him; he was, indeed, a relative of Henry, put on the throne to continue the work of moral reform which Henry had begun in 1046. Henry III had no intention of overturning existing relationships. In a world in which as anointed ruler, he was clearly elevated above any ordinary layman, imperial control of the Church was accepted as the proper order of things. Henry would have acted swiftly against anyone who had opposed him in this and, indeed, it seems that Leo IX shared his views.

The situation changed rapidly in the middle 1050s. Leo died in 1054, Henry in 1056, and his last German appointee, Victor II, in 1057. The German throne was now occupied by a young boy, while the papal curia was filled with zealous reformers gathered there by Leo IX. The most important of these in the period immediately after Victor's death was Cardinal Humbert of Silva Candida. When Leo had died, Humbert had been in Constantinople, the leader of an abortive mission aimed at reconciling the patriarch and the Byzantine Church to Roman primacy, but which had succeeded only in alienating the Greeks more than before. Further evidence of the cardinal's uncompromising nature appeared in 1058 when, in Book Three of his *Libri adversus simoniacos*, he suddenly launched a frontal attack upon the whole relationship of seculars to the Church, giving especial emphasis to the evils allegedly resulting from royal theocracy of the kind which Henry III and his predecessors had so assiduously maintained. In Humbert's view, secular princes who presided over episcopal elections and invested bishops with their ring and staff were making a travesty of the true social order, for such actions meant that 'everything is done in such disorder that the first are

Table 3 Popes (anti-popes in parentheses)

Leo IX	1048–54
Victor II	1055–7
Stephen X	1057–8 (Benedict X, 1058–9)
Nicholas II	1059–61
Alexander II	1061–73 (Honorius II, 1061–64)
Gregory VII	1073–85 (Clement III, 1080–1100)
Victor III	1086–7
Urban II	1088–99
Paschal II	1099–1118 (Theodoric, 1100; Albert, 1102; Silvester, 1105–11)
Gelasius II	1118–19 (Gregory VIII, 1118–21)
Calixtus II	1119–24
Honorius II	1124–30 (Celestine II, 1124)
Innocent II	1130–43 (Anacletus II, 1130–8; Victor IV, 1138)
Celestine II	1143–4
Lucius II	1144–5
Eugenius III	1145–53
Anastasius IV	1153–4
Adrian IV	1154–9
Alexander III	1159–81 (Victor IV, 1159–64; Paschal III, 1164–8; Calixtus III, 1168–78; Innocent III, 1179–80)
Lucius III	1181–5
Urban III	1185–7
Gregory VIII	1187
Clement III	1187–91
Celestine III	1191–8
Innocent III	1198–1216
Honorius III	1216–27
Gregory IX	1227–41
Celestine IV	1241
Innocent IV	1243–54
Alexander IV	1254–61
Urban IV	1261–4
Clement IV	1265–8
Gregory X	1271–6
Innocent V	1276
Adrian V	1276
John XXI	1276–7
Nicholas III	1277–80
Martin IV	1281–5
Honorius IV	1285–7
Nicholas IV	1288–92
Celestine V	1294. Resigned. Died 1296
Boniface VIII	1294–1303
Benedict XI	1303–4
Clement V	1305–14
John XXII	1316–34 (Nicholas V, 1328–30)

last and the last first'. As Humbert saw it, a prince's authority could not encompass any sacerdotal element because of his anointing; from now on the quasi-priestly functions of the early medieval king were to be the target of the reformers' attacks. Here is Humbert setting the hierarchy right in a manner which was to be repeated many times in succeeding generations:

> Anyone then who wishes to compare the priestly and royal dignities in a useful and blameless fashion may say that, in the existing church, the priesthood is analogous to the soul and the kingship to the body, for they cleave to one another and need one another and each in turn demands services and renders them one to another. It follows from this that, just as the soul excels the body and commands it, so too the priestly dignity excels the royal or, we may say, the heavenly dignity the earthly. Thus, that all things may be in due order and not in disarray the priesthood, like the soul, may advise what is to be done. The kingship in turn, like a head, excels all the members of the body and leads them where they should go; for just as kings should follow churchmen so also layfolk should follow their kings for the good of church and country.
>
> (Tierney 1964:41–2)

The election decree of 1059 shows how quickly Humbert's teaching was absorbed in papal circles, thus enlarging the whole scope of reform from concentration on the specific issues of clerical simony and unchastity to a more ambitious attempt to redefine the traditionally accepted relationship between the spiritual and the temporal powers.

To some extent this new papal assertiveness had become possible because of the weakness of imperial leadership, but even so the papacy was not operating in a political vacuum. The return of papal self-respect coincided with the rise of a new and aggressive power in southern Italy, that of the Normans. Since the beginning of the eleventh century, Norman adventurers had been establishing themselves in the south in piecemeal fashion, taking advantage of the fragmented political scene. Initially, Pope Benedict VIII (1012–24), anxious to counteract Byzantine influence in Apulia, seems to have encouraged them, but by the time of Leo IX, their growing power, especially that of the Hauteville family, began to seem threatening. Leo IX believed that the new importance which the reform movement had given to the papal office needed to be safeguarded by the creation of independent territorial power from which military force could be drawn. His exchange of papal rights in Bamberg and Fulda for imperial powers in Benevento, south of Rome, was a step in this direction. Henry III had not been opposed to this policy, for the creation of solid territories under manageable popes was a useful counter to the growing power of his enemy, Godfrey, Duke of Lower Lorraine, who had gained an interest in the area through his marriage to Beatrice of Tuscany in 1054. This was the context within which Leo IX led an army against the Normans in 1053, following complaints from the citizens of Benevento, but the papal army was comprehensively defeated at Civitate (thirty miles north of Foggia) and the pope captured. Civitate showed that, as long as the papacy thought in terms of territorial power in central Italy, the political complexion and territorial aims of the rulers of the south would be issues of vital importance. This helps explain the oscillations of papal policy thereafter. If Norman power could not be overcome, then it might be utilised to provide material support against any threat to the newly established papal independence. To this end Nicholas II reversed Leo's policy and, in the Treaty of Melfi (1059), assumed for the papacy the right to invest prominent Norman leaders with territories in the south in return for their military support.

Nicholas's successor, Alexander II (1061–73) soon began to experience the stresses that the new papal policies would bring in relations with the emperors. Confrontation with Henry IV arose over the see of Milan. The conflict was complicated by problems arising from the riven social structure of Milan. The entrenched clerical establishment, drawn from the most powerful families of the city and fortified by the prestige of participating in the see of St Ambrose, traditionally adopted a stance independent of Rome and followed customs of clerical marriage and purchase of office inimical to the reformers. Opposition to this was centred upon a group of reforming enthusiasts known as the Patarenes, whose attacks on these abuses had by the 1060s increasingly developed from verbal denunciation into physical assaults upon priests. The Patarenes, although they do not represent a revolt from below – their leaders were largely of aristocratic background and their support came from varied social strata – were nevertheless regarded as disrupters of the social order by the dominant city families (Cowdrey 1968). Alexander II had at first been supportive of the movement and had granted them a papal banner, but a growing unease with such groups, especially as they sometimes appeared to be arguing that the validity of the sacrament was determined by the moral state of the priest, led him to put pressure on Archbishop Guido to correct the faults of the clergy under his care. But Guido achieved little and, in 1070, apparently having lost interest in the struggle, he resigned his office, sending his insignia not, however, to the pope but to the German king, Henry IV. Henry promptly invested his own candidate, a priest called Godfrey, whom he persisted in maintaining even when, on Guido's death in 1071, Alexander's legate presided over a new election.

The conflict over Milan illustrates how the papal position had advanced since the time of Leo IX. 'Liberty of the Church' meant not only freedom from outside lay intervention but, more positively, submission to the highest lordship possible, which could be seen only as the papacy (Tellenbach 1940:127–61). A good idea of the progress of this idea within papal circles can be seen by the developing relationship with Cluny. The Cluniacs had, since the early tenth century, been pursuing the goal of monastic reform, protected by the charter of immunity granted them by Duke William of Aquitaine. In practice this meant the freedom to pursue excellence in the monastic life, but it does not seem to have implied any radical change in the nature of existing social relationships in the way that the mid-eleventh century reform was coming to do. However, during the decades after *c.*1060 Cluny came to be seen by the popes as a shining example of what *libertas* had meant for the reformers, an ecclesiastical institution free of all secular influence and directly subject to the see of St Peter (Cowdrey 1970:44–57).

The issues which the reformers sought to resolve were brought to a head in the most dramatic fashion during the pontificate of Gregory VII (1073–85). Gregory was the name taken by Cardinal Hildebrand, after Pope Gregory the Great, his great exemplar. He had been born in Rome, but had become a monk possibly at Cologne, before being brought back to the city as part of the group assembled by Leo IX. In 1073 he was almost the last survivor of this group, with nearly a quarter of a century's experience in the reform movement. He was swept to power by the Roman people in a manner quite contrary to the decrees of 1059, and he was always acutely conscious of his vulnerability on this score during the violent conflict with Henry IV that dominated his reign. Despite this, Henry was initially conciliatory, for he had serious political problems in Saxony. In a letter of September 1073, he lashed himself with reproach:

> Alas for me, guilty and unhappy that I am!… Not only have I encroached upon
> the property of the Church, but I have sold churches themselves to unworthy
> persons, men poisoned with the gall of Simony.
>
> (Emerton 1966:19)

However, with his victory over the Saxons in June 1075, his attitude changed, and he
began once again to invest clerics chosen by himself, including his own candidate,
Tedald, into the see of Milan, in place of Godfrey. Gregory's enforcement, in a series
of synods from 1075 onwards, of the decrees of his predecessors against simony,
unchastity and lay investiture, meant that a confrontation became inevitable. In the
Roman synod of 1078, lay investiture was described as causing the Christian faith 'to
be trampled underfoot'. Any cleric receiving any bishopric, abbey or church in this way
should know that the investiture was invalid and that the recipient would be
excommunicated (Emerton 1966:133).

However, by 1078, events had already taken a decisive turn. Gregory's complaints
about Henry's investitures had been met, in January 1076, with the denunciation of the
pope as a false monk who had forfeited his authority. At the Lenten synod of 1076, the
pope replied by suspending Henry from government, annulling all oaths to him and,
finally, excommunicating him. By this action Gregory was, in effect, suspending the
king by removing the ecclesiastical sanctions without which he could not function. As
such, it certainly had the required effect, for Henry's support quickly evaporated, while
his enemies, particularly the Saxon and south German princes, revived their opposition.
The result was that the princes invited the pope to a meeting at Augsburg, to be
assembled in February 1077, at which the pope would settle the matters at issue.

Gregory VII never produced a consistent abstract formulation of the relationship
between the spiritual and temporal powers, for his reform activity seems to have been
fired more by moral zeal than an interest in legal definitions. As a consequence the
extent of his claims on behalf of the spiritual power has been the subject of much
unresolved debate. It is, nevertheless, important to consider his views, since the issue
remained a central element in the affairs of western Christendom for the whole of this
period. In a series of what seem to be chapter headings for a canon law collection
known as the *Dictatus Papae* (March 1075), Gregory had set out the position of the
papacy. Number twelve contained the bald statement that popes could depose
emperors. The next year, in August, responding to a request from Hermann, Bishop of
Metz, for clarification, he called the notion being put about that kings could not be
excommunicated 'fatuous' and demanded to know whether God excepted anyone
when he gave to Peter the power of binding and loosing. Once again he reinforced the
vision of the earthly hierarchy which was, for him, fundamental to 'right order'.

> Perchance they imagine that royal dignity is higher than that of bishops; but
> how great the difference between them is, they may learn from the difference
> in their origins. The former came from human lust for power; the latter was
> instituted by divine grace.
>
> (Emerton 1966:103–4)

Yet, despite the excommunication Gregory continued to call Henry 'king', while
leaving open the possibility that he could be reinstated. This has led Karl Morrison to
suggest that Gregory believed that Henry should be removed from his office

permanently, but that in the end he did not think that he himself could do more than withdraw the Church's support from one whom he saw as being caught in the toils of Satan (Morrison 1962).

However Gregory VII's position is interpreted, it is evident that the short-term effect of the excommunication was to give the pope the upper hand in the struggle. The king needed, at all costs, to prevent a union of pope and princes at Augsburg; indeed, so anxious was Henry to head off the pope, that he struggled across the Mount Cenis pass in December 1076, despite the severity of the winter and the high altitude (Robinson 1999:159–60). These are the circumstances which led to Henry's famous submission to the pope at the castle of Canossa in the Apennines in January 1077. For three days Henry waited outside the castle as a penitent asking absolution and, finally, Gregory gave in, absolved the king, and restored him to the kingship. The pope acted in accordance with what he believed to be his moral duty, but it was not a wise move politically, despite the symbolic reversal of the early medieval relationship between the *regnum* and the *sacerdotium*. Henry was once again respectable and his supporters returned to the fold, while his enemies, feeling betrayed by the pope, elected an anti-king, Duke Rudolf of Swabia, at Forchheim in March 1077. Gregory's reaction was to declare that the rightful ruler was the one on whose side stood justice, a moral line which alienated both factions.

Gregory's decision in favour of Rudolf in 1080 necessarily led to a second excommunication of Henry IV, an action which Rudolf's death in the same year did nothing to change. But the second excommunication had less import than the first; in the spring of 1081 Henry decided to follow the precedent of previous German rulers and invade Italy, having already created an anti-pope in opposition to Gregory. However, Rome would not yield to him for three years and even when, in the spring of 1084, he was able to install his anti-pope as Clement III and thus gain an imperial coronation, Gregory remained beyond his reach in the great fortress of Castel Sant' Angelo. Moreover, experience since 1050 had taught the popes the value of allies in the region. Although Gregory's relations with the Normans had been uneasy during the 1070s, he could not afford enemies both to the north and south, and the leading Norman, Robert Guiscard, had been allowed to renew his oath of fidelity in 1080. This alliance now came to the pope's rescue, for the threat of Guiscard's Normans persuaded Henry to retreat. The Normans were hardly ideal partners for a pope so concerned to purge sin, for they looted the city before withdrawing. Gregory VII had no option but to accompany them and he died at Salerno in May 1085.

Despite the considerable physical danger in which Gregory had been placed in 1084, force alone could not settle the issues. At heart the conflict was ideological. The reformers knew that they needed to expend considerable energy on a polemical campaign designed to show that secular rulers were no more than officers who could be removed by a superior ecclesiastical power if they failed to fulfil their functions properly. Behind this lay the assertion of the primacy of the see of St Peter, head of an organic hierarchy in which all other elements were assigned their specific functions. In a letter to Hermann of Metz in 1081, Gregory cited, among many others, the most basic of the tenets upon which papal primacy rested:

> Who does not remember the words of our Lord and Savior Jesus Christ: 'Thou art Peter and on this rock I will build my Church, and the gates of hell shall not prevail against it. And I will give thee the keys of the kingdom of heaven

and whatsoever thou shalt bind on earth shall be bound in heaven and
whatsoever thou shalt loose on earth shall be loosed in heaven.' (Matthew
16:19).

(Emerton 1966:167)

Henry IV himself had made the need for such justification so acute through his own
vigorous counterattack. It has been pointed out that forty-two letters survive from the
reign of Henry IV in contrast to a mere four from that of his father, and that all but four
of Henry IV's letters date from after the accession of Gregory VII (Robinson 1978:61),
an output which shows that Henry was as concerned as Gregory to affirm his vision
of the world order. The king was anxious to show that the Gregorians had wilfully
overturned the existing order and thus destroyed the Christian unity that had existed
in the past, shrewdly maintaining that he, like his father, wanted only to see the
episcopal sees filled by worthy men. For Henry, the king was not some lower species
of being, having gained his position, as the Gregorians would have it, because of lust
for power, but a partner with the Church in the proper government of Christian
society.

In the German king's view, Gregory VII's most notorious activities were those
involving the use of military force to further papal ends. Here was obvious evidence of
the disruption of which he accused the pope. For, just as Gregory believed that lay
power could be put to perverse uses in the service of the devil, he also developed the
idea that it could be used in the service of the Lord through His chosen representative
in the see of St Peter. Laymen who fought on papal behalf became *milites Christi*,
gaining salvation by their actions. This policy was evident at two levels: that of the
defence of papal territorial interests within the Italian peninsula and in the wider field
of Christian militancy against Islam in the Mediterranean. In Italy, Gregory particularly
employed the concept of a *milicia Dei* to the forces deployed on papal behalf by his
most loyal lay supporter in Italy, Matilda, Countess of Tuscany. Apart from Tuscany,
Matilda ruled lands further north across the Apennines and into the region of the lower
Po valley, and it was in Matildine territories that the submission at Canossa had taken
place. Her mother, Beatrice, had been a strong supporter of the reform popes since the
time of Leo IX and, after Beatrice's death in 1076, Matilda continued this policy, even
to the extent of making testamentary arrangements for the transfer of her allodial lands
to the papacy (Partner 1972:129). Henry IV's policy in Italy was much hindered by
Matilda's consistent support for Gregory, for control of her lands would greatly have
facilitated any German descent towards Rome. So close was the alliance that Gregory's
enemies alleged that the Church was administered by 'this new senate of women'
(Mommsen and Morrison 1962:149). At the same time the papacy made its presence felt
in the Mediterranean as a whole. In March 1074, Gregory had even declared that he was
preparing to bring aid to the Byzantine Empire, which was afflicted by the attacks of
the Seljuk Turks. Gregory imagined himself leading the expedition, even envisaging that
the Countess Matilda and the Empress Agnes, mother of Henry IV, could be persuaded
to set out too. Although he was never able to put this into practice, it illustrates how
the conception of the *milicia Dei* was becoming an integral part of the papacy's policy
towards Mediterranean politics (see Plate 7). Not surprisingly, Henry IV believed that
the traditional imperial role of military leadership was being usurped.

This wider vision of Mediterranean dominance reflected the reformers' desire to
make papal leadership felt all over Christendom. Papal letters and, sometimes, papal

Plate 7 This scene showing the Cleansing of the Temple by Christ (Matthew 21:12) is one of the illuminations in a gospel book given to the monastery of Polirone (near Mantua) by Matilda of Tuscany, a close ally of Pope Gregory VII, in the late eleventh century. The depiction of this incident reflects Gregory's concept of justifiable Christian violence. (Photograph reproduced by permission of the Pierpont Morgan Library, New York. M. 492, f. 84r.)

legates found their way to places as far apart as Norway and 'Mauretania' (Sitifis, North Africa). The Spanish kingdoms were of particular concern in that because of their relative isolation during the period of Muslim domination of the peninsula in the early middle ages, religious life had developed distinct characteristics which were not in keeping with the uniformity sought by the reformers. Most importantly the liturgy followed a pattern of its own, the Hispanic or 'Mozarabic' rite, as opposed to that of Rome. While the more easterly parts which had ready contact with France were largely brought into line (Sancho of Aragon had even offered his kingdom to the papacy in fief in 1068), León and Castile proved more difficult. This extract from a letter of Gregory VII to Alfonso VI in 1074 shows how uniformity was seen by him as an integral part of the proper world order:

> May you, like the other kingdoms of the west and the north, accept the order and ritual of the Roman Church – not those of Toledo nor any other but of that Church which was founded by Peter and Paul upon a solid rock through Christ and consecrated in blood, and against which the gates of Hell, that is, the tongues of heretics, have never been able to prevail.
>
> (Emerton 1966:29)

An indispensable concomitant of reform therefore was the achievement of uniformity of practice and belief under papal direction.

Gregory's pontificate had immense long-term significance, but in the immediate aftermath of his death in 1085, it did indeed look as if the evil disruption depicted in Henrician propaganda had come to pass. Neither Henry's invasion, nor Norman insolence, helped create a favourable atmosphere for reform, and this was reflected in the year's delay before, in May 1086, Desiderius, Abbot of Monte Cassino, was elected as Victor III. Victor maintained the continuity of reform, but had little time to do much else, for he died after only sixteen months as pope. He was succeeded by Otto, Cardinal-Bishop of Ostia, the former prior of Cluny, who took the name of Urban II. Although no less determined than Gregory, Urban's more calculating approach enabled him to pursue reforming aims without the accompanying Gregorian drama. He was helped by a fortunate conjunction of events. The invasion of Henry IV had sharpened the perception that the papacy needed greater territorial security in Italy and, to this end, in 1089, Urban organised the marriage of the Countess Matilda to Welf, son of Welf IV of Bavaria, who had been deposed as duke by Henry. The aim was to create a buffer against the emperor which extended into southern Germany, but Henry reacted by invading Italy once again, defeating Matilda's forces in 1091, and occupying Rome. But such invasions were very difficult to sustain. Military defeat in 1092, together with the defection of his son, Conrad, left him vulnerable, and when the Lombard cities led by Milan threw their weight behind the papal cause, Henry was trapped in Verona, for the Alpine passes had been blocked by the Bavarians.

Henry did not escape until 1097, leaving Urban free to organise a series of councils through which he could promote reform. The councils at Piacenza and Clermont in March and November 1095 were central to this policy, but they are best remembered for developing Gregory's *milicia Dei* into 'the armed pilgrimages' which became the crusades. By the time Henry IV had managed to return to Germany, armies from northern and southern France, Lorraine and southern Italy, were being organised into the first of the great expeditions to the east which were to become the most explicit expression of papal claims to Christian leadership. In July 1099 these armies captured Jerusalem, but Urban died before the news could reach him.

It was perhaps as well that the German threat had been negated at this time, for the issue of investitures was beginning to generate friction with other countries as well. Relations with the Norman rulers of England provide a useful illustration of the problems. Gregory had allowed William the Conqueror to retain control over the appointment and investiture of clerics since, despite his faults from the Church's point of view, the pope saw him fundamentally as a supporter of reform. Indeed, he had largely been committed by his predecessor's support for William's invasion in 1066, a policy determined initially by what Alexander regarded as usurpation of the see of Canterbury by Stigand, Bishop of Winchester, and supporter of King Harold, William's rival. But in the late-eleventh-century climate such an accommodation could be only temporary, as can be seen by the attitude of William II. William had failed to give recognition to Urban II (the anti-pope, Clement III, still provided a potential alternative), whereas Anselm of Bec, Archbishop of Canterbury from 1093, had already done so before he became archbishop. Given his ambitions in Normandy, where Urban was accepted, William found it politically expedient to allow Anselm to receive the pallium from Urban. But the king's actions thereafter showed no sign of allowing the archbishop more than a very restricted role indeed, even within the see of Canterbury itself, and in 1097 Anselm could tolerate no more and went into exile. The following period was formative for Anselm in that he attended Urban II's Roman synod of 1099, where the pope anathematised all those (lay or ecclesiastical) involved in lay investiture and those clerics who did homage to laypeople. Therefore, when Anselm returned to England after the death of William II in 1100, he refused to perform homage to the new king, Henry I. Caught between king and pope the archbishop went back to Rome, but soon found that, Urban's pronouncements notwithstanding, his stand was of less consequence to the new pope, Paschal II, than the need to find a workable relationship with the English king (Southern 1963:150–80). In 1107 Henry I eventually agreed to desist from investing clerics with the ring and the crosier, so that the outward symbolism of the independence of the ecclesiastical office was established. However, since he was allowed both to receive the homage of bishops before consecration and to be present at episcopal elections, in practice Henry's grip on appointments was not weakened.

This case points the way towards the formula which eventually brought compromise on the investiture question at Worms in 1122, for it makes a distinction between two elements in the see, the *spiritualia* and the *temporalia*. The ground for this had been prepared a few years before, in particular by the careful interpretations of the position offered by the canonist, Ivo of Chartres, and by his pupil, Hugh of Fleury. During this period, similar concessions were made to France and to Sicily. In France, Philip I agreed to abandon investiture and indeed homage, but he retained an oath of loyalty and still disposed of the temporalities of the see, a position which ensured that, at least in northern France, the bishops were elected with his consent, while the lands and movables of their sees were usually exploitable by the monarchy during vacancies. In the south, the Normans, or more specifically the Hauteville family, had extended their dominion onto the island of Sicily, a conquest largely completed by 1091. After Guiscard's death in 1085, his brother, Roger, emerged as the leading figure and it was to him that, in 1098, Urban II granted the title of Apostolic Legate, which apparently meant legates could be appointed only with Roger's approval and that control of ecclesiastical appointments on the island could be exercised only through Roger.

The Empire, however, was still perceived as a direct opponent of the fundamental papal position, a situation exacerbated by the sheer size and power of the German bishoprics and abbeys, so that compromise was far more difficult. Henry IV died in 1106, still excommunicate, but his son, Henry V, had been reconciled to the Church the year before. This made possible the end of the schism caused by Henry IV's anti-popes, but it did not solve the problem of investitures. In these circumstances, when Henry arrived outside Rome in February 1111, the pope offered him a truly radical solution. The Church would hand back to the temporal power its regalia, thus simultaneously freeing ecclesiastics from secular responsibilities and removing the chief motive for lay investiture. Despite the sweeping nature of the proposal, Henry V agreed and it was embodied in a pact at Sutri dated 9 February. In view of the events which followed historians have generally believed that Henry was merely exploiting a naive pope, for when the forms of the agreement were read out as a prelude to Henry's coronation ceremony at St Peter's, the whole proceedings were quickly broken up by vociferous opposition and, three days later Henry withdrew from Rome, taking Paschal and the cardinals with him. Since, in effect, the leaders of the Church were now his prisoners, Henry was able to lever from Paschal both the concession of the right of investiture and an imperial coronation, after which he returned north, apparently leaving the Gregorian position in tatters. In one sense, Paschal's proposal was the logical extension of the reformers' desire to extricate the offices of the Church from material entanglements, but in another it failed to exploit the potential of Cardinal Humbert's declaration of the superiority of the ecclesiastical power, which implied that both rulers and their possessions were subordinate to this higher power.

It was not, therefore, until a new pope, Calixtus II (1119–24), had gained office that a compromise similar to those achieved with other kings was worked out. Under the terms of the Concordat of Worms (1122), Henry renounced investiture of a prelate with ring and staff, but kept the right of investing with the regalia (i.e. the goods and imperial rights held by the bishoprics and abbeys) and with the sceptre. The investiture could take place immediately after the election if it was in Germany, but six months later if it was in an Italian or Burgundian see. In Germany the actual election would take place in the emperor's presence (Tierney 1964:91–2). Just as in their relations with Roger of Sicily and Henry of England, in the end the popes would have to accept that no medieval king could possibly imagine ruling without control over major Church appointments.

The settlement of 1122 removed for a generation the major preoccupation of the papacy with the Empire, but it did not establish a world free from troubles. The election decree of 1059 had been a bold demonstration of the 'proper order', but it had not solved the problems of achieving 'free' papal elections. In December 1124 the election of Teobaldo dei Boccapecorini, Cardinal-Priest of Sant'Anastasia, was overturned even as the ceremonies for his installation were proceeding, for the commander of the papal mercenary guard, Roberto Frangipani, broke into the church and proclaimed Lambert, Bishop of Ostia, as pope. That he was able to take office as Honorius II owed more to the support of the Frangipani and the highly influential papal chancellor, Aimeric, and to the bribery of possible supporters of Teobaldo among the rival Pierleoni family, than it did to the decree of 1059. Not surprisingly, when Honorius died in 1130, these rivalries broke out again, but this time leaving the Church with two popes, a situation which lasted for eight years. Even as Honorius lay dying the cardinals scrambled for position. Within hours of his death on the night of 13 February, Cardinal Aimeric had engineered the election of Gregory Papareschi, Cardinal-Deacon of Sant'Angelo, as Innocent II. He represented the Frangipani interest, but the Pierleoni were not to be outmanoeuvred a second time and, by the morning of 14 February they had persuaded a majority of cardinals to choose Peter Pierleoni, who took the name of Anacletus II. The Pierleoni had become rich helping to finance the expansion of papal power and they made this money tell in buying support. Innocent II, although elected first, soon found his support evaporating. In May he fled, eventually reaching France, while the Frangipani fell in behind Anacletus. Although Innocent managed to array most of Christendom behind him, he was unable to return to Rome until after the death of Anacletus in 1138, for Anacletus had secured the support of the Norman ruler, Roger II, by conceding him the title of king in 1130.

Once re-established in Rome, in April 1139, Innocent assembled a great council to reassert the work of reform, just as Calixtus II had done in 1123. The scope was wide, with decrees ranging from the condemnation of simony as an illegitimate usurpation of office to a prohibition of jousts and tournaments in which, it was said, men were so often killed in consequent danger of their souls. The connecting thread remains a sharp condemnation of materialism, which is seen here largely in terms of the twin evils of avarice and violence. Finally, one further purpose was revealed: Innocent wished to ensure that all of Anacletus's influence on the Church was obliterated (Foreville 1965:187–94). Clause thirty of the decrees: 'The ordinations made by Pierleone and the other schismatics and heretics, we declare null and invalid' (Foreville 1965:194). But despite his desire to wipe Anacletus from the history of the Church, Innocent could not avoid the political consequences of the schism. If the popes wished to maintain residence in Rome, which was the see of St Peter and therefore the foundation of their authority, and if they wished to consolidate their territorial lordship in central Italy in order to protect that position, they were inevitably major players on the Italian political scene. For Innocent II this led to the disastrous attempt to overturn by force the Anacletian settlement with Roger II. But, as with Leo IX in 1053, the Normans were too strong, the papal army was defeated and the pope himself captured; in the ensuing Treaty of Mignano (July 1139), he had no alternative but to confirm Roger's position. Control of Rome proved no easier, for factional conflict was complicated by the growth of communal interests not dissimilar to those already established in the Lombard cities. In the twelfth century larger communes regularly attempted to increase their power over lesser towns within their orbit and, in this case, the immediate cause of the agitation was Innocent's failure to follow up a victory over neighbouring Tivoli in the manner required. After Innocent's death in 1143, this seems to have developed into an attempt to gain control of Roman government by means of a Senate set up for this purpose. To the popes this was a revolt against their authority; indeed, early in 1145 Pope Lucius II seems to have been killed in the fighting which resulted.

In February 1145 a Cistercian abbot, Bernard Paganelli, closely connected with St Bernard, was elected as Eugenius III, and he managed to reach an agreement with the commune in which he recognised the Senate elected by the various regions of Rome, while the Senate allowed the pope to reappoint the Prefect with overall charge of the city. The essential instability of the social life of Rome was, however, quickly demonstrated when Eugenius made the mistake of allowing Arnold of Brescia to enter the city. In 1139 Arnold had been condemned by Innocent II for anti-clerical preaching and, in the following year, expelled from France by King Louis VII, but Eugenius III reconciled him to the Church, probably in 1146, and sent him to Rome to do penance.

The sight of what he believed to be corruption in the papal curia was too much for Arnold; his reaction seems to have combined with the political opposition to the pope to reignite the conflicts in the city. Once more papal residence became untenable. By 1148 Arnold was at the centre of the unrest, advocating the withdrawal of obedience to the papacy, leaving it to exercise spiritual authority only. When Eugenius died in 1153, Arnold still enjoyed widespread support in Rome and it was not until the conjunction of events that led to the coronation of Frederick Barbarossa in June 1155, that Arnold was overcome and executed by the Prefect of the City. Eugenius's problems in Rome were not alleviated by success in the wider world, for his attempts to revive distinctly flagging crusading enthusiasm only met with success when stiffened by the preaching of his mentor, Bernard of Clairvaux. Eugenius had been reacting to the loss of the city of Edessa in 1144, but the Second Crusade which was finally launched in 1147 managed only an abortive attack upon Damascus. Crusading necessarily entailed such risks for papal prestige; only the prominence St Bernard, first in preaching and at later in excusing the crusade, did something to draw criticism from the papacy.

The history of the papacy between the Concordat of Worms in 1122 and the death of Eugenius III in 1153 vividly illustrates that, even without a direct imperial threat, Roman feuds, Norman ambitions and incompetently led crusades could reduce grandiose papal plans to ashes. But nowhere was the growing chasm between reforming idealism and the actual implementation of policy more evident than in the development of papal administration. The popes had soon found that the documentation available to show how the Church should be formed on earth was inadequate, and this had inaugurated the search for past texts, previously neglected or unexploited, which could rectify this. The papal researchers unearthed all kinds of material from papal registers to the writings of the Church Fathers, so that it soon became necessary to find a systematic way of organising these, and from these circumstances there developed what can be described as 'a science of canon law'. One of the earliest examples was the *Collection of the seventy-four titles*, probably the work of Cardinal Humbert, and by the late eleventh century a distinct methodology could be seen to be emerging through the work of men like Ivo of Chartres. In *c.*1140 this new science found its supreme exposition in the great collection produced by the monk, Gratian, known as the *Decretum*. Gratian's application of the dialectical method was so thorough that his work became the standard textbook, the point from which all later commentators started. Gratian's environment was that of the law schools of Bologna, which in the twelfth century became the greatest centre for the study of both Roman and canon law. From here, during the twelfth and thirteenth centuries, emerged a supply of trained lawyers who could staff the papal administration and even aspire to the papacy itself. With the accession of Alexander III in 1159 began a succession of legally trained popes who came to dominate the office in the thirteenth century.

The structure over which they presided had been largely formed by the middle of the twelfth century. By the later eleventh century the popes had begun to organise a proper chancery for the issue of documents, together with a *Camera* or treasury which, by 1140, encompassed the library and archives as well. Under Urban II the papal organisation can accurately be described as the *Curia Romana*, served by a full range of functionaries. The Cardinal John of Gaeta was the key figure in achieving these reforms as papal chancellor from 1089 until he himself reigned briefly as Pope Gelasius II (1118–19). At the same time the cardinals themselves were transformed into a distinct college, for after the 1059 election decree not only did they gain greater individual importance, but also they began to acquire an institutional coherence as well. By Paschal II's time there were settled numbers of cardinals (seven (later six) bishops, twenty-eight priests, eighteen deacons) in the college, which had its own treasury. In the past these positions had largely been filled by local clerics whose duties were primarily liturgical, but in the reform era they were drawn from all Christendom, creating for the papacy an advisory body not unlike a secular ruler's 'court' of vassals (Robinson 1990:16–18).

By the mid-twelfth century, however, these changes had begun to create their own problems. The papal court had become the centre of a great network: streams of decrees, letters and judgements poured out, while the paths to Rome were beaten solid by crowds of litigants. This was why Arnold of Brescia had thought the papal curia was 'not the Church of God, but a place of business and a den of thieves', and why John of Salisbury, who observed the workings of the papal curia at close quarters between 1148 and 1152, commented that when Eugenius III returned to Rome in 1149 he 'received a splendid reception from the nobles, whose noses sensed the gold and silver of Gaul' (Chibnall 1956:49–51). Most famously, St Bernard deeply feared the consequences of the growth of papal power. In a letter to Eugenius, shortly after he became pope, he wrote: 'You have been called to hold a high position, but not a safe one; a sublime position, but not a secure one. How terrible, how very terrible is the place you hold!' He went on to lament the passing of the days of St Peter, 'who would sully his fingers with no gifts and could say with a clear conscience and a pure heart: "Silver and gold have I none"' (B.S. James 1998:278–9). Bernard's lament made little difference. Walter Map, Archdeacon of Oxford in the later twelfth century, who had attended the Lateran Council of 1179, wrote that he had never yet seen a poor man bring back a privilege from Rome, because (quoting Ovid), 'if you bring nothing in hand, Homer, then out you will go' (M.R. James 1983:97). The fact was that all Rome, from the money-changers and usurers attracted by a world in which every sort of currency changed hands, to the curial officials who, not being properly paid or beneficed, were open to bribery, had come to depend upon the papal system.

Even before the death of Eugenius, however, a new and formidable figure had appeared, whose character and policies were to rivet papal attention until his death on crusade in 1190. On 9 March 1152 the Staufen, Frederick of Swabia, was crowned King of the Romans at Aachen. Initially, the new pope, Adrian IV (elected December 1154), had envisaged Frederick taking up what he saw as his rightful place as protector of the Church and, with this in mind, he met Frederick at Sutri in June 1155, preparatory to an imperial coronation in Rome. Adrian had already threatened Rome with an interdict in order to force the expulsion of Arnold of Brescia, and he had shown his view of the Normans by his excommunication of William I for invading the papal territories of Benevento. These actions were in keeping with the Treaty of Constance made two years before in which Eugenius III and Frederick Barbarossa had agreed to co-operate in their policies towards both the Romans and the Normans. But at Sutri there was a brief hiatus before Frederick would perform the traditional ceremony by which he was required to lead the pope's horse into Rome, minor in itself, but in an age so highly conscious of symbolic acts, indicative of Frederick's cast of mind. Moreover, although Frederick refused to have any truck with the ideas of imperial autonomy that had been broached by Arnold of Brescia, he stayed in Rome only long enough for his coronation on 18 June before beginning the journey back to Germany. To the pope, Frederick's protection must have seemed a dubious asset, tinged as it was with the implication of control. From this time relations between pope and emperor began to deteriorate, culminating in a misunderstanding at Besançon in 1157 which, if it was not actually manufactured, owed much to the state of mutual suspicion which had developed by then. The fact was that Frederick's abrupt departure left Adrian isolated, yet it remained essential for the papacy to maintain a firm territorial base in central Italy. In 1156 the pope therefore allowed himself to become involved in a fruitless Byzantine plan to overcome the Normans which ended, as so often before when the popes had ventured south in arms, in Norman victory. Adrian, trapped in Benevento, had no alternative but once more to recognise the Norman kingship, taking William I's homage for Apulia and Sicily in June 1156.

If the Treaty of Benevento exposed the fragility of the papal–imperial relationship, then the quarrel at the imperial court at Besançon brought the issues out into the open. Frederick had been at Besançon for some months when, in October 1157, papal legates, the Cardinals Roland and Bernard, arrived there with a letter from the pope. The ostensible purpose was to rebuke the emperor for not taking more vigorous action against those who had attacked Eskil, Archbishop of Lund, while he was travelling through imperial territory. The tone is that of one who is surprised and a little hurt that, having treated Frederick so affectionately and honourably, he had not had a better response, but the actual words used to express these sentiments gave rise to immediate offence. According to Rahewin, the continuator of Otto of Freising's *Deeds of Frederick Barbarossa*,

> what had particularly aroused them all [i.e. those assembled at Besançon] was the fact that in the aforesaid letter it had been stated, among other things, that the fullness of dignity and honor had been bestowed upon the emperor by the Roman pontiff, that the emperor had received from his hand the imperial crown, and that he would not have regretted confirming even greater benefits [*beneficia*] upon him, in consideration of the great gain and advantage that might through him accrue to the Roman Church.

Apparently they chose to accept what Rahewin calls 'the literal meaning of these words', for memories were still fresh of Frederick's coronation in Rome in 1155 when, first there had been an attempt by the Romans to offer the crown to Frederick, which had been indignantly rejected, and then, many of Frederick's entourage had seen the mural of the Emperor Lothar III in the chapel of St Nicholas in the Lateran on which, Rahewin claimed, was an inscription describing him as 'vassal of the pope', a picture which Pope Adrian had assured Frederick he would have removed (Robinson 1990:452–3). The situation had been further inflamed when one of the legates is alleged to have said: 'From whom then does he have the empire, if not from our lord the pope?' In the ensuing disorder the legates were physically threatened before Frederick had them abruptly hustled from the gathering. In the end Adrian was forced to put a conciliatory gloss on the letter, claiming that in this context *beneficium* meant not 'fief' but 'good deed' (Mierow 1955:183–4, 199), although his explanation seemed far from convincing.

The fact was that the papacy continued to see the Empire as an essentially derivative power. The Carolingians and the Ottonians had been crowned by the popes and this pretension had been supported by reference to the Donation of Constantine, which purported to show that the Emperor Constantine had granted Pope Sylvester I the rule of Rome and its possessions in the west. Although this document was in fact a forgery, probably of the mid-eighth century (and indeed had been exposed as such by Otto III's chancery in 1001), the popes of the eleventh and twelfth centuries apparently believed in it, for its echoes can be discerned in their pronouncements and visual symbolism (Robinson 1990:22–6). For their part the emperors appealed to historical and legal precedent of equal longevity, encompassing not only the Carolingians and Ottonians, but also the Roman Caesars themselves, a claim which necessarily placed as much emphasis on Rome and Italy as did the popes. The emperors backed this up by right of conquest, pointing out that it had been the Franks who had saved the papacy when, in the eighth century, Byzantine power had been crumbling and the Lombards had been threatening Rome.

Ultimately, the extent to which either side could turn theory into reality depended upon the actual military and political balance in Italy. During the next eighteen years Frederick set out to achieve this political control, making four great expeditions to Italy in 1158–62, 1163–4, 1166–7 and 1174–7, apart from his initial appearance in 1154–5. The political power-brokers of Italy could not relish this prospect, especially when, in 1158, he issued a series of decrees at Roncaglia (near Piacenza) which claimed regalian rights in Lombardy so extensive that representatives of the great cities of the north – particularly Milan, Piacenza and Brescia – sought out papal aid. Adrian allowed Frederick forty days' grace in order to rescind these decrees, on pain of excommunication, but on 1 September 1159 he died, before he could put this into effect. However, the pattern was already set: Frederick was determined to impose his imperial rule, while some combination among the papacy, the Italian cities and the King of Sicily was bound to oppose him. With Adrian's death the consequence for the Church was another long and bitter schism.

The election of 7 September 1159 showed once more the vulnerability of the papacy despite the decree of 1059. Although the great majority of cardinals elected Cardinal Roland as Alexander III, a minority with some support within Rome chose Cardinal Octavian as Victor IV. It is improbable that the imperialists from Frederick's court had been directly involved, but the situation which had arisen provided an ideal opportunity for Frederick to demonstrate in practice the ideology which he was vigorously propounding, namely that he was the true successor of the Roman emperors, deriving his power and authority from no earthly institution. Roman emperors had convened synods in order to resolve the problems of the Church; Frederick did the same, presiding over a gathering at Pavia in February 1160. Alexander refused to accept such a pretension, but nevertheless the council, predictably, declared Victor IV to be the rightful pope.

The result was schism, perpetuated by the imperialist creation of two further popes between 1164 and 1178, and by Frederick's invasions of Italy. Despite the support which he enjoyed in the rest of Christendom, Alexander III was forced to take refuge in France between 1162 and 1165, and to retreat to Benevento when Frederick entered Rome in 1167. In the end the constant resistance of the Lombard cities took its toll and when Frederick was defeated at Legnano (between Lake Maggiore and Milan) in May 1176, he decided to settle for peace, embodied in the terms agreed at Venice in 1177. Pope and emperor agreed upon mutual restoration of lands and vassals seized during the schism, while Alexander accepted the ecclesiastical appointments which had been made in Germany. Most importantly, for Christendom as a whole, the imperialists at last recognised Alexander as pope.

This was not a long-term solution, but it did lead Alexander III to reconsider the papal electoral procedure at the Third Lateran Council of March 1179. The pope saw this as a fitting gathering of the universal Church after the divisions created by the schism. At least 300 bishops attended, coming from as far west as Ireland and as far east as the Crusader States, and including extensive representation from the German Church. Alexander set down that a two-thirds majority was necessary within the college with all the cardinals having an equal vote, rather than the graduated system of 1059. This did not, of course, prevent dissension or outside intervention, but it did make it difficult for interested seculars to sustain a credible opposition candidate. This decree was one of twenty-seven canons issued by the council. Prohibitions on simony and clerical unchastity were repeated, and, most strikingly, a number of canons were promulgated intended to shape attitudes towards the Jews, towards a new poverty movement, the Waldensians, towards the Cathar heretics, and towards lepers, as well as regulations on social and commercial relations with Muslims (Foreville 1965:210–23).

When Alexander III died in 1181, he left a delicate balance in Italy, but during the 1180s the increasingly critical state of the Holy Land, culminating in the loss of Jerusalem in October 1187, meant that papal policy could not be governed entirely by narrow territorial interests in the peninsula. These two considerations dominated the relatively short reigns of the next five popes between 1181 and 1198. Lucius III, Alexander's immediate successor, met Frederick at Verona in 1184, but the main outcome was an agreement on the vigorous prosecution of heretics rather than a further clarification of the emperor's Italian plans. The engagement in October of Henry, Frederick's heir, to Constance, aunt of William II of Sicily, did nothing to set the pope's mind at rest, and he refused to crown Henry as co-emperor as his father wished. The election of a known anti-imperialist as Pope Urban III in 1185 seemed to presage a further deterioration of relations, but Urban was overtaken by events in the Holy Land. Both his successors, Gregory VIII and Clement III, now strove for a new crusade; indeed Frederick set out for the east in May 1189, followed by the Capetian and Angevin rulers, Philip II and Richard I, the next year. But the Italian political scene was never static. When William II died without direct heirs in November 1189, Henry determined to incorporate the Kingdom of Sicily into his lands by right of his wife, a situation made more threatening for the papacy by the accidental death of Frederick Barbarossa in Asia Minor in June 1190. In fact, it took Henry VI until 1194 to achieve the conquest of Sicily and the reigning pope, Celestine III, was still stalling on Henry's desire for recognition of the Hohenstaufen hereditary position when the emperor unexpectedly died in September 1197. Once more there was respite for the papacy, for Henry's heir, Frederick, was still an infant.

The election of Lothar of Segni as Pope Innocent III, on 8 January 1198, at 37 the youngest of the cardinals, might at first sight seem surprising. But the twenty-six years since the death of Alexander III had seen five popes, none of whom had lasted as long as seven years and one of whom, Gregory VIII, had reigned for less than two months. All of them had been aged when elected; the last of them, Celestine III, was in his ninety-second year when he died. In choosing Lothar the cardinals seem to have perceived not only his ability, but also the need for a fresh and dynamic figure.

If this was the intention, then Innocent certainly fulfilled expectations. Historians have accepted that this pontificate had more impact on Christian society than any other since that of Gregory VII. The lack of a credible imperial opponent, combined with

Innocent's vigorous restatement of papal authority expressed in his decretals (i.e. judicial decisions of the pope in the papal court) and executed by a host of practical actions throughout Christendom, carried the papacy to a height of power and influence never previously achieved. During his eighteen years as pope, Innocent made and unmade rulers; presided over, at one time or another, as vassal states, the kingdoms of Sicily, Iberia and England, as well as possibly Hungary, Poland and Bulgaria; launched one great crusade to the east and laid the plans for another; inaugurated the Albigensian Crusades against the Cathar heretics of Languedoc; and in central Italy pursued a determined campaign of recuperations which established a formidable papal monarchy in the peninsula based upon the *Patrimonium Petri.* However, his political and crusading activity should not be allowed to obscure his awareness of the need for reform and pastoral care; indeed, he would have seen these actions as a piece. The fierce letters denouncing the Cathar heretics need to be set in the context of his recognition of the value of contemporary poverty movements to the Church: the Humiliati in 1201, some of the Waldensians in 1208, the embryonic Franciscan movement in 1210. The culmination can be seen in the great council which met at the Lateran in November 1215, attended by over 400 bishops and 800 abbots and chapter heads.

Having said this, however, Innocent's failures are as significant as his successes, for they show that even under this pope, the great papal plan for the remoulding of society was, in practice, severely circumscribed. The interventions into imperial affairs never did produce an ideal papal candidate, while Innocent's final choice of the Hohenstaufen Frederick II was to prove, from a papal point of view, a most damaging mistake. The Albigensian Crusade did not eliminate heresy in southern France, let alone deter others elsewhere and, indeed, its capture by self-interested seculars became a continual source of unease to the pope. The great crusade to the east was diverted to Constantinople in 1203–4 and did nothing for the Crusader States and, although Innocent gained a Latin patriarch, this served only to alienate the Greeks even further from the Roman pope. Finally, the creative initiatives taken by Innocent in his treatment of poverty groups met with a lukewarm response within the established Church: the clerics at the Fourth Lateran Council determined that there was no further need for new orders. The pontificate demonstrates how restricted were human agents, even if convinced they acted as God's vicars, in their attempts to rebuild the earthly city. The reformed papacy was fired by a great social ideal based upon what it interpreted as the proper Christian order. Because he had great gifts and energy, deployed in a favourable political environment, Innocent's pontificate is a good test of the extent to which that ideal was ever achievable.

It is evident from Innocent's sermon at his consecration on 22 February 1198, that his conception of papal power was already highly developed before he became pope. The superiority of the spiritual power is set out uncompromisingly in a famous passage. 'To me is said in the person of the prophet, "I have set thee over nations and over kingdoms, to root up and to pull down, and to waste and to destroy, and to build and to plant" (Jeremiah 1:10)' (Tierney 1964:131–2). On the other hand, Innocent had been a pupil of the famous canon lawyer, Huguccio of Pisa, at Bologna during the late 1180s, and Huguccio's world view suggests a duality of powers that concedes independent origin to temporal rule as well as autonomy within its own sphere (Watt 1965:17). This training may well explain Innocent's caution in the forms used to justify his interventions. Confronted by two candidates for the German throne, the Staufen Philip of Swabia and the Welf Otto of Brunswick, both crowned by their adherents during 1198, Innocent set out the papal position in the decretal *Venerabilem* (1202). In this he accepted the electoral rights of the princes, as Huguccio had described, but asserted that, since the pope anointed, consecrated and crowned the emperor, it equally appertained to him to examine the suitability of the candidate and, if warranted, to reject him. He accepted Huguccio's formulation of the duality of powers, but subsumed the temporal into the spiritual to such a degree that he was in effect setting out a hierarchical conception of the world little different from that conceived by Gregory VII.

Innocent's view of the exercise of spiritual power carried with it a second corollary, which was that he had the right to act *ratione peccati* (by reason of sin). Thus, the decretal *Novit*, promulgated on the occasion of Innocent's intervention in the war between the Angevin King John and Philip II, King of France, set down that

> we do not intend to judge concerning a fief, judgement of which belongs to him [i.e. the King of France]... but to decide concerning a sin, of which judgement undoubtedly belongs to us, and we can and should exercise it against anyone.
>
> (Tierney 1964:134–5)

Here again Innocent carefully picks his way around what he accepts to be a purely secular matter, that is a feudal dispute, but still finds justification for intervention. Innocent hardly needed to make an unambiguous assertion about the nature of temporal power appertaining to the Holy See, since the two principles of ultimate jurisdiction and *ratione peccati* were flexible enough to cope with most matters affecting papal interests.

While the creation of a unified and morally purified Christendom remained the papacy's ultimate goal, ever since Leo IX the popes had believed that this could be achieved only from a secure territorial base in central Italy. As a cardinal, Hildebrand was 'custodian of the altar of St Peter' and thus had particular responsibility for this problem, striving to counter the fraud and maladministration that had characterised the government of papal holdings in the pre-reform era, and slowly loosening the grip of the Roman aristocracy on what he regarded as rightfully belonging to the papal patrimony. Because of Hildebrand's efforts it became possible for Cardinal Deusdedit to compile the *Collectio canonum*, which recorded properties and revenues owed to the Holy See. It was by no means complete, but nevertheless was a remarkable achievement in that so lax had been the administration of the previous half-century that there were no documents at all available to the cardinals since the pontificate of Gregory V in the late tenth century. Early investigations such as this enabled much fuller surveys to be compiled, most importantly for Innocent's era, the *Liber censuum*, completed in 1192 by the *camerlengo*, Cardinal Cencio Savelli (Innocent's successor as Honorius III). This provided a comprehensive list of those institutions, both inside and outside the Papal States, that owed *census*, in this way showing their dependence on the apostolic see (Zema 1947:137–53). Until this time, wrote Cencio in the preamble to his book, the Roman Church 'was incurring a large damage and loss', but that his intention was to remedy this and provide 'materials for all my successors' (Lunt 1934:1:38). Innocent's policy of recuperations was an integral part of this process; papal resources in lands and revenues needed to be mobilised in the service of the apostolic see, both by recovery of lands believed to have been lost and by efficient financial administration. He was most successful in the Duchy of Spoleto and in large parts of the March of Ancona, so that, by 1216 the papacy controlled a wide band of territory in which it exercised temporal sovereignty running diagonally across the centre of Italy from coast to coast.

The most pressing reason for the establishment of the Papal State was the need for security. Under Henry VI there had seemed a real danger of a union of Sicily and the Empire, but with Henry's death events largely outside Innocent's control ensured that the link was broken. In March 1198 the German princes elected Henry's brother, Philip of Swabia, as king, but within two months Constance, Henry's widow, had made her infant son, Frederick, a ward of the pope, a move largely dictated by her fervent desire to protect Frederick's Sicilian inheritance from what she saw as German designs. Finally, in July, led by Adolf, Archbishop of Cologne, and financed by the Angevin, Richard I, the enemies of the Staufen crowned Otto of Brunswick, Richard's nephew, thus creating a direct rival to Philip of Swabia. Innocent's assessment of the candidates was based on their attitudes towards papal policy in Italy and Sicily. Otto's apparent willingness to accept the papal view led, in 1201, to a declaration that the pope was prepared to accept him as worthy to be crowned. But the weakness of Otto's position became ever more evident in the years that followed, while Innocent's policy of recuperations in Italy ensured that Philip's ambitions in the south stood little chance of being realised. Moreover, his Sicilian plans became less relevant as Frederick grew nearer to the age when he could come into his inheritance. By 1207 Innocent and Philip were prepared to come to terms, but their moves towards reconciliation were suddenly shattered when Philip was assassinated in June 1208, a private act having nothing to do with these wider issues.

Frederick came of age in December 1208, and Innocent therefore gave up the regency of Sicily, but by that time he had acceded to the sign of God's will which he believed had been shown by Philip's murder, and had once more committed himself to Otto. In June at Neuss, Otto had again made sweeping promises which seemed in keeping with the pope's Italian policy and, accordingly, Innocent crowned Otto IV on 4 October 1209. However, almost at once Otto began to implement plans to invade the Kingdom of Sicily, contravening his promises and compromising the pope's reputation. In little more than a year after crowning his chosen candidate, Innocent was forced to excommunicate him (18 November 1210), just as Otto's forces entered the Sicilian kingdom. As a guardian of the interests of Frederick of Staufen, Innocent had left much to be desired, but by 1211, despite some misgivings, he had no alternative but to promote his former ward. Frederick was crowned at Mainz in December 1212, and Innocent's support was rewarded with the Golden Bull of Eger (July 1213), which accepted the recuperations in Italy and conceded claims over the Church which might legitimately have been pursued under the Concordat of Worms. Otto's declining fortunes became irrecoverable when, as part of King John's anti-Capetian coalition, he was defeated by Philip II at Bouvines in July 1214. Innocent's manipulation of affairs must have seemed complete when, in July 1216, he received Frederick's promise not to unite the German and Sicilian thrones.

The Fourth Lateran Council, assembled in November 1215, only eight months before the pope's death, brought together the various strands of Innocent's many-sided reform activity. Canon twenty-five, for example, took an uncompromising stand on interference in ecclesiastical elections:

> Whoever consents to his irregular election by a secular power contrary to
> canonical liberty will lose the benefice from the election and become ineligible;
> he cannot be promoted without dispensation to any dignity whatsoever. Those
> who have proceeded in such an election, which we declare null *ipso iure*, will be
> suspended from their offices and benefices for three years and during that time
> deprived of their power to elect.

Closely connected to this is canon forty-six, which forbade taxation of clergy by
laymen without first consulting the pope 'to whom it appertains to attend to the needs
of all'. The distinction between the clerical and lay orders was clearly given greater
emphasis by such decrees, but the council treated the needs of the body of the Church
in its widest sense as well. In this respect, canon twenty-one was very significant for it
replaced the previous expectation that the eucharist be taken three times annually, often
disregarded, with the more realistic command that all Christians confess annually and
receive the eucharist at least at Easter, on pain of exclusion from the services of the
Church, including Christian burial. 'This salutary decree will be frequently published
in the churches: thus no one can cover his blindness under a veil of ignorance' (Foreville
1965:359–60, 368–9, 357–8). Innocent's whole attitude towards Christian society is
encapsulated here: evasion and prevarication would not suffice, for Christians were
either committed to the faith, or they were excluded, along with other unbelievers.

The pontificate of Innocent III determined the abiding themes of the reigns of his
thirteenth-century successors: the aims of the popes must be to promote Christian
unity through the crusade and the crushing of internal heretical dissent; to reinforce that
unity through the purification of society, an end which necessarily could be achieved
only if preceded by clerical reform; and to maintain papal independence by ensuring
that Staufen ambitions did not turn the holder of the See of St Peter into the tame
bishop of a new 'Roman' empire. What marked off the three major pontificates which
followed that of Innocent III – encompassing Honorius III (1216–27), Gregory IX
(1227–41) and Innocent IV (1243–54) – was that the last of these themes came, by
stages, to overshadow the other papal goals, leading the popes more and more into
overtly political acts to which the wider aims of the Christian community, even the
crusade, came to be subordinated.

In 1215 Frederick II had taken the cross. Although this had not been at papal
instigation, Honorius III hoped that Frederick would implement his promise by aiding
the Fifth Crusade, which was fighting in the Nile Delta between 1218 and 1221, and this
may account for the pope's willingness to allow the election of Frederick's son, Henry,
as King of the Romans in April 1220, and to provide Frederick himself with an imperial
coronation at Rome in November. In fact, Frederick was too deeply involved in
reconstructing monarchical authority in the Kingdom of Sicily to help the crusaders;
it was the conviction that Frederick intended to extend this form of government into
Lombardy, and thus encircle the papacy, that led directly to the more aggressive policies
of Honorius's successors, Gregory IX and Innocent IV. From this premise arose the
justification for papal policies during the middle decades of the thirteenth century.
Gregory twice excommunicated the emperor in 1227 and 1239, the first time for turning
back from crusade, the second for allegedly contravening the provisions of the Treaty
of San Germano, made when the parties had been reconciled in 1230. After 1239 a new
bitterness pervades the atmosphere, leading in time to papal plans not simply to limit
Staufen power, but quite literally to eliminate the dynasty. Frederick responded to the

excommunication by invading the Papal States, while Gregory attempted to summon a council at Rome which would, he hoped, array Christendom against the heretic emperor. But in May 1241 Frederick seized and carried into captivity some of the prelates travelling to the council. The situation was deteriorating rapidly when, in August, the pope died.

These circumstances tested the election decree of 1179 almost to destruction. After two months of incarceration, the cardinals elected Goffredo Castiglioni as Celestine IV, but ironically the pope who had been produced with so much agony lived only another seventeen days. The dispersal of the cardinals which followed meant that the Genoese, Sinibaldo Fieschi, was not chosen until June 1243, taking the name of Innocent IV. Prolonged negotiations with Frederick followed, but there was no basis of trust. The old wounds were reopened when, in June 1244, Innocent secretly fled, first to Genoa and then to Lyon. Once there, the pope felt free to begin a series of actions which culminated in the deposition of Frederick at the Council of Lyon on 17 July 1245. Innocent had called the council in the previous December, apparently in the same spirit as the great ecumenical assemblies of his predecessors, with the intention of promoting Church reform and of meeting external threats, particularly that of the Mongols, but the abiding memory is of the final decree against Frederick, from which, despite the eloquence of Thaddeus of Suessa, the imperial representative, Innocent was not to be diverted.

The break was accompanied by a violent propaganda offensive, orchestrated by Cardinal Rainier of Viterbo, and this has sometimes led to the view that Innocent's policies so distorted papal objectives that they were directly responsible for a fundamental decline in the power and influence of the papacy in the later middle ages. It seems, however, more reasonable to place him, as he did himself, in the context of previous papal history, a history which he set out more systematically than any previous pope (Watt 1965:59ff.; Tierney 1965). Innocent saw himself as the successor to a long line of ministers of God, stretching back to Noah.

> For we act as a general legate on earth of the king of kings who bestowed on the prince of the apostles, and in him on us, a plenitude of power to bind and loose not only everyone, but everything 'whatsoever'…
>
> (Tierney 1964:147)

Nevertheless, Innocent could not return to Rome until after Frederick's death in December 1250. The chance that determined he should outlive Frederick enabled Innocent to turn papal policies in the following decades towards the total destruction of what he believed was 'a brood of vipers'. With the one exception of Gregory X (1271–6), this became the overriding papal concern during the next three decades.

The popes therefore began a search for an alternative candidate to the Staufen, a candidate who would act as the trusted exponent of papal wishes. After a number of failed negotiations, in 1263 the French pope, Urban IV (1261–4) finally gained the agreement of Louis IX of France to the renewed choice of his younger brother, Charles of Anjou. Until this time the papacy's political schemes had brought little return. Although Frederick's son, Conrad IV, had died in 1254, leaving as his heir his 2-year-old son, Conradin, there existed a formidable opponent in the person of Manfred, an illegitimate son of Frederick II who, unencumbered by the German kingship, had systematically strengthened his rule in the Kingdom of Sicily and had built up alliances among the Italian cities stretching from Genoa to Siena. The papacy was now determined to provide Charles with every facility to oppose what it saw as this new Hohenstaufen menace, even accepting Charles's election as Senator of Rome. Charles proved to be a formidable ally, defeating and killing Manfred at Benevento in 1266, and executing Conradin in 1268 after winning the battle of Tagliacozzo.

But the victories were double-edged, for Charles was now in a position to dominate the papacy. The vacancy of nearly three years, which followed the death of Clement IV in 1268, showed Charles's growing influence, while of the six popes elected between 1271 and 1285, when Charles died, only Gregory X and Nicholas III (1277–80) had either the will or the opportunity to offset Charles's power. The most constructive of these popes was Gregory X who worked to maintain the traditions of reform and crusade which had been overshadowed by the papacy's Italian concerns. He used the vehicle of a general council which met at Lyon in 1274. Here a new crusade was planned involving all the leading Christian monarchs, including the newly elected German ruler, Rudolf of Habsburg. Aid was envisaged from the Byzantine Emperor, Michael VIII, who was deeply concerned about Charles's plans for a Mediterranean empire which would encompass Constantinople itself. Michael's agreement to union of the eastern and western Churches stemmed directly from this fear. Finally, like its predecessors, the council produced a string of reforming decrees, including a tightening of the rules on papal elections in the hope of avoiding deadlocked conclaves. These rules were permanently incorporated into the procedures in 1294. Unlike Gregory, a former Archdeacon of Liège, Nicholas III emanated from the Orsini, an important Roman family, and necessarily concerned himself closely with Italian politics, but he was no more enamoured of Charles's stifling alliance and, in 1278, when the terms expired, he succeeded in persuading him to relinquish the powerful posts of Senator of Rome and Vicar of Tuscany. His continued negotiations with the Byzantines over Church union blocked Charles's expansionist plans in the eastern Mediterranean.

When Nicholas III died in 1280, therefore, Charles exerted himself to secure a more subservient figure. After six months he succeeded in the person of Simon of Brie, who became Martin IV. Under him Charles regained the influence lost in central Italy: the Senatorship of Rome, control of offices in the Papal State, unwavering papal support for the Guelph party in the factional struggles of the Italian cities. Charles was stopped not by the papacy, but by the Sicilian Vespers, a sudden and shattering popular uprising against Charles's rule on the island in 1282. This uprising was consolidated by the prompt invasion of Peter of Aragon, who believed himself heir to Staufen claims through the right of his wife, Constance, a daughter of Manfred. The invasion revived bitter memories for the papacy. Martin excommunicated Peter and proclaimed a crusade against Aragon. When Charles and Martin IV died within three months of each other in January and March 1285, they left the papacy so deeply embedded in the mire of Italian politics that only the very greatest of popes could have transcended the problems.

No such figure appeared. The French crusade against Aragon ended in disaster, claiming the life of King Philip III in October 1285. Neither Honorius IV (1285–7) nor Nicholas IV (1288–92), the first Franciscan pope, could find a solution to the Sicilian problem. Moreover, while Nicholas and his predecessors struggled with the complexities of Italian politics, the universal mission of the Church was faltering, for the Latins in the east were stumbling towards their final debacle. In May 1291 Acre fell to the Mamluks and the Latins evacuated the Palestinian mainland. There were loud recriminations as well as several elaborate plans for the retrieval of the situation, but no new crusade was organised, for when Nicholas IV died in April 1292 the cardinals, split by family faction and conflicting priorities, were unable to produce a new pope for two years and three months.

During the thirteenth century the papacy had defined and systematised its world view, while at the same time taking vigorous practical measures, especially in Italy, to defend itself against those who would turn this grandiose concept into a pious fiction. It was equally important to the papacy that its institutional development could enable it to mobilise the administrative means to accomplish these aims. Canon law provided an authoritative justification for papal actions and the thirteenth-century popes were anxious that it should be effectively codified. In 1234 Gregory IX issued the *Liber Extra* after work commissioned from Raymond of Peñaforte, supplemented in 1298 by the *Liber Sextus* which included collections made since the 1230s. The interaction between the development of papal administration and the compilations was a major element in the consolidation of the hierarchical view of the Church towards which Gregory VII had been struggling. At its apex the pope exercised supreme administrative and legislative power, drawing to himself the right to dispense from laws, as well as, more positively, to fill ecclesiastical benefices, a practice known as papal provisions. This power had developed from the reservation of specific classes of benefice, and had been used by Clement IV from 1265 to appoint to benefices vacated while the holder was at the curia. Although this applied to a tiny proportion only, the principle was established and, under later popes such as Boniface VIII and Clement V, extended to include other classes of benefices as well. However, perhaps the one action which really epitomised the approach of the thirteenth-century popes was the appointment of specialist inquisitors, who were first established during the 1230s. These formed legal tribunals responsible to the papacy, and designed as a systematic means of searching out and, if possible, reconciling heretics to the universal Church.

An increasingly specialist administrative structure implemented papal decisions and drew in papal revenues. The sheer volume of juridical business meant that the pope, sitting in his consistory court of cardinals, was no longer able to cope and it became necessary to subdivide judicial business. Under Gregory IX there emerged a separate *Penitentiaria*, for example, a department particularly concerned with dispensations from censures, vows or penances, which the pope had reserved to himself, while civil and penal cases appertaining to the Holy See were handled by the *Audentia Sacri Palatii*. Finance, organised through the *Camera*, similarly grew with the scope of papal activities. Crusades or sustained political initiatives needed an organised financial bureaucracy capable of collecting and disbursing the many varied forms of revenue claimed by the papacy, as well as presiding over the judicial processes which inevitably arose. Revenues were drawn from the Papal State, from special contributions like Peter's Pence, from gifts and fees paid by prelates who had occasion to visit the Curia, from *servitia communia*, the payment of one-third of a year's income by newly appointed bishops and abbots, from annates, the year's income from lower benefices, and from the *census* owed by exempt ecclesiastical institutions dependent on the Holy See and by certain temporal rulers with feudal links to the papacy. But the pressure continued to grow and Innocent III's temporary expedient of a proportional tax on the clergy in 1198 to pay for the crusade became, during the conflict with Frederick II, a regular impost, while the growth in papal provisions actually increased those liable to *servitia* or annates. Indulgences and fines for offences like usury added to the irregular incomes of the *Camera*. In addition, the cardinals had their own financial administration, although not their own system of collection; in 1289 they were conceded a half-share of revenues collected by papal agents for the *Camera* (Lunt 1934:1:57–136, 26–7).

The man who eventually emerged from the electoral wrangle of 1292–4 was the most extraordinary choice of the entire thirteenth century. On 4 July 1294 the cardinals elected Peter of Morrone, 80 years old and founder of the Hermits of the Holy Spirit of Maiella, whose chief house was at Sulmona, thirteen hundred feet up in the Abruzzi mountains, east of Rome. He himself, having resigned as leader of the order, lived in an exposed hut on nearby Mount Morrone. He was completely out of his depth when suddenly plunged into the papal whirlpool. Most of his thirteenth-century predecessors had been insiders, well versed in Italian politics and legally trained, so that they could manipulate the vast papal administrative and patronage structure. But it was precisely because he lacked these characteristics that he was chosen, appearing to some to represent qualities of sanctity and piety in keeping with the ideas of contemporary poverty movements, and to others, like Charles II, Charles of Anjou's successor, as an eminently malleable instrument, too naive to resist the pressures of the Neapolitan court. In fact, Angevin influence quickly predominated, persuading the new pope, who took the name of Celestine V, to settle in Naples and to appoint cardinals and dispense offices at Charles's behest. Under these circumstances papal government rapidly fell into a state of disorganisation which exceeded that of the previous two years. On 13 December 1294 Celestine resigned his office and ten days later Cardinal Benedict Caetani was elected in his place, taking the name of Boniface VIII (Boase 1933:38ff.).

Boniface had many of the qualities necessary to restore the papacy's position; he was forceful and intelligent and had had wide experience of curial affairs, most recently as legate to France in 1290–1. His Roman background and extensive family connections seemed to fit him to operate in the complex politics of central Italy, while his legal training gave him an understanding of the judicial and financial systems upon which the papacy depended. In some ways the promise implied by these qualities was fulfilled. Despite heavy pressures, when he died in 1303 the papacy had cash reserves in hand; his *Liber Sextus* was incorporated into the legislation of the Church; his bull, *Super Cathedram* (1300), set down balanced and durable regulations on the vexed question of relations between the secular clergy and the mendicants. Yet the best known incident of his pontificate is that which took place at Anagni, the place of his birth when, on 7 September 1303, William of Nogaret, the leading minister of Philip IV of France, and Sciarra Colonna, leader of the family which was the chief rival of the Caetani, tried to seize him. The coup failed, but Boniface died three weeks later.

The attack at Anagni was the culmination of a bitter conflict with the French monarchy which, ironically, at least partly as a consequence of papal policies, had replaced the Empire as the most important monarchy in the west. Boniface certainly continued to try to manipulate events in Germany; in 1298 he asserted his right to determine whether the newly elected king, Albert of Austria, was a fit ruler, before he would agree to his coronation. Equally, he remained deeply concerned about the three-cornered wrangle over Sicily involving Charles II, James of Aragon and his brother, Frederick, now the ruler of Sicily, a situation which, despite Boniface's efforts, looked less and less amenable to a solution. But in the long perspective it was the struggle with France which seems to have presaged a major change in the relative position of the papacy and it was Boniface's conspicuous lack of success in conducting that struggle that has led to the judgement that his pontificate was a great turning-point in the history of the medieval papacy. The vicissitudes of the relations between Boniface and Albert of Austria between 1298 and 1303 bear no comparison to the coruscating clashes between Innocent IV and Frederick II; the real conflict lay with France. It seems likely that, for all his talents, Boniface failed to recognise the fundamental shift in power that had taken place.

Two great confrontations with France occurred in 1296–7 over clerical taxation and in 1301–3 concerning the extent of royal jurisdiction over clerks. The context within which Boniface had to operate during these struggles is important, for his exploitation of his office to aggrandise himself and his family in central Italy quickly enraged the Colonna family, motivated by similar self-interest. The growing hostility between the two clans culminated in May 1297, in the seizure by Stefano Colonna of a Caetani baggage train containing cash for the purchase of certain properties also coveted by the Colonna, thus bringing the quarrel to a head just at the moment of greatest tension with France over the issue of clerical taxation. Boniface's running battle with the Colonna undermined his Italian base and gave a focus to his potential enemies, including the spiritual wing of the Franciscan movement, which resented the removal of Celestine V. Celestine's death the previous year while in papal confinement could easily be depicted in sinister terms. The vilification of Boniface's character which began at this time not only stuck to the name of Caetani, but also undermined the prestige of the office which he held.

The first dispute arose from the situation created by the war which had broken out between Edward I of England and Philip IV in 1294. Both had taxed their clergy to help pay for the conflict; neither had asked for papal consent in accordance with the decree of 1215. The bull *Clericis laicos* of February 1296 contained a general prohibition of this practice, ordering the clergy to withhold all payments unless they had received the authority of the pope. Although the English king eventually complied, the French monarchy reacted by cutting off all exports of gold, cash and bills to the apostolic see, a practical measure which had almost immediate effect.

Tracts, not unconnected with the royal chancery it must be assumed, began to circulate, examining the relationship between lay and ecclesiastical power in such a way as to suggest that it did not behove a spiritual body to concern itself with matters so earthly as taxation. Philip IV discerned very clearly the implications of *Clericis laicos*. A papacy often racked by faction and itself inclined to pursue partisan political policies could not be allowed to determine when the King of France could go to war. At first Boniface stood firm, but in July 1297, in the bull *Etsi de Statu*, he modified his demand to a point where it almost disappeared, declaring that in a case of dangerous threat to the realm, the royal conscience should be the determinant of whether or not the clergy should be taxed. The possible conjunction of Capetian and Colonna had been too strong for papal defences.

A brief period of reconciliation followed; in August 1297 Boniface canonised Louis IX, setting the seal on the title of the most Christian kings which, in their anxiety to counterbalance the imperial threat, the popes had so readily conferred upon the Capetians. But by the end of 1301 Boniface was again deeply embroiled with the French monarchy. This time the challenge had come directly from the French crown, for Bernard Saisset, Bishop of Pamiers, had been tried and imprisoned by the royal courts for treason and heresy, largely on the basis of some wild remarks by the bishop himself and some testimony tortured from his servants. Boniface was invited to confirm the sentence. Once again he overestimated his strength, perhaps made confident by the success of the Jubilee the previous year, which had attracted huge numbers of pilgrims to Rome. In the bull *Ausculta fili* (December 1301) he lectured the French king on the injuries suffered by the Church at his hands and informed him that his misdemeanours would be considered at a council to be held in Rome in November 1302.

The French government reacted by distorting the contents of the bull to make it appear as if Boniface was claiming direct feudal overlordship over France, using a meeting of the Estates in April 1302 as a vehicle for the material. The French clergy, caught between the two protagonists, pleaded with Boniface not to insist on the council, but the pope, mindful of his defeat in 1297, was not to be diverted. The council was duly held and the famous bull *Unam Sanctam* (November 1302) followed, setting out the well-worn arguments for papal supremacy which had been deployed in the past. In the summer of 1303 the pope drew up the bull *Super Petri solio*, which excommunicated Philip IV. It was his intention to proclaim this on 8 September which precipitated the attack at Anagni.

Succeeding popes could not escape this legacy. Benedict XI, elected October 1303, had no opportunity. He was dead within eight months, having barely had time to begin the healing process which he thought necessary by absolving Philip the Fair and reconciling the Colonna cardinals to the Church. The real victim of the circumstances was Bertrand of Got, Archbishop of Bordeaux who, as Clement V, was Benedict's unlikely successor. Bertrand was a sick man, but he was soon to find that prevarication based upon the excuse of illness was about his only defence against the importunities of the French government. He was elected after an eleven-month conclave, an outsider just about acceptable to both the Bonifacian and French parties within the College, because closely attached to neither of them. But from the beginning he was forced to give priority to French affairs. Within a month of his coronation at Lyon in November 1305, he had created sufficient French cardinals to swing the whole balance of the College away from the Bonifacians; in February 1306 he annulled *Clericis laicos* and *Unam Sanctam*. In a pontificate which lasted until 1314 he never felt able to travel to Rome; in March 1309 he set up his residence in Avignon. Popes had often by choice or necessity resided outside Rome, even escaping to France on occasion, but most stayed within the hill-fortresses of the Papal State. Clement's exile was therefore different in kind. Moreover, it endured, leading to a whole succession of popes at Avignon which adhered even after Urban VI's return to Rome in 1378, creating a schism which cut through the universal Church like a deep and septic wound. This schism could not have been maintained had it not been for the secular support received by both lines of popes and here perhaps lies the ultimate significance of events of the pontificate of Boniface VIII, for by the late fourteenth century the popes no longer directed the political powers of the west in the manner of Innocent III, but were themselves subject to the vicissitudes of powerful political entities in a world which much more resembled 'Europe' than 'Christendom'.

Like his predecessors, Clement considered crusade and church reform to be the twin pillars of papal policy, but knew that neither would make much progress without French co-operation. The French persisted with a demand for a posthumous trial of Boniface VIII, a scenario that Clement wanted to avoid at all costs, both because of its effects on the papacy's reputation and because of the doubts that it might cast upon the apostolic succession. This threat necessarily influenced his reaction to other initiatives taken by the French king, such as the arrest of the military Order of the Templars in October 1307. The Templars were charged with heretical crimes, centred upon obscene reception ceremonies, and confessions were tortured out of them by Philip's agents.

Although ostensibly the work of William of Paris, papal inquisitor in France, in reality the impetus had come from a government intent upon seizing the order's wealth. The trial shows clearly the limits of Clement's freedom of action, for his indignation at this attack upon an exempt order could not be translated into anything more than a series of administrative delays, maintained until May 1312 when, at the Council of Vienne, he suppressed the order and transferred its goods to the Hospitallers. Leverage had been brought against him in 1310 when the proceedings against Boniface VIII had actually been reopened; nor did he feel able to resist the French demand for the canonisation of Celestine V in 1313, although just as he suppressed rather than condemned the Templars, he practised a typical evasion by using the name of Peter of Morrone rather than Celestine.

Nevertheless, Clement continued to perceive his role within the context of the high medieval papacy. He remained concerned about reform, as can be seen by his compilation of papal decretals in the decrees promulgated at Vienne (later known as the Clementines). He continued also to pursue papal political interests in relation to the Empire and to Italy. The election of Henry of Luxembourg to the German throne in November 1308 reopened the issue, for Henry was gripped by the belief that imperial destiny lay in the restoration of Italy to peace, and was endowed with sufficient energy to try to put this into practice. Since there was little he could do to stop Henry's proposed expedition, Clement tried to channel it in a direction which suited him, both by sending a legate to accompany it and by extracting a series of promises, in an agreement made at Lausanne in 1310, that Henry would defend the Roman Church, crush heresy, and overcome the enemies of the Church. If by this Clement meant to revert to the old ideal of an emperor in the service of the papacy, he was soon disappointed. In the Italian cities Henry was perceived as a Ghibelline partisan; at the Neapolitan court as a potential conqueror. Although he was crowned emperor by Clement's reluctant cardinals at St John Lateran in June, when he unexpectedly died at Pisa in August 1313 he was indeed planning an attack on Naples. The extent to which Clement had, by this time, abandoned any idea that he might have harboured of a subordinate emperor holding Italy together for him, can be seen in the unequivocal constitution *Pastoralis cura* (March 1314), which restated papal superiority over the empire and repudiated Henry's attempt to establish authority over the King of Naples, who was specifically a papal vassal.

The pontificates of Benedict XI and Clement V did nothing to unify the College of the Cardinals. Indeed, Clement's regime complicated the issue still further by adding a third vested interest, that of the Gascons elevated to the College since 1305. Although Clement died in April 1314, the cardinals were unable to agree on a new pope until August 1316, when they eventually chose James Duèze, Cardinal-Bishop of Ostia, a Cahorsin of advanced years. Perhaps they thought to postpone their conflict during what must have appeared at the outset to be the beginning of a short pontificate. But John XXII proved to be tougher than anticipated, reigning until 1334, longer than any other pope since Innocent III. It was this pontificate which really confirmed papal residence at Avignon and completed that reorientation of papal policy and position within Christendom which the defeat of Boniface VIII had heralded. Politically, this meant preoccupation both with France itself and with the problems arising from the Angevin–Aragonese conflict; in the religious sphere it meant the condemnation of the Spirituals in 1323, overt recognition that the papacy no longer had any real sympathy with the poverty ideals.

5

The crusades

The crusades grew out of the papal reform movement, for they provided the papacy with a means to put its ideas about the regeneration and purification of society into practice. The formation of an army of God had a double advantage in that it provided a means of enforcing papal will and at the same time diverted the warlike activities of the most belligerent classes of society towards papal ends, instead of their preoccupation with internal feuding and attacks upon the clergy or clerical property. In its most dramatic form this entailed the recruitment of large armies to fight an external enemy which, it was claimed, had violently seized the Holy Places, the very sites of Christ's life, death and resurrection, persecuted the Christian inhabitants, and erected idols in place of the worship of the true faith. However, the concept was more flexible than this. Gregory VII had already used papal armies against the enemies of the faith in Italy and had presented them as 'soldiers of Christ' and, although in the twelfth and thirteenth centuries the capture and defence of Jerusalem remained central to the Christian vision of the crusade, the instrument which the papacy had forged could be used in other contexts, apparently with equal validity. Indeed, the original idea of a Christian 'just war', formulated by St Augustine in the pre-Islamic era, necessarily conceived that such force would be used against those who would disrupt Christian society such as heretics, schismatics or men of violence.

Despite an intensive propaganda campaign detailing the depredations of the barbaric Turks, therefore, the origins of the crusades are to be found within the nature of western Christian society in the second half of the eleventh century rather than through any external stimulus. Indeed, although the issue is controversial, there does not seem to be any evidence that Christians were particularly provoked at this time. While it is true that the invasions of the nomadic Seljuk Turks into Asia Minor had increased in scope and frequency since the Byzantine defeat at Manzikert in 1071, nevertheless Islam had held Jerusalem since 638 without producing any western reaction at all comparable to the movement launched at Clermont by Urban II in November 1095. Urban's appeal to aid the eastern brethren received such a huge response because it accorded with attitudes already familiar to his audience's experience in the west.

Western Christians were accustomed to taking part in devotional and, since the eighth century, penitential journeys to the shrines of the saints, particularly that of St James at Compostela in Galicia. If the great increase in the provision of huge churches in many of the small communities along the pilgrimage routes to Galicia is any indication, then growing numbers must have been taking to the pilgrim roads in the eleventh century, sometimes individually or in small groups, occasionally as part of much larger expeditions. The ultimate experience, however, was to visit Palestine itself. To touch and see the places where they believed Christ had actually been present in body was a sensation for which pilgrims were prepared to undergo many hardships and great risks. Such journeys had been especially promoted since the tenth century by the reformed Benedictines who had created the great monastic network of Cluny, so that by 1095 the idea of a Jerusalem pilgrimage was familiar to a wide geographical and social spectrum.

Despite the immense social changes of the twelfth and thirteenth centuries, the conviction that they were taking part in a pilgrimage remained an integral part of the crusaders' self-image, and indeed the terminology of pilgrimage continued to be used. The anonymous author of the *Gesta Francorum*, who seems to have been a clerk rather than, as was formerly thought, a knight (Morris 1993), describes the crusaders who had fought their way across Asia Minor and taken Jerusalem as 'a force of beggars, unarmed and poverty-stricken, who have nothing but a bag and scrip' (R. Hill 1962:96). Almost 150 years later John of Joinville, about to join the crusade of Louis IX in 1248, still went through the pilgrim rituals before departure.

> The abbot of Cheminon gave me my pilgrim's staff and wallet. I left Joinville immediately after – never to enter my castle again until my return from oversea – on foot with my legs bare, and in my shirt. Thus attired I went to Blécourt and Saint-Urbain, and to other places where there are holy relics.
>
> (Shaw 1963:195)

It has been shown that the privileges and obligations of the crusader, as well as the vow which he swore, grew out of these pilgrimage rituals (Brundage 1969:3–29). Like the pilgrim, the crusader received privileges of both a spiritual and material nature. The centrepiece was the indulgence which, in the popular mind at least, meant that those who died on the crusade had guaranteed their place in Heaven, for their sins were wiped clean. Again the author of the *Gesta* expresses the popular attitude when, for instance, describing the siege of Antioch in March 1098, he tells how 'more than a thousand of our knights or foot-soldiers suffered martyrdom, and we believe that they went to Heaven, and were clad in white robes and received the martyr's palm' (R. Hill 1962:40). Modern opinion is that Urban II meant (indeed could only have meant) to offer remission of the penances imposed by the Church in this life, but that this distinction was lost in the tide of popular enthusiasm (Mayer 1988:23–37). Certainly, by the 1140s the Church itself seems to have accepted the popular interpretation, for St Bernard talks of the taking of the cross as if it were an astute deal, for it offered eternal merit for a relatively limited series of earthly acts (B.S. James 1998:462). At a more mundane level the crusader gained a series of legal privileges designed to protect his person and property while on a long journey, as well as his family and possessions at home. Although these provisions became more sophisticated in time, their basis was that of the hospitality owed to the pilgrim. In return the crusader committed himself to the journey to the east as part of a general expedition to the Holy Sepulchre, his adherence reinforced by ecclesiastical sanctions which ultimately rested on excommunication.

The armies which departed from north-west Europe, southern France and Apulia in 1096, however, were clearly not simply pilgrims, for they were heavily armed and quite consciously setting out to do battle for the faith. While there had been instances of pilgrims taking to arms in the past – most notably in the very large German pilgrimage to Palestine in 1064–5 – such clashes had been incidental to the main purpose of the participants. Urban's expedition therefore needed to justify itself within the context of the Christian faith, a faith founded by a man who had, according to St Luke, called upon his followers to turn the other cheek, and whose passivity in the Garden of Gethsemane contrasts with the violence of his leading disciple, Peter. Some churchmen could never see a way to evade this issue. For Peter Damian, there were no circumstances in which it was permissible for a Christian to fight on behalf of the Church. But, in fact, the pass had already been sold under the Emperor Constantine in the early fourth century, for the Church could never have succeeded in becoming the religion of the Roman state nor of reaching the Germanic tribes who settled in the remains of the Roman Empire without compromising on warfare. The warrior cult was so deeply embedded in western society that the Church could do no better than adapt or redirect it, for elimination was an unreachable goal.

Such adaptation, indeed, was what many eleventh-century clerics had tried to do by their promotion of the peace movements in a society in which there was little or no legal restraint upon the violence of the *milites*. Since the last decades of the tenth century, certain bishops, especially in France where royal authority was weak, had called local assemblies at which they had attempted to place certain categories within the populace under Church protection, an idea extended in the 1020s to cover certain specific periods of time as well. It is noticeable that the main support for the First Crusade was largely drawn from areas where the secular authorities had been relatively unsuccessful in keeping order in the past and where ecclesiastical peace movements had therefore become makeshift substitutes. Peace movements were not known, for example, in the Empire or England before 1066 (Matthew 1966:49–50). However, Marcus Bull's view that the peace movements as such were more important as elements in crusade ideology established after the event rather than a direct influence on the generation of the First Crusade itself has some force (Bull 1993b:2–69); their chief influence may have been as a contribution to the creation of a favourable climate of opinion. While the peace councils probably had little practical effect upon the level of violence, they nevertheless did at least underline the concept that the motive of those who fought was of fundamental importance. Fighting for the cause of the Church to overcome those evil-doers who would break the Church's peace could be presented as a world apart from those butchers who killed from malice or greed or pride. The Church could then turn to the Old Testament to justify such action, in particular to the punishment meted out by Moses upon the apostates whom he discovered worshipping the Golden Calf (Exodus 32) and to St Augustine's convenient formulation of the preconditions of just cause, right intention and legitimate authority, before engaging in warfare (F.H. Russell 1975:16–39). Even so, both the pope and the crusade preachers who helped spread his message after 1095 generally sought to present the expedition to the Holy Land as essentially a defensive move occasioned by the aggression of Islam against 'our lands'. Many crusade warriors seem to have understood this within their own terms: as faithful vassals they would rally to their lord when he was attacked, so too could they avenge the violation of God's patrimony (Riley-Smith 1980:7–9).

In these circumstances it is likely that the elements of the idea of an army of Christ's soldiers had been forming in Urban II's mind for some time. He himself was steeped in the ideas of reform; he had before him Gregory VII's own abortive plan of 1074 to lead an expedition to the east; he had been pope seven years already, so his experience of the affairs and needs of the Church at the highest level was already extensive. Most importantly, throughout his pontificate he had been anxious to repair the break in relations between Rome and Constantinople which had resulted in the schism of 1054. The Byzantine emperor, Alexius I (1081–1118), was equally interested in improving relations. In 1089 the patriarch had written to Urban saying that he would consider restoring the pope's name to the diptychs, on which the Byzantine Church inscribed the names of those patriarchs whom it regarded as orthodox and, in March 1095, the emperor sent representatives to the pope's first council at Piacenza. It is not clear if the initiative came from pope or emperor, but whoever was responsible, this action enabled Urban to crystallise a plan to send an army to the east, for Alexius's representatives asked for military help from western knights to combat the incursions of the Seljuk Turks into Asia Minor. Foreign soldiers had been a common sight in Byzantine armies and it is likely that Alexius sought no more than a more systematic recruitment, aiming his request at the pope because he rightly discerned him to be the most prominent leader in the west. In typical Byzantine fashion the message was geared to the audience; the emphasis seems to have been on the persecution of eastern Christians by the Turks rather than on the territorial exigencies of the Empire.

Eight months later at Clermont in the Auvergne, Urban II converted these negotiations into a stirring appeal to rouse the peoples of the west to arms, calling down anathema upon those who committed murder, pillage and arson against God's people, and exhorting them instead, in the words of Fulcher of Chartres, 'to exterminate this vile race from our lands' (Ryan 1969:66). In the rhetoric of the chroniclers he appears to have been turning the peace movements within into a weapon to strike the enemies without. Their ultimate goal was to be Jerusalem, but at the same time he aimed to recreate the bonds between eastern and western Christians in a way which would bring to fruition the negotiations with Emperor Alexius. He may even have cherished a vision that ultimately the whole of the former Christian lands converted by the Apostles would be restored to the Christian faith (Katzenellenbogen 1944).

To a degree the response to this speech was stage-managed. Adhemar, Bishop of Le Puy, quickly offered his services, presumably by prior agreement with the pope, while soon after the council messages came from Raymond IV, Count of Toulouse, with a pledge of his support. The pope himself, as well as designated preachers like Robert of Arbrissel, then set out on a tour of France to spread the word, the message being reinforced (and perhaps reinterpreted) by many unofficial preachers as well. It is unlikely that the pope himself had much idea what the response would be – thus the need for the prepared volunteers – but by any yardstick it was quite astonishing. Within a year expeditions were being prepared by some of the great lords of north-west Europe, including Hugh of Vermandois, the brother of King Philip I of France, Robert, Count of Flanders, Robert, Duke of Normandy, and Stephen, Count of Blois. Even Godfrey of Bouillon, Duke of Lower Lorraine, and his brothers Eustace and Baldwin, vassals of Emperor Henry IV, took the cross. Later in 1096 some of the leaders of the Normans who, during the eleventh century had settled in southern Italy, joined the adherents, led by Bohemond of Taranto and his nephew, Tancred. Many smaller groups attached themselves to these armies: Fulcher of Chartres lists nineteen of them (Bull 1993a:360–1). The total number of participants may have been between 80,000 and 100,000 (France 1994:122–42), a figure quite unprecedented in the eleventh century.

These great lords and their vassals were to be the backbone of the crusade, but the success of the appeal depended upon more than simply the redirection of the nobility's warrior instincts. The pope drew upon deep feelings of popular piety, already stimulated by Church reform and expressed in the boycott of sinful priests, in the peace councils and in participation in pilgrimage. Such piety was not the exclusive possession of any one class, and preachers, often unauthorised, found that they could create an image of Jerusalem, with its needs and rewards, in the minds of large masses of people, many of whom had never carried arms or had any idea of the location of the Holy Land. The first contingents of nobles and knights under Hugh of Vermandois reached Constantinople in November 1096, a year after Clermont but, between these dates, many thousands of people from northern France and the Rhineland had become the first crusaders of all, for, in the winter and spring of 1095–6, with little preparation, they had set out for the east. By the end of September 1096, few of them were still alive, victims of the Turks, the Hungarians, or simply the conditions under which they attempted to travel.

The inspiration of these mass movements was a charismatic preacher called Peter the Hermit, supposedly an ex-monk from the region of Amiens who, dressed in a hair shirt and riding on a donkey, seems to have had the power to stimulate thousands by his preaching. The content of his message is not recorded, but he may have tapped the widespread belief that the poor were specially chosen by God, a theme seen frequently on contemporary church portals in the form of the parable of Dives and Lazarus (Luke 16), and apparently referred to by Urban II at Clermont (Ryan 1969:64) (see Plate 8).

Plate 8 The death of Lazarus, the poor man turned away from the rich man's table. Dogs lick his sores, while above an angel is about to carry him 'into Abraham's bosom' (Luke 16:20–31). South Porch, west side, Abbey Church of Moissac, 1120s. (Photograph reproduced by permission of Auguste Allemand.)

Explanations of sculptural and painted images to those seen as 'illiterates and rustics' was a well-established mode of communicating religious and moral ideas (Camille 1985:32–3). Peter would not have found it difficult to draw parallels between the tormented Lazarus and the lives of the poor in 1096 for, according to the monastic chronicler Ekkehard of Aura, from Corvey on the River Weser, many of the west Franks needed little inducement to leave their homes. For several years they had suffered from local warfare, famine and a gangrenous disease, since identified as ergotism (Ekkehard of Aura 1895:17). Ironically, the harvest of 1096 was an especially good one, greatly aiding the preparations of the armies that were to follow, but too late to be of much help to the popular movements, some of which had started out as early as December 1095.

In the end these popular armies made more impact on the Byzantines and the Jews than they did on the Turks. The armies led by Peter the Hermit and another Frenchman, Walter Sans Avoir, were massacred in western Asia Minor, while a number of German expeditions, largely from the Rhineland, which tried to follow them, attacked the Jewish communities of the great trading and episcopal cities of the region, before themselves being slaughtered by Hungarian troops as they tried to make their way east. To the modern observer this outcome was perhaps quite predictable, but these movements should not be too readily dismissed, for some contemporaries at least saw them as a significant part of the crusade. The author of the *Gesta Francorum*, for instance, describes the Franks as ordering themselves into three armies, the first of which, he says, was led by Peter the Hermit, so he apparently made no clear distinction between 'popular' and 'noble' expeditions (R. Hill 1962:2), while more recent research has emphasised that they contained more nobles and knights than was once thought (Riley-Smith 1986:49–57). Moreover, there was a persistent twelfth-century belief which was certainly in circulation within twenty years of the First Crusade and probably before, that Peter the Hermit was actually the originator of the crusade (Blake and Morris 1985).

By April 1097 the main crusading armies had encamped outside Constantinople. They were unruly and independent of each other, as well as of the Byzantine emperor. They did not represent help in the form that Alexius had wanted, but the emperor made the best of the situation by extracting an oath from the leaders promising to return to the empire lands which it had recently held and to acknowledge Alexius as overlord of any other lands that they might conquer. The process was a difficult one and in the end Raymond of Toulouse could be persuaded only to swear in general terms to respect the person and property of the emperor. The issues raised are indicative of fundamental differences between the crusaders and the Byzantines which were to manifest themselves with increasing frequency in the future. Ultimately the effects of the crusades upon Byzantium were to be much more profound than they were to be upon the Muslim world.

Just over two years after it had gathered at Constantinople, on 15 July 1099, the First Crusade captured Jerusalem. It had taken two great battles at Dorylaeum (July 1097) and Antioch (June 1098) and three long sieges at Nicaea (June 1097), Antioch (October 1097 to June 1098) and Jerusalem (June and July 1099), as well as numerous smaller engagements and sieges. Those who survived the entire crusade travelled in the region of 2,700 miles (France 1994:3). By the time the crusaders took Jerusalem they were in a terrible condition, depleted in numbers by battle, famine and desertions, and they had experienced unimaginable horrors, circumstances which might explain why they massacred the population without mercy. The crusade was a success in the sense that the Byzantines recovered a large part of western Asia Minor, including the key city of Nicaea, as well as laying the foundations for their renewed control of the coastal lands, both north and south, and the important river valleys of the region. It meant, too, that the Latins were able to set up four states in the east: Edessa, Antioch, Jerusalem and finally Tripoli. Jerusalem itself had been liberated from what were seen as the polluted hands of the Muslims and some of the crusaders at least were rewarded not only by spiritual gifts, but by material gain as well. Jerusalem may not have been the golden city of the preachers' imagination, but Fulcher of Chartres describes how it was agreed that, after its capture, whoever first entered a property could hold it as his own, adding that in this way 'many poor people became wealthy' (Ryan 1969:123).

The crusade was a failure, however, in the sense which had meant most to the pope, for it did not promote the reconciliation of the Churches. Quite the opposite had occurred, for the crusaders had, almost from the beginning, conceived a prejudice against the Greeks, whom they were convinced were treacherous and double-dealing, a prejudice reinforced when Alexius failed to come to their rescue during the siege and battle of Antioch in 1098. Bohemond who, with his father Robert Guiscard, had several times invaded the Balkans from their base in southern Italy, found that he could turn this prejudice to his own advantage. Once he had gained control of Antioch with the departure of his rival, Raymond of Toulouse, in January 1099, he threw out the Greek clergy and reneged on his oath to Alexius. In Byzantine eyes this violation of solemn agreements could not be forgiven and, during the twelfth century, the Comnenian successors of Alexius mounted great expeditions to bring Antioch under their control again.

The establishment of the Crusader States committed western Europeans to crusading for the foreseeable future; moreover, the more familiar a feature of life crusading became, the more uses the papacy found for it. Even in the late eleventh century the papacy had seen Islam as presenting a double threat, not only in the east, but in the Iberian peninsula as well; while in 1147 Pope Eugenius III accepted that the campaigns of Henry the Lion, Duke of Saxony, against the pagan Wends in the Baltic lands, could also legitimately be regarded as crusades, complete with full indulgences. Some participants were narrowly concerned with their own expeditions, but other observers did see the movement as a broad front in this way. Helmold, writing in 1167–8, described the Second Crusade as an enterprise in which it was recognised that there was a need to divide the forces into three: to the east, to Spain, and 'against the Slavs who live hard by us' (Tschan 1935:172). After the Fourth Crusade seized Constantinople in 1204, Innocent III and his successors presented the newly conquered lands in Romania and Greece as worthy objects of crusading activity. Innocent was also responsible for turning the crusade against the Cathar heretics of southern France, when he inaugurated the Albigensian Crusades in 1209, while many of his thirteenth-century successors argued that the defeat of papal enemies in Italy was a vital prerequisite for success in the east. This does not mean that Christians regarded all crusades in the same light, whatever the scale of indulgences offered. Indeed, the failure of the papacy to involve more than special interest groups in the campaigns in the Latin Empire of Constantinople and in Greece underlines the fact that most Christians had a hierarchy of crusading priorities in their minds. What it does mean is that crusading expeditions, preaching, taxes and even special military orders became central elements in the life of western Christendom in the twelfth and thirteenth centuries.

Nevertheless, although the scope and variety of crusading expanded, Palestine remained its focal point. Once control of the ports had been established and the Seljuks restricted in their movements, there flowed a constant stream of pilgrims, merchants, legates and, from the 1130s, Templars and Hospitallers, in both directions. Moreover, new crusaders arrived in contingents of varying size, encouraged by the Frankish rulers in the east, who regularly tried to recruit additional forces for specific ventures. Even so, it needed a huge effort to put together an expedition on the scale of the First Crusade and this did not happen again until the 1140s. The Second Crusade was the result of the interweaving of a number of disparate and not altogether compatible strands. To some extent it was a reaction to disaster, for at Christmas 1144, Zengi, Atabeg of Mosul, had seized most of the County of Edessa, the first but most vulnerable of the Crusader States. Responding to pleas from the Franks and Armenians, Eugenius III issued the bull *Quantum praedecessores* on 1 December 1145, addressed to the king and nobility of France. It seems probable, however, that Louis VII had, independently of the pope, already decided upon a pilgrimage to Jerusalem, a plan not entirely in accordance with Eugenius's conception either of the military needs of the east or indeed of the papacy's own role as prime mover of the crusades. In fact, neither pope nor king evoked much response and it took an appeal by Louis to Bernard, the highly influential Abbot of Clairvaux, to fuse the elements into a realisable expedition. Bernard's mediation led to the reissue of the papal bull and in the months that followed he undertook a strenuous preaching campaign throughout France. Indeed, almost single-handedly he put together a crusade which neither pope nor king had been able to launch on their own, and consequently the Second Crusade bears Bernard's stamp. Nor did he confine himself to France. He wrote to the English and the Spanish and, in November 1146, met the German king, Conrad III, in an effort to persuade him as well. Conrad did not give in easily, but at a second meeting, at Christmas, he too succumbed to Bernard's eloquence.

It seems with hindsight that the crusade was dangerously dependent upon the charisma of one man – a man, indeed, who was not able to reinforce it by his actual presence – and this may help to explain the apparent absence of that depth of determination which carried the First Crusade through so many horrific experiences. Neither of the great French or German armies really recovered from setbacks met on their separate journeys through Asia Minor, for they seem to have possessed neither the logistical skill nor the discipline to carry through the difficult feat of moving a large army safely through hostile territory and harsh terrain. In October 1147 the main German army was defeated at Dorylaeum and fell back on the coast in ever-increasing confusion, while a smaller contingent under Otto of Freising was overcome near Laodicea. Few had either the resources or the will to struggle on to Syria, although the leaders did manage to obtain ships and to finish the journey by sea. Louis VII's army fared no better. Only the discipline and cohesion imposed at the king's behest by a contingent of Templars travelling with them, prevented the army from being completely wiped out by the constant Turkish attacks during the winter of 1147–8. Again, only a limited number was able to reach the Crusader States by taking ship from Attalia.

Once in Palestine the conduct of affairs was no better. An assembly held at Acre, in June 1148, decided to attack Damascus, apparently under the influence of the European leaders. Since the Franks of Outremer perceived the threat to be from Aleppo and, indeed, had been in alliance with Damascus since 1139, it is unlikely that they would have advocated this course. It has been argued that the subsequent incompetence with which the plan of attack was carried out was largely due to local sabotage (Mayer 1988:104). Whoever (if anybody) was to blame, the consequence was to alienate the Damascenes who, in 1154, chose to place themselves under the Franks' enemy, Nur-ad-Din.

Not surprisingly, Bernard of Clairvaux received much of the blame for the failure and, judging by his attempts at defending himself, felt much aggrieved as a consequence, but the real losers were the Franks of Outremer, so dependent upon western help which was not provided very readily in the decades that followed. Frequent letters arrived in the west explaining the problems of the Crusader States and especially aimed at Louis VII and Henry II (Smail 1969; J. Phillips 1996). In 1184–5 a full-scale embassy was sent. Yet, although both kings made monetary contributions, neither appeared in person and, in Henry's case, little encouragement was given to his vassals to participate either. The increased co-operation between the Crusader States and the Byzantines, especially during the 1160s, is partly explained by these circumstances. In fact the long and bitter conflicts between the Angevins and Capetians and between Frederick Barbarossa and the Papal–Lombard alliance seldom offered sufficient respite for any of these powers to make proper preparations for crusading, while the Sicilian monarchs had regarded the Kingdom of Jerusalem with hostility since the rejection of Adelaide, mother of Roger II, as queen of Jerusalem by Baldwin I in 1117.

It therefore needed an even greater crisis than the loss of Edessa to stir the Third Crusade. In July 1187 the Franks, undermined by their own divided leadership, allowed themselves to be provoked by Saladin, the Sultan of Egypt, into leaving a good defensive position in order to march to relieve Tiberias. As they struggled towards their objective, they were overcome on the Horns of Hattin within sight of the Sea of Galilee. Most of the able-bodied knights were killed or captured, with the losses among the military orders being particularly heavy. An almost undefended Jerusalem fell at the beginning of October and within a year Saladin had captured most of the important Frankish centres in the Kingdom of Jerusalem and the County of Tripoli. The news could not be ignored. At the Abbey of Bury St Edmunds, for instance, Jocelin of Brakelond noted how, when Abbot Samson heard of the capture of the Cross and the fall of Jerusalem, 'he began to wear breeches of hair cloth and a hairshirt instead of one made of mixed wool and linen. He also began to abstain from meat and dishes containing meat' (Greenway and Sayers 1989:36).

The first help came almost inadvertently, for Conrad, son of the Marquis of Montferrat, after first arriving at Acre in July 1187, in ignorance of both the battle and the fall of the city itself, sailed north to Tyre, where his presence stiffened resistance and probably prevented the collapse of the entire kingdom. By the autumn of 1187 the papacy was actively promoting a new crusade among European monarchs. King William II of Sicily, his fleet already in action against Byzantium, was able to send ships which saved Tripoli; Richard, Count of Poitou (who became king of England in July 1189) took the cross as early as November 1187, followed by Philip II of France and Henry II of England in January 1188, and Frederick Barbarossa in March. Each of these monarchs had the resources to raise a formidable army and the emperor, imbued with an image of himself as leader of western Christendom, set off independently, crossing the Bosporus in March 1190. But it was a false dawn for, although the German army battled its way across Anatolia, the whole expedition fell apart when Frederick Barbarossa drowned while crossing the River Saleph in June 1190.

Richard I and Philip II each departed from Vézelay in July 1190, making their ways to Messina by different routes. In contrast to Frederick, both had organised fleets. Neither king trusted the other and their relations in Sicily were marked by deep mutual suspicion, culminating in their separate departures for the east. One effect of this was that it was Richard alone who, in May 1191, seized the island of Cyprus from its Byzantine governor, thus creating a new Crusader State which more than compensated for the loss of Edessa, although significantly at the expense of fellow Christians. Once in the east the partisan attitudes of the monarchs encouraged the reappearance of the factionalism which had characterised the politics of the Latin settlements before Hattin, with Philip giving his support to Conrad of Montferrat, while Richard backed Guy, the King of Jerusalem who, as a Lusignan, came from a family who were Richard's vassals in Poitou.

Both kings found that the immediate task was the reinforcement of the siege of Acre, begun by Guy of Lusignan in August 1189 in an attempt to re-establish his authority after Hattin. Smaller contingents of crusaders had already made significant contributions, but the two new armies tipped the balance and Acre fell in July 1191. Philip, however, remained in the east only until the end of the month, his total stay in the Holy Land amounting to less than four months. Although he left a substantial French presence, the effective leader was now Richard I. In August he marched south, keeping tight discipline so that the army did not break up like so many of its predecessors, overcame Saladin in battle near Arsuf on 7 September, and retook the key port of Jaffa which had been so vital to the crusaders when Jerusalem was first captured in 1099. But this was the limit of his success; Jerusalem itself proved logistically impractical. Moreover, Richard's affairs in the west could wait no longer and, in September 1192, he made a three-year truce with Saladin, departing the following month.

The achievements of the Third Crusade were concrete, although relatively modest, but the sheer scale of the organisation is impressive and reflects the far-reaching developments which had taken place in the administrations and economies of the west since the time of the First Crusade. Then, the best that individual crusaders could hope for when they needed to raise money was an *ad hoc* arrangement with the local monastery; but by the late twelfth century the military orders, through their network of houses in the west, were often able to provide finance, advice and transport related to the specific needs of crusading. Taxation had become both more sophisticated and more burdensome. In 1188 Henry II and Philip II imposed the so-called Saladin tithe to help pay for the planned expedition, effectively a general tax on income and movables upon those who did not themselves crusade. This was a huge proportion of resources to attempt to extract and, eventually, Philip II was forced to abandon it. The Angevins, however, did not, and such proportional taxes became a permanent feature of their finances (Baldwin 1986:52–4).

Such massive sums of money were needed because by the late twelfth century, methods of transportation and warfare demanded them. Frederick Barbarossa was the last to take the treacherous land route across Asia Minor, for the sea now presented a viable alternative. English and Flemish crusaders had intended this as early as the Second Crusade, but many got no further than Lisbon. In 1190 Richard's fleet sailed from Poitou and Gascony, around the Bay of Biscay to Lisbon, Messina and Cyprus, and eventually to Acre. By this time, too, suitable shipping for loading, carrying and landing horses on long voyages was relatively common, presaging a new era of crusading which could be supplied by sea. These changes saw the appearance of increasing numbers of specialists, both in the art of transportation and warfare. The crusade army of the late twelfth century needed sea-captains, quartermasters, engineers and archers. Such skill had to be bought, further adding to the ever-growing costs.

In many ways the outcome of the Fourth Crusade, for which Pope Innocent III began preparations in August 1198, was determined by these new circumstances. A tax of one-fortieth was levied on clerical income to help pay crusade expenses. A spectacular preaching campaign in northern France by a parish priest called Fulk of Neuilly attracted many adherents, but real progress was made when at a tournament at Ecry in Champagne in November 1199, Theobald, Count of Champagne, and Louis, Count of Blois, and their vassals, took the cross, soon to be followed by Baldwin, Count of Flanders, and his brother Henry. It was decided to approach Venice for transportation. The outcome was an agreement, in April 1201, that Venice would build shipping for 4,500 knights, 9,000 squires, 20,000 foot-soldiers and 4,500 horses. The Republic itself would adhere to the crusade for a year and a day from the date of departure. The total cost would be 85,000 marks. In their approach to both finance and transport the crusaders showed their awareness of contemporary methods but, when they assembled in Venice in the spring of 1202, their inexperience was revealed in one vital area, that of contracting for large numbers, for it was discovered that the estimate of their needs was about three times too high. Geoffrey of Villehardouin, the most important chronicler of the crusade and one of the chief negotiators with the Venetians, was very bitter, claiming that they had been betrayed by the many crusaders who sailed from other ports. 'They were much despised and greatly blamed for this; and as a consequence of their bad conduct they met with much misfortune later on' (Shaw 1963:41). However, modern research has shown that this was not a realistic argument, for it has been estimated that there were only about 14,000 crusaders in total, including both those who went to Venice and those who set out from other ports, well under half the original estimate (Queller and Madden 1997:48). Despite immense efforts the crusaders could raise only an additional 34,000 marks, which was insufficient to bridge the deficit.

From this time the rank-and-file crusaders in particular were caught between a business enterprise that would not forgo its debts and a spiritual leader who would not dissolve the bonds of a solemn religious oath. The crusaders were pushed this way and that by forces over which they had little control and understanding. When, at the suggestion of the Doge, the crusaders did set sail in October 1202, it was to attack the Christian city of Zara on the Dalmatian coast and not the great Muslim power of Egypt. According to Robert of Clari, the Picard knight who was a vassal of Peter of Amiens and the chronicler who was closest to representing the attitude of the ordinary lay crusader, 'the host as a whole did not know anything of the plan, save only the highest men' (McNeal 1936:42). The debt therefore enabled the Venetians to use the crusaders to help them to recover Zara, which they had lost in 1180–1 when the city had revolted and soon after placed itself under Hungarian protection. Despite protests and desertions the city was captured and pillaged in November 1202, and the crusaders spent the winter there. Innocent III, whose calling of the crusade had in itself been meant as a demonstration of papal leadership, now found himself obliged to react to Venetian moves. He had forbidden the attack, but to keep the crusade in being, he lifted his excommunication of the participants, except for the Venetians themselves.

The capture of Zara did not change the fact that the Venetians still held the crusade in their grip, but new possibilities were opened up when it was proposed by envoys from Philip of Swabia, the German ruler, that they take up an offer made by Alexius Angelus, son of the former Byzantine emperor, Isaac II, who had been deposed in 1195 and was now blinded and in prison. Alexius had escaped, probably sometime in 1201, and had visited both the pope and Philip, to whom he was related by marriage. He was touting for help to recover the throne and the crusade seemed to open up an opportunity for him. In return for overthrowing the 'usurper', Alexius III, Alexius Angelus promised to pay the crusaders 200,000 marks of silver and to provide 10,000 soldiers for the war in the Holy Land, an offer which seemed to solve both the crusaders' financial problems and to strengthen the expedition. These were the circumstances which led to the second diversion of the crusade, from Zara to Constantinople.

Once at Constantinople in June 1203, the defects in the plan soon became evident. Although Isaac and Alexius IV were established as joint rulers, the Byzantines had no more chance of fulfilling their promise than the crusaders had of paying their debts. The Greek populace, enraged by Alexius' subservience to the Latins, turned on him and strangled him, elevating Alexius Ducas as Alexius V, while the crusaders, angry and betrayed, resolved to attack the city. Neither side needed much persuasion to believe the worst of the other after a century of deteriorating relations, largely stemming from the crusades themselves. Despite the weakness of the city and the internal problems of the Byzantine Empire, the crusaders did not find its capture easy, for their own forces were no more than 10,000 strong and the city had a double line of walls ten to eleven miles around. Once again the Venetians, the key element in the politics and the economics of this crusade, were the determining force, for it was their military and naval expertise which enabled the crusaders to penetrate the north-west corner along the Golden Horn on 13 April 1204. The next three days were spent in pillaging the richest city in the world, striking a physical and psychological blow from which Byzantium never properly recovered, despite regaining the city fifty-seven years later.

The crusaders were now able to set up a new Latin Empire at Constantinople. Many of the leaders, the most prominent of whom was Boniface of Montferrat, who had been chosen as the secular leader of the crusade in June 1201, carved out lordships for themselves in Thessalonica, Greece, and the Archipelago. Innocent III gained a Latin patriarch and, despite his loss of control over events, talked for a period as if God's miracle had been granted to Latin Christendom, writing enthusiastically in 1205 about the intellectual and material rewards of settlement in these lands. The Venetians, preferring indirect control to the burdens of too great an area of territory, were able to monopolise trade in Constantinople and in the Black Sea by means of a number of important way stations. The coincidence of a crusade which seemed to serve so many interests has led to suggestions that there had been a conspiracy to divert it from its initial objective of Egypt. Belief in this may well be more a matter of temperament rather than evidence, but to date nobody has produced a definitive answer to the question (see McNeal and Wolff 1969). Nevertheless, chronology, geography and the disparate nature of the participants suggest that the idea of a plot is inherently unlikely.

Despite the optimistic tone of his letters of 1205, Innocent III knew very well that the Fourth Crusade had gone disastrously adrift. Yet it was inconceivable that any pope of the twelfth and thirteenth centuries could have turned away from crusading, especially one of Innocent III's outlook. Indeed, to the pope, the threats to the faith continued to be all too evident. In June 1209, he finally managed to launch a crusade against the Cathars of Languedoc, and in July 1212, he had the satisfaction of learning that the combined armies of Castile, Navarre and Aragon had defeated the Berber Almoravides of north Africa at the battle of Las Navas de Tolosa. However, these efforts had unexpected consequences of a quite different kind from those produced by the diversion of the Fourth Crusade. In the spring and summer of 1212, Innocent was confronted by popular movements whose members, setting out initially from Vendôme in northern France and soon after from Cologne in the Rhineland, were apparently determined to succeed where those whom Robert of Clari had called 'the high men' had failed, and regain the True Cross lost at Hattin in 1187. This was, as Gary Dickson describes it, 'the first "peasants' crusade" to be composed solely of peasants', for its distant predecessor of 1095–6 encompassed a much greater social range. As such, it must have been quite impossible to foresee even for such a perceptive pope as Innocent III. In fact, the so-called 'Children's Crusade' included shepherds, rural and urban artisans and labourers, as well as women and children. It seems to have found its origin in the Ile-de-France in May, sparked off by the official preaching and organised processions of 1211–12 intended to kindle enthusiasm for the Albigensian and Spanish expeditions, and then spread to the Rhineland in the course of the next two months (Dickson 2000). In France it coalesced around Stephen, a shepherd from Cloyes, near Vendôme, who claimed to have received letters for King Philip II of France from 'a pilgrim', who was actually Christ in disguise. The letters were handed over to the king at St Denis and examined by the masters of the University of Paris, after which, on royal instructions, most of peasants dispersed. A similar leader emerged in the Rhineland, from the region of Cologne, whose followers headed south in order to sail for the Holy Land, although in the end they progressed no further than the Mediterranean coast. The pope seems to have recognised that the feelings which they represented, however inarticulately, were widespread, and that any new crusade needed to draw on those deep emotions which had moved men to take the cross in the first place, but at the same time he knew that a new expedition needed to be properly prepared and executed so that the failures of the past would not be repeated (Powell 1986:15–32).

Innocent III presented the crusade as everybody's responsibility, for Christ had suffered for the salvation of all. As such, indulgences could be gained by anybody who made a contribution to the crusade, even these manifestly unsuitable as actual participants. However, while for the pope this opened up the benefits of salvation through crusading to society as a whole, the policy of redeeming vows which this encouraged undoubtedly led to the criticism that spiritual rewards were being sold. Moreover, since the crusade was such a positive responsibility upon all, Innocent's policy had the effect of overriding previous conventions: the marriage vow, for instance, had been regarded by canonists as taking precedence, whereas Innocent determined that a man did not need his wife's permission to undertake the crusade (Brundage 1967a). Innocent took equal trouble over the practical aspects of crusade planning, for the Fourth Crusade had foundered because of a lack of professionalism in this area. The papacy took the initiative in organising and collecting funds on a greater scale than ever before and, especially under Honorius III, took significant steps towards its centralisation, while continuous efforts were made to enforce peace movements and agreements to free secular rulers and their vassals for crusading.

The outcome of Innocent's rethinking was the Fifth Crusade between 1218 and 1221, in which his plans were carried through in modified form by his successor, Honorius III. The aim, like that of the Fourth Crusade, was Egypt, without which, it was believed, the defence of Jerusalem would not be viable. In circumstances of great hardship the crusaders gained an initial success when they took Damietta on the Nile Delta in November 1219, but they never received sufficient reinforcements from the west to make a move decisive enough to break the stalemate which followed. In particular, promises that the Emperor Frederick II, who had taken the cross in 1215, was about to appear, were not fulfilled, while at the same time important segments of the army regularly departed for home. Inevitably time itself wore down the crusading force which, devastated by the conditions under which it was obliged to live, fell to internal conflict. Much of this centred upon the abrasive personality of the papal representative, Cardinal Pelagius, whose refusal to accept the offer of al-Kamil, the Aiyubid ruler, to cede Jerusalem in return for the evacuation of Egypt, split the leadership. Nevertheless, the underlying problem remained one of resources and manpower, which were not adequate in the first place and which declined as time went on. James Powell's study shows that the Fifth Crusade simply withered away (1986:168–9). Late in August 1221, the crusaders were forced to relinquish their only bargaining counter of Damietta. An eight-year truce was negotiated with al-Kamil.

Much of the blame fell on the papacy, but in practice it is clear that the determining factor had been the failure of Frederick II to appear in person. During the rest of the century this dependence upon secular powers became ever more acute as the balance of influence between the papacy and secular governments began to shift decisively in favour of the latter. In their different ways, the two most important expeditions of the thirteenth century after 1221 – those of Frederick II in 1228–9 and Louis IX between 1248 and 1254 – both demonstrate the truth of this.

In 1225 Frederick II assumed the title of King of Jerusalem, having married Isabella, the heiress to the throne, and in June 1228, set out on crusade. That Frederick saw the crusade in his own terms is underlined by his willingness to ignore excommunication, imposed on him by Gregory IX for his continual delays, and by his conduct in the Crusader States. In February 1229 he seized the opportunity presented by threats to al-Kamil within the Aiyubid clan, to negotiate the return of Jerusalem to Christian hands, together with associated lands like Lydda and Bethlehem. In doing so he paid scant attention to the sensitivities of the local baronage, whose rights and attitudes meant little to him. His stay in the Holy Land was, however, brief, for the invasion of his lands in southern Italy by papal troops, forced him to return. Nevertheless, by 1231 he had installed his own *bailli* and supporting troops in Tyre, actions which show his serious and continuing interest in the Holy Land. But it was an interest prompted not by the papal world view, but by Frederick's own concept of the imperial destiny.

Louis IX's interest in crusading stemmed from a quite different perception, but it was just as much moulded by the king's own personal views as that of Frederick II had been. According to Joinville, the king took the cross in 1244 after being so ill that his attendants disputed whether he was still alive. As Joinville saw it, the Lord had worked within him both to restore his health and to lead him to take the cross. Between 1248 and 1250 the king mounted the last large-scale expedition to the east in the thirteenth century. It was exhaustively planned and lavishly financed; once again the objective was Egypt. But Egypt proved to be as difficult to take in 1250 as it had in 1218. In June 1249 Damietta fell much more easily than it had thirty years before, and the king set about establishing Capetian overlordship in a manner reminiscent of his predecessors' expansion into Anjou and Toulouse, but consolidating this by further advance proved much more difficult. In February 1250 the king's younger brother, Robert of Artois, won a victory outside Mansourah and, excited by this, led a reckless attack into the town itself which resulted in the deaths of him and most of his companions. In many ways this was the turning-point of the crusade, for the French army was unable to contain renewed Egyptian attack and was forced to retreat. During the withdrawal the king was captured and only released on payment of a ransom of 800,000 *besants* and the cession of Damietta. Despite this disaster the king stayed in Outremer for another four years, rebuilding its defences and making contact with the Mongols, with whom the possibility of an alliance was being canvassed. If Joinville's recollection is correct, Louis stayed in the east in the teeth of almost universal opposition from his relatives and vassals. But even he could not remain permanently. He eventually departed in April 1254, probably because it had become increasingly difficult to finance the crusade since the death of the Regent, the Queen Mother, Blanche of Castile, in November 1252.

After Louis the position of the Latin states, which were coming under great pressure from the Mamluks, who had climbed to power in Egypt during the 1250s, became increasingly desperate. Louis himself longed for another crusade, but was unable to mount an expedition further east than Tunis, where he died in August 1270. Edward of England campaigned briefly in the Holy Land in 1271; after his accession to the English throne the next year, however, he was never in a position to do more than send supplies. Charles of Anjou, after buying a claim to succession from Maria of Antioch in 1277, sent his representatives and regular supplies, but was unable to appear in person. The papacy did not retake the initiative in the way that Innocent III had done, not only because there were no popes of Innocent's calibre in the second half of the thirteenth century, but also because the affairs of central Italy continually preoccupied them. Indeed, the inhabitants of the east constantly complained that the papacy gave priority to Italian affairs at the expense of the Holy Land.

The fall of Acre to the Mamluks in May 1291, and the subsequent collapse of what was left of the Latin states, led to another reappraisal of crusading in the west. Reforms were suggested in the light of thirteenth-century events. Some favoured attempts at conversion, an idea which Francis of Assisi had attempted to put into practice in Egypt in 1219. Others believed that the war machine which had been constructed was itself at fault, both in its components and its use. Such schools of thought advocated measures such as the rationalisation and union of the military orders for more efficient operation or the concentration of resources upon sea power.

No great expedition actually set out in direct response to 1291, but the reaction in the west was not confined to theorists. The French monarchs and their families, for instance, following the path of their predecessors, took the cross, often in elaborate and very public ceremonies that inspired others to follow their example. Philip IV and his sons, Louis X and Philip V, all pledged to go on crusade and began preparations for advance parties, while at the same time levying taxes on both clergy and laity. Almost every year between 1312 and 1320 new vows were taken and the crusade preached widely in northern France. Some observers viewed these actions cynically, seeing only another excuse for taxation in a country whose financial system, vast as it was, obstinately refused to function efficiently. There may be some truth in this view, but it should not be forgotten that between 1315 and 1322 northern Europe was experiencing the huge crisis of 'the great famine' and that northern France was one of the regions most hard hit. Some, on the other hand, such as the participants in the popular movement known as the Pastoureaux which ravaged parts of France and Languedoc for a few months in the spring and summer of 1320, were directly influenced by the crusading atmosphere. The Pastoureaux, like other such movements, had no chance of crusading in the east; instead, they spent their energies on the Jewish communities of south-west France, Navarre and Aragon, often with the complicity of local consulates, before being wiped out or dispersed by royal officials.

Crusading therefore continued to maintain a grip on the imagination of large sectors of society from the top to the bottom. Huge effort was expended on planning, financing and, despite the prevarications of the last Capetians, actually going on crusade, especially under the Avignon papacy (Housley 1986). If enthusiasm for the crusade is measured in terms of this broad effort to defend Christendom rather than specifically to go to recover Jerusalem, then 1291 cannot be seen as the turning-point as it once was. Nevertheless, the trend towards control by secular powers rather than the papacy was reinforced in the fourteenth century and with it a tendency to be prepared to crusade only when the objective was securely planted within the political and economic interests of the ruler concerned. In this sense, the crusading climate had changed. In the past, many rulers, even those of a most evidently self-seeking nature, had overcome their prejudices sufficiently to crusade in the Holy Land. In the fourteenth century, however, it seems that few identified their interests directly with Jerusalem.

Crusading had profound effects upon all who took part; there were no light-hearted participants set on enjoying the climate, the drink and the women. Indeed, there were probably relatively few who set out to make their fortunes as was once thought, for crusading was too expensive and risky to be seen in terms of an investment. There were undoubtedly men who, as Jean Richard (1999:78) sees it, were tempted by the east. In the First Crusade, Bohemond of Taranto and his nephew, Tancred, from the Normans of southern Italy, and Baldwin of Boulogne, younger brother of Godfrey of Bouillon, and his relative Baldwin of Bourcq, from the Rethel family, were intent on gaining lordships. The Italian merchants who bought goods from the east in the markets of Acre or Tyre in order to resell them in the west certainly expected to make a profit. Nevertheless, John of Salisbury, writing about the Second Crusade, assumed that most crusaders could expect to be out of pocket and implied that those who were not had been guilty of corruption. In his account of Arnulf, Bishop of Lisieux, and Godfrey, Bishop of Langres, who accompanied Louis VII's army, both of whom he regarded with contempt, he describes how they 'received large sums of money from the sick and dying whom they attended and absolved in the name of the pope, claiming to be his representatives'. The scale of this was such that 'they are believed to have accumulated more wealth during the expedition than they paid out of their own pockets' (Chibnall 1956:55). It is noticeable that Thierry of Alsace, who went on crusade four times in twenty-five years (1139, 1148, 1157 and 1164) was, as Count of Flanders, ruler of one of the richest fiefs in Europe, flourishing on the proceeds of the cloth trade and the innovations of its agriculture. For most crusaders, therefore, the experience was very special and for this reason many felt compelled to write about it or to dictate their memories to others.

Hardships are common to every account. Ambroise, who wrote a verse account of Richard I's crusade, has a graphic description of the starvation suffered during the siege of Acre in the summer of 1191, a situation which, as a partisan of Richard, he blamed on Conrad of Montferrat:

> My lords, I am not joking, in order that meat should not be totally lacking in the army of God, they skinned the fine horses and eagerly ate them. There was a huge crowd at the skinning [of the beasts] and it was still a costly meat. The

misery lasted the whole winter and the flesh was sold for ten sous the piece. A dead horse was easily sold for more than a live one would have been. The flesh tasted good to them and they ate even the guts. Then they cursed the marquis who had brought them to this sorry pass.... Had it not been for the herbs they planted and the seed they sowed, from which everyone made his mess of pottage, the loss would never have been made up. There you would have seen fine men-at-arms, worthy and valiant men, brought up in riches, reduced by famine and distress that when they saw the grass growing they went to eat and graze it.

(Ailes and Barber 2003:2:90)

The fighting itself was painful in other ways, as Richard of the Temple, a participant and later Augustinian prior of Holy Trinity in London, shows in his description of the battle of Arsuf of 7 September 1191.

There you would have seen our knights who had lost their warhorses walking on foot with the infantry. They were firing missiles from crossbows or arrows from bows at the enemy, returning blow for blow as far as means and strength allowed. Always eager to practise the art of the archer and crossbowman, the Turks for their part pressed on without a pause; bolts rained down, arrows flew, the air hummed. The sun's light was dimmed by the great number of missiles, as it does in winter in thick hail or snow. Horses were pierced by the points of darts and arrows. So many of these missiles covered the surface of the ground all around that anyone who wanted to collect them up could gather at least twenty in one grasp.

(Nicholson 1997:249)

Part of the problem lay with the nature of crusader armies, always carrying large numbers of non-combatants even before the real problems were encountered. Even Odo of Deuil, the St Denis chronicler, whose account of Louis VII's crusade is strongly pervaded by the pilgrimage tradition, nevertheless lamented that it would have been better if the pope had kept such people at home, 'for the weak and helpless are always a burden to their comrades and a source of prey to their enemies' (Berry 1948:95). Some could not stand it and deserted or at least contemplated it. According to Raymond of Aguilers, who was chaplain to Raymond of Toulouse during the First Crusade, there were members of the count's army who were ready to leave even before they had seen a Turk.

While all of our people dreamed of leaving camp, fleeing, forsaking their comrades, and giving up all which they had carried from far away lands, they were led back to such a steadfast strength through the saving Grace of repentance and fasting that only their former ignominy of desperation and desire for flight strongly embarrassed them.

(H. Hill and L.L. Hill 1968:23)

Many, in fact, did desert the First Crusade, including such famous participants as Stephen of Blois and Peter the Hermit. Nor were circumstances always easier for those left behind, especially wives who may have had little idea of the fate of their husbands.

Richard of the Temple gives some idea of the scope of the problem. When, in July 1191, the Turks were about to surrender the city of Acre to the besieging crusaders, as part of their settlement they proposed to hand over 2,000 noble Christians and 500 lesser captives. 'Saladin', they said, 'would have a search made throughout all his lands to find them' (Nicholson 1997:219). By the thirteenth century, canonists were forced to confront the problem of the spouse who had disappeared on crusade, for many women could not know if they were widows. No agreement was reached over the time which could be allowed to elapse before remarriage, for instance. Some commentators set a hundred years, while others, more reasonably, settled for five (Brundage 1967b).

Alleviation could come in both material and spiritual form. When matters went well, the crusaders could gorge themselves on booty. After overcoming the rich army of Kerbogha, Atabeg of Mosul, outside Antioch, on 28 June 1098, Raymond of Aguilers saw an almost childlike celebration:

> The hardships of the encounter were rewarded by the sight of the returning masses. Some running back and forth between the tents on Arabian horses were showing their new riches to their friends, and others, sporting two or three garments of silk, were praising God, the bestower of victory and gifts, and yet others, covered with three or four shields, were happily displaying these mementoes of their triumph.
>
> (H. Hill and L.L. Hill 1968:43)

The fall of Constantinople in April 1204, however, brought the crusaders far more than mere mementoes. Robert of Clari's account has a sense of naive awe that is a completely genuine reaction.

> Not since the world was made, was there ever seen or won so great a treasure or so noble or so rich, not in the time of Alexander nor in the time of Charlemagne nor before or after. Nor do I think, myself, that in the forty richest cities of the world there had been so much wealth as was found in Constantinople. For the Greeks say that two thirds of the wealth of this world is in Constantinople and the other third scattered throughout the world.
>
> (McNeal 1936:101)

Plunder was both a pleasure and a necessity, but it was not sufficient in itself. Many crusaders believed that they or others had visions or religious experiences which showed God's working in the world and his intervention in the crusade. The chroniclers of the First Crusade are a particularly rich source of such experiences. The allegiance of the knightly classes to the warrior saints justified itself at Antioch, for the author of the *Gesta* claimed that there

> appeared from the mountains a countless host of men on white horses, whose banners were all white. When our men saw this, they did not understand what was happening or who these men might be, until they realised that this was the succour sent by Christ, and that the leaders were St George, St Mercurius and St Demetrius. (This is quite true, for many of our men saw it.)
>
> (R. Hill 1962:69)

But the greatest reward of all was the attainment of Jerusalem itself and the associated holy places. William of Tyre described the effects which this had on the members of the First Crusade as he imagined it.

> As the word Jerusalem fell upon the ears of the pilgrims – Jerusalem the city for whose sake they had endured so many hardships – fervent devotion so overwhelmed them that they could not restrain their tears and sighs. Falling upon the ground, they adored and glorified God, who had granted His faithful people the privilege of serving him worthily and commendably, the Lord who had mercifully deigned to hear the prayers of His people and had deemed them worthy, according to their hope, to reach the city so ardently desired.
>
> (Babcock and Krey 1941:1:338)

During the twelfth and thirteenth centuries the crusading movement was responsible for fundamental changes in western Christendom, for to enable tens of thousands of men and women to travel to and from Palestine, Syria, Cyprus, Egypt and Greece, and to move their horses and supplies, involved a revolution in transportation, finance and government so profound that it must be accounted a major reason for the transformation of the nature of western European society and its economy from that of the early medieval world (Constable 1982). Although returning crusaders brought with them a range of products which did much to change the daily lifestyle of at least the upper classes, these influences were less important than the upheaval needed to mount and sustain the crusades in the first place. While the long-term consequences were economic, the crusades nevertheless remained at base a religious movement, promoted by a papacy which could not have activated them without being able to draw on such feelings. These aspirations often took the form of individual quests for salvation and in this way the crusading movement reflects the preoccupation with motive which dominated twelfth-century religious thought. Salvation through crusading, however, necessarily involved an increasing exclusivity among those who saw themselves as the elect. A concomitant of the adoption of this path to salvation was the attempt to purge Christendom itself of elements which were discerned to be internally subversive, in particular, Jews, heretics, schismatics and, in 1321, lepers. This sense of being an elect was present from the very beginning of the crusade movement. In the chronicle of Raymond of Aguilers, considerable space is given to the visions of a humble Provençal crusader called Peter Bartholomew. In one of them, he has a conversation with Christ, who tells him that he hates the Jews

> as unbelievers and ranks them the lowest of all races. Therefore, be sure that you are not unbelievers, or else you will be with the Jews, and I shall choose other people and carry to fulfillment for them My promises which I made to you.
>
> (H. Hill and L.L. Hill 1968:95)

6

Monasticism and the friars

So the cell of Maule rose by the prudence of devoted monks, and through the abundant gifts of worshippers grew and prospered to the praise of God. For the place was very fertile, with vines and rich fields, watered by the river Mauldre which flowed through it, and strongly defended by a great number of noble knights. These during their lifetime gladly made gifts of their lands and other wealth to the church; for the monastic order is honoured by them and in the hour of death it is wholeheartedly sought by them for their souls' good. These knights frequent the cloister with the monks, and often discuss practical as well as speculative matters with them; may it continue a school for the living and a refuge for the dying.

(Chibnall 1972:3:205–7)

This short passage from Orderic Vitalis, describing the growth of a dependency of St Evroult, a small priory, just to the south of Meulan, in 1076, illustrates very clearly how, during the early middle ages, the monastery had come to interact with its social environment. This house had been established through the pious donations of the laity who, in turn, expected their path to salvation to be smoothed by the prayers of the monks and by their burial in the monastery. Equally, during life, they assumed that the monastery would be accessible to them, that they could meet and talk with the monks in the cloister, that a place in the house would be available for those of their relatives who wished to enter and that at least some of their children would receive instruction in letters there. The survival of many thousands of charters recording donations to local monasteries testifies to the importance of these relationships; indeed, some families were so closely associated with a particular house that it became a target for that family's enemies, a situation which led to agreements to defend it when required (Bull 1993b:174–5).

Following the example of the ascetics of Syria, Palestine and Egypt, from the fourth century onwards hermits and monastic communities had begun to establish themselves in the Christianised parts of the Roman Empire in the west. Although ultimately the most important influence was to be the Rule of St Benedict, composed *c*.535 and used by Benedict at the Abbey of Monte Cassino, these communities were, like Maule, established on an individual basis; they did not form orders in the manner that came to characterise the twelfth century. In some, indeed, there was an element of revolt against the increasing institutionalisation of the Church following its adoption by the emperors. As the empire disintegrated, monasteries slowly appeared in the midst of the barbarian kingdoms, spreading from Italy to southern Gaul and the Alpine regions and northwards to Francia, Britain and Ireland. Missions to the Anglo-Saxons in the early seventh century and to the more northerly continental lands such as Frisia, Thuringia and Saxony from *c*.650, were conducted by monks who founded outposts of Christianity in often hostile lands. Monasteries in the early middle ages therefore formed religious, educational and economic centres in a world in which political structures were often crude and unstable and, although between the eighth and tenth centuries some were severely shaken or even destroyed by the Vikings and Magyars while others lost much of their original purpose under stifling lay influence, nevertheless they were sufficiently deep-rooted to remain the dominant cultural force.

Under the patronage of Louis the Pious in the second decade of the ninth century, St Benedict of Aniane had promoted the systematic establishment of the Rule of St Benedict so that it came to be the most important, although not the exclusive, pattern of monastic life. Its essentially moderate nature, conciseness and balance between activities remained attainable for ordinary mortals, despite the vicissitudes of the world in which they lived. This was still the context within which Orderic Vitalis viewed monasticism. Although new ideas and a new spirit brought striking changes in the twelfth century, Benedictine houses like that of St Evroult remained a solid part of the landscape throughout the middle ages. They show a wide variety of forms ranging from cells like that of Maule to great houses like that of Bury St Edmunds.

There is a lively account of the position of Bury within the community by Jocelin of Brakelond, successively chaplain to the abbot and guestmaster in the late twelfth century. Bury had been founded in the 1020s; by Jocelin's time its abbot was one of the leading men of the kingdom, a tenant-in-chief of the king and the possessor of jurisdictional powers equivalent to those of a royal sheriff. As Jocelin describes in detail, his appointment was a matter of considerable importance to the king and Henry II took some care over the election of Abbot Samson in 1182. The extent of the monastery's concern with the wider world comes out very clearly in Jocelin's account of Samson's problems. It had been allowed to fall into a parlous economic plight under Samson's predecessor, for it carried a heavy burden of debt which it took years to pay off. For much of the time, therefore, the new abbot was preoccupied with the restoration of the abbey's position. The following passage conveys something of what the headship of such a great abbey would have entailed.

> When the abbot had taken the homages, he requested an aid from his knights, and they promised £1 each. But they then went into urgent consultation together and subtracted £12 for twelve knights, saying that those twelve were bound to assist the other forty, not only in performing the duty of castle-guard and in rendering scutages, but also in paying the abbot's aid. This made the abbot very angry when he heard it, and he told his close advisers that if he lived he would get even with them by paying them injury for injury.

The abbot's anger at his knights' recalcitrance is hardly surprising, for he in turn owed service to his feudal superior, the king. In 1197 Richard I demanded service of one knight in ten, which in Bury's case meant that four knights were needed to fight in Normandy, but Samson's vassals claimed that they were not required to serve overseas. In the end he went to Normandy himself and arranged for four stipendiary knights to be provided, giving them money for forty days' service. He found, however, that they might be kept for a year or more and therefore he was forced to buy the king's agreement that they should serve for only forty days, an agreement which cost him £100 sterling. When he returned, his attempt to extract this money from his own knights met only with a lower, counter offer, which finally he decided to accept. Not surprisingly, Samson told Jocelin that his many problems caused him misery and heartache, and that 'if he could have returned to the circumstances he had enjoyed before he became a monk, with 5 or 6 marks a year to keep himself at the university, he would never have become a monk or an abbot' (Greenway and Sayers 1989:26, 76–7, 33–4).

While all this seems far distant from the austerities of third-century Syria and Egypt, it can be seen that Samson could not afford to be an other-worldly ascetic if his abbey was to survive and to fulfil not only its secular role but its spiritual function as well. Orderic Vitalis was aware that such establishments were vulnerable to criticism from the zealous, but defended the customs and practices of his own house on the familiar ground of the importance of variety within unity. 'But, as Pope Gregory says, the varying custom of Holy Church does not impede the unity of the faith.' Customs such as the wearing of breeches and the use of lard in place of olive oil were simply sensible adaptations to the northern climate.

> It is true that we are severely criticized by many because we do not engage in daily manual labour; but we openly offer in its place our earnest toil in the worship of God, as we have been taught to do by true masters of former ages, who have proved their worth by their long-continued observance of the divine law.
>
> (Chibnall 1973:4:319)

Despite, or perhaps because of, their secular concerns, the monasteries were very aware of their relationship with the lay world. This consciousness had been greatly sharpened by significant reforms in the tenth century, led by the Burgundian house of Cluny, founded in 909, and the Lotharingian houses of Brogne, founded in 914, and Gorze, reformed in 933. Relations with seculars were not always as harmonious as those that Orderic Vitalis would have us believe appertained at Maule. The piecemeal nature of monastic foundation in the early middle ages, together with the disintegration of royal authority in the ninth century, inevitably meant that many monasteries found themselves excessively dependent upon local lay powers, often to the detriment of their spiritual functions. The real importance of Cluny was the creation of a climate of opinion in which such subservience was seen to be undesirable not only to the monks, but to responsible laymen as well. Cluny's foundation charter, drawn up for Duke William of Aquitaine, granted the house freedom from outside interference both in the election of its abbot and the conduct of its affairs, a freedom successfully used in the tenth and eleventh centuries by the papacy to draw the Cluniacs directly into its orbit. Cluny was not the originator of this trend towards monastic exemption under the papacy, but it soon became its leader (Cowdrey 1970).

During the tenth and eleventh centuries, Cluny's reputation attracted to it an increasing number of dependent houses, creating a network which, by 1109, on the death of Abbot Hugh, numbered in the region of 2,000 and included substantial allegiances not only in France, but also in Germany, Spain and Italy. Other foundations, such as Jumièges in Normandy, and Hirsau in the Black Forest, although not directly linked to Cluny, bore the imprint of this reform. Brogne and Gorze were less strong numerically – Gorze, for instance, was eventually connected to about 154 houses – but were very influential in the more concentrated area of the Rhineland and Lorraine. Once again the interaction with lay society is evident, for the Cluniacs, having broken free from lay dependence, were equally keen to encourage their now receptive patrons to adopt their view of right conduct. Sinners should, therefore, by granting their goods to the monasteries and at some point committing themselves in person, seek the intercessory prayers of the monks; they should desist from violence and rapine in the way demanded by the peace councils which the Cluniacs did so much to promote; they should expiate their sins by penitential acts, which should include not only almsgiving but also large-scale personal sacrifice in the form of long and difficult pilgrimages. By the second half of the eleventh century, Cluniac success was very overt. Cluny had become closely associated with the reform papacy, which liked to present it as an exemplar, and it had drawn in very large numbers of recruits. The Cluniac reform did nothing to lessen the involvement of the monks with contemporary society; indeed it had quite the reverse effect.

Until the beginning of the twelfth century, therefore, Cluny had been the most successful monastic development ever. But, despite its supremacy, changes had been occurring in the eleventh century which, by the 1120s, were to make Cluny look old-fashioned and to force its abbot, Peter the Venerable (1122–56), onto the defensive. Writing c.1120, Guibert of Nogent described a foundation which had been established at La Chartreuse near Grenoble in the Alps. It had been the work of Bruno of Cologne who, for twenty years, had been a master at the episcopal school at Reims, together with two companions.

> After Bruno had left the city, he decided to renounce the world, too, and, shrinking from the observation of his friends, he went on to the region of Grenoble. There, on a high and dreadful cliff, approached by a rough and rarely used path, under which there is a deep gorge in a precipitous valley, he chose to dwell and established the customs by which his followers live to this day.
>
> (Benton 1970:60–2)

The year was 1084 and this was the beginning of the Carthusian Order. The first group lived in some rough huts, but by Guibert's time their numbers had grown slowly and their organisation was more systematic.

> The church there is not far from the foot of the mountain, in a little fold of its sloping side, and in it are thirteen monks who have a cloister quite suitable for common use but who do not live together in cloister fashion like other monks. They all have separate cells around the cloister, in which they work, sleep, and eat.

Guibert describes their modest diet of bread, vegetables and fish and their wine, which was so diluted as to be almost tasteless; their church which had no lavish ornaments;

their clothes which mainly consisted of hair shirts next to the skin. They were administered by a prior, while the Bishop of Grenoble acted in place of an abbot. Their only real accumulation of property was the acquisition of a rich library.

> In that place... the soil is very little cultivated by them for grain. With the fleeces of their sheep, however, which they raise in great numbers, they are accustomed to buy the produce they need. Moreover, at the foot of the mountain there are dwellings sheltering faithful laymen, more than twenty in number, who live under their careful rule. These monks are so filled with zeal for the life of meditation which they have adopted that they never give it up or grow lukewarm, however long their arduous mode of living may last.

Guibert had no direct experience of Chartreuse but, writing in the second decade of the twelfth century, he does reflect contemporary admiration for a development of which contemporaries were well aware: the appearance within the Church of dynamic new monastic orders, reforming and innovative, which were the most vital element within the contemporary Church. Apart from the Carthusians, the late eleventh century and early twelfth century saw the appearance of the Cistercian Order and the military orders of the Hospitallers and the Templars, as well as the adoption of a quasi-monastic life by many cathedral chapters, so that the canons regular, such as the Augustinians, the Premonstratensians and the Victorines, lived under a rule as strict as that of the 'new monks'. The Cistercians grew out of a foundation by Robert of Molesme, a Cluniac who had broken away in 1075, and established himself first at Molesme and then, growing dissatisfied with this too, next at Cîteaux in Burgundy in 1098. Although he was persuaded to return to Molesme after 1098, the community at Cîteaux survived and prospered under successful abbots, Alberic (d. 1109) and, most important, Stephen Harding (d. 1134). By 1113 it was in a position to found a daughter house at La Ferté to the south. Military orders represent a different, but nevertheless related strand of reform. The Hospitallers had, since at least the 1080s, operated as a charitable foundation tending sick and exhausted pilgrims in Jerusalem. With the rise in the number of pilgrims following the capture of the city by the crusaders in 1099, they began to expand their facilities, while at the same time attracting increasing numbers of donations. In 1113, now too large to maintain their original dependency on the monastery of St Mary of the Latins, the Order received papal recognition and the right to elect its own master. The Templars were founded in 1119 by a knight from Champagne, Hugh of Payns, to protect pilgrims travelling between Jaffa and Jerusalem and, at least initially, acted as a complementary organisation to the Hospitallers. In 1129 they received a Rule at the Council of Troyes, heavily influenced by the Cistercians and, during the twelfth century, developed into a formidable force of fighting monks, dedicated to the Holy War. In the 1130s the Hospitallers adopted a military function similar to that of the Templars, but their charitable activities remained fundamental to their existence and, indeed, ultimately outlasted their military role.

Many others, who were never destined to create large organisations, nevertheless found this inspiring. One such foundation was the community at Palmaria, near Tiberias in the Kingdom of Jerusalem, founded before 1130 by Gormund, lord of Baisan, and then handed over to Elias, a local hermit, who had once been a grammar teacher in Narbonne. Although St Bernard himself refused offers to establish the Cistercians in the Holy Land, Elias was determined to imitate their lifestyle, even sending one of his community to the west to bring back a Cistercian monk to show them all the practices of the order, as well as making an unsuccessful attempt to persuade his monks to wear heavy cowls in the Burgundian manner, which were in fact quite unsuitable for the heat of Palestine (Kedar 1983:68, 75; Jotischky 1995:44–6). Even though the community did not thrive, perhaps because of conflict between Elias and some of the monks, and the site was eventually taken over by the Cluniacs, such efforts do reflect the widespread enthusiasm generated by the reformers, even though in this case it had no long-term success.

The origins of these changes must be sought in the eleventh century. In Italy and France in particular there were marked signs of dissatisfaction with contemporary monasticism. This dissatisfaction manifested itself in a search for an older form of religious life which predated the Benedictine Rule, that of the eremitical life of the Desert Fathers. In the course of the eleventh century, individuals and small communities established themselves at Camaldoli, Fonte Avellana and Vallombrosa in Tuscany, at Savigny in Normandy and at Fontevrault and Grandmont in Poitou. These varied ventures do not in themselves represent a coherent movement – and indeed it is evident that the objectives of the successful new orders of monks and canons of the next generation were by no means identical – but they do in their different ways suggest a reaction against the secular entanglements which were becoming all the more obvious as the European economy began to revive. The eremitical life was a means of fleeing the new economy, the growing towns and the tentacles of feudal dependence, and of regaining the life of poverty which men like Peter Damian saw as the highest calling of the monastic vocation. Damian had this advice for newly professed monks:

> Let each substance consider its origin, so that while the flesh is convinced that it is itself no more than the dust which it beholds, the soul, raised up to that which it has lost, may long for it with eager and unfailing desire. Let your poverty and need cause you to favour rough and rugged clothing; in the cold of winter wear poor and despised garments.... Keep away from public places; flee from the sight of men. Search for unfrequented places, go into hidden and remote retreats. For secret prayers storm heaven, and carry off forgiveness when they are poured forth often in the shadows by the light of heaven.
>
> (McNulty 1959:126–7)

In the eyes of many contemporaries existing monasteries fell far short of these fierce ideals. In the vast empire of Cluny, for instance, the monastic day was largely occupied by liturgical activity rather than maintaining Benedict's balance between prayer, learning and manual labour (Knowles 1963). Moreover, Cluny's expansion had been achieved at some cost, for there was a growing tendency to receive novices in large numbers without adequate preparation, which diluted standards. The new orders therefore were partly prompted by reaction against Cluny, and for this reason they tended to exaggerate its defects, but this should not obscure the very positive aims of the reformers. The Carthusians, for instance, achieved a remarkable compromise between the eremitical and the cenobitic life, by creating circumstances in which the individual could live a virtually solitary existence, yet still have the protection of the cloister. The Carthusians met at only a few set times per week; even their water was piped to each individual cell. At the same time, however, the communal structure made a more effective barrier to the intrusions of the outside world than any individual or unorganised group could have achieved. The Cistercians were particularly stirred by their desire to return to what they regarded as the true purity of the Rule of St Benedict, adversely affected, in their view, by the accretions of later centuries. To achieve this they left the populated places and all that established social convention entailed, and set themselves up in what they liked to describe as 'the desert'. Here they supported themselves with the labour of their own hands and, from the 1130s, that of the *conversi* or lay brothers whom they accepted to share in the monastic life. Usually they worked estates consolidated into 'granges', some but no means all of which were established on previously uncultivated or even uninhabited lands.

The new orders were not, however, simply a response to specific monastic needs; their aims were also very much in harmony with a number of contemporary attitudes. These attitudes were not always expressed or channelled in the same way, but they did spring from the same source. During the eleventh century clerical leaders had increasingly involved society as a whole in attempts to improve standards of public morality: episcopal attempts to limit the damage caused by feudal anarchy had led to the calling of the peace councils and this had been followed by the papal drive against sinful priests. At the same time, a growing concentration on the humanity of Christ both provided inspiration and offered new opportunities for emotional commitment. The growing popularity of the expiatory pilgrimage, which had culminated in the mass response to succour the Holy Land through the First Crusade, was one manifestation of this, drawing ecclesiastic and layman alike to visit the places of Christ's life and miracles. The Cistercian retreat from city life, uncluttered by the complicated and time-consuming liturgical practices of the black monks, was particularly attractive to the knightly classes, who became their most enthusiastic donors, some of whom at least were coming to view self-denial as the best route to salvation (Bouchard 1991:192–7). Moreover, the new monasticism not only catered for the social elites, but also responded to popular needs as well by offering a role as *conversi* or, in the case of the military orders as sergeants.

All these forces were harnessed by outstanding leadership: men like Bruno of Cologne, Robert of Molesme, Stephen Harding and, most important of all, Bernard of Clairvaux. Bernard joined the Cistercians in 1113. He did not save the young order from extinction as was once thought, but his great skills as writer and orator and his tireless activity on behalf of the order did provide marvellous publicity. Clairvaux was founded by him in 1115 and had sixty-five daughter houses by the time of his death in 1153. Nor was he exclusively concerned with the Cistercians, for the Templars, insignificant and faltering before the Council of Troyes in 1129, received the benefit of his experience in helping to draw up a proper Rule and the stamp of his approval in his treatise, written in the early 1130s, *In Praise of the New Knighthood*, which provided a justification for the strange new vocation of fighting monk (Greenia 2000). The papacy, too, concerned to expand its own reformist influence, took an increasing interest in these orders, granting privileges which undermined the traditional influence of the episcopacy over the monasteries in their dioceses, and made the orders instead directly responsible to Rome. The Cistercians, for instance, although they never received a general privilege, gained exemption from the payment of tithe on lands cultivated directly by themselves in 1132 and in a series of bulls were virtually freed from episcopal authority (1132, 1152 and 1184).

The success of these orders is the outstanding feature of twelfth-century monastic history, but this success contained an inherent contradiction, nowhere more evident than in the Cistercian Order. If success is to be measured in houses, recruits and incomes the Cistercians must be reckoned the leaders. By 1151 they had 353 houses in every country of western Christendom; down to 1675, 742 different Cistercian foundations existed (Lekai 1977:43–4). Growth had been achieved by the development of a series of 'family' groups with the new foundations linked to the mother house which had originally established them by means of regular visitations from its abbot. In comparison Carthusian expansion had been modest. There were about thirty-seven houses by 1200 and the numbers in each were strictly controlled (Jedin *et al.* 1970:51). However, while the Carthusians could maintain their original ideal with these limited numbers, the Cistercian desire to live in poverty and isolation was put under serious pressure by such growth.

William, monk of Malmesbury in Wiltshire, a sharp observer of the early-twelfth-century scene, devotes several pages of his fourth book on the history of the kings of England to the Cistercians.

> These men ... love bright minds more than gold vestments, knowing that the best recompense of good deeds is the enjoyment of a clear conscience. But if the laudable clemency of the abbot either wishes or pretends to wish to mitigate anything in the letter of the rule, these men strive against it, saying that there is not much time in life, nor will they live as long as they have done already; that they hope to maintain their purpose, and to be an example for their successors in the future, who will sin if they should waver ... the Cistercian monks of today are an example to all monks, a mirror for the zealous, a goad for the slothful.
>
> (Stubbs 1889:2:385)

William wrote this in the 1120s, a period when the formerly predominant Cluniac way of life appeared outmoded and lax by comparison, so that Peter the Venerable, Abbot of Cluny, for all his great intellectual gifts, found it almost impossible to defend his order from the criticisms launched against it by St Bernard in the 1120s. Although he by no means conceded all Bernard's points, Peter nevertheless was forced to consider ways of reforming the Cluniacs, turning upon his own monks and denouncing their comfortable lifestyle and full stomachs in a way reminiscent of St Bernard himself (Knowles 1963:66). Indeed, the debate between St Bernard and Peter the Venerable is only the best known of a whole series of arguments sparked off by the spread of these new varieties of religious life.

Yet, as early as the 1160s, hardly more than a decade after St Bernard's death, Pope Alexander III, no enemy of the Cistercians, was telling the General Chapter that they had abandoned their original institutions in favour of secular activities (Lekai 1977:300–1). By the mid-thirteenth century, just as Peter the Venerable had castigated the Cluniacs, Stephen of Lexington, who became Abbot of Clairvaux in 1243, had reason to tell his monks that they in turn looked to have grown old in comparison with new preaching orders like the Dominicans (Lekai 1977:80). As Abbot of Savigny from 1229 he had already found it prudent to enforce a two-year period of study of the laws and customs of the order upon those who had completed their novitiate, which was an implicit admission of Cistercian ignorance of their original ideals. The fact that sober observers such as these suggest that serious problems were developing within the order is significant, because it shows that the accusations of the more biased critics of the time, like Walter Map, were not entirely based on personal vindictiveness or long-nursed grudges. Map believed that the encroachments of the Cistercians of Flaxley on the revenues of a church appertaining to him had lost him considerable income, and he lashed out at the order for its avarice, its ruthlessness and its fraud. Worst of all, in the midst of all this, it was self-righteous. 'They are making the Kingdom of God somewhat limited, if no one is in the right way but themselves' (M.R. James 1983:87).

These critics reflect a growing hostility towards the order which contrasts with the glowing praise of the early twelfth century and the manifest confidence with which St Bernard had attacked the Cluniacs. The more temperate critics and the obvious enemies were therefore different manifestations of the same problem: for the former the Cistercians were not observing their original institutions and customs, and were therefore hypocrites, for the latter, they were avaricious. The meeting-point lies in the economic role of the Cistercians. Both in the *Exordium Parvum* of the mid-1130s and in the statutes emanating from the chapter meeting of 1134, there is emphasis upon a system of economic support which avoided the secular world so that the ideals of eremitical isolation could be maintained. Their livelihood was to be gained from manual labour aided by lay brothers; they worked granges devoid of the usual apparatus of seigneurial overlordship, such as tithes, villages, serfs and incomes from monopolies like ovens and mills; lands which they held were not to be too close to those of secular lords. Since they rejected tithes for themselves, Innocent II's exemption of 1132 seemed natural.

The extraordinary expansion of the order, however, soon placed these revolutionary economic concepts in extreme jeopardy, for neither economic self-sufficiency nor isolated communities were easy to maintain within, on the one hand, a religious climate that so favoured the order that donations were attracted at an increasingly rapid rate and, on the other, an economic environment that made active involvement in the market and the monetary economy difficult to avoid. The Cistercians, where they had retreated to unoccupied or underpopulated areas, actually served as colonisers, and were soon bringing in income from the sale of wool and wine which were specialist operations well suited to the grange system. Moreover, Cistercian claims to be seeking the 'desert' owe much to what has been called 'the rhetoric of reform' and cannot always be taken literally. In practice, not all Cistercian houses were as remote from major lines of communication and population centres as they claimed, and their isolation should sometimes be seen more in spiritual than in directly physical terms (Constable 1996:120, 217–18), so it is not surprising that they were drawn into the wider economy relatively easily. In twelfth-century Burgundy, where the order originated, there was little in the way of 'howling wilderness' (Bouchard 1991:103) and, from the beginning, their charters show that were engaged in the contemporary landed economy. Although they attempted to minimise their participation in certain aspects of contemporary monasticism such as control of parish churches, the acquisition of serfs and the operation of seigneurial monopolies, they never sought to avoid them completely. Thus, the achievement of the compact granges which appears to have been their ideal, would not have been possible without active involvement in the land market involving purchase and exchange, as well as the passive receipt of gifts (Bouchard 1991:188).

This was not in itself problematical in the early decades, but by the late twelfth century the range and scale of their economic activities, together with their exemptions and privileges, began to appear incompatible with the unrealistic ideals they themselves had created and indeed had emphasised during the twelfth century through their additions to the *Exordium Parvum* and other early documents. Taking an example from

England, which is the best researched area, it has been shown that in a large area extending from north Yorkshire to the Cotswolds, sheep were of primary importance to Cistercian houses, especially between *c*.1175 and *c*.1325. Meaux, in east Yorkshire, for instance, kept about 11,000 sheep during the 1270s and, while few other houses could rival this, nevertheless a contemporary Italian list of wool-producing monasteries in England covering the period 1281–96 shows that about 85 per cent of Cistercian houses were involved to some degree (Donkin 1978:68–102). Symptomatic was the apparent ease with which the Cistercians had absorbed the whole structure of abbeys based on Savigny in Normandy in 1158 which had originated in a reform similar to the Cistercians but which had, from the beginning, taken both tithes and serfs. Since no attempt was made to dispense with these rights, tacit encouragement was given to other Cistercians to continue expansion into areas of existing cultivation with all that implied in the enjoyment of traditional manorial rights and in close contact with seculars. Attempts to avoid this problem only led to equally dubious acts, such as the expulsion of the existing inhabitants from a region taken over by the Cistercians, a step which maintained their theoretical purity, but only at the price of further criticism and, indeed, hatred.

The Cistercians therefore illustrate the central moral dilemma of twelfth- and thirteenth-century Christians in an acute form. Their attempt to escape the materialist environment, because it had proved so attractive to so many people, ultimately led them back to the secular world. Moreover, hard work and frugal living served only to increase the profits. While the twelfth-century expansion loosened the Cistercians' grip on their original ideals, new problems in the thirteenth century exacerbated the situation. They were caught in a vicious circle for, as their popularity began to wane and newer forms of religious life, in particular the friars, began to exercise a stronger attraction, their powers of recruitment began to diminish, especially of lay brothers, many of whom were drawn from a similar social environment to that of the early Franciscans. Without sufficient lay brothers direct cultivation became impossible and it became increasingly common to lease lands to lay tenants instead. In their attempts to stem this decline in the numbers of lay brothers, the Cistercians offered relative independence in the management of the estates upon which they were settled. The consequence was that the lay brothers came to form a vested interest which in turn not infrequently came into conflict with the choir monks. These difficulties and the criticism tended to feed off each other, culminating in the revocation of the tithe exemption in 1215, for it seemed inequitable now that the Cistercian economy so much resembled that of society as a whole. By this time the monks whom William of Malmesbury had described as zealously opposing any change from the strict letter of the rule were now prepared to seek almost any expedient which would ensure economic survival: sales of wool in advance of future delivery, diversification of economic interests into any areas which seemed profitable, even dispersion of the monks to reduce costs. While the condition of the Cistercians should not be exaggerated – the degree of self-awareness shown by men like Stephen of Lexington shows the capacity for reform – it is clear that they were no longer the shining beacon among Christians that they had once been. Instead, their abbeys must have seemed little different from those of St Evroult or Bury St Edmunds.

It is, however, evident that the Cistercian route to reform, although highly influential, was but one of several important monastic innovations. The military orders had, by their very nature, to be very active in the secular world, tending the sick, fighting the Muslims and supplying the crusaders. The reforms adopted by the canons represent another variation, for many among them wished to create a more structured life than had previously been the case. Many canons held prebends, which had tended to work against the maintenance of a communal life, but the adoption of a rule during the late eleventh century created a class of regular canons under a monastic discipline but free to fulfil their obligations as priests in society. The Augustinian or Austin canons followed a rule which they believed to have been written by St Augustine for himself and a fellow group of clerics, although in practice it appears to have been a composite work stitched together from some of his writings. Although there was no single individual founder, increasing numbers of canons were adopting this way of life by the late eleventh century. The success of this rule can be seen by its continuing influence during the high middle ages, since it was by this means that the Dominicans were able to establish themselves after the prohibition on the formation of new orders at the Fourth Lateran Council in 1215. More immediately, the preacher Norbert of Xanten (*c*.1082–1134), who from *c*.1115 had gathered a considerable following, was allowed to establish a community under this rule in 1121 at Prémontré, near Laon, and from this developed the Premonstratensian canons. The value of the Premonstratensians was quickly recognised; in 1124, for instance, at the request of the Bishop of Cambrai, Norbert set up a house of canons at St Michael's Church in Antwerp as a barrier against the revival of heresy in a region which had recently been much troubled by the preaching of Tanchelm of Antwerp (Wakefield and Evans 1969:673). The order gained papal confirmation in 1126.

Contemporaries were well aware of this new variety of religious life. The author of the *Libellus de diversis ordinibus*, who was himself a canon, probably at Liège, set out in the mid-twelfth century to explain 'the many kinds of callings' that had come into being, including that of the canons. He described how 'their order, when the charity of many was cooling, formerly became tepid', but that it was now flourishing.

> One must first understand that this order has three parts now: some are separated from the multitudes entirely by their way of life and habit and dwelling-place as much as possible; others are situated next to men; and others live among men and are thus called seculars....Their task is to teach the people, take tithes, collect offerings in church, remonstrate with delinquents, reconcile the corrected and penitent to the church, and observe other duties also laid down in the old law which are still kept in the church of our day.
>
> (Constable and Smith 1972:3, 57)

Both the Augustinians and the Premonstratensians, through their work in the community from a base established upon a proper rule, fulfilled a role in the twelfth century similar to that which was to be taken up so dramatically in the thirteenth century by the friars. Indeed, the *Libellus* reflects a perception shared by both contemporaries and modern historians, which is that between the mid-eleventh and the mid-twelfth centuries there was a dramatic expansion in overall numbers, perhaps as much as tenfold in some regions (Constable 1996:46–7, 88–94).

In this male-orientated society, it is not surprising to find that provision for women within the Church was and remained essentially piecemeal, reflecting a variety of pressures, not all of which were reconcilable. The misogynistic nature of clerical teaching inevitably coloured male views of women who desired to follow the monastic life. On the one hand, it prompted the belief that, given the inbuilt female moral and physical fragility, it was better to provide carefully supervised houses for those who wanted them, but on the other there was a distinct lack of co-operation, seemingly influenced by the fear that women would in some way dilute the achievement of the male order. Most of the men who gave the matter real thought – such as Robert of Arbrissel, Norbert of Xanten or Bernard of Clairvaux – had the problem thrust upon them, rather than considering it on their own initiative. Both Robert of Arbrissel and St Norbert, just like heretical leaders such as Tanchelm, attracted large numbers of women followers by their preaching, and provision had to be made for them if scandal was to be avoided. In both cases, at Fontevrault and at Prémontré, the solution was to provide them with a claustral life, tightly controlled by clerical supervision, rather than to risk the problems which might have arisen had they continued as followers of wandering preachers. In 1140, the Premonstratensians decreed that in all double monasteries facilities for men and women should be separate, while in 1198 they determined that women should no longer be accepted at all. St Bernard rejected the idea of Cistercian nuns, but he did give his attention to the ideas being developed by the Gilbertines in England, and was instrumental in setting them up as an order. In 1131 Gilbert of Sempringham had established a community for women in Lincolnshire and, although Bernard would not accept their affiliation to the Cistercians, in 1148 he did help Gilbert create an appropriate rule. In practice, however, this shelved the problem only during Bernard's lifetime, since from at least the 1180s female communities which had set themselves up began to call themselves Cistercians, much to the embarrassment of the order. Persistence paid; in 1213, the order was compelled to acknowledge their existence and to try to make provision for them.

Even so, these developments did little to change the fact that in this period men dominated a world which, at least in theory, had once been 'equal in monastic profession'. The Premonstratensian community at Schäftlarn in Bavaria, for example, ignored the decrees of 1140 and 1198; indeed, it seems to have been very convenient to have a ready supply of female labour which was employed in a range of tasks from laundering to copying manuscripts (Beach 2004:109–14,126–7). When separation did take place, this was also disadvantageous, for the increasing clericalisation of the monks (itself a consequence of papal reform) diminished the importance of female houses in the hierarchy, as well as burdening nunneries with the extra expense of paying clerics to provide sacramental services for them (Johnson 1991:165, 225–6).

This does not mean, however, that traditional nunneries, headed by powerful abbesses, and performing important communal roles, had ceased to exist. From St Augustine onwards nunneries had been created by the female relatives of the religious and the powerful, and these constituted almost all such houses in the early middle ages. Even the one female Cluniac house – that of Marcigny, founded in 1055 – came about in this way. This remained true of a significant proportion of female houses in the twelfth and thirteenth centuries as well (Johnson 1991:34–41). A typical example of such an aristocratic house is that described by William of Tyre at Bethany, founded and lavishly endowed by Queen Melisende of Jerusalem, specifically for her sister, Iveta, in 1142. 'It was,' says William,

> consideration for her sister which led the queen to undertake this enterprise, for she felt that it was unfitting that a king's daughter should be subject to the authority of a mother superior, like an ordinary person.... She endowed the church with rich estates, so that in temporal possessions it should not be inferior to any monastery, either of men or women.

Although she initially put it in the care of experienced women, when they died she made her sister mother superior.

> On that occasion, she made many additional gifts.... As long as she lived she continued to enrich the place by her favor, in the interests of her own soul and that of the sister whom she so tenderly loved.
>
> (Babcock and Krey 1941:2:133–4)

As in most female houses the sisters were all of noble origin and, not surprisingly, there were insufficient numbers of Frankish women of the requisite social status living in the east. Nuns therefore included noble ladies who had come initially as pilgrims, but who had then taken vows at Bethany, most notably Sibyl, wife of Count Thierry of Flanders, in 1158, apparently despite her husband's disapproval (Hamilton 1995:699).

Entry into nunneries was not, however, always such a matter of individual wishes. Men who themselves entered a monastery, joined a military order or went on an expiatory pilgrimage, often made provision for wives and daughters to enter a monastic house. In *c*.1120, after the tragic events that led to his castration, Peter Abelard became a monk at St Denis. Although reluctant, his former lover, Heloise, was persuaded to take vows at Argenteuil, an action which her letters show caused her much torment in the years that followed. Through Heloise can be gained some intimation of the state of mind of many such women. In her second letter to Abelard written in *c*.1131 from the Paraclete where her community had been established by Abelard, she shattered Abelard's complacent attitude towards the problems of the monastic life when she told him that she was, despite outward appearance, still deeply affected by the past.

> It is easy enough for anyone to confess his sins, to accuse himself, or even to mortify his body in outward show of penance, but it is very difficult to tear the heart away from hankering after its dearest pleasures.
>
> (Radice 1974:132)

Even Valdès, founder of the Waldensians and promoter of a radical approach to lay piety, fell back upon this traditional solution for the family, sending his daughters to the abbey of Fontevrault. Other women ended up in the claustral life because they were unlucky enough to be married to men who had backed the wrong side in a political struggle. Occasionally, the documents provide a glimpse of the human circumstances which sometimes lay behind entry into such a life. In *c*.1130, for instance, a Burgundian knight called Guido Cornelly discovered that his wife had, 'by secret judgement of God', become afflicted by leprosy. He decided that, as was customary in such cases, they should part, and that he would go to Jerusalem to end his life in the service of God, while his wife and three daughters would be consigned to the care of the Abbey of St Bénigne of Dijon (D'Albon 1913:19). While there was undoubtedly a growth in demand for outlets for female piety not adequately met in the twelfth and thirteenth centuries, it is equally true that monastic houses, both male and female, contained many inhabitants confined by circumstance rather than by choice. Ultimately, in the great majority of cases, the wider needs of family and kin took priority and, indeed, were sufficiently powerful to ensure the continuation of the practice of presenting dowries throughout the thirteenth century, despite the Church's view that such gifts were simoniacal (Johnson 1991:15–27).

Had Guido Cornelly and his wife lived a generation later they might have found more specific provision for those sick with leprosy. Although monasteries remained important centres of medieval life, after the mid-twelfth century donors began to show a marked preference for more specialist foundations, such as hospitals and leper houses. These hospitals were administered by brothers and sisters who lived under a quasi-monastic rule or constitution, often following that of St Augustine, and supervised by the local bishop. The hospital at Angers, for instance, was founded c.1175 by Stephen of Marcay, Seneschal of Anjou, and a rule survives from the late twelfth century. It shows a staff of ten brother clerks, ten lay brothers and ten sisters as a maximum, but no limit on the number of poor who could be taken in because 'the house is theirs'. The rules of these houses reflect this double purpose, that of brothers and sisters seeking their own salvation (about three-quarters of most rules are concerned with their conduct) and that of caring for the sick. When the sick were admitted they were to be given communion and then their needs were always to be given priority. 'No brother or sister', says the Angers rule, 'should dare to complain or murmur about food given to the poor, or offend by word or deed, even if treated in a contemptuous fashion' (Le Grand 1901:22–5).

By the first decade of the thirteenth century, therefore, many Cistercians had become conscious that their distinctive identity as a reformist order had been lost and that their way of life differed little from that of the monks of the older Benedictine houses. At the same time their unique role was further undermined by the very positive attraction of a new reforming movement within the Church, that of the friars. In c.1208 Francis of Assisi, the son of a prosperous Umbrian cloth merchant, became convinced that he should adopt a life of poverty and preaching in the manner which he believed had been followed by Christ and the Apostles. This decision is encapsulated in the famous incident described by his first biographer, Thomas of Celano, who had himself joined the friars in 1215. Francis had demonstrated his commitment to his new life by putting aside all material things, including some money belonging to his father.

> But when his father saw that he could not bring him back from the way he had undertaken, he was roused by all means to get his money back. The man of God had desired to offer it and expend it to feed the poor and to repair the buildings of that place. But he who had no love for money could not be misled by any aspect of good in it; and he who was not held back by any affection for it was in no way disturbed by its loss. Therefore, when the money was found, which he who hated the things of this world so greatly and desired the riches of heaven so much had thrown aside in the dust of the window sill, the fury of the raging father was extinguished a little, and the thirst of his avarice was somewhat allayed by the warmth of discovery.

He then took his son before the Bishop of Assisi and Francis renounced all he had.

> He did not wait for any words nor did he speak any, but immediately putting off his clothes and casting them aside, he give them back to his father. Moreover, not even retaining his trousers, he stripped himself completely naked before all. The bishop, however, sensing his disposition and admiring greatly his fervor and constancy, arose and drew him within his arms and covered him with the mantle he was wearing.
>
> (Habig 1980:240–1)

Thomas's *Life*, written in 1228–9, had been commissioned by Pope Gregory IX, who as Cardinal Ugolino, Bishop of Ostia, had been the cardinal-protector of the Franciscans. As such, it is one of the first signs of a developing cult. In the thirteenth and early fourteenth centuries – and there is some irony in this, given Francis's desire to 'put off everything that is of this world' – this cult was expressed in an ever-increasing quantity of writing, building and painting. It was a cult which influenced very directly the nature of thirteenth-century piety and which in turn was reflected most evidently in the style and subject-matter of Italian art. Moreover, as the canonisation of Francis in 1228 shows, it was from the beginning nurtured by the papacy. Under Innocent III and Gregory IX in particular its value to the institutionalised Church was quickly perceived, while Francis's insistence on the duty of obedience and adherence to the Catholic faith was fully utilised in the conflict with those who assailed the Church for its worldliness and lack of spirituality.

Francis was about 27 when he received his message in the church of San Damiano in Assisi. From that time he devoted himself to a life of absolute poverty in which he preached and cared for the sick, especially lepers, as well as repairing local churches as he believed himself to have been instructed. By late 1210 he had attracted about eleven companions and he sought and was given verbal approval for their way of life by Innocent III, despite some doubts in the curia. At this time he had written a very brief Rule based largely on the Gospels, which has not survived. The first formal Rule dated from *c*.1221 and a revised version, incorporating changes brought about by papal influence, was produced in 1223 (see Plate 9). The original small group lived at the Portiuncula at Assisi, from which at various times they set out on preaching missions. Francis and some of his companions even looked towards the conversion of the infidel and, after two abortive attempts, reached Damietta with the Fifth Crusade. In 1219 Francis actually gained an audience with al-Kamil, the Egyptian sultan, although, predictably in the circumstances, without managing to convince him of the need to become a Christian.

In western Christendom, however, the Franciscans became increasingly popular. By 1217 there were adherents in France and Spain as well as Italy, and the order was divided into provinces. By 1224 there were thirteen of these. Here lay the kernel of a serious problem. Much of Francis's preaching took inspirational form. He spoke 'not in the persuasive words of human wisdom (1 Cor. 2,4)', said Thomas of Celano, 'but with the learning and power of the spirit' (Habig 1980:258). It is clear that Francis could convey his ideas through personal example and through striking verbal images, but that the organisational problems attendant upon rapid growth placed a strain upon him with which he was unable to cope. He was apparently afflicted by dreams centred upon this unresolved dilemma, such as the one in which he was in front of starving brothers whom he tried to feed with bread, only to see the crumbs fall through his fingers (Lambert 1998:36). Yet, within two years of his death in 1226, there was founded at Assisi a basilica in memory of the man who could not be misled by the possibility that good could sometimes be done with money. The driving force behind this was Brother Elias of Cortona, Minister General between 1221 and 1227 and again from 1232 to 1239. Funds were collected and the basis of a double church was completed by 1239 and consecrated in 1253. This building, together with the commissioning of the *Life* by Thomas of Celano, was part of the same desire by the established ecclesiastical authorities to preserve the memory of the saint in the way they deemed most appropriate. Francis had been aware of this, but unable to do anything about it. After

Plate 9 The frescoes in the upper church of San Francesco, Assisi, thought by some to be painted by Giotto's workshop in the 1290s, present the official view of Franciscan history. In this scene Francis receives the revised written Rule from Pope Honorius III in 1223. (Photograph reproduced by permission of Casa Editrice Francescana, Assisi.)

his return from crusade in 1220, exhausted and ill, he handed over the leadership to Peter Cantanii and, after his death in 1221, to Brother Elias. In 1218 he had accepted the need for a cardinal-protector in the person of Cardinal Ugolino; in 1223 it was Ugolino who was largely responsible for revisions made to a new Rule which he had persuaded Francis to draw up. The contrast between these practical steps and the way of life actually followed by Francis during these last years is very pointed. In the late summer of 1224 he retired to Mount Verna in the Apennines which had been granted to the order twelve years before. Here he lived apart from his few companions and in September he received what he believed to be the miraculous imprint of the stigmata. During the last two years of his life the pain from this seems to have contributed to the deterioration of his health, already badly affected by increasing blindness and internal haemorrhaging. He died on 4 October 1226.

Francis's lifestyle was attainable by an exceptional individual and perhaps a small group of followers, but tensions inevitably arose with growth. Although the developments of Francis's later years and after his death have sometimes been seen as a perversion of his ideals, the concerns of a papacy already deeply worried about dissent were understandable. The missions of 1219 are a good example of the problems which could arise from a lack of organisation and planning. In Germany the brothers, unable to communicate in the local language, were taken to be heretics and were stripped and beaten up. In contrast, the trend of papal thinking was underlined in 1230 when Ugolino, now Gregory IX, issued the bull *Quo elongati*, which established that the order could hold buildings, furnishings and books by means of a third party such as the papacy or the cardinal-protector, thus creating a distinction between possession and use which, for the next century, was to be a central concern of all those with an interest in the mendicant orders and their role in society. Stage by stage the papacy remodelled the order: in *Ordinem vestrum* (1245) convenience rather than necessity became the determining reason for third-party retention of money for the order, while *Exiit qui seminat* (1279) recognised that, although the papacy technically remained the owner of the goods, their distribution and control was to be looked after by the order's ministers. Most striking of all, however, was Martin IV's bull, *Exultantes in Domino* (1283), which established proctors for the task of administering the property, but gave the ministers and *custodes* direct control over their appointment, while leaving decisions as to the needs of individual convents to these same ministers. Whatever the other ambiguities of Francis's legacy, it is clear that for him poverty meant no permanent possessions; in the twenty years after his death the papacy, by its increasing resort to intermediaries, reinterpreted this as a repudiation not of all material goods, but rather of the right to own such goods (Lambert 1998:106, 134).

A desire to make full use of the order, as well as perceptions of practical necessities, undoubtedly led the Holy See to steer the Franciscans along this road, but at the same time the popes were acknowledging the existence of marked developments within the order itself. Even before the death of Francis it had been losing the essentially lay character of its earliest devotees. Priests, several of whom were learned theologians already established in the universities, began to join the order; by the late 1220s connections with the important theology schools at Paris and Oxford were solidly established, despite the fact that St Francis had seen knowledge as a form of property (Le Goff 1980:128). By the middle of the thirteenth century the influence of the learned and priestly interest within the order had so increased that each convent had its own rector preparing novices for higher study in much the same way as in contemporary Dominican houses. This element within the order had really won the internal political battle when Gregory IX was persuaded to dismiss Elias of Cortona as Minister General in 1239. Elias had largely dissipated his popular following within the order both by his autocratic methods of government and by his inappropriate lifestyle. Thereafter, ministers like Haymo of Faversham (1240–4) and, most importantly, St Bonaventura (John of Fidanza, 1257–74), ensured that their grip on the order did not slacken. Bonaventura believed that the Franciscans had achieved a unique blend of the qualities and functions of all other types of clerical calling. In order to maintain this he saw a sound organisation based on settled convents and well-stocked libraries as an essential prerequisite; the wandering life of the unlearned mendicant had, in his view, no future.

As such he vigorously rebutted criticisms of the order's large convents and the friars' evident disinclination to engage in manual labour, while at the same time, in the Constitutions of Narbonne of 1260, issuing a series of statutes designed to correct the abuses which such a conventual life had tended to encourage. Symptomatic was the clause allowing the order to employ servants; the Franciscans were now a clerical order who needed others to fulfil the mundane tasks of everyday living for them.

Such distinctive traits did not develop unchallenged. The attitudes of the secular clergy towards privileged orders had already been shown in 1215; the clericalisation of the Franciscans provided an almost model demonstration of why they thought in this fashion. In the form in which the papacy and Bonaventura envisaged them the Franciscans were, both explicitly and implicitly, a living criticism of the seculars. Their permanent convents, their right to bury seculars in their own cemeteries (granted 1250), and their increasing popularity as confessors, seemed designed to mock the role of the secular clergy, which already felt itself undermined by increasing papal centralisation. Their occupation of university chairs and their increasingly frequent appointments to bishoprics encroached still further on existing vested interests. Strong protests were made at the Council of Lyon in 1274, but with little effect. Indeed, *Ad fructus uberes* of 1281 reasserted the right of the mendicant orders to preach and hear confessions and, as if to underline the extent of the seculars' defeat, Franciscan appointments to bishoprics shot up after 1274, reaching fifty-six by 1311 (Moorman 1968:307). Thereafter papal policy seemed to oscillate on this issue, probably reflecting the continuous lobbying of both interests at the curia. The problem never disappeared, but at the Council of Vienne in 1311–12, Clement V did manage to reimpose the compromise set out in the bull *Super cathedram* (1300), which allowed the friars to continue to preach, hear confessions and bury those who desired it, but placed quite specific restrictions on the exercise of these functions.

The privileges of the Franciscans, however, not only offended outsiders, but also drove a wedge deep into the fissures within the order itself. By the mid-thirteenth century it was evident that there were two parties: the Conventuals, who followed the path being mapped out by the papacy, and the Spirituals, who presented themselves as the true followers of St Francis, committed to an ideal of poverty which they believed was disappearing. Despite the efforts of Bonaventura, dissent persisted and by the 1290s there were strong Spiritual groups in Provence and Italy. In 1294 these groups experienced a brief taste of triumph when the hermit, Peter of Morrone, was unexpectedly elected pope as Celestine V. Celestine's natural sympathy for the Spirituals led him to create a new order for them called 'The Poor Hermits of Pope Celestine'. The Poor Hermits did not last long. When Celestine resigned in December 1294 they fled, dispersing to the Greek islands, for they knew they would get little sympathy from Boniface VIII. Further efforts to hold the order together by Clement V between 1309 and 1312, culminating in the legislation promulgated at the end of the Council of Vienne in May 1312, did not outlast his pontificate (Lambert 1998:197–214). The real drive against them, however, began under John XXII (1316–34). In a series of bulls between 1317 and 1323 he brought the full weight of his authority to bear. Four 'Fraticelli', as he called them, were burnt to death as heretics in 1318, while in the bull *Ad conditorem canonum* of 1322 he maintained that the distinction between use and possession was artificial and withdrew the Church's intermediary role. Just under a year later, in *Cum inter nonnullus*, he declared heretical the idea of apostolic poverty. The bull symbolises the end of an era; papal interest in movements of spontaneous evangelical piety was totally absent in the later middle ages.

That piety had not only appealed to men. In March 1212 a 17 year old called Clare fled from her noble relatives in Assisi and joined Francis and his companions. Francis placed her in a local Benedictine house and no amount of pressure by her kin could shake her. Indeed, she was soon joined by her younger sister, Agnes. Francis helped establish them and their companions in a small community at the Church of San Damiano and in 1215 drew up a rule for them. By 1219 there were at least four similar houses in existence and they applied to the papacy for confirmation. Papal reaction shows that a female apostolate was not considered appropriate; the rule given them by Cardinal Ugolino was largely Benedictine, making them into strictly closed communities. Through Francis's intervention San Damiano did obtain the so-called 'Privilege of Poverty', which made it distinct from other female houses in that it was allowed to dispense with settled incomes and lands. Clare clung to this privilege until her death in 1253, but successive popes were equally determined to prevent what they regarded as the peculiar position of San Damiano from spreading to other communities of female religious. Like the Cistercians and the Dominicans, the Franciscans were not over-enthusiastic about attached female houses; in 1263 Urban IV created a separate cardinal-protector for the Clarisses and removed the obligation on the Franciscans to provide these houses with a chaplain. Once again the conventional monastic outlook outweighed innovation in the thirteenth-century Christian community, for the massive growth in beguinages, including some that developed as semi-monastic communities from Franciscan tertiaries, is clear evidence of the extent of contemporary demand for female houses.

From the 1230s onwards the fresco cycles and ecclesiastical buildings connected with the Franciscans increasingly reflected the papal and Conventual view of the order's history, while many Franciscans became absorbed into the structure as bishops, inquisitors and university theologians. The change can be illustrated by the great Franciscan church of Santa Croce in Florence. Founded in 1294–5, the ground plan shows a building 380 feet long with ten chapels flanking the choir. The artistic representation of Francis's life, such as the great fresco cycle in the upper church at Assisi dating from the late 1290s, similarly reflects the establishment view, being based on the *Life* compiled by Bonaventura in 1263 which, although heavily dependent upon Thomas of Celano's two lives of 1229 and 1247, subtly altered the emphasis to underplay Thomas's depiction of Francis's unease with developments in his later years. At Assisi the order is depicted as strongly linked to the institutionalised Church.

Men like Bonaventura and the leader of the opposition to Elias, Haymo of Faversham, were upright and honourable but, rather like the Cistercians a century before, the effect of these developments was to remodel the Franciscans into a body which resembled a conventional monastic institution. Given their licence to preach and to travel and their papal privileges, it is not surprising to find that the extent of hostility could sometimes be as strong as the cult. Matthew Paris, writing under the year 1247, saw the appearance of two Franciscan brothers collecting on behalf of the pope, as an opportunity to attack two targets at the same time, castigating them as hypocrites, humble before the king, but proud and extortionate once they had gained his permission to gather in procurations (Luard 1880:4:599).

Dominic of Guzman was a direct contemporary of Francis of Assisi and the two men, together with the orders which they founded have, as a consequence, often been the objects of comparison and contrast. The clear differences in background and early career are indeed reflected in the distinctiveness of the two orders, but at the same time there are common features in the impulses which drove them, features evidently discerned by both men when they eventually met in 1221. Dominic was born in the village of Caleruega in Old Castile in *c.*1172. Caleruega was a recently colonised hill settlement, largely dependent upon its pasture and its vines, set within the harsh landscape of the Upper Duero valley, but Dominic himself came from a relatively privileged background, for his parents were members of the locally prominent noble families of Guzman and Aza. His parents were therefore able to provide for a clerical career and he received his elementary education under the auspices of an uncle who was both a priest and a rural dean, before leaving home for the famous cathedral school of Palencia, where he studied the liberal arts and theology. While at Palencia he gained a reputation for austerity and selflessness, culminating in the sale of all his possessions (including his much-valued books) in order to relieve those suffering from famine. By 1196 or 1197 he had been noticed by Diego of Acebo, prior of the chapter at the cathedral of Osma where, at the invitation of the bishop, he became a canon. Osma was an influential community following the Rule of St Augustine, and Dominic quickly rose to prominence, successively holding the positions of sacristan (1199) and sub-prior (1201).

The real transformation in his life, however, came after he had begun to travel beyond Castile, in particular when, in 1203 and 1205, he accompanied Diego, who had become Bishop of Osma in 1201, on two missions to Denmark, which were part of the diplomatic and marriage plans of the Castilian ruler, King Alfonso VIII. Experiences undergone at this time must have been profound, for both Diego and Dominic seem thereafter to have been powerfully driven by the desire to evangelise, seeing the need both to combat heresy in the Toulousain, where the dualist heresy of the Cathars was deeply rooted and, further north, to convert the pagans of the Baltic lands. The two men therefore visited the pope in Rome in 1206, partly because they needed papal action to conclude certain aspects of the royal affairs, but at the same time because they hoped to gain from Innocent III a commission to preach among the Slavs. The pope would not grant permission, apparently because he considered the work to be done in Castile to be too important, but he did encourage them to make contact with the Cistercians, who were primarily responsible for the conduct of the papal mission to combat the heresy of the south of France. In the spring of 1206, after visiting Cîteaux itself, they met the papal legates at Montpellier. The legates had had little success and to Diego it seemed that to have any impact they themselves needed to adopt the apostolic life of preaching and poverty which the heretics used so effectively to convince potential adherents. To this end he impulsively sent back to Castile his entire baggage train and following, and set about the task of evangelisation as a poor beggar, accompanied only by Dominic, and two of the legates, themselves apparently converted to the idea despite some initial reluctance. Papal permission for this approach, seemingly based on ignorance of the steps already taken, did not transpire until some six months later. For many Dominican writers these were the first steps in the foundation of what was to become the Order of Preachers.

During the year 1206–7 they perambulated the Midi, engaging in public disputations with the heretics and preaching to the populace. Dominic himself established a base at Prouille, between Fanjeaux and Montréal, to which were attracted a number of women who had been converted by the efforts of the preachers. From the spring of 1207 there began to form here the rudiments of a community which eventually became an important convent, acting as a centre for female orthodoxy in the region. There is little direct evidence available to trace Dominic's activities during the next four or five years. Diego died in December 1207, while the onset of the Albigensian Crusade against the heretics in the summer of 1209 overshadows the preaching campaigns in contemporary accounts. Simon of Montfort, who was appointed crusading leader in August 1209, strongly supported Dominic's work, but there does not seem to have been a direct association between the crusaders and the preachers as such. By 1213–14 Dominic had attracted a small group of like-minded men and, by the beginning of 1215, at the request of the papal legate, they had set themselves up in a small hospice in Toulouse granted to them by Bishop Fulk, with the aim of re-establishing the faith in the city after the ravages of the war years. They were further strengthened when, in April, a prominent citizen called Peter Seila joined the group, bringing with him three houses which from then on acted as a centre from which they could work. In effect, this was the first Dominican house.

Their position was confirmed by Bishop Fulk and they were granted one-half of the third part of the tithe in perpetuity, deemed appropriate as the proportion of the tithe normally set aside for the poor (Vicaire1964:171). Here, in embryonic form, was a preaching order rather than a delegation sent out for a set period or purpose. This, however, was on only a local scale, but as can be seen from the plans which Diego and Dominic had presented to Innocent III in 1206, Dominic envisaged a broader field than this. The obvious step was to approach the pope to confirm the order: the meeting of the Fourth Lateran Council in November 1215 seemed the ideal opportunity. Canon thirteen of the council declared, however, that, 'for fear that too great a diversity of religious orders should introduce serious confusion into the Church of God', there should be no new orders and that anyone wishing to establish a house in the future should adopt an existing rule (Foreville 1965:354). This canon, which reflected the views of the secular clergy rather than those of the pope, is a pointer to future problems, but in 1215 it was not the serious setback to the Dominicans which has sometimes been suggested. Confirmation was not incompatible with canon thirteen; Dominic seems to have been quite prepared to adopt the Augustinian Rule, with which he was already familiar. Dispensations, which in the original meaning of the rule were largely on health grounds, were used to obtain time for the brothers to preach and to study. Limited numbers of lay brothers were allowed to help free the priestly class for their central aims. Innocent III's death in 1216 did nothing to hinder the order, for his successor, Honorius III, proved equally supportive. M.H. Vicaire calculates that between 1216 and Dominic's death in 1221 he issued more than sixty bulls, letters or privileges in favour of the Dominicans (Vicaire 1964:222).

Between 1215 and 1221, therefore, Dominic established an order of a highly innovatory kind, in that it was charged with the specific task of preaching, a task for which its members were granted remission of sins just like crusaders. After the Lateran Council, Dominic set about expanding the scope of this enterprise, despite the reluctance of some of his companions. By 1219, either through dispersing the brethren in groups or by personal intervention, he had set up houses in Paris, Bologna, Rome, Madrid and Segovia. The next year he assembled the order's first General Chapter at Bologna, in which he established a layered organisational structure which proved to be remarkably durable. The General Chapter which, from the following year, would meet alternately at Bologna and Paris, would consist of representatives of the order's priories.

In this form it would legislate for the order, and to this end Dominic set down a series of constitutions which, apart from some reorganisation by the third master, Raymond of Peñaforte, in 1241, have remained in force throughout the order's history. A basic provision of these constitutions was that a priory should consist of a minimum of twelve Dominicans and must include a prior and a master of theology who would teach the novices. This was a prelude to the second Bologna Chapter where the order was now in a position to promote an orderly expansion upon this framework. During 1221, individual houses were established in Germany and in Sweden, and brethren were sent to England, Poland, Hungary and Latin Greece. The Dominicans were now sufficiently numerous to set up five distinct provinces in Lombardy, Provence, Spain, France and Rome. A papal bull of May 1219, which conceded the Dominicans the right to portable altars, greatly facilitated this expansion, since it enabled new priories to be created in even the most temporary accommodation, dispensing with the need to seek out facilities within an existing church in the town concerned (Vicaire 1964:340–1). In many ways this privilege symbolises both the commitment of the Holy See to the Dominicans and the inbuilt resistance of some secular clergy to the growth in exempt orders.

By 1221 there were twenty-one houses for men, but Dominic's experience at Prouille had also shown him that there existed a huge potential response among women as well. Part of the reason for the success of Catharism had been that network of female devotees had been attracted by the willingness of the sect to accept women as *perfectae* or ministers. Prouille, in the very centre of the Cathar *pays*, provided an orthodox counter. By 1212 piecemeal donations had provide it with permanent buildings and, in 1216, the community was given a proper rule of observance. Two years later a papal privilege officially linked it to the Dominicans. In the same year, while on a visit to Madrid, Dominic had accepted a further group of sisters into the order. Meanwhile, during the later months of 1219 and during 1220, Dominic battled to establish another female house at Saint Sixtus in Rome. This was done largely on papal initiative, for Honorius III wanted to follow up Innocent III's unfinished plan to set up a 'model' reformed house for nuns in the city. In the face of some determined and occasionally violent resistance from some of the Roman aristocratic families, many of whose daughters lived in the existing, less rigorous houses of Santa Maria in Tempula and Santa Bibiana, Dominic succeeded in consolidating them into a fully closed community under his order's supervision. According to the Dominican Inquisitor, Bernard Gui, writing in 1303, there were 141 convents under Dominican supervision by that year (Hinnebusch 1965:1:377), which was a massive expansion in the context of the limited numbers of female houses in general.

Dominic succumbed to the pressures of the life which he had been leading even earlier than Francis. He died in August 1221, weakened by dysentery and an inadequate diet and exhausted by constant travelling. The differences between him and Francis have often been stressed, both by contemporaries and by later historians. William, rector of Puylaurens, who was from Toulouse and a contemporary of the first generation of inquisitors established by Pope Gregory IX to seek out heretics, believed that the authorities added a Franciscan to a tribunal made up of Dominicans in order to seem to temper rigour with mercy (Duvernoy 1976:152–3). Indeed, to the papacy the organised and systematic approach of the Dominicans, together with their theological training, made them obvious appointees as inquisitors. Dominic provided a firm overall structure within which new priories could be established. They could not be set up without meeting certain specific criteria, most evidently the minimum size of twelve and the provision of educational facilities. The choice of Paris and Bologna, the two greatest intellectual centres of the time, as the first two establishments of the order after Toulouse demonstrates the importance that Dominic attached to the systematic training of preachers before they could be allowed to begin their apostolate. The spontaneous preaching of St Francis must have produced a quite different impression on the audience. This planned approach dominated the thinking of the order's leaders after Dominic's death. William Hinnebusch points to the way that the order settled itself in England according to a predefined programme, first going to Oxford in 1221 and London in 1224, followed by a steady geographical expansion, the stages of which can be identified by successive implantations in major centres like Norwich and York. The contrast with the abortive Franciscan expedition to Germany in 1219 is painfully evident. The Dominicans consequently founded fewer establishments than the Franciscans, but they were generally of a larger size. By 1277 they had about 450 priories, whereas the Franciscans had 1,538 communities of very uneven size. According to the list of 1303 this had risen to 590 priories by the early fourteenth century in eighteen provinces. Hinnebusch estimates total membership at about 20,650 (1965:1:261–3, 279, 330–1).

Admirers of the Dominican approach can, however, be too easily seduced by this image of calm orderliness, especially in view of the self-inflicted wounds of the Franciscan Order during the later thirteenth and early fourteenth centuries. In fact the two orders by no means represent such a radical polarisation between reason and passion as such a view might suggest. Innocent III and Cardinal Ugolino saw in both a fundamental compatibility of aim which was very much in keeping with the early-thirteenth-century environment. Both orders set out to preach and save souls and to both founders the need to shed material encumbrances and to follow the apostolic path of poverty was of fundamental importance. As early as the 1190s, over a decade before Francis's dramatic renunciation at Assisi, Dominic had demonstrated his scale of values when he sold all his possessions to feed the victims of a famine. Moreover, when he wished to organise a proper order, he too came up against the practical problems, complicated in his case by long-established Church laws which forbade priests to attempt to live without proper means of support. His earliest priories existed on rents and alms, but by the time of the General Chapter of 1220 he had, quite unambiguously, rejected not only property, but revenues as well, leaving the order to exist through its priories, the sites of which it did own, and periodic 'questing' for alms when needs became acute.

Nor should it be assumed that the development of the Dominicans throughout the thirteenth century was without its problems, although the order never split in the spectacular manner of the controversy between the Spirituals and the Conventuals. Despite the extensive educational provisions there were still complaints that the friars set out inadequately prepared; despite the careful delineation of territories within which each priory was allowed to seek alms, there were still quarrels between houses and disputes with seculars who objected to obtrusive begging methods; despite the prohibitions on property, the regulations were sufficiently relaxed in 1239 to allow the storage of food and, soon after, the collective possession of books. Moreover, the latent resentment of privileged orders which existed among sections of the secular clergy was never far from the surface. In the 1250s it manifested itself most clearly at the University of Paris where the secular masters, led by William of Saint-Amour, made a determined attempt to dislodge the friars from the chairs which they held. Although this represented a general attack on the mendicant orders, the Dominicans, to whom theological study was so central, were especially vulnerable. For a brief period in 1254 the opponents of the mendicants even managed to gain the ear of Innocent IV, although his revocation of their privileges was quickly overturned by his successor, Alexander IV. In 1256 William produced his *Perils of the Last Times*, in which he attacked not only the friars' position at the university, but also their whole *raison d'être*. William was in the end defeated in that he was condemned by the pope and forced to retire from the controversy, but the quarrel nevertheless shows that although the friars succeeded because their ideals were in tune with so many of the religious aspirations of the century, there were, too, many enemies who would seize on any weakening of their position. Indeed, for all the organisational skills of Dominic and his immediate successors as master-general, by the last quarter of the century the Dominicans did begin to experience the problems of expansion, acquiring property under one guise or another and becoming increasingly involved in daily Church affairs. Indicative of the change is that in 1283 they were allowed to appoint proctors to represent them in court cases dealing with litigation over property and money.

The success of the friars stemmed from the fact that they touched deep-rooted needs in thirteenth-century Christian society, needs felt particularly strongly in the commercially orientated cities of the Italian peninsula. Apart from the Franciscans and the Dominicans, these attitudes found other outlets. Soon after, there appeared other groups of friars, such as the Carmelites, and, in Florence, 'The Order of the Slaves of the Blessed Mary' or the Servites. The Carmelites were themselves strongly influenced by the prevailing climate, much to the regret of some of their members, for they were in origin a group of hermits who, in the second half of the twelfth century, had established themselves on Mount Carmel, near Haifa. In the 1230s they had begun to settle in the west, a move which led to the adoption of a mendicant life, more city-based than eremitical. Lay religious fraternities were also established, like the Franciscan Tertiaries, the Brethren of the Order of Penance, largely Dominican in inspiration, and religious militia like the Milizia di Geso Cristo, founded in 1245 to combat heretics. It is no coincidence that anti-materialistic heretical groups like the Waldensians and the Cathars also proliferated in these circumstances.

The economic and political environment of urbanised Christendom in the thirteenth century, especially in the city-states of Tuscany and Umbria, encouraged an active and participatory civic life. The message epitomised by the Franciscans was ideally suited to this, contrasting as it did with the monastic, contemplative world which required those who would be saved to cut themselves off from the outside. If the crusades, as Guibert of Nogent had claimed in the early twelfth century, provided a new path to salvation for the secular knighthood, then the friars, a century later, offered a means by which the inhabitants of the new urban agglomerations, afflicted by the guilt induced by the nature of their occupations, might seek intercession for their sins.

7

Popular religion and heresy

One of the most striking and detailed descriptions of the medieval 'visionary imagination' can be found in Book Eight of Orderic Vitalis' *Ecclesiastical History*. Writing in *c.*1131, he tells the story of 'Hellequin's Host', derived from an account of a priest called Walchelin who claimed that it had happened to him while returning from visiting a sick parishioner on the outskirts of the village of Bonneval in the diocese of Lisieux on the night of 1 January 1091. Orderic accepted this as fact not because he believed every story of this kind that he heard, but because he thought that he had a trustworthy witness. He started from the assumption that visions, miracles and supernatural events were perfectly possible, were, indeed, an integral part of the world in which he lived, but that, like any other story, they needed to be treated critically. But Walchelin's story is interesting not only for the way that it demonstrates contemporary perceptions of the world, but also because its content is the basis of similar stories found elsewhere in western Christendom. It therefore has more than a local significance (Chibnall 1973:4:237–51).

The priest heard what he took to be the approach of a great feudal army and his first reaction was to hide, since he assumed that such troops quite casually pillaged and that he would be robbed. However, a huge man carrying a mace appeared and blocked his way, and thus he was forced to witness the passage, not of human knights rushing to a siege, as he had thought, but of a terrible and ghostly procession. First there appeared a great crowd carrying items of plunder, among whom were various neighbours who had recently died, complaining bitterly of the agonies that they suffered because of their sins. Then came bearers carrying biers on which sat dwarfs with huge heads, followed by two Ethiopians carrying a tree trunk on which was tied a priest called Stephen, who had died before completing his penance for murder. Stephen lay screaming and bloody while a demon tortured him with red-hot spurs. Next a huge troop of women appeared riding saddles 'studded with burning nails' on which the wind caused them to rise and then fall back onto the points. 'Indeed it was for the seductions and obscene delights in which they had wallowed without restraint on earth that they now endured the fire and stench and other agonies too many to enumerate.' Walchelin recognised various noblewomen here and, ominously, a number of riderless horses belonging to women still alive. Nor were ecclesiastics spared, for priests and monks, bishops and abbots, were next, including 'many of high repute, who in human estimation are believed to have joined the saints in heaven'. Finally, there came a great army of knights enveloped in 'blackness and flickering fire', and again Walchelin was able to pick out individuals, sentenced to torments for their crimes. One knight in particular importuned Walchelin, demanding that he take messages to his wife and son that they might right the wrongs for which he was being punished, wrongs which included unjust judgements, seizures of other people's property, and usury. The priest's attempt to seize one of the passing horses to take as proof of what he had seen served only to increase the horror of the occasion, for it drew attention to him and nearly caused him to be slain and dragged into the procession as well. He was saved only by an appeal to the Virgin Mary, who caused his dead brother to appear and drive off the knights who were threatening him. Walchelin at first refused to accept that it was his brother, but eventually gave in and was compelled to listen to an account of how his brother had suffered 'unspeakable torture' for his sins.

> Remember me, I beg: help me with your prayers and compassionate alms. In one year from Palm Sunday I hope to be saved and released from all torments by the mercy of my Creator. Take thought for your own welfare: correct your life wisely, for it is stained by many vices, and you must know that it will not be long enduring.

No complex theology was necessary for comprehension of such a tale. Men must do penance for their sins in hope of avoiding such a sentence; nothing would save them if they did not genuinely repent in their hearts, whatever their social rank. Above all the love of the material world was the greatest curse; in Walchelin's vision, avarice and lust are the two most prominent vices. Walchelin himself was ill for a week after the experience and only then was he able to go to Gilbert, Bishop of Lisieux, and receive from him 'the remedies he needed'. Not everybody would undergo so personalised and vivid a trauma as this, but the message was accessible to all in powerful visual form, prominently displayed in the sculpture and painting of cathedrals and churches.

Many charters testify to the effect these perceptions had on individuals. Departure on pilgrimage or crusade was a particularly stressful time, both for participants and for those who remained at home. Two early-twelfth-century charters record donations to the abbey of La Grasse. While evidently expressed in the style of the monks who drafted them, it is unlikely that they misrepresented the donors' feelings. In 1101, Ermengarde, Viscountess of Béziers, and her son, Bernard Aton, were about to set out on a pilgrimage to the Holy Sepulchre, and they gave to the abbey the village (*villa*) of Cazilhac (near Carcassonne) and the church of St Hilary within it,

> fearing the magnitude of our sins and considering how we ought to be able to find mercy before the severe and dreadful judgement of God, accepting the advice for salvation from the Lord himself, who says in the Gospel: 'Give alms and behold all things are clean unto you.' [Luke, 11.41].

In return they asked that the monks never cease praying for them. Eight years later La Grasse received from Agnes, Countess of Roussillon, the ruined monastery of St Andrew of Sorède (near Argelès), in order to restore it and to re-establish the Benedictine Rule there.

> And, I, Agnes, Countess, bear witness before God and the saints that, if my lord
> Gerard, through the bountiful mercy of God, should return from the Holy
> Sepulchre, I shall cause him to approve and confirm this charter of donation
> > (Magnou-Nortier and Magnou 1996:226–7, 246–7)

Some clerics were not above exploiting such feelings, as can be seen in the phenomenon of the cult of the carts which appeared in Normandy and the Paris Basin in the 1140s. Two Norman abbots, Haimon of Saint-Pierre-sur-Dives and Robert of Torigny of Mont Saint-Michel, described how there was general participation in rebuilding of churches regardless of the traditional functional divisions of society. 'Who has ever heard tell,' asks Haimon,

> in times past, that powerful princes of the world, that men brought up in honor
> and in wealth, that nobles, men and women, have bent their proud and haughty
> necks to the harness of carts, and that. like beasts of burden, they have dragged
> to the abode of Christ these waggons, loaded with wines, grains, oil, stone,
> wood, and all that is necessary for the wants of life, or for the construction of
> the church?
> > (E.G. Holt 1957:49–50)

Robert of Torigny identified Chartres as the starting-point, but says that it spread to Normandy and other places in France so that one saw

> everywhere humility and suffering, everywhere penance and remission of sins,
> everywhere lamentation and contrition. You might have seen women and men
> dragging themselves on their knees through deep marshes, beating themselves
> with whips, everywhere miracles repeatedly occurring, chants and hymns of
> praise being rendered to God.... It might be said, that the prophecy was
> fulfilled: 'The spirit of life was in the wheels.'
> > (Howlett 1889:150–1)

It is not surprising to find that Suger, ever competitive, claim similar efforts being made on behalf of St Denis, especially in the quarry at Pontoise from which the abbey took most of its good quality stone. Suger says that 'nobles and common folk alike' tied ropes round their chests like draft animals and hauled stone from the bottom of the quarry (Panofsky 1979:93).

This was only one manifestation of such communal action, however, for it could take a variety of forms. Often the impetus can be found in an attempt to avert or overcome crisis, as can be seen on the eve of a battle (especially in a crusading context) or in the face of natural disaster. The cult of the carts was rather cynically manipulated towards essentially local objectives, but just over a century later, in 1260–1, the Flagellant movement, beginning in the Umbrian hill town of Perugia, had a much wider influence, spreading first to Rome and then north to Lombardy, Provence, Germany, Hungary and Poland. Barefoot and stripped to the waist, the flagellants lashed themselves on the upper shoulders in series of public penitential rituals, all the time chanting and singing. As they moved from town to town they attracted increasing numbers of adherents, as well as inspiring the foundation of many penitential confraternities of laymen. The crisis which had originally ignited the movement had arisen from the coalescence of a number of elements. The year before, Perugia had been on the losing side in the battle of Montaperti between Florence and Siena, the city itself was torn by conflicts between magnates and *popolo*, and the prevalent atmosphere of prophetic upheaval had been given a focus by a frightening stories of the Mongol threat, an aspect which took on greater immediacy when the processions reached eastern Europe. Although in its later stages the movement experienced considerable clerical hostility, there is no doubt about its orthodox origins, nor about the disciplined nature of its rituals (Dickson 1989).

Some popular enthusiasm was often the consequence of loyalty to a local saint. They were a familiar part of everyone's world, since their feast days punctuated the year. In the early fourteenth century this was formalised in the synodal statutes of the diocese of Cambrai, under which priests were ordered not to give permission 'for the use of the plough, of horses, [or] of animals' on thirty-five days throughout the year, as well as on all Sundays. There were another thirteen minor feasts on which it was licit to plough and cart (Avril 1995:175). More dramatically, on occasions, the relics and shrines of the saints could draw great crowds, for the saints were seen as powerful intercessors for the sinful in the heavenly court and as workers of miraculous cures in the terrestrial world. Occasionally instant sanctity brought forth an instant cure as, according to Galbert of Bruges, one man found after the murder of Charles the Good in 1127.

> For while the sick and crippled were lying under the bier in the midst of the tumult, a lame man, who was born with his foot attached to his buttocks, began to cry out and bless God who, through the merits of the pious count, had restored his natural capacity to move, in the sight of all the bystanders. And so the news of the miracle quieted everyone.
>
> (Ross 1982:139–40)

With the spread of popular preaching in the thirteenth century such miracle stories became standard material. According to James of Vitry, successively Bishop of Acre and then cardinal, writing in the 1220s and 1230s, so great was the healing power of St Martin that men were restored even when they did not want to be. Playing on the popular prejudice that lazy men exploited infirmities to avoid work, he gives the following tale in his *exempla*.

> Although, indeed, poverty and other tribulations are good, nevertheless certain men misuse them. Thus we read that when the body of St Martin was carried in procession it healed all the sick who met it. However, near the church there were two vagabond beggars, one of whom was blind, the other crippled. They spoke together and said, 'Look the body of St Martin is now being brought in procession and if it catches up with us we shall be healed at once and from then on no one will give us alms, but we will be obliged to work and labour with our own hands.' The blind one, however, said to the cripple: 'Climb up on my shoulders, since I am strong and you who can see well can lead me.' When they had done this they intended to take flight, but the procession overtook them and because of the crowds they could not run away and were healed against their will.
>
> (Crane 1890:52)

The most powerful and merciful intercessor of all was the Virgin Mary; around her grew an immensely popular cult that reached its height in the thirteenth century. An index of its growth was the use of the apocryphal stories of her death, assumption and coronation on church portals, where they begin to appear instead of the traditional depiction of the Last Judgement. The first complete porch to be devoted to the Coronation of the Virgin was probably that at Senlis, north of Paris, dating from the early 1170s, although this same theme incorporated into capitals at Reading Abbey about forty years earlier suggests that the cult was beginning to take hold well before this. The Cistercians and the Franciscans made her the special object of their devotion, but in the popular mind she was the universal mother whose charity could be sought by all. A graphic illustration of this can be seen in the set of popular poems or songs known as the *Cántigas de Santa María*, written in Galician-Portuguese, and dating from the reign of Alfonso X of Castile in the third quarter of the thirteenth century. These consist of over 400 poems, most of which are illustrated by six miniatures each with an explanatory caption. These poems and their illustrations help to compensate for the lack of direct evidence of popular ideas. The stories are told in terms of a battle between the forces of good and evil for individual souls, often shown in very literal form with devils and angels struggling and arguing. Since it was generally accepted that an unconfessed person could not reach Heaven, many of the stories concentrate upon death and the period immediately preceding it. Here the Virgin is able to circumvent the problem of death before confession for her devotees, in one case even reconstituting a decapitated man so that he might confess. These stories are remote indeed from the formal rules laid down by, for example, the episcopacy at the Fourth Lateran Council of 1215, where the sacramental nature of penance was emphasised by the requirement of universal annual confession and absolution by a priest (MacKay and McKendrick 1979). One hundred and fifty years after Orderic Vitalis believed that the priest Walchelin had been saved from a similar unconfessed end by invoking the Virgin, the *Cántigas* demonstrate the enduring popularity of that belief.

While the Virgin and the saints became the focus of popular devotion and adoration, one group – the Jews – was forced to perform the opposite function, that of popular scapegoats, to such an extent that one historian has suggested that Christians were actually projecting upon them their own doubts and guilt (Little 1978:54). It has already been shown how ecclesiastical legislation and princely exploitation created a context for these attitudes. Within this context depictions of the Jews in both visual and written form served to build up a popular image. Guibert of Nogent, for instance, was one of the first to show the Jews as in league with devilish forces. Guibert tells the type of story that easily caught popular imagination. A monk had fallen ill.

> Because of this, to his sorrow, he had occasion for talking with a Jew skilled in medicine. Gathering boldness from their intimacy, they began to reveal their secrets to one another. Being curious about the black arts and aware that the Jew understood magic, the monk pressed him hard. The Jew consented and promised to be his mediator with the Devil. They agreed upon the time and place for a meeting. At last he was brought by his intermediary into the presence of the Devil, and through the other he asked to have a share in the teaching. That abominable ruler said that it could by no means be done unless he denied his Christianity and offered sacrifice to him.
>
> (Benton 1970:115)

Crusading did more than anything else to turn prejudice into violence. Crusading preparation incited high religious excitement and, since it usually took place in the spring, at or near Easter, the possibility of violence against the Jews, who were presented as a deicide people, was even greater. When such excitement combined with economic resentments, perhaps exacerbated by the financial stresses which crusading placed on participants, then it comes as no surprise to learn that Christians were easily convinced that the non-believers in their midst were as much enemies of God as the Turks in Syria and Palestine. Terrible massacres of the Jews in the Rhineland and in some parts of France took place in the First and Second Crusades, in England during the Third Crusade, and during the crusade of Theobald of Champagne in 1239. The popular religious movements known as Pastoureaux of 1251 and 1320 were similarly accompanied by attacks on the Jews. Indeed, in 1320, the widespread slaughter of the Jews in Aquitaine and Languedoc became the chief feature of the movement.

The Jews themselves came to see these persecutions within their own historical context; their suffering and martyrdom would precede the Messianic Age. Some chose to kill themselves and their families rather than suffer forcible conversion, while others believed that the coming of the Messiah would be brought forward by these events (Goldin 1997). Albert of Aachen, describes how, during the First Crusade, seeing the destruction wrought by the Christians, the Jews

> turned upon themselves and their companions, on children, women, mothers and sisters, and they all killed each other. Mothers with children at the breast – how horrible to relate – would cut their throats with knives, would stab others, preferring that they should die thus at their hands, rather than be killed by the weapons of the uncircumcised.
>
> (Edgington 2004)

There are equally graphic accounts of these crusades by Jewish chroniclers. Particularly important is Solomon bar Simson, who had close knowledge of events in Mainz up to 1140. The following passage, again referring to the First Crusade, conveys some sense of the Jewish outlook in these circumstances.

> However, God, the maker of peace, turned aside and averted His eyes from His people, and consigned them to the sword. No prophet, seer, or man of wise heart was able to comprehend how the sin of the people infinite in number was deemed so great as to cause the destruction of so many lives in the various Jewish communities. The martyrs endured the extreme penalty normally inflicted only upon one guilty of murder. Yet, it must be stated with certainty that God is a righteous judge, and we are to blame.
>
> (Eidelberg 1977:25)

The fundamental reason for this Christian hostility was religious prejudice, which was to be found at all levels of society. Judaism was an ancient religion and civilisation which most Christians made little effort to comprehend; the determined efforts of the Jewish communities to maintain their own identities, centring their life upon the synagogue, served to sharpen this prejudice. Sculptural representations of the synagogue in its blindness reinforced this attitude and the debates between priests and rabbis did nothing more than consolidate entrenched positions. When King Louis IX of France had set up such a confrontation at the University of Paris in 1240, he was predictably not convinced by the Jewish arguments and established a commission to examine the matter. On the basis of its report he decided, in June 1241, to burn all Talmudic writings, which were seized from synagogues throughout France. On the other hand, Louis was eager to see Jews or Muslims converted and in October 1269 gathered a great assembly of his vassals at the monastery of St Denis to witness the baptism of a Jew who wished to become a Christian (Riquet 1976:345–50). Louis, moreover, despite the book burnings, ensured that direct attacks on the Jews were rare during his reign, for he kept a tight grip on the realm. Church leaders were equally opposed to violence, as St Bernard's condemnation of the massacres of 1147 during the Second Crusade demonstrates. Zeal for God's glory was praiseworthy, he agreed, but cautioned that it needed 'the timely restraint of knowledge'. By this he meant that the Jews should not be persecuted because they existed for a purpose important to Christians.

> The Jews are for us the living words of Scripture, for they remind us always of what our Lord suffered. They are dispersed all over the world so that by expiating their crime they may be everywhere the living witnesses of our redemption.

Moreover, the Apostle said that at the appropriate time, the Jews shall be saved. 'If the Jews are utterly wiped out, what will become of our hope for their promised salvation, their eventual conversion?' (B.S. James 1998:462–3).

Nevertheless, whatever may have been their intentions, kings who burnt books and abbots who emphasised the Jewish 'crime' could serve only to strengthen popular religious prejudice and, at this level, it is evident that contemporary Jews were identified with the events of the Passion in the most direct way. Solomon bar Simson expressed the essence of this attitude.

> The enemy unjustly accused them of evil acts they did not do, declaring: 'You are the children of those who killed our object of veneration, hanging him on a tree; and he himself had said: "There will yet come a day when my children will come and avenge my blood." We are his children and it is therefore obligatory for us to avenge him since you are the ones who rebel and disbelieve in him. Your God has never been at peace with you. Although He intended to deal kindly with you, you have conducted yourselves improperly before him. God has forgotten you and is no longer desirous of you since you are a stubborn nation. Instead, He has departed from you and has taken us for His portion, casting His radiance upon us.'
>
> (Eidelberg 1977:25)

During the twelfth century the belief in 'evil acts' referred to by Solomon bar Simson came to centre upon two specific issues: the accusations of ritual murder and desecration of the host. The first alleged incident of ritual murder seems to have occurred at Norwich in 1144 when the body of a 12-year-old apprentice called William was found in Thorpe Wood. Popular belief, led by his hysterical mother, ascribed his death to the Jews, although it did not develop into a cult until the story was written up by a monk at Norwich called Thomas of Monmouth, who purported to present 'proofs' of Jewish guilt. Thomas of Monmouth explained the murder in terms of a widespread Jewish conspiracy, claiming that a converted Jew, who had become a monk, had told him that every year at an assembly held at Narbonne, the Jews selected a particular area where their co-religionists would be required to find a suitable victim, since the blood of a Christian was needed for the Passover service. In 1144 the choice had fallen on Norwich (Jessopp and James 1896). Thereafter the ritual murder accusation appears in a number of different locations across Europe, although it apparently remained a fixed idea in Norwich for, according to Matthew Paris, in 1240 it nearly happened again. At this time the father of a young boy who had been seized and circumcised preparatory to crucifixion, found the boy imprisoned in a Jewish house. All the Jews of Norwich were arrested and four of them executed for this crime (Luard 1880:4:30–1).

The accusation of sacrilege seems to have arisen partly from the circumstances created by the Jews' economic role for, among the items pledged as security for loans, were various ecclesiastical vessels of high intrinsic value. According to Rigord of St Denis, among the reasons for Philip II's expulsion of the Jews was their pollution of such objects. Their children ate and drank from chalices, while a gold cross studded with gems, a Gospel decorated with gold and precious stones, and some silver cups and vases, were found in a bag which the Jews had placed in a ditch used as a latrine (Delaborde 1882:1:25, 27). The idea that the Jews desecrated the host was an evident manifestation of this attitude, gaining particular strength during the thirteenth century after the decree of the Fourth Lateran Council of 1215 had laid down that the consecrated host should be publicly worshipped. The depiction of a figure digging his knife into what appears to be a large host on the lintel of the tympanum at the cathedral of Autun, dating from the 1120s, suggests, however, that the belief was entrenched well before 1215.

By the early fourteenth century popular anti-Semitism was deeply ingrained in western Christendom. Preaching, together with widespread participation in popular religious movements like crusading, had accustomed Christians to the idea of Jewish responsibility for crimes against the faith. Outbursts of violence, varying in scale and ferocity, had become commonplace. The protection of the secular authorities, never greatly effective, also began to diminish at this time, as the economic role of the Jews began to decline. By the late thirteenth century most Jews involved in money-lending were concerned largely with small-scale loans to the lower classes and with pawnbroking, a situation which had the disadvantage of creating even more hostility among the elements in the population most likely to turn to violence, while at the same time removing any interest the secular authorities might have had in protecting them. During the fourteenth century, therefore, Jewish evil was held to be responsible for many of the disasters that struck that society, most notably for the spreading of the Black Death. This, however, had been preceded by an outburst in France in 1321 in which the Jews were accused of masterminding a plot to overthrow all Christian authority by killing off the population by poisoning the wells. Their agents were alleged to have been the lepers, since suspicion would have fallen too easily upon them if they had been seen near wells or public fountains. Their backers were supposed to have been the Muslim rulers of Spain and north Africa, a coalition that brought together in one great conspiracy all the main elements of a popular nightmare (Barber 1981).

Widespread involvement in the Marian cult and the attacks upon the Jews were in fact two sides of the same coin for, since the launch of the clerical reform programme in the 1050s, some popes and Church leaders had played upon popular sensibilities in an effort to encourage wider involvement in a campaign to boycott priests guilty of simony and incontinence. Indeed, there was some justification for Henry IV's jibe that Gregory VII had gained for himself 'acclaim from the mouth of the rabble' (Mommsen and Morrison 1962:150). By the late eleventh century the Christian populace had become accustomed to participation in mass religious activity which encompassed not only the negative act of ignoring sinful priests, but also the more positive steps of participating in peace councils, pilgrimages and, eventually, crusades. The potential for social upheaval that this issue contained can be seen in the spread of the movement of the Patarenes from Milan to the other north Italian cities of Brescia, Piacenza and Cremona during the 1050s and 1060s, where they condemned what they saw as 'tainted' priests, while the incident at Cambrai in 1076 when the servants of the bishop burned to death a priest called Ramihrdus, who had refused to take communion at the hands of clerics 'up to the neck in simony and other avarice', indicates the degree of risk involved in Gregory's aim to achieve a 'pure' Church. The fact was that the reformers had unleashed a power that they could not easily control for, although neither the Patarenes nor Ramihrdus were unorthodox, the drive for clerical reform inevitably stimulated criticism and debate about the Church and, consequently, provided a means through which social discontents could surface, often in the form of anti-clericalism or even heresy.

The Church first became seriously troubled by dissent in the early decades of the twelfth century when a series of self-appointed leaders succeeded in arousing enthusiasm and support on a scale sufficient to sustain itself for several years. The hostility of the clerical writers testifies to the unease or even fear which these movements aroused. The first to attract widespread attention was a man who may have once been a priest himself, Tanchelm of Antwerp, who preached extensively in the Netherlands between *c.*1110 and 1115, when he was killed by a priest with whom he had been arguing. Although imprisoned for a short time during this period, he had not been deterred from a series of violently anti-clerical campaigns. According to a letter from the canons of Utrecht, he was supposed to have described the churches as brothels and the sacraments as pollutions, from which it followed that no tithes should be paid. He seems to have had a large and mixed following, for he was popular both in Zeeland, which was primarily rural, and in cities like Antwerp. The canons believed that he had a band of 'disciples', apparently as a kind of bodyguard, and that he had 'married' an image of the Virgin Mary, a device used to encourage the credulous to provide offerings. The full horror of this man's behaviour, as far as the canons were concerned, was the sexual excess which he encouraged. A follower of his, a blacksmith called Manasses, had formed a fraternity

> composed of twelve men, representing the twelve apostles, and a woman as St Mary. They say that she used to be led round the twelve men one by one and joined with them in foul sin, a gross insult to the Holy Virgin, as a sort of confirmation of their fraternity.
>
> (Moore 1975:30)

Here the canons were building on a well-established tradition, for accusations of immorality, often in the form of sexual perversions, had customarily been thrown at critics of the established order and were not specific to the Christian era.

Tanchelm's activities were relatively short-lived, but they were not unique, as can be seen by the movements begun by Henry the Monk, from Lausanne, and Peter of Bruys (in the French Alps), who both led his own movement and had some influence on Henry. Henry is first known from some disturbances at Le Mans in 1116 and lasted until 1145, when St Bernard came to Toulouse to confront him, after which nothing further was heard of him. Peter was active from *c.*1119 until he was burnt to death by a mob in front of the church of St Gilles in *c.*1136. Once again the theme of a corrupt Church and clergy is central. Henry put on a hair shirt and inveighed against a venal hierarchy, whose sinfulness invalidated the sacraments. Indeed, he taught that there was no use for an institutionalised Church at all, and he rejected the fundamental concepts of original sin and infant baptism. The true Church was not dependent upon such things, but consisted only of the faithful who obeyed Scripture. Peter of Bruys was even more radical; all the externals of worship were condemned, including crosses, church buildings and religious music, the Old Testament was not acceptable, and the Eucharist was a fraud, for the transformation of the Body and Blood took place once only, at the Last Supper. Both men found a ready response and, even more worrying for the ecclesiastical and secular authorities, the presence of both seemed to incite violence. At Le Mans, for instance, the Henricians began a series of physical attacks upon the clergy, while Peter of Bruys died when he was pushed into his own fire, where he had been burning crosses.

The most famous of the anti-clerical agitators of the first half of the twelfth century was Arnold of Brescia who, unlike the others, came from an educated and noble background. Moreover, also unlike the others, although his verbal assaults upon the Church were uncompromising, it is difficult to find the directly heretical statements attributed to men like Tanchelm, Henry and Peter. He began preaching on the need for a return to the poverty of the Apostles in *c.*1119, was condemned by Pope Innocent II in 1139, and expelled from France by Louis VII in 1140. In *c.*1146 he submitted to Pope Eugenius III, who sent him to Rome, apparently as a means of keeping a watch on him. Here, however, between 1146 and 1155 he gained great popularity on the basis of his view that the power and property of the Church should be abolished and, possibly, for questioning the validity of the sacraments, although this may have been an extrapolation of his abolitionist views. However, Arnold was different from the other popular preachers of the time in one further way, for his preaching carried a political dimension. He believed the emperor to be superior to the pope in temporal matters and urged Frederick Barbarossa to come to Rome to claim his position. In Rome itself a commune was declared and the pope twice driven out (in 1146 and 1150). The threats to established authority were obvious. Otto of Freising says that Frederick refused to take notice of 'fables of this sort', and in 1155 Arnold was taken and executed, having been handed over by the emperor to the Prefect of the City of Rome (Mierow 1955:63).

By the 1140s and 1150s, therefore, heresy had, in the eyes of the clerical authorities, reappeared as a major problem on a scale not experienced since Arian beliefs had captured the allegiance of the Goths and Vandals in the fourth and fifth centuries. There had been, it is true, manifestations of dissent in the early middle ages, particularly in the first half of the eleventh century, when some chroniclers thought that they discerned heretical movements, but in practice these could hardly be called popular heresies, for in some cases the 'heretics' were so self-effacing as to be almost invisible. Among the more identifiable were heretics at Châlons-sur-Marne (in *c.*1000 and *c.*1048, but with no apparent connection between them), Orléans (1022), Arras (1025) and Monteforte, near Turin (*c.*1028). Neither geographically nor socially is it possible to determine a pattern, while the sources upon which most of our information is based need careful analysis if they are not to mislead the modern reader.

There is here then little to contradict the view that the real stimulation to dissent appears to have come from within the Church itself, which provoked the debate about materialism and spirituality as well as defining the boundaries of that debate. However, the reasons for the scale of popular response are not exclusively and unambiguously religious. The preachers spoke to a society in which a developing economy was undermining the old order and stimulating both social and physical mobility. It is likely that those most affected by these forces were also most susceptible to what Janet Nelson calls 'a crisis of theodicy', that is a sense of dissonance between experience and received knowledge or belief (Nelson 1972). This does not mean that heresy was a form of social protest by the underprivileged, for this sense of displacement could be felt at all levels of society, particularly in the towns where the manifestations of change were most evident. Heresy was not of course exclusively urban, for men like Tanchelm could draw an audience in town or country alike, while, as will be seen, the adherents of the dualist heresy of Catharism could be found among all classes and environments. Nevertheless, it was in the towns that the turnover of population was most rapid, for the towns were largely dependent upon immigration to maintain and increase their populations and, in the twelfth century, contained a populace of which perhaps a third or even a half were first generation immigrants facing such problems of dislocation.

Movements like those of the Henricians and the Petrobrusians had seemed dangerous while they had lasted, but within a relatively short time they had burnt themselves out. Nevertheless, from the mid-twelfth century the Church had to face the fact that heresy was becoming not only increasingly common, but also more durable. There was considerable diversity, but two central themes can be discerned: first, movements which were founded upon the idea of a return to a life of apostolic poverty which, when they became heretical, were often marked by anti-clericalism and anti-sacerdotalism, occasionally becoming millennial in their aspirations; and second, Catharism which, in its most developed state, offered a form of absolute dualism which amounted to more than doctrinal deviation or resentment of the clergy, but to a coherent set of alternative Christian beliefs founded upon a solid and far-reaching organisation. Like earlier movements, both strands of dissent shared an abhorrence of materialism, especially when ostentatiously embraced by churchmen, but they sought solutions to the problems by very different paths.

The hunger for a return to an age of simplicity manifested itself in myriad forms, especially in regions like Tuscany and Lombardy, where the stark contrasts of urban wealth and poverty provided an appropriate stimulus. Four examples can serve to illustrate these varied approaches, which involved both men and women: the Waldensians, the Humiliati, the Beguines and other pious lay women, and the Spiritual Franciscans. The Waldensians had the widest appeal, for the movement spread from its origins in Provence to most regions and ultimately was the only one of the heresies of the high middle ages to survive into the period of the Reformation. In about 1173 a merchant and money-lender from Lyon called Valdès decided that his way of life was wrong and that he should follow the scriptural injunction in Matthew, Chapter 19: 'If thou wilt be perfect go sell what thou hast and give to the poor and thou shalt have treasure in heaven. And come follow me.' He made provision for his family and then gave away all he had, in order to begin a life of poverty and preaching, preaching based on Scripture which he had translated into the vernacular. These actions were not in themselves heresy, but they did create an unstable situation, for Valdès was a layman, taking upon himself the clerical task of preaching and interpreting Scripture, which at the very least could be seen as an implicit criticism of the clergy. Moreover, from the mid-1170s there is evidence of female Waldensians actively preaching, although they played no part in the leadership of the movement (Biller 1996). Not surprisingly, many clerics were hostile.

In 1179 Valdès therefore appealed to Pope Alexander III at the Third Lateran Council. The pope was cautiously welcoming, appreciating the devotion to voluntary poverty, but at the same time he insisted that Valdès and his followers be examined by a commission of theologians. They found the religious knowledge of the Waldensians defective, striking a direct blow at Valdès's chief *raison d'être* which was preaching. The pope therefore gave permission for the Waldensians to preach only if licensed to do so by the local clergy which, in the context of clerical hostility, amounted to a virtual ban. Although for at least a generation the Waldensians occupied an ambiguous position on the fringes of the Church, these were the first steps which were to drive a wedge between Valdès's followers and the orthodox. The possibility that the movement could be kept within the Church is shown by Valdès's willingness to make a profession of faith at the Council of Lyon in 1180 and, indeed, over a quarter of a century later, in 1208, when the split with the Church had become more evident, by the reconciliation of a group of Waldensians under Durand of Huesca, taking the name of the Poor Catholics.

By 1208, however, a fragmentation had developed which reflected varying shades of opinion about the relationship with the Church. In 1184 Valdès had been placed under anathema by Lucius III, while the spread of his followers into Lombardy, the Rhineland and Austria left the Church with less and less control over their activities. The Lombard Waldensians rejected both the clerical organisation and the sacraments administered by unworthy priests, actually creating their own ministers instead. Not all the Waldensians were prepared to accept this, but a conference held at Bergamo in 1218 failed to reconcile the different groups, and by the mid-thirteenth century they contained variations ranging from the idea of a priesthood of all believers to those who organised themselves into a type of 'Church', with two classes, brethren and associated lay communities. In the twelfth and thirteenth centuries the Waldensians, although not strictly a movement of doctrinal opposition, presented a real challenge to the Church, a challenge not met from within but by another and in many ways similar impulse, that of the Franciscans.

While the Waldensians developed into a movement with a very broad appeal, the Humiliati and the Beguines catered for more specific needs, those of the family and those of lay women. Neither set out to be unorthodox but both adopted patterns of life which were sufficiently radical to provoke criticism and hostility from some elements within the Church. The Humiliati were largely confined to the towns of northern Italy, where they lived simple lives in family groups, supporting themselves from their own manual labour and withdrawing from the normal social bonds by refusing to take oaths. Their attempts to gain papal recognition failed when they could not be persuaded to stop preaching, during which, according to some indignant clerics, they disparaged the clergy. Eventually, the majority were reconciled by Pope Innocent III, who allowed them to preach on condition that they avoided doctrinal issues. In 1199 he organised them into three orders, consisting of laymen living with their families, laymen and women living in communities of a quasi-monastic kind, and a clerical order, including monks and priests (Bolton 1972).

The spread of beguinages – houses of religious women living continent lives and, like the Humiliati, supporting themselves by their own labour – was almost contemporary, for they first appear in the second and third decades of the thirteenth century. They were particularly attractive to women of urban, non-noble background, since nunneries remained primarily aristocratic in composition, despite the acceptance of some women from the burgher class in the twelfth and thirteenth centuries. This partly explains why beguinages were most commonly found in northern Europe, especially in the towns of the Low Countries and the Rhineland. It has been suggested that a possible reason for their appearance may be found in the greater average life expectancy of females in this period in comparison with the early middle ages, which may have left a surplus of women without husbands (Herlihy 1975:12), but it is equally likely that others joined these communities for precisely the opposite reason, that is to escape marriage to a partner chosen for them by the family. However, many had far more positive motives than this, for there is much evidence to suggest that, in the changing environment of the thirteenth century, women were seeking a means of expressing their deeply held beliefs in forms that differed markedly from the limited opportunities provided by the traditional female monastic houses. The strength of these feelings is reflected in the numbers involved: in Cologne in 1320, for example, despite their attempted suppression at the Council of Vienne in 1312, it is estimated that about 15 per cent of the adult female population lived in these communities (Bynum 1987:13–30). Their existence created similar problems for the Church to those presented by the Waldensians and the Humiliati. On the one hand they attracted praise for their devotion. Fiery moralisers like Fulk, Bishop of Toulouse, and James of Vitry, were highly enthusiastic. On the other hand, many were doubtful that they were or could remain orthodox, seeing them as open to heretical influences such as Waldensianism, or even Catharism. This reaction was perhaps not unconnected with their attempt to find their own answer to the religious needs of women, independent of the male hierarchy and without a set and written rule, and it is not surprising to find that those houses which became most acceptable to the Church were those on which clerical supervision was imposed. This trend became more and more common in the late thirteenth century, often accompanied by an almost routine reference to the canon of 1215 which had placed a ban on the foundation of new religious orders.

However, not all pious women lived in groups. Some exceptional individuals attracted widespread attention through ascetic feats and visionary experiences which went far beyond the cognisance of the average beguine community. It has been shown by Caroline Walker Bynum (1987) that a significant proportion of these women used food practices, most importantly extreme forms of fasting and food adulteration, as means of achieving control of their own lives and of manipulating the lives of others, thus giving them power and opportunities that would not otherwise have been available to them. Some claimed to live on the eucharist alone by which they could achieve what they believed was a fusion with Christ. More mundanely, on occasion, they were able to expose the deficiencies of the institutionalised Church by their physical inability to receive the host administered by a corrupt or immoral priest, a circumstance which has distinct donatist overtones reminiscent of the conflicts of Gregory VII's pontificate. The reaction of the orthodox ecclesiastical establishment to them was as ambivalent as it was to the beguinages, but there is no doubt that, whatever the misgivings of the authorities, together they formed a significant element in the spiritual attitudes of the high and late middle ages, quite distinct from earlier centuries.

The Spiritual Franciscans represent the most extreme manifestation of the poverty movement for, as the conflict within the Franciscan Order became more sharply defined in the later years of the thirteenth century, their views became entwined with distortions of Joachimite prophecy in such a manner as to make potential reconciliations such as those engineered by Innocent III quite impossible. Joachim of Fiore was a Cistercian abbot in Calabria who had died in 1202. His prophetic ideas, however, outlived him, for he had believed that there were three epochs of history corresponding to the three Persons of the Trinity: the Age of the Father, or the Old Testament, the Age of the Son, corresponding to the New Testament and still in being in Joachim's own time, and the Age of the Spirit, still to come. The Age of the Spirit would be heralded by a new order of monks, there would be an increase in persecutions and two Antichrists would appear. The extremists within the Franciscan ranks who saw themselves as the faithful keepers of the doctrine of poverty in the face of persecution, were very attracted by this structure, adapting it to fit their view of the world in which they were the new order presaging the new age. In particular they interpreted opposition to Peter John Olivi, a Franciscan from Narbonne, in this light. Olivi was much admired by the Spirituals for he had worked out a strict doctrine of poverty, the *usus pauper*, which centred on the repeated use of goods by the friars, which he interpreted as a mortal sin. While Olivi himself could not be classed with this group, it is clear that many of his supporters were. The Spiritual Franciscans therefore foresaw the imminent destruction of existing institutions, including, above all, the corrupt Church of the Second Age, thus turning a disciplinary dispute within the Franciscan order into radical doctrinal deviation (Lambert 1998:157–95).

As in the early twelfth century, these poverty movements had an obvious and direct religious impulse, provided by Scripture such as that in Luke, 'For it is easier for a camel to go through a needle's eye, than for a rich man to enter the Kingdom of God.' In the thirteenth century the preaching of the friars added fuel to the fire, as they expostulated upon the sins of lust and pride, but most of all on avarice, a sin to which there was no limit, expressed most graphically in the image of the usurer (A. Murray 1972) (see Plate 2). Men and women who were concerned about their salvation in such a society turned to an imitation of the apostolic life, but they did not necessarily become heretics. Some occupied a shadowy area between orthodoxy and heterodoxy, a fact recognised by contemporaries other than Innocent III. Even Peter of Les Vaux-de-Cernay, the highly orthodox chronicler of the Albigensian Crusade, said that the Waldensians 'were evil men, but much less perverted than other heretics [i.e. Cathars]; they agreed with us in many matters, and differed in some' (Sibly and Sibly 1998:14).

To the Church, however, there was no such ambiguity about Catharism which, in the first half of the thirteenth century, seemed to present a terrible challenge. Most information on Cathar belief comes either from Catholic polemicists or from inquisitorial depositions, and inevitably any modern description suffers from this bias in the sources. Nevertheless, it is important to attempt to reconstruct it in order to see why the Church regarded it as such a serious threat. Catharism aimed to offer a solution to the fundamental religious and philosophical problem of the existence of evil. How could a God, omnipotent and timeless, have created a world in which evil so manifestly stalked? The answer was to be found in the existence of two principles, that of Light or the good God of the Spirit and that of Darkness or the evil God of material things. The good God was the creator of everlasting and eternal things, the evil God creator of the material world, of visible and transitory things. Initially, Cathars in western

Christendom believed in mitigated dualism. Many myths and stories were woven around this, but the essence was that Satan, or the evil principle, was originally either a son of God or a fallen angel, who had conspired against God and had been expelled from Heaven as a consequence. He had taken with him the angelic souls which he had involved in the conspiracy, so that the souls had become separated from their guardian spirits. They had since been prevented from returning because they were entrapped in the world of matter which Satan had created after his fall. The similarities to the Catholic version of the Fall are evident, but in the late 1160s absolute dualism had penetrated the west, probably spread by missionaries from the Bogomil Church, which had entrenched itself in the Balkan provinces of the Byzantine Empire. Absolute dualism postulated the existence of two quite separate and co-eternal deities, rather than the derivative idea of the mitigated school.

The implications, if not always the practice, of these beliefs were far reaching. Since the material world was evil, then Jesus Christ could not have taken human form, could not have died on the cross nor have been resurrected. Some absolute dualists thought that these events did occur in what they called the 'Land of the Living', which was the 'new earth' created by the Good God, an idea which arose from their belief in the existence of two quite separate creations (Hamilton 1999:8–11). Nevertheless, their view of the appearance of Christ in the world meant that, as far as the Catholic Church was concerned, they denied the fundamental doctrines of the Catholic Church of the Incarnation, Redemption and Resurrection. Christ had come to earth to re-establish contact between the guardian spirits and the lost souls entrapped in matter, a mission which he had accomplished by establishing the True Church, that of the Cathars, by which the imprisoned souls could be consoled and salvation gained. Satan, wrongly believing that Christ had a material body which could be crucified, had established a false Church, pretending that it was the work of Christ. This was the Catholic Church with its fraudulent sacraments. The Cathars could not accept the continuity and consonances of the Old and the New Testaments therefore. The Jehovah of the Old Testament was the evil creator who dealt in disaster and revenge, and the prophets were the agents of Satan, but the New Testament represented the world of the spirit. In the Cathar Church the souls achieved their return to their guiding spirit by means of a ceremony known as the *consolamentum*, a baptism of the spirit, conducted by the laying on of hands by one of Christ's ministers, called *bonhommes* or *perfecti*, who formed the Cathar spiritual elite. The *consolamentum* could be received only by those who had faith and was therefore denied to children. It contrasted with baptism by water, which was material and corruptible, and which was given to the unknowing infant, as well as to the converted adult. The *bonhommes* lived rigorously ascetic lives in an attempt to make a progressive renunciation of the material prison of the body. Chastity was essential, for each birth represented another victory for Satan, entrapping another soul in its vile prison, and diet was strictly controlled so that, when they were not fasting, they ate foods considered to be less material, such as fruit, fish and vegetables, rather than the products of warm-blooded animals like meat, eggs and cheese. They did not believe in killing or carrying arms and they renounced all lies and oaths, as manifestations of the materialistic lifestyle. The renunciation of oaths was considered to be particularly significant by their Catholic opponents, who often used this as a means of testing the faith among suspects. Since Carolingian times the oath of fidelity was interpreted not only as a specific allegiance to a monarch, but also as a promise to support Christian society as a whole and any man who betrayed these interests would be considered *infidelis*. The *bonhommes* had no property of their own, but lived a wandering life of poverty and preaching or, in some cases, especially among female ministers, followed a more settled life of contemplation and manual labour in one of the houses kept for them by their supporters.

The *bonhommes*, however, formed only a small minority of those who adhered to Catharism. Between *c.*1200 and *c.*1250 when the heresy was at its strongest in southern France, there are unlikely to have been more than 3,000 in total, for most followers could not hope to aspire to the full rigour of the life. These followers were known as *credentes* or Believers, who lived in ordinary society and were not required to undertake the abstinences of the *bonhommes*. When they met a *perfectus* or *perfecta* they performed a ritual greeting known as the *melioramentum*, bowing three times and asking for a blessing and a prayer that they might end their life having been consoled, a ceremony which, indeed, was often performed when a believer knew that death was near. Some absolute dualists believed in transmigration or metempsychosis. For the unconsoled salvation would be delayed, but if they sympathised with the Cathars their next incarnation would be in a being of less material content, whereas if they were evil persons they would reappear as a lower creature.

It is clear that this heresy was well established in western Christendom by the 1160s, but its origins have long been a matter of dispute, for the passage of ideas, especially those concerned with such inherent problems as that of the existence of evil, is very difficult to trace. Until recently the view most widely held was that Cathar doctrines are likely to have become established in the west between 1140 and 1160. However, the subject remains controversial, as some historians would argue for an earlier date, perhaps around 1100, or even during the first decades of the eleventh century (Hamilton 1994; C. Taylor 2000). External influences seem to have been important, for the Bogomils, believers in mitigated dualism, had been established in Bulgaria and Macedonia since at least the 940s, and in Thrace and Constantinople from the last decades of the eleventh century. There are reports of Cathars in Flanders and northern France, as well as in the Rhineland between the 1140s and the 1160s, while in 1166 German Cathars, apparently from Cologne, were discovered at Oxford (Biller 1999b). In 1145 there appear to have been dualists in Toulouse and by 1165 it was possible to hold a debate between Cathar *perfecti* and orthodox clergy at the castle of Lombers, near Albi. About ten years later, between 1174 and 1177, the Cathars held a council at the village of Saint-Félix-de-Caraman, to the south-east of Toulouse, at which Nicetas, Bogomil Bishop of Constantinople, divided the Mediterranean territories into bishoprics. It was probably at this time, too, that the westerners became convinced of the truth of absolute dualism (Hamilton 1978). Under this new organisation each bishop had an 'elder son' and a 'younger son' who represented an order of succession, while beneath them were deacons. Even so, such apparently solid organisation did not prevent splits, for doctrinal divisions were frequent, especially in Italy where, by 1190, there were six separate churches, five of which adhered to mitigated dualism and one of which retained the absolute dualism brought from Constantinople twenty years before (Wakefield and Evans 1969:162–3). The appearance of dualism in so many different places suggests that there were several different points of entry, although Peter Biller argues strongly for the chronological primacy of Francia or northern France from which he believes the heresy spread to Languedoc (Biller 1999a).

It seems unlikely, nevertheless, that Catharism was entirely the result of transmission from outside, despite the fact that mutations of Persian Manichaeism can be seen to have spread from the east to Asia Minor in the form of the Paulician heretics and thence to the Balkans. The fact is that the problems with which dualist belief is concerned are so fundamental that latent dualism almost certainly existed before the 1140s. It is not difficult to imagine that dualism could arise from the belief of the existence of an evil force, led by the Devil and his minions. Moreover, the elite members of the Christian Church itself, the monks, shunned material things, mortified the flesh and abstained from procreation. The description of the death of St Evroult, the founder of his community, given by Orderic Vitalis, suggests an attitude of mind not dissimilar to that of the *bonhommes*, who refused to take steps to prevent their deaths. 'Falling sick with fever,' says Orderic,

> he was not seen to take any food for forty-seven days, except sometimes the sacrament of the body of Christ.... And when men of religion from near by came to visit him, and begged him with tears to agree to take something from the alms that had been offered to restore his body, he said, 'Peace, peace, my friends; do not weary me by asking what I utterly reject.' For he who was nourished by the Holy Spirit within had no need of earthly food.
>
> (Chibnall 1972:3:299)

The most likely explanation for the spread of Catharism is that Bogomil missionaries activated forces inherent in the Christian society and environment of the twelfth century and that, just as in Catholic belief, they found a response at a variety of levels ranging from a superstitious fear of the dark to a subtle appreciation of an alternative doctrinal and intellectual system.

If it is accepted that dualism was indeed latent, then it seems probable that Catharism became strongest where the crust of repression was thinnest, that is in regions where the clerical and secular authorities failed, for one reason or another, to act sufficiently in concert to prevent heresy breaking through that crust. This means that there is no set pattern or social model; heresy spread or was opposed for different reasons in different areas and communities. In northern Italy, the Rhineland and Flanders, communal upheavals had disrupted traditional structures of authority centred on the bishopric. These regions suggest a dislocation of the structures of power which might allow heresy to spread or be tolerated, while at the same time their proximity to international trade routes facilitated the spread of ideas as well as goods.

Contemporaries, however, believed that Catharism was strongest in Languedoc, especially in the County of Toulouse, for it was against this region that the Albigensian Crusade was directed from 1209, and it was in this region that the most systematic operation of the inquisitors can be seen from the 1230s. As in Italy, Catharism evidently found much support in Languedocian towns, especially Toulouse, the largest of them. Nevertheless, in this case the importance of towns can be exaggerated, for the region west of the River Orb was much more affected by Catharism than the east, yet was much less urbanised, with proportions of 3 per cent and 11.3 per cent respectively (J.C. Russell 1972:154–9, 162–3). Catharism in the south in fact had very firm roots in rural and even isolated areas. Evidence for peasant interest is inevitably hard to obtain, although it is probable that certain tithes, in particular *carnalages*, the tithes on slaughtered beasts, provoked resentment against the Church. What is clear is that the lesser nobility, which was both stable and rural, lent much support to the Cathar *bonhommes* who, in times of trouble, often found shelter in their castles and protection through the network of relatives created by noble intermarriage. While in northern France a recognisable hierarchy, based on the inheritance of the fief through male primogeniture, was emerging by *c.*1200, the south was much more diversified, for the fief had a much less precise connection with military service and obligations to one's lord, and partible inheritance rather than primogeniture was the rule. Moreover some of the more important lordships were based in very rugged country in the Black Mountains and the foothills of the Pyrenees. The lords of almost inaccessible castles like Cabaret or Termes were not easily brought under superior control. It had been difficult enough for the Capetian Louis VI to subdue his vassals in the rolling country of the Ile-de-France in the first three decades of the twelfth century; the problem was much greater in the more mountainous parts of the south, with the consequence that strong comital or monarchical authority was lacking in the late twelfth century, a time when Catharism was at its most effective as a religious force. It may even be that in certain lordships Catharism replaced Catholicism as the main element of religious cohesion in society.

Such a social structure seems to have allowed greater female influence than feudal society with its emphasis on military prowess, with the result that Catharism spread through noble family connections, especially under the influence of a dominant matriarchal figure. In many cases the first known adherent to Catharism within the family was just such a figure and the careers of several of these women, all born between 1160 and 1180, have been shown to bear remarkable similarities during the next generation. Under their influence family members were brought up in a tradition which made adherence to group attitudes almost inevitable and marriage into families of similar mind obvious. When, in 1243–4, royal forces eventually came to besiege Montségur which, under its lord, Raymond of Péreille, had been a Cathar centre since its construction at the beginning of the thirteenth century, 40 of the 415 inhabitants appertained to the Mirepoix-Péreille clan, ranging through four generations from the 70-year-old Marquésia Hunaud of Lanta down to her baby great-grandson, Esquieu of Mirepoix (Roquebert 1985:226–7).

Reactions to heresy in society at large were by no means uniform. Despite the religious context within which medieval people lived their lives, there were many who were largely indifferent to such issues. Friars inveighed against those who attended church infrequently, while the decree of 1215 laying down that all should take sacramental confession at least once a year suggests that they did not do even this (A. Murray 1972:94). In some regions, too, the populace could be quite tolerant of deviation. Several witnesses who appeared before the inquisitors in the 1230s and 1240s recalled the easy-going days before the crusaders came to Languedoc in 1209, when they grew up with Cathars and Waldensians and apparently thought nothing of it. Sometimes there was a refusal to take them seriously. Some thought that Valdès had gone out of his senses when he gave up all his property and material comforts and left his family, while in the case of the Breton, Eon de l'Etoile, who came before the Council of Reims in 1148, the ecclesiastical authorities seem to have accepted that he was not responsible for his actions or for the wild belief that he shared the government of the universe with God (Moore 1977:228–9, 69–71).

Usually, however, heresy was perceived as a serious threat, and indeed was often presented as a disease which could easily spread and destroy society. Eckbert of Schönau, a canon of Bonn, writing in 1163, said that the Cathars have multiplied in every land, so that the Church of God is suffering great danger from this most evil poison, which flows against it from all sides; for their message crawls like a cancer, and spreads far and wide like the progress of leprosy, corrupting the precious members of Christ.

(Migne 1855a:14)

During the twelfth century, therefore, the Church tried to isolate the disease by excommunication and anathema, using the church councils as its vehicle for condemnation. This was accompanied by a determined campaign of persuasion. St Bernard led a preaching mission to Languedoc in 1145 which appears successfully to have confounded Henry of Lausanne, and a successor of his, Henry of Clairvaux, led two missions to the same region in 1178 and 1181, although he was much less successful at combating the Cathars than St Bernard had been with the Henricians, despite the presence of an armed following. Innocent III sent almost annual legations to Languedoc between 1198 and 1208. But, at the same time he was heir to half a century of frustration, for there is little doubt that during this period Catharism had actually grown stronger in the region. For this reason his language grew increasingly militant. He frequently demanded that the secular powers give the Church more vigorous aid in combating heresy, especially the reigning count, Raymond VI of Toulouse, and when he could gain little concrete commitment from him he appealed to his overlord, King Philip II, but with no more success. He was equally determined to activate the local clergy, the inadequacies of some of whom had helped heresy to spread in the first place, but his attempts to remove the man whom he believed to be the keystone of the clerical edifice in the region, Berengar, Archbishop of Narbonne, were frustrated until 1212 (Emery 1941:55–60).

Then, in 1207, the pope broadened his appeal to include not only the French king but also a number of leading French lords. The heretics of Languedoc, he said, were insensible to peaceful arguments and therefore the Church was obliged to call on the secular arm. By this means 'the sectaries of perfidious heresies, ground down by the strength of your power, shall be led back to the knowledge of the truth through the afflictions of war' (Migne 1891:1247). This inaugurated an era of force in dealing with the Cathars, although the spark which actually ignited the Albigensian Crusade was the murder of the papal legate in Languedoc, Peter of Castelnau, in January 1208, by a vassal of Raymond of Toulouse. In 1209 a crusade of the north French, Flemings, Normans and Germans descended along the Rhône and cut through the south, rapidly capturing Béziers and Carcassonne but, having completed a set period of service and gained the indulgence offered by the pope, most of them then withdrew. These were the circumstances which led to the choice of an ambitious lord from the Ile-de-France, Simon of Montfort, as leader. During the next four years he proved to be tough and resourceful, as well as extremely cruel. His activities brought him into conflict with most of the leading powers in the area, culminating in his defeat and killing of Peter II of Aragon at the battle of Muret in 1213. However, Count Raymond and his son, encouraged by a papal judgement in the Lateran Council of 1215 protecting the rights of the young Raymond, returned to the offensive in 1215, and in 1218 Montfort was killed while besieging Toulouse. No effective leader was found to replace him and there followed a resurgence of southern resistance which, by 1224, had led to the retreat of the north French. After fifteen years of war, the crusade appeared to be a failure both as a conquest and as a means of eliminating heresy, but in 1226 a second invasion which this time was led by King Louis VIII proved too much for an exhausted land. In 1229 Count Raymond VII, who had succeeded his father in 1222, capitulated and signed the Treaty of Paris which effectively established the power and influence of the French crown in southern France.

The Albigensian Crusades demonstrated two fundamental points to the popes in the fight against heresy: first, that the secular power upon which they relied could and did use the weapon largely for its own ends, and second, that the crusades were too impermanent, too dependent upon the quality of individual leaders and on the limited periods of service fulfilled by the French knights. The roles of Peter II and Simon of Montfort epitomised these weaknesses. Peter II had intervened to protect his political interests north of the Pyrenees, having seen the crusaders as conquerors rather than heresy hunters. He himself was completely orthodox; he had indeed been one of the heroes of the great Christian victory over the Moors at Las Navas de Tolosa the year before his death. Similarly, while Simon of Montfort lived, the crusade was ruthlessly driven on, but with his death the conquests rapidly disintegrated. It was evident that a more systematic means was needed to fight heresy and from this period both secular and ecclesiastical authorities can be seen to be seeking just such a solution.

Not all secular rulers had been as uncooperative as the Counts of Toulouse, as can be seen by the enactments against heresy in England in 1164 and in Aragon in 1194 and 1197. Moreover, on particular occasions secular rulers had seen it as their duty to execute heretics found in their lands: Robert II of France in 1022 and Henry III of Germany in 1052 are cases in point. However, the fathers at the Fourth Lateran Council of 1215 tried to establish a more systematic approach, enacting canons which laid down that secular rulers take action against heretics identified by the Church. Acting on these principles, in 1224 the Emperor Frederick II established harsh penalties for convicted heretics, ranging from cutting out the tongue to death by burning. In the Constitutions of Melfi of 1231 he set down the thinking behind this.

> Heretics try to tear the seamless robe of our God. As slaves to the vice of a word that means division, they strive to introduce division into the unity of the indivisible faith and to separate the flock from the care of Peter, the shepherd to whom the Good Shepherd entrusted it.

The penalty should be death and confiscation of goods just as in the crime of high treason. Suspected heretics should be sought out and examined by the Church and if they were found to persist in deviating from the faith they should be condemned 'to suffer the death for which they strive' (Powell 1971:7–9). These laws reflect the prevailing climate of the thirteenth century. The Castilian *Siete Partidas* of the 1260s, although not officially accepted as law at this time, nevertheless are a measure of contemporary opinion. Here heretics are described as 'a species of insane people' and 'worse than beasts', and it is stressed that they do great injury to a country by endeavouring 'to corrupt the minds of men' The penalty for the obstinate must be death by burning (Scott 2001:5:1443). The evident perception of heresy in the laws of both Frederick II and Alfonso X is therefore of a threat not simply to the Church, but to the whole fabric of society, a perception which underlines the artificiality of seeking to explain heresy as if religious and social issues were entirely separate phenomena.

The assembly at the Fourth Lateran Council was not, however, prepared to leave the matter solely to secular rulers. Until this time the means available to hunt out heretics had largely been derived from antiquated laws of the Roman era: denunciation by a person in authority, accusation by a member of the community, or inquiry by the local bishop. While these procedures may have been viable against individual heretics, they were little use against a heresy like Catharism which had communal support. The meeting between Pope Lucius III and the Emperor Frederick I at Verona in 1184 was a consequence of this failure and resulted in the promulgation of the bull *Ad Abolendam* which set up a type of episcopal inquisition by giving the bishops the duty of an annual visitation and inquiry into parishes where they suspected heresy. Innocent III strengthened this by giving papal legates inquisitorial powers as well, but the system remained inadequate while heresy hunting was regarded as just one of a range of duties such prelates were expected to perform. Even the most conscientious could not be expected to cope with popular heresies on this basis. The deployment of specialist inquisitors by Pope Gregory IX therefore arose from these circumstances. Gregory created inquisitors whose exclusive duty was to search out heretics, attempt to reconcile them to the Church and to impose upon them penance appropriate to the offence. The inquisitors usually operated in pairs on a set circuit and when they arrived in a region preached a sermon on faith in front of the clergy and people, before issuing two decrees, the edict of faith, which made it the duty of everyone to denounce all suspected heretics under pain of excommunication, and the edict of grace, which allowed a period, which seems to have varied from a week to thirty days, for heretics themselves to come forward.

Hitherto it had not been difficult for communities which harboured Cathars to counter often half-hearted episcopal inquires and to intimidate potential informants. The inquisitors, however, were more subtle, for the names of witnesses were not revealed, thus creating a sense of unease in a community which had something to hide. The possibility that the inquisitors already held denunciations delivered in secret during the period of grace encouraged others to defend themselves in the same way. Once the façade of community solidarity could be cracked and the inquisitors had names and places to hand, then the search could begin in earnest. Individuals brought before the inquisitors were being directed in one way, that is along the path of confession, penitence and reconciliation. They had no legal defender, no knowledge of those who had denounced them, and only a précis of the evidence. Their only line of defence – admittedly used quite frequently – was that witnesses were acting from malice. From 1252 torture could be used in certain cases, although it does not seem to have been a feature of the Cathar inquiries. Once guilt had been admitted, sentence was pronounced in the form of a general sermon held in public, often presented in quite a theatrical manner. Heretics believed to be genuinely repentant were reconciled to the Church, their excommunication was lifted and a penance imposed. Penances varied from a monetary fine for minor transgressions to harsh imprisonment, chained in irons, fed only a diet of 'the bread of sadness and the water of tribulation'. The accused who were not prepared to retract were deemed 'obstinate' and handed over to the secular arm which, as laws such as those of Frederick II indicate, usually meant death by burning, confiscation of property, and a prohibition on office-holding by the heirs, often for at least two generations. The inquisitors did not, however, create circumstances which led to mass burnings, for only a small proportion of the accused were actually handed over to the secular arm.

The effectiveness of the inquisitors is difficult to measure. They did establish a bridgehead for the forces of orthodoxy in predominantly hostile regions like the

County of Toulouse, but in the course of so doing it provoked bitter opposition. The reckless massacre of the inquisitors at Avignonet in 1242 by partisans of Peter-Roger, lord of Mirepoix, is only the most serious of a whole series of incidents in the region. Moreover, they were dependent upon secular support just as the crusade had been and where this was lacking or enfeebled, the inquisitors found it difficult or impossible to operate. In the Capetian lands such support was forthcoming, especially under Louis IX, but this too could create problems, for in such cases the machinery might be manipulated for secular purposes as happened under Philip IV in the trial of the Templars between 1307 and 1312. If the elimination of Catharism was the main objective, then this had largely been achieved by 1321, when William Belibaste, the last so-called *perfectus*, was tricked into returning to Toulouse from his exile in Catalonia and burnt to death. By this date Catharism, apart from a brief revival in the County of Foix under Peter Autier, a notary from Ax, and his brother, in the first decade of the fourteenth century, had been declining since the fall of its important base, the castle of Montségur, to royalist forces in 1244.

The inquisitors did not accomplish this on their own for, in the decades after 1229 the economy of the south revived more rapidly than might have been expected, helping to reconcile many to the new circumstances, while the Church had continued to make determined attempts to re-establish itself as an effective force in Languedoc by preaching campaigns and by the founding of monastic houses in areas where they had previously been sparse. St Dominic's establishment of the nunnery at Prouille in 1206 is one such case, representing a recognition by the Church that it had failed to make proper provision for the religious needs of the populace in certain areas. Prouille is particularly important in that needs of women, who had been so active in the Cathar network, were at last appreciated. Such foundations became more common after 1229 as northern influence in the south increased. In some cases, orthodox northerners displaced southern seigneurs who became exiled *faidits*, no longer able to provide support for their Cathar clients, while sometimes former Cathar supporters like Oliver of Termes were persuaded to abandon their resistance and to enter Capetian service. Oliver eventually took the cross and participated in both Louis IX's crusades in 1248–54 and in 1270 and was rewarded with a partial restoration of his lands (Peal 1986). In other cases families had simply been eliminated: the great Mirepoix-Pereille clan had contained thirty-three known *perfecti* and *perfectae*. In a space of fifteen years, ten of these were burnt to death, eight of whom were women. Families lost their 'directrices de conscience' and their personnel. The inquisitorial records left by Pons of Parnac and John Galand between 1273 and 1289 show little sign of the great extended families seen in the inquiries of Bernard of Caux and Ferrier thirty years before (Roquebert 1985:239–41). In one way or another, therefore, the structure which had nourished Catharism in the past was broken up and the continuity of heretical tradition lost. Hunted by the inquisitors and deprived of secure bases, the *bonhommes* found it increasingly difficult to maintain a hold on the population, their support and status dwindled and the intellectual and doctrinal content of their message was diluted and distorted. William Belibaste was not the last proud representative of a line of Cathar leaders, but a fugitive of no real learning, whose best hope had lain in keeping quiet.

Part III

Political change

8

The Empire

But since immature age inspires too little fear, and while awe languishes, audacity increases, the boyish years of the King excited in many the spirit of crime. Therefore, everyone strove to become equal to the one greater than him, or even greater, and the might of many increased through crime; nor was there any fear of the law, which had little authority under the young boy-king.

(Mommsen and Morrison 1962:106)

When Henry III died in October 1056, his heir, Henry IV, although crowned King of the Romans two years before, was under 6 years old. The words above, from the anonymous *Vita Heinrici IV imperatoris*, although not written in a spirit of disinterested objectivity, nevertheless accurately encapsulate what was to happen during the long minority which was to follow. By the time Henry came of age in 1065, he had experienced the full range of blows described by his anonymous partisan. In 1062 he had been kidnapped by Anno, Archbishop of Cologne, and for the next two years exploited in the interests of this most ambitious prelate, while his mother, the Empress-Regent Agnes, had been forced to retire into monastic seclusion in Italy. Then Anno, while away in Rome applying his manipulative talents to the papal succession, was himself displaced by an equally overbearing personality, Adalbert, Archbishop of Hamburg-Bremen, whose influence lasted until Henry dismissed him from his counsels in 1066. But the striving 'to become equal to the one greater than him' was not confined to the great ecclesiastical princes, for the lands to which Henry acceded had seldom resembled a coherent entity. The duchies which made up the kingdom were based on traditional and deep-rooted divisions into peoples and accepted, only with reluctance, a higher level of authority. Moreover, this partly conceals another layer to the problem, for within the duchies themselves the real strength lay with those leading families possessed of large tracts of allodial land – land owned in full proprietary right – and with the holders of fiefs which, for various reasons, they could treat as if they were allodial lands (Gillingham 1971:12–14). At this level – particularly as a consequence of fundamental economic and social changes taking place in the late eleventh and twelfth

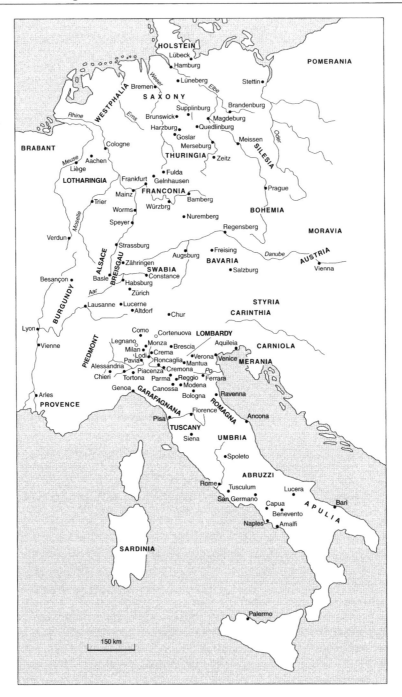

Map 2 The Empire

centuries – there was an ever-shifting kaleidoscope of power, so that matters were rarely stable. Most restless were the Saxons, once the favoured duchy when their duke gained the kingship in 919, but under the Salian dynasty in the eleventh century increasingly disgruntled. This underlying discontent – by no means confined to the reign of Henry IV – fanned by the intrigues of other dukes, erupted into rebellion in 1073, a rebellion which took two years to suppress, and not before the rebels had desecrated the burial places of Henry's son and brother at the royal castle of Harzburg in 1074. In short, the great families had been slow to accept the idea of a 'German Kingdom' and control of their intrigues made the government of Germany a complex and unpredictable task at the best of times (see Map 2).

But Henry IV did not come to the throne at the best of times. Not only had his minority and the weak rule of the Empress Agnes undermined the monarchy's position within Germany, but also during the same period the growing assertiveness of the reform popes had crystallised into a view of the world order quite at odds with that held by his father and in turn by Henry himself. The papal reform affected all rulers, but it was more important to the German kings than to any of the others because it was upon them that the imperial inheritance had fallen (see Table 4). The east Frankish rulers who had emerged from the debris of the late Carolingian Empire in the tenth century could never see their exclusive field of action in Germany. The weakness of the west Frankish rulers had given their Saxon neighbours the opportunity to grasp the imperial legacy of Charlemagne, and the military victories of Otto I (936–73) had shown the world that they were appropriate heirs. The occupant of the German throne

Table 4 Rulers of Germany and the Empire

Henry III, Salian	1039–56. Imperial coronation 1046
Henry IV, Salian	1056–1106. Imp. coron. 1084. Deposed 1105
Henry V, Salian	1106–25. Imp. coron. 1111
Lothar III of Supplinburg	1125–37. Imp. coron. 1133
Conrad III of Hohenstaufen	1137–52
Frederick I of Hohenstaufen	1152–90. Imp. coron. 1155
Henry VI of Hohenstaufen	1190–97. Imp. coron. 1191
Philip of Swabia, Hohenstaufen	1198–1208
Otto IV of Brunswick, Welf	1198–1214. Imp. coron. 1209
Frederick II of Hohenstaufen	1212–50. Imp. coron. 1220. Deposed 1245
Conrad IV of Hohenstaufen	1237/50–4
Henry Raspe of Thuringia	1246–47
William of Holland	1247–56
Alfonso X of Castile	1257–75
Richard of Cornwall	1257–72
Rudolf I of Habsburg	1273–91
Adolf of Nassau	1292–8. Deposed 1298
Albert I of Habsburg	1298–1308
Henry VII of Luxembourg	1308–13. Imp. coron. 1312
Louis IV of Bavaria	1314–47. Imp. coron. 1328

in the eleventh century therefore saw himself both as the apex of Christian society and as ruler over territories which included not only Germany, but the Kingdom of Burgundy and the Italian peninsula as well. He believed too that this entitled him to be crowned in Rome and thus to determine the appropriate holder of the Bishopric of Rome. For Henry IV and his successors, this element of their inheritance was as deeply ingrained as their desire to govern Germany and to control the duchies.

In the decade after he came of age, Henry struggled to reassert royal power. He saw the need to strengthen and enlarge the royal demesne, particularly in the Salian lands in the Rhineland and in the Saxon lands inherited from the Ottonians. The use of *ministeriales* as royal officials, already deployed by predecessors like Conrad II (1027–39), is evidence of his intention here. Equally, it was natural to expect him to continue to try to control ecclesiastical appointments, for the support of the Church, both spiritually and materially, had been an essential element in the Ottonian governmental system. Moreover, the growing economic power of the towns, especially those of the Rhineland, offered Henry new opportunities, as at Christmas 1073, when the populace of Worms expelled the bishop and welcomed Henry IV. The result was a privilege which conceded the citizens freedom from tolls in a range of German towns on the grounds of their 'extraordinary fidelity' to the Crown, especially 'while all the princes of the realm were raging against us' (B.H. Hill 1972:235–6).

Chief among those raging against him was the Billung family, holders of the Dukedom of Saxony since 936 who, in combination with powerful Saxons such as Otto of Northeim, attempted to block royal entry. Otto had a very personal reason for rebellion since in 1070 Henry had controversially deprived him of the Duchy of Bavaria on the disputed grounds of treason. However, Saxon opposition ran deeper than the grievances of individuals, for Henry's policy of 'recuperations' following losses sustained during his minority, was seen in the duchy as oppression and as a threat to the possessions of all Saxon lords. The construction of a series of royal castles (some unprecedentedly large), mostly manned by Swabians, served only to strengthen the developing image of Henry as a tyrannous ruler. Moreover, the Saxon peasantry were also in revolt, their resentment provoked by the material consequences of royal success in the form of taxation and services, and by the unrestrained pillaging of Henry's Swabian garrisons (Robinson 1999: 63–104). Henry's defeat of these forces in a bloody three-hour battle at Homburg on the River Unstrut in June 1075 owed much to the divisions between these opponents, who had little in common. It has sometimes been argued that the apparent removal of the Saxon menace made Henry over-confident in his dealings with the pope, that indeed a decisive flaw in his character was his lack of patience which led him to undertake too many actions at the same time. Yet the Empire was a vast and complex inheritance in which problems seldom presented themselves in neat chronological order; the challenges faced by its ruler were greater than those which confronted any other contemporary. A new conflict between Henry and Gregory VII was almost certain to arise, in which the political problems of German government became entangled with the papal challenge to imperial authority. 'I am aware,' Henry wrote bitterly to the pope in 1075, 'that almost all the princes of my realm rejoice more in our discord than in our mutual peace' (Mommsen and Morrison 1962:143).

This interweaving of events can be clearly seen after Henry's defeat of the Saxons, for this was followed by his defiance of Gregory early in 1076, the pope's retaliation by excommunicating the king at the Lent synod soon after and then, in January 1077, Henry's submission at Canossa, intended to protect his political position in Germany by preventing the conjunction of his enemies. Because of this submission, the election of Duke Rudolf of Swabia as king by his German enemies in March 1077 did Henry far less damage than it might have done, while Gregory's recognition of Rudolf in 1080 and his second excommunication of Henry were much less effective than the papal actions of 1076. Therefore, with Rudolf's death as a result of wounds received in the battle with Henry's forces at Hohenmölsen in October 1080, Henry felt confident enough to begin the invasion of Italy in 1081 which led to his coronation by the anti-pope Clement III in 1084 and Gregory's enforced retreat from Rome in the company of the Normans. After this, Henry proclaimed in triumph to Bishop Theoderic of Verdun:

> Know that this Hildebrand has been cast down by the legal judgement of all the cardinals and of the whole Roman people and that Clement has been elected our pope and exalted to the Apostolic See by the acclamation of all the Romans.
> (Mommsen and Morrison 1962:166)

Although the Normans prevented Henry from establishing his position in Rome in 1084, the king had nevertheless recovered much of the ground lost during the late 1070s. He now tried to consolidate his hold over his potential enemies in Germany and Italy in the hope of re-establishing the kind of supremacy achieved by his father. The coronation of his son, Conrad, in 1087, was a step towards this end, an act intended to secure the succession and to deter any repetition of the events that led to the election of Rudolf of Rheinfelden in 1077. But, as has been seen, the claims of imperial ideology and the territorial scope that this encompassed meant that apparently disparate events in different parts of the Empire were always liable to become intertwined, so that there were often opportunities for those who wished to thwart the imperial dream. This was never more evident than during the last two decades of Henry's reign. The Saxons refused to accept the removal of bishops who did not support Clement III, as Henry wished; this was no mere whim on Henry's part, since his status as emperor depended upon the acceptance of Clement III as the legitimate pope. Rebellion and military defeat for Henry followed, and in 1089 he was obliged to accept a much greater degree of independence for Saxony than had seemed probable in 1075. Peace did not last long; within a year he was forced to intervene in northern Italy to tackle what to him must have looked very like a conspiracy against him orchestrated by Pope Urban II. It was centred on the Countess Matilda of Tuscany, whom the *Vita Heinrici IV* describes as 'that grasping woman who was laying claim to almost all of Italy' (Mommsen and Morrison 1962:118), but it included Welf IV, Duke of Bavaria, whose son had married Matilda and, in 1093 and 1094, Henry's son, Conrad, and wife, Praxedis. Despite initial success when, in 1091, he captured Mantua, this coalition was too strong for him, and it was 1097 before he could extricate himself from Verona, where he had been trapped by his enemies, and return to Germany. A settlement was patched up when the marriage between Welf, son of Welf IV, and Matilda, contrived as it had been by the papacy, broke up.

But Henry's misfortunes had one further course to run for, in 1104 his son, and by this time designated heir, the future Henry V, became deeply involved in what Henry later described as a 'horrible betrayal, unheard-of to all ages' (Mommsen and Morrison 1962:189). In 1098 Henry had been created heir at his father's insistence, Conrad having been disinherited because of his plotting, but here too the king's faith had been misplaced. 'Whence may one assure himself of security when he is not safe from him whom he begat?' laments the author of the *Vita* (Mommsen and Morrison 1962:118). Henry is supposed to have been concerned at the decline of royal authority in his father's later years and, while this may be so, he found ready allies among the German aristocracy, who must have felt considerably less sympathy with this point of view. The *Vita* portrays him as a man seduced into rebellion by his father's opponents, for they told him 'that he would at last have sanctified himself if he made void the vow vowed to an excommunicate'. The motivation of these men, according to the *Vita*, was to overturn Henry IV's *Reichsfriede*, or 'imperial peace', issued the previous year, which had been an attempt 'to bridle the evils which came into being before that time', that is to control internecine warfare and robbery. 'But I waste my time,' says the author of the *Vita* in disgust, 'I ask the ass to play the lyre: bad customs grown usual are never removed or, if so, with difficulty' (Mommsen and Morrison 1962:122, 120–1). The damage is manifest. I.S. Robinson has measured the ebbing of confidence in the effectiveness of Henry IV's government over the half-century of the reign. Diplomas (grants of land or rights), unlike letters, were issued in response to petitions and not on royal initiative, so that they are a good indication of the credibility of his government. The decline from an average of 22 per annum in the first decade of the reign to only four per annum in the last decade is very striking; in contrast, during Henry III's admittedly much shorter reign, the average was 22 per annum throughout (Robinson 1999:12–13). In 1105 in a final humiliation, Henry was tricked into putting himself into his son's hands and imprisoned. Although he escaped the following year and at once began a vigorous campaign to re-establish himself, he lived only a few months longer, dying at Liège in August 1106. He died excommunicate and his body was left for five years without Christian burial.

Henry V's accession, however, did nothing to change the nature of the fundamental problems which, from now on, all aspirants to the imperial throne would have to face, problems which centred on the definition of the emperor's relationship with the divergent forces of his world: the reformed papacy, the ever-changing pattern of the Italian political scene, the discontented and often rebellious aristocratic families of Germany. Initially, his prospects seemed more favourable than those which had faced his father in 1065. He had gained power as an adult, reconciled with the papacy, and was supported by a substantial section of the German nobility. The most threatening of the duchies – that of Saxony under the Billung family – had, in 1106, fortuitously fallen to his gift when Duke Magnus died without male heirs. Henry invested Lothar of Supplinburg, a relatively minor noble, but long-term enemy of his father, as the new duke. Marriage alliances linked the new king with the Duchy of Swabia and the March of Austria. In these circumstances he felt confident enough to mount an expedition to Italy where, in 1111, he accepted Paschal II's sweeping grant of the regalia of the Church in return for the renunciation of lay investiture. In April he was crowned at St Peter's. But, like emperors before and after him, furore broke out once he had left, and the pope's concessions were cancelled.

Control of Germany proved to be equally illusory and elusive. When Henry tried to take over vacant fiefs in Saxony, a natural concomitant of his policy of extending crown lands in the region, he found that Lothar was no more co-operative than previous Saxon dynasts, his enmity made more formidable by the support of Adalbert I, Archbishop of Mainz. Adalbert had been Henry's chancellor, but now, motivated by an inextricable mixture of personal ambition and a desire to protect ecclesiastical independence – indeed, he seems to have identified the two – he began to orchestrate German opposition. Adalbert proved to be a determined and persistent antagonist; his final triumph was achieved in 1125 when, on Henry's death, he thwarted the king's hopes for the succession, thus ensuring that the elective principle with its accompanying emphasis on the role of the great ecclesiastical and secular princes remained very much alive. Ultimately this was to produce a crystallisation of dynastic faction in Germany which dominated its politics for the rest of the century and beyond. In 1113, however, it was Henry who gained the upper hand, capturing Adalbert and defeating the Saxon rebels near Quedlinburg. Soon after, in January 1114, he consolidated his reputation by effecting an alliance with Henry I of England through marriage to his daughter Matilda.

These successes proved to be fragile, since they offered no real solutions to persistent problems. Henry's refusal to present Adalbert for judgement simply provided another pretext for disaffection, especially in Saxony and Lotharingia, led by Duke Lothar. This time the king was twice defeated and, in 1115, forced to release Adalbert, who promptly excommunicated him in a censure issued jointly with another great German prelate, Frederick I, Archbishop of Cologne. Henry's situation at this time aptly encapsulates the imperial dilemma, since with the problems presented by Lothar and Adalbert still unresolved, Henry felt obliged to embark upon a second expedition to Italy with the double aim of gaining control of the Matildine lands, which fell to him on the countess's death in 1115, and of achieving a second coronation, this time in conjunction with his new wife. The coronation was indeed achieved, but not at the hands of the pope, who fled at the emperor's advance. The Archbishop of Braga performed the ceremony in 1117 and was excommunicated as a consequence. As so often, an imperial incursion into Italy proved to be the pursuit of shadows.

The compromise over investitures at Worms in 1122 grew out of these circumstances. The accession in 1119 of a more determined pope in Calixtus II, together with a strong desire for a settlement among even the secular German nobility, brought Henry to the agreement and therefore once more into the fold of the Church. But Henry could achieve no such working compromise with either Lothar or Adalbert. In Henry's last years Lothar acted as if royal authority was of no account, preventing the king from placing his own candidates in two vacant margravates in east Saxony (which Henry had a right to do), and then, in 1124, failing to appear before the imperial court at which he was to explain himself. The extent of Henry's authority was also demonstrated when the king, encouraged by his father-in-law, Henry I of England, threatened to invade Champagne. Surprisingly, in August 1124 his forces were rebuffed when a substantial part of the north French nobility temporarily sank their differences and rallied behind King Louis VI. Henry decided that confrontation was less than prudent and withdrew without courting battle. It was an inglorious end for the last of the Salian emperors. Nevertheless, the problems of the last years can lead to an underestimation of Henry's achievement. Humiliation had not been heaped upon him in the manner that he had inflicted it on his father, while, despite the problems created by the perennial regional rivalries of Germany, the crown had actually emerged from the Investiture Controversy in a better state than many of its enemies. In May 1125, he died, leaving the imperial treasure and insignia in the hands of his wife, Matilda, but no direct male heir.

Henry left a clear if indirect indication that his successor should be Frederick II, Duke of Swabia. He seemed the obvious choice. Frederick was Henry's nephew, son of his sister Agnes and Frederick of Hohenstaufen, who had died in 1105. Duke

Frederick had spent the reign building up Hohenstaufen power in his duchy, yet had shown no tendency towards disloyalty. He had taken part in Henry's first Italian expedition, and in 1116 the king had been confident enough to leave authority in his hands when he had once more set out for Rome. He had made Frederick's brother, Conrad, Duke of eastern Franconia. Moreover, the Hohenstaufen were also linked by marriage to the other great family of Germany, the Welfs, for Frederick was married to Judith, daughter of Henry the Black, Duke of Bavaria. But the chosen candidate who emerged from Mainz at the end of August was not Frederick but Lothar of Supplinburg, a result preferred by Adalbert of Mainz, who dominated the proceedings. In the encyclical of the princes, headed by Adalbert, they chose to emphasise 'the oppression which had afflicted the Church and the whole kingdom until the present time' (Weiland 1893:1:165). The key to his success had been the adhesion of Henry the Black, who by this act revived the feud between the two most powerful families among the German dukes, the Welfs and the Staufen. This rivalry, which had existed since 1079, had originally centred upon their respective spheres of influence in Swabia, but it was to have a significance for the crown which transcended this. Even so, it was hardly unique; German regional politics was founded upon shifting sands, and the relations between the dukes and the monarchy tell only part of the story.

The election of 1125 is explicable in terms of the German political structure. By the end of Lothar's reign two of the five original duchies of Saxony, Franconia, Swabia, Bavaria and Lotharingia were held by the Welfs. They were the most powerful family in Germany, for Henry the Proud had succeeded his father in Bavaria in 1126, and the following year had married Gertrude, Lothar's only child. In addition, in 1137, Lothar may have granted Saxony to Henry the Proud; at the least the Welfs had *de facto* possession. The status of the March of Austria, which was a Bavarian fief held by the Babenberg family, who were closely related to the Staufen, made little material difference. Four other duchies had been created during the tenth century: Upper and Lower Lotharingia, Carinthia in the south-east (again largely dependent on Bavaria) and Bohemia, which was regarded as a duchy within the German structure. Equally important were the great ecclesiastics, the archbishops of Cologne, Mainz, Trier, Bremen-Hamburg, Magdeburg and Salzburg. The first three in particular were often able to play key roles in the election process.

The chosen candidate was regarded by law as the King of the Romans and the designated emperor, and would normally expect to go to Rome to receive an imperial coronation, although whether this coronation was substantive or merely confirmatory remained a contentious issue. Apart from Germany, the Kingdoms of Burgundy and Italy also appertained directly to the emperor. The German rulers had held Burgundy since the era of Conrad II, although they did not exercise any great authority there until Frederick Barbarossa's marriage to Beatrice of Burgundy in 1156. Italy was a different matter. Here the political structure was, if anything, even more complex than that of Germany. As heirs to the Frankish conquest of Lombardy, the east Frankish rulers considered themselves the rightful kings of Italy, entitled to be crowned with the iron crown of the Lombards at the ancient capital of Pavia, or on other occasions at Monza or Milan.

But reliance on possession of the Italian kingdom would have left the German rulers with a much more restricted concept of their rights in the peninsula than they quite evidently tried to exercise in practice. As claimants to the imperial throne they were naturally drawn to Rome and thus to a much wider view of their Italian heritage, a view which not only encompassed Lombardy, but also brought them into territorial conflict with both the developing Papal State in central Italy, and the nascent Norman kingdom of the south. A further complication was that a marked characteristic of the northern and central parts of Italy had been the appearance of the urban communes; all emperors from the time of Henry IV had to reckon with and adapt to their existence. By *c*.1100 all of northern Italy with the exception of Piedmont had seen the development of governmental institutions in the towns based on a consulate drawn from the most powerful urban groups which, in various ways, now shared power with the more traditional authorities of count, duke, marquis and bishop. In addition, Venice, with its doge and council, while nominally Byzantine, was in practice an independent power. In the early twelfth century the emperor who ventured over the Alps therefore entered a world even more politically fragmented than that of the German kingdom. Growing cities competed with each other and with the local feudal and episcopal powers. Cities like Milan were so powerful that they could cow their immediate neighbours; in other places feudal agglomerations such as the assemblage controlled by the Countess Matilda of Tuscany held sway. The Matildine inheritance that Henry V had sought included a large part of the Apennines south of Reggio, Modena and Bologna, parts of the Lower Po region including the counties of Mantua, Reggio and Ferrara, and the Tuscan lands of the Garfagnana, the upper valley of the Serchio and Versilia. Small wonder that they were coveted by the papacy, desperate to ensure its territorial security in central Italy.

The dynastic rivalry which could so easily flourish in circumstances such as these was immediately apparent after the election of 1125. While the elective principle predominated, contention over the definition of crown lands, as opposed to the private property of the family of the previous monarch, was almost certain to ensue. The lands of the Salian house were claimed by the Hohenstaufen, but Lothar did not accept that the crown lands of Henry V appertained to the family as well. This was the pretext for the imperial ban placed upon Frederick of Hohenstaufen at Christmas 1125. Two years later relations between Lothar and the Hohenstaufen had deteriorated to the point where Conrad, Frederick's younger brother, set himself up as a direct rival. In December 1127, he was proclaimed king by an assembly of Swabian and Franconian lords, an action which was followed by his excommunication by Honorius II. The ensuing events demonstrate how anachronistic it is to see the medieval empire in national terms, for Conrad's rebellion soon drew in a much wider circle of interested parties. Early in 1128 he crossed the Alps and, at Milan, received the iron crown of Lombardy from the archbishop. Both parties had their own objectives: Conrad was laying claim to the Matildine lands left to Henry V, while the archbishop was demanding that the pope comply with the ancient right of the see of St Ambrose that the pope send him the *pallium* rather than he travel to Rome to receive it. But the forces ranged against the Hohenstaufen were too great. In the schism that followed the death of Honorius II in 1130, both papal candidates, seeking wider European support, condemned Conrad. In Germany itself the combined weight of Lothar supported by the Welfs proved too much for Frederick to resist. By 1132 it appeared that the Hohenstaufen threat had been overcome; Lothar was free to take on the imperial mantle and descend into Italy.

Unlike the invasions of the peninsula by his two predecessors, Lothar's expedition was positively encouraged by a pope who needed imperial support to re-establish himself in Rome. Lothar had, in March 1131, accepted Innocent II as legitimate pope, but his rival, Anacletus, still held Rome. This expedition came close to the papal ideal that the emperor should act as the secular arm of the Church. With Lothar's backing, Innocent was able to enter Rome, but could not gain access to St Peter's. Lothar's coronation took place therefore at the Lateran on 4 June 1133. Four days later Innocent conceded the emperor rights over German churches in considerably vaguer terms than those delineated at Worms, and at the same time enfeoffed him with the Matildine lands in return for an annual *cens* of 100 *livres* of silver. But within a week Lothar had begun the long journey back to Germany and Innocent, unable to sustain his position, was forced to retreat to Pisa. Lothar's rapid withdrawal demonstrates once again that it was, in fact, rarely possible for the German ruler to bring pressure to bear in central and southern Italy for any sustained period. Ultimately only political control of the south could achieve this.

It was not long before Lothar was prevailed upon to try again. The new expedition looked distinctly more promising than Lothar's previous effort. His armies were large enough to divide into two, Lothar taking the route along the Adriatic coast, Henry the Proud leading troops into Tuscany and the Papal States. They reassembled at Bari in May 1137. The threat certainly seemed real to the Normans of the south. King Roger II of Sicily, his Apulian vassals in revolt, prudently retreated to the island. But the pope's assumption that he could invest Apulia upon Rainulf of Alife, Roger's long-standing enemy, was quickly challenged by Lothar, whose whole attitude seems to have hardened since his first visit to Italy. In the end the investiture was performed jointly by the two powers, but the potential for future conflict was clear and Lothar's death in December 1137, as he travelled back from this expedition, probably saved Innocent II from a more serious confrontation.

The memory of Lothar's last expedition must have influenced Innocent II in his attitude towards the new election in Germany. On his death-bed Lothar committed the royal insignia to Henry the Proud. But the papacy did not respond to the obvious inference and instead, worked to secure the election not of Henry but of Conrad of Hohenstaufen. An assembly was hastily convened at Coblenz in March 1138, where Conrad was elected, but the Bavarians and the Saxons were not present. Conrad naturally feared the overwhelming preponderance of the Welfs; consequently he declared that Duke Henry could not hold both duchies at the same time. In July 1138 he followed this up by confiscating first Saxony, which he granted to Albert the Bear, Margrave of the North March, and then, in December, Bavaria, ceded to his half-brother, Leopold, Margrave of Austria and leader of the rising family of the Babenbergs. Although Henry the Proud died in October 1139, leaving an heir, Henry, only 10 years old, there was no possibility that Conrad could make such sweeping changes permanent. The Saxon nobility, mobilised by the boy's grandmother, Richenza, quickly drove out Albert, and in 1142 Conrad was obliged to accept Henry as Duke of Saxony. In Bavaria, Welf fortunes could not be restored so rapidly. When Leopold died, Conrad granted both Austria and Bavaria to Leopold's brother, Henry Jasomirgott, consolidating the arrangement by marrying Henry to the widow of Henry the Proud. But Henry the Lion, although he had seemed ready to concede Bavaria, had not in fact given up hope. In 1147 he reclaimed it, and in 1149 his uncle, Welf VI, returning from crusade through Sicily, broadened the base of the opposition to Conrad with the help of financial aid from Roger II, who was anxious to avoid a repetition of Lothar's invasion in 1136–7. Roger, as usual, had calculated shrewdly for, although Conrad had tried while on crusade to assemble an alliance against the King of Sicily in concert with Manuel I, the Byzantine emperor, he was never afterwards free to put it into effect. His only success had been the election of his young son, Henry, as king at Frankfurt in March 1147, shortly before departing for the crusade. But here too he was frustrated. Henry died in 1150, predeceasing his father. When Conrad died in 1152 he recommended for the succession not his other young son, still only 6 or 7 years old, but his nephew, Frederick of Swabia.

Frederick's position was strengthened in comparison with his immediate predecessors by apparently unanimous electoral support. Here is Otto of Freising's explanation:

> There have been hitherto in the Roman world, within the borders of Gaul and Germany, two renowned families: one that of the Henrys of Waiblingen, the other that of the Welfs of Altdorf. The one was wont to produce emperors, the other great dukes. These families, eager for glory as is usually the case with great men, were frequently envious of each other and often disturbed the peace of the state. But by the will of God (as men believe), providing for the peace of his people in time to come, it came about that Duke Frederick, the father of this Frederick, who was a descendant of one of the two families (that is, of the family of the kings), took to wife a member of the other, namely, the daughter of Henry, duke of the Bavarians, and by her became the father of the Frederick who rules at the present time.
>
> The princes, therefore, considering not merely the achievements and the valor of the youth already so frequently mentioned, but also this fact, that being a member of both families, he might – like a cornerstone – link these two separate walls, decided to select him as head of the realm.
>
> (Mierow 1955:116)

This extract is taken, not from *The Two Cities*, but from *The Deeds of Frederick Barbarossa*, Otto's account of the beginning of the reign, covering the years 1152–6. Although it would have been inconceivable for Otto to have abandoned his structural view of world history, the tone of the *Deeds* is decidedly more optimistic than that which pervades *The Two Cities*. Otto thought that he perceived at last, in Frederick, a prince truly worthy to succeed the Romans and Charlemagne, and he set about imbuing his nephew with a sense of imperial destiny more intense than any seen since the days of the Ottonians. 'Things', says Otto in the prologue to the *Deeds*, 'have changed for the better' (Mierow 1955:27). Otto would have appreciated the illustration taken from the *Historia Welforum*, *c*.1170, in which Frederick sits enthroned, his sons, King Henry, and Frederick, Duke of Swabia, on either side, beneath the caption, 'In the midst of his offspring sits the imperial father' (see Plate 10). Frederick is father in a double sense, both to his own sons and to the wider imperial family of Christendom, while the presence of the two generations illustrates the continuity of the imperial institution of which Otto speaks. Although Otto died in 1158 this ideology ultimately determined Frederick's outlook, infusing his actions both within the territories claimed directly for the empire and his relations with the wider world.

Five years after his election, in 1157, at Otto's request, Frederick set down in a letter what he considered to have been the principal achievements of his reign to that point, the intention being that the incidents described should, in the emperor's words, be 'amplified and increased' by Otto's 'renowned skill'. He described his anointing and crowning at Aachen in April 1152, the general assembly at Merseburg at Whitsun of the

Plate 10 Emperor Frederick Barbarossa, flanked by his sons, Henry and Frederick, portrayed as the imperial father. From the *Historia Welforum, c.*1170. (Photograph reproduced by permission of Hessische Landesbibliothek.)

same year where he had sat in judgement on the Danish succession dispute and received the homage and fealty of King Svend, and his control of the Church, shown by his transfer of Wichmann, Bishop of Zeitz, to the Archbishopric of Magdeburg. He had then crossed the Alps into Lombardy in 1154, overcoming those cities which opposed him, and celebrated his victory at Pavia. This had been an urgent task 'because this land, on account of the prolonged absence of the emperors, had become arrogant and, conscious of its strength, had initiated rebellion'. As a result, he continued, 'we were wroth and destroyed almost all its strongholds' (Mierow 1955:17–20). He then marched south into Romagna and Tuscany, met the pope at Sutri and, despite opposition, was crowned in Rome, on 18 June 1155. He took Ancona and Spoleto from the Normans before returning north, winning a victory at Verona en route. Back in Germany, in September 1156 he completed a settlement between the two most powerful dukes, Henry the Lion and Henry Jasomirgott. The court held at Besançon the following year in October could be regarded as a fitting assembly for such a ruler, not only arbitrator of the affairs of Germany and Italy, but also accepted as the superior of the Duchy of Bohemia and the neighbouring realms of Denmark, Poland and Hungary. The choice of Besançon in itself reflected the great increase in direct control that he had gained over Burgundy by his marriage to its heiress, Beatrice, in June 1156, a link which not only extended his influence over Burgundy, the Viennois, Provence and the Arelate, but also completed imperial domination of the Alpine passes into Italy.

Frederick's account of his achievements, while hardly objective, can be seen to have considerable justification. Not only had he made his presence felt in Burgundy, but also he had exploited the widespread support that he had received at his election to try to resolve long-term conflicts that had dogged the reigns of his predecessors. His appointment of Wichmann to the Archbishopric of Magdeburg in 1152 testified to his determination to enforce the provisions of the Concordat of Worms in Germany. Equally important were his relations with the lay nobility. The settlement between the two Henrys referred to in his letter was intended to terminate the quarrel between them over the Duchy of Bavaria, the loss of which Henry the Lion had never been able to accept. Under the terms of the so-called *privilegium minus*, Henry the Lion was given back the Welfs' traditional duchy with no diminution of his rights in Saxony, while, 'in order that this matter does not seem in any way to diminish the honour and glory of our most dear uncle', the March of Austria was converted into a duchy to be held and disposed of by Henry Jasomirgott by hereditary right. Moreover, Henry's powers within the new duchy were sweeping, for 'no person, great or small, may presume to exercise any jurisdiction in the government of the duchy without the consent or permission of the duke', while the duke himself was to owe no service to the empire, except to royal courts held in Bavaria, and was to have no obligation to serve on military expeditions 'except those which the emperor happens to ordain in the kingdom or provinces adjoining Austria' (Appelt 1975:10(1):255–60).

The settlement of 1156 shows Frederick very much as he imagined himself as, in Otto's phrase, 'Father of his Country' (Mierow 1955:169), presiding over a united Christian community. Indeed, Frederick had already shown how he conceived of the government of his German lands in the publication of his *Landfriede* (probably in 1152), a series of twenty provisions for the peace of the land. In the preamble he declares that 'we, wishing both divine and human laws to remain strong… proclaim, by royal authority a peace, long desired and necessary before everything in the land, to be established throughout all parts of the kingdom' (Appelt 1975:10(1):39–44). The great princes of the realm were men of dignity and power and had every right to be treated accordingly. Two years after the agreement with the two Henrys, for instance, Frederick rewarded the loyalty of Vladislav II, Duke of Bohemia, by elevating the dukedom into a kingdom, at which Vladislav 'returned rejoicing and accoutered himself for the Italian expedition, that as king he might set forth, together with the emperor, in regal splendor' (Mierow 1955:189). Moreover, Otto records that Frederick had taken particular pleasure in the 1156 agreement, for Henry Jasomirgott had initially been very reluctant to accept it, and had not been finally persuaded until the previous June. 'The prince prized this more highly than the successes of all his other undertakings: the fact that, without the shedding of blood, he was able to bring to friendly relations princes of the realm so mighty and so closely related to himself' (Mierow 1955: 163–4).

In one vital respect, however, Frederick's letter seriously distorts the degree of his success: this is in his description of the expedition to Italy in 1154–5. The claim that he had destroyed 'almost all the strongholds' of the Lombard cities actually meant only the submission of Rosate, Chieri and, after much toil, Tortona, and did not include the leaders of the communal movement like Milan. Accordingly, in July 1158, accompanied by the largest army that he ever mustered, Frederick once more set out to regain what he believed to be the customary imperial rights in Lombardy. The key to Lombard resistance was Milan and this time the sheer weight of Frederick's army was too much for the city, and it capitulated within a month. It was a natural step thereafter for Frederick to turn his mind to the overall government of his Italian kingdom. Just as he had settled German affairs in his *Landfriede* and by his negotiation of accords between the leading princes, so too he set about putting Italian affairs in order through the decrees of Roncaglia of November 1158. Here, it was made clear that the position of the consuls, the fealty of the populace, and the regalian rights, all ultimately stemmed from the emperor. Frederick evidently saw these provisions as a natural corollary of his role and his dismissal of a large part of his army suggests that he thought others would see them in the same light. Like the papacy, Frederick believed that it was his task to restore 'the right order' of society, lost sometime in the past. Moreover, 'right order' coincided with economic advantage, for the powers of which the cities were now deprived brought great financial gain to the emperor. Frederick was driven to Italy by both ideology and profit.

But just as the papacy had to contend with obstinate forces which did not share its vision of the terrene hierarchy, Frederick too was to find again and again that the structure of his ideal imperial order was undermined. Within two months of the issue of the decrees, Milan once more refused obedience, and was joined in an attack on the pro-imperial towns of Lodi and Como by Crema and Brescia. Frederick had once more to embark upon arduous military operations, which entailed a six-month siege of Crema between July 1159 and January 1160, and an even longer conflict with Milan, which was worn down only in March 1162. Now equipped with his own pope in Victor IV, he was ready to move south again, but Alexander III had anticipated him, having fled to France in April.

The pattern of Frederick's relations with the powers of Italy was therefore set, but he never again attained such a position of dominance with the pope in exile and Milan brought down. In October 1163 he reappeared as arbiter of disputes, only to find that there was little real depth of loyalty to the imperial cause. No military demonstration was attempted, since only Pavia, Como and Lodi, all fearful of Milan, could have been depended upon. However, in November 1166 he began his fourth expedition, comparable in scale to the army of the late 1150s, and aimed at Rome itself. As in 1158, when Frederick marshalled all his resources, he was a formidable power. By late July 1167 he had captured Rome, forced Alexander III to retreat to Benevento, and been recrowned with his wife by a new pope of his own creation, Paschal III. Since William I of Sicily had died the year before, leaving a minor to succeed, the possibility was now open to fulfil the aims of 1155 and remove the upstart Normans from the south. But, as in 1155, disease ravaged the army, and retreat was inevitable. Almost at once his enemies fell upon the wounded giant. An alliance of cities, the Lombard League, had been formed earlier in the year, and its adherents had become so numerous that Frederick extricated himself from the peninsula only with great difficulty. Not until early in 1168 was he able to pick his way back, in disguise and without his army.

The crucial and decisive confrontation for Frederick in Italy began when he set out for the fifth time in the autumn of 1174. He took a powerful force, but there was one notable absence, that of Henry the Lion, upon whose contingents Frederick had so often relied in the past. Henry had, however, grown in both power and ambition, seeking to expand his territories in Nordalbingia and eastwards along the Baltic. Helmold of Bosau reckoned his power, ten years earlier, as having 'increased beyond that of all who were before him', and described him as 'a prince of the princes of the earth'. Nobody could expect to oppose him. 'He trod upon the necks of rebels and broke up their strongholds; he extirpated the men who had revolted and made peace in the land; he built very strong fortresses and possessed an exceedingly great heritage' (Tschan 1935:264–5). Not surprisingly, when Frederick ran into difficulties in Italy in the autumn of 1175 he turned to Henry for reinforcements. However, at a meeting between the two at Chiavenna (north of Lake Como) in January or February, 1176, Henry asked as his price for support in Lombardy the cession of the imperial advocacy of Goslar, once the chief city of the Saxon rulers and an imperial possession ever since (K. Jordan 1986:160–4). Negotiations continued even after Frederick had returned to Lombardy, but the emperor could not bring himself to accede to such a demand.

The lack of Henry's troops certainly weakened Frederick, but it is difficult to judge how far they really influenced the outcome of the expedition, since the Italian cities were much stronger than they had been in the 1150s. They had even built a new city as the League symbol, that of Alessandria, south-west of Milan, on which Frederick spent six months of vain effort. Most of 1175 passed in cautious manoeuvring, but on 29 May 1176 the Lombards caught Frederick at Legnano, coming from Como with reinforcements he had just met from Germany and, despite being rocked by the German cavalry, inflicted the heaviest defeat that he had ever suffered. After Legnano he had to settle with the world as it was rather than the way imperial theorists believed that it should be.

It was not a world so unfavourable to Frederick's position as the defeat would suggest. Eighteen years of conflict had stretched papal resources, which probably explains Alexander III's willingness to compromise on the issue of ecclesiastical appointments in the Peace of Venice of July 1177. Peace was also confirmed with William II of Sicily, to last fifteen years, and with the Byzantine Emperor Manuel, but relations between Frederick and the Lombards remained sensitive and, for the time being, he settled for a six-year truce. By the time that the truce had run out, both sides were prepared to compromise. Under the Peace of Constance of 1183 the cities accepted Frederick's overlordship, and the magistrates took an oath of fealty on behalf of their own city. They did, however, retain regalian rights (which included control over a wide range of jurisdictions from military service to tolls) and the collection of certain taxes, as well as the election of their own magistrates, all powers which the emperor had tried to regain. Significantly, from the point of view of the imperialists, the towns accepted investiture of the regalia from the imperial representative (Appelt 1990:10(4):68–77). The 'proper' order had been retained, but the changes in the distribution of power within it, caused by the rapid increase in the economic and political strength of the Lombard cities from the mid-eleventh century, could not be erased. The seal was set on these complicated settlements when the accord with the Sicilian crown was confirmed by the marriage of Frederick's son and heir, Henry, to Constance, aunt of William II, at Milan in January 1186.

In Germany, Frederick had largely maintained his image as father of the realm, but the problems presented by Henry the Lion were not amenable to the methods of arbitration used in the 1150s. Henry's attempts to blackmail Frederick into conceding Goslar undoubtedly helped change the emperor's attitude towards him, but it was the bitter opposition of the Saxon and Rhineland nobles and bishops to both the style and substance of Henry's government which brought matters to a head. In January 1179 Frederick was reluctantly compelled to summon Henry to appear before a royal court meeting to answer charges brought against him by almost the entire Saxon aristocracy and Church. Henry failed to respond both to this and to two further summonses, which led Frederick to pronounce against him as a recalcitrant vassal. On 13 April 1180, by the terms of the so-called Gelnhausen charter, Henry's northern fiefs, including Saxony, were redistributed on the grounds that he had oppressed the liberties of both churches and nobles, and had refused to answer to a legitimate feudal summons on three occasions (Appelt 1985:10(3):360–3).

The key to Henry's fall lay in the combination of the emperor and the nobility. Henry had faced opposition before, but then he could rely on Barbarossa's support. Helmold believed that noble discontent in Henry's lands in 1166 broke out precisely because in October Frederick had set out for Italy and they were no longer restrained by his presence. When Frederick returned he imposed peace at Würzburg in the late spring of 1168 in a manner which Helmold saw as very much favouring Henry: 'he accused them [i.e. the princes] of violating the peace and declared that the sedition in Saxony had given the Lombards occasion for defection'. In the settlement which followed, 'Everything turned out as the duke wished and, without any loss on his part, he was saved from being encompassed by the princes' (Tschan 1935:265, 273). In 1179–80 that support was withdrawn and Frederick realised that he had to side with Henry's many enemies.

Most of Henry's territory was regranted. The Saxon duchy was divided between Philip, Archbishop of Cologne, and Bernard of Anhalt, who received the Saxon ducal title, while Otto of Wittelsbach became Duke of Bavaria. The Welfs, however, retained their allodial lands, centred on Lüneburg and Brunswick, despite the three-year exile imposed on Henry himself which began in 1182. By the time of Frederick Barbarossa's death in 1190, the structure of the Kingdom of Germany was no longer built upon the old duchies. New political entities had come into being which were to determine the realities of German government in the future. Bohemia was now a kingdom and the new duchies of Westphalia, Styria, Austria, Brabant, Pomerania, Merania, Würzburg and Zähringen had been established.

Throughout his reign Frederick had conceived of himself as emperor and had acted accordingly. The Kingdoms of Burgundy and Italy were not 'foreign', nor were the journeys to Rome merely for shallow display. The agreements with the German princes were not 'concessions' wrung from a reluctant centralising monarch, but legitimate settlements by imperial judgement. The successful accumulation of resources for the Staufen heirs was more than just an insurance policy against losing the kingship, but represented one means to acquire the power and prestige that he thought appropriate to his position. In the end the sheer size of the dominions which imperial tradition imposed upon Frederick severely limited the degree of success that he was able to achieve, just as it had with his predecessors. He simply did not have the means. Thus, Frederick did not attempt to establish a uniform system of communicating with the myriad variety of local powers contained within the polity; although the language of the *Landfrieden* conveys much about Frederick's self-image, there is little evidence that the actual provisions could be consistently implemented (Vollrath 1996). Nor did he have a chancery in the sense that it was understood in England or Sicily. Indeed, the fragility of his administrative resources can be demonstrated by examining the effects of the disastrous Italian expedition of 1166–7. Karl Leyser has pointed out that between August 1167 and June 1168 no diplomata were issued by the imperial notaries and scribes, which suggests that they too had been among the victims, thus depriving the emperor of expertise which could not be quickly replaced (Leyser 1994a:119–21). Beneath his enthusiasm for the 'most famous of the Augusti', Otto of Freising had known this well enough. Describing Frederick's return to Germany after his expedition to Italy in 1155, he commented, 'Now, when the prince returned to the transalpine regions, just as his presence restored peace to the Franks, so his absence deprived the Italians of it' (Mierow 1955:167). It was perhaps appropriate that Frederick should have died on crusade – an institution which, in the twelfth century, best demonstrates both the universalist aspirations of Christendom and the massive difficulties to be overcome by those who would seek to give them reality.

The death of William II of Sicily seven months before, without direct male heirs, gave the imperialism of Frederick's son, Henry VI, an extra dimension, for his marriage to William's aunt, Constance, in 1186 reinforced, although it did not in itself justify, the continuing imperial claim to the Kingdom of Sicily, drawing him south and emphasising to the papacy that Hohenstaufen ambitions were becoming more and not less threatening to its autonomy. By his invasion of the Norman kingdom, Henry condemned the Italian peninsula to long-drawn-out and increasingly bitter warfare, more damaging even than Barbarossa's campaigns before 1176. Moreover, once established in Sicily after 1194, Henry was attracted by wider Mediterranean ambitions, taking up with vigour the old Norman antagonism towards the Byzantine Empire.

It was this compelling ambition to conquer Sicily that led Henry to make a hasty settlement with Henry the Lion in the Treaty of Fulda (July 1190), as well as alienating imperial rights in Lombardy in order to finance his plans. On 14 April 1191 he gained an imperial coronation from the new pope, Celestine III, reluctantly abandoning the town of Tusculum, hitherto loyal to the imperial cause, to its Roman enemies, apparently to enable the pope to fulfil a promise made by his predecessor. From Rome he turned south, for the Sicilians had chosen Tancred of Lecce, an illegitimate son of Roger of Apulia, eldest son of Roger II, as king. Alliance with Pisa and Genoa, who would provide naval aid in return for trading privileges, completed Henry's rapid preparations. But, by late August, Henry had been forced to retreat, for disease had cut into his army and, to make matters worse, his wife Constance had been captured and handed over to Tancred. In June of the following year, Pope Celestine, deeply relieved at his escape from this new Hohenstaufen threat, invested Tancred as King of Sicily.

Celestine's judgement may well have been vindicated but for two unforeseen events: the capture of the Angevin Richard I, in December 1192, while returning from crusade, and his delivery into Henry's hands and, a year later, the death of Tancred. These two men had been the focus of opposition to Henry, for in 1191, in the course of his journey to Palestine, Richard had allied with Tancred, thereby reviving the Welf–Hohenstaufen rivalry, for he was brother-in-law to Henry the Lion.

When Richard fortuitously fell into his hands, Henry was facing an increasingly widespread revolt in north-west Germany, having alienated not only the Welfs, but also the nobility of the lower Rhineland and Westphalia, who had risen in opposition when he had tried to force his own candidate into the Bishopric of Liège. When Albert of Louvain, elected by the majority of the chapter and consecrated by the pope, was murdered by three German knights in November 1192, the blame fell on Henry, who had been his most bitter opponent. The capture of Richard meant that he could use Angevin influence in the region in his own favour and thus split up the opposition. Richard did not obtain his freedom until February 1194, and then only when he had accepted Henry as his overlord and had paid a large ransom. But Richard had been free for less than three weeks when Tancred died, and the way was clear for Henry to mount a new expedition, this time successfully. He was crowned at Palermo on Christmas Day 1194 (see Plate 11). He quickly set about imposing his rule. The extent of this German presence can be seen by the titles granted to Markward of Anweiler, a former *ministerialis*, who was made Marquis of Ancona, Duke of Ravenna and Romagna and Count of the Abruzzi. A brief revolt shortly after Henry's coronation did nothing to shake this new power.

In 1195, however, Henry was still a relatively young man and the scope of his ambition did not stop with Sicily. His tutor, Godfrey of Viterbo, had imbued him with grandiose concepts of universal monarchy. Henry's actions and attitudes suggest that he believed himself chosen for imperial power far wider in scope than that possessed even by his father. Here is the link between the *Realpolitik* that persuaded him to exploit the capture of a crusader, supposedly under the protection of the Church, and apparently puzzling actions such as the granting of the Kingdom of Arles to the captive Richard, for Henry saw himself as the distributor of kingdoms and the leader of Christendom at the same time as he felt the need to act ruthlessly to achieve these ideological ends. It is not surprising to find such a man taking the cross, as he did at Bari in March 1195. At the same time he began to threaten the Byzantine empire, becoming even more clearly a rival to be eliminated. When he entered Palermo he found there Irene, daughter of the Byzantine Emperor, Isaac Angelus, destined to be married to a son of Tancred. Now he saw the opportunity to force his way into the panoply of claimants to the Byzantine throne by marrying her to his brother, Philip of Swabia. The sudden deposition of Isaac II by his elder brother, Alexius, on 8 April 1195, provided such a pretext. For the next two years the weakened Byzantine Empire was forced to pay out a form of 'protection money', but sooner or later Henry's combination of crusading fervour and universalist aims was likely to translate into direct military action.

However, before his expedition could set out, Henry determined to set the seal on his plans by gaining acceptance of the hereditary succession of the Hohenstaufen. Now securely in possession of the hereditary kingship of Sicily, this could tie the two crowns

Plate 11 The Emperor Henry VI receives the symbols of Fortitude and Justice from the Virtues, while below his rival for the throne of Sicily, Tancred of Lecce, lies twisted beneath the Wheel of Fortune. Peter of Eboli, *Liber ad Honorem Augusti*, *c.*1195–6. (Photograph reproduced by permission of Burgerbibliothek, Bern.)

in a bond of dynastic union and ensure Hohenstaufen dominance of the empire for the foreseeable future. Largely because they had been able to provide a succession of male heirs crowned during the lifetime of their predecessors, hereditary progression had been achieved subtly by the Capetians, in Henry's eyes a dynasty minor in comparison with his own. But Philip II was the eighth member of his family in the direct line. Henry was only the second of the Hohenstaufen in direct line, but Otto of Freising had held that the Staufen were indeed the true imperial successors of both the Carolingians and the Salians. Henry now had a son, Frederick, born at Jesi on 26 December 1194. It seemed obvious that proper arrangements for the succession should be made before his departure on a crusade from which he might never return. But the German princes, led by Archbishop Adolf I of Cologne, took a stand on the tradition also clearly explained by Otto of Freising, that it 'is the very apex of the law of the Roman empire, namely, that kings are chosen not by lineal descent but through the election of princes' (Mierow 1955:115). Henry offered concessions, such as hereditary succession in both lines for lay princes in their fiefs and suppression of the rights of spolia (the property of deceased clerics) and regalia taken from ecclesiastical benefices during a vacancy. It seems that most princes were prepared to agree, but Adolf's opposition (for reasons of his own) held up proceedings and, at the end of 1196, Henry, anxious to begin crusading, settled temporarily for the acceptance of the succession of his son Frederick only. His crusading plans were not brought to fruition either, blocked first by a serious revolt in Sicily in May 1197, and then ended by Henry's unexpected death on 28 September, aged 31. His son, Frederick, was not yet 3.

Institutional development had transformed methods of government during the twelfth century, but the changes had not negated the importance of individual rulers. Kings still needed to be peripatetic, their subjects still regarded them with greater awe and respect when their proximity demanded it than when they were at the other end of their lands. Otto of Freising remarked that the Italian cities were obedient to the emperor only if they sensed 'his authority in the power of his great army' (Mierow 1955:127), an observation particularly pertinent to the medieval empire, both because of its vast size and diversity and because there were fewer institutional substitutes for the ruler's personal presence than there were in some other contemporary governments. A smooth transition of government was hardly to be expected after Henry VI's death.

Frederick's mother, Constance, had been alienated from her husband and his German vassals and officials since at least 1194. While Archbishop Adolf of Cologne, determined to promote the primacy of his own see at the expense of Mainz, scrambled for power in Germany, she tried to remove her husband's partisans, and made Frederick himself a ward of the new pope, Innocent III, placing Sicily back in its feudal dependence on the papacy. Frederick was crowned in May 1198, but in November Constance herself died, so for the time being at least little account was likely to be taken of a small boy. Meanwhile, in Germany, peace among the German princes, so fervently and genuinely desired by Frederick Barbarossa, seemed as far away as ever: in March, seeing little hope for the child Frederick, most of them had elected Philip of Swabia, Henry VI's younger brother, but in June, a rival group led by Adolf of Cologne, whose city's commercial interests were closely bound up with England, chose Otto of Brunswick, the third son of Henry the Lion, and nephew of the Angevin, Richard I. This rivalry evidently weakened monarchical power in Germany, for both sides sought to buy military support from tenants-in-chief who, were, in fact, already legally obliged to provide it under the terms of their feudal relationship with the crown (Krieger

1996:166–8). As for Frederick, it was 1206 before he was actually handed over to the papacy and another two years before papal forces could drive out the Germans from the Sicilian kingdom. Then, on 26 December 1208, when Frederick was 14 and therefore officially of age, Innocent formally transferred the government of Sicily to him.

Until this time papal policy had been determined by the need to prevent any reunion of Sicily and the Empire. For this reason Innocent had accepted Otto in 1201 in preference to the apparently less co-operative Hohenstaufen; the powers of northern and central Italy, freed from the threat of Henry VI, had lined up on either side, with Milan and its Lombard League allies supporting Otto, while Cremona and its partisans accepted Philip. But Otto found it difficult to maintain his support. Even Adolf of Cologne began to lose faith in the value of this alliance, especially after the blows dealt to the Angevin cause by Philip II of France during his conquest of Normandy in 1203 and 1204. On 6 January 1205 he therefore crowned Philip of Swabia at Aachen, thereby providing him with the proper ceremonial to reinforce his possession of the imperial insignia and thus making him a far more convincing candidate than Otto.

However, a possible papal accommodation with Philip which both sides seemed to be moving towards in 1207 was overturned by Philip's assassination in June 1208 and, for a brief and disillusioning period, the pope turned back to Otto IV. A marriage was arranged between Otto and Beatrice, the eldest daughter of Philip of Swabia, which would effectively transfer the Staufen lands to Otto, and Otto promised the pope what he wanted to hear, giving territorial guarantees not only for the Papal States, but also for the Matildine lands, Ravenna, Spoleto, Ancona and Tuscany, as well as ceding royal rights over ecclesiastical appointments, including those of spolia and regalia, over which there had been so much contention during the twelfth century. On 4 October 1209 Otto IV was crowned at Rome. The reconciliation did not last long. Otto's invasion of the Sicilian kingdom, in disregard of all papal aims, so alarmed Innocent that, in November 1210, he excommunicated him.

With Philip of Swabia dead and Otto IV excommunicate, Frederick II decided to gamble on grasping for himself what he undoubtedly saw as his rightful inheritance. He was encouraged in this by Innocent III and by Philip II, united now in their determination to be rid of Otto. For his part Frederick was ready to give the pope the guarantee that he required, including the confirmation of Sicily as a papal fief and the crowning of Henry, Frederick's 1-year-old son, as King of Sicily. Frederick's later indifference to papal concerns about the union of the northern and southern kingdoms of the empire may well have stemmed from his knowledge that Innocent provided him with support only when it was convenient for papal policy. By the autumn of 1211 he judged that he had enough support in Germany to risk the journey north. He arrived in April 1212 and in November met Prince Louis, Philip II's heir, at Vaucouleurs, where he agreed not to conclude any peace with Otto, King John or their allies without first consulting Philip. In return Frederick received 20,000 *livres*, invaluable for extending his support. He was crowned at Mainz on 9 December. Otto of Brunswick, nevertheless, still had adherents in the Rhineland and Saxony, but when he was defeated at the battle of Bouvines in 1214, his position became untenable. Frederick's status was confirmed by a recrowning at Aachen on 25 July 1215.

Henry VI's invasion of Sicily meant that his son had spent his disturbed childhood in the south, and only in 1212 was he able to enter Germany after a series of events over which initially he had had no control. This environment determined that Frederick, although as strongly imbued with the ideology of empire as his father and grandfather, necessarily gave that empire a different territorial emphasis. Nevertheless, his approach to the government of Germany did not differ fundamentally from that of his predecessors. From the very beginning when, in 1212, he confirmed the privileges which Philip of Swabia had granted to Otakar of Bohemia, making Bohemia a kingdom with little real feudal relationship to the empire, and, in 1214, when he ceded Nordalbingia to Valdemar of Denmark, a region over which Valdemar had extended his control in 1203, it is evident that he envisaged his German kingdom as a confederation of lay and ecclesiastical princes in the traditional manner. While these were arrangements with individual rulers, Frederick's agreement with the ecclesiastical princes, the *Privilegium in favorem principum ecclesiasticorum* of April 1220, was a generalised privilege, confirming rights that they already possessed. The eleven articles show the same cast of mind that Frederick had manifested in his dealings with Otakar and Valdemar. He abandoned claims to spolia; he granted safeguards to prelates who held minting and toll rights, in origin regalian but at various periods absorbed by the Church; he strengthened ecclesiastical jurisdiction over dependants who tried to escape to the cities; he issued guarantees against the depredations of lay advocates (once given to churches and monasteries by the monarchy for their protection and the administration of their estates but by the thirteenth century often seen as exploiters of church property); he conceded the right to dispose of fiefs fallen vacant either by confiscation or death; and he granted support to sentences of excommunication issued both by refusing excommunicates access to his courts and by imposing a sentence of outlawry upon persons not absolved within six weeks (Weiland 1896:2:86–91).

In September, Frederick left Germany for Rome where, on 22 November, he received the imperial crown from Honorius III. Within a few days he had returned to the Kingdom of Sicily where, after an eight-year absence, he set about the process of recovering lost royal rights. For the next five years the Sicilian kingdom became the centre of his attention, beginning with the issue of the Assizes of Capua in December 1220, which laid down that all privileges had to be given up for official verification, and continuing with the destruction of castles built since 1189, the abolition of the commercial privileges of outside maritime powers like the Genoese, and the forced resettlement of rebellious Muslims at Lucera.

The differences in his approach to the government of Germany and Sicily seem stark, but they remain compatible with the Hohenstaufen approach to their imperial inheritance. It was as evident to Frederick as it had been to his predecessors that he could not apply consistent methods of government throughout the varied imperial lands which he considered directly under his rule; indeed, for a traditional legalist like Frederick the differences between his rights in Germany and Sicily made this obvious. If Frederick seems to have been over-considerate to the great princes of Germany, then it was not only because of his natural interest in the south from which he came, but also because there were severe limits to what he could achieve, limits imposed both by the circumstances which already existed in 1212 and by the approach to government which had characterised past German kings. In comparison, the governmental structure of Sicily, created by the Norman rulers, offered far greater possibilities for a more centralised form of government, despite the losses which had occurred since 1197.

By the mid-1220s Frederick had re-established powerful monarchical rule in the south. Then at Easter 1226, he convened an imperial diet at Cremona. Since this city was the leading enemy of Milan, it now seemed as if he intended to enforce what he saw as imperial rights in the north. Certainly Milan and its allies saw it that way: in March the Lombard League was reformed. The accession of Gregory IX in 1227 set the pattern which endured for the rest of the reign, for neither the pope nor the majority of the Lombard cities could accept an imperial Italy any more than their predecessors could have done. Moreover, the conflict with the papacy was given additional edge by Frederick's approach to the crusade and to the reconquest of Jerusalem, where he pursued policies independently of a papacy which had always seen the crusade as a symbol of its own leadership of Christian society. Frederick's taking of the cross in 1215, his marriage to Isabella, daughter of John of Brienne, King of Jerusalem, and his crusading expedition of 1228–9, were all driven by the same ideological imperative, for no material advantage could be derived from them. In Frederick, the tradition of crusading, which had been established by his predecessors since the time of Conrad III, remained a powerful influence upon his view of the world. The crusade was indeed the occasion of an overt break with the papacy, leading to Frederick's excommunication when he was forced to turn back in 1227 and to his self-coronation in Jerusalem in 1228 while still excommunicate. Moreover, in 1229, Frederick was obliged to return from the east in order to drive out the papal troops which had invaded his Sicilian kingdom. Frederick's military strength pitted against Gregory's spiritual censures seem to have forced a compromise, embodied in the Treaty of San Germano/Celano of 1230, in which Frederick showed himself willing to concede papal powers over the Sicilian Church in return for the lifting of the excommunication.

The accord with the papacy was followed by the pursuit of his goals with a greater intensity than ever before. The differing patterns of government in Germany and Italy can be illustrated by a comparison between two documents from 1231: the *Constitutio in Favorem Principum* in May (issued by King Henry (VII), Frederick's son, and confirmed by Frederick the following year) and the *Liber Augustalis* (Constitutions of Melfi) in August. The documents have one common aim: they both show a powerful intention to prevent the growth of urban independence. But there is a fundamental difference too: whereas the *Constitutio* confirmed princely rights, especially in the face of royal officials, the *Liber Augustalis* reflects an intense desire to enforce the imperial will as the source of all political power. In the *Constitutio*, both ecclesiastical and secular princes in Germany were confirmed in an extensive range of juridical, monetary and commercial powers, which both codified previous practice and, at the same time, severely restricted their exercise by the imperial cities. The expansion of the cities, in some ways not dissimilar to the earlier growth of the Lombard communes, was restricted in order to ensure that the interests of the princes were not damaged: clauses two and four, for instance, forbade the creation of new markets to the detriment of existing ones and the diversion of ancient roads except at the wish of travellers. Most strikingly, though, the constitution was very restrictive where imperial intervention might have occurred: clause one, for instance, decreed that 'we should not build any new castle or city to the prejudice of the princes', while clause seventeen conceded that 'we will strike no new coinage in the land of any prince, which might damage that prince's coinage' (Weiland 1896:2:418–20). The *Liber Augustalis*, on the other hand, was the culmination of Frederick's legislative activity in the Kingdom of Sicily, which had begun with the Assizes of Capua. These constitutions were an attempt to impose a systematic and centralised system of administration and justice upon the kingdom. Thus title XXXI:

It was not without great forethought and well-considered planning that the *Quirites* (Roman citizens) conferred the *jus et imperium* for establishing law on the Roman *Princeps* by the *lex regia*. Thereby the source of justice might proceed from the same person from whom their defense proceeded, who was the ruler of the people by the power committed to him by the dignity of Caesarean fortune.

(Powell 1971:32–3)

The emperor therefore had no intention of allowing his plans in Italy to be disrupted by conflict in Germany; in 1232, at Aquileia, he obliged his son, Henry, to take oaths regarding his future conduct, for Henry seems to have been trying to build up his own party in Germany in a manner which Frederick saw as contrary to imperial authority. But the problem was not solved: in 1234 Henry went into open revolt and the next year made an agreement with the Lombard League as well. Frederick returned to Germany and at Worms in 1235 deposed Henry as king; Henry spent the last six years of his life in various places of captivity. When he committed suicide in 1242, Frederick portrayed the episode as the sacrifice of family for empire, unavoidable because of this higher calling. A few days after Henry's submission, Frederick had taken as his third wife, Isabella, sister of Henry III of England. This was a prelude to reconciliation with the Welfs, traditionally linked with the English crown, for Otto of Brunswick, nephew of Otto IV, received the fiefs of Lüneburg, Brunswick and other Welf lands, together with the title of duke. This was followed by the issue of the *Constitutio Pacis*, designed to enforce the peace of the land and to regulate and systematise criminal procedures (Weiland 1896:2:241–63). In 1235, at Mainz, Frederick came closest to the concept of empire exemplified by Frederick I, the imperial father dispensing justice and healing rifts within the Christian family.

But not all were equally enthusiastic members of that family; the war in Italy, signalled by the revival of the Lombard League in 1226, dragged on, sordid and enervating. None of the League cities attended Frederick's diet at Ravenna to which they had been summoned in 1231, and resistance continued even after the military successes of Frederick and his ally, Ezzelino III da Romano, ruler of Verona, in 1236 and 1237, which culminated in the imperial victory at Cortenuova. Moreover, Frederick's successes revived papal anxieties; the emperor did nothing to calm them by marrying his natural son, Enzo, to the heiress of Sardinia, an island claimed by the papacy as part of the Donation of Constantine. It was evident that the accord of 1230 could not endure and Gregory again excommunicated Frederick in 1239. The breakdown in relations was complete when, in May 1241, prelates sailing to a papal council in Rome were captured by Pisan ships and handed over to Frederick. Innocent IV was no more accommodating. In July 1245 he deposed Frederick at the Council of Lyon and the next year engineered the election of a new king, Henry Raspe of Thuringia, while in Italy a papal army stood ready to invade Frederick's lands after a plot to murder Frederick had been hatched at the imperial court itself. Meanwhile, the war in Italy ground on: imperial setbacks in 1248–9 were followed by fresh victories in 1250. There was no suggestion that Frederick's ambitions were diminished when, on 13 December, he died.

The reign and personality of Frederick II have impressed both contemporaries and historians more deeply than any other ruler of the period. The Franciscan, Fra Salimbene of Parma, was so affected by him that when he died, he records how for many days I could scarcely believe that he was dead, until I heard it with my own ears from the mouth of Pope Innocent IV when he preached to the people of Ferrara on his return from Lyon.... For I was a Joachimite and believed and expected and hoped that Frederick would do greater evil than he had done so far, although he had done a great deal.

(Scalia 1966:251)

By this he seems to have been equating Frederick with Antichrist, whose presence presaged the Messianic Age, a structure of history adhered to by followers of the writings of the Calabrian Abbot Joachim of Fiore (d. 1202). Salimbene's disappointment lay in the dashing of his prophetic hopes of the appearance of the new age. Matthew Paris was equally fascinated: to him belongs the famous passage, entered under the year 1238, in which he says that there were rumours that Frederick was wavering in the faith, that he was reported as saying the people had been seduced by three skilled and cunning impostors, namely Moses, Jesus and Mohammed, whose aim had been to gain domination over the world (Luard 1880:3:520–1). Modern historiography has been equally lively. In 1927 Ernst Kantorowicz (1957a) created a furore by his depiction of Frederick as, it was alleged, a hero-figure, set to dominate the world. While Kantorowicz's critics claim that he allowed an outward veneer of imperial ideology and propaganda to blind him to contemporary political realities, Frederick's admirers deplore the attempts to reduce a man they see as the wonder of his time to the mundane level of any other ruler, struggling for survival in the hard world of medieval politics (Abulafia 1977; Gillingham 1976).

Kantorowicz, suggests Karl Leyser, saw the emperor 'as he wished to be seen, through the preambles of his letters, his constitutions, his charters, his book on falconry and the iconology of his buildings' (Leyser 1982:270). These materials are indeed saturated with a consciousness of imperial destiny and cannot be dismissed as a mere manipulation of language invented to conceal Frederick's political objectives in Italy. Moreover, the image projected is not that of Matthew Paris's 'three impostors' passage, but one of defender of the faith against deviation, an objective carried through in practice as well as theory. Nevertheless, although legislation like the *Liber Augustalis* shows a belief in the imperial mission which characterises both the Salians and the Hohenstaufen in one form or another, it does not indicate a legislator of great originality or enlightenment. Indeed, his 'modernity' can be exaggerated. His belief in astrology was almost obsessive, while his devotion to the memory of his young relative, St Elizabeth of Hungary, who was canonised in 1235, suggests an addiction to the cult of saints and relics more intense than certain more cynical contemporaries suggested of him. There is no doubt that for nearly forty years Frederick was the dominating figure in the politics of the medieval west, exceptional both in the scope of his ambitions and in his extraordinary mental capacities. But there is no doubt too that he was rooted in the traditions of his time, in his ideology, in his laws, and in his personal beliefs. He was no new Messiah come to free the Christian world from the bonds of conflict, but a ruler who conceived of his rule as truly imperial, expending his life in an effort to make this a reality.

Between Frederick's death in 1250 and the accession of Henry of Luxembourg to the German throne in 1308 the popes succeeded in their most coveted political ambition, for during that time the King of Germany was prevented from effective intervention in Italy. Conrad IV died less than four years after his father, leaving a son, Conradin, only 2 years old, although Conrad's intervention in Apulia had already provoked

Innocent IV into excommunicating him in February 1254. His real successor in the south was Frederick's illegitimate son, Manfred, who, in 1258, seized on a rumour that Conradin was dead to have himself crowned King of Sicily. In Germany the electors disregarded Conradin, but could not agree among themselves: in 1257, upon the death of William of Holland (1247–56), they produced two candidates, Richard of Cornwall, brother of Henry III of England, and Alfonso X, King of Castile. In the midst of this proliferation of claimants there was little chance of a significant imperial revival. The popes, nevertheless, were determined to free Italy from the Hohenstaufen; between 1266 and 1268 the papal champion, Charles of Anjou, defeated and killed both Manfred and Conradin.

Richard of Cornwall was marginally the more credible of the two candidates who had been elected to the German throne in 1257 and he had been recognised by the papacy. But in 1272 he died and Pope Gregory X began to exert pressure on the electors to find a suitable replacement. Gregory's preferred candidate seems to have been Otakar of Bohemia, who had been extending his power into Silesia in the north and Austria and Styria to the south, but in 1273 the German electors chose a less powerful contender, Rudolf of Habsburg, a Swabian count with a solid landed base in Upper Alsace, in the Rhine and Aar valleys, and around Lake Lucerne. Although in many ways he can be seen as the political heir of the Hohenstaufen, the options available to Rudolf were much more limited. In the west he faced pressure from French expansion into the Low Countries and Lorraine; in the east Otakar of Bohemia refused to accept defeat in the struggle for the kingship. The encroachments of Philip III of France affected him less than the challenge of Otakar: the pronouncement at Speyer in December 1273, that all crown lands which had been illegally usurped were to be returned, was aimed primarily at Otakar. In 1276 Rudolf seized Austria and Styria from Otakar, and two years later killed him in battle, conferring the confiscated duchies upon his own sons in 1282.

The consolidation of this power, however, meant little to Rudolf without the establishment of hereditary succession and, to this end, he was prepared to conciliate both the French king and the papacy. Such plans ran quite contrary to the interests of the powerful ecclesiastical electors of the Rhineland, and at Frankfurt in 1291 Rudolf was not even able to persuade them to accept the succession of his son, Albert, as King of the Romans. Indeed, when Rudolf died in 1291, the electors chose another relatively minor noble, Adolf of Nassau. The aim was to secure a ruler who would resist French encroachment in the west, still more insistent since the accession of Philip IV in 1285. Adolf's alliance with Edward I of England in 1294 was made with this in mind. In fact Rudolf's policy proved to have been more realistic, for Philip IV was soon intriguing with the Habsburgs to bring about Adolf's removal. In 1298 the conspiracy came into the open: the electors deposed Adolf in June and, in the next month, he was killed in battle.

The crown now returned to the Habsburgs and Albert took up again the policy of his father. In a meeting with Philip IV in 1299 he ceded to the French the lands that they had acquired west of the Meuse. But hereditary plans needed papal support and here Albert found himself drawn into the quarrel between Boniface VIII and Philip IV. He could not please both of them: his alliance with the papacy in 1303 led to French links with Bohemia in an effort to undermine him, just as he and Philip had undermined his predecessor. Boniface's death in October 1303 effectively cut the ground from beneath Albert's feet. In the remaining years of his reign he concentrated upon building up family lands in Meissen and Egerland (1305) and in Moravia and Bohemia (1306), for there was little opportunity to cast his eyes towards the wider horizons of the emperorship. The contrast between the relative positions of Albert and Philip the Fair and those of Frederick Barbarossa and Louis VII a century and a half earlier in itself reveals the changes which had occurred in the political balance of the west.

Nevertheless, the medieval empire remained an integral part of the Christian structure. On 27 November 1308 the German electors chose Count Henry of Luxembourg, whose court was French-speaking, as the new King of the Romans. He had lands between the Moselle and the Meuse, but they were less extensive than those of the Habsburgs. Yet this apparently insignificant figure, who does not seem initially to have had ambitions for the throne, quite unexpectedly launched himself upon the first serious attempt to re-establish the empire since the death of Frederick II. When he died from malaria near Siena on 22 August 1313, he had established imperial vicars in many Lombard towns, including Milan; had been crowned emperor in Rome on Pope Clement V's instructions; had determinedly but unsuccessfully besieged Florence, leader of his opponents among the cities, for several months; and was en route to begin a campaign to dethrone the Angevin, King Robert I of Naples, who had backed the Florentines. Yet he had also encountered the perennial problems of northern invading armies in Italy: obstructionist city leagues, huge military costs, weary and disease-ridden troops. Although he seemed at first to have reconciled Lombardy to the new order, when he was in Genoa in the winter of 1311–12, there were serious revolts in Brescia and Cremona; when he marched from Pisa to Rome in May 1312, he found Angevin troops blocking the way to St Peter's; and when he besieged Florence during the winter of 1312–13 the combined diplomatic forces of the pope and the French and Angevin kings were conspiring against him. He died portrayed by his Florentine enemies as a Ghibelline tyrant of which Italy was well rid, yet another victim of the diseases of the peninsula, as were his queen and cousin before him.

Henry had begun with high aspirations. In 1309 he had even secured papal support in return for promises to respect the integrity of papal lands in Italy. He seems genuinely to have believed himself to be above the party strife of Guelph and Ghibelline (labels applied to the nominally anti-imperial and pro-imperial factions in the Italian cities since the 1240s) (Waley 1978: 15–26), but this was not how others saw him or wanted him to be seen. Consequently, it is difficult to see Henry VII as on the verge of success when he died. If the past experience of the Hohenstaufen, much more liberally endowed with time, money and troops, is any guide, then Henry was only at the beginning of a long-drawn-out series of wars from which he could never emerge as permanent victor. Henry's reign showed that the imperial idea was not dead and could indeed be revived in one of its more idealistic forms, despite the cynicism shown in many quarters and the progress of more compact political entities. As William Bowsky has shown, city rulers still found it worthwhile to take the title of imperial vicar, those condemned as rebels by Henry still struggled to have the stigma removed, and Florentine resistance could be co-ordinated only on the basis of Henry's 'injustices', which invalidated his claims to overlordship (Bowsky 1960:183). Even after the double election of October 1314, which brought forth Louis, Duke of Bavaria, as the Luxembourg choice, and Frederick, Duke of Austria, as candidate of the Habsburgs, Pope John XXII, elected in 1316, refused recognition to either of them, for he had no wish to see imperial plans in Italy revived. His fears were well grounded; the German rulers of the fourteenth and fifteenth centuries remained obsessed with the possibilities of empire.

9

The Kingdom of Sicily

Roger II, son of Count Roger I of Sicily, and grandson of Tancred of Hauteville-le-Guichard, a minor noble from the region of Coutances in Normandy, was crowned King of Sicily, Calabria and Apulia in a grandiose ceremony at Palermo on Christmas Day, 1130. This, according to Roger's diplomata, was not an innovation, but a restoration, for a monarchy had existed at Palermo in Antiquity (Houben 2002:50–7). Three months earlier Anacletus II, desperate for support in the schism which had developed after the disputed papal election in February, had granted the crown to Roger and his heirs in perpetuity, receiving from Roger the homage and fealty which previous popes had regarded as their legitimate right (Douglas 1976:45–7, 83–7).

The core of Roger II's power lay in the island of Sicily which his father had first attacked in 1060–1, when he had made an unsuccessful expedition against Messina. From 827 the island had been conquered by the Arabs who, during the next 150 years, had steadily colonised it. They did not, however, obliterate all the signs of previous Byzantine rule established there since the time of Justinian's reconquests in the 530s. The Normans made another attack in 1062 when Roger of Hauteville combined with his elder brother, Robert Guiscard, and they succeeded in gaining a base at Messina from which they began a piecemeal conquest of the northern parts of the island. The ruling Zirid dynasty, based in north Africa, had no real control over the warring Muslim emirs and, by exploitation of these circumstances, the Normans forced their way across the island, reaching Palermo in 1072. Ships and men freed by the capture of Bari, the last Byzantine city in Apulia, in the previous year, helped them to gain a city which, at this time was, with the outstanding exception of Constantinople, the largest city on the northern Mediterranean shore. Guiscard held on to Palermo for himself, together with half of Messina, while Roger did homage to him for the remainder of the island. Although Guiscard was clearly the senior partner, having already both defeated and allied with popes and driven the Byzantines from southern Italy, his death in 1085 left Roger as the main beneficiary, and led ultimately to the establishment of his progeny as kings of Sicily rather than those of his elder brother. In 1091 Roger took Noto, the last Muslim town which had resisted him (see Map 3).

Count Roger died in 1101, leaving sons who were still children and a regency under his tough and resourceful Italian wife, the Countess Adelaide (see Table 5). Roger II became his heir when his elder brother, Simon, died in 1105, and ruler in his own right

Map 3 The Kingdom of Sicily

when he was probably 16 years old in 1112. His independence was underlined when, in 1113, his mother arranged to marry King Baldwin I of Jerusalem. Baldwin I had no children and a condition of the marriage was that Roger should succeed to Jerusalem as well if the marriage produced no offspring. It did not, but the project turned sour in 1117 when Baldwin, under pressure from the Church, repudiated Adelaide on the grounds that his previous wife was still living. The affair poisoned relations between Sicily and Jerusalem for many decades, but it is significant in suggesting the scope of the ambitions of the Sicilian rulers, for Roger II realised very well the potential of his position. The expansion of trade between the Italian ports and the Levant, together with the growing Christian assertiveness seen in the crusading movement at both the eastern

Table 5 Rulers of Sicily

Robert Guiscard, of Hauteville	1059–85. Duke of Apulia
Roger I of Hauteville	1062–1101. Count of Sicily
Simon of Hauteville	1101–5. Count of Sicily and Calabria
Roger II of Hauteville	1105–54. Count of Sicily and Calabria. Crowned king 1130
William I of Hauteville	1154–66
William II of Hauteville	1166–89
Tancred of Hauteville	1189–94
William III of Hauteville	Feb.–Nov. 1194
Henry I (VI) of Hohenstaufen	1194–7
Frederick I (II) of Hohenstaufen	1197–1250
Conrad I (IV) of Hohenstaufen	1250–4
Conrad II of Hohenstaufen (Conradin)	1254–8. Deposed 1258
Manfred of Hohenstaufen	1258–66
Charles I of Anjou	1266–85. Deposed in Sicily 1282
Naples	
Charles II of Anjou	1285–1309
Robert I of Anjou	1309–43
Island of Sicily	
Peter I (III) of Aragon	1282–5
James I (II) of Aragon	1285–96. King 1290
Frederick II of Aragon	1296–1337

and the western ends of the Mediterranean, meant that Sicily occupied a key geographical position. Moreover, the proximity of a papacy which had inaugurated the crusades and was therefore itself deeply involved in the politics of the Mediterranean, had in the past been a distinct asset to the Normans, and was to prove to be so in the future, despite the vicissitudes of relationships with individual popes.

More immediately important to Roger was the south Italian mainland, ruled by Duke William of Apulia, who had succeeded Roger Borsa, Guiscard's son by his second marriage to a Lombard wife, in 1111. Guiscard had left no proper governmental institutions, nor had he solved the underlying political and social tensions within these lands. Neither Roger Borsa nor William had been able to suppress the resentments of other Normans settled in the south who, having been forced to accept Guiscard's supremacy, had reasserted their independence after 1085. Although Roger Borsa had established his authority in Salerno his rule had been strongly challenged in Apulia and Calabria. He had been particularly troubled by his half-brother, Bohemond, Guiscard's son by his first wife who, until his departure on crusade in 1096, was a fierce rival. Bohemond's revolts had indeed forced Roger Borsa to concede him a quasi-independent principality based on Taranto in the former Byzantine region of the east.

Guiscard's preference for Borsa seems to have derived from a desire to reconcile the Lombard population to Norman rule, but it had done nothing to curb Norman rivalries, nor had it satisfied the Lombards whose hatred of the Normans frequently manifested itself, especially through urban revolts. In these circumstances William had found it necessary to buy Roger II's help in 1122 by ceding him Calabria and, when William died in 1127, Roger claimed that he was his designated successor, despite the fact that Bohemond II, ruler of the crusader principality of Antioch, was actually a closer relative. William, in fact, does seem to have agreed to Roger's succession in 1125, but this had never been formally ratified, for it appears that William had made other, contradictory promises (Houben 2002:41–7).

From Calabria, Roger quickly extended his control over Apulia in the east and over the western ports of Salerno, Naples and Amalfi. Opposition, ineffectively co-ordinated by Pope Honorius II and led by Robert of Capua and Count Rainulf of Alife, failed to deter him, and in 1128 Honorius decided to accept him as ruler of Apulia and Calabria. Roger, who until then had been fairly liberal with concessions, especially to towns like Salerno, whose support he had bought, now asserted his overlordship. In September 1129 he held a great court at Melfi, where he extracted oaths of fealty to himself and his sons from the assembled vassals and issued a series of decrees aimed at enforcing ducal peace (Jamison 1987:238–43). Assertion was followed by action. Early in 1130 he set about gaining direct military control over the towns, beginning with Salerno. The coronation of 1130 therefore drew together what was, in essence, a new but as yet undeveloped political entity.

Roger's achievement is a truly striking example of social and political mobility. Small groups of Normans, mostly from the minor noble families of the Cotentin and western Normandy, which were the poorer parts of the duchy, had begun to appear in southern Italy as early as 999. By 1016 they had become actively involved in the complex politics of the region, in particular providing military help to a Lombard called Melo, in revolt against Byzantine rule. Driven by land hunger, by political rivalries in Normandy, and by the desire (and, indeed, in the eyes of the Church, need) for penitential pilgrimage, they found military employment in this divided world, although the sporadic rebellions made little headway against Byzantine rule until the local commander, George Maniaces, was killed while attempting to seize the imperial throne in 1043. By this time Byzantine government had entered upon a catastrophic decline under the feeble and warring successors of the Macedonian Emperor, Basil II, who had died in 1025, a decline which was not halted until the 1080s and 1090s. But by the late eleventh century it was too late for Byzantium, for the chance of effective rule in Italy had disappeared for ever in the interim, leaving the house of Hauteville as the predominant power.

Byzantine decline occurred at the same time as the rejuvenation of the papacy. Although initially the Norman presence had seemed a useful means of undermining the Byzantines, by the 1050s the papacy was beginning to see the Normans as a threat to its regional security. The consequence was Leo IX's disastrous foray against them which resulted in his defeat and capture at Civitate in 1053. Although when Leo died the next year he was still implacably opposed to the Normans, this confrontation emphasised that they had the military power which the papacy lacked, while the popes could provide them with respectability and standing. Indeed, the papal need for military support was demonstrated in 1058, when Richard of Aversa sent a large force to aid the reform party against the Roman nobility. This was recognised by Nicholas II who, in the Treaty of Melfi in 1059, came to an agreement with the two Normans who had emerged as the most important, Richard of Aversa, and Robert Guiscard, eldest survivor of the Hauteville clan. The papacy, abrogating to itself rights of questionable validity, granted Capua to Richard, and Apulia and Calabria to Robert, with the hope that, in the future, with the help of God and St Peter, Sicily would be added to this largesse as well.

Guiscard and Roger then set about making papal grants a reality. By 1067 they had overcome all the other Normans except for Richard of Aversa, and the next year they attacked Bari, which finally fell in 1071. In 1077 they took the equally important port of Salerno on the opposite coast. The extent to which Guiscard was rising in the world can be gauged from the fact that, in 1074, he could seriously contemplate a marriage link with the Byzantine imperial house which, although it presided over an empire which had come down in the world, nevertheless continued to regard itself as the highest expression of Christian organisation on earth. In that year, Guiscard's daughter was betrothed to a son of the Emperor Michael VII, but the deposition and death of Michael in 1078 put an end to this project in that form. Instead, Guiscard now used this as a pretext for an attack on the Empire itself, using an impostor whom he claimed was the Emperor Michael. From this time, Norman ambitions extended across both shores of the southern Adriatic as well as southwards to Sicily, and in 1081 Guiscard and his son Bohemond took Corfu and Durazzo. This policy was to leave an enduring legacy of rivalry between the rulers of southern Italy and the Byzantines which was to reappear constantly during the twelfth and thirteenth centuries, forming a strand which links Norman to Hohenstaufen and Hohenstaufen to Angevin.

Gregory VII, when he became pope in 1073, could not be blind to Norman ambitions, but he had no real alternative to the Norman alliance. In 1080, with Richard of Aversa dead and relations with the German Emperor, Henry IV, continuing to deteriorate, Gregory accepted the renewal of Guiscard's oath on the 1059 terms. This was the prelude to the infamous 'rescue' of the pope in 1084 when, following Henry IV's occupation of Rome, the Normans sacked the city and removed Gregory to Salerno. With the death of both Gregory and Robert Guiscard in 1085, leaving the mainland possessions of the Normans split between the rivalries of Roger Borsa and Bohemond, Count Roger emerged as the dominant figure, ultimately opening the way for his son's triumph in 1130.

Roger II's alliance with Anacletus II was a mixed blessing for his kingship. While it is quite possible that he really believed Anacletus to be pope, since he had a majority in the cardinals' college and enjoyed the support of many south Italian churchmen, it soon became clear that other Christian rulers, orchestrated by Bernard of Clairvaux, did not. During the 1130s Bernard mounted an intense propaganda campaign in favour of Innocent II, presenting Roger II as 'the tyrant of Sicily' against whom it was the Christian duty of all rulers to take action (Wieruszowski 1963). The exigencies of his position meant that Roger provided the raw material for this campaign, for resistance to his expansion onto the mainland was put down with great ferocity, largely by the Muslim mercenaries whom he employed. Moreover, Roger exhibited no public remorse for what could be presented as the oppression of Christians, and many were convinced that he was indeed a tyrant in the sense of a ruler who behaved without legal restraint. An index of the extent to which this idea had taken hold can be seen by its reflection in a comment of Orderic Vitalis who, writing perhaps shortly before 1141, commented on how Roger had 'flourished for many years in great prosperity, though he is stained with so many crimes that he ought by right, in my opinion, to expiate them with great sufferings' (Chibnall 1978:6:433). Deeper thinkers than Orderic presented Roger's rule within an historical context. Otto of Freising saw his rise in the following way.

> At that time, upon the death of Rainulf, Roger entered Apulia, then without a ruler, drove out Rainulf's brother [actually his cousin], the prince of Capua, and many other nobles, and regained possession both of Apulia and of Campania. He visited its inhabitants with many afflictions and oppresses them even to this day. He cruelly despoiled of its many ecclesiastical ornaments the monastery of the blessed Benedict, situated on Monte Cassino, an object of veneration to all the world. Report has it that in his first invasion, when he captured the city of Bari [actually Troia, 1139], he perpetrated a cruel and monstrous deed. When he had captured the city he not only persecuted the living with various kinds of torture but vented his fury even on the dead: he ordered the corpse of Duke Rainulf to be exhumed and to be dragged through the streets. These and other works of cruelty, patterned upon the deeds of the ancient Sicilian tyrants – acts told of him in uncountable numbers – we omit since they are [now] known to well nigh everyone.
>
> (Mierow 1966:432)

For some, political self-interest powerfully reinforced moral indignation, for Roger's successes impinged upon the claims of both the western and eastern emperors, Lothar III in Germany and John Comnenus in Constantinople. Both saw Italy as a former centre of imperial power which appertained to them, but of which they had been temporarily deprived. Moreover, the Venetians, strongly linked to Byzantium, could not view with equanimity the possibility that Roger II's navy might come to dominate the southern Adriatic and central Mediterranean. St Bernard therefore somewhat disingenuously encouraged German invasion of Italy, and in 1133 Lothar, accompanied by a small army and supported by the Norman 'rebels', Robert II of Capua and Rainulf of Alife, who had defeated Roger the year before, was crowned in the Lateran Church at Rome by Innocent II. Lothar, however, was beset by problems in Germany and it was not until the summer of 1136 that he was in a position to make a really serious attempt to overcome Roger. For the better part of a year he looked as if he might succeed. Roger was forced to retreat to Sicily and Innocent and Lothar granted Apulia to his chief opponent, Rainulf of Alife. But at this point a small but significant dispute disrupted the unusual harmony between the papal and imperial powers, for Lothar refused to allow Innocent to invest Rainulf with these lands. Eventually, they compromised and agreed to a joint investiture, but the incident illustrates Roger II's most important advantage, which was that his most formidable enemies were unable to unite against him for long. The fundamental conflict of interest between the two claimants to universalist power was always liable to reassert itself to the advantage of the kings of Sicily.

The alliance between Innocent and Lothar, although it restored Innocent to Rome, did not provide the pope with the material backing that he needed for more than a few months in 1137. When Lothar retreated in September, Innocent was left to defend himself from his own resources. At the Lateran Council of April 1139, he excommunicated Roger, and then gathered an army intended to put an end to the 'tyranny'. But Roger had been actively campaigning on the mainland since the autumn of 1137 and his forces crushed the papal army and captured the pope. The death of Anacletus in January 1138, therefore, was not the disaster for Roger that it might have been. By the terms of the Treaty of Mignano of 1139 Innocent was forced to concede to Roger his title and position. There were moments during the 1130s when Roger's conquests on the mainland hung by a thread, but with Mignano he was able to take another significant step towards the acceptance of his rule as the 'normal' state of affairs in southern Italy.

However, neither Innocent nor his immediate successors reconciled themselves to Roger's rule. Between 1140 and 1153, when Eugenius III died, the popes were reluctant to enter into more than temporary agreements, making truces for set periods rather than a proper peace. 'The crafty king of Sicily', as John of Salisbury later called him (Chibnall 1956:67), was therefore obliged to sustain continuous diplomatic activity, both by subsidising the Welf opponents of Lothar's successor, Conrad III, and by attempting to ally with the Byzantines. For a short time the calling of the Second Crusade took the pressure off him, for all his potential opponents were fully absorbed by its demands. Roger himself took the offensive, seizing Corfu from the Byzantines in 1147 and consolidating his hold on north Africa from a base established in Tripoli the previous year. The respite was brief for, although Roger was able to exploit the disasters of the crusade to convince some of its main supporters, notably the French monarchy and Bernard of Clairvaux, that Byzantine treachery had been responsible, Conrad III, returning west through Constantinople, formed an unlikely alliance with the Emperor Manuel against an opponent whom they both perceived as a usurper. Only Conrad's death in February 1152 saved Roger from a repeat of the crisis suffered during Lothar's invasion in 1136–7.

Seen from the outside these perceptions of the danger presented by Roger II were quite justified, for there is much evidence that his ambitions were vast in scope. His policy towards north Africa is a case in point. In 1127 he took Malta which, apart from being an important source of cotton, was also turned into a valuable naval base, from which he could attack Muslim pirates who disrupted the Mediterranean trade. Thereafter, Sicilian grain gave him an economic weapon by which he could extend his influence in the divided world of Zirid Tunisia, where the land was already torn by war and famine. Soon this was taken a stage further: he took Jerba (1135), Tripoli (1146) and Mahdiya (1148), while Tunis seems to have been controlled indirectly through a Muslim governor. There is no sign that he saw these conquests as a religious war; rather they served his political and economic interests. Taken in conjunction with his links with Fatimid Egypt they extended his range from eastern Algeria to the Levant and gave him control of many of the caravan routes along the coast and from the interior. Similarly, his brief alliance with Ramón Berenguer of Barcelona in 1128, in which he planned to send ships to help in the Valencian campaign, in return for which he would receive a share of the gains, and his later attacks on the Byzantine Empire, stemmed not from crusading ardour, but from a desire to expand his conquests (Abulafia 1985). No more than the Angevin Henry II, could he conceive of his lands as 'sufficient'.

Although Roger II's political position was never completely secure, the triumph of 1130 was not overturned. When he died in 1154 he was still King of Sicily and he was able to hand on the title to his son, William, whom he had had crowned in 1151, despite the opposition of Pope Eugenius III. The reasons for his survival and, indeed, prosperity do not lie simply in his diplomatic machinations and his Muslim mercenaries, for he displayed too a remarkable ability to adapt the diverse institutions of his polyglot lands into a coherent administrative structure which was at least the equal of any of his royal and princely contemporaries. It is significant that Otto of Freising, writing in the 1140s, continues his description of Roger's 'tyranny' by conceding that

> there are those who say he does these things in the interests of justice rather than of tyranny, and claim that he is more than all other rulers a lover of peace; and they assert that it is to preserve peace that he holds rebels in restraint with such severity.
>
> (Mierow 1966:432)

Roger's desire to enforce his rule is most evidently demonstrated by his legislative activity, seen in the Peace of Melfi of 1129 and the assizes which he promulgated during the 1140s. The essence of these enactments was the overriding need to establish the superiority of his justice, forcing vassals to swear fealty to him and his sons, punishing private warfare and the violation of his peace, in particular attacks on the non-noble classes, and reserving important criminal cases for first the ducal, and then, after 1130, the royal courts. The introduction of a new royal coinage at Ariano in 1140 emphasises these objectives, for control of minting was, in the twelfth century, seen much more as evidence of political authority than as a means of economic regulation. Under the supervision of his very able chief minister, the Admiral George of Antioch, who presided over Roger's administration from c.1126 until his death in 1151, Roger began to put in place an administrative machinery to enforce his laws. He regarded the island of Sicily and Calabria as the foundation of the kingdom, administering these regions directly from central institutions based at Palermo, a method facilitated by the relative weakness of the aristocracy of these regions. In the autumn, 1144, he reinforced his authority in these regions by ordering all his vassals to renew their privileges, a process which was costly for them both in the payments that must have been demanded and in the encroachments which such an inspection would have made possible for royal officials. Jeremy Johns estimates that about 120 privileges were renewed in a period of intense activity at the royal chancery in 1144 and 1145 (Johns 2002:115–18). However, in Apulia and Capua it was evidently necessary to create some form of provincial administration. In 1134 and 1135 he first introduced justiciars and chamberlains, following his defeat of a series of rebellions, while in the face of Lothar's invasion of 1136–7 he divided the lands into military districts, each with a constable at the head of the feudal levy of the region, centred on the most important local fortress or town. Originally Roger seems to have envisaged that his sons would act as overall governors of these mainland provinces, and indeed, they do start to appear in this role from 1137 onwards. However, by 1149 all of them except for his ultimate successor, William, had met early deaths, and there was no alternative but to revert to the use of officials like the chancellor, as he had done while his sons were still children. Recognition of the greater strength of the mainland nobility is, however, evident from the fact that the counts were not subordinated to these officials, for they continued to exercise jurisdiction over their own tenants provided that they recognised their ultimate loyalty to the crown; indeed, in some cases they themselves undertook such offices in the royal service (Jamison 1987: 252, 270–82).

This increasingly systematic organisation of administration was, however, geared to the achievement of his political aims, rather than to the economic well-being of his lands, for the survival and consolidation of Roger's rule was achieved only by immense expenditure, which in turn led to a policy of stifling fiscality. Most of the products of the island of Sicily, like wheat, salt, timber, fruit, tunny fish, dyestuffs, minerals and silk, were kept under royal control, sometimes in the form of monopolies. On the mainland potential economic centres, like Naples, Amalfi and Salerno on the west and Bari on the east, might have developed like their urban counterparts in central and northern Italy, but their independence was subordinated to Roger's system and their rebellions put down with a savagery and destructiveness which precluded the kind of capitalistic growth which typified Tuscany. Meanwhile, the Norman kings themselves made vast profits from the export of raw materials but, with the exception of silk, they apparently did not think in terms of promoting manufacture. Indeed, foreign merchants were encouraged to bring in finished products from outside. Although merchants like the Venetians and the Genoese were sometimes granted concessions, this operation too was a source of profit. On imports alone foreign merchants paid taxes on anchorage, on transportation from ship to shore and from market to city gate and out into the country, among other imposts. A good example of the king's outlook can be illustrated by the trade in wheat with Tunisia which was largely aimed at gaining supplies of gold from beyond the Sahara, gold which was eventually used for Roger II's coinage (Abulafia 1983). According to Otto of Freising, there were those who thought that this was the nub of his rule, claiming that in his love of money 'he has surpassed even all western kings' (Mierow 1966:432).

A similarly tight control was exercised over the Church, a control made all the more imperative given the lack of trust between Roger II and the popes of his era. This became particularly evident during the 1140s when Roger, well aware of the continuing precariousness of the kingdom, tried to develop further his military resources. One important measure taken in 1142 was the establishment of a much larger number of fiefs owing service directly to the crown. In order to maintain their value he forbade alienation to the Church, while at the same time attempting to extract military service from existing Church lands, especially in the Abruzzi region, which was often the first area to face attack from the north. In contrast to the eleventh century, when churches and monasteries had relied largely on a policy of self-help, they were gradually being brought within the crown's own military structure (Loud 1983). The power of the Norman kings over the Church has often been traced to the grant of 'legateship' made to his father, Count Roger I, and his heirs, in 1098 by Urban II. This grant appears to have restricted papal intervention in the ecclesiastical affairs of the island by channelling it through the count only, a restriction which left both ecclesiastical appointments and the enforcement of papal enactments in the count's hands. This circumscription of ecclesiastical power was not, however, peculiar to Sicily. All popes had to make a realistic assessment of the extent to which their influence could be exercised at any particular time and in any particular region; they were, at various periods, equally restricted in their relations with other countries, including Germany, England, Spain and Hungary (Ménager 1959:317–18).

John of Salisbury shows very clearly how the situation could vary with circumstances. First he describes the past as he sees it.

> For the king, after the fashion of tyrants, had reduced the church in his kingdom
> to slavery, and instead of allowing any freedom of election named in advance the
> candidate to be elected, so disposing of all ecclesiastical offices like palace

appointments.... As an added injury, the king would suffer no papal legate to enter his territory, except at his summons or with his express permission.

(Chibnall 1956:65–7)

John admits, nevertheless, that the effects on the Sicilian Church were not necessarily bad. 'It is true that in making appointments to churches he was held guiltless of open simony and took pride in presenting decent men wherever they might be found.' In these circumstances, in 1150 Eugenius III, under pressure from disturbances in Rome, and Roger, anxious to secure official sanction for his episcopacy, sought to compromise. Roger apparently agreed to free election to Sicilian benefices, reinforced by papal examination of those elected, and the pope reciprocated by approving most of the appointments which had been made. This kind of compromise was often made by the papacy in the twelfth century and, given the political circumstances, would have been likely irrespective of the matter of legatine authority.

Roger II's political success can be measured by the fact that by the mid-twelfth century his activities affected every power that had Mediterranean interests. Despite external enemies which, on occasion, threatened to develop into a coalition of almost the entire Christian world against him, he maintained the territories which he had won by 1130 and, indeed, even extended them across the very centre of the Mediterranean into north Africa. Moreover, despite the diversity of race and culture within these lands, he imposed an administrative system which both maintained royal justice and filled the royal coffers, while at the same time essentially leaving local institutions, languages and religious observances intact. But care must be taken not to overstate the case. Roger II acted in a way which was consistent with the establishment of his power in a given set of circumstances. This meant the imposition of his rule, sometimes by ruthless and bloody military terrorisation and the extraction of monetary resources regardless of the long-term economic effects. He was equally pragmatic in his administration, where his frequent use of Saracen eunuchs, whose offices were prominently placed in the royal palace, enabled him to distance himself from unpopular measures, while at the same time exploiting their skills. If, on occasion, this meant sacrificing them, as in the case of his former favourite, Philip of al-Mahdiya, who, in 1153, was executed on the grounds that he was a secret Muslim, there was nothing they could do about it (Johns 2002:215–19, 286–9). Alexander, Abbot of St Salvatore in Telese (near Benevento), describes Roger in very favourable terms, as might be expected of a chronicler commissioned for this purpose by Matilda, the king's sister, but he nevertheless makes it very clear that Roger was 'both in public and in private restrained in familiarity, affability and in mirth, so that he never ceased to be feared' (Houben 2002:177).

Roger's death did not change the political situation of his kingdom, for by 1155 William I too was faced with an array of his father's old enemies. Byzantine money made a significant contribution to a rebellion of his vassals which in turn helped Pope Adrian IV's attempt to restore Robert of Capua, while for the first time there was a revolt on the island of Sicily itself. Byzantine and papal troops began to carve up southern Italy. In north Africa the rise of the Almohades led to widespread defections from Norman rule and Tripoli was lost in 1154, followed by Mahdiya in 1160. William's reaction was much like his father's, pounding the rebels with considerable violence (including the blinding of Robert of Capua) and overcoming his external enemies in separate land and sea battles. For the third time the papacy was forced to come to terms.

In the Treaty of Benevento of 1156 William was confirmed in his titles and all the Hauteville conquests were finally recognised, while the pope was accepted as overlord. There was too a realistic recognition of mutual interests in ecclesiastical affairs, already presaged in the later years of the reign of Roger II. Adrian IV agreed (as Urban II had done) that papal legates could not enter the island of Sicily without a royal request, although this concession was not to apply to the mainland. In practice, however, the popes exercised this right on the mainland only four times between 1156 and 1189, which was itself a reflection of the fact that Roger II's successors generally protected the Church in the kingdom as well as restricting their direct interventions in appointments to the small number of sees that really mattered to them (Loud 1982). The culmination of the conflict coincided with a distinct cooling of relations between Fredrick Barbarossa and the papacy and when Alexander III was elected in 1159, William I was among his most solid supporters. Pope, Sicilian king and Lombard communes now saw all too clearly that the chief danger lay in the German invasions. In these circumstances the African provinces could not easily be retaken and William I never risked sending an army against a power as formidable as the Almohades.

However, although the revolts of 1155 had been put down, the reasons for internal discontent remained. George of Antioch had been replaced as admiral by Maio of Bari and the revolts had in part been a rejection of Maio's increasingly centralised and exclusive rule. Maio's introduction of the new posts of master captain and master chamberlain as overall governors of Apulia and Calabria between 1156 and 1158 is indicative of his approach, while the Catalogue of Barons, which was a new list of fief-holders and their military obligations to the crown, first compiled in 1150–2, must have facilitated a redistribution of fiefs after the rebellions of 1155. Although the baronage expected to play their part as advisers to the monarch, the increased professionalisation of the administration continued to diminish their role. In November 1160, Maio was assassinated and in the following year a revolt in Sicily led to the destruction of land registers presumably detailing obligations and fiscal burdens. Like the others, this revolt was overcome and William presided over a peaceful realm until his death in 1166. Nevertheless, the frequency of these expressions of discontent does reflect what many of his subjects saw as a repressive regime, the roots of which went back to the time of Count Roger. The anonymous contemporary author known as 'Hugo Falcandus', who was evidently an administrative insider, hated this style of government. His view, although laced with extreme personal abuse of Maio, whom he called a 'beast' and a 'repellent pest', nevertheless reflects a wider resentment of the kind of autocratic regime which he believed had been created. 'Maio excluded everyone else, and would confer with king alone each day; he alone dealt with the affairs of the realm, and turned the king's mind in whichever direction he pleased' (Loud and Wiedemann 1998:60). If Maio was indeed 'the true successor of Roger II' (Jamison 1987:260), then the willingness to revolt and conspire which characterises both the Norman-Sicilian baronage and the south Italian cities can be readily understood.

This underlying discontent, which is as central a theme of the history of the Norman-Sicilian kingdom as is that of the success of its kings in creating their new state, reasserted itself as soon as William died. His son, William II, was not of age and the regent, the Queen Mother, Margaret of Navarre, had little option but to conciliate the baronage and the cities. Political exiles were allowed to return and the tax imposed on the cities by William I was removed. In 1168 Stephen of Perche, Margaret's chancellor, was forced to relinquish his post and for a time the kingdom was ruled by a Council of Ten, although this was largely made up of bishops and administrative officials rather than nobles. When William came of age in 1171 he dismantled this apparatus, but he does seem to have held back from pushing Roger II's methods through to their logical conclusion in the manner of Maio of Bari, so that the incipient development of an absolutist regime, apparently favoured by his father, never came to fruition. Under William II there were no more omnipotent *amirati*, but, instead, a group of *familiares regis*, usually between three and five in number, who made up an inner council (Takayama 1993:123, 164).

Frederick Barbarossa's defeat at Legnano in 1176 and the Peace of Venice which followed the next year did much to secure William's position since, for the first time, the emperor recognised the Sicilian king. Of Sicily's outstanding opponents, only Byzantium remained an enemy, partly because William had been personally affronted by the failure of negotiations for his marriage to Maria, daughter of Manuel Comnenus, in 1172. William had his revenge in 1185 when he launched violent attacks on Durazzo and Thessalonica. Unlike his predecessors, he took an interest in the Crusader States, which had received no help from the Sicilian kingdom since Queen Adelaide's humiliation in 1117. His shipping had already attacked the Egyptian coast in 1169 and 1174 and it was William's fleet which saved Tripoli after Saladin's devastating campaign following the Christian defeat at Hattin in 1187. At the time of his death in 1189, William was planning to join the Third Crusade himself. William had accepted that there was little that he could do about the Almohades and he had made peace with them in 1180, but it seems that he was particularly worried by the possibility that the Aiyubids might extend their control further to the west.

During the 1170s and 1180s the kingdom probably came nearest to the picture sometimes painted of it as a flourishing, multicultural idyll. The Spanish Muslim pilgrim, Ibn Jubayr, landed there while sailing back from the east in 1185 and, despite his hostility to all things Christian, was deeply impressed.

> Their King, William, is admirable for his just conduct, and the use he makes of the industry of the Muslims.... He has much confidence in Muslims, relying on them for his affairs, and the most important matters, even the supervisor of his kitchen being a Muslim; and he keeps a band of black Muslim slaves commanded by a leader chosen from amongst them.... The King possesses splendid palaces and elegant gardens, particularly in the capital of his kingdom, al-Madinah [Palermo]. In Messina he has a palace, white like a dove, which overlooks the shore. He has about him a great number of youths and handmaidens, and no Christian King is more given up to the delights of the realm, or more comfort and luxury-loving. William is engrossed in the pleasures of his land, the arrangement of its laws, the laying down of procedure, the allocation of the functions of his chief officials, the enlargement of the splendour of the realm, and the display of his pomp, in a manner that resembles the Muslim kings.

Ibn Jubayr can think of no greater compliment than to describe the island as 'a daughter of Spain' (Broadhurst 1952:339–41). Even then tensions still existed below the surface, as increasing numbers of Latin Christian immigrants from the mainland began to settle on the island, leading to sporadic violence in communities which, half a century before, had been almost exclusively Muslim and Greek (Loud and Wiedemann 1998:12).

Such an exotic court appears, on the surface at least, to have owed more to the Greek and Arab presence than it did to the external influences of Latin and French culture, thus raising the question of the real nature of the regime created by the Normans in the south. The consequence has been a debate about the extent to which Byzantine and Muslim appearances are merely a superficial veneer upon a king, court and government which fundamentally differed little from northern society, the society from which Count Roger and Robert Guiscard had originally come. Historians have come to sharply different conclusions, producing a rich and complex historiography, but within the space available here, the polarisation of views can perhaps best be presented by examining the arguments of two notable contributors to the debate, Antonio Marongiù and Léon-Robert Ménager (Marongiù 1963–4; Ménager 1959). According to Marongiù, Roger II's monarchy was 'similar in kind and authority to the dignity and power of the ancient Romano-Byzantine emperors, a monarchy which knows no superiors, no institutional limitations and no concessions to its subjects'. In contrast Ménager claims that 'In the spheres of royal action, the Norman state of Italy did not apply any new solution. It continued again the most simple and logical of western traditions.'

Marongiù is particularly interested in the iconography of the Norman regime. Between 1143 and 1151 there was founded at Palermo by the Admiral George of Antioch, the Church of the Martorana. It contains the famous mosaic which shows Roger II being crowned by God, the iconography of which, in Marongiù's view, is close to that of a Byzantine coronation of the tenth century (see Plate 12). The king receives his crown directly from God and not through the Church, which is subordinate to the state; indeed, God is made manifest in the king by the facial resemblance between Christ and Roger in the mosaic (Kantorowicz 1957b:65). Roger himself wears the vestments of a Byzantine emperor, while his crown is a special type known as the *camelaucon*, the closed-in crown which, according to Marongiù, had, until this time, been exclusively connected with the Byzantine autocrator. The continuity of the image can be seen in a similar mosaic in the cathedral at Monreale, to the west of Palermo, built between 1174 and 1182. Here the walls are covered by about 8,000 square feet of Byzantine-style mosaic, including a version of the coronation of William II which incorporates the same iconographic details shown in Roger II's case.

This coronation included the singing of a special litany known as the *laudes*, which have been studied by Ernst Kantorowicz (1958). The *laudes* were an acclamation of the king which, by this period, had taken set forms in different monarchies. They began with the words *Christus vincit, Christus regnat, Christus imperat,* that is an invocation of Christ as victor, ruler and commander. Equally, then, through Christ, His royal vicars on earth conquer, rule and command the order of the present world, a world set out in all its hierarchy by the *laudes*. The formulary of the *laudes,* as chanted in the thirteenth-century Kingdom of Sicily, is closely modelled on that of the Gallo-Frankish lands, a point of little help to Marongiù's argument. However, the unique feature of the Sicilian *laudes* is the absence of any acclamation to any other human power, including the pope. The *laudes* of Palermo could therefore be seen as representing the king as absolute within his own kingdom, as an autocrator after the Byzantine fashion.

If the Sicilian king set out on his reign in a quasi-imperial fashion, then it might also be said that he ended it in the same tradition. A study by Elizabeth Hallam (1982a) shows that in the monarchies of England and France there was only a slow development of ceremonial around royal burials. The way that the corpse of Henry I was stripped and pillaged in 1135 is indicative of attitudes towards the dead king. In

Plate 12 Roger II of Sicily, dressed in imperial vestments, receives his crown directly from Christ and not through the mediation of the Church. However, the significance of the symbolism can be overemphasised, given the relatively small Greek community for which it was apparently designed. Church of the Martorana, Palermo, 1143–8. (Photograph reproduced by permission of Alinari.)

contrast, the German emperors were laid to rest at Speyer with lavish ceremonial and it does seem as if the Sicilian kings were anxious to adopt the imperial pattern. Hallam sees Roger II as a conscious rival to the Byzantine emperor, John Comnenus, who was buried in great splendour in 1143. Two years later, Roger II gave two porphyry sarcophagi to his own monastic foundation at Cefalù, to the east of Palermo, of which one was intended to hold his remains, the other to be in his memory. Monreale, with its elaborate setting and buildings, was similarly intended as 'a family pantheon' for the Sicilian kings when it was founded by William II.

To the artistic images and ceremonial stagecraft of the Sicilian kings, Marongiù would add their view of themselves as law-givers. He sees Roger II not only in the traditional role of the king whose function was to maintain justice, a role prescribed by the ecclesiastical theorists, but also as a king who set out actively to legislate. The affirmation of the supremacy of legislation is a sign of the king's supreme power, deriving from the authority given him by God. The claim to such authority was previously seen as the exclusive possession of the imperial majesty.

Ménager, on the other hand, is well aware of the famous mosaic portraits of Roger II and William II, but he does not believe that they bear much relation to the reality of kingship in twelfth-century Sicily. In practice the Sicilian rulers, even when they became kings, continued to take oaths of homage and fealty to the papacy, a process which can be traced from Robert Guiscard in 1059 to William II in 1188. This is a very different picture of the kings' relationship to ecclesiastical authority from that presented by the mosaics. Nor is the evidence of the *laudes* very decisive, for it dates from the period of Frederick II, by which time Ménager believes that the nature of the monarchy had radically changed. There is in fact no contemporary evidence of the twelfth-century *laudes* in Sicily, but the reality of papal overlordship would seem to contradict a projection of thirteenth-century practice back into Roger II's time.

The messages conveyed by the outward forms of crown, dress and court ceremonial are no more helpful: the *camelaucon*-style crown was used by parties as diverse as the pope and cardinals on the one hand and by the Lombard princes of Salerno of the late tenth century on the other; royal dress shows signs of Byzantine influence, but then that could be expected following the acquisition of the techniques of the Byzantine silk industry in 1147; and the ceremony of prostration before the ruler, so often associated with eastern absolutist regimes, can again be found earlier at the Lombard court of Salerno. Ménager concedes that the artistic representation and symbolism of twelfth-century Sicily is heavily influenced by Greek art, but suggests that this is because Roger had Greek and Arab advisers, while he himself had never been north of Monte Cassino. This does not mean that they reflect juridical reality. Indeed, even Kantorowicz's point about the facial resemblance between Christ and Roger in the mosaic may not be very relevant, since art historians like Kitzinger deny that a Byzantine artist would have used such a device. To have done so would have provoked deep-rooted conflict within Byzantium, as the iconoclast controversy, generated by fear of idol-worship, had shown in the past (Kitzinger 1976:320–6). For Ménager, therefore, the essence of Roger II's court is feudal, in that the king took a coronation oath of a Carolingian kind, and he issued charters and diplomas witnessed by Franco-Norman prelates and barons, just like his contemporaries in the north. He thinks that it is dangerous to analyse what he calls 'the exterior signs of royalty' in juridical terms, for there is a world of difference between the position of the Lombard princes of Salerno – for whom a case could be made that they had imperial pretensions based on external symbolism – and the emperors of Byzantium.

The fact is that the twelfth-century Kingdom of Sicily was a land full of paradoxes, since it was a centre for the intermingling of different religions and cultures. Architecture is a case in point: the evident Greek decoration seen at Monreale, the Martorana and Cefalù, can be balanced by the Church of San Giovanni degli Eremiti with its eastern dome, or by the Church of San Nicolà at Bari, which has been seen to resemble eleventh-century Norman romanesque. It may be, therefore, that both views are too heavily influenced by the tyranny, not of Roger II, but of historical 'constructs' (E.A.R. Brown 1974), such as 'Byzantine autocracy' and 'French feudal kingship', by which they measure a regime which, at base, seems primarily concerned to consolidate and extend its conquests by whatever means presented themselves. Evelyn Jamison's explanation of the nature of justiciars makes a good illustration, for the use of these officials suggests a knowledge of their existence under Henry I in the Anglo-Norman lands, but their actual functions were derived much more directly from the former Byzantine structure in Calabria (Jamison 1987:306). Equally striking is the introduction of the royal *diwan* on the island of Sicily in March, 1132, soon after Roger II's coronation at Christmas, 1130. This was a specialised office, established by George of Antioch, which issued documents in Arabic or Arabic and Greek. George, who had many links with Egypt, had apparently used a Fatimid model, itself the consequence of a reform in 1107–8. The office had a double advantage, serving both a practical purpose and helping the king to present an appropriate image to his Muslim subjects. The elaborate calligraphy of its documents made them instantly recognisable as royal artifacts in the same way as his coinage. As Jeremy Johns points out, these Sicilian kings were the only Mediterranean rulers in the twelfth century to rule on a trilingual basis, a situation which the creation of the *diwan* helped make possible (Johns 2002:257–300).

William II's reign brought peace to the Sicilian kingdom for the first time under the Normans, but the respite was short-lived, for he died without direct heirs. In Sicily and Calabria, a group of leading magnates engineered the coronation of Tancred of Lecce, the illegitimate son of William I's elder brother, Roger, Duke of Apulia, but perhaps indicative of the enduring unpopularity of the Hauteville monarchy on the Italian mainland, in Apulia the barons chose Roger of Andria. More threatening to Tancred was the evident determination of the Emperor Henry VI to make good the imperial claim to southern Italy and Sicily. The emperor's position was perhaps further strengthened by the fact that in 1186 he had married Constance, aunt of William II, which gave him a claim through the hereditary right of his wife. However, it seems unlikely that any of the parties concerned, except for Constance herself, saw the marriage in this light, for it is clear from the privileges issued by Henry in regard to the kingdom between 1191 and 1197 that he saw the region as a legitimate part of the empire since ancient times and not therefore dependent upon his marriage link with the Norman kings. Similarly, the papacy could not have approved of such a union on these grounds either, for the obvious reason that it regarded the Sicilian rulers as its own vassals, a claim accepted by the Normans, but never by the emperors (Clementi 1953–4:328–35). As for William II himself, he seems to have used the marriage as a means of consolidating his peace with Frederick Barbarossa, thus helping to ensure the continued stability of Italy, while he concentrated his attack upon Byzantium. The eventual conquest of Sicily by Henry in 1194 owes more to Henry's imperial ambitions than to any subtle German plan dependent upon the marriage to Constance.

Tancred was not greatly helped by the arrival of the armies of Richard I and Philip II, en route to the east, in September 1190. Although Richard should have been his natural ally, there was friction over Tancred's treatment of Joanna, Richard's sister and William II's widow, for Tancred had retained both her dowry and a legacy left by William II for the crusade. Although the issues were resolved, Richard's eventual alliance with Tancred was of no direct use in the face of the impending threat of Henry VI. His first attempt at invasion in 1191 had had to be abandoned, but by 1194 Henry was in a position to try again. Tancred died in February 1194, leaving his young son to succeed as William III. This was a thin defence against such a formidable power, and on Christmas Day Henry was crowned at Palermo, a success which underlines how fortunate previous Sicilian rulers had been in never having to face a sustained Hohenstaufen attack. The nature of the new regime was summed up in a deadpan passage by the English chronicler, Roger of Howden. After the coronation,

> the emperor caused the bodies of King Tancred, and his son, King Roger, to be dug up from the ground, and despoiled them of crowns and sceptres and other regalian ornaments, saying that they were not kings by law, but on the contrary were usurpers of the kingdom and perpetrators of violence... and he blinded and castrated King William, son of King Tancred.
>
> (Stubbs 1870:3:270)

Ménager does not, however, argue that his view of twelfth-century kingship holds good for the whole history of the Sicilian kingdom in the middle ages. He too sees distinct absolutist tendencies under Henry VI and Frederick II, since for him the Hohenstaufen represent the real imperial period, when there is seen 'the end of the juridical ethic linked to the traditional norms of the feudality'. If this was Henry VI's true intention he had little time to implement it, for in September 1197 he died. Nor had his new subjects been very amenable. A few months before, like his Norman predecessors, he was faced with widespread revolt in Sicily and, again like the Normans, he had put it down with great savagery. Noble independence, together with William II's divided political inheritance, had forced the kingdom into 'German' and 'Norman' camps, recreating once again the political instability which had characterised Norman Italy before 1166.

Henry left only the 3-year-old Frederick as his heir and he was promptly made a ward of the papacy by his mother Constance who, as a descendant of the Normans, saw this as a natural alternative to a German domination which she had come to hate. Constance herself died in November 1198, and Frederick spent his childhood in Sicily, vulnerable to sudden changes in the political climate about which he could do nothing. When he came of age in December 1208 he received from the pope the government of lands which had fallen into anarchy of a kind that Roger II and the two Williams had struggled for two generations to overcome. Symptomatic was the reappearance of urban independence which had been so violently crushed by Roger II, while the northern maritime cities seized the chance to enlarge their trading privileges in the key cities. In 1204 Genoa actually took over Syracuse (Powell 1962:439–51). There was little immediate possibility that Frederick could alter the situation, for his main goal between 1208 and 1212 was survival. In 1210 the kingdom nearly suffered an invasion from Otto of Brunswick, while Frederick's departure from Sicily in March 1212, in the hope of gaining a coronation in Germany, was a massive gamble which could easily have gone disastrously wrong. However, by this time Otto's star was waning; in July 1214 Bouvines came as the final blow. A year later Frederick was crowned again at Aachen by the papal legate, but it was not until he had completed over five years of intensive work in Germany, culminating in the great privilege to the ecclesiastical princes in 1220, that he was able to return to the south. Having received the imperial crown from Honorius III, in late November he re-entered the kingdom which was to become the subject of his most intense governmental supervision.

Almost immediately Frederick set about restoring rights on the Norman model, issuing a series of assizes at Capua in December 1220 which aimed at re-establishing the position of the monarchy as it had been in 1189. Central to these laws was the relationship of the crown to two key elements, the nobility and the towns. He used the old but effective method of demanding that all privileges be resigned and re-presented for examination. Any concessions which had been made since William II's death were withdrawn, including those made by Frederick himself in more desperate times. His aims can be identified with those of the Norman kings: acceptance of royal overlordship and the superiority of royal justice; suppression of adulterine castles and the prohibition of private warfare; and the subordination of the towns to royal officials, eliminating any incipient signs of self-government in the form of consuls or *podestà*. Frederick, however, differed from the Normans in the extent to which he intended to develop this control. Some, as Otto of Freising had reported, had thought Roger II chiefly motivated by the love of money, but Frederick's wider plans in the Italian peninsula as a whole were to consume resources on a scale never dreamed of by the Normans. Driven by the double spur of ideology and financial need, at Capua Frederick began a process which was to turn the Kingdom of Sicily into the most tightly regulated monarchy of the thirteenth century.

For Frederick, therefore, the Capuan assizes represented no more than a much needed repair. In 1231 the *Liber Augustalis* or the Constitutions of Melfi, in their detailed regulation of almost all aspects of life under the monarch, set down Frederick's concept of government in a far more refined form than ever before. He began from the position taken by Roger II, itself taken from Justinian's *Codex*. 'No one should dispute about the judgment, plans, and undertakings of the king.' To do so 'is comparable to sacrilege'. Central to that judgement was that a general peace should be established within the kingdom and that grievances should be pursued not by means of private warfare and vengeance, nor through self-governing communes, but through the courts and officials provided by the king, since although the king could not always attend personally, 'we... believe that we are potentially present everywhere'. Within this structure the nobility continued to enjoy their right to be judged by their peers 'so that due honour may be completely preserved for each and every noble of our kingdom', while ecclesiastical dignitaries were permitted a considerable degree of independence from royal officials, provided that they did not violate the king's overall authority.

Acceptance of the king's juridical position, however, was not enough in itself, for Frederick's imperial ambitions involved him in wars in northern Italy which became increasingly expensive to maintain. The most detailed control of all, shown both in the *Liber Augustalis* and in later enactments was applied to the kingdom's economy, for Frederick needed to extract the maximum possible in taxation. According to the *Liber Augustalis*, a sufficient number of officials had been established to enable everyone to obtain justice and therefore attempts by the towns to create their own system of officials, in whatever form, could be interpreted only as treason, punishable by death. Usury was declared illicit, with the prominent exception of the Jews. Regulation of the crafts, elsewhere commonly incorporated in urban statutes, was included in the *Liber Augustalis*, as the ruler's responsibility (Powell 1971:11, 21, 46, 12–13). Control gave access to taxation. Extraordinary taxes like the *collecta*, used sparingly by the Normans, became quite regular by the late 1230s; monopolies over iron, pitch, hemp and dyeing, among other products, were developed into a system far more complete than that of Roger II; manufactured goods and raw materials were heavily taxed both at source and through port dues if they were exported. Even this was not enough; foreign loans had to be raised, something to which the Norman kings had not resorted. Despite the ban on usury, Frederick's own constitution permitted the Jews to make loans at 10 per cent, while penalty clauses in contracts that Frederick made with Roman and Sienese bankers show that he himself paid interest on external loans. As the scope of his wars in Lombardy increased, loans seem to have been raised in anticipation of taxation (Powell 1962:478, 482).

The long-term effect was the perpetuation of a society in which the nobility, although subordinate to the monarchy, remained powerful landlords, but had little interest or opportunity for economic enterprise of the kind seen in the north. The tendency seen under the Normans towards the creation of an economy based on the export of raw materials, especially foodstuffs, but with little development of finished products or financial services, was therefore exacerbated. Native merchants found themselves in a weak competitive position in the wider world, since privileges in foreign ports were difficult to obtain without active monarchical support. In contrast, the merchants of Marseille, Venice, Genoa and, above all, Pisa, could often gain exemptions in Sicilian ports, at least when political circumstances persuaded Frederick of the necessity of granting them. Monetary reform did nothing to alleviate this; Frederick's issue of the gold *augustales* in 1232 seems to have been more concerned with the promotion of his own imperial image than with the practical needs of commerce (Powell 1962:491–513). Norman and Hohenstaufen rule hampered the development of cities like Palermo, Messina, Naples and Amalfi, turning them into monetary conduits within the royal demesne, disgorging taxation for Italian wars.

In July 1220, while manoeuvring for a papal coronation, Frederick II had written to Honorius III to explain that any idea that he was aiming to unite the Kingdoms of Germany and Sicily was quite unfounded, for such a thing would not be fitting (Huillard-Bréholles 1852:804). Subsequent events had proved to the papacy's satisfaction that this was an empty promise and explain why the papacy searched so determinedly for a client king for Sicily after Frederick's death in 1250. After the disappointments associated with Richard of Cornwall and Edmund of England, the banner was finally taken up by Charles of Anjou, younger brother of Louis IX of France. The early death of Frederick's successor, Conrad IV, in 1254, and Charles's victories at Benevento in 1266, in which Frederick's illegitimate son, Manfred, was killed, and at Tagliacozzo in 1268, which was followed by the execution of Conradin, Frederick's grandson, ensured that the papal plan could actually be implemented.

The Kingdom of Sicily was therefore once again the subject of outside conquest, for its key position in proximity to Rome and in the central Mediterranean as a whole inevitably made it a fulcrum of the politics of the high middle ages. Reaction to this new invader was not favourable and, repeating a pattern so often seen before, revolt broke out even before Charles had secured his position. Stirred up by partisans of Conradin, by late April 1267 all of the island of Sicily, with the exception of the great cities of Messina and Palermo, was in rebellion. Discontent spread to Calabria and even as far north as Lucera, where the Muslim colony was joined by Christian opponents of Charles on the mainland. However, Charles's victory at Tagliacozzo isolated the rebels and by the end of 1269 he had forced capitulation both at Lucera and on the island. Savage repression followed, with many deaths.

If, in these respects, the new regime resembled those that had gone before, so too did the governmental structure erected by Charles. In the past, Normans and Germans had imposed themselves as a new ruling class. Under Charles the great majority of the fief-holders and officials were drawn from his other lands in Anjou, Maine and, most of all, Provence. Fiefs were made available because of confiscations and flights following the defeat of the Sicilian revolt in 1269, while in the following year Charles declared that grants of land made by Manfred, Conrad or Frederick after 1245 (when he had been deposed by Innocent IV) were invalid. All other fief-holders had to produce their titles to be verified and confirmed, just as their predecessors had done before Frederick II in 1220. One innovation, however, was that any fief-holder who absented himself from the kingdom for more than a year automatically lost his fief, a neat method of confiscating the lands of political exiles who had left in the face of Charles's victories.

The establishment of a French upper class was accompanied by an equally thorough takeover of the administration of the kingdom. There was no great institutional change, especially in the system of administering the two key areas of justice and finance. The central administration which, despite Charles's peripatetic lifestyle, tended to settle at Naples, was theoretically placed under seven main officials whose functional roles were clearly marked, but in practice the grand justiciar and the grand admiral emerged as the dominant officers. At regional level the division of the land into eleven provinces, each with a salaried justiciar, again resembled the structure employed by previous regimes. In 1277 it was determined that French should be the language used in treasury accounts and in mandates to officials, but this did not fundamentally change the nature of an administration largely taken over from the Normans and the Hohenstaufen.

Although Charles did not bring any great innovation to the government of the *Regno*, he did apply a characteristic meticulousness and attention to detail to its actual operation. For those of his subjects exposed to criminal attack this was a laudable quality, but for the far greater number severely affected by what they came to see as his financial oppression, it was a source of deep resentment. In many ways Charles's government represents the culmination of the fiscal system established and refined by first the Normans and then Frederick II. The characteristics which had ground money from the *Regno* in the past were now exacerbated by Charles's efficiency and political ambition. The *subventio generalis* which Frederick II had turned from a feudal aid into a regular tax, the *collecta*, was maintained, despite being lifted by a repentant Frederick on his death-bed and despite Charles's promises not to reimpose it. The huge burden of indirect taxation, especially in the form of customs, harbour and warehousing dues, and duties on both raw materials and finished products, was maintained as before, its effects sometimes worsened by the abuses of officials, who held rights to collect this taxation as a farm. The economic consequences were similar to those seen under Frederick II, for native merchants had little opportunity to expand their activities. Indeed, Charles's need for money led to the continued encouragement of outside financiers, although through the great Florentine firms rather than the Pisans who had been favoured by Frederick II. By 1270 Charles's influence in Tuscany at the head of a Guelph League in which Florence was the most prominent city was secure. The Florentines provided loans in return for control of a large part of the profitable grain trade of Apulia and Sicily, a pattern which emphasised the trends of the past, making the *Regno* a land producing large quantities of valuable raw materials, but little in the way of its own manufactures (Abulafia 1981).

Charles's relentless financial pressure arose from the wider ambitions that had so often gripped the rulers of Sicily. His interest centred on Byzantium, where Constantinople had been repossessed by the Greeks under Michael Palaeologus in 1261, and from as early as 1267, when he formed a very favourable alliance with the exiled Latin Emperor Baldwin II, he began assembling resources. In 1271 the marriage arranged between his daughter, Beatrice, and Philip, Baldwin's son, took place. But Charles was to be continually frustrated in his plans, first by Conradin's invasion in 1267–8, then by the need to aid his brother, Louis IX, on the crusade to Tunis in 1270 and, most importantly, throughout most of the 1270s by the determined efforts of Michael Palaeologus to neutralise him by gaining papal support. Byzantine agreement to Church union at the Council of Lyon in 1274 made a direct attack by Charles impractical at that time. Meanwhile, Charles was always looking for an opportunity to extend his influence in the Mediterranean, especially by involvement in the complicated politics of the Latin and Greek states of the Balkans and Greece. The Tunisian crusade also revived interests of past Sicilian rulers for, although the expedition brought only suffering and death to his brother, Charles emerged with an advantageous ten-year treaty with the Tunisian ruler. Moreover, in 1277 he bought a claim to the crown of Jerusalem, reflecting an interest in the Crusader States which he had been pursuing for some years before this. All these activities were extremely expensive. Despite the loss of the greater part of the Angevin archives, there is still ample evidence to show that Charles sent a steady stream of aid to his clients and allies in the eastern Mediterranean, exporting large quantities of arms, horses, clothing and food supplies, as well as direct subsidies. A fourteenth-century Greek chronicler, Nicephorus Gregoras, aptly summed up Charles of Anjou as a man who dreamt of restoring the monarchy of Julius Caesar and Augustus and who had the strength and ability to turn thought into deed in a manner far superior to his predecessors (Migne 1865:259–62).

However, while he pursued these far-reaching schemes Charles seems to have taken the island of Sicily for granted. The island had been the centre of government under the Normans, but under Charles the core of the monarchy was seen as the mainland with the seat of the treasury at Naples. Sicily itself was useful for its additional revenues, its grain supplies, and the deep-water facilities at the port of Messina, where shipping could be assembled for the assault on Byzantium. It was, nevertheless, Sicily's latent discontents that provided a lever for Charles's enemies, notably Michael Palaeologus and Peter of Aragon who, as the husband of Constance, Manfred's daughter, was the focus of discontented Hohenstaufen exiles. The extent to which there was a widespread conspiracy to unseat Charles remains a matter of dispute, but it seems clear that these exiles maintained contacts with Constantinople.

In fact, the rising which is known as the Sicilian Vespers, which began in Palermo on Easter Monday, 30 March 1282, seems initially to have been a spontaneous popular outbreak concentrated upon dislike of the French who, both in their personal behaviour and in the conduct of their public functions, paid little regard to the susceptibilities of the populace. The spread of the revolt and its sustenance in the days that followed, however, was perhaps the consequence of a more organised response, leading to the establishment of communes at Palermo and, a month later, in the key port of Messina. Even so, this does not fully uncover the layers of discontent, for many

Sicilian barons had been adversely affected by the presence of Angevin fief-holders, and they too soon found it in their interest to sustain and, to some extent, manipulate the revolt. Given the frequency of uprisings on both the mainland and the island, it can be seen why at first it did not appear to be any different from those of the past, all of which had been repressed with varying degrees of difficulty. Charles set about preparations to end it, but his counter-attacks in August and September failed in their immediate objectives and when he learned that Peter of Aragon had landed at Trapani at the end of August he realised that he was facing a long struggle. Moreover, the loss of Sicilian grain supplies did not make his task any easier, since they were important in enabling him to obtain Florentine loans which financed his war effort. Nevertheless, he did have the consistent support of the pro-French pope, Martin IV, and he did mobilise resources from Provence as well as Apulia, but still failed to retake the island. Indeed, he died in January 1285 in the bitter knowledge that his naval expedition of the previous year had been defeated by Admiral Roger of Lauria, and his son and heir, Charles of Salerno, taken captive.

The division of the *Regno* between the Angevins and the Aragonese created circumstances which kept the emissaries of half a dozen courts busy for the next twenty years, as well as giving further stimulus to the market for mercenaries, since from the Vespers in 1282 until the settlement agreed at Caltabellotta in 1302 the striving of the interested parties to mould a recalcitrant world to their will drove forward a complex series of military manoeuvres and diplomatic initiatives. At the heart of the problem was a papacy which, since the time of Robert Guiscard, regarded the disposal of southern Italy and Sicily as very much its own concern and, consequently, was deeply reluctant to accept the permanence of the Aragonese occupation. This papal attitude led to the disaster of Philip III's crusade against Aragon in 1285 and to the continuing promotion of the cause of Charles II after he had obtained his release in 1288. The Papal-Angevin cause was strengthened by divisions within the Aragonese royal house, for when Peter III died in 1285 he left Aragon to his first son, Alfonso, and Sicily to his second son, James, and when James succeeded Alfonso in Aragon in 1291, he left his younger brother, Frederick, as his representative in Sicily. Thereafter, there was always the possibility that Frederick could be isolated, for King James might be tempted by appropriate offers from the Angevins. This seemed to have been achieved in June 1295 when James agreed to give up Sicily in return for a marriage alliance with the Angevins and compensation in the form of the island of Sardinia. Frederick was to marry Catherine of Courtenay, titular heiress to Constantinople, and would be free to pursue continuing Latin claims to the city. In the end, like so many initiatives of this period, this carefully constructed edifice fell apart, for it had little connection with reality. Frederick did not marry Catherine; instead, he was crowned King of Sicily at Palermo in December 1295. Despite the number of opponents that this created, there was little coherence in their attacks, and finally Charles had to settle for peace.

The Treaty of Caltabellotta of August 1302 accepted Frederick as King of Sicily during his lifetime – although Boniface VIII maintained that he could be called only King of Trinacria – and a marriage alliance was to be made with the Angevins. The treaty did not solve the problem in that in the long term neither side acted as if they intended it to be permanent. Frederick set up his son as his heir in 1314 and had him crowned co-ruler in 1328; King Robert, who succeeded Charles II in 1309, restarted campaigns against the island, making five major attacks between 1314 and 1342. The fact was that the peace of 1302 was more a result of external events, in particular

Boniface VIII's preoccupation with Philip IV of France and Charles II's pursuit of a claim which his dynasty had to the Hungarian throne.

The effect on the south itself, however, was to exacerbate already existing tendencies. Charles continued the fiscal policies of his father, raising huge sums in taxation and through monopolies, as well as continuing to encourage outside bankers and merchants such as the Florentines, in return for access to Apulian raw materials like grain and oil. On the island the change of regime, as might be expected, altered the pattern of government relatively little, for the Aragonese continued to need the *collecta*, while Catalan merchants replaced Florentines in the exploitation of the grain trade. In their turn some of the Sicilian barons grew discontented as the number of Spanish fief-holders on the island grew, but in general the nobility benefited from the change, since Frederick could not survive without baronial support. The coronation of 1295 had been accompanied by a promise to hold annual parliaments, which could give or withhold consent to warfare and taxation. The two kingdoms which emerged in the early fourteenth century may have been political and economic rivals, but they shared certain common characteristics: monarchical rule based upon a powerful baronage which drew its strength from its jurisdictional and economic powers over large rural estates, and which faced relatively weak competition from native mercantile and urban interests.

10

The Italian city-states

In his letter of 1157 describing the first five years of his reign, Frederick Barbarossa had laid great stress on the results of his intervention in Lombardy, which he presented as a rebellious land now restored to its proper position of imperial subordination. But in fact the letter represented wish rather than reality, and his continuing attempts to reshape the Italian political structure into the imperial mould became a major preoccupation of his reign. In taking on the Italian cities, Frederick had come up against one of the most dynamic forces of twelfth-century Christendom, that of the communal movement which, far more than anywhere else, manifested itself in Lombardy and Tuscany.

Cities had been important in Roman Italy, but their administrative and cultural continuity had been broken in the late sixth century by the invasion of the Lombards who, unlike their Gothic predecessors, had little sympathy with or interest in the Roman way of life. Although eventually the Lombards and, from the late eighth century, the Carolingians, had restored a degree of political coherence, especially in the north and the centre, it had not been firmly based. The late Carolingian Empire had no administrative means of controlling its representatives in Italy or indeed, anywhere else, so that the counts and viscounts soon entrenched themselves as local seigneurs in the areas where they supposedly exercised delegated authority. By the early tenth century no discernible unified political structure existed and it is not surprising to find that the Magyars were able to penetrate deeply into Lombardy even though they were unable to overcome walled settlements. Important changes can be discerned from the second half of the tenth century when the Ottonians tried to use the bishops, over whose appointments they exercised considerable control, as a means of governing, and in so doing created the nearest approximation to a political 'system' in Italy since Charlemagne's time. These bishops tended to equate the diocese with the counties into which the old imperial marquisates had been divided in the past and by the mid-eleventh century most of them were claiming a quasi-comital authority. Moreover, although the Italian peninsula had been as disrupted as anywhere else in the period between the sixth and the ninth centuries, it had been so profoundly shaped by the Roman past that even this prolonged upheaval could not erase it. Both the concept and the reality of the *civitas* had survived in a manner quite unique in the west, which meant that the general demographic upsurge had its most immediate effects in the peninsula

(P. Jones 1997:73–92). Nevertheless, the picture remained confused, for there were many secular lords, powerful on a local or even regional scale, who could rival the bishops or who held specific jurisdictions within the cities, while at the same time the quickening tempo of economic life had begun to stimulate agriculture and reinvigorate the cities and towns, encouraging the gradual appearance of 'a middle class', whose position was founded upon newly created wealth.

The communes emerged from these circumstances, but their origins are generally obscure. It is clear that they were sworn associations of men seeking to establish their power and that their activities can be discerned in both large cities and quite small communities. Membership was probably a mixture of descendants from older comital families and newer men who had begun to benefit from economic growth and who were themselves promoters of that growth. The participation of members of the rural nobility is evident, attracted by the increasing range of economic and political opportunities available in the cities at a time when a high birth-rate appears to have been exercising pressure on their traditional landed resources. These associations sometimes presented themselves as representatives of the 'people', seeking to connect themselves with more traditional civic assemblies, but they were not in origin public bodies as such. In some cases confrontations with the bishops followed; in others the bishops were absorbed, helping to give a veneer of legitimacy and a focus of loyalty.

The greatest opportunities for these embryonic city-states occurred from the middle of the eleventh century onwards as the struggle between empire and papacy intensified. Reform agitation frequently shook the foundations of episcopal rule in Lombardy, Emilia and Tuscany on which the emperor relied, and he soon found it convenient to buy support with juridical concessions to the leading men of certain cities, concessions which in turn formed the basis of Tuscan city-republics like Pisa and Lucca (see Map 4). The appearance of a ruling consulate followed soon after. Between *c*.1085 and 1125 there is evidence of the existence of a consulate in Pisa, Biandrate, Asti, Milan, Arezzo, Genoa, Pistoia, Cremona, Lucca, Bergamo, Bologna and Siena, and it is probable that Piacenza, Mantua, Modena, Verona, Florence and Parma can be added to this list (Waley 1978:27).

However, the accession of Frederick Barbarossa in 1152 brought to the imperial throne a ruler determined to regain what he regarded as lost imperial rights and inaugurated a century of political struggle, the effect of which were felt long after the death of Frederick II in 1250. The campaign of 1154 demonstrates the issues at stake: 'For it is an old custom,' says Otto of Freising,

> maintained from the time that the Roman empire passed over to the Franks even down to our own day, that as often as the kings have decided to enter Italy they send ahead certain qualified men of their retinue to go about among the individual cities and towns to demand what pertains to the royal treasury and is called by the natives *fodrum*.... Likewise, another right is said to have found its source in ancient custom. When the prince enters Italy all dignities and magistracies must be vacated and everything administered by his nod, in accordance with legal decrees and the judgment of those versed in the law. The judges are said also to accord him so great authority over the land that they think it just to supply for the use of the king as much as he needs from all that the land customarily produces that is essential for his use and may be of advantage to the army, only excepting the cattle and the seed devoted to the cultivation of the soil.
>
> (Mierow 1955:129)

Map 4 The Italian city-states

Milan was the city which most blatantly contradicted this view of world. As early as 979 there had been an anti-episcopal rising and by the 1090s communal rule had been clearly established. As a consequence, Otto claimed, it was 'elated by prosperity' and 'puffed up to such audacious exaltation that [it]... recently even dared incur the anger of the prince, standing in no awe of his majesty' (Mierow 1955:129).

The detailed provisions of the decrees of Roncaglia of November 1158, after Milan had been defeated, show the nature of the regalian rights which Frederick believed had been usurped. Four distinguished Roman lawyers from Bologna were employed to draw up a list. They were very thorough, setting out that the emperor was entitled to military service; had authority over all roads and navigable waterways; held rights over ports, tolls, minting, fines, vacant fiefs, and confiscated property; was entitled to *corvées* of cartage and furnishing of boats, and to extraordinary taxation for royal expeditions; had the right to establish magistrates and to build palaces in certain cities; controlled mines, fisheries and salt-pans; was entitled to the property of those condemned for *lèse-majesté*; and to all or half of any treasure discovered in these lands or on church property, depending on the circumstances. Moreover, the Lombards were obliged to pay annually both a head and a property tax which, in theory at least, would have provided massive returns (Arnold 1997:168). Having established that these powers stemmed from the emperor, Frederick was then prepared to regrant them to those who could furnish proof of their rights, a concession of benefit particularly to ecclesiastical institutions, but of much less value to the towns and cities whose power had developed piecemeal and indeed had sometimes been seized from the bishops. Frederick's conception of his position in relation to the cities was further emphasised by his prohibition of private wars – in keeping with his view of the function of the lower orders in his *Landfriede* – and by the edict which set down the need to obtain the permission of the overlord before fiefs could be alienated or partitioned. All males between 18 and 70 had to swear to maintain the peace (Appelt 1979:10(2):27–9, 32–6). The sense that the past was being restored was emphasised by the transfer of the coronation seat from Milan to Monza.

Not surprisingly, Milan thereafter was in the forefront of Lombard opposition to the Hohenstaufen, for it was prime mover in the formation of the Lombard League in 1167 and in its revival in 1226 when a new threat arose from Frederick II. In Tuscany the cities were slower to organise themselves, but they too formed an alliance in 1198, the year after the death of Henry VI. In the end, after the defeat at Legnano in 1176, Frederick Barbarossa had been obliged to come to terms. By the Peace of Constance in 1183 he accepted that the cities had the right to elect their own consuls, that they could build fortifications, and that they could enjoy the customs of the past, although Frederick was still sufficiently formidable to ensure that they paid heavily for these powers and that they recognised that the exercise of them was under the overall umbrella of imperial jurisdiction.

Frederick II's hostility to civic independence was even more intense than that of his grandfather, for in him the imperialist view was reinforced by the inheritance of Norman administration in Sicily where the cities had been 'forced back into the position of demesne towns' (Jamison 1987:235). The cities of the north and centre resisted Frederick so determinedly because they knew well what to expect from observation of his government in Sicily where, between 1220 and 1225, all resistance was crushed and royal rights lost during the interregnum after 1197 were re-established. His view of communes, as expressed in the *Liber Augustalis* of 1231, was quite unambiguous.

> We abolish the illegal usurpation that has prevailed in certain parts of our kingdom and command that from now on they [i.e. the towns] should not create podestas, consuls or rectors in any districts. Also, no one should usurp any office or jurisdiction for himself by authority of some custom or by election of the people. We desire that everywhere through the kingdom there should be only those officials established by our majesty or by our command.... But if any commune establishes such officials in the future it should suffer perpetual desolation, and all the men of that city should be held as perpetual forced laborers. But we order that anyone who has received any of the aforesaid offices should be punished by death.
>
> (Powell 1971:48–9)

Milan led the opposition because it would have been the main loser if Frederick had successfully followed up his victory at Cortenuova in 1237.

The communal view of such imperial pretensions was captured with neat economy in the lowest register of the great integrated scheme in the Scrovegni Chapel at Padua painted in the early fourteenth century by the famous Florentine artist Giotto di Bondone. Here are set out the Virtues and Vices, the overall purpose being to link with the Last Judgement on the west wall. Justice and Injustice are painted in communal terms. Justice is an enthroned queen with scales in each hand: on her right an angel crowns the righteous, on her left the criminal is executed. Along the bottom are the legitimate activities of a well-governed and peaceful state, including hawking, dancing and trading. The symmetry of the setting emphasises the objectivity of her judgements. Injustice, on the opposite wall, is shown as a bent judge, his one-sided pose and talon-like hands indicating the double corruption of favouritism and bribery. His left hand rests on the hilt of his sword. Around him are a broken gate and city walls, fissured and collapsing, while outside the crops are torn up before they can come to fruition. Below, the effects of misgovernment are evident: warfare, rape and robbery (see Plate 13). For the Guelph cities who opposed imperial rule, such chaos was the inevitable consequence of the appearance of any imperial army. The emperor usually enforced his demands for *fodrum* or taxation of the cities by this method, as Otto of Freising believed that he had every right to do.

> Hence it comes about that, on the prince's arrival, most of the cities, towns, and strongholds that attempt to oppose this right by absolute refusal or by not making full payment are razed to the ground to give evidence of their impudence to posterity.
>
> (Mierow 1955:129)

Papal manoeuvrings too had their effects on the cities. With Frederick II's death in 1250, the papal dream of eliminating the Hohenstaufen was given substance by the invitation to Charles of Anjou to take on the mantle of papal champion. Charles arrived in Rome in 1265 with the object of attacking Manfred, Frederick II's illegitimate son, who was the effective ruler of the Kingdom of Sicily. Manfred had allied with the Ghibellines of Siena in 1259, an alliance which had sharpened the traditional rivalry with Florence, thirty miles to the north. The result was the battle of Montaperti in 1260, in which the Sienese were victorious, a famous victory long remembered. But in practice its effects were short-lived, for Charles overcame his Hohenstaufen rivals at Benevento (1266) and Tagliacozzo (1268), and the next year the Florentines gained their revenge over Siena at Colle di Val d'Elsa, establishing a Guelph dominance to which Siena was forced to conform. The Angevin success gave coherence and substance to anti-imperial sentiment in Tuscany which in the past had failed to create effective city leagues in the Lombard manner.

The depth of this sentiment was very fully demonstrated between 1309 and 1313 when Henry VII made one more attempt to re-establish imperial in rule in Italy. Since initially he had the backing of the pope he presented himself as the impartial arbiter of the endemic city disputes, and to this end in the spring of 1310 he sent legations to Lombardy and Tuscany to announce his intentions. As soon as he had crossed the Alps he began to implement this policy, most importantly in Milan, perennial centre of resistance to German armies, where he reconciled two bitter rivals for its control, Guido della Torre and Matteo Visconti, in December 1310. He was then crowned King of Italy at Milan on 6 January 1311, and a few days later he appointed his brother-in-law, Amadeus of Savoy, as his Vicar-General in Lombardy. Other towns had their

Plate 13 Giotto's portrayal of the effects of Justice and Injustice in the bottom register of the Scrovegni Chapel, Padua, c.1303–6. (Photograph reproduced by permission of Scala.)

governments, whatever their form, replaced by imperial vicars. But the image of a ruler above party proved impossible to sustain, for he was, after all, trying to impose imperial rule in a land in which the great majority of the cities were now Guelph in adherence, while financial pressure constantly tempted him to abandon his disinterested stance. The Florentine government had already made up its mind well before his arrival. According to Dino Compagni, a contemporary actively involved in Florentine politics until his party lost power in 1301:

> They showed themselves to be enemies of the emperor in every way, calling him a cruel tyrant and saying that he allied himself with the Ghibellines and did not want to see the Guelphs.... They removed the imperial eagles from their gates and from wherever else they were carved or painted, setting penalties for anyone who painted them, or did not erase those already painted.
>
> (Bornstein 1986:97)

By the time that Henry had reached Pisa (his most ardent Italian ally) in February 1312, the Florentines had convinced neighbouring cities that he represented a danger which had to be resisted at all costs. In December of the previous year these cities had made a pact of mutual aid at Bologna, swearing to resist Henry until he was either dead or driven out (Bowsky 1960:142).

Although he saw them from a traditionalist point of view, Otto of Freising was shrewdly aware of the nature of these city-states. Writing in the 1150s, he describes the people of the Lombard communes as being

> so desirous of liberty that, avoiding the insolence of power, they are governed by the will of consuls rather than rulers. There are known to be three orders among them: captains, vavasors, and commoners. And in order to suppress arrogance, the aforesaid consuls are chosen not from one but from each of the classes. And lest they should exceed bounds by lust for power, they are changed almost every year. The consequence is that, as practically the entire land is divided among the cities, each of them requires its bishops to live in the cities, and scarcely any noble or great man can be found in all the surrounding territory who does not acknowledge the authority of the city.

Otto therefore picks three salient characteristics: they are governed by elected consuls who hold office for a short duration; the centre of power is the urban unit; and the surrounding area, or *contado*, is subject to that urban government. Not surprisingly, Otto did not approve, seeing the commune as a means by which traditional social and political values were overturned. The crux of the matter was that

> forgetful of their ancient nobility [referring to the Romans], they retain traces of their barbaric imperfection, because while boasting that they live in accordance with law, they are not obedient to the laws. For they scarcely if ever respect the prince to whom they should display the voluntary deference of obedience or willingly perform that which they have sworn by the integrity of their laws, unless they sense his authority in the power of his great army.
>
> (Mierow 1955:127–8)

Fundamental to Otto's objections was what he perceived to be their instability, since without the rule of outside princely or episcopal power, these urban governments were subject to rapid change, both in composition and structure. The communal oath of mutual dependence had enabled its members to act in concert and this oath remained at its core, repeated each time the consuls or ruling body were changed. Moreover, officials employed by the commune were similarly required to take an oath to the government when they entered their posts. As Kenneth Hyde has pointed out, this produced considerable fluidity, for changes and additions might be made to laws and regulations on any of these occasions, leading to greater experimentation in governmental form and administration than was to be found elsewhere in western Christendom (Hyde 1973:97–8). The relatively high degree of literacy and numeracy required by citizens for their commercial activities provided the means for these changes, for laws were written down and archives created, and more and more aspects of life were regulated. This in turn meant that considerable political control could be exercised by these governments, although the consistency with which they were able to do this was inevitably tempered by the instability which Otto so deplored. This, then, is what Otto meant when he made a distinction between being obedient to law on the one hand, and *the laws*, that is those of the imperial power representing the proper order, on the other.

Otto of Freising's perception of these cities was in most respects an accurate one, but in his anxiety to demonstrate how they had overturned the right order of things he greatly exaggerated their democratic nature. While it is true that they were 'desirous of liberty'- indeed, the Florentines maintained their outward adherence to republican values despite Medicean dominance in the fourteenth and early fifteenth centuries – it would be unrealistic to expect that the foundation and maintenance of the communes owed much to the socially deprived in revolt against the ruling classes. Siena, for example, had had a consulate of some kind since at least 1127 and had always been controlled by a narrow oligarchy, although the regime of 'The Nine', established in 1287, had been preceded by the wider representation of 'The Twenty-Seven'. The cities of Genoa and Florence, which were different in so many other respects, nevertheless exhibited these same oligarchic characteristics. In Genoa, seigneurial lords like the Embriaco and the della Volta, the basis of whose wealth had originally been in land, accumulated capital from tolls, market dues and the *census* on land, and invested in the trade in cloth, spices and alum. By the early thirteenth century these families were the most powerful in Genoa, far out-distancing those seigneurs who had remained lords over the agricultural lands of the Genoese hinterland. The real wealth of Genoa thereafter lay in the exploitation of its harbour rather than the steep hills behind it (Renouard 1949:46–55). In Florence, many of the dominant families had emerged from the lords of the *castelli* of the surrounding countryside. They, too, looked to the city as a means of investing seigneurial profits. Communal control over the *contado* was not a simple process in which there was a slow extension outwards from the city, for the most powerful urban figures retained their original grip on their rural lordships (Plesner 1934), nor indeed was that communal control always complete. Even in cases where communal force was used directly to subordinate the power of the rural nobility, they re-emerged in urban guise. In 1135, according to Giovanni Villani, the noble family of the Buondelmonte had been forced by the Florentines to destroy their castle close to the city, which they had been using to extract tolls from passing travellers. Nevertheless, the family was allowed to retain its other possessions on condition that they came to live in the city, and during the twelfth century they quickly became one of the most powerful of the Florentine magnate clans (Villani 1969:1:182).

Venice was one outstanding Italian city that did not entirely fit this pattern, for it had no *contado* to speak of, being largely dependent upon its sea-borne commerce and its colonial outposts. The early medieval settlements around the lagoons had been subordinate to Byzantium, but in the twelfth and thirteenth centuries the Venetians cultivated the idea that the Republic had always been an independent entity ruled by its doge and protected by its patron, St Mark. The exploitation of the legend of St Mark in particular showed a precocious awareness of the value of propaganda in developing the city-state, comparable to the cult of St Ambrose at Milan. Mark was regarded as the apostle of the northern Adriatic and was informed by an angel that his body would eventually be laid to rest in Venice. Accordingly, his relics were brought to the city from Alexandria, apparently in the early ninth century, and by 836 the doge had completed a church to receive them. The present church is the third, built largely during the 1060s and 1070s and perhaps first consecrated in 1084–5. In the course of the twelfth century an extensive programme of mosaic decoration was undertaken in which the story of St Mark's life was prominent. The capture of Constantinople in 1204 infused the Venetians with even grander ideas, as well as increasing the means to fulfil them, and led to a further programme of mosaic decoration, hastening the transition of the church from ducal chapel to state basilica, a focal point for the community as a whole (Demus 1988:1–15). Identification with the basilica necessarily marginalised the bishop and his cathedral, so that revolt against episcopal rule, so common in communal development elsewhere, played no part in the establishment of the Venetian state.

The doge himself was elected by the *Arengo* or General Assembly, a body in practice dominated by a relatively small number of leading families, some of whom liked to claim dynastic origins going back to the late Roman period. In the early middle ages the doge had exercised quasi-regal powers, although he often appears to have been no more able to control feuding nobles than any other contemporary monarchs (see Table 6). By the late twelfth century, however, the Venetians had achieved a degree of governmental stability quite unknown in other Italian city-states. This rested upon the slow development of a series of checks and balances, initially deriving from a desire to restrict ducal power. Signs of this can be seen as early as 1032, but the culmination of this process occurred in the crisis of 1172 when the reigning doge, Vitale II Michiel, was assassinated. His family had already held office three times before in the twelfth century and Vitale's nepotism had provided a focus for opposition, but the catalyst was his failure to gain revenge upon the Byzantines after the attack upon the Venetian colony in Constantinople the previous year. Although the new doge, Sebastiano Ziani, was quick to dissociate his regime from his predecessor's murder, it is evident that these events provided the opportunity to set up a nominating committee which could choose the doge from among their number. Thereafter, new elections were usually accompanied by additions to the oath of office, hedging the doge with further restrictions (Lane 1973:90–2). Nevertheless the doge was not eclipsed, for powerful personalities like Ziani himself and Enrico Dandolo (1192–1205) continued to exercise great influence (Queller and Madden 1997:9–10), while the failure of contemporary experiments with the *podestà* in other cities underlines the importance of the continuity of Venetian ducal government.

The doge sat at the head of a series of bodies, running upwards from the General Assembly, through the Great Council and the Quarantia or 'The Forty' to the Privy

Table 6 Doges of Venice

Domenico Contarini	1043–70
Domenico Selvo	1070–84. Deposed
Vitale Falier	1084 or 1085–96
Vitale I Michiel	1096–1102
Ordelaffo Falier	1102–18
Domenico Michiel	1118–29. Abdicated
Pietro Polani	1130–48
Domenico Morosini	1148–56
Vitale II Michiel	1156–72
Sebastiano Ziani	1172–8
Orio Malipiero	1178–92
Enrico Dandolo	1192–1205
Pietro Ziani	1205–29
Jacopo Tiepolo	1229–49. Abdicated
Marino Morosini	1249–53
Ranieri Zen	1253–68
Lorenzo Tiepolo	1268–75
Jacopo Contarini	1275–80
Giovanni Dandolo	1280–9
Pietro Gradenigo	1289–1311
Marino Zorzi	1311–12
Giovanni Soranzo	1312–28

or Ducal Council. At each stage there was a greater concentration of power, although during the thirteenth century it was upon the 300–400 members of the Great Council that the structure was founded, since elections to the many committees and magistracies responsible for the actual running of the Republic began here. Judicial appeals and preparatory work on legislation were considered in the more compact body of the Quarantia, three of whose members were elected to serve on the Ducal Council. The Ducal Council was a committee of ten, presided over by the doge and incorporating the three *capi* of the Quarantia and representatives from each of the six *sestieri* or districts of Venice.

In comparison with many cities the ruling elite who filled these bodies was relatively numerous, but still amounted to only about 150 families in a total city population of about 120,000 (Lane 1973:18–20). In 1297, moreover, after a number of false starts, the procedures for election to the Great Council were reformed, entrenching the old established families even more securely than in the past and emphasising the aristocratic nature of the government. Membership of the Great Council for the previous four years now entitled consideration by the Quarantia for a further term, with twelve ballots needed for confirmation. Loss of one's place through being abroad (which must have been a frequent occurrence because of commercial commitments) entitled the same consideration from the Quarantia on return. Provisions could not be revoked without the approval of five members of the Ducal Council, twenty-five members of the Quarantia and two-thirds of the Great Council, while the Quarantia could not approve anyone's election to the Great Council unless thirty or more of their number were assembled. New members could gain membership of the Great Council if their names were proposed to the Quarantia by a committee of three electors (changed annually) and then approved by at least twelve votes (Romanin 1853:342–4). This last provision served to enlarge the numbers on the Great Council without in practice absorbing many men from outside the circles of the leading families, and the institution of tighter controls on entry during the next twenty-five years came close to making membership of the Great Council hereditary.

Within this structure considerable effort had been expended to avoid the formation of factions so characteristic of the other Italian cities. In the Ducal Council no family could be represented by more than one member, while among the committees responsible for administering vital services such as the Mint and the Arsenal, a complex series of checks and overlapping jurisdictions made the capture of power by any one clan very difficult indeed. In this period the structure was only once seriously threatened, when in 1310 a revolt led by Marco Querini and his son-in-law Bajamonte Tiepolo attempted to overthrow the doge, Pietro Gradenigo. Both men harboured personal grievances, exacerbated in Querini's case by his belief that he had been made a scapegoat for the failure that year of the Republic's attempt to seize Ferrara from papal overlordship. Although some forces reached the Piazza San Marco, the attempted *coup* was frustrated and its leaders either killed in the fighting or exiled. A new Council of Ten was then created to monitor the exiles with the aim of preventing them becoming a focus for further revolt (Lane 1973:114–16).

Narrow as they often were, these city elites nevertheless liked to see themselves as governing in accordance with the Church's teaching that the individual could not take precedence over the general welfare of society (Thrupp 1941). In fact, these ideas had little practical effect, for the Church seemed unable to apply its abstractions to the actual tasks of urban government, while both the governments themselves and the guilds interpreted 'common good' in the quite specific sense of protecting the interests of their own members. Great intellectual effort was expended on the issue of usury, but the chief consequence in the city-states was the extraction of donations and patronage in expiation rather than its prevention. Governmental policies on prices and wages were equally self-interested: the control of bread prices and the stockpiling of food in case of famine were determined by fear of social unrest, while restriction of wage levels had more to do with cutting costs than protecting the consumer. Moreover, the larger the city and the more developed its economy, the less likely was there to be a response to wider social needs, for participants in international commerce and large-scale manufacturing were more affected by the fluctuation of the market than by the generalised teachings of the Church. Villani probably reflects the opinions of his class most accurately when he describes the defeat of the French by the Flemings at Courtrai in 1302 as the abasement of 'the flower of chivalry ... by the most vile people there were in the world, weavers, fullers, and workers in other vile arts and crafts' (Villani 1969:2:68).

As Otto of Freising perceived, most of these governments controlled not only the city itself, but also the *contado*. Just as demesne land was a fundamental part of monarchical and princely power, so too the *contado* was needed to supply food, tax and soldiers. A large section of Ambrogio Lorenzetti's famous painting of Good

Government in the Palazzo Pubblico in Siena, dating from the late 1330s, shows the hills around the city covered by neatly cultivated fields, vines and olives, and dotted with animals, while the roads are filled with merchants and peasants going about their business. Most of the powerful within the city possessed considerable rural interests, either because they owed their original wealth to their lordships in the countryside, which they had not relinquished, or because they had invested money made elsewhere in the *contado*. Governments made up of such men were well aware of the *contado*'s importance, and this is reflected in the communes' efforts to extend their domination by the conquest of smaller neighbours, the negotiation of agreements for mutual defence, or by the purchase of important estates.

Some areas, especially uplands nominally within the *contado* remained largely under seigneurial control, but generally the effect upon rural communities was to break up what remained of the manorial structure, dissolving the bonds of serfdom, but maintaining a considerable jurisdictional and economic hold over the peasantry. Most landlords, especially if they were town-based, exercised control through various forms of leases, of which the *mezzadria*, or share-cropping contract, became the most common. The commune itself exerted its power through its system of officials, often putting in a *podestà* or rector over dependent *castra*, small towns and villages, backed up by a panoply of regulations. These reflect the force that urban governments could bring to bear, compelling peasants to bring land under cultivation, issuing decrees against collective action, imposing heavy tax burdens, sometimes in the form of a requirement for free grain supplies, and even shifting sections of the population about. Even so, not all cities found their *contado* adequate for their needs, as the example of thirteenth-century Florence shows. The proper provisioning of the city remained essential to the communal government, if only to keep prices at a level at which disorder would not be provoked. In Siena, storehouses for food were created for this purpose, backed by laws forbidding the export of foodstuffs at particular times. As a result, conflict with powerful vested interests, such as the butchers and animal-dealers of the Maremma, which was one of the areas of the *contado* where Sienese control was weakest, was not unusual, for high profits could be made selling to towns whose *contado* contained inadequate pasture (Bowsky 1981:207).

Moreover, the *contado* supplied not only food but also men, for the city-states needed soldiers to defend themselves within the complicated politics of medieval Italy. Although they sometimes employed mercenaries, for most of this period the land-based city-states relied on a militia drawn from the populace. This militia consisted of horse as well as foot, and another reason for Otto of Freising's disdain of the commune was the habit of knighting men whose social background he believed made them unfitted for such an honour (Mierow 1955:127–8). Recruitment for the militia, however, often spread the net wider than those who possessed horses and the associated equipment. The famous Florentine artist Coppo di Marcovaldo was captured at the battle of Montaperti, apparently while serving in the very menial role of setting up shields for archers and crossbowmen, while the Sienese artist, Duccio, chosen by the commune to paint its greatest icon of the Virgin, nevertheless was supposed to serve in the army. In 1302 his apparent refusal to do so led to a fine of 18L. 10s. (White 1979:21). In fact, although in the later Middle Ages the Italian peninsula became a lucrative field of operation for the *condottieri* or mercenary captains, who hired out themselves and their companies to the city-states, this trend was not very evident until the late thirteenth century. Venice, as ever, was something of an exception, but as the Fourth Crusade demonstrates, it had instead an enormous ship-building capacity. For this crusade the Venetian yards may have turned out as many as 50 galleys and 450 transports within about eighteen months (Queller and Madden 1997:17).

However, in monarchical states, even when a dynasty had taken root and hereditary succession was fully established, there was always the possibility of internal conflict at danger points such as minorities or regencies. Otto of Freising, as an experienced politician, was well aware that the city-states were much more vulnerable to such upheavals, for there were many more possible factional combinations than were likely under a monarchy. Personal and family rivalries, some perhaps finding their origins in their seigneurial background, were characteristic of the cities, creating a townscape overshadowed by fortified towers. Even in a town as small as San Gimignano, which is unique today in retaining as many as thirteen of these towers, only a sketchy impression is conveyed of the outward appearance of the cities, for it is believed that in the thirteenth century there were more than seventy-six of them.

The nature of the struggles, to which the communes never found an effective answer, varied from city to city. In Genoa, for instance, an aggressive individualism, typified by members of the Zaccaria family, prevailed. Its most famous member was Benedetto Zaccaria who, born in 1248 into one of the most prominent Genoese aristocratic dynasties, was already involved in the eastern trade by 1259. During the next half-century he made money from alum, mastic, shipping and banking. He conducted his own diplomatic policies in aid of his activities, receiving a number of monopolies within the Byzantine Empire as a consequence of his friendship with the Emperor Michael VIII. When he returned to Genoa he took a prominent part in the city's politics, becoming Constable of the Commune (Renouard 1949:96–100). In the great Tuscan cities like Florence and Siena, the struggles more often crystallised around the Guelphs and the Ghibellines, purporting to represent the pope and the emperor respectively, although they sometimes had as much relevance to internal faction as to external allegiance. When the Guelphs became dominant in central Italy after the invasion of Charles of Anjou in 1265, there occurred further fragmentation among them into the 'Blacks' and the 'Whites'. From the mid-twelfth century many towns granted power for limited periods to a *podestà*, an outsider believed to be uninvolved in local conflicts, in an effort to achieve stability. In Florence, according to Villani, this occurred in 1207, when such an appointment was thought necessary because of the increase in inhabitants and consequent growth in crime. The *podestà* was to administer justice for a year in co-operation with the judges and thus, it was hoped, would establish a system which would not be prone to bribery, threats or malice (Villani 1969:1:212).

The relative failure of this experiment can be judged by the growth of organised corporations of the *popolo*, which are evident in many cities in the course of the thirteenth century. The *popolo* did not encompass the mass of the population, but rather those whose economic success had brought them an increasing stake in society and who believed themselves unfairly excluded from power. In cities where power had been largely wielded by members of families of noble origin, the *popolo* movement gives the impression of class conflict, but the struggles which this provoked were more concerned with gaining control of communal government than effecting any revolutionary change in its nature. A fairly typical pattern can be seen in Villani's description of the first establishment of the *popolo* in Florence in 1250, when they rose up against the dominant pro-Ghibelline Uberti family, setting up instead a popular government under an elected captain, Uberto da Lucca, supported by twelve *anziani*, or elders, two from each *sesto*. Twenty standards were then distributed to act as rallying points in case of any counter-move (Villani 1969:1:261–4). In these circumstances the *podestà* often found that he was obliged to share his powers with the *Capitano del Popolo*, while by the late thirteenth century anti-magnate legislation, excluding certain families from office and imposing heavy penalties for breaches of the peace, was being introduced. The *popolo* movement was widespread, even in the first half of the thirteenth century. Lauro Martinès shows that between 1197 and 1257 they gained a share in power in Milan, Mantua, Cremona, Lucca, Piacenza, Lodi, Verona, Bologna, Modena, Bergamo, Siena, Pistoia and Parma (Martinès 1980:58–60).

These general characteristics can be seen in the specific case of the Tuscan city of Siena. Siena has one of the most compelling focal points of any Italian city with its sweeping central piazza, the Campo. Dominating this piazza, on its south side, is the Palazzo Pubblico, the town hall built in stages between 1293 and 1360, largely by the communal government known as the *Noveschi* or 'The Nine'. The central block has four storeys and, at this period, the two wings had two storeys each. By 1341 the Torre del Mangia had been completed. No tower in the city outstripped this one, not even that of the cathedral. Siena is built on three hills, a topography which determined its division into the districts of the *terzi*, and the Palazzo Pubblico itself is sited in a position which was intended to avoid the appearance of favouring any one district or faction. From here the *Noveschi*, which had gained power in 1287 and lasted until 1355, ruled the city, issuing a stream of decrees which included planning regulations governing the buildings around the Campo which, from 1297, had to conform to certain standards in order to preserve the unity of the space. Although by this date the city was in theory ruled by its *podestà*, the real power remained with the *Noveschi*. These were drawn from the *popolo grasso*, who had made their fortunes from international trade and banking, wool manufacture, dealing in dyes and other pharmaceuticals, and retailing (Bowsky 1981:20). They had acquired one-third of the communal offices as early as 1147 and a half of the positions within the governing oligarchy of 'The Twenty-Four' by 1233 (Hook 1979:14). They served for two-month periods, during which they actually lived in the Palazzo Pubblico, an even shorter period of office than that seen by Otto of Freising as being unstable. Although the *Noveschi* ruled the city, they often did so in consultation with the other 'orders', the four Provveditori of the Bicherna or financial magistracy, the four consuls of the Mercanzia or merchant guild, and the three consuls of the Knights or 'Captains of the Party' (which after 1271 meant the Guelphs) (Bowsky 1981:23, 54–6). In practice, the same names and families recur so that the sense of discontinuity suggested by regulations governing tenure of office is not an entirely accurate reflection of reality.

At its height the population over which the *Noveschi* governed may have reached 50,000 in the city itself, with perhaps another 62,000 in the *contado*. The *contado*, a mixed region broken up by hills, valleys and swamps, covered an area about thirty miles' radius from the city, but it did not include any navigable rivers or ports and in 1303 the government tried to extend its control to the small port of Talamone to compensate for this. The government's apparent failure to maintain safe communications with this new acquisition shows that communal control over the countryside had its limitations. This political unit seems to have reached its maximum practical size. This, indeed, was a general characteristic. Hyde estimates that up to one-third of communal populations lived within the sound of the council bell and that all of the population was accessible in about one day's riding, circumstances which must have encouraged the imposition of a regulatory approach to government (Hyde 1973:94). Despite the failure of the Talamone initiative, Siena had considerable resources within the *contado*, including pasture, vineyards, olives, grain, fruit and mineral deposits.

Within the Palazzo Pubblico the *Noveschi* habitually met in the Sala della Pace (dei Nove), decorated on three sides from 1338 to 1339 by the allegory of justice, common good and tyranny painted by Ambrogio Lorenzetti. This is a complex and very rich painting which has been analysed in detail by several authorities, but the central lesson which it conveys is that the oligarchy conceived of itself as ruling for 'the common good', its authority emanating from the community and its probity watched over by the Virgin, the protector of the city. The central panel is dominated by two figures, on the right the enthroned monarch representing Siena itself and on the left, the female figure of Justice. Around them a series of further figures represents the Virtues, and connected by a cord to them both are the citizens who are the governing body of the commune. On the right wall the allegory merges into a more realistic observation of the effects of good government, in which town and countryside are at peace, their inhabitants going about their various occupations unhindered by the horrors which afflict the world depicted on the left which is ruled by Tyranny and subjected to warfare, rape and murder, its structure rent apart by conflict.

In Siena, as in other Italian city-states, there are evident signs of the government trying to put its concept of rule into practice, especially in efforts to ensure provisioning of the populace and control of prices in times of famine; in improving public safety through the creation of communal police and firefighters; in maintaining the cleanliness of the city through laws concerned with sanitation and the industrial use of residential premises; and in works of public charity such as support for and control of the Hospital of Santa Maria della Scala. However, such extensive governmental activity had to be paid for and the Sienese, like other communal governments, attempted to do this by establishing often relentless tax-gathering machines. Direct taxes based on hearths and indirect taxes on goods and services, known as gabelles, pressed heavily on the populace. By *c*.1330 the gabelles had become increasingly important, providing the commune with at least one-third of its revenue, covering, as Philip Jones expresses it, 'almost everything but air and water' (P. Jones 1997:390–401). Here, it can be seen that the *Noveschi* had a distinctly restricted view of the common good, for they naturally believed that it depended upon the preservation of their own regime. In the end the inability of governments like that of Siena to absorb the message of their own propaganda may well have led to their downfall. The oligarchy of the *Noveschi* fell in 1355 at least partly because of financial dishonesty, suggesting that concern for personal profit ultimately engendered an inability to manage communal finances.

Otto of Freising, however, would not have regarded control, both economic and legal, over the lives of the mass of populace, as anything other than natural. What he found worthy of comment was the way that both nobility and Church were subordinated as well. In Siena, as in other great cities like Florence, by the late thirteenth century the great magnate families were specifically excluded from office. From 1277 they could not be elected to the consulate, at least partly because of fears that a powerful noble family or individual might seize power and overturn communal institutions. Nevertheless, this did not represent such a polarisation of power between the *popolo grasso* and the *casati* as has sometimes been suggested, for in Siena at least the nobility held power in other capacities, as castellans, ambassadors, war captains and judges, among other roles, and it is clear that they took part in the various councils of the commune, even though unable to serve as members of the Noveschi. Their role was circumscribed rather than eliminated.

Apart from the Palazzo Pubblico, Siena had a second key building, equally important to its life, that of the cathedral. As such it is not surprising to find that the commune enveloped religious affairs just as it did every other aspect of existence in the city. By the 1280s many activities, once the preserve of the Church, had been laicised, including jurisdiction over criminous clerks. The Church itself, indeed, was largely filled by members of the families of the powerful, so that, as William Bowsky (1981:110) describes it, it was in many ways pre-Gregorian. The cathedral itself, begun in 1196, was an object of pride to the commune, and the decision to enlarge it in 1285 was partly provoked by rivalry with other cathedrals in central Italy. The state of the cathedral therefore was largely a political concern, controlled by the commune through a board of works, the *Opera di Santa Maria di Siena* (Larner 1971:66). It followed that the commune should see its fate as closely bound up with its patron saint, which in Siena meant the promotion of the cult of the Virgin. The Sienese believed that their victory over Florence at the battle of Montaperti in 1260 had been directly attributable to the Virgin, and the commissioning by the commune of a new painting of the Virgin by the great Sienese artist, Duccio di Buoninsegna, in 1308, emphasised the importance attached to the cult. In June 1311, Duccio's completed masterpiece was carried through the streets in a great procession from his workshop to the cathedral.

The cathedral extension and the new painting of the Virgin emphasised the growth of communal pride. Duccio's *Maestà* replaced the so-called *Madonna degli Occhi* by an unknown Sienese artist and probably dating from the second decade of the thirteenth century, upon the high altar. The contrast in style, scope, technical skill and cost is striking. The *Madonna degli Occhi* is painted on a small wooden panel from which she stares straight ahead with the Child held frontally in a Byzantine pose. He shares no human relationship with the mother and there are few additional details beyond the two angels above. On the other hand Duccio's *Maestà* was a huge project, demanding the erection of a large framework of highly skilled carpentry and, with its twenty-six scenes of the Passion on the back, encompassing a programme equivalent to the sculptural facades of the French cathedrals. The costs of the materials, especially the gold leaf, and the labour – for the Sienese government signed the Duccio shop on an exclusive three-year contract – suggest that quality rather than price determined the nature of the commission.

Siena is a prime example of the Tuscan commune, proud of its history and republican institutions, but over a century before the fall of the Noveschi there had been signs in many cities, especially in the north, that republican forms of government were finding it difficult to survive. Sometimes a 'tyrant' became dominant such as Ezzelino III da Romano in the Trevisan March, to the north of Venice, in the 1230s and 1240s. Ostensibly allied to the imperial cause, much of the time he was involved in what has been called a pointless drive for power, apparently uninterested in titles or the establishment of a hereditary dynasty (Larner 1980:129–31). It may be that the Veneto region was promising territory for such takeovers, for cities like Ferrara and Mantua never really developed as communes in the Florentine or Sienese manner at all. Nevertheless, the transition was not necessarily inevitable, for it could even be reversed. Thus Padua, dominated by Ezzelino from his base in Verona between 1237 and 1256, managed to restore communal government and until *c*.1310 grew and prospered, never being seriously shaken by internal division or external threat. But even Padua succumbed when put under pressure, significantly from Verona under the regime of a *signore*, Cangrande della Scala. By 1318 the Paduans had come around to the idea of a single governor to protect them from the Veronese threat. This bought time, but did not save the city; in 1328 the dynasty of the Carrara established itself with Veronese support (Hyde 1966:1–3).

In the long term, the activities of men like Ezzelino presaged the crumbling of the communal form of government, although it was replaced not by men like him, but by *signori* who were actually given specific grants of power, which came to be passed along the hereditary line. In Lombardy, the first such grants were made in the 1260s; by the early fourteenth century some of the best known dynasties of the later Middle Ages were establishing themselves, such as the Visconti of Milan, where they received official sanction from the Emperor Henry VII in 1311. In Tuscany, the ground had been prepared by the rise of the Angevins; a number of cities, including Florence and Lucca, granted the power of the *podestà* to Charles of Anjou for set periods. The threat of Henry VII combined with that of their own exiles served to strengthen this trend. According to Villani, the Florentines

> gave themselves to King Robert for five years, and then renewed it for three, and thus for the following eight years King Robert would have the *signoria*, sending them his vicar every six months, and the first was Messer Giacomo di Cantelmo of Provence, who came to Florence in the month of June, 1313. And soon after in a similar way the Lucchesi, the Pistolesi, and the Pratesi gave the *signoria* to King Robert.
>
> (Villani 1969:2:181)

In Villani's opinion, this was the saving of the Florentines, who would otherwise have torn each other apart.

The emergence of the *signoria* in so many city-states by the early fourteenth century would have confirmed Otto in his belief that the governmental structures of the commune were inherently unstable. In the end the communal buildings and art do not seem to have been outward symbols of a deeper loyalty. It has been suggested that this failure helps to explain the continued attraction of an authority figure, despite the bad experiences that had arisen from imperial invasions in the past. Even the personification of the Common Good in Lorenzetti's fresco, which is represented by a crowned figure seated on a throne, was more likely to be perceived as a prince than as a symbol of the republic (Hyde 1972:305). Moreover, the commune contained conveniently inflammable material which could both justify a takeover and make it possible. The urban-based nobles, for example, were seen as a disruptive force, but this awareness did not prevent them creating an example of violent behaviour which others, seeking to protect their positions, were not slow to follow (Martinès 1972:337). The nobles themselves, adversely affected by the partial or even complete loss of access to the positions of power and profit within the commune which had resulted from the rise of the *popolo*, were sometimes willing to allow the establishment of a dictatorship which would restore such offices to them. Where they still formed a clearly identifiable element therefore – as, for example, in Milan – the potential for the establishment of the *signoria* was that much greater. In addition, the same circumstances that encouraged the spread of heresy provided a context for social and political discontent, for the towns inevitably contained large numbers of people lacking roots in the community. The aspirant *signore* had plenty of exploitable resources.

The Italian city-states were unique in the high middle ages. A measure of this can be gained by assessing the extent of urbanisation achieved, unmatched by any other parts of Christendom. Tuscany is perhaps the best example, defined by Josiah Russell as a region centred on Florence, bordered by the Mediterranean on the west, the Apennines on the north and east, and on the south by Orvieto, where it reached the edges of the Papal States (J.C. Russell 1972:40–52). In *c.*1200 Pisa was the largest city of the region, with a population of about 20,000, followed by Florence with about 15,000 and Siena with about 10,000. By the end of the thirteenth century Florence had seen a dramatic growth, becoming the leading city of Tuscany without serious challenge. By this time Florence had about 96,000 inhabitants, Siena 52,000 and Pisa 38,000. All had high densities, with Florence reaching about 150 per hectare and Pisa as high as 205. While these urban populations are quite exceptional, the surrounding *contadi* were not especially densely populated, averaging about thirty to the square kilometre. This made the relative proportions between town and country quite different from elsewhere. According to Russell's researches, the top city of most medieval regions would contain only about 1.5 per cent of that region's population, while the top ten cities would make only 4.7 per cent. Yet, in the Florentine region, even in the early thirteenth century, these cities made up 10.8 per cent of the total, a figure which had grown to 26.3 per cent by the end of the century. Although the cities were themselves very varied in size and development and although their relationship with the countryside can now be seen to be more complex than had once been thought, their characteristic feature was the extent to which this urbanisation determined the nature of government and society, producing a political structure in which the city was not simply a part of the larger whole, but was itself the fundamental unit.

11

The Capetian monarchy

Robert the Monk, former Abbot of Saint-Rémi at Reims, writing after the capture of Jerusalem in 1099, portrays Urban II at Clermont as appealing primarily to the Franks.

> Race of the Franks, race beyond the mountains, race chosen and beloved by God, as is manifest in your many labours, set apart from all other peoples as much by the situation of your lands as by your Catholic faith and honour paid to the Holy Church: to you our sermon is directed and to you our exhortation is extended.
>
> (Robert the Monk 1866:727)

This idea that the Franks were a chosen people in whom the Christian virtues were inherent, was to have a long life, for it was the foundation of a highly successful piece of dynastic image-building. While the Angevins were portrayed by Gerald of Wales as the devil's brood, their origins clouded by sinister witchery (Warner 1891:301–2), and individual monarchs who crossed the papacy had their reputations besmirched by clerical propaganda, leaving Roger II of Sicily as the 'tyrant king' (Wieruszowski 1963) and the Emperor Frederick II as an heretical blasphemer with perverted sexual tastes (Van Cleve 1972:420, 481), the Capetians emerged as the true defenders of Christendom, 'the most Christian kings' as the popes called them, protectors of the papacy, valiant crusaders and hammers of heretics and Jews (see Table 7).

From the 1120s the centre of the cult was the venerable Benedictine monastery of St Denis, eleven miles to the north of Paris, which, under Suger and his successors, created a tradition of pro-Capetian historiography unmatched by any contemporary dynasty. The nearest equivalent in England – the chroniclers of St Albans – never identified with the ruling dynasty in the same way and, indeed, in their portrait of King John, created the archetypal opposite of the 'good' King Philip, his Capetian contemporary (Southern 1970:150). Suger moulded the image from an incident that was, in reality, a non-event. In August 1124, the Emperor Henry V diverted a planned expedition against Duke Lothar of Saxony in the direction of western Francia, in particular towards territory in the vicinity of Reims (see Map 5). His reasons for doing this have been disputed, but the encouragment he received from his father-in-law, Henry I, King of England and ruler of Normandy, suggests that Suger was right to believe that they were acting in concert. The stage was set for a dramatic conflict

Table 7 The Capetian kings

Hugh	987–96
Robert II	996–1031
Henry I	1031–60
Philip I	1060–1108
Louis VI	1108–37
Louis VII	1137–80
Philip II	1180–1223
Louis VIII	1223–6
Louis IX	1226–70. Canonised 1297
Philip III	1270–85
Philip IV	1285–1314
Louis X	1314–16
John I	November 1316
Philip V	1316–22
Charles IV	1322–8

involving the three most important political powers of northern Europe, with the weakest of the three, Louis VI, about to be crushed between two powerful adversaries. In fact, nothing actually happened, for Louis was able to rally support not only from the royal demesne in the Ile-de-France and its immediate vicinity, but also from the great lords who were his tenants-in-chief, the Dukes of Burgundy and Aquitaine, the Counts of Anjou and Flanders, and even from Theobald, Count of Blois-Chartres, an old enemy of his house. Faced with this show of unity, Henry V decided to avoid battle and withdraw.

Suger used this unpromising material with consummate skill, narrating how Louis VI had, in this hour of crisis, gone to the abbey and prayed to St Denis, and then had received the banner of St Denis, to be borne into battle with him. This was, in fact, the standard of the French Vexin which Louis's predecessor, Philip I, had held in fief from the abbey, but in this more elevated guise it could be presented as a symbol of the kings' vassalage to the Apostle of France. Since the time of Charlemagne the royal flag or *oriflamme* had customarily been deposited at the abbey, a flag supposedly presented to the emperor by Pope Leo III. By the late twelfth century, the *oriflamme* and the banner of the Vexin seem to have merged in people's minds, so that thereafter this standard was seen as the protector of the French king and people in battle (Spiegel 1975:58–9). After receiving the banner, Louis convoked the great assembly which had apparently intimidated Henry V, and immediately after the emperor's retreat, in a donation to the abbey, he affirmed that the French monarchy had been placed by providence under the protection of St Denis and his companions. In practice, there may have been more mundane reasons for Henry V's change of policy, for he had recently received news of a rebellion at Worms, which he now turned back to crush (Leyser 1994b:109–12), but this did nothing to undermine Suger's presentation of the episode.

The process continued under Louis VII and Philip II. Odo of Deuil, who was to

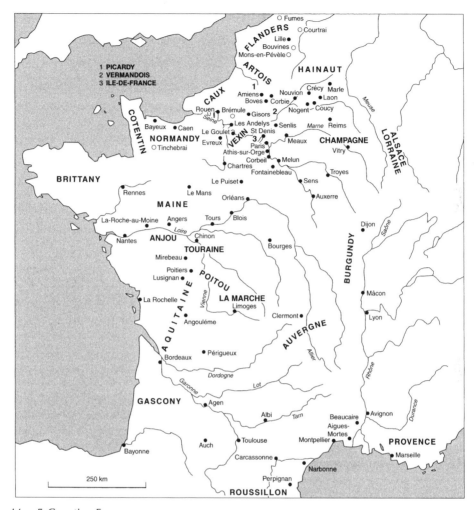

Map 5 Capetian France

succeed Suger as Abbot of St Denis, wrote up an account of the Second Crusade of 1147–9 supposedly to furnish Suger with material for his life of Louis VII. In the midst of this disaster, Odo portrays Louis as a saintly king whose first concern is his duty to God.

> Amid so many hardships his safe preservation was owed to no other remedy than his religion, for he always took communion before he went to attack the enemy forces and on his return requested vespers and compline, in such wise always making God the alpha and omega of his deeds.
>
> (Berry 1948:143)

Not surprisingly, when the Capetian dynasty really did have something to boast about, with Philip II's crushing victory over the coalition assembled by the Angevin King John at Bouvines in 1214, the chronicler William the Breton presented the event in what Georges Duby sees as 'manichaean' terms of absolute good and absolute evil (Duby 1990:13–30).

However, while it is true that the Franks indeed responded in great numbers to the calling of the First Crusade and that, in future generations, they came to see the crusades as primarily 'Frankish' expeditions, in the early twelfth century the practical manifestations of God's favour are harder to discern than Robert of Reims claims. The reigning monarch, Philip I, was the fourth in his family in the direct male line to rule Francia since the election of Hugh Capet in 987. The royal demesne was relatively small and landlocked and, until the purchase of Bourges some time between 1097 and 1102, contained only two important towns, Paris and Orléans. The paucity of distinguished buildings emphasises its lack of prestige. When Abbot Suger came to rebuild the abbey-church of St Denis in the 1140s, his architect drew upon constructional elements not from the Ile-de-France, but from the rich architectural traditions of the Capetians' neighbours in Normandy and Burgundy. Like all great lords, the kings attempted to augment their demesne and Philip I did indeed manage to acquire the Gâtinais, the Vexin and Corbie (Fawtier 1965:103–5). Nevertheless, although the region contained rich grain lands, the kings were unable fully to tap potential resources, for their control over many parts was tenuous. Castellans, who had emerged as effective local powers in the later Carolingian era, often defied the efforts of the king to undermine their autonomy, for the early Capetians lacked the military means to sustain their campaigns or the institutional power to bring offenders to the royal court. In 1079 Philip I's forces were actually put to flight by one such lord, Hugh of Le Puiset, who remained a thorn in the king's side until his death in 1094 (Cusimano and Moorhead 1992: 85).

At the same time, the great lords who, for at least some of their lands, were vassals of the king, had, in the eleventh century, taken progressively less interest in royal affairs. The attendance of these men at royal assemblies had gradually diminished, for they had concerns of their own, both in attempting the difficult task of consolidating power within their own fiefs, and in determining their own relations with each other. One of them, William, Duke of Normandy, effectively overshadowed the French king after 1066, for his conquest of England gave him access to resources that considerably outweighed those of Philip I. In the north, the Flemish counts had benefited from the increased revenues derived from growing trade, so that by 1100 they could probably assemble a force of vassals about 50 per cent greater than that which the Capetian demesne could supply (Ross 1982:9). Although the counts had been fief-holders of the French crown since the late ninth century, they had since expanded their control across the Scheldt so that in 1056 they became imperial vassals as well. Such men could pursue policies quite independently of the king; the Flemish counts married into the Danish royal house when it suited them, since it strengthened their position in the midst of the swirling English and imperial rivalries. Equally independent were the Counts of Anjou and of Blois-Champagne. The Counts of Anjou had, by 1060, become formidable rulers, having absorbed neighbouring counties like Touraine, and extended their influence through far-reaching marriage links, while the Counts of Blois-Champagne had acquired such extensive interests in northern France that their lands seemed to hem in the Capetians. Certainly, neither Robert the Pious nor Henry I had been able to rule with any comfort while the restless and aggressive Count Odo II (d. 1037) had been alive. To the south-east, the Duchy of Burgundy had been held by a brother of Hugh Capet until his death in 1002, but through persistent effort Robert II had managed to take it over. He does not, however, seem to have intended it to become a permanent part of the royal demesne, for his arrangements for the succession made provision for it to be granted to a younger son, a condition fulfilled in 1032 after the king's death (Lewis 1982:26–7).

These great lords could not ignore the kings, for their very proximity involved them in the ever-shifting political rivalries of north-west Europe, but the other great fiefs supposedly appertaining to 'the Kingdom of the Franks' seemed remote indeed. Brittany, Aquitaine and Toulouse were quite distinct from Francia in language and culture; the French king seemed of little relevance to them. Norman–Angevin rivalries were far more important to Breton politics than any actions of the Capetians, while the whole orientation of the Counts of Poitou who, since the early tenth century, had been trying to justify their title as Dukes of Aquitaine, a sprawling and diverse region stretching to the Pyrenees and the Massif Central, was towards the south. Even further away was the County of Toulouse, which had also begun to take shape in the tenth century and which encompassed claims both beyond the Pyrenees and in Provence. Robert of Reims may have believed that Urban II's appeal was primarily to the chosen race of the Franks, but no small part of the motivation of Raymond IV, Count of Toulouse from 1093, in joining the First Crusade, was a belief that he was entitled to be regarded as its secular leader.

Weak as these kings appear in comparison with the German emperor or even the king of England, they were not, however, entirely without advantages, for in practice these great lords presented less of a threat than might appear at first sight. Their interests were usually too diverse and their own rivalries too intense to combine against the king, an act which, even had it been possible, would have been of dubious utility, for the Capetians did not greatly impinge upon them. Moreover, the Capetian problems within their own demesne were not unique. Only the Dukes of Normandy and the Counts of Flanders had made appreciable progress in imposing their will upon their unruly vassals and even in these lands the fragility of the peace is made all too evident in the writings of Orderic Vitalis and Galbert of Bruges. Orderic's description of the anarchy and violence which consumed the Duchy of Normandy under Robert Curthose in the late eleventh century shows how much still depended upon the personality of individual dukes, while Galbert's account of the murder of the Count of Flanders, Charles the Good, while at prayer in his own castle chapel at Bruges in 1127, reveals deep currents of discontent within the county, extending well beyond the immediate group of conspirators responsible for the murder (Ross 1982).

Therefore, although the first four Capetians had made little perceptible political progress, the success of their putative rivals should not be exaggerated either. Moreover, for well over a century, the Capetians had maintained a grip on the throne itself. Between 888 and 987 four of Hugh Capet's ancestors had held the throne at one time or another; after 987 the family succeeded in permanently obstructing a Carolingian revival. By the early twelfth century, this grip had already shown itself firm enough to withstand the dynastic rivalries of the reign of Henry I (1031–60) and the minority of Henry's son, Philip, only 8 years of age when he succeeded. It is noticeable that the struggle which occurred among the sons of Robert the Pious after 1025, when the eldest, Hugh, predeceased his father, was an internal family conflict which implied no change of dynasty whoever had succeeded, while in 1060, despite the evident dangers of a minority, the baronage accepted the validity of Philip's coronation the previous year. It has been shown that when Hugh Capet was elected in 987, he was already the head of an 'entrenched *Geschlecht*' with a son 15 years old, and that the contemporary power-brokers of Francia would not have failed to realise the long-term implications of the election. Hugh Capet, of course, continued to promote dynastic interests, just as his predecessors and contemporaries did in their own fiefs. Anticipatory succession – the crowning of the king's son within the father's lifetime – which has often been stressed as the key to Capetian survival, was common practice within other feudal dynasties. It was calculated not only to ensure the succession of the eldest son, but also to be part of more comprehensive arrangements for the orderly disposition of the family's property when the old king died. It is therefore not surprising to find that the 'elections' of both Philip I and Louis VI in 1059 and 1100 were largely a matter of formal ratification following the presentation of his heir to the assemblies by the reigning monarch. Philip I even accentuated this trend further when, for the first time, he bequeathed not only the family demesne to the heir, but acquisitions made during his lifetime as well, acquisitions which had traditionally gone to cadet branches (Lewis 1982:1–77).

Occupation of the throne, however, important as it was, did not in itself make a monarchy. Sacred rites made a king distinct from his subjects. The attribution of magical qualities to a leader found its origins in a time long before there were means to record it. As Germanic society became Christianised, the Church took an increasingly important part in the development of what became a monarchical mystique. In return for promises by the ruler to fulfil certain Christian duties, the Church provided, within the striking visual framework of the consecration ceremony, a powerful reinforcement of the belief that the monarch was marked out by special qualities conferred by God. In the case of the Capetians, this took the form of an elaborate coronation ceremonial either at the Abbey of St Rémi at Reims or, more frequently, at the cathedral. During this ceremony the king was anointed, quite consciously after the manner of Saul and David, by holy oil supposedly brought to St Rémi by a dove from Heaven at the time of the baptism of the Merovingian king, Clovis, in *c.*496 (Lot and Fawtier 1958:2:29–32). The oil was kept in a reliquary in the shape of a dove and was supposed, miraculously, never to diminish. Among the statues which once adorned the west front of the rebuilt façade of St Denis were Old Testament kings whose virtues, it may be surmised, Suger intended to be seen as inherent in the Capetians (Katzenellenbogen 1959:28ff.).

The support and approval of the Church was essential if the sacral attributes of kingship were to be exploited, a support theoretically available only to those rulers prepared to implement a programme consistent with the clerical social and political concepts. Clerical writers in the early middle ages had created an image of the just king who made lawful use of his divinely granted authority by displaying the qualities of piety, justice and mercy. This was not necessarily very helpful to the establishment of hereditary right, since the Church might not discern that the nearest male heir had the relevant qualities, but in the case of the Capetians, despite a long wrangle over Philip I's adultery, the stability offered by dynastic continuity amidst the turbulent noble conflicts of north-west Europe, soon began to outweigh any advantage that a change of dynasty might have brought, even had the Church found that this was a practical proposition in the late eleventh century. The papacy, in particular, would hardly have found it politic to seek a direct confrontation with both the French and German rulers simultaneously, and indeed tended to favour the French king as a counter to imperial pressures. When the presence of the emperor in Italy became too overbearing, France was needed as a refuge. Consequently, the attempts by the reform papacy to desacralise monarchy, a policy in keeping with the sharp separation of things spiritual from things secular which the reformers insisted upon, was not applied with any force against the French kings (Kern 1948:36).

Louis VI succeeded to the throne in 1108, but had effectively been king for some years since his father, overweight and inert, had apparently lost the capacity to rule. This may explain why Louis was the only Capetian who was not consecrated before the death of his father, an omission which made his succession slightly fraught, for his half-brothers had their eyes on the throne. Nevertheless, they seem not to have constituted a long-term threat; much more evident was the need to exercise authority within the royal demesne itself, a continuing struggle by no means resolved by Philip I. Two men have been seen to epitomise the resistance of the castellans to Louis VI: to the south in the vicinity of Chartres, Hugh of Le Puiset, and to the north, around Laon, Thomas of Marle. They seem perhaps more important than they actually were because their activities have been so graphically described by two contemporary authors: Hugh of Le Puiset by Suger (Cusimano and Moorhead 1992:84–90, 94–104), and Thomas of Marle by Guibert of Nogent (Benton 1970:184–8, 198–205). In fact, there were numerous other lords whose activities must have been scarcely less damaging to royal authority. Moreover, neither abbot was equipped to give a disinterested picture, for Suger was concerned to glorify the achievements of the monarchy, while Guibert, his observations affected by a mixture of prurience and genuine horror, was more concerned with his own inner feelings than with news reporting. Nevertheless, despite their distortions and exaggerations, these accounts are interesting because they do reflect at least some part of contemporary opinion and therefore must have helped mould views of a king who had managed to come to grips with these problems.

Hugh III of Le Puiset was the grandson of Hugh I, who had defeated King Philip's forces in 1079. Suger saw him as even worse than his ancestors, a man in whom the evil of generations had become concentrated. In 1109 he succeeded to the castellany where he became 'elated for having gone unpunished while he brutally tyrannised needy churches and monasteries'. Next,

> since he did not think much of either the King of the universe or the king of the French, he attacked the most noble countess of Chartres and her son Theobald.... He ravaged their land all the way to Chartres, delivering it over to plunder and fires.

Their attempts to fight back made little impact since, Suger says, they could seldom get closer to his castle than eight or ten miles, a typical radius which a single stronghold could dominate at this period. Eventually, Theobald of Chartres turned to the king, stating his case, according to Suger, very much in terms of the enforcement of the Peace of God, for he appealed for the king to 'end the persecution of the churches, the plunderings of the poor, and the ungodly hardships endured by widows and orphans whenever Hugh ravaged the land of the saints and its cultivators'. Moved by the complaints which he had received, in 1111 Louis attempted to exercise his right of overlordship by summoning Hugh to appear at his court at Melun. His failure to do so – not apparently unexpected, judging by the military preparations already undertaken – was followed by a royal campaign against a recalcitrant vassal, which succeeded in taking Hugh prisoner and in destroying the castle. The campaign is presented by Suger as a holy task undertaken to restore to the Church its rightful possessions despoiled by the lord of Le Puiset, for the king acted as God's vicar. The respite was short-lived, however, for Hugh was released in 1112, only to return to his previous ways. Significantly, he was able to rebuild his castle, which gave him an effective base to raid the surrounding region. It was another six years before the king finally overcame him; in 1118 he followed the course set by his father, who had taken part in the First Crusade. In the Latin East he joined other members of the family and it is a measure of Louis VI's success that the Le Puiset clan perceived there to be more opportunities in the Kingdom of Jerusalem, where they were related to King Baldwin II, than in the Ile-de-France (A.V. Murray 1992:16–19). Hugh never returned from his journey of expiation.

With the disappearance of Hugh of Le Puiset, the royal demesne to the south of Paris was largely drawn within royal control, but north of the city the problem proved less tractable. Thomas of Marle was the son of Enguerrand of Coucy, Count of Amiens, who died in 1116, and with whom Thomas carried on a long-standing feud which, in Guibert's view, terrorised the countryside and despoiled the churches. Guibert has nothing favourable to say about him, dwelling on the tortures that he was supposed to have inflicted on those unfortunate enough to become caught up in the running conflicts of the region. Thomas, in fact, features so prominently in Guibert's narrative because of his support, from 1112, for the hated commune of Laon, which the abbot regarded as inherently evil and disruptive of the proper order of things, and it is not now possible to judge how far Thomas can be regarded as exceptionally cruel, even by the standards of his peers, or whether his reputation is a product of an over-heated imagination. Nevertheless, it is evident that Thomas, using his castle at Marle as a base, was as independently aggressive in the northern parts of the demesne as Hugh Le Puiset was in the south.

At length, Louis gathered an army with the aim of forcing Thomas to restore certain properties that he had seized from the monastery of St Jean-de-Laon. By the spring of 1115, the king had overcome Thomas's castles at Crécy, Nouvion and Marle, and Thomas was forced to come to terms, paying compensation to the king and the injured ecclesiastical institutions and, as a consequence, becoming reconciled to the Church. Although the parties concerned had gone through the conventional moves, Louis evidently was still not strong enough to impose a permanent solution. Thomas of Marle remained a power in the area, becoming even more entrenched with the acquisition of his paternal inheritance of Coucy and Boves in 1116. It was 1130 before Louis, in concert with Raoul, Count of Vermandois, was able to mount a decisive attack, eventually capturing and imprisoning him.

While he struggled to establish an effective base in the Ile-de-France, Louis was simultaneously forced to accommodate himself to the activities of neighbours in the surrounding fiefs. Neither Hugh of Le Puiset nor Thomas of Marle had confined their activities exclusively to the royal demesne, as the involvement of the Counts of Blois and Vermandois shows, so Louis was bound to be drawn into the politics of the powers around him even if his ambitions did not extend beyond his own demesne. One overshadowed all the others, that of the Anglo-Normans. King of England since the death of one elder brother, William, in 1100, Henry I had become master of Normandy following his capture of the other, Robert, at the battle of Tinchebrai in 1106. The existence of this formidable ruler, whose personality towered over those of his contemporaries, meant that Louis's scope for practical action outside the royal demesne was quite limited, whatever Suger tried to convey by his presentation of the events of

1124. Inferior in resources and gaining little advantage from his kingly attributes when in conflict with another king, Louis struggled against Henry with small success.

A reliable index of the relative strength of the two monarchies throughout the twelfth century was the degree of power that they could wield in the key frontier area of the Vexin, within which lay the formidable fortress of Gisors. Measured by this standard, Henry retained the upper hand, despite the vicissitudes of his reign. After Tinchebrai, Louis adopted the view that Henry was a usurper in Normandy and acted accordingly. It was a policy that produced sporadic fighting and political manoeuvring for the rest of the reign. Despite promises to the contrary, Henry occupied Gisors, and Louis, rather unconvincingly acting the part of feudal overlord, summoned him to appear at his court in 1109. Henry did not respond and the two kings were at war until 1113, when a peace was made in which Louis recognised Henry as overlord of Brittany and Maine. Louis had not been helped when Theobald, Count of Blois, had changed sides, so that he was faced with the opposition of both the powers with lands immediately adjacent to his demesnes. The low point in Louis's fortunes came in 1119 when, in another venture into the Vexin, he was defeated at the battle of Brémule, north of Les Andelys. His appeal to Pope Calixtus II, then holding a council at Reims, against Henry, made little practical difference, and in the following year he was forced to concede the unfavourable terms that Henry's son, William, should do homage to him for Normandy, despite the fact that hitherto he had supported Robert's son, William Clito, as the legitimate heir, and that Henry should hold Gisors, even though he had fought for a decade to prevent this.

Louis's problems were compounded in 1125 when Theobald of Blois succeeded to the county of Champagne, which meant that he controlled territories not only to the south-west of the royal demesne, but to the east as well. He was equally unsuccessful in Flanders, following the murder of Charles the Good in 1127. For a few months it looked as if he would be able to impose his own candidate, William Clito, but opposition, especially from some of the stronger towns, steadily eroded his support. The account of Galbert of Bruges conveys very strongly the sense of power slipping from William Clito's grasp as former supporters deserted to the camp of the other claimant, Thierry of Alsace. Fortunately for Louis, fear of the stifling presence of Henry I led Thierry to accept Capetian overlordship.

Yet, despite his problems, Louis left his heir a far more promising legacy than he had received from Philip I. Although his eldest son, Philip, had died in 1131, he had a second son, Louis, whose marriage in 1137 to Eleanor, heiress to the vast fiefs in the south-west over which William, Duke of Aquitaine, claimed overlordship, suddenly opened up great new horizons for the dynasty. Nor did the Capetian patrimony itself look so modest as it had once been for greater political control of the demesne meant that its potential resources could be more effectively exploited. John Benton (1967) has shown that by the 1170s the royal demesne was as profitable as any of the great fiefs which surrounded it, with an annual income of at least 60,000 *livres parisis*. In contrast, Henry I's plans had been shattered by the death of his son, William, in the White Ship disaster of 1120. With no other legitimate male successors, in 1127 Henry declared his daughter, Matilda, widow of the Emperor Henry V, to be his heir, and soon after married her to the heir of the county of Anjou, Geoffrey Plantagenet. These arrangements, however, could not prevent the succession crisis which followed Henry I's death in 1135. The rapid seizure of the English throne by Stephen of Blois, younger brother of Theobald, left England divided from Normandy, and Anjou and Blois in conflict.

Moreover, Louis VII was heir to an increasingly potent ideology. It would be an exaggeration to say that the difference between Philip I and Louis VI was that the latter had Suger to write up his exploits, but it is true that a seductive Capetian propaganda began to exercise a strong influence on contemporaries from Suger's time. Suger does not seem to have attended the abbey school at the same time as the future Louis VI, as was once thought, but he was certainly involved with the Capetian court from at least 1112, some years before he became abbot (Grant 1998:78–9, 86). It is not therefore surprising to find that Suger, who so fervently identified St Denis with the cause of the Capetian monarchy should, especially in the later years of the reign, have attained a position of great influence, largely displacing the traditional royal officers such as the seneschal and the chancellor. Indeed, the increasing grip on the royal demesne exercised by the monarchy was accompanied by a decline in the importance of these offices, which had customarily been dominated by prominent seigneurial families from the Ile-de-France like the Rochefort and the Garlande clans. When, partly as a result of pressure exerted by Bernard of Clairvaux, Stephen of Garlande lost control of the seneschalsy in 1127, the trend towards reliance on a body of unofficial advisers linked more closely to the reigning monarch was considerably strengthened.

Louis VII's twelfth-century reputation, however, was not entirely dependent upon the image of the French monarchy built by Suger under his father. At Christmas 1145, Louis made public his resolve to journey to the east. It is likely that he had already decided upon an expiatory pilgrimage, even before the fall of Edessa the previous year and, indeed, in June 1147, shortly before his departure, he made a special journey to St Denis to see and kiss the relics of the saint, before receiving the satchel, symbol of the pilgrim (Grabois 1985). The expedition itself was a painful failure and, by the autumn of 1149, at the urgent request of Suger, Louis was back in France. In retrospect, like others of Louis's initiatives, the crusade can be seen to have been incompetently led and poorly planned, but contemporary opinion was much kinder to the king than later historians have been. John of Salisbury describes how, when the pope greeted the king at Tusculum on Louis's return from the east in October 1149, 'one would have said that he was welcoming an angel of the Lord rather than a mortal man' (Chibnall 1956:61–2). Although there was widespread disappointment at the failure, it was the Byzantine Emperor Manuel who was cast in the role of scapegoat, a view given currency by Odo of Deuil, whose account of the expedition was written partly to show Greek responsibility and partly to exalt the king. For twelfth-century men, Louis became the pious and just crusader king of simple tastes. Indeed, in 1169, Frederick, Archbishop of Tyre, on a mission to the west, offered Louis 'the keys to the city of Jerusalem', evidently not intending that he replace Amalric, the reigning king, but rather inviting him to assume some kind of protectorate over the holy places (J. Phillips 1996:190–2). From this time, despite the fact that Philip I had taken little notice of the First Crusade, the dynasty was indissolubly linked to crusading: the next four Capetians were all directly involved, while Philip IV and his sons were constantly preoccupied with planning projects.

Buttressed by improved material resources, a brilliant new marriage and effective ideology, it might be thought that Louis VII was well set to make a real political impact in northern Europe and, indeed, in the early years of his reign he pursued an aggressive policy which suggests great confidence in his own power. In Normandy, he invested Eustace, son of King Stephen of England, as duke; in Toulouse, where he had a claim through Eleanor, he launched an attack on Count Alfonso-Jordan; and in the archbishopric of Bourges he tried to impose his own man, even though the chapter, backed by the papacy, had chosen a different candidate. But none of these ventures enhanced either the power or the reputation of the king. Geoffrey of Anjou was alienated by the Norman investiture and steadily encroached upon the duchy until, by 1144, when he captured Rouen, he had largely gained control; intervention in the south proved to be beyond Louis's military scope at this time and, in 1141, the king had to retreat; while the dispute over the archbishopric of Bourges drew in Theobald, Count of Blois-Champagne, for he supported the opposing candidate, Peter of la Châtre. The situation was further complicated by the king's support for Raoul of Vermandois, the royal seneschal, who had put aside his wife, a niece of Theobald. Some bitter military campaigns in Champagne in 1142 and 1143 followed, including a notorious incident in which some 1,500 people were burnt to death in a church at Vitry. While it now seems unlikely that the holocaust at Vitry played any significant part in changing Louis's policy, as has sometimes been thought, by the next year he does seem to have recognised that there was little future in sustaining a conflict which had lost him the support of the papacy and Bernard of Clairvaux, as well as leading to the struggle with Count Theobald. It therefore may have been at this time that he formulated his plans for the pilgrimage to Jerusalem. In any event, in 1144 he withdrew on all fronts which, together with his crusading activities, restored the papal goodwill he had been in danger of losing. When Louis and Eleanor were about to depart from Tusculum after their meeting with Eugenius III in 1149, John of Salisbury describes how

> though he [the pope] was a stern man, he could not hold back his tears, but sent them on their way blessing them and the kingdom of the Franks, which was higher in his esteem than all the kingdoms of the world.
>
> (Chibnall 1956:61–2)

In the years that followed, Louis needed all the allies he could find, most especially the papacy, for in 1154 the effects of Henry I's marriage of his daughter Matilda to Geoffrey of Anjou finally worked themselves out, creating a concentration of power in the hands of his grandson on a scale not even Henry himself could have envisaged. In December, in accordance with his agreement with the late King Stephen, Henry of Anjou, Duke of Normandy since 1150 and Count of Anjou since his father's death in 1151, was crowned King of England. While there was little that the French court could have done to prevent this, the pill was made even more bitter by the fact that Henry's queen was Eleanor of Aquitaine, whom he had married in May 1152, less than two months after her marriage to Louis had been nullified on the grounds of consanguinity. The marriage, sealed without the permission of Louis as overlord, made Henry lord of vast lands stretching to the Pyrenees.

Although these events have sometimes been viewed in romantic terms, all three parties had very practical reasons for their actions. The break between Louis and Eleanor had been likely for some time, for one of the main reasons for the meeting between Louis and Pope Eugenius in 1149 had been the growing rift between the king and queen, supposedly the consequence of an affair between Eleanor and Raymond of Antioch, her uncle, during the crusade. According to John of Salisbury,

> He [the pope] reconciled the king and queen, after hearing severally the accounts each gave of the estrangement begun at Antioch, and forbade any

future mention of their consanguinity: confirming their marriage, both orally and in writing, he commanded under pain of anathema that no word should be spoken against it and it should not be dissolved under any pretext whatever. This ruling plainly delighted the king, for he loved the queen passionately, in an almost childish way. The pope made them sleep in the same bed, which he had had decked with priceless hangings of his own; and daily during their brief visit he strove by friendly converse to restore love between them.

(Chibnall 1956:61–2)

It may have been true that, as John of Salisbury says elsewhere, the king loved Eleanor 'almost beyond reason' but, as the events of 1152 show, the pope's efforts as a marriage guidance counsellor were fruitless. The truth of the matter was that Eleanor had provided the king with no male heirs and the continuity of the line was endangered, a priority which, for the Capetians, nothing else could override. Eleanor, for her part, needed to look after herself in the vulnerable position in which she was left after the divorce. Henry was the most powerful protector around. As for Henry, although the move was dangerous, the prospect of Aquitaine in the hands of another lord could not be contemplated with equanimity by a man whose own county bordered on that of Poitou. Suddenly, it was the French succession that looked in danger, with the prospect of civil war after Louis's death, just as England had been afflicted during the previous generation. It was not until Louis's third wife, Adela of Champagne, gave birth to the future Philip II in 1165, that this possibility diminished.

Despite his failure to foresee or prevent Eleanor's remarriage, Louis had done what he could to counter the Angevins both by supporting Eustace in Normandy and by active intervention himself, pressure which gained for him the cession of the Norman Vexin in return for the king's recognition of Henry as duke in 1151. Therefore, despite Louis's limited influence over Henry's actions, the tie of vassalage remained, a tie which, in more favourable circumstances, could be exploited to the advantage of the suzerain. For the remainder of his reign, Louis's chief preoccupation outside the demesne was inevitably with Henry II, a struggle which he pursued by armed conflict, diplomacy and marriage alliance, sometimes employing a degree of duplicity that belies his pious image, but in practice seldom gaining any decisive military or political advantage.

The years 1158–60 are worth closer examination as an illustration of the nature of the considerations which governed relations between Capetian and Angevin. Although Henry had renewed his homage in 1156, he was not satisfied with the status quo, for it is evident that he did not regard the loss of the Norman Vexin as permanent, since it did not accord with his guideline, which was the restoration of the rights possessed by his grandfather. It was to this end that he negotiated a marriage alliance with Louis in August 1158, when Louis's daughter, Margaret, was betrothed to Henry's son and heir, Henry the Younger, with the Norman Vexin as dowry. Since both the parties were still infants, the Vexin would revert to Henry only when the marriage actually took place. But the strands of Henry's policies were multifold and his ambitions not limited to the Vexin, for since his brother Geoffrey, who had a claim to Brittany, had died the previous July, Henry wanted that duchy as well. The meeting of 1158 was therefore designed not only to cement the marriage alliance, but also to head off possible interference by Louis as Henry began to pursue his brother's claims.

By the next year, Henry's focus had shifted to a third area which abutted onto his massive domains, that of the Toulousain, claimed through right of his wife. Here, Louis gained a small but significant triumph, for when Henry gathered a great army to attack Toulouse, Louis took his forces south and, at the request of Count Raymond V, occupied the city. Henry was therefore frustrated, for Louis's overlordship could not be directly flouted by an attack, if he himself wished to retain credibility as overlord of a kingdom and many great fiefs. In the end, albeit reluctantly, he withdrew. There was, however, a price to pay for Louis, as Henry, who had both Henry the Younger and Margaret in his custody, now arranged their marriage and therefore, in November 1160, took over the Norman Vexin. Louis, for his part, was already repositioning himself, for when his second wife, Constance of Castile, died, he hastily remarried, taking as his new wife, Adela of Champagne. This meant a complete reorientation of policy, for it ended the long-standing enmity with the house of Blois, and clearly established that the co-operation between Capetian and Angevin of 1158 was little more than a temporary hiatus in an inevitable fundamental rivalry between the two dynasties.

This kind of manoeuvring characterised the rest of the reign. Sometimes Louis gained small advantages, especially when the murder of Becket in 1170 brought universal condemnation upon Henry and praise for Louis, the king who had sheltered the archbishop after his flight from England in 1164. Moreover, the Angevin lands, although vast in area and resources, were not a coherent unit. They could be prized apart, and in 1173–4 Henry was faced with a rebellion so serious and widespread that, for a time, it looked as if he would never regain the dominance of his early years. Although the driving force behind the discontent was that of Henry's sons, particularly Henry the Younger, Louis was involved in its promotion. Its failure was, indirectly, another sign that he could not really inflict serious damage on Henry II. The reality was that Louis had neither the military competence nor the resources to do more than contain Henry and that ultimately the sheer size of the Angevin lands presented greater problems to Henry than did the activities of his overlord.

The reigns of Louis VI and Louis VII changed the Capetians from a relatively insignificant local dynasty into a power to be reckoned with, even by men like Henry II, but there is nothing to alter the traditional view that the really decisive period of the Capetian era was that spanning the four decades straddling the year 1200, the period of the rule of Philip II, 'Augustus', 1180 to 1223. It was during this reign that France changed from, in Joseph Strayer's words, a Bohemia or Bavaria, into one of the dominant political and cultural forces of thirteenth-century Christendom. From the very beginning of the reign, although still only in his mid-teens and lacking any experience in government (he had been crowned only towards the end of his father's life in 1179), Philip II had set out to accumulate territorial jurisdiction by whatever means came to hand. At this time his most significant gains were substantial interests in Artois and Vermandois, acquired through the right of his first wife, Isabella of Hainaut, who died in 1182. However, the core of his success was the conquest of Normandy, achieved by July 1204, a triumph which was followed by the seizure of other Angevin lands during the next two years, including Anjou, Maine, Touraine, Brittany and, temporarily, Poitou and the Auvergne.

Philip II set about developing his power more systematically than any French king had ever previously done. The essence of this preparation was the king's remarkable skill in extending royal influence through the manipulation of the complex feudal relationships of northern France. The centrepiece of the network was the king's claim to ultimate suzerainty, a claim which grew out of Suger's dictum that the king could be vassal to no one, ultimately implying a feudal hierarchy which devolved from the king.

It has been shown that under Philip II there was a great increase in the issue of royal documents which in some way addressed the question of the king's rights as overlord (Bisson 1978:470–4). Even Henry II found it necessary to concede homage for his continental lands to Louis VII, an action not taken by either of his two predecessors while they were crowned rulers of England. If the Angevins were drawn into the system, it is not surprising to find other great territorial princes, like those of Flanders, Champagne and Burgundy, also offering their homage, the vicissitudes of the shifting feudal alliances of the north notwithstanding. The following pledge by Ferrand, Count of Flanders, made in 1212, shows how the decentralised Carolingian world had been transformed into a 'feudal system'.

> I, Ferrand ... make known to all that I am the liege man of my lord Philip, the illustrious king of France, against all men and women ... and I have sworn to him that I will render good and faithful service, nor will I desert him as long as he wishes to render justice to me in his court. If, however, I were to be wanting in good and faithful service to him, I concede that all my men, barons as well as knights, and all the communes and communities of the towns and fortified places of my land, may help the lord king against me and may do as much harm as they can to me, until amends are made to the lord king for his goodwill. And I wish and command that all the aforesaid, barons as well as knights and others swear and guarantee this to the lord king. If, however, there are any who do not wish to swear this I would render all the harm I could to them, I would have neither peace nor truce with them in any way, unless it was through the wish and good pleasure of the lord king.
>
> (Warnkoenig 1835:345)

As this document shows, the establishment of such a hierarchy strengthened an existing trend, that of the attendance at the royal court of the important territorial lords and their acceptance of that court's jurisdiction, a trend which can be traced from the late 1140s. The idea of the court as the ultimate fount of justice and thus the possessor of appellate jurisdiction can be seen to be an intrinsic part of this, so that the rear-vassals had access to the king's court if they could argue that they had been denied justice at the hands of their immediate lord. It is evident that Ferrand's vassals, as well as the count himself, were expected to 'swear and guarantee' their loyalty first and foremost to the king. Not surprisingly, royal officials found more and more pretexts for the intervention of royal justice, creating a climate in which it was accepted that any matters involving royal officials or in which one party appealed to royal judgement should be under the jurisdiction of the king's court (Mitteis 1975:274–9). At the same time, although the most evident effects of these changes were felt by the nobility, the system had the advantage that it was flexible enough to accommodate other, newer social elements as well, most particularly the increasing number of towns and groups of villages claiming communal or quasi-communal status. Here the king granted charters of privileges, but again reserved ultimate jurisdiction for the royal court and ensured that the military and financial returns justified the concession.

All this meant royal officials in increasing numbers; Philip II was the first of his line to preside over a government which could properly be called bureaucratic. With the main offices of state often left vacant, from the early 1190s Philip relied upon a small group of *familiares* of relatively obscure background, who loyally served him throughout the reign (Hollister and Baldwin 1978). Lesser officials were equally modest in origin, but nevertheless effective in intervening not only in matters connected with the royal demesne, but also in other fiefs and ecclesiastical lordships whenever the opportunity presented itself, thus giving the king wedges of influence well beyond the areas which, by 1223, can legitimately be shaded in on a map as royal demesne. However, the most striking changes in Philip's government can be seen in the administration of that demesne, for as the whole scope of government began to expand in the 1180s and 1190s, it became more necessary to define specialist departments, with a broad division emerging between the secretariat, justice and finance. By the time of the first known Capetian 'budget' in 1202–3, for instance, the royal officials were already meeting three times per year at the house of the Templars in Paris, where accounts were checked and reviewed. By that time too the most important of these accounts were those provided by the *baillis*, omnicompetent regional officials introduced in 1184, and largely modelled on Norman institutions. Although the king did not abolish the older *prévôtés*, whose holders farmed their offices (indeed the numbers of *prévôtés* actually increased), the use of *baillis* gradually established a structure of salaried and regulated officials whose presence became indispensable to the administration of the royal demesne in northern France.

However, because the king was establishing himself at the apex of French feudal society and because his demesnes were larger and better governed than ever before, it does not follow that the conquest of Normandy was part of an inevitable long-term process in which the scales became ever more obviously tilted against the Angevins. Indeed, until the unexpected death of Henry's heir, Richard I, in 1199, Philip had been conspicuously unsuccessful in gaining territory from his rivals, despite his attacks on the Angevin lands in the years between 1191 and 1194, while Richard was on crusade and in captivity. The turning-point for Philip came with the acceptance of Richard's younger brother John in Normandy and England in April and May 1199, for the Angevin lands were torn by a disputed succession. While John received support in the north, Arthur of Brittany, the 12-year-old son of Henry's fourth son, Geoffrey (d. 1186), was acclaimed in Anjou, Touraine and Maine, as well as Brittany itself, lands which included the key cities of Angers and Tours. Philip II, in keeping with his policy of trying to bring the great fiefs into direct subordination to the crown, seized the opportunity not only to exploit the Angevin quarrels, as he had done so often in the past, but also to detach Brittany from dependence on Normandy. He therefore received Arthur's homage for these lands and began to make preparations for war with John.

Although both claimants could make out a case in law, John, using soldiers and money recently collected by Richard, possessed the force. He marched swiftly into Anjou where the key figure on Arthur's side, William des Roches, Constable of Anjou, negotiated peace between him and Arthur. Meanwhile Philip, under some pressure from the papacy because of his failure to honour his marriage to Ingeborg of Denmark, suddenly came to an agreement with John, embodied in the Treaty of Le Goulet (May 1200). Under its terms John was recognised by Philip, in return for which he accepted Philip as his overlord for his continental lands and paid a relief of 20,000 marks to enter into the inheritance. Moreover, various lands, the most important of which was the County of Evreux, were ceded to Philip. Arthur was abandoned. Philip renounced suzerainty over Brittany and all rights over Arthur, who was acknowledged to be John's vassal. The treaty was consolidated by the marriage of Philip's son, Louis, to Blanche of Castile, John's niece. Accordingly John was received at Angers in June and the lands of his father and brother submitted to him. As many historians have said, Philip extracted harder terms from John than ever before, but at least John could now enter peacefully into his lands.

The situation was, however, disrupted by John himself in the affair of the Angoulême marriage. John probably first saw Isabella of Angoulême, then aged 14, on 5 July. He was betrothed to her on 23 August, married to her on the 30th, and on 8 October she was crowned at Westminster. The marriage involved both the dissolution of John's existing marriage and the breaking of Isabella's engagement to Hugh, lord of Lusignan, son of the Count of La Marche. This was certain to alienate the Lusignan family, the most powerful clan in this key region of Poitou, but John, far from conciliating them, set about seizing their castles. The following Easter the Lusignans retaliated by making war on John and by appealing to the court of John's overlord, Philip II. There now unfolded a classic example of a dispute of a feudal kind, in which the rear-vassal appealed to the court of the ultimate suzerain. In the exploitation of such disputes lay Philip II's greatest skill.

The dispute ultimately gave Philip a legal pretext to invade Normandy; he had no special interest in protecting the Lusignans. Indeed, it was some time before he found it convenient to act. He was, however, greatly helped by John's behaviour for, despite being cited three times, John failed to appear at Philip's court. In April 1202 the court accordingly informed the king that John should be deprived of all his lands as a contumacious vassal. As was pointed out long ago by Achille Luchaire, cases of complete disinheritance were rare (1901:129). The judicial forms provided only a thin cover for Philip's ambitions which, after all, had been frequently enough displayed in the past. As for John, a good case can be made for the Angoulême marriage on strategic grounds in that this region of Poitou was important in the communications of the Angevin lands. The houses of Angoulême and Lusignan were often rivals and the king needed the allegiance of at least one of them. Nevertheless, John's failure to take proper account of the consequences of the marriage drew him into a far more significant confrontation than he must have anticipated.

In June, Philip began his invasion of Normandy, while Arthur took his chance to attack in Poitou, taking Mirebeau and blockading Queen Eleanor in the town's keep. The relief of Mirebeau and the capture of Arthur and the Lusignans at the end of July showed that John did have energy and military ability, despite many opinions, both contemporary and later, to the contrary. John did not, however, defend Normandy with such resource. In the spring of 1203, Philip began a new offensive against both the Seine and the Loire valleys. John's attempt to hide behind an appeal to Pope Innocent III failed, for Philip informed the pope that it was a feudal matter in which the pope could not interfere. Meanwhile, John blundered further by alienating William des Roches, who held the key to support in Anjou, by refusing to hand over Arthur as promised. Indeed, by the winter of 1203–4 rumours were circulating that Arthur had been murdered. Philip continued to press into Normandy and when, after a long and bitter siege during the winter of 1203–4, Château Gaillard fell, the way was opened to Rouen. In the meantime John had left for England in October 1203, and he did not return throughout Philip's conquest. When Rouen capitulated in June 1204, having been offered very favourable terms by Philip, Normandy was lost, and during the next two years massive defections among the baronage led to the acquisition of the adjoining Angevin fiefs.

In retrospect, 1204 was decisive, but King John could hardly be expected to accept the loss of Normandy with equanimity. During the next decade he expended immense administrative and diplomatic effort in an attempt to recover what he had relinquished with so little apparent resistance. It was not an impossible project, for there was no shortage of disaffected lords willing to listen to John's overtures, their interest quickened by the English king's financial backing. Even in Normandy itself, which has so often been presented as defecting to Philip with relatively little difficulty, there were complaints about his monetary exactions and discontent over the loss of trade with England which the conquest had caused. By 1213 a formidable coalition had been assembled which included, apart from Otto of Brunswick, linked to John by blood and marriage, Renaud of Dammartin, one of the most powerful lords of northern France, a former ally of Philip with whom he had since quarrelled, and Ferrand of Portugal, Count of Flanders, alienated by Capetian pressure on the fief. Many other lords from the Low Countries, like the Count of Holland, were keen to see the Capetian checked. John had hoped to make a junction with their forces by approaching from the south, but the whole structure started to fall apart when, on 15 July 1214, he was beaten back by Prince Louis at La Roche-au-Moine. Twelve days later his allies were defeated in a battle fought on the plateau near the village of Bouvines in south-east Flanders. Otto of Brunswick fled, Renaud and Ferrand were thrown into captivity and John had to make peace, which he did at Chinon in September. He then returned to England to face the political consequences of his financial exactions which led to Magna Carta in the summer of 1215 and the civil war of 1215–16. Even then, John was not free of Capetian pressure for, in 1216–17, Prince Louis invaded England, tempted by some of the baronage who led him to believe that they preferred him to John. The outcome was still uncertain when John died, leaving Louis in the invidious position of contesting the throne with the legitimate heir, John's infant son, Henry. Faced with baronial opposition and the disapproval of the papacy, Louis decided to cut his losses.

Bouvines was therefore a battle with very tangible political consequences, not only for the Angevin cause in Normandy and in England, but also for Flanders, where Capetian officials now inserted themselves, and for the Empire, where Otto IV's fading claims in the face of Frederick II were now finally extinguished. But, for the Capetians, as has been seen, Bouvines had a further value, for in the pro-Capetian writings it became one of the central elements in the dynasty's image, serving to mask the unheroic reality of Philip's character. Although a crusader king in 1190–1, he had not cut an impressive figure, for he had departed from the Holy Land as soon as was practically possible, and he had used Richard I's continued participation in the crusade as an opportunity to attack his lands. Moreover, his relations with the papacy were far from harmonious, for the popes were not prepared to accept his repudiation of his second wife, Ingeborg of Denmark, in favour of Agnes of Méran, whom he supposedly married in 1196. The land of the king of the chosen race was even put under interdict by Innocent III for a time in 1198 during the course of this dispute which was not settled to papal satisfaction until 1213.

In many ways the reasons for Philip's success in conquering Normandy are implicit in the narrative of events. John's political and military errors, combined with almost inexplicable periods of inertia, often at crucial moments, lie at the heart of the matter. These errors were compounded by Philip II's ability to exert so much military pressure on the Angevin lands that ultimately they could not pay for their own defence. In 1202–3 Normandy received over £18,000 from the English Exchequer to supplement an annual income of about £24,500, but there do not seem to have been any equivalent payments coming from the more southerly parts of the Angevin possessions (J.C. Holt 1984). If anything, additional revenue was needed in the south, for Philip attacked not only along the Seine, but the Loire as well. Past payments added to the burden: the Norman contribution to Richard I's ransom had been £4,000 (1194–5) and Château Gaillard and its surrounding works, Richard's great castle on the Seine, had cost £11,500 by the end of 1198. Moreover, John depended increasingly on mercenaries, the cost of which had multiplied threefold since the 1160s (P. Harvey 1973:13–14). A telling illustration is provided by Sir Maurice Powicke, who showed that in 1197/8 the cost of hiring 890 foot-soldiers at Château Gaillard for eight days was so great that if they had been maintained for a year the total would have reached £3,000 (Powicke 1961:331).

The comparative size of the lands ruled by Philip II and John is not therefore such an obvious indicator of their relative financial positions as it might appear at first sight. The Angevin lands were vast, but difficult to govern and defend, while the Capetian demesne, reorganised by Philip under a new financial system during the 1190s, yielded a 72 per cent increase in revenue between 1179 and 1203 (Baldwin 1986:248, 114–51). This did not mean that the task was an easy one for Philip, or that his resources were overwhelmingly superior. The inadequacies of Louis VII's legacy are all too evident in the early years of the reign, when Philip was forced to any expedient that came to hand in order to raise money, coming down heavily on the Jews and, more dangerously for a dynasty so dependent upon ecclesiastical approval, upon the clergy as well. It was these problems which made the centralisation of demesne finances so important, for the economic prosperity of the Ile-de-France, experiencing booms in both agriculture and building during Philip II's reign, must have been obvious to the observer, even if impossible to quantify. The administrative reorganisation and the military conquests paid off handsomely: between 1204 and 1221 the new acquisitions added another 69 per cent to Capetian revenue, making an absolute increase of 80,000 *livres parisis* per annum, truly a different world from that of Louis VII.

During a reign of forty-three years Philip II was almost entirely preoccupied with events in northern France just as, with rare exceptions such as the expedition of 1159, his predecessors had been. Languedoc was a land of different language and culture, its lords theoretically linked to the French monarchy by feudal ties, but in practice largely beyond the range of its experience and interest. Philip II therefore had no intention of being diverted from his conflict with King John by Innocent III's appeals for help against the southern heretics and the successes achieved by the Albigensian Crusades between 1209 and 1218 were largely the work of his vassals. But Simon of Montfort's death in 1218 put these gains in jeopardy and Pope Honorius III once more tried to draw in the king. Philip remained cautious, and it was not until his son succeeded as Louis VIII in 1223 that new plans were made for subjugating the south. He had played a prominent part of the Angevin wars for a decade before his accession, so that his invasion of Poitou in 1224 was simply an extension of these policies, but he differed from his father in taking a marked interest in the south. He had already led expeditions in 1215 and 1219 and in 1225 he finally persuaded the papacy to part with the money that he demanded for a new crusade. The next year, at the head of an army which was probably twice the size of the original Albigensian Crusade in 1209, he moved down the Rhône, took Avignon, and precipitated another collapse of the southern nobility. His early death in November 1226, leaving a minor to succeed, may have mitigated the effects upon the house of Toulouse, but even so, in 1229, Raymond VII was forced to accept the Treaty of Paris which allowed him to retain only a proportion of his lands during his lifetime. Jeanne, Raymond's daughter, was to marry a younger brother of Louis IX, later named as Alphonse of Poitiers, on whom the bulk of these lands would devolve.

The arrangements made for the division of territory shown in this treaty were in keeping with Louis VIII's provisions for disposing of the other huge areas which had now fallen into Capetian hands. In his will of 1225 his dispositions for the cadet branches were quite similar to those envisaged by Henry II in the twelfth century. In common with contemporary feudal practice, he left the inherited lands, together with the coveted Normandy, to his successor, the maternal lands to his second son, and the other conquests to the third and fourth sons. Any further sons were to go into the Church (Lewis 1976). By this means Artois, Anjou, Maine, Poitou and the Auvergne went to these younger lines as *apanages*, just as Toulouse was to do after Count Raymond's death. The king's stated aim was to secure a peaceful succession and prevent family disputes but, as Henry II's sons showed only too clearly, there was no guarantee that this would be successful. The only certainty was that if no provision were made for the younger sons, the family would not remain at peace for long.

In fact, it was the Capetians' good fortune that their reigns remained relatively free of the internecine strife that had so damaged the Angevin cause, so that the imagery of Christian kingship so assiduously cultivated by the writings of Suger and William the Breton continued to develop untrammelled by the need to gloss over struggles for the throne which might imply a diminution in the purity of the blood. The ultimate success of this propaganda was achieved in August 1297, when Pope Boniface VIII presided over the canonisation of Louis IX. In Louis VIII's eldest son, only 12 years old when he succeeded to the throne in 1226, the image and the reality of medieval kingship came closer to complete juxtaposition than at any other time. The canonisation was the peak of a campaign begun as early as 1272, but heavily promoted by Louis IX's grandson, Philip IV, to honour his predecessor, for at the same time he lavished his patronage upon a wide variety of religious houses connected with Louis, as well as establishing and endowing a Dominican nunnery at Poissy, place of Louis's birth and baptism. The cult received further impetus with the production of laudatory biographies, most notably that of William of Saint-Pathus, a former confessor of Louis's queen, Margaret of Provence, written in 1302–3, and that of John of Joinville, the knight from Champagne who became Louis's close friend, in 1309 (Hallam 1982b). Such cults, which had received a considerable setback in the face of the desacralising policies of the popes of the reform era, had nevertheless been regaining strength in the twelfth and thirteenth centuries, especially as monarchies like those of France, England, Sicily and Iberia consolidated their material power. One index of this was the increasingly elaborate ceremonial accompanying a royal burial for which an appropriate setting had been provided by the series of effigies of Capetian predecessors, including both Merovingians and Carolingians, and their tombs, carefully arranged beneath the rebuilt crossing of the church at St Denis between 1264 and 1267 (Hallam 1982a:372). Moreover, Louis IX seems to have been the first of the Capetian kings who regularly touched sufferers from the disease of scrofula, who thereby hoped to receive a miraculous cure, and this too was continued by Philip IV (Barlow 1980; M. Bloch 1973:11–48).

There is no doubt that this cult was promoted by Philip IV for good political reasons and with considerable effect, but it was the character of Louis IX himself that made it all possible. Joinville, who, for all his admiration for the king, was well aware of his faults, seems to have encapsulated his view of his duties as king when he described how, as Louis lay ill at Fontainebleau, he urged his son

> to make yourself loved by all your people. For I would rather have a Scot come from Scotland [apparently the most outlandish idea that he could conceive] to govern the people of this kingdom well and justly than that you should govern them ill in the sight of all the world.
>
> (Shaw 1963:167)

This desire to adhere to an ideal of kingship was paralleled by a personal life in which he pursued a regime of stringent asceticism combined with a deep devotion towards the religious and the afflicted. Much of his time was therefore occupied with the foundation and refurbishment of religious houses and with charitable work. This involved practical participation rather than simply symbolic acts or the granting of charters. One story among the many told by his hagiographers was that of his visits to the Cistercian abbey of Royaumont, where a brother named Légier was isolated from the others because he was almost devoured by leprosy. Légier's nose was eaten away, he had lost his eyes, his lips had burst, and his body streamed with pus, yet it was to this man that the king directed his attention. Even the abbot later admitted that such visits filled him with horror (Daunou and Naudet 1840:96–7).

His character seems largely to have been formed by his mother, Blanche of Castile who, as regent during his minority, steered him through the baronial discontents of the first decade or so. In the 1220s, ambitious northern lords like Philip Hurepel, Louis's uncle, tried to wrest control of the young king from his mother, so that at various times in the 1220s and 1230s discontent was stirred up in Picardy, Champagne, Burgundy and Brittany, which in turn was complicated by the attempted invasions of Henry III of England seeking to regain his father's patrimony, and by the revolts of the southern lords of 1240 and 1242, still resentful of the imposition of royal and inquisitorial authority. This was the most turbulent period of Capetian history since the early years of the reign of Louis VI, but it seems improbable that, given the disparate nature of the parties involved, there was any serious threat to the monarchy itself. It may well be that the most important effect of the *frondes* of the king's youth was to reinforce his determination, evident throughout the reign, to impose his interpretation of the obligations of royal authority regardless of persons. The disaster of the crusade seems to have strengthened rather than undermined his faith and when he returned to France in 1254, he began a programme of internal administrative reform and external arbitration of outstanding differences with other Christian powers that more than ever before represented a coherent attempt to apply his moral and religious principles to the task of government.

The centralisation and specialisation of what were becoming major departments of state, already evident under Philip II, continued to develop. Regular sessions of the *parlements*, for instance, were held to hear litigants. By the mid-century they had a staff of about thirty in almost permanent session in Paris, fortified by legal records and royal decrees, and thus slowly developing a body of legislation. It was, however, at local level that the mass of the populace was most likely to feel the effects of the king's rule and it is in his attempts to improve the quality of administration in the provinces that Louis was most active. By this time the royal lands had been organised into a series of distinct administrative districts: in Francia, the *prévôté* of Paris and the *bailliages* of Senlis,

Vermandois, Amiens, Sens, Orléans, Bourges, Mâcon and Tours; in Normandy, the *bailliages* of Rouen, Caen, Cotentin, Caux and Gisors, and in the south, where the terminology was different, the *sénéchaussées* of Beaucaire and Carcassonne.

For many local communities, however, greater systematisation of government was equated with more efficient oppression and it was to counter such attitudes that Louis introduced a circuit of itinerant commissioners, known as *enquêteurs*, often drawn from the Franciscan and Cistercian orders, to investigate and remedy complaints against royal officials. They first appeared in 1247, before his departure on crusade, and the information which they gathered led to the ordinance of 1254 which set down regulations for the conduct of royal officials. Most of the complaints concerned officers at a very local level, for here the opportunities for petty tyranny were almost unlimited. Some had little justification, like the man who, imprisoned for hitting his wife, agreed that he had done it, but 'not beyond measure', but many were more serious. William Païen, a clerk, for instance, had had all his movable goods seized, and had been tortured so severely that he was now a cripple, having been accused of pillaging some episcopal treasure (Langlois 1901:348–51). The king's attempted remedy can be seen in the ordinance of 1254, which set down that the royal officials 'will do justice to all, without respect of persons, to the poor as to the rich, and to men from other countries as to those who are native-born'. In order to achieve this, the *baillis* were not to have ties in the region which they administered, were to be moved at regular intervals and, when they left office, were to be answerable to any complaints that might be laid against them (Shaw 1963:337–41). The impact of these reforms should not be exaggerated; they perhaps reveal more about the king's view of government than about its actual operation. Some offices, for instance, despite the regulations, tended to develop a familial character, while the king implicitly accepted the venality of the minor office-holders, concentrating instead upon whether the functions of the office were performed rather than the fact that it was bought and sold (W.C. Jordan 1979:48).

The underlying theme of Louis's reign was his determination to adhere to his coronation oath to uphold the law; Joinville's anecdotes provide a number of homely illustrations of the way that he gave his personal attention to this. Such stories provide the raw material of popular sanctity, but an important practical concomitant was the enforcement of monarchical peace which, in particular, meant emphasising the ultimate judicial superiority of the crown. Ordinances against judicial duels, private warfare and the holding of tournaments, together with restrictions on the carrying of arms, reflect a general attitude which found specific application in cases such as the trial of Enguerrand of Coucy in 1259. Enguerrand's servants had hung three young French nobles who had inadvertently trespassed in his woods, an act which provoked complaint both from the neighbouring abbey of St-Nicholas-au-Bois, where they had been staying, and from Giles le Brun, the royal constable, to whom one of them was related. Enguerrand was the leader of one of the most important baronial clans, closely allied to the powerful counts of Dreux and confident of his position within the circles close to the king. It was therefore a shock both to him and others when his claim that he need answer only before his peers received scant sympathy from the king, who first imprisoned him and, then, following a royal inquest, fined him a total of 22,000 *livres*. It is typical of the king that most of the fine was spent on the provision of buildings for the Franciscans and Dominicans in Paris (Richard 1992:212–13, 228–9).

Despite his panoply of clerical advisers, the king could be equally tough on the Church, itself a vested interest. It is clear, for instance, both from the evidence of a number of specific disputes and from references by Joinville that he would not back excommunications without evidence of their necessity, on one occasion being told by the Bishop of Auxerre that because of this attitude 'the honour of Christendom is declining in your hands' (Shaw 1963:332). Nor was he reluctant to move against clerics who infringed what he saw as royal rights, engaging in a number of lengthy disputes, not always clearly resolved. His taxation of the clergy, especially for crusades, brought further waves of protest, but these appear to have done nothing to divert him from his course. At the same time, however, the French Church needed the king as a shield against the increasingly intrusive policies of a papacy intent upon gathering taxation for its struggle with the Hohenstaufen and, from the 1260s, frequently intervening in specific sees on the grounds of its plenitude of power.

The application of Christian principles to practical government therefore exempted no one from the king's higher duty to God's law. This logically involved an attempt to bring peace among Christians, while attempting to combat any machinations of the devil which might serve to undermine that Christian society. The crusade was central to this view of his role but equally it involved sustained campaigns against what were seen as alien elements within Christian society, the blasphemous and the irreverent, heretics and Jews. His two most outstanding external problems were with his neighbours in Aragon and in England, problems which he tried to rectify in the treaties of Corbeil (1258) and Paris (1259). The agreement with James of Aragon was perhaps less contentious than the question of his relations with Henry III. James and Louis agreed on a mutual renunciation of claims in areas where their jurisdictions conflicted, so that James retained only the lordship of Montpellier in southern France. For his part, Louis withdrew claims to Roussillon and Catalonia that had their origins in Carolingian times. With Henry, Louis was anxious to regularise the conquests of the past and, in order to gain recognition of their legitimacy, confirmed Henry's right to Gascony, which became a fief of the French crown.

Louis died a martyr's death outside Tunis in August 1270, while on his second crusade. Charles of Anjou, now attempting to build a Mediterranean empire from his base in Sicily, has been seen as influencing the choice of Tunis, but recent opinion suggests that it was not directly relevant to his ambitions. Once again therefore it was the king's will which prevailed, although he seems to have intended the Tunisian campaign to have been the first stage of an operation which ultimately would have taken the crusade to Syria and Egypt (Richard 1992:319–24; Dunbabin 1998:195–7). Here, indeed, is the key both to Louis IX's reign and the use to which it was put thereafter. In a significant sentence Joinville commented that

> when anyone consulted him on a certain matter he would not say: 'I will take advice on this question'; but if he saw the right solution clearly and plainly he would answer without reference to his council, and at once.
>
> (Shaw 1963:331)

Not surprisingly, contemporaries were not always as uncritical as some of the hagiographical writing after his death.

As he lay dying, Louis IX is supposed to have set down instructions to his son, Philip. In Joinville's version they read like a blueprint of the reign that was just ending: suffer any torment to avoid mortal sin, accept adversity or prosperity with equanimity, maintain good customs and abolish bad ones, ensure that you have wise counsellors and confessors, punish any disparagement of God or humans, provide equitable justice, ensure that all live peacefully, honour the Holy Church, beware of wars against other Christian princes, appoint good officials and keep a close check on them, and finally, have masses and prayers said for Louis himself after his death (Shaw 1963:347–9). But it is too much to expect that any other ruler could emulate Louis IX, however much he might strive to do so. The new king, Philip III, was pious and brave, but his reign was bound to seem, both to contemporaries and later historians, as a sad contrast to that of his father. Louis IX's reign soon began to take on the aura of 'a golden age', the 'good customs' of which the royal subjects found increasingly convenient as a reference point when the tentacles of royal power seemed to be embracing them too firmly. Philip IV found ways of coping with this problem, most evidently by appropriating the role of successor to St Louis for himself and exploiting it against those who would resist royal power, but Philip III had no such opportunity or, perhaps, ability.

Philip III found it difficult to ride out the pressures applied by those who wished to dominate the government, in particular by Charles of Anjou. Charles was the central figure in the two key issues of Philip's reign: the territorial rights of the crown and the crusading tradition of the Capetians. In the first he failed to get his own way, but in the second he set in motion events which brought his nephew to military disaster and finally death in pursuit of objectives which could only have benefited Charles. In each case Philip failed to follow his father's instructions: in the first, to dispense justice equitably, in the second, to beware of wars with fellow Christians. The territorial issue reflects changes which had already started to take place under Louis IX, for it concerned the status of the *apanage* of Poitou and Auvergne, held by Alphonse of Poitiers. When Alphonse died without issue in 1271, it was claimed by his brother, Charles, as the nearest relative. Although the Treaty of Paris of 1229 determined that Toulouse would revert to the crown, there was considerable ambiguity about the status of Alphonse's *apanages* received under the terms of Louis VIII's will. Andrew Lewis has shown that Louis VIII's thinking was very much in tune with that of most twelfth- and early-thirteenth-century nobles regarding the disposal of their lands, but by the later thirteenth century, despite the continuance of the *apanage* system, the Capetian kings seem much less willing to allow large parts of their territorial acquisitions to be granted to cadet branches. Louis IX was by no means as generous as his father in his provision of *apanages*, while Philip III's arrangements seem positively mean in comparison with those of Louis VIII. In 1284, after a long legal battle, characterised by considerable shifting of ground on the royal side, the *parlement* decided that Alphonse's lands did not devolve upon Charles as the nearest heir, since they were a royal gift and not an inheritance, a decision quite contrary to the custom hitherto followed (Lewis 1982:174–8). These kings may have been moving tentatively towards a concept of France as a territorial entity, in which the granting of *apanages* seemed less natural than it had to Louis VIII. It is noticeable, for example, that Louis IX, in contrast to his grandfather, made considerable efforts to establish the monarchy in the Mediterranean both through his marriage to Margaret of Provence and his establishment of the royal port at Aigues-Mortes.

Charles of Anjou was also instrumental in drawing Philip into the disastrous crusade against Aragon, although the actual campaign took place after his death. When the Sicilian Vespers overthrew Angevin rule on the island, and Peter of Aragon seized the chance to invade, Pope Martin IV excommunicated him and began to activate the French connection. His offer of the crown of Aragon to Charles of Valois, a younger son of Philip, was accepted in February 1284, and a crusade called in its support that summer. In May 1285 the French army invaded but, although Philip succeeded in taking Gerona, the annihilation of his fleet cut his communications and his army, afflicted by disease as well, was forced to retreat. The Aragonese chronicler, Bernat Desclot, who was probably a nobleman in Peter's entourage, believed that this destroyed Philip, describing him not unsympathetically as so 'grievously afflicted by sadness in his heart that his strength failed him and came not again' (Critchlow 1928:357). He died on the return journey at Perpignan in October 1285.

Philip IV came to the throne at the age of 17, just over a century after his famous predecessor, Philip II, had succeeded at a similar age. The contrast to the situation in 1180 is striking. Huge additions had been made to the royal demesne, most spectacularly in Normandy and Toulouse. By the late thirteenth century these two fiefs combined yielded nearly half of the king's ordinary annual revenue (Strayer 1969:3). Central administration was crystallising around clearly defined departments of state, and the main local administrators, the *baillis* and the *sénéchaux*, were salaried officials, closely accountable. The papacy continued to look to the French monarch as its chief protector in times of adversity, while the French Church, at least in the north, was closely bound to the ruling house. The notion of the French king as the most Christian ruler, presiding over a new chosen people, was already firmly implanted, as well as being personified by Philip's honoured grandfather. For these reasons the reign has often been seen as a crucial stage in French history; in particular some nineteenth-century French historians, such as Thierry and Michelet, saw Philip IV, powered by the drive of the lawyers who served as his chief advisers, begin a process which ultimately led to the destruction of the traditional medieval forces and thus opened the way for the development of the French national state (Pegues 1962:7–21, 221–5). More recent writing has rejected this view as excessively schematic, but even so its influence lingers, for the reign is still often seen in terms of the victory of embryonic national monarchy over the universalist powers, an appropriate culmination to two centuries of Capetian development.

Yet, when Philip IV died in November 1314, he left his son, Louis, a heavy burden of problems: a league of discontented nobles, two great unsolved and long-running crises in relations with Flanders and the English crown, and the smell of a series of scandals, including the attacks on Boniface VIII in 1303 and the Order of the Templars between 1307 and 1312, which had provoked both shock and cynicism among his contemporaries. He left too the legacy of crushing military defeat at the battle of Courtrai in 1302 and the memory of a series of financial crises in which the government seemed to be lurching from one expedient to the next, crises by no means alleviated by the elaborate bequests and donations to which he committed his son for the safety of his soul (E.A.R. Brown 1976:379). These apparent contradictions make it necessary to look more closely at the reign, especially with a view to discovering the extent to which Philip or his advisers were to any conscious extent acting differently from previous rulers.

The central theme is one of finance, for while the French king's incomes had indeed increased dramatically, so too had the scale of the problems. Philip III left his son a huge debt from the Aragonese war, which perhaps cost in the region of 1.25 million *livres tournois*, and, although Philip IV never allowed himself to be drawn into such ventures or to become tangled with the schemes of the Angevins, he too needed massive sums, for he was as resolute as his predecessors in his desire to enforce monarchical power. None of his neighbours found proximity comfortable. Determined as he was to reach a settlement over the Aragonese affair, there were still outstanding territorial questions as late as 1295, despite a general agreement in 1287, while French influence in Iberia remained through his control of Navarre, whose links to France had been secured by Philip's marriage to its heiress, Jeanne, in 1284. Equally, along the eastern and north-eastern borders French officials continually encroached upon contiguous territories (the important city of Lyon, for instance, had been gained by the end of the reign), and the king himself tried to promote the candidature of his son to the imperial throne. Most of all, however, he continued the Capetian policy of bringing pressure to bear upon the great fiefs, where his exemplar seems to have been, not Louis IX, but Philip II. Four of these remained important: Burgundy, Brittany, Gascony and Flanders. The first two were to feature prominently in the problems faced by the Valois in the late fourteenth and early fifteenth centuries, but the last two presented obstacles that were more immediate. Relations with Edward I at first seemed promising, for at the beginning of Philip's reign he had come to Paris to do homage for Gascony. However, the feudal relationship was an uneasy one, for the French king's policies suggest very strongly an unwillingness to accept the status quo created by his grandfather. Appeals from Edward's Gascon vassals to the *parlement* of Paris were encouraged and French officials exploited the indeterminate frontier as much as possible. In fact, most of the Gascon lords remained attached to the English crown, but there were always some whose interest could be attracted, especially in the border region of the Agenais. The techniques used by Philip IV in his dealings with Gascony seem to have much in common with Philip II's policy towards the Angevin lands, and it is difficult to avoid the conclusion that his ultimate aim was to deprive the English king of the fief, just as Philip II had taken Normandy from King John. The costs of such an operation seem, at least initially, to have been of less concern to him, for they certainly outweighed what Philip could have gained from the duchy had he conquered it.

Not surprisingly, these tensions soon escalated into open warfare. In the early 1290s sea battles involving Norman, Gascon and English sailors led Philip to cite Edward to appear before the *parlement* in his capacity as duke. Edward sent his brother, Edmund, to answer in Paris, and it was proposed that French officials occupy certain Gascon fortresses for forty days while the matter was being investigated. Predictably they were dilatory in restoring them when the period ended, with the result that in the years 1294 to 1296 relations deteriorated into serious warfare which was not brought to an end until a truce was arranged by Pope Boniface VIII in 1298. In the hope that peace would be consolidated, a marriage was arranged between Isabella, Philip's daughter, and Edward, Edward I's heir.

The position of Flanders was interwoven with that of Gascony and England. The French king had long coveted the region and the reigning count, Guy of Dampierre, looked to England, with which the county had strong commercial and political ties, as a counterbalance. Edward, for his part, had subsidised those fiefs and minor princedoms that lay to the north and east of France. Flanders was the chief among these and, indeed, in 1294 the link had been strengthened when Guy had married into the English royal family. Again Philip applied pressure which seemed to have the aim of eventual annexation: a tax of one-fiftieth on Flemish towns, invasion, and defeat for the Flemings at Furnes in 1297. Although there was some respite with the truce of 1298, when it expired in 1300 the French again invaded and occupied the towns. In 1301 the king himself made a grand tour of the county. Neither he nor his officials, however, showed much awareness of the class tensions that existed in this highly urbanised region. The deep divisions between the pro-French urban oligarchies and what the

Annales Gandenses calls 'the commonalty' led to the revolt of May 1302, known as the 'Matins of Bruges' (Johnstone 1951:23–5). French attempts to bring the county back under control resulted in the pitched battle at Courtrai in July in which, to their great shock, the French forces were defeated. Courtrai did not settle the matter, but it was an immense blow to Capetian prestige – in a sense the reverse image of Bouvines – and entailed even greater material costs than had hitherto been incurred, since an attempt would have to be made to recover lost ground. Some of this was indeed regained in August 1304, when the Flemings were obliged to retreat from the field at Mons-en-Pévèle, a victory followed by the imposition of the Treaty of Athis-sur-Orge (June 1305), which ordered the destruction of urban defences, the payment of a large indemnity and the undertaking of an expiatory pilgrimage by the people of Bruges. The inability of the French to enforce these sweeping provisions eventually led to preparations for a new Flemish campaign in 1313, following a series of abortive conferences and piecemeal annexations. The financial strain that this involved helped precipitate the opposition of 1314. When Philip died at the end of November, neither Gascony nor Flanders was securely under his control.

Philip IV's attempts to absorb these two fiefs drew his administration into a frantic search for money, bringing immense pressure on the government and leading to collision with both the Church and the baronage. Unlike Philip II, he failed to recoup his losses or rebuild his treasury by the outright conquest of either Gascony or Flanders, so that financial crises continued to recur. Joseph Strayer has shown the various forms of taxation which were tried with greater or lesser success or frequency: feudal aids, proportional subsidies for the defence of the realm, clerical tenths and annates, forced loans (becoming gifts so frequently that they amounted to a form of taxation), the *maltôte* on commercial transactions, and various occupational taxes (Strayer 1939:7–21). The clergy above all were exploited, especially after the capitulation of Boniface VIII on this issue in 1297. So aggrieved did they become that in 1303 and 1304 the king was faced with clerical opposition that came close to a complete programme of reform. There are signs that an attempt was being made to reorganise the financial administration when, in the early 1290s, the Templars, who had been responsible for Capetian demesne finances for most of the period since Philip II, were relieved of most of this responsibility which was taken over directly by royal officials. However, the government appears to have been unable to sustain this, for in 1302 the order was once more in partial control of royal finances.

There were, in addition, alternatives or supplements to taxation. Coinage debasement was a frequent resort during the 1290s and the early 1300s, causing price inflation and deep social discontent. The return to the 'good money' of St Louis in 1306 did nothing to stabilise the situation, for the pain of debtors and tenants now suddenly faced with at least a threefold increase in payments manifested itself in rioting in Paris so serious that the king found it necessary to hide in the Templar fortress just to the north of the city until it died down. Moreover, the 'reform' of 1306 was soon undermined by a further series of debasements. Others, apart from the clergy, were also vulnerable. Italian merchants and bankers, 'the Lombards', advanced money against taxation, arranged loans and, between 1291 and 1311, several times suffered seizures of their goods, and assets. The Jews, victims of Philip II's financial needs in similar circumstances, were subjected to a series of spoliations, culminating in their expulsion in 1306. Finally, most audaciously of all, the government turned on the Order of the Templars, whose members in France were suddenly arrested in October 1307, and charged with a range of heretical crimes. Whatever Philip may have convinced himself about the extent of their alleged depravity, there can be no doubt that a desire to control their lands and banking deposits was a central reason for their arrest. In the end the monarch failed to gain a permanent hold on the Templar property, for in 1312 Clement V arranged for their assets to be transferred to the Hospitallers, but meanwhile considerable profits had been extracted from the administration and leasing of the order's estates and later from quittances squeezed from the Hospital.

Important as they are, however, a study of financial exigencies presents only a one-dimensional view of a king whose personality is complex and elusive. Unlike St Louis, Philip failed to inspire any credible contemporary portrait. His chief ministers – Peter Flote, William of Nogaret and Enguerrand of Marigny – seemed to be conducting policy and in turn it was they who suffered the consequences: Flote being killed at Courtrai in 1302, Nogaret excommunicated and Marigny executed through the machinations of his enemies at court after Philip's death. Yet Joseph Strayer nevertheless believed that Philip was the guiding hand of the reign, having a clear concept of his rights and the means by which he could pursue them, well before Flote, the first of the apparently dominant ministers, appeared in 1289. The ministers themselves were picked by the king, mostly from outside the circle of Parisian administrators from which it might otherwise be expected that they would come, and protected by the crown when pressure mounted for their removal. His analysis of routine governmental letters too shows that the king took a personal interest in about 50 per cent of the total, suggesting that such an active ruler could hardly have been uninvolved in the great issues of the reign (Strayer 1980:15–35). On the other hand, Robert-Henri Bautier, using the same body of documents, has placed an entirely different interpretation upon them, seeing the matters in which the king took a close interest as being narrowly concerned with grants to his close advisers and family, and with pious activities such as grants to favoured religious institutions. Moreover, his itinerary shows him preoccupied not with affairs of state, but, in his early years particularly, with hunting and, increasingly, after the death of his wife in 1305, with a form of mysticism centred on personal austerities. This was a state of mind which, Bautier believes, Nogaret in particular could exploit at will, so that the king could, for example, be persuaded to believe the charges against the Templars, unlikely as they appeared to many contemporaries (Bautier 1978). Such differing views stem from the conflicting elements within the king's own character. Elizabeth Brown sees him as driven by 'a stubborn and impractical idealism' and a censorious morality, derived from an identification of his policies with the cause of God. To some extent the great dramas of the reign can be linked to these attitudes: the conflicts with Boniface VIII, the wars with the Flemings, the trials of the Templars and the bishops of Pamiers and Troyes, and the treatment of the lovers of his daughters-in-law and of the women themselves. Yet, at the same time, she suggests that he was subject to profound self-doubts and guilt feelings. The roots of both aspects of his personality can be traced back to the experiences of a childhood in which he was indoctrinated with a set of rigid principles and traumatised by personal losses and the atmosphere of his father's court, experiences in no way offset by any real human contact or warmth (E.A.R. Brown 1987).

It is equally difficult to place the reign in the long perspective. In the conflicts with the papacy and the great fiefs has been seen the genesis of the modern state, sovereign within a set of defined borders. Some contemporary writers like the Dominican, John of Paris, did indeed argue that the secular state could not possibly be derived from the spiritual power, being a natural formation in existence long before the papacy; such views often gained a favourable hearing, for the ground had already been well prepared by the development of secular power in the course of the thirteenth century (Watt 1971:76–7,124). Nevertheless, such an interpretation of the reign can be overstated. Philip IV's attitudes and policies seem to accord more with the Capetian cult so assiduously fostered by his predecessors than with any idea of modern statehood, although it is possible that by so doing he created circumstances which encouraged the French to see themselves as a new elect people replacing that of the corrupt Jews which, ultimately, forged some sense of national identity (Strayer 1971; Menache 1980). In the early fourteenth century, however, 'France' lacked many of the main attributes of nationality. Philip himself travelled with any regularity only in certain limited areas and he had no maps to guide him, while his subjects show a distinct reluctance either to attend his meetings of the Estates-General, despite the fact that they were assembled six times between 1290 and 1314, or to pay tax on a regular annual basis without a perception of some distinct crisis, or to speak the same language and follow the same customs. The king himself, harsh as he was in his treatment of Boniface VIII and Clement V, could not conceive of a world in which the papacy did not have an important role. He wanted his own way over the condemnation of the Templars, but he went to immense and – if nationality mattered more than the Christian commonwealth – irrelevant trouble to coerce Clement V into agreeing to this, an end which was finally only partially successful. Finally, it is difficult to see the reigns representing the crystallisation of long-term development, for he left a series of problems which confounded his successors, both his three sons who followed between 1314 and 1328, and the Valois after them, which emphasises that the difficulties of the Valois were by no means all of their own making.

The extinction of the Capetian dynasty after fourteen kings and nearly three and a half centuries was unexpected and undistinguished. None of Philip's sons, Louis X, Philip V or Charles IV, was able to provide a male heir (except for Louis's son, John, who lived only five days) and none ruled for more than six years. Each struggled with financial problems, abortive crusade plans and social discontent, with noticeable lack of success, while the prolonged famine of 1315 to 1322 deepened the atmosphere of crisis. Their own superstitious fears added to problems over which they had little control. It is salutary to conclude with an image to set against the Sunday of Bouvines and the canonisation of Louis IX. It is that of Philip V at Poitiers in 1321, ordering the arrest and torture of lepers, whom he apparently believed had been killing Christians by poisoning the wells, not only in France, but also throughout Christendom (Barber 1981).

12

The Kingdom of England

When William, Duke of Normandy, was crowned King of England by Ealdred, Archbishop of York, at Westminster on Christmas Day 1066, he could reflect that he had within his grasp a prize so glittering that it outshone the gains made by any other eleventh-century military commander. If, indeed, as William of Malmesbury later claimed, he was accustomed to pump up his courage by telling himself that it would be dishonourable to appear any less brave than Robert Guiscard – a Norman of inferior rank and relative penury who, nevertheless, had established his dominion in a large part of Apulia – then, on that Christmas Day, he had cause to believe that he had outstripped even Guiscard's achievement (Jamison 1938:247). The actual invasion had been a very great risk; only the scale of the pickings had made it worthwhile. The need to cross the Channel meant that England could not have been conquered by attrition, nor could it have been invaded in secret. To gain England William had had to assemble a formidable and expensive army, ship it across to Sussex, and defeat Harold Godwinson, a man who was William's equal in courage and energy and who had, moreover, the advantage of fighting on his own ground, backed by the resources of a rich country.

The circumstances which had led William to take this gamble stemmed from the succession crisis created by Edward the Confessor's failure to provide a direct heir. In England such a crisis had been made all the more likely because its immediate past connections with Scandinavia and Normandy made external intervention all but inevitable. It has been pointed out that well before the Norman Conquest the continental threat to England had been exacerbated by the evident co-operation of the Normans and the Vikings, a situation which had not occurred in the early phases of Viking expansion (Matthew 1966:32–4), so that a keen appreciation of Norman politics was necessary if England was not to be left very exposed. To some extent Edward the Confessor had subsumed this threat within his own person since, as the son of Aethelred and Emma of Normandy, he had the appropriate mixed descent, but unless he had a clearly designated heir the solution was essentially temporary.

This was the context of his apparent promise of the succession to Duke William, which probably occurred early in 1051. Edward had been brought up in Normandy and always retained strong Norman sympathies, while William had already shown evident qualities of leadership. He had survived a turbulent minority between 1035 and

1044 and had re-established ducal authority in a series of shrewd and clear-sighted military and diplomatic moves, which included the crushing of a serious revolt in 1047. Moreover, Edward may have intended the offer as a counter to the growth in power of the family of Earl Godwin of Wessex, whose role in English politics had become particularly prominent in the early years of the reign. Indeed, an abortive revolt by Godwin in the early autumn of 1051 was probably connected with the offer to William, although the chronology of these events remains obscure. Godwin, faced with the opposition of the other earls as well, fled, but was allowed to return the following year.

In practice, therefore, the events of 1051 did no more than give William a claim to the English throne, for manoeuvrings concerning the succession continued. This point is underlined by one particularly murky episode, the meaning of which will probably never be entirely disentangled. After Godwin's death in 1053, his son Harold seems to have been a party to an invitation to Edward the Aetheling to return to England, together with his three children. Edward was the son of Edmund Ironside, briefly king in 1016 and grandson of Aethelred, and therefore a possible future claimant to the throne. However, he had lived in Hungary for forty years and was therefore unfamiliar with English conditions, and it is a reasonable supposition that Harold, while not necessarily aiming for the crown himself, nevertheless saw in Edward a king much more amenable to control than William of Normandy. If that was his plan it came to a premature end when Edward suddenly died in 1057 in circumstances which are far from clear. His son, Edgar, was no more than six at this time, and therefore not a credible candidate in opposition to William.

Whatever his previous plans, in 1064 Harold found himself pushed towards the Norman succession. Probably in that year he set out to cross the Channel. The reasons for this journey are not known for certain, but most historians have assumed that he was sent by Edward to confirm William's succession, and that he had, by this time, accepted it as inevitable. If this is so, he arrived in Normandy by a circuitous route since, apparently because of adverse weather, he landed in Ponthieu, was captured by Count Guy, and then ransomed. Once in Normandy he took an oath of fealty to William and apparently agreed to do all in his power to establish William on the throne after Edward's death. These curious events meant that, when Edward died in January 1066, both Harold and William could put their own construction on them, for Harold could argue that promises had been made under compulsion, while William could allege that Harold's seizure of the throne was the act of a perjurer. William's version was more widely accepted partly because he was represented at the papal court and Harold was not.

Moreover, as Harold must have been acutely aware, William was not the only other claimant. On 20 September 1066 a great army led by Harald Hadrada, King of Norway, and Tostig, the deposed Earl of Northumbria and Harold's own brother, defeated an English army near York and took the city. Harald Hadrada claimed the throne on the basis of an agreement with Hardaknut, Knut's son and successor in England until his death in 1042, and Magnus, King of Norway, who died in 1047. Harold therefore marched north, although he knew very well that William was only awaiting a favourable opportunity to invade in the south. Harold defeated and killed his opponents at Stamford Bridge on 25 September, only to learn that William had landed at Pevensey in Sussex on the 28th (see Map 6). It is difficult to believe that there had been a massive conspiracy against Harold centred on Tostig with his many

Map 6 The Kingdom of England

contacts on the continent. Harold's fleet had been waiting for William throughout the summer and its disbandment at harvest time may have been William's opportunity. In any event, Harold responded with his usual vigour and by 13 October was in position to fight William near Hastings. Despite the views of armchair critics since that time, neither side had much option but to fight, and in the end William's superior generalship won the day. Harold was killed and the way was open for William to gain the English throne, for there was no other credible candidate left. Many of the English earls, Edgar the Aetheling and Archbishop Ealdred of York, accepted this in a meeting at Berkhamsted and with this rather grudging support William proceeded to his coronation.

In the 1120s Orderic Vitalis wrote of the Normans that they

had subdued a people that was greater, and more wealthy than they were, with a longer history: a people moreover amongst whom many saints and wise men and mighty kings had led illustrious lives, and won distinction in many ways at home and on the battlefield.

(Chibnall 1969:2:269)

Table 8 Kings of England

William I, the Conqueror	1066–87
William II, Rufus	1087–1100
Henry I	1100–35
Stephen of Blois	1135–54
Henry II of Anjou	1154–89
Richard I	1189–99
John	1199–1216
Henry III	1216–72
Edward I	1272–1307
Edward II	1307–27

This assessment of the country which William had gained would find favour with most modern historians, for the England which William took over offered an institutional structure for government unequalled elsewhere, and certainly far in advance of the Norman administration. A comparison between the position of the kings of England (see Table 8) and those of France emphasises the point. The early Capetians had little power and less respect, their estates were landlocked and weakly controlled, their great vassals no longer came to their assemblies, and their administration consisted of little more than they could cart around in their wagons. In England the earls held vast estates which in practice had become hereditary, but the concept of public authority still existed and the earls continued to act as channels for the transmission of royal commands. Indeed, the effects of Viking attack had been to weld England together under the monarchy of Wessex, whereas in Gaul it had done quite the opposite, exposing the deficiencies of royal administration and forcing the localities into a form of self-help which paid little attention to central government.

Two reliable indicators of the English king's authority are his ability to levy *danegeld* (*heregeld*), which in the late tenth and early eleventh centuries had been used to buy off the Danes, and his use of the writ, a concise order granting a privilege or a property, sealed with the royal seal, a device which the Anglo-Norman monarchy was to find ideally suited to its style of government. The ability to collect and account for some of the royal revenues at a fixed treasury at Winchester at a time when most other rulers viewed their finances almost entirely in domestic terms is a measure of this developed authority. At a local level the division of the land into shires and below them into hundreds, together with the device of inquiring into matters by means of the sworn testimony of local men, offered the potential for an effective system of courts. Moreover, the deputies of the earls, the shire-reeves, provided the prototype for the royal sheriffs by means of whom the Norman kings were able to extend their influence throughout the country.

Nevertheless, the Normans did not inherit a finished system; their problem was to govern England in ways which consolidated the Conquest. The difficulties were severe. To begin with, regional differences remained quite marked, especially between the Danelaw on the eastern side and the remainder. Mercia and Wessex continued to be conscious of their separate past, while some areas, like Kent, retained distinct characteristics throughout the middle ages. Northern England had not been moulded into a structure of shires to anything like the degree achieved by the Anglo-Saxons in the rest of the country. Most importantly, the early years of William's reign were marked by rebellion, the crushing of which hastened the process by which the English aristocracy was replaced by the Normans. Between 1068 and 1071 revolts involving Edgar the Aetheling, most of the English earls, and outside opportunists like Malcolm of Scotland and Svend of Denmark, all had to be overcome. In 1068 the fall of Exeter compelled the west to come to terms, while in the north savage repression followed the revolt of the earls in 1069, leaving long-lasting marks upon the people and the landscape. Then, in 1072, in a bold and extremely risky campaign, William penetrated to the heart of the Scottish kingdom, and forced Malcolm III to recognise his conquest of England and to stop harbouring English dissidents.

Although no overall leader of the English presented himself, these revolts do demonstrate that neither the Normans nor the English conceived of William's invasion as a harmonious exercise in power-sharing. The account of the Norman priest, William of Poitiers, shows very clearly the viewpoint of conquest.

> But neither kindness nor fear was sufficient to persuade the English that peaceful tranquillity was preferable to things new and disordered. They did not dare to take up arms and revolt openly, but they engaged in perverse, local conspiracies through which they might find an opportunity of doing harm. They sent messengers to the Danes or to others, wherever they could hope to find any help. Some fled the realm into exile, so that they might free themselves from the power of the Normans, or so that they might return against them with the help of foreign forces.
>
> (Foreville 1952:264)

Although William the Conqueror avoided blatant dispossession of those English lords who remained quiescent, he did need to satisfy his warriors, not only because they expected reward, but also because he depended on them to hold the country thereafter. Moreover, the success of a warrior's enterprises was customarily demonstrated in a very tangible way by the exhibition and distribution of plunder. William of Poitiers leaves no doubt about the massive extent of this in his description of how William carried the rich spoils through Normandy in the spring of 1067 (Foreville 1952:222–8, 254–62). The English earls did not need to possess exceptional perspicacity to discern that there was little future for them under the new monarchy.

The distribution of lands and favours began almost immediately, probably under the supervision of a small inner council which included men like William's half-brothers, Odo of Bayeux and Robert of Mortain. Relatively compact lordships were granted to those who occupied vulnerable areas, especially on the frontiers of Wales or in areas exposed to possible invasion from Ireland, but most others received lands scattered in several counties, like the royal demesne itself. These men became his tenants-in-chief and they were required to provide the king with knights when he needed them. They in turn enfeoffed others from which they provided service or alternatively used their incomes to hire the men they owed. William does not appear to have interfered with these latter arrangements, but it was vital that he did not lose contact with these rear-vassals as had happened in France under the early Capetians, who recovered their position slowly and painfully only in the course of the twelfth century. Throughout the reign he emphasised his majesty in three great annual feasts attended by his important lords, secular and ecclesiastical, and many of their vassals, and in 1086 he was careful to ensure that all important rear-vassals did direct homage to him at a great assembly at Salisbury. Again, the contrast with the eleventh-century Capetians is telling, for the presence of the great lords in the witness lists of their diplomas is conspicuously lacking. The Norman land settlement was reinforced by castles, which had been relatively rare in Edward the Confessor's time. In the first five years of the Conquest about thirty-three castles were put up; by 1086 the number had risen to at least eighty-six (Renn 1973: maps B and C, 13, 15). At the same time William introduced a new type of law into England, that of the forest, governed by its own courts, which preserved vast tracts for the royal hunt by a heavy blanket of restrictions upon the designated areas. At the upper levels these changes proceeded very rapidly. By 1076 William felt confident enough to leave England for four years; ten years later the Domesday survey shows that the English aristocracy had almost completely disappeared. The same process can be seen in the Church. Stigand, Archbishop of Canterbury, condemned by the papacy as long ago as 1052, was at last deposed in 1070, conveniently demonstrating William's commitment to reform without damaging his power, and replaced by Lanfranc, Abbot of St Stephen's, Caen. Effectively, control of the episcopal sees was left in William's hands; the result was that by 1070 only three bishops of English birth remained (Barlow 1999:75–6). In the monasteries William was more inclined to let nature take its course, but the long-term effects were the same.

The degree of success achieved by William is exemplified by the most famous document of the reign, the two great volumes which surveyed the land and inhabitants of England known as Domesday Book. At a time when Philip I of France was incapable of overcoming unruly vassals like Hugh of Le Puiset in his own demesne lands, William was able to order a survey so detailed that it even itemised domestic livestock. He decided on the survey at Christmas 1085, as a consequence of his desire to have a more exact knowledge of the resources available to him, a desire apparently prompted by the abortive invasion of Knut IV of Denmark earlier in the year. The mechanics of the operation demonstrate how effectively William utilised the Anglo-Saxon structure, for preliminary surveys were made at local level through the use of sworn juries, then checked by specially appointed commissioners, and finally sent to Winchester, where a digest of the information was produced. The survey was not absolutely complete, for London, Winchester and four northern counties were omitted, and the material from the eastern counties was never summarised, but even so William was, within a few months, provided with far more information on his financial resources and on the tenure of the land than any other contemporary monarch. Even the Norman rulers of Sicily, inheritors of the Byzantine and Muslim administrative traditions, were probably not as well informed until the 'Catalogue of Barons' of *c*.1150, while comparable data were not available to the French monarchy until Philip II's reorganisation of the royal administration in the 1180s and 1190s.

Moreover, it is doubtful if the French kings had such a clear grasp of the extent of their realm even by the early fourteenth century.

However, admiration for Domesday is easier to evoke now than then. The monk called 'Florence of Worcester' followed his description of Domesday with the comment that 'the land was vexed with many misfortunes as a result' (B. Thorpe 1849:2:19), a phrase which supports the view of those historians who argue that the chief purpose of the survey was to enable William to tax England more effectively than he had hitherto been able to do. The Anglo-Saxon kings had taken *geld* country-wide, but by 1086 the assessments for particular areas often bore little relation to real resources, if indeed they ever had done, and Domesday showed this. However, having made this elaborate survey, no action was taken to adjust the assessments in the light of its information. This may have been partly due to William's death in September 1087, but perhaps also because it was not easy to make the Anglo-Saxon system of government work in the way that the Normans wanted. Indeed, it has been argued that William and his successor, William Rufus, were in fact living on 'borrowed time', relying on the expertise of English moneyers, sheriffs' officers and stewards to keep the system going (Warren 1984). The problem eventually had to be faced by Henry I, who gained the throne when this generation of English functionaries had largely died out, but it is reasonable to speculate too that these men never tried too hard to help the Normans in the first place.

This sense of foreign occupation must have been heightened by the continuing interest taken by the Norman kings in continental politics. William himself died of wounds sustained while campaigning against Philip of France; his sons too found their fortunes heavily entangled with the affairs of Normandy and its neighbours. Initially William left a divided inheritance: Normandy to his eldest son, Robert, England to the next, William Rufus, and a monetary legacy to the third, Henry. Such an arrangement was inherently unstable, especially given Robert's already proven incompetence in government, which acted as a permanent temptation to Rufus. Moreover, the Conquest had left a web of cross-Channel ties among nobles and churchmen, which could not be readily cut so soon after 1066.

As soon as he had crushed an ineffective rising in favour of Robert, which he had achieved by autumn 1088, William Rufus therefore set out to break his elder brother. As holder of the richer part of his father's domains, he could draw on superior resources and he inaugurated a series of heavy exactions to finance this policy, rigorously implemented by Ranulf Flambard, his Keeper of the Seal and chief minister. In particular, his extraction of payments from individuals as a consequence of exploiting his feudal rights of relief and wardship and his development of the profits of justice, foreshadowed the way that Norman, and later, Angevin government was to develop. Moreover, he demanded payment of reliefs in money rather than in the traditional form of military equipment, a method which gave him much greater flexibility in his military activities. He used the money to harass his brother, first between 1089 and 1091 when, under pressure from a Scottish invasion, he came to an agreement with him, and again between 1094 and 1096, when Robert decided to go on crusade, pledging Normandy to William for 10,000 marks. With Robert out of the way he restored his father's rule, and in 1098 even extended his power into the neighbouring County of Maine. He may have been planning an even more grandiose scheme, for in 1099 he began negotiations with William IX, Duke of Aquitaine, apparently for a similar pledge to finance a crusade by William. His unexpected death while hunting in the New Forest in August 1100 leaves his intentions tantalisingly unclear. Robert, however, was returning from a successful crusade, complete with a new bride and matching dowry acquired in Sicily, and William could not realistically have hoped to hang on to Normandy in the face of a brother who had restored both his reputation and his finances, at least in the short term. As for Poitou, distance made this a difficult if not an impossible objective.

William Rufus was not well remembered because he did nothing to cultivate the contemporary keepers of monarchical reputation, the monastic chroniclers. The monasteries had contributed heavily towards his military exploits, while his standing was further undermined among ecclesiastics because of his prolonged conflict with Anselm of Bec. Anselm was foisted on him as Archbishop of Canterbury in 1093, but quarrelled with him in 1097 after a series of minor disputes, none very important in itself, but which nevertheless seems to have convinced him that the king had no intention of allowing him any real freedom of action as archbishop. The quarrel led to the archbishop's exile. This was compounded by William's failure to recognise either Pope Urban II or Paschal II, except for a short period during the last four years of Urban's pontificate. Particularly galling for the clergy seems to have been his readiness to view them as fallible human beings rather than a race apart. This attitude was summed up by Orderic Vitalis in the following account of the king's comments on Serlo, Abbot of Gloucester's apparently well-intentioned warning that he should improve his treatment of the Church.

> I wonder what has induced my lord Serlo to tell me such things, for I believe that he really is a good abbot and a sensible old man. Yet he is so simple that he tells me, when I have so much real business to attend to, the dreams of snoring monks, and even has them written down and sent across several counties to me.
>
> (Chibnall 1975:5:289)

When Rufus died, his younger brother Henry was hunting in the same party. Since Winchester with its royal treasury was only a few miles away and Robert was still travelling back from the east, it would have taken superhuman modesty or incredible indolence not to have acted at once to seize the throne. Such an action does not in itself implicate Henry in William's death despite the suspicious circumstances; had he even considered it for a moment, the option of doing nothing was not open to him. The other political heavyweights in England knew that any help they gave Henry would have to be reciprocated after he became king. Thus William died on 2 August and within three days Henry had been crowned at Westminster by the Bishop of London, supported by the late king's household and by important baronial families such as the Beaumonts and the Clares.

The new king at once set about consolidating his position. Like his brother, he issued a charter at his coronation which, although it was much cited at the time of Magna Carta, cannot be regarded as very extraordinary in 1100. It was, not untypically, largely concerned with the alleged abuses of the previous reign, most of which were the common policy of any kings with pretensions to strong rule. Most of the clauses did not press with any weight upon Henry's conscience in the years that followed. To the Church he conceded 'freedom' and the removal of unjust exactions, in particular the exploitation of episcopal and monastic demesnes during vacancies. To the baronage he moderated the demands made by his brother for feudal incidents, promising to take only 'lawful' reliefs on inheritance, not to charge for the marriage of heiresses, not to force widows to remarry, and to allow widows and other relatives the wardship of minors. Free disposal of movable property was granted to the relatives of barons who died intestate, while pledges of movable property for offences committed should relate to the extent of the offence and not be unlimited. Knights who owed military service were quit of *gelds* and 'all works'. For the towns and shires he abolished what was called 'mintage', apparently a payment taken by the king to cover the costs of depreciation of the coinage. To the population as a whole he forgave debts and pleas owing to Rufus, he remitted murder-fines owed up to the day of the coronation, and he granted an amnesty to those who had seized any property since William's death, provided that it was at once returned. The general tone of the document is summed up in clause thirteen: 'I restore to you the law of King Edward together with such emendations of it as my father made with the counsel of the barons.' The one area in which he made no concession, perhaps significantly in view of what they symbolised about the imposition of Norman power, was in the forests, which were to be retained 'in my own hands as my father did before me' (Douglas and Greenaway 1981:432–4). Soon after, in late September, Anselm responded to Henry's entreaty to return and within three weeks the archbishop had reluctantly (since she had once lived in the community of nuns at Wilton) solemnised his marriage to Eadgyth, who was sister of the king of Scotland and descended from Alfred on her mother's side. She took the name of Matilda. Louis of France, son of King Philip I, but effective Capetian ruler by this time, gave public recognition when he visited Henry at Christmas, while the following summer, after an initial spat, Robert too accepted Henry as king by the terms of the Treaty of Alton.

These deals served to solidify Henry's opportunism, but he did not intend them to freeze the situation permanently. Some barons would still be disaffected; relations with Anselm were unlikely to be any easier than they had been under Rufus, especially as the archbishop had, since 1099, become imbued with a much more rigid line on investiture; Duke Robert remained a serious rival; and the Capetians would continue to try to undermine Anglo-Norman power by whatever means came to hand. A baronial rebellion, in which Robert of Bellême was prominent, did indeed break out in 1102, but was effectively suppressed. Anselm was less easy to deal with and eventually, in 1106–7, the king compromised by giving up investiture with staff and ring, but insisted that prelates who had done homage to him should be consecrated. Henry, though, lost nothing in terms of control of appointments and feudal overlordship. In Normandy, Robert's competence as a governor and military leader had not been improved by his crusading activities. In June 1106 Henry caught him at Tinchebrai, north of Domfront, and, according to a good contemporary witness, defeated him in only an hour (Douglas and Greenaway 1981:329–30); the imprisonment which followed lasted for twenty-eight years until Robert's death in 1134. As has been pointed out, Anglo-Norman continuity was mostly maintained between 1066 and 1204, not because there was a settled succession, but because no co-heirs were prepared to accept division. Moreover, so long as both the Church and the baronage maintained strong cross-Channel links, there was likely to be support for whoever could grab the whole (Le Patourel 1979:106).

This success had wider implications, for it inevitably made Henry into a key figure in the politics of northern Europe, a role which he took on without any hesitation. Throughout the reign it seemed to him quite natural to spend much of his time out of

England implementing these wider ambitions. This particularly brought him into conflict with Louis VI of France, who purported to believe that Henry had usurped Normandy. In the course of this prolonged conflict Henry did achieve a striking success in defeating Louis at Brémule in 1119, but this could never be as decisive as Tinchebrai. Indeed, it was partly offset in 1124, when invasion by Emperor Henry V, to whom Henry's daughter Matilda had been married in 1114, was outfaced by Louis and his leading vassals in northern France.

Normandy's other powerful neighbour and traditional rival was Anjou, where the frontier in Maine was as sensitive as that of the Vexin in the face of the Capetians. Fulk V, who became count in 1109, was particularly formidable and, contrary to the instincts of the Norman baronage, Henry seems to have been interested in neutralising the threat by means of a marriage link rather than through outright warfare. In 1119 William, Henry's heir, was married to Fulk's daughter. The project was destroyed by the drowning of William in the White Ship disaster of November 1120, but Henry's belief in this policy was maintained despite the need to remodel his plans for the succession. The year after the Emperor Henry V died in 1125, Matilda returned to England and Henry persuaded the barons to accept her as his heir. He then arranged for her marriage to Geoffrey Plantagenet, Fulk's son, which took place in 1128. When Fulk himself left for Jerusalem, in which he had a long-standing interest, in order to marry Melisende, heiress to the kingdom, Geoffrey gained Anjou, and then looked ambitiously towards Normandy. But Henry was reluctant to let go. When Henry died in December 1135 it was in the knowledge that Geoffrey had invaded the duchy, reviving all the old Norman fears and hatreds.

Henry's efficient – in some senses ruthless – organisation of English administration, was therefore necessary, not only to help finance this policy, but also because he needed a governmental system upon which he could rely when he was away. The reign is characterised by the professionalisation of the royal administration, epitomised by the appointment of Roger, Bishop of Salisbury, a Norman in origin, as chief justiciar, from *c.*1109. The chief justiciar presided over the Exchequer court, an institution which was probably created during the reign of William Rufus. From at least 1116 it held annual sittings, at Easter and Michaelmas, in which accounts were audited. The collectors and exchequer officials sat around a table on which was laid a chequered cloth, and by moving counters in what was in effect a huge abacus the mechanics of the financial administration were clarified in a way never previously achieved, and many of the more cumbersome aspects of a system of Roman numeration minimised. Record was kept upon long rolls of accounts, the Pipe Rolls, which survive in almost continuous succession from 1155, but of which there is a single example in 1130, so that they evidently predate this. Such a system needed trained and loyal personnel, whom Henry drew both from established families, accustomed to an active role in government, and from men less prominent in the social hierarchy, whose skills he needed to utilise. It seems likely that one reason for the avoidance of a major confrontation between the government and the nobility was because of what Warren Hollister and John Baldwin call this 'meld of wealth and service' (1978:890). Perhaps, too, the contemporary perception that his aims were essentially conservative masked the innovatory nature of the methods used to achieve them, thus gaining for Henry a reputation as a king imbued with the traditional virtues of peace and justice (Hollister and Baldwin 1978; Hollister 1985).

This approach could not, however, have been effective without strong links at local level based on the sheriffs who, in turn, were overseen by itinerant justices checking their activities through general eyres (visitations) and taking evidence from juries. The system had its rough edges – it was, for instance, difficult to prevent the development of dynasties of sheriffs with their own vested interests – but its logical and systematic methods did enable the king to begin to tap the resources of a country, already rich in the mid-eleventh century, and now visibly responding to the expansive economic climate. Henry's promises in his coronation charter could not long survive in these circumstances. Quite contrary to its provisions he was soon manipulating his rights of feudal overlordship to maximise his cash income, including the translation of reliefs into money and the frequent taking of scutage (monetary payments) in lieu of direct service. There is indeed a distinct edge to the verdict of Orderic Vitalis upon Henry: 'After thorough study of past histories, I confidently assert that no king in the English realm was ever more richly or powerfully equipped than Henry in everything that contributes to worldly glory' (Chibnall 1978:6:100–1).

By the end of the reign the elements of the English system of administration, so useful to William the Conqueror, had been assimilated to such an extent that their Anglo-Saxon origin was now irrelevant. A concomitant of this was the submersion of Anglo-Saxon culture as an element in its own right. Indeed, it has been argued that Orderic Vitalis and William of Malmesbury were so alert to the Anglo-Saxon past precisely because it was disappearing within their lifetimes (Matthew 1966:296). Henry responded to the need to build a structure no longer reliant upon servants with knowledge of pre-Conquest days. Symbolic of this was the ambitious attempt to codify English law in the so-called *Leges Henrici Primi*, assembled by an anonymous cleric early in the reign. Although in places it is confused and ambiguous, it is important in implying that in a world largely characterised by local custom and practice, England was unique in having a country-wide legal structure. The picture of uniformity and control which he draws is undoubtedly exaggerated, but the stability of the coinage in Henry's time does go some way to substantiate it, in that the contemporary French monarchs, for instance, were unable to control the circulation of local, often poor quality, currencies.

Despite his success in achieving 'everything that contributes to worldly glory', Henry I remained acutely conscious that in William of Malmesbury's words, 'nothing can remain unshaken for long, even with the greatest labours' (Stubbs 1889:2:385). His own personal feelings of insecurity are well documented, both in his nightmare of rebellion, told and illustrated under the year 1130 by the monk John of Worcester (Weaver 1908:32–3 and frontispiece), and in observations by shrewd politicians like Abbot Suger, who describes how Henry frequently changed the position of his bed, as well as sleeping with his sword and shield next to him (Cusimano and Moorhead 1992:114). The White Ship disaster seems to have emphasised this streak in his character; many of his actions after this time, like the foundation and lavish endowment of Reading Abbey, can be at least partly explained by a belief that not even the most powerful kings could expect their plans to survive divine displeasure (Kemp 1986:13–19). With William's death, Henry's plans for the succession collapsed; the tragedy, says William of Malmesbury, caused an extraordinary change in circumstances (Stubbs 1889:2:497) and led first to Henry's attempt to produce a new legitimate heir through remarriage and then, when this failed, to his reconstruction of the Angevin alliance through the marriage of Matilda to Geoffrey of Anjou. But, despite his attempts to consolidate these arrangements by elaborate ceremonies of oath-taking, his new structure was much less convincing than the old and it cannot have been altogether surprising to many contemporaries that it was upset immediately after Henry's death. With great speed, Stephen, Count of Mortain and Boulogne, younger brother of Count Theobald of Blois and, like Matilda, grandchild of the Conqueror in that he was the son of William I's daughter, Adela, crossed the Channel and seized the throne. Less than a month after Henry's death, on 22 December 1135, he was crowned king by the Archbishop of Canterbury.

Both at the time and in the years immediately following, Stephen's coup seemed to have been successful. Within eighteen months he had apparently settled the usual uncertainties and discontents that accompany a change of regime: 'freedom of the Church' was promised at the Council of Oxford (April 1136), the barons and the prelates swore oaths to him at Westminster at Easter, and even Robert of Gloucester, Matilda's half-brother, accepted him soon after, although his oath of homage was explicitly conditional, while Henry, son of King David of Scotland, did homage for his father's English fiefs. In Normandy, Geoffrey of Anjou's invasion of 1136 was destructive but politically inept, and by March 1137 Stephen had been accepted there too. His elder brother, Theobald, was bought off with a pension and in May King Louis VI of France recognised him as well. The problem of alleged perjury stemming from Stephen's oath to support Matilda at Christmas 1126, was bypassed by the usual method of claiming duress, an excuse accepted by Pope Innocent II. Moreover, Henry I had built up support by granting to what contemporaries described as 'new men' lands seized from his opponents, in particular from the supporters of William Clito, the son of Duke Robert of Normandy. Naturally, such opponents had gravitated towards Geoffrey of Anjou; Henry's 'new men' therefore had a vested interest in keeping Stephen on the throne (Davis 1967:8–10, 14). Two of Stephen's three predecessors had seized the throne in the face of other claims created by the lack of a legitimate male heir, and both had established themselves successfully despite rebellion and discontent. In 1136–7 there seemed no reason why Stephen's reign should not settle into these patterns of the recent past.

But Stephen never quite managed to put out all the fires of rebellion simultaneously and, as they flickered and flared across Normandy and England in the late 1130s, both partisans and opportunists began to sense that the civil wars which Henry I's death had initially seemed to presage were not far beneath the surface. Stephen's credibility began to waver in the face of these challenges, for the oaths by which Henry had tried to control the situation after his death would not go away, nor did Stephen show himself as very capable of handling the conflicting pressures which arose from these circumstances. 'It was,' says the author of the *Gesta Stephani*, a chronicler very sympathetic to Stephen, 'like what we read of the fabled hydra of Hercules; when one head was cut off two or more grew in its place' (Potter 1976:68–9). At first the threats came from the borders, north and south. David of Scotland had been the first to swear support for Matilda while, at the same time, he coveted the earldom of Northumbria. Although his forces were defeated by an army assembled by Archbishop Thurstan of York at the Battle of the Standard in August 1138, it was still necessary to try to stabilise the position and a treaty was made at Durham which enfeoffed his son Henry with the earldom. Two months before, Geoffrey had again invaded Normandy and this time he was supported by the man who was to become the key figure on the Angevin side, Robert, Earl of Gloucester.

Events like these weakened confidence in Stephen's ability to control the situation and discontent began to spread to England itself: Ranulf, the powerful Earl of Chester, saw the agreement with Scotland as a threat to his plans to regain his family's patrimony in the borders, lost under Henry I, while Stephen's brother, Henry of Blois, Bishop of Winchester, and the man generally accepted by contemporary chroniclers as being crucial to Stephen's success in the first place, was alienated and alarmed by the king's sudden arrest, in June 1139, of Roger, Bishop of Salisbury and chief justiciar since at least 1109, and his relations, Alexander, Bishop of Lincoln, and Roger, the chancellor. This was followed by the siege of Nigel, Bishop of Ely, in the castle at Devizes. There may have been reason to suspect the loyalty of these men, but nevertheless Henry, who had become papal legate the previous March, could not ignore such a blatant attack on leading prelates, contrary both to the liberty of the Church and to Stephen's own promises at his coronation in 1136. Henry therefore used his legatine powers to summon Stephen before a council at Winchester, but this failed to resolve the matter. At the same time, Stephen's rapid multiplication of earldoms among his friends, especially those linked to his closest confidant, Waleran of Meulan, suggested a determination to insert his own men into the regions, which Henry must have seen as a threat to his own influence (Davis 1967:33). The rift between the brothers weakened Stephen just at the point when the Angevin threat was beginning to intensify. Stephen did not help his cause by his incompetent handling of an attempted invasion in support of Matilda in September 1139. He failed to prevent Robert of Gloucester reaching his west country base and then, despite pinning Matilda in Arundel, allowed her safe conduct to link up with him. Stephen seems here to have acted on the advice of Henry of Blois, whose motives must be suspect, despite the favourable interpretation put on them by some modern authorities (Davis 1967:40). The sigh of frustration at this is almost audible in the writing of the now elderly Orderic Vitalis who had, by this time, been chronicling the evils of slack government for more than three decades.

> In granting this licence the king showed himself either very guileless or very foolish, and prudent men must deplore his lack of regard for both his own safety and the security of the kingdom. He could easily have stamped out the flames of terrible evil that were being kindled if he had acted with the foresight characteristic of wise men.
>
> (Chibnall 1978:6:535)

At a time, therefore, when he should have secured his position beyond serious challenge, Stephen found himself having to struggle against opposition which was strong enough to disrupt his rule, but had insufficient support to supplant him. This was clearly shown when Stephen was captured in battle with Ranulf of Chester near Lincoln in 1141. Matilda herself entered London, supported by Geoffrey of Mandeville, whose position as Earl of Essex was a vital element so close to the city. But even with his help, Matilda could not consolidate her position. Her arrogant conduct, combined with the Londoners' preference for Stephen who had granted them communal rights, quickly undermined her and she was forced to retreat. When, in turn, Robert of Gloucester was himself captured in September 1141, the only solution was an exchange of prisoners; Stephen returned, insisting that he had remained king throughout, and Henry of Blois reappeared at his side.

During the 1140s Stephen continued to meet a series of seemingly endless but uncoordinated challenges. The Angevin cause was itself disjointed, since Geoffrey of Anjou concerned himself with Normandy rather than helping his wife and Robert of

Gloucester, a policy which paid off in that by 1144 he had gained the duchy. Once again the instability of the Anglo-Norman connection was demonstrated. But this did not help the Angevins in England: Matilda only just managed to escape from Oxford when Stephen besieged it in 1142, while her 14-year-old son, Henry, made a farcical invasion in 1147. Indeed, Robert of Gloucester's death later that year removed the one figure of stature behind Matilda and she left England in 1148. Henry tried again in 1149, hoping to combine with discontented barons, but again failed to make any progress. From time to time the Angevin opposition overlapped with baronial discontent, but this was never a consistent pattern. In 1144, for example, there were separate revolts by the relatives of Robert of Gloucester, by Geoffrey of Mandeville and by Ranulf of Chester.

It is, however, difficult to estimate the effect of the fighting on the country as a whole. A detailed chronological account of Stephen's reign leaves the impression of the almost constant movement of armies, the devastation of crops and prolonged sieges. This must have been more damaging than the previous period of orderly government under Henry I. Certainly, contemporary chroniclers, whatever political viewpoint they represented, believed that the country and its people were suffering. Both William of Malmesbury, whose *Historia Novella* is dedicated to Robert of Gloucester (Potter 1955:40–2), and the author of the *Gesta Stephani*, claim that past tranquillity had been replaced by present disorder and pillage (Potter 1976:152–7). This view is dramatically highlighted by the author of the Anglo-Saxon Chronicle at Peterborough who, in a famous passage, alleges that

> I have neither the ability nor the power to tell all the horrors nor all the torments they inflicted upon the wretched people in this country; and that lasted the nineteen years while Stephen was king, and it was always going from bad to worse.
>
> (Douglas and Greenaway 1981:210)

There is no reason to regard these authors as hysterical and it seems likely that the West Country, parts of the Midlands and the Fens in particular were at various times badly afflicted, but equally it should also be seen that the chroniclers' viewpoints were regionally selective, and areas like Kent, for example, were only marginally affected. Moreover, their concern to show the effects of human sinfulness lends their descriptions a certain stylised quality, which means they need to be read with caution. Even in those areas where royal authority had been rendered ineffective, some measure of order was provided by local authority, often protected by agreements between lay and ecclesiastical magnates of the region. Anarchy existed more in the sense that, under Stephen, England was in a state of political confusion rather than one of total social disintegration (Cronne 1970:1–25).

Despite the loss of Normandy, Stephen did not give up hope of recovering his position. He tried hard to have his son, Eustace, crowned in an attempt to imitate the successful establishment of dynastic continuity achieved by the Capetians, but Archbishop Theobald and his colleagues refused to co-operate since it had been forbidden by the pope. Eustace died in 1153, still unconsecrated. In contrast, Henry of Anjou had begun a dramatic rise which was to transform him from a minor irritant in the complex English conflicts of the late 1140s into a dominating figure of European politics of the second half of the twelfth century. At the end of 1149 he had received Normandy from his father; in May 1152 he married Eleanor of Aquitaine, less than three months after her divorce from Louis VII; and in June 1153 he once again invaded England. The plain style of the Peterborough annalist sums up the outcome.

> Then he went with a big army into England, and won castles, and the king went against him with a much bigger army, and all the same they did not fight, but the archbishop and the wise men went between them and made an agreement that the king should be liege lord and king as long as he lived and after his day Henry should be king; they should be as father and son; and there should be peace and concord between them, and in all England.

The relief was almost tangible, 'and it soon became a very good peace, such as there never was before' (Douglas and Greenaway 1981:214). As a consequence, when Stephen died in October 1154, there was no repeat of the cross-Channel dash; Henry was able to wait until 19 December before being crowned.

Stephen made a bold and apparently decisive bid for a disputed crown, but in contrast to William the Conqueror and Henry I he had neither the political judgement nor the ruthlessness to consolidate it. To some men, forced to survive in the shifting sands of the reign, it became evident that their first priority must be the protection of the family patrimony, while to others the anarchy was simply an opportunity to make what profit they could. Either way there could be no stability in England.

In one sense Henry II's succession represented a return to the Norman past. He was an undisputed heir who could show ancestors both Norman and Anglo-Saxon and, from the beginning, he insisted on the restoration of the situation in England as it had existed at the time of his grandfather's death. This was accompanied by a reunification of the Anglo-Norman polity, lost when Geoffrey of Anjou had gained the duchy in the mid-1140s, but in the past always renewed by the Norman kings whenever the opportunity presented itself. However, in another sense, Henry's arrival represented a new conquest which some have seen as important as that of 1066 (Le Patourel 1979:114), for he was an Angevin as well as a Norman, and this brought with it much wider continental perspectives than either Rufus or Henry I had ever contemplated, with consequent important long-term repercussions in England. The possession of Anjou, Normandy, Aquitaine and England did not satisfy Henry; according to Gerald of Wales, he once said that 'the whole world was too small for one brave and powerful man' (Warner 1891:157). In 1157 Malcolm IV of Scotland did homage to him for his earldom of Huntingdon, while an expedition into north Wales forced the leading princes to accept his suzerainty. During the winter of 1171–2 he took an army to Dublin, where both the Irish kings and the Norman settlers submitted. The deaths of his brothers, Geoffrey (in 1158) and William (in 1164), eliminated potential sibling rivalry. Brittany was left largely isolated and succumbed to Henry's pressure in 1166, when his third son, Geoffrey, was betrothed to the heiress, Constance. Although forced back from Toulouse in 1159, Henry nevertheless received the homage of Count Raymond V in 1173. By 1174 he was lord of a vast conglomerate of lands which stretched from Scotland to the Pyrenees and from the Atlantic to the Auvergne. His English lands provided him with his royal title, but he was bound to view England itself as only one part of this wider 'empire', centred as much upon the great historic route-centres of Angers and Tours as upon London. Twenty-one of his thirty-four years as King of England were spent outside the kingdom.

From the first he was concerned to ensure the continuation of this dynastic success.

Less than four months after his own coronation he arranged for the succession of his son, William, to the English throne. In 1156 he himself did homage for his continental fiefs to the French king, Louis VII; this was soon followed by the betrothal of his infant son, Henry (his heir after William's early death in 1156), to Louis's daughter, Margaret. Nor had he failed to learn the lessons of the debacle of Henry I's succession arrangements. Reliance on the survival of one son was evidently foolhardy, yet a king with many sons needed to satisfy them all. Henry II's approach to the problem was obvious and natural for his time. His lands would be divided, not into rival slices in the Carolingian fashion, but around a central core of patrimonial lands, which meant Anjou, Normandy and England, to be settled on the eldest son, Henry, with the remainder divided among the others. To this end, Henry was crowned in 1170, Richard was invested with Aquitaine in 1167, Geoffrey married Constance of Brittany in 1181, and Henry had John proclaimed Lord of Ireland in 1177. This distribution between inherited and acquired territories was already evident among the baronage in the later years of Stephen's reign; here was the same principle applied on a massive scale (J.C. Holt 1972). Daughters were used to create a network of alliances unmatched by any contemporary ruler: in 1168 Matilda married the Welf, Henry the Lion, Duke of Saxony; in 1176 Eleanor married Alfonso VIII, King of Castile; and in 1177 Joanna married William, King of Sicily.

The sheer scope of Henry II's plans is breathtaking; it is certainly comparable in scale and vision with Barbarossa's attempts to revive imperial dominance. Moreover, it was, as will be seen, accompanied by a much firmer grasp of administrative needs than Frederick Barbarossa ever managed. But inevitably he could not accomplish this without challenge, and this challenge came most dangerously from within the family itself. Serious rebellions in 1173–4, in which the young Henry, Richard and Geoffrey were involved, and in 1183, largely instigated by Henry, were unsuccessful, but in 1189, in the face of a new revolt led by Richard and backed by John, he was forced to capitulate, days before his death in July. The Capetians, Louis VII and Philip II, unable to inflict any decisive damage themselves, naturally took the opportunity to exploit the Angevin rivalries.

The history of the Kingdom of England in the second half of the twelfth century cannot be seen in isolation from these events. Just like Henry I, his grandson needed a system which could run without his continual personal supervision. This could be partly achieved by rebuilding Henry I's governmental structure, but the world had not stood still since 1135 and Henry II had at his disposal far better means of developing his administration. Most noticeable was the availability of many more clerks whose education and familiarity with systematic legal procedures could be readily utilised. The investigation of local government by itinerant justices in 1170 may have been partly prompted by a desire for a similar professionalisation at county level. The end result was the dismissal of a large number of sheriffs and their replacement by men of a similar background to those already employed in the Exchequer. It was men of this administrative background who produced two treatises which aimed to explain the workings of the key elements of finance and justice. Books such as these would have been irrelevant if there had not existed a whole administrative class who could appreciate and understand them. The *Dialogue of the Exchequer*, completed in 1179, was written by Richard FitzNigel, Bishop of London and royal treasurer between c.1160 and 1198, while the treatise on the *Law and Customs of England* was produced in c.1190, probably by Ranulf 'de Glanvill', chief justiciar between 1180 and 1189.

The efficiency of Henry's financial system is reflected in the reappearance of the Pipe Rolls, which do not seem to have been kept under Stephen, but for which there is a continuous series from 1155. No regular system of annual taxation was conceivable at this time, but income could be accumulated from many sources. Henry drew on demesne revenues, rights of feudal overlordship, profits from the administration of justice, income from selling favours and, from the 1160s, proportional taxes on movables, the most famous being the so-called Saladin tithe of 1188 for the crusade. Scutage and fines for exemption from service came to play a larger role in military provision, reflecting both the increased tempo of monetary circulation and the marked tendency towards the patrimonialisation of fiefs, a development which sometimes left them in the hands of those unsuitable for personal participation in warfare. The king's attempt to find out the numbers of knights owed in each honour in 1166, apparently with the aim of bringing the rating up-to-date, did not meet with much success in this climate; Henry could not reverse the steady change from feudal host to paid army which marked the later years of the twelfth century. Indeed, Henry's command of a vast network of fiefs which included a very long coastline could be more usefully exploited in a much more modern fashion, for the growing trade produced a healthy income from customs dues, especially from the links between the Atlantic coast of the continent and the ports of southern England (Gillingham 2001:63).

Henry was equally interested in his juridical administration. Walter Map, who had an intimate knowledge of the working of Henry's government, says, 'He had discretion in the making of laws and the ordering of all his government, and was a clever deviser of decisions in unusual and dark cases' (M.R. James 1983:476–7). Map's comment is significant, for Henry's reign is characterised by a whole series of 'assizes' designed to expedite legal procedure, with an increasingly professional judiciary using evidence taken from juries. Some of these procedures, such as those embodied at Clarendon (1166) and Northampton (1176), were aimed mainly at criminal activity, but the greater and more effective part of his judicial reform was concerned with title to land, aiming to provide speedy means of establishing rightful possession. The problems inherited from Stephen's reign, combined with a determination by families to keep a grip on their inherited lands, provided the impetus for assizes like *novel disseisin* (1166), which aimed at restoring lands unlawfully seized, *mort d'ancestor* (1176), which regularised the heritability of land, and the Grand Assize (1179 or 1182), which enabled the possessor to have his rights unequivocally reaffirmed by jury. The cumulative social effect of such measures was to place an emphasis on primogeniture through impartible inheritance, leaving the younger sons of free tenants to seek sustenance in other occupations. The increased numbers of those who sought the king's justice testifies to the success of these reforms, while at the same time adding powerfully to the royal income. The king used the same methods to enforce his own rights: the Assize of Arms (1181) made explicit the obligation of all freemen to do military service if required, and the Assize of Woodstock (1184) set down the laws of the forest, which all kings had so jealously guarded since the Conqueror's time.

Such a relentless drive towards administrative clarity inevitably entangled the Church. Henry looked back to a restoration of conditions which he alleged had existed in his grandfather's time; the Church, on the contrary, had continued to develop and define its position in canon law. The Constitutions of Clarendon were the result of an investigation into the Church's past position. Under pressure, Thomas Becket, Archbishop of Canterbury since 1162, agreed to the sixteen articles thus set down, and the English bishops, hitherto firm in their opposition, then followed, only to find that Becket withdrew his consent when Pope Alexander III condemned most of the Constitutions. Although Becket had been Henry's friend and chancellor, he would not accede to what he called 'customs' which he considered to be incompatible with the Church's 'freedom'. In particular, he was opposed to barriers to access to the pope, as seen in clauses four and eight, and most famously, to clause three, which set out the king's interpretation of the respective rights of the clerical and secular authorities over clerks convicted of criminal activities. Becket believed that degradation by a clerical court was sufficient punishment; Henry argued that such a man, having been stripped of his clerical status, should then be handed over to the secular courts and punished accordingly.

Faced with an attempt by Henry to bring charges of embezzlement against him, arising from offences allegedly committed while he was chancellor, Becket fled to France in October 1164. His strength was the king's need, sooner or later, of the services of the archbishop in order to perform certain essential tasks of government. By the late 1160s, the most pressing of these was the coronation of the king's son, Henry, and his wife Margaret, a matter of crucial importance given the problems created by succession crises in past reigns, but when a meeting with Becket at Montmartre in November 1169 proved futile, Henry went ahead by having the ceremony performed by the Archbishop of York in June 1170. As the king had presumably intended, this brought matters to a head. Pope Alexander III granted Becket the power to suspend and excommunicate the bishops involved and to place England under interdict, but the king now offered peace again, which was accepted by Becket at Fréteval (July 1170). For Becket, the issue of the primacy of Canterbury, threatened by the action of the Archbishop of York, seems to have completely overshadowed the Constitutions of Clarendon, which were not even mentioned. Both men seem to have thought they had won.

Not surprisingly, therefore, such a peace did not last for long. When Becket heard that Henry had immediately started to fill vacant bishoprics, his distrust of the king was once more aroused. He therefore promulgated the bulls given him by the pope and in December 1170 crossed to England to assert his authority. He refused full absolution to the bishops involved in the coronation on the grounds that this appertained to Rome and they went to Normandy to protest to the king. In a moment of exasperation Henry apparently asked, not for the first time, why nobody would rid him of Becket. Four knights took him at his word and on 29 December 1170 murdered Becket in his own cathedral. This act transformed the wrangle between king and archbishop into a famous drama. It turned Canterbury into the centre of one of the greatest cults in medieval Europe, for in 1173 Becket was canonised. It left Henry at such a moral disadvantage that he had to agree, at a meeting with papal legates at Avranches in 1172, to penance and reparation through crusade, and eventually, in 1176, to allow clerical appeals to Rome and clerical immunity. Henry's ability to gain bishoprics for his own nominees was, however, not impaired, a comment perhaps on the extent to which the conflict had been the consequence of a clash of personalities rather than one of high principle, as Becket had liked to portray it.

Richard's last revolt in 1189 had, at its root, Henry's refusal to confirm him unequivocally as his successor. Once the old king had been forced to capitulate, Richard abandoned him, apparently cursed by his dying father. When Henry died on 6 July, Richard succeeded without any overt opposition. He was invested as Duke of

Normandy on 20 July and crowned King of England on 3 September. But Henry had not died in peace; the inheritance brought Richard the full range of his father's problems. The crusading vow remained unfulfilled, rivalry with Capetian France under Philip II continued to sharpen, the fear of family intrigue had not abated with the change of kings, while at the basis of it all lay the vast task of administering the Angevin Empire.

By 1189 the crusade had taken on much greater urgency than it had had when Henry had first taken the cross, for the battle of Hattin two years before had destroyed the army of the Frankish settlers, and in the aftermath Jerusalem and a large part of the Christian conquests had been lost. Richard set about the double task of arranging the government of his lands in his absence and the raising of money to pay for the enterprise. He did this at great speed: he stayed in England for less than four months, between August and December 1189, and by early July 1190 he was already on his way to the east. In England he left the government in the hands of William Longchamp, who had been his chancellor in Aquitaine and was elected Bishop of Ely in September 1189, and Hugh du Puiset, Bishop of Durham. Longchamp was chancellor as well as joint chief justiciar with Hugh du Puiset. Experienced seneschals were appointed or confirmed in Normandy, Anjou, Poitou and Gascony. His younger brother, John, was given lands commensurate with his status; in addition to his County of Mortain, he was allowed to marry the heiress to the Earldom of Gloucester, and granted large blocks of territory in the West Country and the east Midlands. His half-brother, Geoffrey, a man with known secular ambitions, was forced into the Archbishopric of York, apparently against his will. Both men were forbidden to enter England for three years, although John was quickly released from this restriction. Money was raised by well-tried methods, but with a distinct preference for those which yielded the most rapid results. In particular, lands, offices and privileges were sold. The treatment of the sheriffs provides a good example: only six of the thirty-one sheriffs survived the Michaelmas accounting session, the positions of the rest going to those who could pay for them, while three of the remaining six paid for additional offices or privileges (Appleby 1965:20). Equipped with these resources, Richard was able to deploy his exceptional military talents in a theatre which was to give him lasting fame. In 1191 and 1192 he made a greater contribution to the position of the Franks in Outremer than any other outside leader managed during nearly two centuries of their existence. However, he could not crown his achievement with the recapture of Jerusalem; in September 1192 he was forced to settle for a three-year truce with Saladin.

One reason for this settlement was that the king had received news of the breakdown of his administrative arrangements in England. A combination of Longchamp's arrogance and John's ambition had factionalised the kingdom, resulting in the enforced flight of Longchamp in October 1191. The situation was exacerbated when Richard was captured on his return journey from the east while attempting a circuitous route via the Adriatic and Austria, a route taken to avoid interception by his enemies in the western Mediterranean. He was handed over to the Hohenstaufen emperor, Henry VI, and spent the period between December 1192 and February 1194 in captivity, until Henry had both negotiated a very large ransom of 150,000 silver marks and had extracted maximum political capital from the affair.

Richard at last returned to England in March 1194. Given an absence of over four years from England and only a little less from his continental lands, Richard's arrangements had stood up reasonably well. Only minor losses of territory had occurred, despite John's intrigues with Philip II which had included a promise to cede most of northern Normandy in January 1194. In England, despite chroniclers' complaints that Longchamp 'made up for his shortness of stature by his arrogance' and that John and Geoffrey of York shared a quality of 'innate perversity', the routine of government had apparently continued. The itinerant justices conducted eyres, while the exchequer accounts do not appear to be disrupted, despite the wholesale change of sheriffs in 1189 (Appleby 1963:9, 40). Moreover, it did not take Richard long to make good the cracks which had appeared. In the two months which he spent in England (mid-March to mid-May), he overcame the resistance of John's supporters, cleared out most of the sheriffs and resold their offices, and emphasised his authority in a great processional crown-wearing at Winchester Cathedral. Most important of all, although Longchamp remained chancellor, he left the highly efficient Hubert Walter, Archbishop of Canterbury since 1193, as chief justiciar.

Even more than his father, Richard's outlook emphasis that England was seen as only part of the wider domains. His suppression of John's rebellion was only his second visit to England and, because of his early death in 1199, his last. If Henry II had really designed royal administration in England to function without a monarch's presence, then Richard's reign was his most successful legacy. Under Hubert Walter, a general eyre was set in motion in the summer of 1194, aimed at eliminating abuses which had developed while Richard had been absent and at dealing with the backlog of outstanding cases. The justiciar's detailed guidelines for its conduct incorporated the jury of presentment as a permanent part of procedure. The next year, in the *Edictum regium*, all men over the age of 15 were required to swear on oath to keep the king's peace. Knights were appointed to receive these oaths, a role which can be seen as a precedent for the office of justice of the peace (Appleby 1965:151–2, 180). At the same time Hubert Walter continued the relentless drive for money, for the king's needs for the defence of his continental fiefs were endless. A central reason for the eyre of 1194 was the income expected in fines from wrongdoers; scutages were taken four times between 1189 and 1196; tallages were taken on towns and boroughs; inquiries were conducted into embezzlement by officials; and there was even a change in the royal seal in 1198, invalidating documents sealed with the old one and thus forcing payment for renewal. In 1198 an immensely ambitious inquiry was undertaken to survey all land under tillage with the aim of taking an aid on each carucate or hide. There is little evidence that it was ever completed; if it had been it would truly have merited the title of the new Domesday.

The bottomless pit into which this money was being thrown was the expense of Richard's wars against Philip II in Normandy and Anjou. Richard had already paid 24,000 marks towards Philip's 'costs' in 1189, when Henry II had been forced to capitulate. In two prolonged periods of conflict between 1194 and 1196, and 1196 and 1199, when Pope Innocent III negotiated a five-year truce, Richard slowly regained most of the lands lost in his absence. He did so by energetic and attritional campaigning rather than by outright battles, and by constructing a string of castles in eastern Normandy, the most spectacular of which, Château Gaillard, built in 1197 on the river cliffs of the Seine at Les Andelys between Paris and Rouen, was by far the most expensive European castle built to that date. At the same time, like his father, he created a European-wide system of alliances extending from Castile and Navarre in the south to Flanders and the Rhineland in the north, while in 1198 his nephew, Otto of Brunswick, was elected King of the Romans, following the death of Henry VI. When

Richard was killed by a sniper while besieging Chalus in the Limousin in April 1199, the Angevin 'empire' looked, from the outside at least, as formidable as it had done at any time since 1154.

Richard's early death has not made it any easier to form an objective estimate of his capacities as a ruler (see Appleby 1965 and Gillingham 1999 for contrasting views). Henry II had nearly thirty-five years as king in which to gain his triumphs and make his mistakes; Richard lasted less than ten, although they were ten years of almost frenetic activity. Some historians have seen him as irresponsible, pointing to the haste with which he arranged matters before his departure for crusade, his massive expenditure and his failure to ensure that the succession was properly secured either in 1189 or 1199. Others point to the fact that it was only in England that the arrangements of 1189–90 broke down and then not disastrously, that the administration of England under Hubert Walter was at least as logical and efficient as it had been under Ranulf Glanvill, and that the failure of his marriage to Berengaria of Navarre to produce an heir was a matter of bad luck rather than bad policy. Nevertheless, it is not even clear how far Richard can be credited with the successes of Hubert Walter's administration. Richard himself could not have learned much about its workings during the short time he spent in England, nor had he much administrative experience of his own from his earlier years in Aquitaine, a duchy with an administration which was primitive compared with that of England. No historian denies the high cost of his reign, involving colossal expenditure on crusade, ransom and warfare with Philip II. Yet, as the reign of John, his successor, shows, he had not bankrupted England, for John continued to extract large sums, which in some years reached record levels. The Angevin perception that there was considerably more wealth to be tapped from England was accurate, although frequently denied and naturally deeply unpopular. Indeed, the very inflation which made the cost of John's armies so much higher than those of his father was a symptom of the rapid economic growth of a country which, relatively speaking, was already rich when it had been seized by the Conqueror. When Richard entered London after his captivity in Germany, the imperial nobles who accompanied him in the elaborate procession through the city were taken aback by the wealth on display. According to the Yorkshire chronicler, William of Newburgh, one of them told Richard that if Henry VI had realised this 'he would not easily have believed that England's wealth was exhausted, nor would he have released you except for an intolerable amount of ransom' (Howlett 1884:406).

John continued Richard's policies: heavy taxation to pay for the military needs, but under John the problems inherent in defending the 'empire' in this way came to a head dramatically and quickly. Although he overcame the difficulties of the succession dispute with his nephew, Arthur of Brittany, and was able to buy Philip II's compliance in the Treaty of Le Goulet in May 1200, he failed to provide the dynamic military leadership of which his brother was capable and he compounded this failure by a series of political errors, the effects of which were exacerbated by his almost pathological suspicion of treachery. The circumstances of these failures have already been explained. By 1206 the apparently solid edifice of seven years before had collapsed; John had lost Normandy, Maine, Anjou and Brittany. These losses were of crucial importance to England, for John now pressed upon its wealth by using every known method of raising money to finance his planned recovery of the fiefs. Increased frequency of taxes and high rating were particular features. Therefore, for example, he took eleven scutages during the reign, while the proportional tax of one-thirteenth, taken in 1207, pulled in the astonishing sum of £60,000 (Warren 1987:148–9) from a country where the crown's normal annual income was nearer £24,000. His biggest windfall resulted from his quarrel with Pope Innocent III who, following the election of rival candidates to Canterbury after Hubert Walter's death in 1205, tried to introduce his own man, the English cardinal, Stephen Langton. John's refusal to accept him led to a papal interdict on the country which lasted for six years between 1208 and 1214, during which John was quite unrestrained in his exactions from the Church, an action from which the chroniclers never allowed his reputation to recover. When John did finally accept Langton in July 1213, it was only because of his forthcoming confrontation with Philip. The capitulation in turn was costly, for not only did John turn England into a papal fief, but also he had to agree to compensate the Church for its losses to the extent of 100,000 marks before Innocent would lift the king's excommunication. Fiscal despotism such as John's could never be popular, but opposition to it was exacerbated by the fact that ties with the continental fiefs were much weaker than they had been in the past, and there was, consequently, less inclination to defend them. The prospect of a permanent division between England and Normandy was far less alarming to the baronage in 1204 than it had been in 1087 or 1100.

The cumulative effects of a quarter of a century of war financing finally hit John after Bouvines, resulting in the domestic crisis that led to Magna Carta in June 1215. This financing had, in turn, been possible only because of the administrative structure developed by Henry II and in that sense the rebellion of 1215–16 was aimed not simply at John, but at the 'Angevin tyranny' as a whole. In fact, such policies were not peculiar to the Angevins (J.C. Holt 1992:24–6), but they had taken them further than any other rulers, especially under Ranulf Glanvill, Hubert Walter and John himself. Moreover, Richard's and John's habit of selling privileges added a further dimension, for the barons' desire to consolidate and extend their hold on these added further strength to the movement of 1215. Leaders of the baronial opposition like Robert FitzWalter and Geoffrey of Mandeville were themselves descendants of leading royal administrators. The Angevin administrative system combined with succession traumas and absentee rulers had produced a highly politicised baronage.

In the first months of 1215 John refused baronial demands for restoration of what were claimed to be the customs of Henry I but, at the same time, perhaps restrained by Langton, failed to take decisive action. This might have been the right course to take but for the fact that London fell in the hands of the barons in May and John found himself in a corner. His agreement at Runnymede (15 June) may therefore have been a temporary expedient; what emerged were 'the articles of the barons', later embodied in the Great Charter. The sixty-three clauses reflect both the opposition to the Angevin attempts to increase revenue and, closely connected to this, their use of arbitrary action rather than due legal process to reinforce this. In the first case there were clauses to protect both church and lay vassals against what were seen as abuses of the king's powers of wardship, marriage and custody; a limit was set on the size of reliefs; methods used to distrain debts owed to the Jews were regulated; and the taking of scutage forbidden except by 'common counsel of our kingdom'. The second case is epitomised by clause thirty-nine, which insisted on lawful judgement by equals or 'by the law of the land' for all free men. Most clauses were formulated by a nobility with its own position clearly in mind, but there was too a recognition of the importance of mercantile interests, especially of the key role of London, which had frequently been a vital element in past political conflicts. The 'ancient liberties and free customs' of London and 'all other cities, boroughs, towns and ports' were guaranteed, as well as a set of standard weights and measures. Charters, however, had been granted and ignored before; clause sixty-one created a council of twenty-five barons to ensure that its terms were kept (Rothwell 1975:316–24).

In fact, the arrangements for the enforcement of the Charter quickly broke down, since neither side was prepared to trust the other to act in good faith. By the time that Innocent III had finally caught up with events in August, when he annulled the charter, both sides were already preparing to fight. With papal backing and superior military force, John had restored himself to virtual control by the spring of 1216. A measure of the desperation of the opposition can be seen by the invitation to Prince Louis of France, who invaded in May and June. John was in the process of attempting to cope with this when he contracted dysentery and died at Newark on 19 October 1216. John's death removed the main barrier to compromise, since his son, Henry, was only 9 years old and could play no effective monarchical role. Henry was crowned at Gloucester on 28 October and then, on 12 November, a regency council, dominated by William, Earl Marshal, and Ranulf, Earl of Chester, reissued the charter in modified form, taking care to remove clause sixty-one which set up the baronial committee of twenty-five. The modified charter therefore appeared almost as if it were a grant of the king's own making, the usual remedy for abuses at the beginning of a new reign. In May 1217 the rebels and the French, their support now cut from under them, were defeated at Lincoln, while in August Louis's fleet was wrecked before he could be reinforced. In September, with the ending of the French threat, Magna Carta was again reissued, together with a Charter of the Forest. The Charter of the Forest was an expanded version of the clauses concerned with operation of the forest laws contained in Magna Carta, in which John promised to abolish 'evil' forest laws, restricting their extent and modifying the punishments for violations. Henry himself confirmed the charters in 1225 while still a minor, at which time they took their final form.

According to the *History of William the Marshal*, the bearing of the young Henry, vulnerable but dignified, had so impressed the magnates who had come to collect him after John's death that they were all moved to tears (Rothwell 1975:82). But Henry, encouraged by his assertive justiciar, Hubert of Burgh, did not remain a small boy for long; in 1220 he received a new coronation at Westminster and by 1223 he had used his father's submission to the papacy to gain the support of Honorius III for the personal use of his seal. Four years later he obtained a letter from Gregory IX declaring that his minority was at an end, for 'he already has assumed a manly spirit and has gained ground in age and wisdom' (B. Wilkinson 1963:1:92).

Indeed, it was soon clear that Henry fully intended to pursue the policies of his predecessors. In 1227, perhaps influenced by the example of Frederick II, he demanded that all those who held royal grants should show by what warrant they were entitled to them; in 1230 he invaded Brittany with the aim of starting to recover his father's losses. The campaign was a failure for which Hubert of Burgh received the blame, but this made no substantial change to Henry's governmental style. Henry believed in his right to choose his own advisers and to pursue his own policies in the Angevin tradition (see the differing views of Clanchy 1968 and Carpenter 1985). The Poitevins, Peter des Roches, Bishop of Winchester, and Peter des Rivaux, replaced Hubert of Burgh as the chief influence on government and when, in 1236, Henry married Eleanor of Provence (sister of Louis IX's queen, Margaret), a number of the queen's Savoyard relatives were also rapidly elevated to positions of power. In 1238 a Frenchman, Simon of Montfort, who had come to England seeking to make good his family's claim to the Earldom of

Leicester, was allowed to marry the king's sister in secret. In 1242 Henry attempted an invasion of Poitou, but this ended even more ignominiously than the previous effort, with defeat at the battle of Taillebourg and retreat to Saintes. Henry eventually had to come to a settlement with Louis IX embodied in the Treaty of Paris of 1259, under which he agreed to hold Gascony by liege homage as a vassal and a peer of France, but the remainder of the old Angevin conglomerate was confirmed in Capetian hands. These failures in France, however, did not rob him of his conviction of his importance on the European stage, for he was not simply King of England, but also grandson of Henry II. In 1250 he took the cross and in 1254 agreed to finance his son, Edmund, as a candidate for the Sicilian throne on behalf of a papacy bent on ridding itself of the Hohenstaufen.

However, by the time of the Sicilian candidature, Henry had already received several warnings that he could not continue his very personal style of government without opposition. The magnates' perception of their role in government had been clarified by the events of 1215–25, while their attitude towards the monarchy's continental interest had cooled even further. In Henry I's time self-interest might have encouraged them to defend Normandy, but for Henry III's baronage the Poitevin campaigns were quite remote from their experience or loyalties, while Henry's elevation of men perceived to be 'foreigners' served only to strengthen these feelings. In 1233 a quarrel over Henry's use of Poitevin advisers had led to the dismissal of the counsellors the following year, while in 1244 the barons had attempted to gain permanent representation on the king's council. The Church too believed that its interests were being damaged by the imposition of foreign prelates upon English sees and the exaction of what many saw as excessive papal taxation. Although the matter is controversial, it seems probable that Pope Alexander's threat, in the spring of 1258, to excommunicate the king for not providing the promised financial support for Edmund's Sicilian candidature brought these matters to a head. A sworn association or commune of magnates, led by Richard, Earl of Gloucester, and Roger Bigod, Earl of Norfolk, persuaded the king to agree to the appointment of twenty-four barons to reform the realm, whose proposals, the *Petitio Baronum*, resulted in the Provisions of Oxford (June 1258). These created a council of fifteen which

> shall have the power of advising the king in good faith concerning the government of the kingdom and concerning all matters that pertain to the king or the kingdom, and for the purpose of amending and redressing everything that they shall consider in need of amendment or redress. And they shall have authority over the chief justice and over all other people.
>
> (B. Wilkinson 1963:1:139)

This council would consult with a committee of twelve barons in Parliament which was to meet regularly, three times per annum. Every freeman, from the king downwards, was required to take an oath to support these provisions. As in 1215, lack of trust between king and magnates led to an attempt to restrict the king's freedom of action. But the reformers went much further than clause sixty-one of Magna Carta, for they set up a baronial council intended to govern rather than simply oversee the Provisions.

Nevertheless, the barons soon found themselves accused of double standards; the reforms which they wished to effect in royal government should also, in the view of the knights of the shire, apply to the barons' administration of their own lands, an attitude which was accepted in the 'Provisions of Westminster' of October 1259, which were particularly concerned with procedures in magnates' courts. Matters like this emphasised differences in outlook among the barons, differences which the king could exploit. Henry III, indeed, was far from being the simpleton of baronial propaganda. For more than thirty years he had evaded attempts to pin restrictions on him and he was no more prepared to accept them than his father had been. He gave way in 1258 in the face of the armed force of the baronage, but for the next three years he used every manoeuvre he could to extricate himself and in 1261, again like his father, he obtained papal release from the oath sworn in 1258. The oath, said Alexander IV, had been 'to the diminution of your power and to the depression of your royal liberty' (Treharne and Sanders 1973:241). Simon of Montfort had not played a leading role in drawing up the Provisions – indeed, at the time he was in France negotiating on behalf of the king – but on his return he quickly emerged as the king's leading opponent, displaying that combination of self-righteous religious zeal for a cause and drive for political dominance which had characterised his father. Simon's leadership and Henry's intransigence polarised opinion; in these circumstances it is not surprising to find the pattern of 1215–16 repeating itself, inducing a spiral of events which eventually left Montfort dead and dismembered on the battlefield at Evesham in August 1265.

Despite the widespread support for reform, Montfort found it difficult to maintain himself in the face of royal opposition, backed by papal censure. This may have induced him to appeal to Louis IX for arbitration, presumably in the hope of legitimising his position, but in the judgement known as the Mise of Amiens (1264), he found Louis totally committed to the monarchy. The judgement led to war which brought victory to Montfort at Lewes (May 1264), but his dominance of the government thereafter served only to confirm the suspicion of those who believed that he was more interested in personal power than reform. A situation which was already slipping out of his control was resolved by the victory of the royalist forces at Evesham. The battle did not, however, in itself settle the issues; indeed, fighting continued for some time afterwards. Only slowly during the next two years was it possible to work out a settlement: the Dictum of Kenilworth (October 1266) set out ways in which those disinherited as a result of Montfort's defeat could regain their lands, and the Statute of Marlborough (November 1267) reaffirmed the Provisions of Westminster and the confirmation of Magna Carta of 1225.

Edward I (1272–1307) has often been contrasted with his father and grandfather; to Louis Salzman (1968:13) he seems to have had more in common with Henry II than his immediate forebears. But differences in personality and competence should not obscure the essential continuities of the period. Edward strove both to assert his overlordship of Wales and Scotland and to defend himself from a similar claim by his own lord, Philip IV of France, in Gascony. He did so with greater efficiency and consistency than Henry III or John, but his successes – quite striking up to 1290, but less impressive after that date – look greater than perhaps they were when compared with the almost total military failure of his two predecessors. Moreover, warfare on this scale did not come cheaply; he needed to raise huge sums of money which he took from every conceivable source. In 1297 this provoked a major crisis, just as it had in the past. Above all, these conflicts show Edward to have had the same highly developed sense of his own prerogatives as had his predecessors, a sense perhaps sharpened by his experiences during the Barons' War. Under Edward this expressed itself most clearly in the application of his judicial supremacy, not only in his dealings with the Welsh and

Scottish rulers, but also in his promotion of legislation designed to define and apply the monarchy's rights as he saw them.

Eastern and southern Wales had been colonised by the Normans; by Edward's time these regions had many connections with England and were often the means by which the English crown exercised its influence in the regions beyond. However, neither John nor Henry III had made much further progress. On the contrary, the crises of 1258–67 had enabled Llywelyn ap Gruffydd to extend his power in northern and central Wales, gaining recognition as Prince of Wales from Henry III in the process. When Edward became king, Llywelyn felt secure enough to avoid doing homage, a provocation which led Edward to set out to enforce his overlordship in a manner which suggests that he had learned a great deal from previous mistakes, both his own and those of his predecessors. Llywelyn was forced to renew his vassalage in the Treaty of Conway in 1277 and then, during a new revolt in 1282, was killed. The Statute of Rhuddlan (1284) established direct royal control in the north and west, which were divided into shires on the English pattern, while coastal castles and fortified towns, extending from Flint round to Aberystwyth and built to the latest designs, were established as centres of authority. Their practical value was reinforced by imperial symbolism; Caernarvon, for example, had polygonal towers like Constantinople and, from 1317, imperial eagles as well. The Welsh did not remain quiescent – there were further revolts in 1287 and 1294–5, timed to coincide with Edward's campaigns in France – but they did not substantially affect the conquest.

In Gascony, however, the situation was reversed; here Edward was subjected to harassment and double-dealing not dissimilar from his own treatment of the Welsh. The strategies of the two sides continued those pursued by their predecessors: Edward attempted to build up alliances in the Low Countries (having already acquired Ponthieu by right of his wife in 1279), while Philip IV encroached upon his rights in Gascony at every opportunity. A sea battle between sailors from Normandy and the Cinque Ports in 1293 provided Philip with an opening rather like the Lusignan appeal against John; the French king cited Edward to appear before his *parlement*. Although the case was not heard, the matter led to negotiations in which Edward was persuaded to hand over the duchy to French officials for a set period, only to find that Philip the Fair had no intention of returning it. Three expeditions were mounted against Philip between 1294 and 1297, but they were continually interrupted by problems in Wales and Scotland and eventually by the crisis of 1297, itself a consequence of the strains imposed by Edward's wars. A settlement was achieved in 1303, as a result of which Gascony was returned, and the peace was consolidated by arranging marriages between Edward and Philip's sister, Margaret, and between the king's son, Edward, and Philip's daughter, Isabella. The return of the duchy was, however, more a consequence of Philip IV's defeat by the Flemings at Courtrai in 1302, than any pressure Edward had been able to exert.

If the problems in the British Isles had been confined to Wales, it might have been possible for the king to have continued to struggle with France, but they included the much tougher problem of Scotland as well. Here, although it had not been formally conceded by any Scottish king since William I in 1212, Edward acted as the overlord from whom ultimate authority descended, first proposing to marry his son, Edward, to Margaret, the infant heiress of Alexander III, and then, when she unexpectedly died, arbitrating on rival candidates, choosing in 1292 an Anglo-Scottish nobleman, John Balliol, as king. But Westminster was to provide the final court of appeal and Balliol's objection to this in practice led him into alliance with France. Edward's reaction was to begin a series of campaigns which he expected would subdue Scotland as they had Wales. But Scotland proved intractable. Each time he seemed near victory, as after the battle of Falkirk in 1298, new resistance undid his work; when he died in 1307 he was preparing yet another campaign against his latest enemy, Robert Bruce.

In England, from the beginning of his reign, Edward tried to generalise the principle of *quo warranto* which his father had insisted upon after his minority, enacting this in the Statutes of Westminster (1275), Gloucester (1278) and *Quo Warranto* (1290). In 1274–5 a great inquiry into both royal rights and abuses by royal and private officials had been carried out, producing a mass of material known as the Hundred Rolls. Further large-scale inquiries followed in 1279 and 1285, intended to provide details down to every village, hamlet and tenement. However, the relative lack of interest in these operations shown by chroniclers implies a certain cynical resignation about them. The land was not again 'vexed with violence' as it had been at the time of Domesday. Edward adopted an equally systematic approach towards the confusions of feudal tenure which had developed since the Conquest, for tenure bore on the provision of military service and scutage, and a lack of clarity arising from the complexities of a fluid land market was likely to have a detrimental effect upon the rights of both king and lords. The Statute of Mortmain (1279) forbade alienation of property to the Church without the lord's permission, the Statute of Westminster II (1285) defined rights of parties in matters concerning the granting of land and the requirements of service, while *Quia Emptores* (1290) laid down that when a lord granted out an estate, the beneficiary should hold from the ultimate lord of the fief and not become a sub-tenant.

Just as the barons who formulated Magna Carta implicitly accepted that the development of royal justice had its advantages for them, so too did Edward's barons recognise the constructive nature of his legal reform, but they were, also like their predecessors, considerably more recalcitrant in the face of the king's financial exactions. Despite the immense sums they raised, both Edward I and Philip IV were faced with acute financial problems arising from the scale and nature of their wars. Edward could draw on demesne revenues, on profits of justice, on purveyance (by which he could requisition supplies for his army at cheap rates) and on tallages taken from royal boroughs. He could also take more general taxes such as proportional levies on laymen and clergy and customs duties on the export of wool, known as the *maltôte*, which he did with increasing frequency as expenses mounted. Proportional taxes on movables, for instance, were taken nine times in the reign, seven of them after 1290. Even this was not enough. Huge debts to Italian bankers were accumulated, most of which were still outstanding in 1307. The king's relations with Parliament can usefully be employed as a measure of the changes of the 1290s. The word had first been used in 1236 to describe the combined meetings of the royal council and courts, although King John had in fact assembled representatives of all the counties twenty years before. Such assemblies were part of the royal system of government and were not connected with any idea of consent (J.C. Holt 1981). For the first twenty years of his reign Edward employed them successfully in the same way: biannual meetings used for legislation, judgements, the receipt of complaints, and the discussion of external matters. But during the 1290s the financial pressures of warfare began to change the nature of such meetings; Parliament was used to express discontent with royal taxation policies and, soon, as an opportunity to do something about them. While Edward's exploitation of his crown rights was resented, the focus of discontent was bound to be on the 'extraordinary' taxes which, it was generally argued, required the consent of the subjects concerned. For many this meant Parliament, often in the form which extended it to knights and burgesses, already seen in Henry III's reign, as well as prelates and nobles. Nevertheless, there was no set form for the consent; Parliament represented only one possibility.

These pressures came to a head in 1297: the clergy had been forbidden to pay without papal consent by the bull *Clericis laicos* of the previous year; laymen were aggrieved by the king's attempt to make all landholders with an annual income of over £20 liable for military service; the nobility, reluctant to serve overseas at all, objected to the demand that they campaign in Gascony while the king was going to Flanders. The conflict was intensified by the personal grievances of Roger Bigod, Earl of Norfolk, and Humphrey of Bohun, Earl of Hereford, respectively the royal constable and marshal, and by the inexperience and rigidity of Robert of Winchelsey, the new Archbishop of Canterbury, but at base lay the scale and methods of royal taxation compounded by the king's sometimes cursory approach to the matter of consent. Edward's initial reaction was typically high-handed. According to the Yorkshire chronicler, Walter of Guisborough, the king was enraged at the earls' opposition, while he reacted to the Church by placing it outside royal protection (Rothwell 1975:226). In August the king went ahead with the Flanders campaign anyway.

The outcome was less serious for Edward than it had been for his predecessors, for the pope, under pressure from Philip IV, backed down on the issue of clerical taxation, while Edward's *Confirmatio Cartarum* (November 1297), reaffirming Magna Carta and the Forest Charter of 1217 and agreeing to seek consent before the taking of all but the customary aids, took the sting out of the lay opposition. But it is clear that the king was not trusted: a further confirmation of charters was made in 1299 and the next year Parliament extracted the *Articuli super cartas*, which incorporated a further twenty clauses regulating resented royal actions like purveyance. Yet in 1303 the king assembled representatives of the towns in an attempt to force them to pay additional customs duties which, although unsuccessful, nevertheless violated the *Confirmatio* of 1297, and in 1305, again just like John and Henry III, Edward sought to use the papacy to escape, obtaining a bull from Clement V releasing him from his oath given in 1297. Soon after, he had Winchelsey suspended and summoned to answer charges before the pope. For many contemporaries the unreliability and vindictiveness that Edward had shown as a young man still marred the character of the mature king.

Edward II received a troubled legacy from his father. An unresolved Scottish war, together with huge debts of over £200,000 owed to foreign bankers, combined with a deeply discontented nobility, an embittered and intransigent Archbishop of Canterbury, and a Parliament in which some had become accustomed to oppose royal government, did not offer the new king the kind of fresh start available to Edward I when he returned from crusade in 1274. Distrust of the king was evident from the beginning of the reign. In February 1308, in a significant addition to the coronation oath, Edward was obliged to swear 'to maintain and preserve the laws and rightful customs which the community of the realm shall have chosen' (Rothwell 1975:525). The imposition of this new clause emphasised an old problem: the fear of the magnates that a king given either to reneging on his agreements or to the promotion of 'favourites' would deprive them of the manifest advantages which stemmed from their social and political position. Edward I had been threatening for the first reason; they knew both from his past record and from the immediate elevation of his friend Piers Gaveston to the Earldom of Cornwall, that Edward II would try to govern by means of the second.

Edward II was therefore in conflict with the magnates from the outset. Although he was obliged to banish Gaveston in May 1308, he was back by the next year, leading to a build-up of opposition which culminated in an attempt to place upon the king a comprehensive set of controls. In 1310 Edward had to accept a committee of twenty-one 'to order and establish the state of his household and of his realm', for it was claimed that otherwise the crown would lose its lands in Gascony, Ireland and Scotland and that there would be rebellion in England (Rothwell 1975:527). This resulted in the Ordinances of 1311 which not only exiled Gaveston once again, but also, in an attempt to deprive the king of both administrative and financial power, determined that his chief officials were to be appointed only with parliamentary consent, his Italian bankers were to be expelled, and the customs duties on foreign merchants, which had been a lucrative source of income since 1303, were to be abolished. But the Ordinances, although often referred to in subsequent years, were observed by the king only when under constraint. He allowed Gaveston to return within two months and engaged new bankers from Genoa to replace those expelled.

The failure to make the Ordinances stick led to open warfare. Gaveston was captured and handed over to the Earl of Pembroke from whose custody he was seized by the most prominent member of the opposition, Thomas of Lancaster, who had him executed. For Edward this was a deep personal loss, but it actually benefited him politically, for the favour shown to Gaveston had been a major reason for the opposition to him. But the king's political recovery did not last long; in May 1314 he was heavily defeated by Robert Bruce at Bannockburn, a disaster which was only the most spectacular manifestation of Edward's continued failure to defend the north against the Scots. Edward now lost what semblance of control he had hitherto maintained, for Lancaster emerged as the dominant figure, while personal rivalries, some of which were unconnected with the monarchy, exacerbated disorder and feuding. Since the years 1315–17 were also a period of severe famine in northern Europe, the misery of much of the populace must have been acute, especially in northern England, where there was little to check the regular Scottish raids. Nor were any of the problems which had plagued the reign ever close to a solution, despite a superficial reconciliation between Edward and Lancaster. Indeed, from 1318 the days of Gaveston seem to have returned with the ascent to the position of Chamberlain of the Household of a new and more ruthless favourite, Hugh Despenser, a minor noble who had come to notice through his father's friendship with both Edwards. Despenser's grasping policies provoked the opposition of both Lancaster and the Marcher lords led by Roger Mortimer, who were particularly affected by Despenser's efforts to expand his interests in the region. A compromise in 1321 in which Edward agreed to the exile of the Despensers was not accepted by the king for long. The ultimate result was direct confrontation in the battle of Boroughbridge (1322). Lancaster was captured and executed, and Edward was able to pass the Statute of York (1322), which repealed the Ordinances and forbade such attempts by subjects to place constraints on royal powers. But Edward could not maintain himself in power by these means for long. His reign had allowed the development of a depth of bitterness and hatred for which ultimately he paid a higher price than any of his predecessors. In 1326 a combined invasion of his wife, Isabella, alienated by the power of Despenser, and Roger Mortimer, was joined by the rebel earls, and Edward and Despenser were captured. Despenser was executed almost at once; Edward was deposed by an assembly of parliamentary estates in January 1327, and replaced by his young son. Nine months later Edward was murdered. This was the first deposition in English history. In one sense, it showed the strength of the crown, for, despite his political ineptitude it had not proved possible to contain Edward permanently except by taking this most drastic step. In another sense it showed the changing relationship between crown and subjects, in particular the leading role played by the magnates in the 'politicisation' of Parliament and the emergence of the Commons as an element to be summoned whenever major issues were at stake.

13

The Iberian kingdoms

Between the reigns of Ferdinand I (1035–65) and Ferdinand III (1217–52), Kings of Castile-León, and Alfonso I (1104–34) and James I (1213–76), Kings of Aragon, Christian reconquest transformed the Iberian peninsula. Since the defeat of the Visigoths between 711 and 715 and the establishment of the Umayyad Emirate in 756, Iberia had become largely Islamic in government and religion, but multicultural and multiracial in composition. During the twelfth and thirteenth centuries it emerged as a land all but dominated by what thirteenth-century Christian chroniclers liked to call 'the five kingdoms', leaving only the dependent Emirate of Granada in the south-east under Muslim control. The unifying theme of the period, therefore, is the attention paid to the ever-changing frontier, the southward movement of which, seen from the point of view of a world inspired by papal ideology, represented a triumph unmatched elsewhere in Christendom. However, it was a triumph achieved only by forging a mentality largely incompatible with the previous relationships which had existed between Christian, Muslim, Mozarab (Christians who had assimilated Arabic customs) and Jew. The cost was seen in the creation of deep-seated internal tensions – political, social, economic and religious – which, in the later middle ages, began to corrode any steps towards acculturation and assimilation which had been, consciously or unconsciously, taken. The reason for this was that Christian success was achieved only fitfully, unevenly, and with many serious setbacks. The major invasions from north Africa of the Almoravides in 1086 and the Almohades in 1146 both seemed, each in its own generation, to have decisively reversed the tide of Christian progress, while even after the much-vaunted Christian victory at Las Navas de Tolosa in 1212, there was still considerable life in the Muslim cause, expressed both in internal revolts against new Christian overlords and in the very troublesome attacks of the Marinids of Morocco after 1275, sometimes skilfully exploited by the rulers of Granada (see Map 7). Moreover, despite the general increase in the population of western Christendom, the natural pressures for more space were far from overwhelming and, with the exception of a few favoured areas, the repeopling of the newly conquered terrain proved to be a daunting task beyond the resources of the Christians. To counter Muslim resistance and offset demographic deficiencies, the Christians had to develop a political and military ruthlessness and a spiritual harshness which, when the frontier could expand no more, turned in upon itself to leave a society riven by political and social conflict.

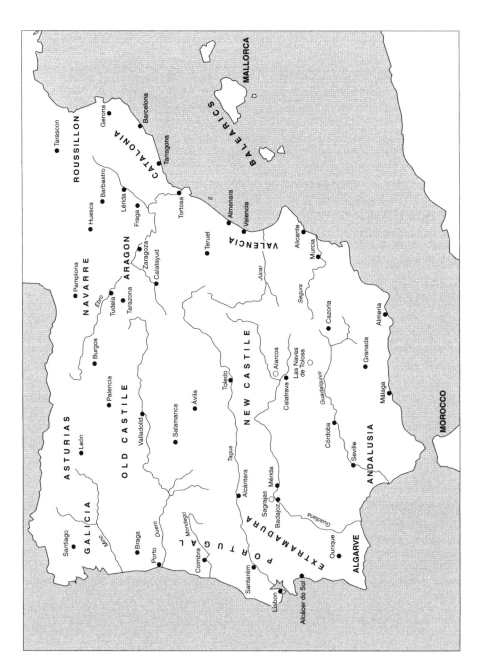

Map 7 The Iberian kingdoms

The crystallisation of Spain into two distinct camps originally arose from the volatile situation created by the collapse of the Caliphate of Córdoba. The caliphs, established since 929, although sophisticated and rich, had found political control of the many regional potentates elusive. The last real power in al-Andalus (Muslim Spain) had been al-Mansur, the vizier, who died in 1002. The struggle which followed left a series of petty rulers, the Taifas or party kings, politically unstable, weak in their faith, but economically prosperous and often culturally diverse and open. Therefore, by 1031, when the Caliph was driven out by a popular revolt, his title had no meaning in any case. The northern Christian rulers were not slow to take advantage, extracting tribute or *parias* in return for 'protection' on an ever-increasing scale (MacKay 1977:15–26), tribute used by the more successful rulers such as Ferdinand I of Castile and Ramón Berenguer, Count of Barcelona, as much to extend their power over their Christian neighbours as to expand the frontier.

The novelty of this temporary Christian ascendancy should not be exaggerated, for resistance to the Muslims had been evident since as early as 716, so that in the ninth and early tenth centuries in particular the Umayyads had been forced to give some ground to the Asturian (later Leonese) rulers, kings apparently motivated not only by the usual need to demonstrate their qualities as warrior leaders, but also by a wider consciousness of the Visigothic past and, to some extent, of the cause of Christianity embodied in the cult of St James emanating from Compostela (Lomax 1978:27–43). Nevertheless, in the political kaleidoscope of the mid-eleventh century, alliances across religious lines were common and there was little sign of the crusading spirit. Christian progress towards the Duero River and even beyond had been more a matter of moving into empty spaces than seizing Muslim territory and it is doubtful if Ferdinand I gave any greater weight to this than he did to his dominance over Navarre, whose ruler, Sancho IV (1054–76) was forced to cede to Castile his lands west of the Ebro River before he could inherit the kingdom with any degree of security (see Tables 9 and 10).

The career of Rodrigo Díaz de Vivar, the Cid of later epic, was moulded by these circumstances. Born into the minor Castilian nobility in *c.*1043, he first came into prominence in the entourage of Sancho II, Ferdinand's successor in Castile, but when Sancho was murdered in 1072, leaving his brother Alfonso VI as master of both Castile and León, Rodrigo found himself slipping from favour, and in 1081 he was exiled by a king angered by freelance military exploits which threatened to undermine royal policy along the frontier (Fletcher 1989:125–42). In the years that followed, he carved out a notable career in the eastern parts of the peninsula, in particular in the pay of the Muslim ruler of Zaragoza in the early 1080s and, between 1089 and his death in 1099, as virtually a free agent in Valencia where, by a combination of military skill and political manoeuvring he contrived to dominate a region in the frontline of the powerful Almoravide advance. In June 1094 he captured the city of Valencia itself where, despite its isolation from other Christian territories, he successfully beat off an Almoravide attack in October of the same year. During this time he was twice reconciled with Alfonso, in 1086–7 and 1090–1, but there never developed a lasting trust between the two men, and there was therefore no possibility that the Cid could rely on a permanent landed base in Castile. Although a remarkable soldier, Rodrigo's success was equally due to his skilful manipulation of the system of *parias*, without which he could not have financed his military ventures. Despite the evident development of a more systematic concept of the Holy War during the twelfth century, this exploitation of the opportunities presented by the frontier remained a feature of Spanish society. The

Table 9 Rulers of Castile and León

Ferdinand I	1036–65 Castile
	1037–65 León
Sancho II	1065–72 Castile
Alfonso VI	1065–1109 León
	1072–1109 Castile
Urraca	1109–26
Alfonso VII	1126–57
Sancho III	1157–8 Castile
Ferdinand II	1157–88 León
Alfonso VIII	1158–1214 Castile
Henry I	1214–17 Castile
Alfonso IX	1188–1230 León
Ferdinand III	1217–52 Castile. Canonised 1671
	1230–52 León
Alfonso X	1252–84
Sancho IV	1284–95
Ferdinand IV	1295–1312
Alfonso XI	1312–50

Table 10 Rulers of Navarre

Sancho IV	1054–76
Sancho V (I of Aragon)	1076–94
Peter I (I of Aragon)	1094–1104
Alfonso I (I of Aragon)	1104–34
García V	1134–50
Sancho VI	1150–94
Sancho VII	1194–1234
Theobald I, Count of Champagne	1234–53
Theobald II, Count of Champagne	1253–70
Henry I, Count of Champagne	1270–3
Jeanne, Countess of Champagne	1274–1305
Philip I Capet (IV of France)	1284–1305
Louis I Capet (X of France)	1305–16
Philip II Capet (V of France)	1316–22

following extract from the *Historia Roderici*, probably written not long after 1102, conveys some sense of this world. It took place in 1084 while Rodrigo was in the service of al-Mu'tamin, ruler of Zaragoza.

> Meanwhile King al-Mu'tamin ordered Rodrigo Díaz to gather his troops and invade the land of Aragon with him to lay it waste. They ravaged the land of Aragon and stripped it of its riches and led off many of its inhabitants captive with them. After five days they returned victoriously to the castle of Monzón. The Aragonese king Sancho was indeed present at that time in his land and kingdom but in no manner did he dare to resist Rodrigo. After this Rodrigo fell upon the land of al-Mu'tamin's brother al-Hāyib, and ravaged it. He wrought much damage and destruction there, especially in the mountains of Morella and thereabouts. There was not left in that region a house which he did not destroy, nor property which he did not seize. He campaigned too against the castle of Morella, and fought his way up to the gate of the castle and inflicted great damage on it. Al-Mu'tamin asked him by means of letters and a messenger to rebuild the fortress of Olocau, over against Morella. He at once rebuilt and fortified it and stocked it well with all necessary provisions, and men and weapons.
>
> (Barton and Fletcher 2000:109–110)

The Cid died in July 1099, the same month that the armies of the First Crusade took Jerusalem. Although material gain was never far from the forefront of the minds of the crusaders, the expedition could not have succeeded without the driving force of religious conviction, indeed of religious fanaticism, as the blood-bath that followed the fall of Jerusalem demonstrated only too graphically. According to the author of the *Gesta Francorum*, 'No-one has ever seen or heard of such a slaughter of pagans, ... and no-one save God alone knows how many there were' (R. Hill 1962:92). While such attitudes would have been alien to the Cid, it is significant that during his lifetime this spirit had begun to pervade Iberia just as it had inspired the Normans and the Provençals, the Flemings and the Lorrainers, to overcome unbelievable hardship to reach the Holy Sepulchre. Urban II was as insistent on the need to counter the Muslims in Iberia as he was about the east. In a letter to the Languedocian baronage, written between 1096 and 1099, he urged them to recover the city of Tarragona 'for the remission of sins'. Mindful of the response at Clermont he wrote:

> If the knights of other provinces have decided with one mind to go to the aid of the Asian Church and to liberate their brothers from the tyranny of the Saracens, so ought you with one mind and with our encouragement to work with greater endurance to help a church so near you resist the invasions of the Saracens.

There was, said the pope, no virtue in rescuing Christians from the Saracens in one place, only to expose them to their tyranny in another (Riley-Smith and Riley-Smith 1981:40).

Outside influences were therefore beginning to penetrate the peninsula from Rome, Languedoc, Burgundy and Francia in particular. Symptomatic was the triumph of the Roman liturgy over local traditions, a victory consolidated at the Council of León in

1090, while French influence began to show at court, for three of the five wives of Alfonso VI were French and both his daughters married Burgundian nobles. These changes were part of a wider movement, for the popularity of the pilgrimage to Compostela, together with Cluniac promotion of the route, brought growing numbers of outsiders to Spain, especially soldiers for whom St James was seen as special protector and ally (Ward 1982:111–13). Even though it seems likely that Cluniac influence has been exaggerated, nevertheless pilgrims, monks and traders provided a channel through which a new outlook was transmitted to a country hitherto largely isolated from wider European movements. There are even signs of outside military intervention. In July 1064 a Catalan army, reinforced by French and Norman nobles, took and pillaged Barbastro in the Muslim Kingdom of Zaragoza and massacred many of its inhabitants. Although the city was back in Muslim hands by April of the next year, many of the northerners had already returned home spreading tales of the wealth and booty to be obtained (Ferreiro 1983). The rapid loss of Barbastro does show, however, that in the long term practical help from outside was to be much less important than the implantation of an idea.

But the changing attitudes were not exclusive to the Christian side. In 1085 Alfonso VI had seized the rich prize of Toledo, a capture which opened out the prospect of control of the Tagus valley and with it the acquisition of even greater sums of tribute. This success had great importance for his own lands for it established a permanent ascendancy of Castile over León, in contrast to earlier centuries, but its more immediate effect was to panic al-Mu'tamid, the ruler of Seville, into inviting from north Africa a new and predatory 'protector' in the form of the Almoravides under Yusuf ibn-Tashfin. The Almoravides had risen to power about half a century before, propelled by a puritanical religious zeal based on a literal interpretation of the Koran. By this time they had conquered Morocco and were conveniently close to the straits. Their entry into Spain transformed the lethargic world of al-Andalus. In October 1086, Alfonso's forces suffered a crushing defeat at Yusuf's hands at Sagrajas, near Badajoz, and there was

Table 11 Rulers of Aragon	
Ramiro I	1035–63
Sancho I	1063–94
Peter I	1094–1104
Alfonso I	1104–34
Ramiro II	1134–7. Abdicated
Petronilla of Aragon and Ramón Berenguer, Count of Barcelona	1137–62
Alfonso II of Barcelona	1162–96
Peter II	1196–1213
James I	1213–76
Peter III	1276–85
Alfonso III	1285–91
James II	1291–1327

inaugurated a period of Muslim fanaticism which matched that of their crusading counterparts in the Christian world. Although Christianity was not actually proscribed in al-Andalus, churches were destroyed, individuals and communities were deported, imprisoned and bullied, and before long increasing numbers of Mozarabs began to find their way north into Christian territories. The hardening of the frontier into a religious divide had begun. The taifa kingdoms of the south-west, especially Badajoz and Seville, now fell under Almoravide control, while in the east only the skill and adaptability of the Cid preserved Valencia. Even here, in 1102, three years after Rodrigo's death, this too was abandoned by Alfonso as untenable. Fortunately for the Christian kingdoms, the Almoravides were particularly concerned to establish control over the taifa kings, co-religionists whose weakness in the faith they regarded with contempt. In 1110 the last independent taifa ruler, in Zaragoza, fell to the Almoravides, bringing them within reach of the Ebro River.

The year before, Alfonso VI had died aged 79. Since 1077 he had been using the imperial title, a claim rooted in the Kingdom of León, which had been given greater resonance by the capture of Toledo in 1085. However, after the defeat of 1086 he had struggled to maintain himself in the face of the Almoravides, and from the beginning of the twelfth century the Christian initiative had shifted to his much younger contemporary, Alfonso I, King of Aragon and Navarre, known as 'the Battler', whose mentality had been formed much more by the crusading outlook (see Table 11). Alfonso's father, Sancho Ramirez (1063–94), had actively sought to stimulate papal interest in the reconquest when, in 1068, while on pilgrimage to Rome, he had agreed to become a papal vassal. In the long term this subservience was to become both an embarrassment and an irritation to the Aragonese kings, but in Sancho's time it may have seemed a shrewd method of gaining outside help for a relatively small kingdom which, until then, had not been conspicuously successful in expanding its territory at Moorish expense.

Certainly, Alfonso I seems to have been stimulated by the ambition to play his role on a wider stage, for in 1109 he had married Urraca, the heiress of Alfonso VI, and soon after began to call himself 'Emperor of Spain'. But the marriage was not a success, and by 1114 Alfonso had decided to accept earlier papal nullification, leaving Castile to a decade of dynastic struggle. Nevertheless, although his more grandiose plans had been frustrated, Alfonso continued the war against the Muslims, actively seeking French recruits, including hardened crusaders like Gaston of Béarn. Zaragoza, Tudela, Tarazona and Catalayud were all taken between 1118 and 1120. Vibrations from this war were felt far afield; Orderic Vitalis knew of Normans who had taken part in these campaigns and who had sought new lands to settle. He expressed his satisfaction that the Africans had been 'sent to the infernal regions by Christian weapons' (Chibnall 1978:6:401). These successes opened access to lands south of the Ebro, even tempting Alfonso, in 1125, into a dramatic but ultimately fruitless march as far south as Granada and Malaga. His crusading enthusiasm was more marked than any previous Spanish king; Alfonso was the first Spanish ruler to see the value of the military orders, organising the Confraternity of Belchite in 1122.

Alfonso died in 1134, apparently leaving his lands to be divided between the military orders of the Hospital and the Temple and the canons of the Holy Sepulchre, an eccentric will which was never carried out and perhaps was never intended to be (Lourie 1975). In Aragon, Ramiro, Alfonso's younger brother and a monk since 1093, emerged from his monastery, married, begat a daughter who was married to Ramón

Berenguer IV, Count of Barcelona, and withdrew again into the cloister. Ramón Berenguer was accepted as the new ruler, thus establishing an enduring federation between Aragon and the counties of Catalonia, despite disparate languages, institutions and traditions. Ramón's predecessors had, for most of the century, been consolidating their power in Catalonia and the events of the 1130s provided the opportunity to establish the dynasty's supremacy in eastern Spain. Meanwhile, the Hospital and Temple were generously compensated for their loss, thus ensuring that they remained an integral part of the Reconquest.

By the end of the 1130s, Christian resistance to the Muslims can be discerned on three fronts: in the east the new dynastic union of Aragon and Catalonia; in the centre Castile-León, now ruled by Alfonso VII (d. 1157), who had established himself in 1126 after a period of instability; and to the west Afonso Henriques, Count of Portugal, was taking the first steps in a process which eventually resulted in the formation of a separate kingdom. Castile-León remained the most powerful, a pre-eminence which received public recognition in 1135 when Alfonso VII was crowned emperor in the cathedral at León. These powers now began to take advantage of the crumbling of Almoravide power, undermined both by uprisings in north Africa and by the laxity of its leadership. Even at the height of the Almoravide threat, the key city of Toledo had been retained, reinforced by the resettlement policies of Alfonso VI, who had placed the responsibility for defence upon city militias who would not readily give up the advantages of the grants of privileges which they received. In 1147 Alfonso VII took Almería and in the following year Ramón Berenguer I gained Tortosa, in the latter case greatly reducing threats to Christian shipping. With Tortosa in his hands, Ramón Berenguer could open up the lower Ebro Valley and Lérida and Fraga fell soon after. Despite mutual suspicions, the two rulers signed a treaty of co-operation, that of Tudellén, in 1151 which, optimistically as it turned out, shared out future conquests in Muslim Spain.

One Christian ruler, however, conspicuously avoided such agreements. Building on a grant of lordship over the lands between the Rivers Miño and Duero made by Alfonso VI to his father, Henry of Burgundy, Afonso Henriques had set about creating an autonomous power in the southern parts of Galicia (see Table 12). From the time when he seized power from his mother, Teresa, in 1128, until the end of his very long reign in 1185, his rule was characterised by careful planning combined with a shrewd eye for the main chance. In the 1130s, using Coimbra as a base, he began a series of attacks upon the Muslims in the Tagus Basin. Grants to the Templars and Hospitallers

Table 12 Rulers of Portugal

Henry I of Burgundy, Count of Portugal	1094–1114
Afonso I Henriques	1114–85
Sancho I	1185–1211
Afonso II	1211–23
Sancho II	1223–45. Deposed. Died 1248
Afonso III	1245–79. King from 1248
Diniz	1279–1325

helped to secure the hill country between the Mondego and the Tagus, and in 1139 he won an important victory at Ourique. At the same time, in a policy which recalls that of the Aragonese in the 1060s, he cultivated links with the papacy both through Joao Peculiar, Archbishop of Braga, who had become the metropolitan in 1138, and the monastery of Santa Cruz de Coimbra, which had placed itself under papal protection. After Ourique he began to call himself king, while according Alfonso VII the title of emperor, a move which seems to have reconciled Alfonso to his growing pretensions. However, if Alfonso believed that this subordination involved any practical consequences, he was to be disappointed, for the papal connection was used to declare himself a vassal of the Holy See in 1143, thus preventing Alfonso from making any decisive move against him. It took until 1179 before the popes actually used the royal title in documents, but in practice Afonso Henriques had effectively secured his independence from León thirty years before. By skilful exploitation of forces both inside and outside the peninsula and by sound military planning, Afonso had brought into being an embryonic kingdom that had neither geographical coherence nor an historic basis in either the Roman or Visigothic eras.

By the time that the Second Crusade was being preached in 1146 and 1147, Afonso was ready to attack the Tagus River basin. In March 1147 he captured Santarém, less than fifty miles up river from Lisbon at the river's mouth, the big prize which he was seeking. But to have a reasonable chance of success he needed naval forces and here local interests fortuitously coincided with the European events because in June there put into Porto, at the mouth of the Duero, a combined northern fleet containing Anglo-Norman and Flemish crusaders bound for Outremer in response to the pope's call for crusade. There is an anonymous account of the experiences of these crusaders, probably written by a priest at Lisbon in October 1147, which tells how the Bishop of Porto preached a sermon in an effort to persuade them to stay.

> Therefore, be not seduced by the desire to press on with the journey which you have begun; for the praiseworthy thing is not to have been to Jerusalem, but to have lived a good life while on the way; for you cannot arrive there except through the performance of His works.

What mattered, the bishop explained, was their motive for fighting, and in the crusade against the Moors they undoubtedly had a just cause.

> In you the Lord hath smitten Saul and raised up Paul. The flesh of Saul and Paul was the same, but not the disposition of the mind, for it was completely transformed.

The bishop told them that Afonso had already begun his expedition against Lisbon and would reward those who would help him in the enterprise 'so far as the resources of the royal treasury will permit'.

Attracted by the potent combination of religious zeal and material gain so characteristic of the crusade, the northerners sailed to Lisbon and, after some debate, agreed to help in the assault on the city. Lisbon, says the anonymous author, contained 'the most depraved elements from all parts of the world', for they 'had flowed together as it were into a cesspool and had formed a breeding ground of every lust and abomination'. There is here a striking similarity to the anti-Turkish propaganda that helped stimulate the First Crusade; its injection into the wars of Iberia shows how outside influence had changed the atmosphere since the days of the taifas. Not surprisingly, when the city fell in October, after four months bitter fighting, promises that Muslim lives and property would be spared were ignored.

> Thereupon the men of Cologne and the Flemings, when they saw so many temptations to greed in the city, observed not the bond of their oath or plighted faith. They rushed about hither and thither; they pillaged; they broke open doors; they tore open the innermost parts of every house; they drove out the citizens and treated them with insults, against right and justice, they scattered utensils and clothing; they insulted maidens; they made wrong equal with right.

They even murdered the Mozarab Bishop of Lisbon by cutting his throat, according to the anonymous author. Only the Anglo-Normans restrained themselves, he claimed in self-righteous tones, although his allegation that the pillagers 'secretly snatched away all those things which ought to have been made the common property of all the forces', perhaps offers a reason for the virulence of his criticism (David 1976:79, 83, 95, 177).

Preoccupied as he was with the activities of the crusading fleet, the author of the *De Expugnatione Lyxbonensi* shows no apparent awareness of events beyond his immediate concerns. But while the Christians tore Lisbon apart, new and formidable African forces were consolidating their hold over the remnants of the Almoravides in southern Spain. These were the Almohades, followers of a self-styled *mahdi*, who claimed descent from the Prophet and who, from the 1120s, had proclaimed a holy war against the Almoravides. Initially the Almohade attack favoured the Christians, for the Almoravides were ill equipped to fight both enemies at the same time. Therefore, when the Almohades invaded Muslim Spain in 1147, taking Seville and Córdoba, Alfonso VII was able to take Calatrava and soon after to reach as far as Almería. But it was a false dawn for the Christians, for even before Alfonso's death in 1157 the Almohades had conquered Granada (1154) and retaken Almería (1157). They did not, however, turn their religious zeal directly against the Christians of the Tagus Valley until 1174, by which time the Christians were better able to withstand the shock than they had been in the 1150s and 1160s, when all the states except Portugal had been seriously weakened by disputed succession and minorities.

By the 1170s the Christian kingdoms had regained some of their former strength. Afonso Henriques of Portugal, the most experienced ruler in the peninsula, continued to add to his domains by taking Alcácer do Sal and Badajoz in 1158 and 1169 respectively, while in the other front-line kingdoms by 1179 Alfonso VIII of Castile and Alfonso II of Aragon were confident enough of the future to make the Treaty of Cazorla, setting out their spheres of influence. The new treaty favoured Castile territorially – and for this reason provided cause for future resentment – but it did have the advantage for the Aragonese of releasing them from the tie of vassalage which had bound them to Castile since the 1130s. During the same period a growing awareness of the dangers of the new Islamic *jihad* prompted the formation of three new military orders specifically Spanish in origin, those of Calatrava, San Julián del Pereiro (later called Alcántara) and Santiago, which received official papal approval in 1164, 1175 and 1176 respectively. These orders, especially that of Santiago, became particularly important to Castile-León, kingdoms where the Hospitallers and Templars had never rooted themselves as firmly as they had in the east of the peninsula.

For all their military might and religious fanaticism, therefore, the Almohades did less damage to the Christian conquests than might have been expected. Nevertheless, this perception was less easy to make then than it is now, for there were some alarming parallels with the situation a century before. Once again, Islam seemed to have been revivified at both extremities of the Mediterranean. Saladin's crushing victory over the Latins at Hattin in 1187 and his conquest of large parts of the Crusader States during the next two years was only partially offset by the Third Crusade. In contrast to the conquest of Lisbon in 1147, crusaders sailing to the east to join that crusade failed to prevent the Almohades seizing the lands south of the Alentejo between 1189 and 1191. Moreover, in July 1196 near Alarcos, the Caliph al-Mansur inflicted on Alfonso VIII a defeat on a scale not experienced by the Christians since the battle of Sagrajas in 1086. The danger was exacerbated by the quarrels of the Spanish kings. Most striking was the evident hostility felt towards Alfonso VIII, against whom the other rulers had united in 1190–1, apparently fearing Castilian domination as much as the Almohade *jihad*. The marriage in 1197 between Berenguela, daughter of Alfonso VIII, and Alfonso I, who had succeeded Ferdinand II in León in 1188, was part of an attempt to patch up these self-inflicted wounds. Indeed, there is good reason to believe that *The Poem of the Cid*, which presented Rodrigo Díaz as an authentic Castilian hero, devoted to the cause of the Church and the war with Islam, was composed at about this time (Fletcher 1989:192–5).

Coming when memories of Saladin's successes were still fresh, the defeat at Alarcos galvanised the papacy into a determined effort to recreate the crusading spirit in the peninsula, for the hard-won gains of the twelfth century looked to be in real danger. As might be expected, the chief promoter of this policy was Innocent III, who issued a stream of injunctions to his legates to excommunicate quarrelling kings and those who made agreements with the Saracens. Early in 1211, at the request of Alfonso VIII, he sent letters to the Spanish archbishops offering remission of sins to those who would participate in the Holy War and bringing anathema down on the heads of those who hindered Castilian plans. The next year, in April, he claimed that 'not only do the enemies of God aim to destroy all of Spain, but they threaten other Christian lands: they wish to abolish the Christian name', and to reinforce his point spectacular penitential processions were organised by him in Rome to supplicate God's help (Luchaire 1908:44–7). Meanwhile, in Castile itself systematic preparations for the campaign against the Almohades were already well in hand, and by the summer of 1212 these were sufficiently advanced for an exceptionally large Christian force, combining the armies of Alfonso VIII and Peter II, King of Aragon since 1196, together with a large contingent from Languedoc and even from further afield, to be assembled. Rodrigo Ximénez de Rada, Archbishop of Toledo, had been particularly energetic in bringing this about, negotiating peace between Castile, Aragon and Navarre in 1206, and travelling tirelessly through France, Germany and Italy to raise crusading forces. The Christians set out from Toledo in June, and although most of the French abandoned the cause before the decisive moment, the army was still strong enough to win a devastating victory over the Almohades under al-Nasir at Las Navas de Tolosa on 16 July. This victory was undoubtedly the most famous of the entire period. Even the Cistercian annalist of the house of Waverley in Surrey, largely concerned at this time with the dramas of King John's reign, thought it important to incorporate a letter from Arnold Amaury, Archbishop of Narbonne, giving a detailed account of events (Luard 1865:271–3), while Innocent III was moved to an eloquent reaffirmation of the all-pervading power of God.

> God, the protector of those who hope in him, without whom nothing is strong, nothing firm, multiplying his mercy on you and the Christian people and pouring out his anger on races that do not acknowledge the Lord and against kingdoms that do not invoke his most holy name, according to what had been foretold long ago by the Holy Spirit, has made a laughing stock of the races which rashly murmured against him and a mockery of peoples thinking empty thoughts by humbling the arrogance of the strong and causing the pride of the infidels to be laid low.
>
> (Riley-Smith and Riley-Smith 1981:59)

The battle of Las Navas de Tolosa has traditionally been seen as the great watershed of Spanish medieval history, for the Muslims never again presented a threat as serious as that posed by the Almohades. After 1212 Muslim Spain once again began to disintegrate into a number of rival principalities, the most important of which were Valencia, Murcia, Seville and Granada, while latent rivalries between the Muslim population of Andalusia and the Almohade outsiders began once more to surface. Innocent III appears to have believed that the major part of the work had been completed for, in calling a new crusade in the east in 1213, he revoked the remissions and indulgences for the crusades in Spain and against the heretics of Languedoc,

> chiefly because these were conceded to them in circumstances which have already entirely passed and for that particular cause which has already for the most part disappeared, for so far affairs in both places have gone well, by the grace of God, so that the immediate use of force is not needed.
>
> (Riley-Smith and Riley-Smith 1981:122)

Innocent III's optimism might, however, have been proved premature had it not been for the emergence of two outstanding monarchs in the next generation of Spanish rulers, Ferdinand III of Castile (d. 1252) and James I of Aragon (d. 1276). In fact, the situation remained one of potential rather than actual fulfilment. These rulers were still left with an immense task. As has been pointed out, Ferdinand III conquered more Islamic territory than any other Christian ruler (Lomax 1978:156), while James I turned a loose confederation into the dominant power of the western Mediterranean, encompassing not only Aragon and Catalonia, but Valencia and the Balearics as well. It gives a false perspective to Spanish medieval history to see these achievements merely as a type of 'mopping-up' operation after Las Navas.

Ferdinand III was the son of Berenguela of Castile and Alfonso IX of León. His parents' marriage had been dissolved by Innocent III in 1204 on the grounds of consanguinity but, largely through his mother's determination, he was accepted as King of Castile in 1217, following the death of his grandfather, Alfonso VIII, in 1214, and his uncle, Henry I, three years later. Then in 1230, when his father, Alfonso IX died, he successfully pressed his claim to León, so that the kingdoms were once more united, although it was now clear that Castile rather than León was the dominant partner. In his last years Alfonso had exploited the increasing confusion in Muslim Spain to push down to the middle reaches of the Guadiana, finally taking Mérida and recapturing Badajoz in 1230. The Portuguese had already retaken Alcácer do Sal in 1217 by the now traditional method of combining with a Christian fleet en route to the crusade in the east, so that the frontier in the west had been rolled back to a point where it roughly accorded with the territories conquered in the centre as a consequence of Las Navas. In June 1236 Ferdinand crowned these successes when, after a dramatic and dangerous journey south in the depths of winter and a gruelling siege in the heat of summer, he took Córdoba, a city so long associated with the Muslim power in Spain. The Guadalquivir valley now lay open, beckoning him towards Seville, the greatest prize of all. Seville was one of the most important cities in Europe, a great commercial and cultural centre, matched in size in Spain only by Barcelona. It did not fall easily, but careful planning which included a river blockade, together with a deep determination to overcome the hardships of the siege, eventually brought its complete capitulation in December 1248. Unlike his policy towards some of his earlier conquests, Ferdinand III expelled all the Muslims and under his successor there followed a systematic division or *repartimiento* of the rich property in and around the city.

The similarities between Ferdinand III and his slightly younger contemporary in France, Louis IX, have often been pointed out. Both were heavily influenced by mothers whose piety was matched by their political acumen and both saw the application of Christian morality to the task of government as the central function of kingship. Equally, both conceived the promotion of the crusade as the ultimate realisation of this duty and, finally, both were canonised. The chief difference lies in concrete, territorial achievement. For all his moral greatness, Louis's two crusades were both disastrous, but on his death-bed in 1252 Ferdinand could, with truth, tell his heir, Alfonso, that he would have greater wealth in lands and vassals than any other ruler in Christendom (Menendez Pidal 1955:2:772).

The crusading ardour of James I was equally powerful, but his sexual immorality and his sometimes brutal attitude towards the Church precluded any possibility that he would achieve the saintly status of Ferdinand III or Louis IX. He was only a child of 5 in 1213 when his father, Peter II, was killed at the battle of Muret by the forces of Simon of Montfort, a catastrophe which James later alleged was a consequence of his father's exhaustion brought about by the previous night's debaucheries. However Peter II's defeat is to be explained, the unexpected death of one of the heroes of Las Navas left a crisis in Aragon which James was not able to surmount until he took full control in 1227. By this time he had been fully educated in a hard political school in which his struggles with the factionalised and often disloyal baronage of his lands taught him lessons which were of inestimable value in his later conflicts with the Moors.

Some indications of James's attitudes can be gained from his own chronicle, which he probably dictated to a scribe. Here he describes his first important expedition under the banner of the cross to Mallorca in 1229–30. When the fleet set out his captains were less than confident of success. With the wind veering unfavourably they tried to persuade the king to put back to port, but he overruled them. In his own account he tells frankly of his fear of desertions, but this was not his only motivation.

> And we set out on this voyage in the faith of God and for those who do not believe in Him, going against them for two reasons: to convert them or to destroy them, and to return that kingdom to the Faith of Our Lord. As we go in the name of God, we are confident that he will guide us.
>
> (Smith and Buffery 2003:79)

He was rewarded by the capture of the island, thus securing the western Mediterranean for Catalan shipping and in the long term emphasising the difference between his lands and those of Castile-León, which was becoming essentially a land-based power.

During the 1230s James was preoccupied above all with the capture of Valencia, once briefly held by the Christians through the extraordinary military ability of the Cid, but in Muslim hands since 1102. His account of the campaigns which eventually led to the city's fall in 1238 serves to illustrate the continued difficulties which had to be overcome by the reconquest. Although James was a formidable warrior, he spent at least as much of his time in parley and negotiation as in direct fighting. Here is how he describes the fall of Almenara.

> On seeing our pennon, they [the Muslim representatives of the town government] came to our presence. Then we asked them to signal the day on which they could surrender Almenara. And they said to us that the castle of Almenara was such that, for the service that they would do us, we should do great things for them, since, as soon as the other Moors of the territory heard that we held Almenara, all the country, from Teruel to Tortosa, would surrender to us.
>
> But we said to them it was better that they should hurry to do so before the others, as other castles were negotiating their own surrender; and that if they had the advantage over the others, they would receive better treatment from us for the good beginning they had made.
>
> Each of them asked us for an inheritance of three *jovates* of land each, apart from what they possessed at Almenara, and that we should give to their relatives who would help in this deed, thirty *jovates*, and that all those *jovates* were to be taken from the alguebers, that is to say, from those who had abandoned the place and fled; and that we should give them two hundred cows and a thousand sheep and goats, and that we should give scarlet cloth to forty of their relatives to wear, who would participate with them in the deed, and that we should give to the two of them a rouncy each, in lieu of knights' horses.
>
> (Smith and Buffery 2003:210–11)

It was an effective method for, when a town or castle had been isolated by military invasion, its government could usually be brought to see the advantages of a negotiated surrender. However, one consequence was that many Muslims or *mudéjars* remained settled within Christian territory, especially in the southern parts of Valencia, where James frequently complained about the lack of Christian settlers prepared to colonise the region. This meant that despite agreed settlements like that at Almenara there remained a fundamental tension which, in the second half of the thirteenth century, increasingly expressed itself in *mudéjar* revolt in both Castile and Aragon. James faced revolt in Valencia in 1248, while in 1266 he helped Alfonso X of Castile overcome discontent in Murcia. On his death-bed he is supposed to have told his son

> that he should direct the war well and forcefully, and especially that he should expel all the Moors from the kingdom of Valencia, as they were all traitors, and they had proved it to us many times, for, though we had done good to them, they always looked to do us harm and to trick us if they could; and they would do the same to him if they remained in the land.
>
> (Smith and Buffery 2003:379–80)

In fact, by the later years of his reign 'the war against the Moors' had lost much of its significance. After Murcia had been taken over by Castile in 1243, James and Ferdinand had reached agreement over their respective spheres of influence in the south, agreement which they embodied in the Treaty of Almizra of 1244. This left little scope for further landward expansion by Aragon and during the later years of his reign James's interest turned towards the Holy War in the east. He had, in 1268, received envoys from the Mongols, who offered an alliance for the conquest of the Holy Land. Despite the cautious advice of Alfonso X, who wondered whether the Mongols would keep their word and actually provide the promised aid, James saw himself as elected by God for the enterprise. 'And it seems that God wills it; and since God wills it, we cannot receive harm' (Smith and Buffery 2003:334–5). In the autumn of 1269, therefore, James set sail, but from the outset the fleet was dogged by bad weather and made little progress. After two months of struggle the king allowed himself to be convinced by the Bishop of Barcelona and other leaders that, in fact, the crossing was not agreeable to the Lord, and reluctantly the enterprise was abandoned. Even so, James was the only European monarch to appear at the Council of Lyon in 1274, organised by Pope Gregory X largely to promote the cause of the crusade, where it is clear from his own account that he felt the other powers of Christendom, both secular rulers and military orders, were insufficiently committed to the cause. He himself offered to provide five hundred knights and two thousand foot. In the end, nothing came of the proposal, for the king had wanted to be crowned by the pope as his father had been, but the price demanded by the pope – the renewal of a tribute from the Kingdom of Aragon – was more than James was prepared to pay. 'And we said that we had not come to his court to place ourselves under tribute, but rather so he could concede us freedoms' (Smith and Buffery 2003:366).

James died two years later. By 1276 the political geography of Spain had been considerably simplified. Both Castile and Aragon had reached the limits of their expansion until the fifteenth century, while James had also settled outstanding territorial problems between himself and Louis IX in the Treaty of Corbeil of 1258, the two monarchs largely renouncing their claims on either side of the Pyrenees. French interest in Iberia was not, however, excluded, for the Kingdom of Navarre, largely shut out from any important part of the reconquest by Castile and Aragon had, since the late twelfth century, a strong Capetian connection through Theobald, Count of Champagne, husband of Blanca, daughter of Sancho VI (1150–94). In 1234 his descendants had been accepted as kings by the Navarrese in preference to their predatory neighbours, a fear which seems to have persuaded the widow of Henry I (d. 1274) to marry her daughter, Jeanne, to Prince Philip, the future Philip IV of France. In Portugal, under Sancho II (1223–48) and Afonso III (1248–79), despite internal power struggles, the future shape of the country was also being established, for the penetration of the Algarve isolated the Muslims of the south-west which, in combination with Ferdinand III's successes in Córdoba and Seville, ensured Portuguese domination of the west coast. Here, as with Aragon in the east, the beginnings of Portuguese maritime power can be seen emerging. The only substantial Muslim state to remain was that of Granada under the Nasrid dynasty which, protected to some extent by the mountainous nature of the region, was able to use its economic strength to buy political support in north Africa. Clinging to this ambiguous position, it survived until the late fifteenth century.

As this narrative of the Iberian reconquest has shown, one evident characteristic of Christian Spain in the two-and-a-half centuries after 1050 is the dominant role played by so many of its kings, their power enhanced by the prestige gained as war-leaders and by the economic strength derived from booty, tribute and the extension of their territories. Indeed, in circumstances of almost continuous warfare, the personality and charisma of the king was of crucial importance. James of Aragon was well aware of this. During the siege of Valencia he was wounded by a crossbow bolt – the circumstances are reminiscent of the death of Richard I – but he said that he 'went along laughing so that the army would not be alarmed'. In the privacy of his tent his face and eyes became very swollen, but when 'the swelling on my face had gone down, we rode through the whole camp, so that the people were not completely disheartened' (Smith and Buffery 2003:221). In Castile and León however, the aura of kingship was consciously reinforced by exploitation of the Visigothic past in a way similar to the Capetian emphasis on the house's connection with the Carolingians. In 1270 Alfonso X ordered the production of a comprehensive history of 'Spain', the *Primera crónica general*, in which the Goths are presented as the saviours of the country by divine will, but are punished for the sins of their rulers by the Moorish invasion (C.C. Smith 1988:1:18–19). Although the Spanish kings never claimed that they could heal by touch, they did enjoy the advantages conferred by a holy anointing, a ceremony which enhanced their legitimacy and consecrated their battles.

All these kings ruled through their *curia regis* which, as in contemporary Christian kingdoms, steadily developed more specialist functions during the twelfth and thirteenth centuries. By this time the itinerant domestic officers and their small staff of clerks had been remodelled into permanent departments, serviced by a hierarchy of salaried professionals, each operating within a functional division of government based on secretarial, judicial and financial duties, although the titular heads might still be important prelates or nobles and the distinction between household and public duties less clearly defined than, for example, in thirteenth-century England. As territories expanded, local administration developed appropriately, with the appearance in Castile and Portugal of the *merino mayor* or *adelantado mayor*, who were ceded governmental responsibility for tracts of land often considerably larger than previous comtal divisions. In Aragon the main parts of the federation each had a *procurador general*, while at a lower level judicial officials (*veguers* in Catalonia and Mallorca, *justicias* in Aragon and Valencia) were appointed (O'Callaghan 1975:434, 445–6).

However, the development of the frontier greatly complicated the relationship between the king's government and his subjects, preventing the apparently neat hierarchical structure described above from being applied with any consistency. Most particularly frontier needs made huge demands on demographic and military resources, which could be met only in a variety of ways. In areas remote from important centres, therefore, where it was difficult to attract population, immunities were often granted to great nobles or to the military orders. The lands captured by Portugal around the Guadiana River in the 1230s and 1240s never gained many settlers and instead huge ranching domains were ceded to the military orders (Lomax 1978:144). By the late middle ages the growth of powerful vested interests deriving from this period was to become a major government problem. However, this structure was not true of all frontier lands, for in many areas urban settlement was of central importance, either in newly established defensive burgs or in great and historic cities already established for centuries and now recaptured from the Moors. Here, after conquest, the *repartimiento* generally left much less opportunity for the creation of the huge estates or *latifundia* once thought to typify the Spanish frontier.

The governmental and constitutional implications were considerable, for kings, their personal and symbolic importance notwithstanding, had to take account of all these interests. As in the lands to the north the idea that the king ruled through the advice and consent of his subjects was deeply rooted, and was given practical expression through the periodic meetings of the *cortes*, assemblies of estates which were initially expanded versions of the royal council. The great prelates and nobles were always prominent, but the increasing importance of the towns as providers of tax and militias for frontier defence meant that they too were represented from as early as 1188 in León and 1218 in Catalonia. With the ever-growing expenses of warfare, the kings had recourse to these assemblies for extraordinary taxation such as the *petitum* and the *moneda forera*, and were sometimes forced in return to make promises limiting their power over the important right of minting. Afonso III of Portugal, for instance, was granted the tax called the *monetágio* by the *cortes* of 1254, but only on condition that he did not debase the coinage for the next seven years.

However, the *cortes* were not necessarily always restrictive; the interests of the crown and its privileged subjects often coincided, since many of the latter were already tax-exempt. Generally, the effects of the concept of contract between king and subjects were more marked in Aragon and Catalonia than in Castile. In the north-east of the peninsula the influence of feudal institutions was much more evident, where conflict was sharpened by the attempts of the Aragonese kings to replace traditional customs with codes based on Roman law. In Castile and León, although terms like 'fief' and 'vassal' frequently appeared in documents, they had a much less precise meaning than, for instance, in the territories between the Loire and Rhine. Vassals simply meant subjects, rather than specifically fief-holders owing homage and fealty (MacKay 1977:97–8).

The divergent paths of the two major reconquista powers can be seen most clearly under Alfonso X (1252–84) and Peter III (1276–85), respectively the successors of Ferdinand III and James I. In 1268 Alfonso had, according to James I's own account, tried to dissuade the Aragonese king from setting out for the Holy Land.

> Even so, he well understood that, if Our Lord wished to guide us there, for no king had ever before done so good and honourable a deed, the entire holy land of Outremer and the Sepulchre could be won. Yet he was unable to advise us on it in any way.
>
> (Smith and Buffery 2003:335)

Alfonso was quite right in his perception of the impracticality of the old king's dreams, but paradoxically he never applied such common sense to his own far-reaching plans. Soon after his succession he attempted to make good alleged rights in both Navarre (1253) and Gascony (1254), but he was unable to bring either to fruition. In the south he saw his destiny in north Africa and in 1260 crossed the straits and pillaged the town of Salé in Morocco. This time the consequences were more serious than his meddling in Gascon politics, for a new dynasty, the Marinids, had established itself in the later 1250s and, from this time, began to interest itself in a counter-attack, an interest encouraged by the Nasrids of Granada who saw in the interplay of these two powers a means of self-preservation. When they took Marrakesh in 1269, which finally overcame Almohade power, the Marinids were free to invade southern Spain, which they did on three occasions (1275, 1277, 1282) during the last decade of Alfonso's reign

(O'Callaghan 1975:362, 364, 375–6, 380). It was not until 1338 that this north African threat was finally smothered.

On the last incursion by the Marinids in 1282, they had actually been paid by Alfonso to help overcome internal opposition. This opposition had, in part, been provoked by the greatest and wildest of Alfonso's ambitions, which was his claim to be emperor. Alfonso was here not so much reviving Leonese pretensions, the practical implications of which had largely been confined to the Iberian peninsula but, as the son of Beatrice of Swabia, granddaughter of Frederick Barbarossa, he saw himself as the representative of the Hohenstaufen tradition. From the double election of himself and Richard of Cornwall in 1257 to Richard's death in 1272, he spent much of his energy and his subjects' money on this chimera, only to find in 1275, when he met Gregory X at Beaucaire, that the papacy never had any intention of accepting his candidacy and had indeed already approved the election of Rudolf of Habsburg in 1273. After its experiences with Frederick II, the thirteenth-century papacy could never find acceptable a candidate who, in its eyes, was tainted by association with the Hohenstaufen cause. Not only did Alfonso fail to make any headway with his imperial design, but also he found that the financial demands which his candidacy entailed provoked opposition in the *cortes*, most notably at Burgos in 1272. The conflict gained further bite when Alfonso's attempts to introduce a code of law derived largely from Roman ideas ran into determined opposition from the nobility. The king found that he had no real alternative but to confirm the traditional privileges of the nobility, with the consequence that the most famous legal codification of this period, the *Siete Partidas*, introduced in the 1260s, did not actually become law in Castile until the 1340s (MacKay 1977:99–100).

In the end, the papacy was able to see off Alfonso's imperial candidacy with relatively little trouble, but it was to find that Aragon, although less imbued with global ambitions, was a much tougher nut to crack. Under Peter III the Mediterranean orientation of Aragon was turned into direct intervention in Sicily on a scale which inevitably upset papal attempts to determine the political complexion of Italy. For Aragon, the gains of the twelfth and thirteenth centuries had opened up a long Mediterranean coastline, containing large and prosperous ports like Barcelona, Tortosa and Valencia. Increasingly, Catalan shipping in particular had made its presence felt in the western Mediterranean. James I had led successful expeditions to the Balearics; in 1269 he had imagined that his fleet could take him to conquer the east. In 1282 this naval power made its most decisive intervention so far when, following the rising of the Vespers against Charles of Anjou in Sicily at Easter, Peter III's fleet moved in quickly to prevent Charles recovering the island that he had so dramatically lost. By September Peter had been proclaimed king at Palermo, despite being excommunicated by Charles's French pope, Martin IV. Peter's ambitions had been fired by his connections with the Hohenstaufen for, in 1262, he had married Manfred's daughter, Constance, and after the execution of Conradin in 1268 he purported to consider her the heiress of the Kingdom of Sicily. Charles's insensitive rule in Sicily provided Peter with an ideal opportunity which he could exploit, but at the same time it drew Aragon into a damaging conflict with Angevin, Capetian and papal interests, which ultimately served to erode the credibility of all four powers.

For Peter the consequences of his intervention quickly made themselves felt. His excommunication was followed by the papal offer of the Aragonese crown to Charles of Valois, younger son of Philip III of France, an offer which was accepted in February

1284. Preparations for an invasion of Aragon followed. In the summer of 1284 the pope proclaimed the projected expedition a crusade and finally, in May 1285, a formidable French army set out for the south. The situation had unwittingly been complicated by James I for, like so many Spanish kings, he had divided his lands: the Balearics and the lands north of the Pyrenees, most importantly Roussillon, had been left to Peter's younger brother, James, but he had never been satisfied with the subordination to Peter which this entailed and took advantage of the crisis to ally himself with the French.

The war which followed is described in detail by the Aragonese chronicler, Bernat Desclot. His account reveals a conflict of great bitterness, marked by atrocities on both sides. For a period it looked as if the expedition might succeed, for Philip III forced his way over the Pyrenees and besieged Gerona. In September, despite the guerrilla tactics of the Aragonese and the spread of disease within the army, the city fell, but it was a short-lived victory, for almost simultaneously Peter's masterly and ruthless admiral, Roger of Lauria, wiped out the French fleet and therefore cut off the army's supplies. There was no alternative but to retreat. As the army struggled back over the mountains, many men died of starvation, disease and wounds. For Desclot there was a grim satisfaction in this.

> Thus in this wise the French paid dear for their deeds of arrogance and for the wrongs which they had wrought against the noble King of Aragon Don Pedro, inasmuch as they had trespassed upon his realm without right and unjustly.
>
> (Critchlow 1928:367–8)

Peter III's problems with an external enemy contributed to governmental difficulties which he had to face in the kingdom itself. During the war, the king had been considerably hampered by deep-seated discontent among his own vassals. Although the Aragonese barons tried to exploit the French invasion, the roots of this discontent predated it. There had been open war between Peter III and some of his Catalan vassals in 1280 when he had tried to abrogate certain noble privileges. The faithful Desclot saw it largely from the king's side.

> Now the king sought to do away with these privileges of the realm which were harmful and to wipe them out therefrom and desired to have the others subject to his will. Wherefore the barons of Catalunya were exceeding wroth with the king and sent their messengers to him with cartels of defiance sealed with many seals of all the barons of Catalunya.
>
> (Critchlow 1928:11)

Three years later the Aragonese nobility were similarly rebellious; their defiance took the form of a defensive Union. The king, facing severe external pressure at the same time, had therefore to make a series of concessions to the nobility of the various constituent parts of his lands, at Zaragoza, Valencia and Barcelona. The concessions took the form of the confirmation of traditional *fueros* and usages, the abrogation or limitation of certain types of taxation (the Aragonese had particularly objected to the extension of the Catalan *bovatge* to their lands) and restrictions on military service owed. Built into these concessions was acceptance of the demand for regular meetings of the *cortes* which from this time were definitively established as part of a government seen, far more than in Castile, as being based upon a contract between the king and his more powerful subjects (O'Callaghan 1975:388–9).

By the late thirteenth century, therefore, a combination of circumstances prevented the reconquest from being the first priority in either Castile or Aragon. Nevertheless, both retained ambitions in the south. In 1291 Sancho IV of Castile (1284–95) and James II of Aragon (1291–1327) agreed upon a division of the spoils following a conquest of north Africa, the first partition treaty to apply to this region. This was in keeping with the known aims of previous rulers, particularly Ferdinand III and Alfonso X of Castile, but in practice they had yet to overcome Granada, which they were to find was highly resilient. The geography of the region made access particularly difficult, for rugged mountain ranges pierced only by narrow passes faced Castile, while on the seaward side the few harbours such as Almería and Málaga opened no ways into the kingdom for the Aragonese. It took an immense combined effort, involving ten years of struggle, before Granada was overcome in 1492.

The reasons for the slowing of the reconquest are not, however, to be found entirely in the geography of Granada or the shrewdness of its rulers, for the constitutional problems which confronted Peter III were symptomatic. In both Castile and Aragon internal crises, sometimes exacerbated by outside intervention, greatly weakened the ability of the Christians to deliver a decisive blow against Granada. There were no more great victories like Las Navas or spectacular submissions like Seville or Valencia. The chief problem in Castile centred on the succession and dated back to the reign of Alfonso X. When his eldest son was killed fighting the Moors in 1275, the throne was disputed between Alfonso's grandson and Sancho, his second son. Although Sancho was recognised by the *cortes* in 1278, the struggle continued to plague the kingdom during Alfonso's later years and to provide the Aragonese crown with exploitable opportunities even after Sancho's accession in 1284. Indeed, government was heavily handicapped for the better part of fifty years between 1275 and 1325, for both kings who succeeded Sancho, Ferdinand IV (1295–1312) and Alfonso XI (1312–50) came to the throne as young children, leaving Castile with minorities lasting six and thirteen years respectively. The temptation was too much for James II of Aragon who, contrary to the previous treaty terms, invaded Murcia in 1296. Although the territory was not annexed permanently to the Aragonese crown, nevertheless when James withdrew in 1314, substantial areas in the north – notably in the region of Alicante – were never returned to Castile.

In respect of the succession, the Aragonese crown was more fortunate, but Peter's successor, Alfonso III (1285–91) found that noble opposition to the crown was unrelenting. In 1287, in the so-called *Privileges of the Union*, he was forced to agree to an annual assembly at Zaragoza in which royal councillors were to be chosen and to accept too that the crown's right to judicial action against nobles was abrogated unless the consent of the *justicia* of Aragon was obtained first. Since 1265 the monarch had accepted that this post should be held by a noble, who saw his functions very much in terms of the protection of traditional privileges (MacKay 1977:114). Alfonso's difficulties were compounded by his father's legacy. Although the French crusade had collapsed ignominiously the complicated political problems which arose from the Sicilian question remained. It seems clear that Alfonso decided to cut his losses and, with the permission of his younger brother, James, now ruling Sicily, he negotiated the peace of Tarascon in 1291. However, he died before it could be implemented and, although James succeeded him and was similarly inclined, the Sicilian crown devolved upon a third brother, Frederick, who was persuaded that the arrangements would not be in his best interests. Under the terms of the Treaty of Anagni of 1295, the Aragonese crown agreed to give up Sicily to the Holy See and to receive Sardinia instead, but Sicilian pressure led Frederick to resist and instead of retiring he was crowned in September 1295. Although he now had a strange melange of opponents, Frederick succeeded in holding his own and eventually terms were made and embodied in the Treaty of Caltabellotta of 1302, a treaty which left Frederick king until his death, when his heirs would receive Sardinia or Cyprus and Sicily would revert to the Angevins.

The reconquest did not end with the death of Ferdinand III and James I, for their successors retained far-reaching ambitions. Ferdinand IV and James II signed another partition treaty in 1309 intended to be a prelude to the dismemberment of Granada, and the Castilians actually took Gibraltar in that year, only for it to be lost again in 1333. Equally, the reconquest did not begin with the capture of Toledo in 1085 or the papal exhortations to crusade after 1095, for Islam had been barely established in the peninsula before the first signs of resistance began to manifest themselves. Nevertheless, the kingdoms of Iberia were in substance created in the twelfth and thirteenth centuries in the long and bitter conflicts with the Almoravides and Almohades. These wars, and the ever-changing frontier which was their concomitant, were the greatest formative influence upon the Iberian kingdoms, determining their territorial and political structure, forging their cultural and religious outlooks, and entrenching social attitudes of lasting significance.

14

The states of eastern and northern Europe

In April 1075 Pope Gregory VII wrote to Boleslaw II the Bold, Duke of Poland, expressing his satisfaction that

> Your Excellency is sincerely devoted to St Peter, prince of the Apostles, and that you are showing your reverence with eager enthusiasm, namely, the fact that you have desired to make him your debtor by honoring him with liberal offerings and, as we trust in God, have earned this reward.

The letter, he said, was accompanied by papal representatives who would confer with him on the best ways of improving the care and organisation of the Church in his lands, which he believed to be as yet inadequate, for the bishops were too few for a region of such size. Give heed to their advice, warns Gregory, for the time will soon come when Boleslaw will have to render account before God for the way that he has exercised the power vested in him (Emerton 1966:77–8). The papal legates were evidently impressed by Boleslaw's co-operation, for at Christmas 1076 he was crowned king by Bogumil, Archbishop of Gniezno (see Table 13). The Polish Church was reorganised with Gniezno re-established as the metropolitan see, presiding over the four dioceses of Poznań, Cracow, Wrocław and Plock.

Gregory's relations with Poland in 1075–6 accorded well with the pope's view of right order, for the pope saw himself as presiding over a family of peoples, all of whom had their part to play in the Christian community. It was of particular importance that this concept was recognised by those lands which had only recently been drawn into the Christian orbit. To this end, Gregory's correspondence shows his preoccupation not only with the major struggle with Henry IV and his concerns with the well-established Christian rulers of Iberia, France and England, but also with more remote regions in which the Christian message might still be ignored, suppressed or misunderstood: Poland, Bohemia, Hungary and Scandinavia (see Map 8).

The spread of Christianity in Poland had begun just over a century before, when in 966 Mieszko I of the dynasty later known as the Piasts, had been baptised, a year after his marriage to Dobrawa, daughter of the Christian ruler of Bohemia, Duke Boleslaw I. Just as Gregory the Great had begun the conversion of England through its rulers, so too did the tenth- and eleventh-century popes grasp the opportunity offered by the

Map 8 Poland and Hungary

Table 13 Rulers of Poland

Casimir I the Restorer	1034–58
Boleslaw II the Bold	1058–*c*.1082. Crowned 1076. Deposed *c*.1082
Wladyslaw I Herman	*c*.1082–1102
Boleslaw III Wrymouth	1102–38
Wladyslaw II the Exile	1138–46. Died 1159
Boleslaw IV the Curly	1146–73
Mieszko III the Old	1173–7. Deposed. 1201–2
Casimir II the Just	1177–94
Leszek II the White	1194–1227. Deposed 1200, 1201, 1206
Mieszko III the Old	1201–2
Wladyslaw III Spindleshanks	1202–6. Deposed
Boleslaw V the Chaste	1227–79
Leszek III the Black	1279–88
Boleslaw VI	1288
Henry IV Probus	1288–90
Przemysl II	1295–6. Crowned 1295
Wladyslaw IV the Short	1296–1300. Deposed. 1306–33. Crowned 1320
Waclaw I of Bohemia	1300–5. Crowned 1300
Waclaw II of Bohemia	1305–6

willingness of the Piast dynasty to receive representatives of the Christian Church. Mieszko's baptism was followed up with missionary bishops aiming to establish the ruler's conversion on a wider base. Precisely because of the Church's contacts with Poland, it is at this time that the country emerges from historical obscurity. As Mieszko and his successors well knew, the papacy provided a link with the culture of the Mediterranean, past and present, previously largely inaccessible, while at the same time announcing to the world the legitimacy of the dynasty and the independence of its lands within the wider Church.

In fact, as has been pointed out, Mieszko, although an able and perceptive ruler, did not himself create Poland (Emerton 1966:42). The country had been slowly evolving since at least the fourth century when population pressure had started a series of migrations by the Slavs from their original areas of settlement between the Carpathians and the Middle Vistula. As a consequence, they came to inhabit a much wider area than previously, spreading out eastwards into Russia, southwards into the Balkans and westwards towards the Oder and Elbe Rivers. During the tenth century, the arrival and settlement of the Magyars south of the Carpathians established a new racial and linguistic group in the midst of the Slav bloc, largely cutting off the Poles from the Balkan Church. The Christianisation of the Russian Slavs by the Byzantines in the late tenth century tended to delineate a different type of boundary to the east for, despite Gregory VII's efforts, the region thereafter remained within the cultural hegemony of the Eastern Church. By the time of Mieszko I, therefore, the Polonians settled in the plain between the Oder and Vistula formed a distinct Slav group, with a well-established agrarian economy, an active iron-smelting industry, and trade links with the Rhineland and the Low Countries to the west and with Russia to the east. As in other regions of the Latin West, the population was growing steadily, although initially settlement was concentrated along the two great rivers and along the coast (Górecki 1992:11–12). The Christian representatives found a religion based on worship of the forces of nature, depicted in stone and wooden images. Although perhaps originally a society of free farmers, the more typical late-tenth-century social grouping was centred upon a *castrum* (or *gród*) from which local lords exercised their power over the surrounding area. Such castles tended to attract concentrations of population; by Mieszko's time Gniezno and Cracow were particularly prominent.

It is a truism that Poland's only natural boundary is the Carpathian range to the south. The consequence has been that the country has constantly fluctuated in size. Mieszko's rule saw an expansion into the north which took in most of Pomerania, reaching the Baltic coast between the Oder and the Vistula, and into the south, encompassing an area from Silesia in the west to the upper Wieprz River in the east. In the year 1000 these lands gained further credibility as a political entity when Otto III, the imperial ruler, visited Gniezno, and recognised the independence of Mieszko's successor, Boleslaw I the Brave (992–1025). Both pope and emperor approved the creation of an ecclesiastical structure based upon a metropolitan at Gniezno. Otto may even have conceived of Poland as a kingdom within the empire, similar to Italy, Germany and Burgundy, although if such a concept ever existed it was destroyed by the emperor's early death in 1002. Thereafter, relations with the empire reverted to the ambiguity which had originally prompted Mieszko to seek papal approval, for he had realised that the papacy could provide a useful counter to German ambitions. For their part, most German rulers were concerned to prevent the rise of powerful states to the east in Poland, Bohemia and Hungary, and their policies were therefore aimed at encouraging divisive internal forces and at encroaching upon any territory gained. In Poland they met with some success in the eleventh century, especially during the 1030s, when many of the achievements of Mieszko and Boleslaw were undermined; the policies of Boleslaw II during the 1070s arose from these circumstances (see Table 13).

It may be, therefore, that Boleslaw II's fall in *c.*1082 was a consequence of pro-imperial intrigue, although the exact circumstances have never been satisfactorily explained. In 1079 Boleslaw had Stanislaw, Bishop of Cracow, executed, apparently because he was implicated in a plot to overthrow him in concert with the king's younger brother, Wladyslaw Herman. The discontent which this represented, however, was not extinguished by the death of the bishop, and eventually Boleslaw was forced to take refuge in Hungary, leaving the way clear for Wladyslaw to gain power. Wladyslaw represented imperial interests, as was confirmed in 1088 when he married Judith, sister of Henry IV, but it is unclear whether this coup was connected with the death of Stanislaw, around whom later hagiographers have wound a cocoon of stories intended to show Boleslaw in a bad light, for the bishop was canonised in 1253. Whatever the reasons for the conflict, imperial interests were well served, for Stanislaw's execution effectively broke the connection with Gregory VII. Under Wladyslaw, Poland was drawn into the imperial sphere; it is significant that no attempt was made to have him crowned.

Wladyslaw died in 1102 leaving an inheritance divided between his sons, Zbigniew and Boleslaw. Boleslaw proved the stronger in the ensuing conflict, beating back an invasion by Henry V on Zbigniew's behalf in 1109, and about three years later executing his brother on the grounds of treason, an act which he later tried to expiate. Boleslaw III the Wrymouth took up the plans of his more dynamic predecessors, most crucially regaining lost ground in Pomerania, where pagan practices and the aggression of the local tribes provided him with pretexts for intervention. By 1121 he had re-established Polish power on the Baltic coast with the capture of Stettin (Szczecin); eight years later he had regained the line of the Oder. A useful index of expansion is the appearance of a class of ducal servants called *perticarii* or 'pole-men', responsible for setting up tents for the itinerant dukes, who could no longer rely on reaching urban centres in a day's journey (Gasiorowski 1977:140–3). However, there was a limit to westward expansion, for it was opposed to the interests of both lay and ecclesiastical power in Germany, represented most forcibly by Lothar of Saxony, who was intent upon overcoming the Obodrites living east of the Elbe, and by Norbert, Archbishop of Magdeburg, who had ambitions to subordinate the Polish Church to his see. Boleslaw met similar resistance in the south, where he failed to exploit the succession problems in Hungary in the early 1130s to his own advantage. In 1135, therefore, he was obliged to make a settlement with Lothar, now emperor, at Merseburg; Pomerania was to be held as an imperial fief. Nevertheless, despite this tangible sign of imperial authority, the agreement did accept the Polish conquest of Pomerania.

Boleslaw III was blessed with seventeen children from his two marriages. In an apparent effort to avoid the violence which had marred his own ascent to the throne, he attempted to make comprehensive provision for his five sons by means of which Poland was divided between them, but with the eldest, Wladyslaw, as the senior ruler, based at Cracow, an arrangement sometimes known as the Seniorate. In addition, Wladyslaw was given suzerainty over Pomerania, thus adding a sixth part to the division. The situation seems to have arisen at least partly as a result of pressure exerted by increasingly powerful lay and ecclesiastical lords, although the act of 1137 by which Boleslaw established the division has not survived in its original form and the exact circumstances remain controversial (Grudzinski 1974). This structure collapsed almost immediately after Boleslaw's death in 1138, culminating in direct conflict between Wladyslaw II and the second brother, Boleslaw. In 1146 Wladyslaw was forced into exile in Germany, but Boleslaw IV the Curly soon found himself under extreme pressure from the German rulers, Conrad III and, after his death in 1152, Frederick Barbarossa. The imperial invasion of 1157 is a case in point. According to Rahewin, Otto of Freising's continuator, Wladyslaw had been unjustly driven out by his tyrannical brothers, who had defied imperial requests for his restoration. Rahewin gives no hint that Poland might be regarded as an independent power. 'By such acts,' he says, 'they were openly declaring that they had seceded from the empire and were planning not a secret but an open rebellion.' Frederick Barbarossa could in no way countenance such insults and mounted a great expedition across the Oder, forcing the Poles to retreat, burning their fortresses as they went, and finally bringing Boleslaw to submit at Krzyszkowo, near Poznań. Rahewin, basing himself closely on Frederick's own letter to Wibald, Abbot of Corvey, describes this triumph in truly imperial terms.

> With many prayers, tears, and promises he [Boleslaw] sought to merit return to the yoke of Roman dominion and to the favor of the prince, prudently abandoning his rebellion in the face of irreparable disaster. He might disdain lesser lords, but not him under whose sway lay the Roman empire.

Frederick accepted Boleslaw as ruler, but extracted from him a large indemnity, an oath of fealty and a promise to take part in the forthcoming Italian expedition. In the end Rahewin claims that Boleslaw had no intention of going to Italy, but even so the point had been made that Poland was a subordinate element within the empire (Mierow 1955:175–7).

Some historians see 1138 as the beginning of a new phase in Polish history (Davies 1981:62). Until then, for all its vicissitudes, the Polish state had been held together by a single line of the Piast dynasty, extending at least two generations before Mieszko I. After 1138 Boleslaw III's many progeny, while maintaining Piast domination, split power between several branches and a prolonged period of political disintegration followed. By the late twelfth century the pattern was already set. When Boleslaw IV died in 1173 a third brother, Mieszko III the Old, tried to seize full power, only to be defeated by a younger, probably posthumous son of Boleslaw III, Casimir the Just (d. 1194), who had not been provided for in the original arrangements. Mieszko the Old made a brief comeback in 1201, but in 1202 he too died, the last of Boleslaw's sons. Polish political history in the early thirteenth century can therefore be seen much more clearly in term of the largely separate dukedoms: Leszek the White (1202–27) in Little Poland in the south, Conrad I (1202–47) in Mazovia and Kujawy, Wladyslaw III Spindleshanks in Great Poland in the north-west, all grandsons of Boleslaw III, while in Silesia the deaths of his father (1201) and uncle (1211) left the region under Henry I the Bearded (d. 1238).

Nevertheless, although Poland lacked an overall ruler, the individual dukedoms were generally effectively governed. The population continued to grow and there was extensive agrarian colonisation as well as the establishment of many chartered towns; trade links with Germany, the Low Countries and Hungary were strengthened; and Polish students attended the universities and schools of the West, especially Paris and Bologna. Despite the political divisions, a concept of Poland as a whole remained, particularly cohering around the cult of St Adalbert (Wojciech), who was martyred in Prussia in 997. This was given striking visual expression in the mid-1170s in the installation of the bronze doors in the south door of Gniezno cathedral where eighteen panels depict scenes from the saint's life (Gieysztor 1959) (see Plate 4). It is noticeable that the dukes of Greater Poland made great efforts to ensure that they were in Gniezno on 23 April, Adalbert's feast day (Gasiorowski 1977:147). At the same time Poland began to become more widely known. The English secular canon, Gervase of Tilbury (died after 1211), for instance, who travelled extensively in Italy, the Empire and France in the two decades around 1200, incorporated material on Poland in his *Otia Imperialia*, perhaps acquired from the Polish chronicler, Wincenty Kadlubek (Master Vincent, d. 1223), in Paris or Bologna, or even from visiting the country himself (Banks and Binns 2002:244–5, 272–3, 684–5). Even so, Germany remained the chief point of contact with the older areas of Christendom, and during the thirteenth century German settlement in the more accessible parts of Poland, particularly western Pomerania and Silesia, increased. A measure of this influence was the growth in the acceptance of colonisation under 'German law' (even when the settlers were actually Polish) under which set privileges were granted including personal freedom, juridical immunities and fixed rents (Górecki 1992:193–284).

In the thirteenth century two powerful new external forces, one from the west, the other from the east, impinged upon this structure: the Teutonic Knights and the Mongols. The Teutonic Knights were called in by Conrad of Mazovia. They had developed from a German field hospital, founded near Acre in 1190. Eight years later, they established themselves as a military order, modelling their rule upon that of the Templars, and, during the next thirty years, benefiting particularly from imperial patronage, had steadily expanded their possessions both in the Mediterranean and in Germany. In 1226 Conrad offered them the district of Chelmno (Kulm) on the Vistula, just to the north of Kujawy, in return for help against the pagan Pruthenians against whom he had been struggling for more than a decade. It is probable that the offer was made on the basis that the region was held under Conrad's overlordship, but Hermann of Salza, Grand Master of the order, quickly exploited his contacts with both pope and emperor to obtain privileges from both authorities which, in effect, conceded the order the right to all conquered Prussian lands, irrespective of Duke Conrad. During the thirteenth century the Teutonic Knights set about the methodical conquest of Prussia, reinforced by German and Polish crusaders, and consolidated by the settlement of German knightly and peasant families. Initially they established fairly primitive earth and wood fortifications, but by the late thirteenth century they were building much more formidable brick and stone structures around a main courtyard, the so-called 'convent castles', which became their military and administrative power bases. Here they were influenced by the Order of the Swordbrethren (the Militia of Christ of Livonia), which, on papal instruction, had been taken over by the Teutonic Knights in 1237. However, the Knights took the concept much further, creating a whole network of commanderies at strategic points along major routes, supplied with produce from their own estates and horses from their stud farms (Ekdahl 2002). Despite Pruthenian revolts in 1242 and 1261, by 1283 the Knights had established themselves very firmly in a great wedge of territory extending east of the Vistula along the Baltic seaboard. Pomerania, lying to the rear of the Teutonic Knights, remained a Polish sphere of influence, but in 1308 a revolt threatened the port of Gdańsk and the Polish ruler, Wladyslaw IV, agreed to ask the order for help. As in 1226, the Knights saw off the enemy, but then exploited the situation to their own advantage, seizing Gdansk for themselves in 1309 and then spreading out from there into eastern Pomerania. This cut off Polish access to the Baltic and created a permanent source of friction. The same year, the Teutonic Knights moved their headquarters from Venice to Marienburg, just to the east of the Vistula, leaving no doubt about their long-term intentions.

The appearance of highly mobile Asiatic nomads from Mongolia in southern and central Poland in 1241 was more dramatic and certainly more fearsome but, although raids continued as late as the eighteenth century, was probably of less ultimate significance. However, the first shock was immense, for the Mongols struck deep into the country, crossing the Oder and confronting Henry the Pious, Duke of Silesia, near Legnica. Henry was killed but the fortress itself held out. Although the brunt of Mongol attacks was sustained by Russia and Hungary, Poland continued to be threatened. The year 1259 was a particularly bad one, for Lublin, Sandomierz, Cracow and Bytom were largely destroyed. The sense of doom which this provoked is graphically demonstrated by the appearance of Flagellant processions in Hungary and Poland in 1261 (Dickson 1989:249).

While the Teutonic Knights and the Mongols were new arrivals on the Polish scene, they were not the only external forces to trouble Poland during the thirteenth century. More traditional neighbours were equally anxious to exploit the prevailing political fragmentation. Although the Teutonic Knights put an end to the Pruthenian raids, they could not prevent the incursions of other pagan Baltic peoples. Attempts to convert the

Lithuanians and the Sudovians in the 1250s were markedly unsuccessful. The Lithuanians were especially aggressive, inflicting severe damage on the towns along the line of the Vistula in particular; the establishment of Warsaw in the 1290s was largely stimulated by the need to defend the river route from these attacks. Poland's western neighbours were equally predatory. The Margraves of Brandenburg, established under the descendants of Albert the Bear from 1150, in the area between Pomerania and the River Warta, frequently threatened to destabilise a vulnerable region; indeed, it was their attack upon Gdańsk in 1308 which had brought in the Teutonic Order.

However, in the late thirteenth century it was the Kingdom of Bohemia in the south-west which most affected Poland. Although Bohemia was a distinct political entity with a predominantly Slav population and with crowned rulers since 1198, it had remained much more clearly a constituent part of the Empire than Poland and German influence was much more evident. As such, the Poles often saw Bohemian expansion as a surrogate for imperialist ambitions, especially during the reign of Otakar II (1253–78), the most ambitious of the Přemyslid dynasty. For a short period Otakar seemed to have the empire itself almost within his grasp. By 1269 he had gained Austria, Styria, Carinthia and Carniola. Such territorial power made him a real threat to Silesia, which had been disputed between Poland and Bohemia ever since it had been seized by Mieszko I in the late tenth century. Otakar was stopped not by the disunited Poles but by Rudolf of Habsburg, whose election as King of the Romans in 1273 Otakar had refused to accept.

Otakar's death in battle in 1278, however, proved to be only a temporary respite. Rudolf of Habsburg, anxious to prevent his son Waclaw I (1278–1305) taking up his father's ambitions in Austria, encouraged Bohemian expansion to the east, a task made easier by the death of the last of the Silesian dukes, Henry IV Probus, without direct heirs in 1290. Waclaw's path to domination of Poland was cleared further when the ruler of Greater Poland, Přzemysl II, descended from Mieszko the Old, was assassinated in 1296. The year before, the Polish monarchy had been revived for the first time since 1076 when Přzemysl was crowned, but neither Henry of Glogów nor Wladyslaw the Short, the Piast dukes who claimed to succeed him, could muster enough support to prevent Waclaw from seizing the opportunity. In 1300 he was crowned king, supported by the German ruler, Albert of Habsburg. But the Bohemian line failed to maintain itself on the Polish throne. It may be that Waclaw's favourable policy towards Germany helped to consolidate what some historians have regarded as a developing Polish sentiment, but such feeling is difficult to discern, except in the light of later national attitudes. At this period the Church was the only institution which continued to see Poland as an entity, for its organisational structure had been established at a time when the Polish monarchy still existed. The emergence of Wladyslaw the Short as Polish ruler therefore seems to owe more to his own rather dogged determination on the one hand and the deaths of his rivals, Waclaw II in 1306 and Henry of Glogów in 1309, on the other. By 1314 Wladyslaw had established himself in Greater Poland and in 1320 he was crowned king at Cracow. The coronation could not solve the problems of Poland's relations with its myriad neighbours, but it at least defined the Polish political structure. Under Casimir III (1333–70) it became possible for the monarchy to act as a countervailing force to the regionalism which had characterised Polish history during the thirteenth century.

During the ninth century, Slav occupation of the lands between the Baltic and the Balkans was disturbed – as it had so often been in the past – by the intrusion of nomadic invaders from further east. These were the Magyars, a people of Finno-Ugrian stock, originally from the region of the middle Urals, east of the Black Sea. Under pressure from Asiatic nomads, they had been moving westwards since the fifth century, but it was not until the 890s that they began to have a serious impact upon Latin Christendom. At that time they crossed into the great oval of land around the Middle Danube which forms the Carpathian Basin. They met no resistance either in the steppe land of the Alföld, where the previous tribe which had occupied the region, the Avars, had been eliminated by Charlemagne in the late eighth century, or even west of the Danube in the rolling country known to the Romans as Pannonia (Dunántúl), for the Carolingian rulers were weakened by internal divisions. The Magyars quickly took advantage of this situation and during the first half of the tenth century launched a series of raids deep into the Latin West. Although they established no permanent occupation, nowhere was safe from their sudden forays in search of booty, slaves and tribute: some indication of their mobility can be seen by the fact that they attacked places as far apart as Bremen, Cambrai, Nîmes and Pavia. Gradually, however, the German rulers began to retaliate: in 933 the Magyars were defeated by Henry I near Merseburg and, more decisively, in 955 by Otto I at the Lechfeld, near Augsburg.

Not all the tribes were present at the Lechfeld, but the defeat nevertheless put the existence of the Magyars in jeopardy. None of the eastern nomads established in the Carpathian Basin in the past had survived a determined onslaught from the west and it may have been his realisation of the danger that led the Magyar leader, Géza (970–97), to seek accommodation with Otto I in 973. Christian missionaries were allowed into his lands and his son, Vajk, baptised as Stephen, was married to Gisela, daughter of Henry of Bavaria in 996. Géza was the fifth direct descendant of Árpád, one of the two main leaders who had taken the Magyars west in the late ninth century; his imposition of Christianity and his forceful crushing of dissident clan chiefs ensured the continuance of this dynasty as Hungarian rulers. His son, Stephen, benefited from the same conjunction of events that helped his Polish contemporary, Boleslaw I, for in August 1000 he was crowned king with both papal and imperial approval. As in Poland, this established him as an independent ruler whose legitimacy and power were reinforced by the sanctions of the Church. Stephen took full advantage of his position, ruthlessly crushing opposition and hastening the change from a structure based upon the clan and pagan belief to one centred upon monarchy and Latin Christianity. When Stephen died in 1038 he left a country organised into between forty-five and forty-seven counties (Fügedi 1986:39), administered by royal officials, the *ispáns*, and an ecclesiastical structure consisting of two provinces, of which Esztergom was the head, and eight bishoprics. In 1083, after it had been claimed that miracles had occurred at his tomb at Buda, he was canonised.

Stephen's son, however, predeceased him, and there was no smooth transition of power. Indeed, the era of Árpád rule was characterised by chronic dynastic instability; between 1038 and 1301, when the Árpád line came to an end, there were twenty-two different rulers (see Table 14). In contrast to the Capetian dynasty in France, primogeniture was never fully accepted, while the persistence of the idea that the kingship belonged to the family as a whole was recipe for dynastic feuding (Rady 2000:16–17). The problems which this involved inevitably drew in outsiders, including Germans, Bohemians and Poles, as well as the Byzantines under Manuel I (1143–80). The conflicts which followed Stephen's death were particularly violent, for the throne was disputed between his nephew, Peter Orseolo, and his son-in-law, Samuel Aba. For

Table 14 Rulers of Hungary

Stephen I	997–1038
Peter Orseolo	1038–46
Samuel Aba	1041–4
Andrew I	1046–60
Béla I	1060–3
Salomon	1063–74. Deposed
Géza I	1074–7
Ladislas I	1077–95. Canonised 1192
Koloman	1095–1116
Stephen II	1116–31
Béla II	1131–41
Géza II	1141–62
Stephen III	1162, 1163–72
Ladislas II	1162–3
Stephen IV	1163
Béla III	1172–96
Imre	1196–1204
Ladislas III	1204–5
Andrew II	1205–35
Béla IV	1235–70
Stephen V	1270–2
Ladislas IV the Kuman	1272–90
Andrew III	1290–1301
Wenceslas Przemysl	1301–5. Abdicated
Otto of Wittelsbach	1305–7
Charles Robert (Carobert) of Anjou	1301–42

a time the independence of the monarchy was threatened, for both Peter Orseolo and Salomon (1063–74), who was the son of Stephen's nephew, Andrew, conceded imperial overlordship in return for military help. The link was emphasised in 1058 when Salomon married Henry IV's sister, Judith. In 1074 he received a sharp letter from Gregory VII alleging that the country had been surrendered to the Holy See by King Stephen and that Salomon had 'degraded the right and honor of St Peter' by accepting the kingdom as a fief of the Germans (Emerton 1966:48–9). As a consequence, the papacy had to rely on Salomon's successors, his cousins, Géza I (1074–7) and Ladislas (1077–95), sons of Béla I (1060–3), for the restoration of its authority. Ladislas's support for the papacy against Henry IV provoked an unsuccessful German invasion in 1080 (Kosztolnyik 1981:92–105).

However, the appearances created by such dynastic conflicts can be deceptive. Although Hungary was underdeveloped in comparison with Germany or Italy, it was nevertheless a land of great potential. In the middle of the twelfth century Otto of Freising described it as a very broad plain seamed by rivers and streams. It has many forests filled with all sorts of wild animals and is known to be delightful because of the natural charm of the landscape and rich in its arable fields. It seems like the paradise of God, or the fair land of Egypt.

(Mierow 1955:65)

In Otto's time the lands west of the Danube were the most developed, for the climate was temperate and the land fertile. A clear linear border with the German princes was already evident. East of the Danube the kingdom encompassed the Great Hungarian Plain; here the effects of the heat of summer were mitigated by the River Tisza and its tributaries. The mountains to the north, east and south-east were mainly forested. Both the plain and the forests had great economic resources although, in the twelfth century, they were thinly inhabited compared to the west. Not surprisingly, there was no defined eastern frontier, but rather a porous zone, open to other peoples moving westwards (Berend 2001:25–8, 40). Unlike the minority rule imposed in contemporary Sicily and the Crusader States, the Magyars had settled this land as a people. A Slav population remained and, indeed, influenced language and institutions, but it no longer made up the majority. Otto of Freising, perhaps influenced by traditional stories of past Magyar destruction, could scarcely believe that God had allowed such a beautiful land to be occupied by what he regarded as an appalling people. He saw them as 'of disgusting aspect, with deep-set eyes and short stature', who were 'caricatures of men', true successors of the barbarous Huns and Avars (Mierow 1955:66).

Yet whatever Otto may have thought of them, it was the depth of Hungarian settlement which gave the country the coherence it needed to survive the Árpád quarrels. Indeed, although western Hungary was occupied by Henry III's forces in 1044, much more territory was gained in the eleventh and twelfth centuries than was lost, while the resources which Otto described began to be effectively exploited. Ladislas I pushed south-west into the Slavonian lands between the Drave and the Save, and Koloman (1095–1116) capitalised on this by taking over Croatia and parts of Dalmatia in 1097, lands for which he received a separate crown in 1102. For a period, Hungary held important cities on the Dalmatian coast, including Spalato, Zara and Traù, acquisitions which led to long-term conflict with Venice at the head of the Adriatic. In 1202 the Venetian use of the Fourth Crusade to recover Zara from King Imre, who had himself taken the cross, caused deep dissension in the crusader army and brought papal censure down upon it. Under Béla II (1131–41) the adjoining Byzantine provinces of Bosnia and Serbia were also added to Hungarian territory, provoking Byzantine intervention in Hungary's habitual dynastic struggles and eventually leading to the reoccupation of the provinces by Manuel I. Manuel, indeed, had wider ambitions in the west which included the reincorporation of Italy into what he regarded as its proper place in the Roman imperium, but his conquests lacked depth. His defeat by the Turks at Myriokephalon in 1176 exposed the deficiencies of his rule, while in Hungary his former protégé, Béla III (1172–96), with a French wife and papal backing, was reabsorbed into the western sphere. In 1182 Béla regained the lost Byzantine provinces. Venice remained Hungary's chief rival in the region. The Hungarians also made systematic efforts to colonise the hitherto thinly populated regions to the east and north-east in Transylvania and the Carpathians. In 1188 Béla III ventured beyond these lands into Galicia (Halicz), exploiting the weaknesses of contemporary Russian principalities, a policy continued by his son, Andrew, who mounted fourteen campaigns into the region between 1205 and 1233 (Engel 2001:89).

Moreover, the forceful policies of the first Géza and Stephen and, after them, Ladislas and Koloman, left the monarchy with impressive powers. Otto of Freising believed that such princes could not easily be contradicted; those who opposed the king but failed to overcome him were summarily punished. The bulk of the resources too lay in the king's hands:

> although the aforesaid realm is divided into seventy or more counties, from the proceeds of justice two thirds go to the royal treasury and only one third remains to the count; and in so vast an area no one but the king ventures to coin money or collect tolls.
>
> (Mierow 1955:67)

Otto's view of royal power is confirmed by modern research: in the twelfth century there is no record of any castle in private hands, lay or ecclesiastical (Fügedi 1986:39, 48–9). By the reign of Béla III there began to emerge, as in contemporary western monarchies, a more defined and specialist administration: the establishment of the Chancery in 1185 is symptomatic of the increased attention being paid to the creation and preservation of written records, while the growth of minting profits and mining and salt monopolies into major elements of royal income suggests a rapid spread of a more monetarised economy than hitherto (Engel 2001:62–3). In the thirteenth century the increased importance of the *loca credibilia* (an institution unique to Hungary), located in certain abbeys and cathedral chapters, in which charters were authenticated, reflects the perceived need for better and more precise documentation (Rady 2000:64–78).

During the last decades of the twelfth century, the development of a western-style monarchy, however, brought with it internal problems familiar to such regimes. In the world of Duke Géza in the tenth century, the internal political struggle had largely been with tribal and clan chiefs, but by *c.*1200 opposition had begun to coalesce around powerful vested interests intent upon establishing their juridical and military power at the expense of crown rights. Both baronial families, grown wealthy on the new resources available in the twelfth century, especially from colonisation, and royal servants with delegated power like the *ispáns* (or counts) and the *servientes* (or royal soldiers) sought to entrench themselves in their castles and lands by undermining the extent of royal control over these emergent lordships. These developments first became evident between 1196 and 1235, during the reigns of the sons of Béla III, Imre and Andrew II. For most of his reign Imre was engaged in a struggle for power with his brother which, for a period in the late 1190s, left Andrew as a quasi-independent ruler in the south. Andrew himself gained the throne in 1205, following the deposition and early death of Imre's son, Ladislas. In these conflicts the need for support dissipated considerable crown resources, but the situation was exacerbated by Andrew's own costly and unsuccessful adventures into Galicia and his participation in the Fifth Crusade in 1217–18. Financial and military needs led both to the concession of castles and landed estates to barons and knights in a manner quite contrary to previous monarchical policy and to the farming out of royal monopolies, often to Muslim and Jewish agents, in an effort to raise lump sums quickly. In addition, the increasingly frequent levying of extraordinary taxes provoked discontent across the entire social spectrum.

In 1222 a combination of disaffected barons and royal *servientes* forced Andrew to issue a charter of privileges known as the Golden Bull. The bull concerns itself particularly with the grievances of the *servientes*: none should be seized or destroyed 'in favour of any potentate' unless first cited and convicted by proper judicial procedure, they should have free disposal of their lands even if they had no direct male heirs, they should not be obliged to serve outside the kingdom except at royal expense. General dislike of royal governmental methods is reflected in clauses eleven, fourteen, twenty-three and twenty-four: foreigners could not be promoted to office 'without the advice of the realm', any count not fulfilling his office properly and who brought ruin to the people of his *castrum* to be deprived of his office and forced to make restitution, the king's new money to be observed for a year from Easter to Easter and the coins to be 'as they were in the time of King Béla', and Jews should not be allowed to hold any office involving financial administration. Cap. thirty-one, the last clause, laid down that copies of the charter, 'confirmed by our gold seal', were to be deposited with seven different authorities, the pope, the Hospital, the Temple, the king, the Chapters of Esztergom and Kalocsa, and the Count-Palatine. The king conceded that if he or any of his successors tried to revoke these clauses the nobles and prelates of the realm would have the freedom 'to resist and oppose us' without stigma of any infidelity (Marczali 1901:134–43). It is however, apparent that the Church which, despite vicissitudes, had retained a strong influence in Hungarian government ever since the tenth-century conversions, was dissatisfied with the redistribution of power which the bull seemed to reflect. In 1231 a revised version was issued which, significantly, replaced the last clause on justifiable resistance in favour of enforcement by excommunication of the king by the prelate of Hungary, the Archbishop of Esztergom. Two years later the papal legate, Jacob of Pecorara, Cardinal-Bishop of Palestrina, negotiated the oath of Bereg, which was meant to protect ecclesiastical privileges and incomes (especially from salt) from lay interference, as well as to reinforce previously neglected prohibitions on the employment of Muslims and Jews in government (Berend 2001:158–9).

For different reasons, therefore, in the thirteenth century in both Poland and Hungary there was a marked trend towards the restriction of monarchical powers. Equally, in the late 1230s both countries were subjected to the attacks of the Mongols, but the impact on Hungary, which lay more directly in the Mongols' path, was far greater and more traumatic than it was in Poland. Béla IV (1235–70) seems to have had the intention of reconstructing monarchical power after the damage inflicted under his father, but he had little time to do it. East of Hungary lay a tribe of Kipchak Turks known as Kumans, who had migrated to the area during the eleventh century from the region of the Jaxartes River beyond the Aral Sea. In 1223 and again in 1239 they had been attacked by the Mongols; on the second occasion the remnants of the tribes fled into Hungary. This represented a sizeable migration: it is estimated that they made up 7–8 per cent of the population of Hungary in the second half of the thirteenth century, settled mostly in the central region (Berend 2001:68, 134–9). The country was quite unprepared to meet the challenge. The Kumans were pagan and regarded by the Hungarian populace as barbarian. Conflict culminated in the assassination of Kötöny, the Kuman leader, and the Kumans moved on into the Balkans, pillaging the land as they went. In the spring of 1241 the Mongols themselves arrived and in April nearly wiped out the Hungarian forces at Mohi on the River Sajo. In the next few months they ravaged most of the lowland parts of the kingdom, including Vác, Pest, Várad and Csanád, reaching as far as the Dalmatian coast. King Béla first fled to Frederick, Duke of Austria, who took the opportunity to extort three border counties from him, and then suffered the ignominy of being forced to take refuge on an island off the Dalmatian coast. Most of the inhabitants, however, had no such option: the probable population loss has been estimated at 15–20 per cent (Berend 2001:36–7). The unexpected retreat of the Mongols in the summer of 1242 owed nothing to Hungarian resistance, but was probably a consequence of the succession crisis in the Mongol Empire following the death of the Great Khan, Ögödai, in December 1241.

Detailed study of Hungarian defences in the thirteenth century has pinpointed both the reasons for the failure to counter the Mongols and the consequences this had for the country. Few castles were built of stone; most were 'shard castles' with walls of fired ceramics or constructed in the form of timber boxes filled with earth. Even these were not usually situated on elevated sites or along the eastern frontiers. Defence in the past had relied upon the deliberate establishment of waste land, reinforced by obstacles, behind which mobile forces of archers were deployed. None of these methods proved effective; only six of the seventy-two comital castles known to have existed in the area occupied by the Mongols managed to hold out (Fügedi 1986:47). When Béla returned to Hungary after the Mongol retreat, he therefore embarked upon a campaign of castle-building and reconstruction on an unprecedented scale. Between 1242 and 1270 fifty-five new castles were built and thirteen reconstructed in stone. But he could not undertake this immense task alone; inevitably he was obliged to make grants to lords to help, further entrenching their power. Thirty-four of the fifty-five new castles were non-royal foundations (Fügedi 1986:53–6).

The Mongol invasion therefore destroyed Béla's attempt to reverse the oligarchic tendencies of Andrew II's reign. In 1267 Béla appears to have been attempting to counter the power of the baronage by strengthening the position of the minor nobles. Two or three from each county were to attend the annual assembly at Székesfehérvár in a system which has some echoes of the policies of the French monarchs in providing access to their courts for their rear-vassals. If this was the intention, it had little effect. The pattern of castle-building remains a good index of baronial independence: only nine of the seventy-two castles built between 1271 and 1290 are known to have been royal constructions, and there are no examples at all after 1281. By 1300 only a quarter of Hungary's castles were held by the king and many unlicensed castles were being built (Fügedi 1986:54, 78). By this time many of the minor nobles had become the *familiares* or vassals of the barons.

The rise of powerful baronial families backed by large estates and their own castles made the habitual dynastic conflict of the Árpáds more dangerous than before. In the later years of Béla IV's reign the opposition of his son, Stephen, factionalised Hungarian politics, and in 1266 came close to partitioning the country. These struggles drew in the predatory King of Bohemia, Otakar II, for after Béla's death in 1270 his help was sought against Stephen by the Köszegi family, whose chief strength lay adjacent to Bohemia in the north-west. Indeed, Erik Fügedi has shown that the great majority of the castles built in the last decades of the thirteenth century were concerned with the vicissitudes of border warfare in the west rather than the threat of nomads from the east (Fügedi 1986:59). Hungarian and Kuman troops therefore formed a significant part of the army which defeated and killed Otakar at the Marchfeld in 1278.

Béla had also tried to strengthen his own position by encouraging the Kumans to return after the Mongol retreat. They were given lands on the Tisza River and Stephen was married to a Kuman princess. But under Ladislas IV (1272–90) known as 'the Kuman' because of his mother, this policy had disastrous consequences, pulling the country into a bloody civil war which culminated in the murder of the king. Ladislas's attempts to continue to use the Kumans to bolster his position served only to unite opposition in a country which had already shown its resentment of the Kumans in the past. Ladislas's problem lay not only with the baronage but with the Church as well, which was offended by Kuman paganism, and the king was eventually excommunicated by the papal legate for refusing to impose Christianity on the Kumans. There followed a struggle of will in which Ladislas renounced his wife and took a Kuman instead, but the barons retaliated by overcoming the Kumans in battle in 1280. Ladislas was not reconciled and in 1285 he was even accused of obtaining Mongol help in the struggle. In 1290 he was murdered by Kumans apparently acting for some of the barons.

Ladislas had died childless and in 1290 the only credible Árpád claimant was Andrew, grandson of Andrew II through his third wife. Andrew lived abroad, having married into a Venetian family, but was brought back to Hungary through the efforts of Ladomer, Archbishop of Esztergom. Ladomer was particularly concerned to fend off a number of outside claimants, including the favoured papal candidate, Charles Martel, the eldest son of the Angevin Charles II of Naples, whose wife was Maria of Hungary, sister of Ladislas. Andrew III, though, could not change the now deeply entrenched developments of Hungarian politics and he accepted restrictions on the monarchy similar to those of his thirteenth-century predecessors: no appointments without the consent of the Royal Council, annual meetings of the prelates, barons and nobles, and no major decisions without consent.

Andrew's reign only postponed the Angevin succession. He died in 1301, outliving Charles Martel but leaving a daughter only. The Angevin cause was now in the hands of Charles's son, Charles Robert, but he did not obtain recognition in the face of other foreign candidates until 1308 and even then it took him until 1321 before he could begin a serious policy of recuperation against baronial usurpations. Private castle building continued to predominate: only eleven of fifty-five constructions between 1300 and 1320 were royal (Fügedi 1986:54). Significantly though, ten of these were built between 1310 and 1320, an indication of Charles's growing strength. He was fortunate too to profit from the discovery of gold which provided him with incomes his predecessors lacked. With the relative decline of powers that might threaten Hungarian independence – the Empire, Byzantium, the Mongols – the fourteenth century saw the revival of monarchy in Hungary, even though it was no longer in the hands of the Árpád dynasty.

Like the Magyars, the inhabitants of the Scandinavian countries were chiefly known to the Carolingian world for their attacks upon it. During the ninth and tenth centuries they were feared throughout the north-west not only because of their slaughter, destruction and looting, but also because of their aggressive paganism. Yet this should not obscure the fact that settlement and, more slowly, assimilation, were taking place almost simultaneously. As they created permanent links with the British Isles, Francia and the Empire, the Danes and the Norwegians in particular began to absorb the predominant cultural characteristics of Latin Christendom and to carry back these attitudes to their homelands (see Map 9). The key was the spread of Christianity. Missionaries of the eighth and ninth centuries had penetrated the Saxon world and some had attempted to spread the word into Denmark as well, but they had had very little success. As with eastern Europe, real progress was made in the late tenth century only with the conversion of the Scandinavian rulers. In about 966 Harald Bluetooth,

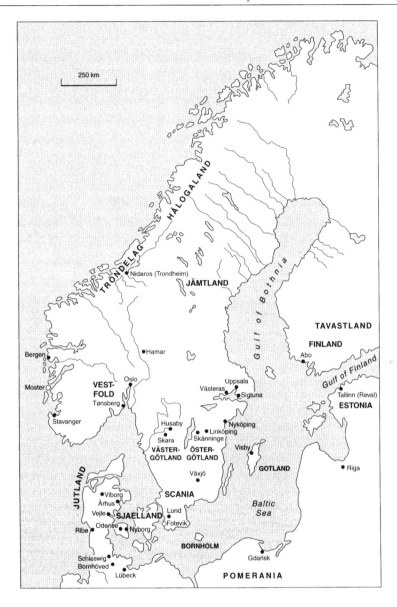

Map 9 Scandinavia

the Danish ruler, was baptised, following the entry of missionaries into the country under his father, Gorm the Old. Both were influenced by the need to avoid giving the emperor, Otto I, an excuse for intervention. Although Svend (d. 1014), Harald's son, had revolted against him, he in his turn came to see the advantages of an alliance with the Church. In Norway the establishment of the Yngling family in the Vestfold region of the south-east, especially under Harald Fairhair at the beginning of the tenth century, similarly provided a means of introducing Christianity. Even so, most members of the family continued to adhere to paganism, and it was not until 995–1000 under Harald's supposed great-grandson, Olaf Tryggvason, a former Viking who had been baptised in England, that Christianity began to be established in an organised fashion. After 1016 the process was accelerated by Olaf Haraldsson, another descendant of Harald Fairhair, who was also heavily influenced by English Christianity. Olaf established Christian practices in the south without too much disruption, but employed force to impose it in the more stubbornly pagan regions of Tröndelag and Halogaland on the north-west coast. By 1024 it was possible to hold an assembly at Moster, which set down regulations for the Norwegian Church. Olaf, however, feared the threat presented by the expanding North Sea Empire of Knut, King of Denmark and England, and his son, Svend. His fears proved justified for Knut was too strong for him and, despite allying with Sweden, in 1028 Olaf was forced to take refuge in Novgorod. Two years later he was killed trying to regain power. Orchestrated by the Englishman Grimkell, Bishop in Norway, a cult developed almost immediately, providing the Norwegian Church with a famous martyr. There were, too, missions to Sweden as early as the 820s, but the first baptism of a king took place sometime before 1010 when Olaf Sköttkonung was received into the Church.

The early pattern of Christian conversion was therefore similar to contemporary events in Poland and Hungary, but the full effects took longer to work through than they did in the east, for Scandinavia was the true fringe of western Christendom; many parts were both difficult to reach and strongly pagan in belief. Norway, for example, was a huge country, over a thousand miles long and, according to Adam, Canon of Bremen, writing in the 1070s, it took at least a month to cross (Tschan 1959:202), for except for a limited region in the south-east it was dominated by forbidding mountains and forests. In the west only the sea provided a sense of unity, linking up the otherwise isolated fjord communities. Moreover, the seafaring skill which this had nurtured created even more far-flung settlements, not only in the island groups around the north of Scotland, in the Isle of Man and in Ireland, but even beyond into what Adam of Bremen described as a terrible and limitless ocean which encircled the whole world (Tschan 1959:215). Iceland was largely settled between 870 and 930, and Greenland colonised from the 980s. Briefly, Norsemen even attempted settlement in 'Vinland' (now identified as L'Anse aux Meadows, Newfoundland), although this seems to have been abandoned by c.1030. Even so, voyages from Greenland across what has since become known as the Davis Strait (only 200 miles at its narrowest point) seem to have continued with the purpose of acquiring timber and furs, and it is possible that at least temporary settlements existed, opening up the intriguing possibility that papal subjects in the twelfth century may have included inhabitants of the New World (Seaver 1996:16–36). Gregory VII's imagination was clearly taxed by the distances involved, for in 1078 he described Norway as being placed 'at the farthest end of the earth' (Emerton 1966:136). Yet the Faroes, Iceland and Greenland were sometimes cut off even from Norway; in 1187, for example, the year in which most of Latin Christendom was devastated by the news of Saladin's victory at the battle of Hattin, no ships at all reached Iceland (Seaver 1996:66). Not surprisingly, adherence to paganism remained strong in many of these communities. Although missions sent by Olaf Tryggvason had established Christianity on an official basis in Iceland by the year 1000, many pagan customs continued to be followed for at least half a century afterwards, while Adam of Bremen describes the great temple at Uppsala in Sweden in which sacrifices were made to the deities of Thor, Wotan and Frikko and where many Christians fell back into their old ways (Tschan 1959:207–8). Over a century later pagan raiders from Estonia destroyed the ancient Swedish town of Sigtuna (just to the south of Uppsala) and even though the Swedes retaliated soon after, there was no permanent Christian presence in southern Finland until the mid-thirteenth century (Musset 1951:237–9). Henry Mayr-Harting's (1972:30) description of the struggle between Christianity and paganism in seventh-century England as 'the genuine engagement of two life principles' applies equally to Scandinavia in the eleventh century.

The distinctiveness of eleventh-century Scandinavia lay therefore not in its political unity, which did not exist, but in its common linguistic heritage and social customs. The Germanic pattern of chiefs (called *herses* or *jarls*), free farmers and slaves still predominated. Local autonomy continued to be centred upon the religious and political assembly known as the *thing* and, while many *things* came to be dominated by the family of the local chief, this was a slow process and became evident only in the later twelfth century. The free peasantry had, indeed, very evident status, shown by their role in the *thing*, their relatively high *wergilds* and, in Norway and Iceland, their frequent possession of *odal* land, held by hereditary right within the kindred group. Kings, on the other hand, while holding an important place in the pagan myths, were more restricted in practice, limited both by the problems of communications and the deep local consciousness. They held demesne lands and they could deploy the *hird*, their personal guard, but their wider powers were confined to the calling out of the *leding* (over which they seemed to have gained a hold after about 1035), which was an amphibious naval force, the collection of certain fines, and the enforcement of limited forms of *corvée*. In such a society and environment the economy remained fairly basic, centred upon farming even among those involved in trade and shipping as well. Climate restricted the growth of wheat to Denmark and southern Norway; beyond there, barley was the staple crop, and even this failed in Iceland which, like Greenland, was often dependent upon imports from outside (Musset 1951:86–119). Only the Lapps or Sami, most of whom lived in the Arctic or sub-Arctic, were linguistically and ethnically separate from the rest of the Scandinavian population (Sawyer and Sawyer 1993:35–6).

Denmark, which was the most accessible, fertile and populous of the Scandinavian countries and had already been heavily involved with England during the reign of Knut (d. 1035), was affected most thoroughly by outside influences. By 1042 Knut's sons were dead, but until 1074 Denmark was ruled by Svend Estridsson, Knut's nephew, and then successively by his sons, Harald Hen (d. 1080), Knut (d. 1086), Olaf (d. 1095), Erik I Ejegod (d. 1103) and finally Niels (d. 1134) (see Table 15). The strengthening connection with the Church can be seen both in the canonisation of Knut in 1101, following his murder in the church of St Alban at Odense, and in Erik's pilgrimage to Jerusalem, during which he met his death. Although an aggressive military leader, who had twice tried to invade England, Knut had been generous to the Church, as well as enforcing tithe payments. This, together with the manner of his death, led to the clerical promotion of his sanctity; by 1095 it was claimed there had been miracles at his tomb. Not surprisingly the cult was encouraged by Erik, whose authority was enhanced both by possession of a saintly father and by the perception of God's approval (Sawyer and Sawyer 1993:215–16). Under Niels there can also be seen the emergence of an aristocracy more characteristic of general western practice: the title of duke was first used, while in the battle of Fotevik in 1134 mounted heavy cavalry were much in evidence. At the same time the king himself began to increase his overall authority, gaining the right to fines for failure to serve in the *leding*, to proceeds from shipwreck, and to control of vacant inheritances.

Table 15 Rulers of Denmark	
Knut the Great	1018/19–35
Hardaknut	1035–42
Magnus the Good	1042–7
Svend II Estridsson	1047–c.1074
Harald Hen	1074–80
Knut IV	1080–6. Canonised 1101
Olaf III Hunger	1086–95
Erik I Ejegod	1095–1103
Niels	1104–34
Erik II Emune	1134–7
Erik III Lam	1137–46
Svend III Grathe	1146–57
Knut V	1147–57
Valdemar I the Great	1157–82
Knut VI	1182–1202
Valdemar II Sejr	1202–41
Erik IV Plovpenning	1241–50
Abel	1250–2
Christopher I	1252–9
Erik V Glipping	1259–86
Erik VI Menved	1286–1319

However, it would have been surprising if the succession of the sons of Svend had not produced rivalry between different branches of the family, and in the later years of Niels' reign this centred upon Knut Lavard, eldest son of Erik I, and Magnus, son of Niels. When Magnus assassinated Knut in 1131 the rivalry degenerated into a civil war which lasted until the accession of Valdemar I the Great in 1157. The conflict enabled imperial power to gain a foothold in a country previously independent, for Magnus gave homage to Lothar III in return for support against Erik Emune, Knut's half-brother. It did him little good, for both Magnus and Niels were killed in 1134 and the kingship continued to oscillate among the different branches of the family. Erik II ruled until 1137, his nephew, Erik III Lam, until 1146, and then Denmark was virtually partitioned between Knut V, son of Magnus, supported in Jutland, and Svend III, son of Erik Emune, whose power lay in Sjaelland and Scania. Again, the German ruler benefited, for both parties looked to Frederick Barbarossa for help and at Merseburg in 1152 Svend renewed the oath of homage and fealty taken by Magnus. Otto of Freising, anxious to emphasise imperial authority, implies that Frederick's arbitration was definitive (Mierow 1955:118), but in fact the conflict went on. Svend attempted to eliminate his rivals, Knut and his cousin, Valdemar, but was only partially successful. Knut was killed, but Valdemar escaped and raised forces which defeated and killed Svend in 1157.

Valdemar's long reign of twenty-five years saw the consolidation of the changes which had been transforming Danish government and society during the twelfth century. The legacy of the civil wars was involvement in German affairs; Valdemar renewed the oath to Frederick Barbarossa in 1158 and supported Frederick's anti-pope, Victor IV, thereafter. But he was equally determined to protect Danish territory from encroachment, building an elaborate combination of walls and fortresses west of Schleswig during the 1160s in order to deter his German neighbours, Adolf of Holstein and Henry the Lion, and inaugurating a policy of expansion along the Baltic coast. The participation of the Danish nobility in the Wendish campaigns in fact proved to be a useful outlet for the growing ambitions of this class. At the same time he strengthened the monarch's alliance with the Church, although his pro-imperial stance initially led to conflict with the metropolitan, Eskil, Archbishop of Lund (1137–77), during which the archbishop went into exile at Clairvaux. Victor IV's death in 1164 took the bite out of the controversy and Eskil returned to Denmark in 1167. Eskil's support for the canonisation of Valdemar's father, Knut Lavard, achieved in 1169, and his willingness to crown his young son Knut (b. 1162) as co-ruler in a ceremony based on western rites, suggests a conception of a monarchy modelled more upon the contemporary French example than upon the Viking past. Valdemar's development of a more systematic administration centred upon a chancery indicates the establishment of a western-type royal household in substance as well as style. In 1231 this chancery was capable of carrying out an inventory of the fiscal value of Danish lands.

Under Valdemar's two sons, Knut (d. 1202) and Valdemar II Sejr (d. 1241) Danish power re-emerged more strongly than at any time since the era of the Anglo-Danish empire, although in the end it could not be sustained. Knut VI was largely dominated by Absalon, who had succeeded Eskil as Archbishop of Lund in 1177. Absalon broke the ties with the Empire and negotiated instead the ultimately abortive alliance with France when, in 1193, Ingeborg, the king's sister, married Philip II. The most spectacular impact, however, was made by Valdemar II who, having tried and failed to seize power in 1192, gained the throne in 1202 on his brother's death. Absalon had died the year before. Valdemar's accession coincided with the German dynastic upheavals following the unexpected death of Henry VI in 1197, and the Danish king took full advantage, seizing Holstein and Lübeck in 1201, occupying Hamburg in 1216, and establishing troops in Tallinn (Revel) in Estonia in 1219. The intention seems to have been to gain control of the sea routes in the Gulf of Finland, for the lucrative fur trade, which had expanded massively in the twelfth century, emanated mainly from the markets of Novgorod (Sawyer and Sawyer 1993:66–7, 154). Ultimately, however, he could not hold these lands and during the 1220s he steadily lost his grip on them, culminating in his defeat by forces from Holstein at Bornhoved (near Neumünster) in 1227.

Valdemar II's reign effectively marks the end of what Lucien Musset calls 'la grande politique' (1951:188), although his successors maintained similar aspirations down to 1319. Valdemar attempted to regulate the succession, again using the French model: the eldest surviving son, Erik, was designated king, the other two sons, Abel and Christopher, received apanages. But, unlike the French royal family, the cadet branches could not be relied upon. Erik, already facing revolt because of his heavy taxation, was assassinated in 1250 and Abel seized power. Two years later he too was killed in a conflict with Frisia. Most significant, though, was the reign of the third brother, Christopher I (d. 1259). Under Christopher the nobility came to meet regularly in an assembly called the *Danehof* at Nyborg, while in 1256 at Vejle the Archbishop of Lund, Jacob Erlandsson, issued a series of decrees laying down heavy penalties for interference with the Church. These developments presaged the restriction of royal power not at grass-roots meetings of the *thing*, as in the past, but by powerful lay and ecclesiastical vested interests. Moreover, the devolution of Schleswig upon the descendants of Abel in 1253 began a process by which the duchy became virtually detached from Denmark and dependent upon Holstein instead. In 1282, under Erik V Glipping (d. 1286), Christopher's son, the aristocracy consolidated its position in a sweeping series of concessions: the *Danehof* was to hold annual sessions; the king could not imprison anyone who had not confessed, not been legally condemned, or caught red-handed; royal tribunals could not levy fines or other pecuniary penalties that were heavier than those allowed by provincial laws; arrangements which had been made in 1256 giving the king the power to confiscate property if his commands were not obeyed were mitigated; the king was to recognise the so-called 'laws of Valdemar' (Musset 1951:192).

By the late thirteenth century, therefore, the Danish political structure had evolved from one in which rights and power were vested in the community in the *thing*, through a monarchical structure in which many of those powers became the prerogative of the crown, to one in which the monarchy in turn had come to be restricted by the aristocracy and the Church. Under Erik VI it is evident that the monarchy had lost the support upon which it had relied since the days of the conversion. Between 1289 and 1310 Erik was involved in a long and sometimes violent confrontation with the Church over the decrees issued at Vejle in 1256, which he was unable to resolve; when he died in 1319 he left an impoverished and weakened monarchy. One of the first acts of his successor, his brother Christopher II (d. 1332), was a confirmation of the judicial and fiscal privileges of the Church, a promise not to force the nobility to provide military service outside the kingdom, and the concession of commercial liberties to the burghers.

The spreading influence of Latin Christendom in the north followed a broadly similar pattern in Norway and Sweden, although in both countries the process was slower than in Denmark. In Norway the Yngling dynasty had overcome its chief rivals in the south-west as early as the time of Harald Fairhair, but the lack of a definite law of succession inevitably induced conflict over the throne, especially as all the previous king's male descendants, including the illegitimate, could present a claim if they could muster enough support. Moreover, although Norway's harsh terrain made it difficult to conquer, it also hindered attempts to wipe out opposition; guerrilla warfare could continue for many years, as can be seen by the case of the *Birkebeiner* (the Birchlegs) in the later twelfth century. Judging by the opposition to his return, it seems that Olaf Haraldsson had been extremely unpopular while he had lived, but the Danish regime that followed his death in 1030 quickly turned the past into a golden age and Olaf into a saint. It was to throw off the Danes that Magnus, an illegitimate son of Olaf, was brought back from Russian exile in 1034 (see Table 16). He seems to have been known as 'the Good' or 'the Peaceful' largely because he was persuaded to leave the landowners of Trondheim in relative independence, but this arrangement was disrupted in 1042 when Harald Hardrada, a half-brother of Olaf, returned to Norway after a career that had taken him across half the known world. Harald's ruthless establishment of his rule, including the harrying of Trondelag, earned him his nickname of 'the Severe', but his wider claims to the Danish and English thrones were brought to an end with his death at Stamford Bridge in Yorkshire in 1066.

Nevertheless, Harald's coup did establish his line on the Norwegian throne for the next three generations until 1130: his son Olaf Kyrri (d. 1093) and grandson,

Table 16 Rulers of Norway

Knut the Great and Svend	1028–34
Magnus I the Good	1034–46
Harald Hardrada	1046–66
Magnus II	1066–9
Olaf III Kyrri	1066–93
Magnus III Bareleg	1093–1103
Olaf IV	1103–15
Eystein I	1103–22
Sigurd I Jerusalemfarer	1103–30
Magnus IV the Blind	1130–5
Harald IV Gilchrist	1130–6
Sigurd II Slembe	1136–9
Sigurd III Mouth	1136–55
Ingi Hunchback	1136–61
Magnus Haraldsson	1142–5
Eystein II	1142–57
Haakon II	1161–2
Magnus V Erlingsson	1162–84
Sverri	1184–1202
Haakon III	1202–4
Guttorm	1204
Ingi Baardsson	1204–17
Haakon IV the Old	1217–63
Magnus VI Lawmender	1263–80
Erik II Priesthater	1280–99
Haakon V	1299–1319

Magnus Bareleg (d. 1103), followed by Magnus's three sons, Eystein (d. 1122), Sigurd Jerusalemfarer (d. 1130) and Olaf (d. 1115), who ruled jointly, although Olaf's youth and early death and Sigurd's crusade left Eystein the dominant figure for much of the period. These kings enjoyed the immense influence in the northern seas which was the legacy of the Viking past, but at the same time their attitudes were slowly being reshaped. An index of the change can perhaps be seen in the careers of Magnus Bareleg, killed fighting in Ulster after a reign largely spent ranging through the Norwegian lands in the manner of his ancestors and his son, Sigurd, whose wandering was channelled into the purposes of the Latin Church through the long pilgrimage undertaken between 1107 and 1111. Harald Hardrada may himself have lived in the Viking tradition, but in Norway he continued the sporadic and violent subjugation of the quasi-independent chieftains, while under his successors the attention paid to the administration of the royal demesne and the expansion of towns like Oslo, Bergen and Nidaros (Trondheim) reflects the influence of Latin Christendom on what had once been a world apart.

It was not, however, until well into the thirteenth century that Norway was able to achieve any dynastic stability. The lack of an established formula for the succession opened the way for men like Harald Gilchrist who, arriving from Ireland in the 1120s, claimed to be the illegitimate son of Magnus Bareleg, and in 1135 seized the throne after blinding Magnus IV, Sigurd's son and designated successor. Harald Gilchrist's activities inaugurated a series of wars, exacerbated by regional interests and personal hatreds. Between 1130 and 1162 there were eight kings, all of who died violent deaths; Harald himself was murdered by Sigurd Slembe (who had also claimed to be a son of Magnus Bareleg) the year after he had gained the throne. It was these circumstances that enabled the regent Erling Wryneck to persuade Eystein Erlendsson, Archbishop of Nidaros, to crown his 5-year-old son as Magnus V in 1163. The ceremony emphasised the sanctity of the occasion by presenting Magnus as the true vicar of St Olaf, while at the same time promoting the role of the archbishop whose see had been freed from dependency on Lund ten years before. A case could be made for Magnus, for his mother, Christina, was the daughter of Sigurd Jerusalemfarer. At the same time, Erling and Eystein attempted to establish a regular system of succession, based on transmission to the nearest legitimate male relative and, failing this, on the decision of an assembly of higher clergy, the *hird* and twelve laymen from each diocese, nominated by the bishops (Gathorne-Hardy 1956:58–62). Again, as in Denmark, there are signs that the community of local assemblies or *things* and the society of free farmers which this represented would eventually be superseded by the government of an anointed king based upon an increasingly influential body of prelates and leading nobles.

At this time, however, the change was more symbolic than real, for pretenders to the throne continued to appear, often gaining support from a disparate collection of discontented elements known as the *Birkebeiner*. In 1177 they found an effective leader in Sverri 'Sigurdsson' from the Faroes, who alleged that he was the son of Sigurd III Mouth, killed in 1155. By 1184 Sverri had overcome the opposition, killing both Erling and Magnus in battle and forcing Archbishop Eystein into exile. Not surprisingly, it was difficult to reconcile the ecclesiastical authorities to this change. Although Eystein died in 1188, the leading Norwegian bishops would not accept Sverri and their opposition eventually escalated into a serious civil conflict known as the Baglar or Crosier War. They reinforced their opposition by excommunication and the threat of interdict. But Sverri was a vigorous and effective ruler, combatting his opponents both in battle and in written propaganda such as his polemic of c.1199 justifying the powers of the monarchy, and his commissioning of a history of his reign, written in saga form by Abbot Karl Jónsson (Sephton 1899). Indeed, between 1190 and 1230 there was a noticeable increase in the production of sagas and histories, most of which were intended to promote the cause of one party or another (Sawyer and Sawyer 1993:219–22, 230–2). When he died in 1202 the conflict remained unresolved; only slowly did the Baglar come to accept the conciliatory efforts of his son, Haakon III (d. 1204). The last remnants of these rivalries did not peter out until the 1220s and the last pretender was not overcome until 1240.

The next century of Norwegian history presents a marked contrast to the internecine conflicts of the years after 1130. Only four kings occupied the throne, all direct descendants of Sverri: Haakon IV the Old (1217–63), Magnus VI Lawmender (1263–80), Erik II Priesthater (1280–99) and Haakon V (1299–1319). Musset has compared the period of the reigns of the first two to that of the era of Valdemar the Great in Denmark, although seeing Norwegian development as over fifty years behind (Musset 1951:206). These kings paid particular attention to the succession. Haakon IV designated first his son, Haakon the Younger, and when he predeceased him in 1257, his next son, Magnus. In 1273 and 1302 detailed laws were drawn up, laying out the exact order of succession and, if necessary, the nature of the regency council. Haakon IV himself was illegitimate, but in 1247 he at last obtained dispensation from Innocent IV. In July, in the cathedral at Bergen, he was crowned with great ceremony by William of St Sabina, the papal legate. Moreover, in the past, pretenders had found support by appealing to regional sentiment; the thirteenth-century kings worked to establish a monarchy in which law and administration descended from the crown rather than ascended from the *things*. Under Magnus VI the old system of *wergilds* was abolished and in the years 1274–6 local assemblies accepted the jurisdiction of royal officials in criminal proceedings. A concomitant of these changes was the development of institutions which could make such a system function. By the thirteenth century, the chancellor had become the most important administrative figure, significantly replacing the much more characteristically Scandinavian position of staller whose most important function had been to act as intermediary between the king and the local assemblies (L.M. Larson 1908:476–8). The rise of the chancellor reflects both the concentration of greater power in the hands of the royal administration and the relative increase in the use of written records rather than oral communication.

It was, too, during Haakon's reign, probably in *c.*1250, that an anonymous author who was perhaps a cleric at the royal court, wrote the treatise known as *The King's Mirror*. Unlike the sagas, this was quite overtly a didactic tract, set down in the form of questions and answers, originally intended to discuss the position of the four orders of Norwegian society – the merchants, the king and his retainers, the clergy, and the peasantry – although in fact the author completed only the first two themes (L.M. Larson 1917:6). It not only reflects the importance of trade in thirteenth-century Scandinavia, but also is equally significant in the views expressed on kingship, for here it bears a close relationship to Sverri's declaration of royal powers presented in the face of the clerical assault of the 1190s. The author was deeply influenced by what he saw as the evils of the past: joint kingship and clerical claims to supremacy. For him the king possessed quasi-absolute powers:

> The king represents divine lordship: for he bears God's own name and sits upon the highest judgment seat upon earth, wherefore it should be regarded as giving honor to God Himself, when one honors the king, because of the name which he has from God. The son of God himself, when he was on earth, taught by his own example that all should honor the king and show him due obedience; for he commanded his apostle Peter to draw fishes up from the depth of the sea and to open the mouth of the fish that he caught first, and said that he would find a penny there, which he ordered him to pay to Caesar as tribute money for them both.
>
> (L.M. Larson 1917:247–8)

Haakon IV's reign needs to be seen in this light, for while he wanted the legitimacy of sacral kingship, equally he was not prepared to accept the subordination to the Church implied in the oath sworn by Magnus V in 1163. While this development of the ideology of kingship in Norway can be exaggerated – the king remained a social being and his 'bureaucracy' numbered no more than 300 men at the outside – there was, evidently, in this period, a distinct cultural shift from the past emphasis upon the personal qualities of the king to a new focus upon the monarchical office, expressed in the symbolism of the coronation and depicted upon seals and coins (Bagge 1993a).

As in Denmark during the thirteenth century, the nobility emerged as a distinct class, a trend reflected in the more formal court hierarchy and in the adoption of the titles of duke, baron and knight during the reign of Magnus VI. However, the assembly of magnates (the *herremote*) failed to establish a regular pattern of meetings or to acquire clear institutional characteristics, making it possible for Haakon V to reverse his father's policy when, in 1308, he reserved the highest titles for the royal family only. The Church was relatively more powerful, but compromise was reached in the Concordat of Tønsberg (1277) in which the king gained virtual control over ecclesiastical elections, in return for the concession of immunities from some of the burdens imposed by the raising of the *leding*. The Church still retained the ability to resist, nevertheless, defending itself against what was interpreted as the anti-clerical policy of the regents during Erik II's minority. In 1290 Erik needed to renegotiate the agreement with the Church.

Perhaps the best indication of the prestige of these monarchs was their impact on the outside world, a world far more aware of Norway than at any time since the Viking era. Relations were maintained with England, Scotland, the Empire, France, Castile and Novgorod. Matthew Paris, who visited Norway himself in 1248, claims that Louis IX of France, hearing that Haakon had taken the cross during the coronation ceremonies of 1247, wrote offering to entrust his entire crusading fleet to the Norwegian king (Luard 1880:4:650–2). Alliances with their northern neighbours were attempted through marriage links to Denmark, Scotland and Sweden. Although in 1266 Norway was forced to concede control of the Hebrides and the Isle of Man to Scotland, first Greenland in 1266 and then Iceland the following year accepted Norwegian authority. But few dynasties enjoyed the longevity of the Capetians. In 1319 Norway accepted the succession of the child, Magnus of Sweden (b. 1317), son of Erik, brother of King Birger of Sweden, and Ingebjorg, daughter of Haakon V, thus creating the dynastic union of the two countries.

For nearly two centuries between 1060 and 1250 the Swedish throne had been disputed by powerful families from the south. One line descended from Stenkil, whose base was in Västergötland, and held power until *c.*1130, when it was replaced by Sverker the Old, from Östergötland. When Sverker was assassinated in 1156, the crown was seized by Erik Jedvardsson (Saint Erik), whose origins are not known, but who may have been linked to Stenkil's line by marriage. Thereafter these two families contested the throne, their rivalries complicated by interventions from Danish claimants (see Table 17). Not until 1250, when the Folkungar, a family of *jarls* who had increasingly acted as 'mayors of the palace', took the throne for themselves, did one family hold power in continuous succession, but the Folkungar in turn dissipated their power in family conflict. No figure like Valdemar I or Haakon IV emerged, and by the early fourteenth century an increasingly powerful aristocracy had come to dominate Swedish society. These struggles were complicated by the Church, which could exploit the need of both sides for its support, but which nevertheless was obliged to commit itself to a long campaign to eradicate remnants of paganism more durable than in either Denmark or Norway.

Almost inevitably, Erik Jedvardsson was challenged by Sverker's sons, and in *c.*1160, the eldest, Karl, who was married to a niece of Valdemar of Denmark, utilised the support of the Danes to regain power for his family. Erik was killed at Uppsala and both the manner of his death and the Danish intervention contributed to his later sanctity, which in turn served as a focus for Swedish independence. But the Church was unable to prevent continuing dynastic rivalries: Karl was killed in 1167 by Knut

Table 17 Rulers of Sweden

Stenkil Ragnvaldsson	1056/60–*c.*1066
Two Eriks, killed	*c.*1066/76
Halsten Stenkillson, deposed before	*c.*1076
(Anund) Ingi Stenkillson	*c.*1076–80. Deposed
Håkan the Red	*c.*1081/85
Ingi again, opposed by	
Blot-Sven	*c.*1090/1100
Philip Halstensson	*c.*1110–1118
Ingi II Halstensson	1118–*c.*1130
Ragnvald Knaphuvud	*c.*1130?
Magnus Nielsen, of Denmark	*c.*1130–*c.*1134
Sverker I	*c.*1134–56
Erik Jedvardsson, the Saint	*c.*1150–*c.*1160
Magnus Henriksen, of Denmark	*c.*1160–*c.*1161
Karl Sverkersson	1161–7
Knut Eriksson	1167–95
Sverker Karlsson	1196–1208. Deposed
Erik Knutsson (first crowned king)	1210–16
Johan Sverkersson	1216–22
Erik Eriksson Läspe (the lisper)	1222/3–9, 1234–50
Knut Johansson Långe (the tall)	1229–34
Valdemar Birgersson	1250–75. Deposed
Magnus Birgersson Ladulås (barn-lock)	1275–90
Birger Magnusson	1290–1319

Eriksson, but it was a member of the rival family, Sverker II the Young, who succeeded Knut in 1196. Erik Knutsson, a grandson of St Erik, then forced Sverker II into exile in 1208; two years later Sverke was killed trying to regain the throne. Neither house could establish even one generation of hereditary succession. Until 1250 they ruled alternately: Johan, son of Sverker II (1216–22) and Erik Eriksson, the last of St Erik's line (1222–50), with Johan's son intruding between 1229 and 1234.

No king could create a powerful monarchy in these circumstances and for the previous half-century at least power had been increasingly concentrated in the hands of the Folkungar, originally from Östergötland, who had consolidated their position by marriage links with both the contending families. In 1250, when Erik Eriksson died without heirs, Birger Jarl had his son, Valdemar, created king. Birger died in 1266, but rivalry between Valdemar and his brother, Magnus, led to the latter gaining the throne in 1275. Magnus Ladulas was succeeded by his son, Birger, in 1290, but the reality of power lay with Torgils Knutsson, effectively the regent, a situation overturned in 1305 by Birger's younger brothers, Erik and Valdemar, when Torgils was killed. Erik seized power for himself in 1306, capturing the king. But Birger escaped and by 1310 had regained sufficient support to partition the kingdom with Erik. Then, in 1318, in an apparent effort to restore peace, Birger invited his brothers to his castle at Nyköping. There he had them arrested, perhaps killing them at once or leaving them to starve in prison. His victory was short-lived, for he was overturned by an aristocratic uprising. He died in exile in 1326; his son, Magnus, was executed in 1320. In that year the nobility of Norway and Sweden found it convenient to accept Magnus, Erik's infant son, as king.

The king-making of the Swedish nobility reflects its relative power. In the twelfth century the provinces had retained considerable autonomy under their *lagmän*, often drawn from a local dynasty. Their concept of kingship still owed more to the Viking past than to that of the developing monarchies of the west. Under the Folkungar the kings were influenced more strongly by contemporary Scandinavian trends, issuing decrees without consulting the *things* and employing their own officials more extensively than had been done in the past, but they did nothing to curb aristocratic power. Indeed, in the ordinance of Alsnö (1279), Magnus cemented aristocratic support by granting fiscal immunity to those who served on horseback, while from 1284 both lay and ecclesiastical lords met in the annual assemblies of the *Hodvagar*, the role of which increased still further during Birger's minority in the 1290s. In 1303 the passing of a law tying the peasantry to the estates of the great proprietors underlined the social and economic predominance of this class.

The Church, too, although unable to create a stable monarchical succession in Sweden, nevertheless progressively gained ground. Sverker gave particular support to the reformists as represented by Archbishop Eskil of Lund, an interest reflected in the establishment of the Cistercians in Sweden in 1143. Ten years later, the papal legate, Nicholas Breakspear, held a synod at Linköping which passed a series of decrees regulating the conduct of the clergy. Royal attachment to the papacy was demonstrated by permission to collect Peter's Pence. In 1164 Alexander III, following up Breakspear's initiatives and anxious to gain support in the conflict with the empire, created the Archbishopric of Uppsala, leaving Lund's primacy little more than symbolic. However, in 1248 another papal legate, William of St Sabina, convened a synod at Skänninge, reinforcing the reform decrees of clerical celibacy and freedom from lay patronage, which seems to confirm Musset's view that the Scandinavian Church was more successful at establishing its political influence than in effecting moral reform (Musset 1951:154). By the thirteenth century the most obvious area for further expansion of the Latin Church lay not in Sweden but in Finland, which remained largely pagan. The papacy had designated Finland a mission area in *c.*1105, but the activities of the Swedes in this land during the twelfth century are clouded by legend. In 1157–8, the later saint, King Erik, may have raided Finland, and a Swedish bishop called Henry was axed to death by a Finnish convert, possibly for taking provisions without asking for them. These two ill-attested happenings became the basis of cults encouraged by the Finnish Church which developed in the thirteenth century under a bishopric at Åbo (Turku), obedient to Uppsala. Expeditions under Birger Jarl (1240) and Torgils Knutsson (1293) brought central and some of eastern Finland under Swedish control, and confined Russian influence to Karelia: these, and other wars, were authorised by papal legates as crusades from 1237 onwards.

15

The Crusader States

Fulcher of Chartres, writing towards the end of his life in the mid-1120s, described conditions for those Latins who had settled in the Kingdom of Jerusalem in the following way:

> For how could they constantly endure such labors, those who were able to rest in their homes for scarcely a month? Certainly one has a hard heart who is not moved by compassion for those who live around Jerusalem, who day and night endure much suffering in the service of the Lord, and who also, when they go from their homes, wonder in fear whether they will ever be able to come back. If they go far they of necessity go loaded with provisions and utensils. If they are poor men, either peasants or woodsmen, they are captured or killed by the Ethiopians in ambush in ravines and forests. On this side the Babylonians [Egyptians] suddenly attack them by land and sea; on the north the Turks take them by surprise. Here in fact ears are attentive to the sound of the trumpeter if perchance the tumult of war shall have been noised abroad.
>
> (Ryan 1969:278)

In this passage Fulcher conveys very strongly the most striking psychological trait of the Latin societies settled in the Levant in the wake of the crusades, which is a sense of living on their nerves, never certain by what means they would survive or what new dangers might threaten. Here, the clerical cliché that catastrophes were punishments by God for men's sins took on an immediacy that it often lacked in other parts of the Christian world (R. Hill 1979). It is not, therefore, surprising to find that the council of king, barons and clerics held at Nablus in 1120, following a series of natural disasters, was noticeably interested in the correction of moral faults lest, for example, adulterers or homosexuals brought God's wrath upon society as a whole. This feeling of insecurity persisted into the thirteenth century. An incident relating to the early 1250s recorded in the Rule of the Templars is symptomatic. Two Templars, out after dark following a late meal, were attacked by Muslims almost within the environs of Acre; one was killed and his horse stolen, the other seriously wounded (Curzon 1886:317–18). It was admitted by an authoritative contemporary that before the 1240s, when the Templars rebuilt the huge castle of Safad overlooking the route between Damascus and Acre, that 'the Saracens, the Bedouins, the Khorezmians and the Turcomans, frequently made attacks as far as Acre and throughout the rest of the lands of the Christians' (Huygens 1981:43). Safad appears to have prevented the penetration of raiding parties, but the mugging of the two Templars shows that castles could not change the fact that the Latins lived in a land where the great majority of the population remained Muslim. Moreover, the respite from larger-scale attack was short-lived, for Safad fell to the Mamluks in 1266. Despite maintaining settlements in Palestine and Syria for 192 years, the impression of a society living on borrowed time never entirely disappears from the sources, even during the brief periods when the crusaders seemed reasonably secure and confident.

After the emotional intensity of the capture of Jerusalem, solutions had to be sought for these practical problems. The first and most obvious of them, even to clerics imbued with the ideology of ecclesiastical superiority, was the provision of effective defences, for the crusaders held only the port of Jaffa and the inland town of Ramla in the entire three hundred miles that separated them from Antioch, although Baldwin of Boulogne had already made considerable progress in carving out a principality for himself at Edessa, north-east of Antioch (see Map 10). It was essential that the coastal cities be captured both to maintain contact with the west and to control the valuable trade which was to become the settlers' most important source of income. Ascalon, further to the south, added to their discomfort, as it acted as a base for Egyptian forces. But the coastal cities would not in themselves suffice, for the crusaders needed to impose themselves upon the hinterland as well, in particular upon the fertile coastal plain and behind this the mountain ranges from the Nosairi and Lebanon mountains in the north, sometimes rising to as high as 9,000 feet, to the Palestinian highlands in the south, less formidable but still in places reaching over 3,000 feet. Behind these ranges lay the earthquake area of the rift valley containing the River Jordan and the Dead Sea, and beyond that the powerful Muslim cities of Aleppo, Hama, Homs, Baalbeck and Damascus. Initially, the possession of these cities was not as vital as those of the coast, but the crusaders' long-term failure to take any of them was eventually to provide the opportunity for a well-organised enemy to encircle the Latin settlers.

At first sight the Latins were ill equipped for this immense task. Most of all they lacked sufficient manpower, having suffered immense losses during the First Crusade, losses compounded by the departure of some of the most important magnates and their retinues for the west after Jerusalem had been taken. The massacre of the local population of Jerusalem left the city largely uninhabited, a situation that had hardly improved by 1115–16 when King Baldwin I offered special privileges to Syrian Christians living in the Transjordan to come and settle there (Prawer 1952:495–7). Albert of Aachen, who was well informed about the army of Godfrey of Bouillon, presents this in the form of a dream by a canon of St Mary's at Aachen. Godfrey was elected first ruler of Jerusalem on 22 July 1099, only eight days after the capture of the city. 'The duke took a seat in the sun. . . . The birds of heaven were gathered around the seated duke, like those from all Christian lands, great and small, noble and lesser people, who were joined with him and subject to him. The birds flew away, as the very great number of pilgrims returned to the land of their birth with the duke's permission' (Edgington 2004). Godfrey had to rely mainly on his household officials and vassals from Lorraine, reinforced by a limited number of nobles from elsewhere such as Galdemar Carpenel from Lyon, who had originally been part of the army of Raymond

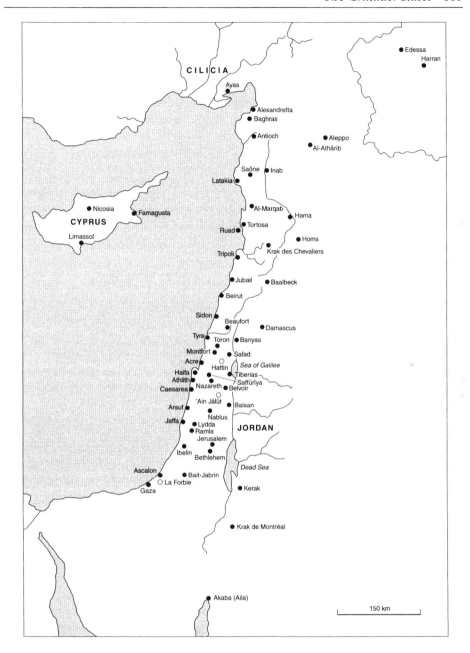

Map 10 The Crusader States in the Near East

of Toulouse (Riley-Smith 1983:724–30). Yet the Franks did experience considerable military success under the first two rulers of Jerusalem, Godfrey of Bouillon, who died in July 1100, and his younger brother, Baldwin, who was crowned first King of Jerusalem (see Table 18). They did so because the Muslims were in an even worse condition than they were, disunited and lacking the sense of unity behind the faith

Table 18 Rulers of Jerusalem

Godfrey of Bouillon	1099–1100
Baldwin I	1100–18
Baldwin II	1118–31
Fulk of Anjou and Melisende	1131–43
Melisende and Baldwin III	1143–52
Baldwin III	1152–63
Amalric	1163–74
Baldwin IV	1174–85
Baldwin V	1185–6
Sibyl and Guy of Lusignan	1186–92. Sibyl d. 1190
Isabella and Conrad of Montferrat	1192
Isabella and Henry of Champagne	1192–7
Isabella and Aimery of Lusignan	1197–1205
Maria of Montferrat	1205–10
Maria of Montferrat and John of Brienne	1210–12
Isabella II and John of Brienne	1212–25
Emperor Frederick II and Isabella II	1225–8
Conrad II (IV of Germany)	1228–54
Conradin	1254–68
Hugh I (III of Cyprus)	1268–84
John	1284–5
Henry I (II of Cyprus)	1285–1324

which had pushed the crusaders on despite the horrors of the First Crusade. By 1110 the Latins had gained control of most of the important coastal cities, including Acre in 1104, which had a safe harbour on a coast singularly deficient in natural protection for shipping. Thereafter, access for western shipping was relatively straightforward as the lack of a coastal base at which water could be obtained meant that the Egyptian galley fleet no longer had the range to reach northern shipping lanes (Pryor 1988:112–34). Only Tyre, taken in 1124, and Ascalon, which held out until 1153, eluded the Christians at this time. The essential prerequisite was that the cities be blockaded from the sea as well as besieged on land. For this the crusaders secured the help of the maritime cities of Italy, in particular Genoa, which by this means first established itself in the eastern Mediterranean, and Venice which, in response to appeals from both the pope and Baldwin II, in 1123 sent a formidable fleet which included forty galleys, twenty-eight chatz (which William of Tyre explains were larger than galleys and powered by one hundred oars) and four even larger ships for carrying baggage and equipment (Babcock and Krey 1941:1:548–9). In return the Italians received extensive trading privileges in these cities, which gave them virtual immunity from customs charges and allowed them to establish quarters which were, in practice, colonial enclaves. All this was achieved with only a small core of fighting men of perhaps between 250 and 300 knights for most of the reign of Baldwin I, although at the battle of Ramla against the Egyptians in

August 1105, there appear to have been as many as 500 (A.V. Murray 1989:282–3).

However, the flanking cities of the east remained in Muslim hands, despite a determined attempt to take Aleppo in 1125 by King Baldwin II and the disjointed efforts of the armies of the Second Crusade against Damascus in 1148. The Fatimids hung on to Ascalon until 1153, blocking expansion to the south-west, and Egypt came only briefly within the Frankish range during the campaigns of King Amalric in the 1160s. The majority of the Franks, therefore, lived in the cities or in the castles which they built or adapted to their purposes, although recent research shows that the Franks established themselves in the countryside more extensively than was once thought, especially in areas of former Byzantine settlement north of Jerusalem as far as Sinjil, and in western and northern Galilee (Ellenblum 1998:30–8, 213–76). Elsewhere in Palestine most of the local population remained Muslim, devoid of political influence or the means for public worship, its role a source of supply of food, labour and taxation obtained via Muslim stewards who had no option but to implement the demands of their Frankish overlords (Mayer 1978:175–87). The exploitative nature of the Italian colonies adds to this impression, for they did not settle outside the coastal cities in which their privileges enabled them to tap the lucrative eastern trade.

During the first generation the Franks established four states, three of which, the Kingdom of Jerusalem, the County of Tripoli and the Principality of Antioch, lay along the seaboard, while the fourth, the County of Edessa, was a landlocked territory east of Antioch extending towards Mesopotamia. Jerusalem included inland areas around Galilee to the Jordan, part of which had been conquered by the Norman Tancred, who had been aiming to carve out a principality for himself in the region. The capture of his uncle Bohemond in 1100 by Danishmend Turks, however, drew him north to take over the regency of Antioch, thus stifling the new political enclave in the south at birth. Bohemond never really profited from his enterprise and ruthlessness in seizing Antioch. He gained his release in 1103, but the next year suffered a serious defeat at the hands of the Turks near the fortress of Harran, south-east of Edessa. In the face of the determination of Alexius Comnenus to close in upon him from the north-west, he decided to leave for Italy and recruit forces to attack the Byzantines in the Balkans as he had done in the past. He never returned to the east. The attack was a failure and Bohemond was obliged to sign the Treaty of Devol in 1108 with the Emperor Alexius in which he agreed to hold Antioch as a fief of Byzantium. This treaty had no immediate practical effect, but it did show what a large wedge the Norman seizure of Antioch had driven between the Christian allies of the First Crusade. Between Jerusalem and Antioch lay the tiny state of Tripoli, founded by Raymond of Toulouse, although Tripoli itself was not taken until 1109, four years after Raymond's death.

Paralleling the problem of defence, the Latins needed to construct viable governmental systems in these new states; the matter was felt particularly acutely in Jerusalem, where the emotive significance of the city and the necessity of defining the relationship between the patriarch and the lay ruler greatly complicated deliberations. The first ruler to be elected was the Lorrainer, Godfrey of Bouillon, although the leading crusaders had initially offered the rulership to Raymond of Toulouse. Raymond was by far the richest and most powerful of the barons who had stayed in the east, but at this time was unpopular because of views which the crusaders perceived to be pro-Byzantine. It is possible that he was reluctant to take the offer because he knew that he lacked support, but hoped that ultimately the crusaders would see that they had no alternative. A means of doing this was to refuse to take the title of king, thus making it difficult for any other candidate to do so either. This may be unjust to him. His house chronicler, Raymond of Aguilers, states that 'he shuddered at the name of king in Jerusalem' (H. Hill and L.L. Hill 1968:129), and this piety may have been perfectly genuine. However, whatever the reason, Godfrey seems to have evaded the problem by declining to be crowned either.

The extent to which Godfrey would be able to exercise his new role, however, was called into question with the arrival in Palestine of a new papal legate to replace Adhemar of Le Puy, who had died in 1098. This was Daimbert, Archbishop of Pisa, who refused to confirm the newly elected Arnulf of Chocques as patriarch and instead had himself enthroned at Christmas 1099. It is clear from his actions and his letters that Daimbert intended to establish himself as effective ruler, less for ideological reasons than because of personal ambition. With the backing of the Pisan fleet and the support of Bohemond, for a period he looked likely to succeed, especially when Godfrey died unexpectedly in July 1100. But from then on circumstances conspired against him: the Lorrainers seized the citadel in Jerusalem and called in Godfrey's brother, Baldwin, from Edessa, while his chief supporter, Bohemond, disappeared into captivity. When Baldwin arrived in November, Daimbert was in no position to offer resistance; Baldwin was crowned King of Jerusalem at Christmas 1100, at Bethlehem.

The Crusader States in Palestine and Syria were not alone in their position on the frontiers of Christendom, but they were unique in their role as guardians of the city of Jerusalem and the surrounding holy places. The kingship established by Baldwin I therefore was unlike any other in Christendom in that, although he held demesne lands and presided over the mosaic of lordships held by his vassals in the same manner as western rulers, he was also king of a country which was an emotional focus for all Christians and which was therefore also seen as the common heritage of the entire community of the baptised. Added to the problems of defence and governmental structure, therefore, were those created by the links with the west, since all Christians were encouraged by the Church to contribute to the well-being of the holy places by going on crusade and pilgrimage. Indeed, a stream of letters from the east shows how dependent were the Latin settlers upon these contributions, but the attentions of the westerners were at the same time a mixed blessing, since a successful appeal for help might bring a huge, temporary influx which often had significant effects upon the relations between the residents and their Muslim neighbours well beyond the period of the actual crusade. Moreover, crusades led by men who were regarded as major leaders in the west often took their own course, paying insufficient attention to local advice. Indeed, in *The Play of AntiChrist*, an anonymous work of *c*.1160 closely connected with Hohenstaufen court circles, the King of France is shown as temporarily resisting the emperor, but, significantly, the King of Jerusalem is portrayed as being glad to concede imperial primacy (J. Wright 1967:70–3,76). More than any other country in the twelfth and thirteenth centuries, the Crusader States were dependent upon the perception of them by the other powers of western Christendom and their people.

Between 1100 and 1131 the forceful personalities of the first two king of Jerusalem, Baldwin I and, after 1118, his cousin, Baldwin II, contributed significantly to the survival of the Crusader States. Baldwin I was particularly successful at making the Frankish presence felt through the capture of the coastal cities, active intervention in Syria, and expansion southwards to Akaba and the Red Sea. In 1118 he even invaded Egypt. Baldwin II maintained the pressure on specific important objectives, in particular Tyre and Aleppo. Both rulers were greatly helped by divisions within Islam.

The Muslim world, rent by the schism between Sunnite Baghdad and Shi'ite Cairo, was even more fragmented at the local level, for the Seljuk sultans failed to impose any degree of political and military unity in Syria, while the Fatimid forces were relatively ineffective in the face of Frankish cavalry. It was never easy for those Muslim rulers most affected by the Franks to persuade their neighbours that they needed help. Ibn al-Qalanisi, the Damascene chronicler, described how, in February 1111,

> a certain Hāshimite sharīf from Aleppo and a company of Sūfīs, merchants and theologians presented themselves at the Sultan's mosque, and appealed for assistance. They drove the preacher from the pulpit and broke it in pieces, clamouring and weeping for the misfortunes that had befallen Islām at the hands of the Franks, the slaughter of men, and enslavement of women and children. They prevented the people from carrying out the service, while the attendants and leaders, to quieten them, promised them on behalf of the Sultan to dispatch armies and to vindicate Islām against the Franks and the infidels.
>
> (Gibb 1932:111)

As a consequence of such appeals the Seljuk sultan supported Maudud, ruler of Mosul (1108–13), who formed a rather uneasy alliance with Tughtigin, Atabeg of Damascus (1095–1128), as part of an attempt to weld together a wider coalition against the Franks. But Maudud's death in 1113 and the victory at Danith (on the borders of Tripoli and Antioch) by Roger of Antioch, Tancred's nephew and successor as regent since the latter's death in 1112, put an end to these efforts.

These fundamental weaknesses among the Muslims enabled the Franks to survive serious set-backs like Roger's defeat and death by the Artukid Turk, Il-Ghazi, in 1119 near al-Atharib between Antioch and Aleppo (the so-called 'Field of Blood'), and in 1123–4 the capture of Baldwin II himself by Belek, Il-Ghazi's nephew. But in 1125 Baldwin's siege of the key city of Aleppo failed to bring about its capitulation, and in some ways this may be seen as a turning point, for in 1127 'Imad-ad-Din Zengi came to power, the first of three outstanding Muslim leaders of the twelfth century who, imbued with an increasingly powerful adherence to the *jihad*, initially forced the Franks onto the defensive and then came close to eliminating their presence on the Palestinian and Syrian mainland altogether. Zengi had been made Atabeg of Mosul in 1127. In the following year he was accepted in Aleppo as a direct consequence of previous Frankish pressure. Beyond this, however, his room for manoeuvre was in fact rather limited, since behind Antioch lay the apparently menacing presence of Byzantium under the Emperor John II Comnenus, while further progress to the south was blocked by the Christian alliance with Damascus. His really significant success came when he captured the relatively isolated Frankish outpost of Edessa at Christmas 1144, seizing the opportunity presented by the deaths of John Comnenus and King Fulk of Jerusalem the previous year.

Zengi was assassinated in 1146, but his Syrian lands fell to his second son, Nur-ad-Din, who took up the cause of Islam with equal fervour. He was greatly helped by the incompetence of the leaders of the Second Crusade who, during 1148 and 1149, achieved nothing apart from alienating the Christians' Damascene ally. The failure of this expedition opened the way for Nur-ad-Din's attack first on the Antiochene lands, which culminated in the defeat and death of Raymond of Antioch at Inab in 1149, and then on Damascus itself, which he took in 1154. Once again, however, the Byzantine influence in Syria restricted his progress. In 1158–9 Manuel I mounted an expedition to Cilicia and Antioch which was sufficiently impressive to deter Nur-ad-Din from any decisive confrontation.

Although a heavy burden of the responsibility for the loss of Edessa rested upon the shoulders of the count, Joscelin II, who was not present in person to resist Zengi, nevertheless the crusaders did not lack able leaders during these years. The throne of Jerusalem in particular continued to be occupied by committed and vigorous kings. Baldwin II had no male offspring, but in 1129 he secured the marriage of his daughter, Melisende, to Fulk, Count of Anjou, who had a long-standing interest in the crusade and who, on a previous visit to Jerusalem, had become an associate of the embryonic Order of the Templars. Fulk succeeded jointly with Melisende in 1131 and, despite problems with a section of the Jerusalem nobility and conflict with his wife over the actual exercise of power, proved to be an effective successor of the two Baldwins. In the north he consistently combatted Zengi and in 1137 he was rewarded by an agreement with Damascus which, according to Ibn-al-Qalanisi, committed both parties 'to take common action and support one another, and to unite and join forces in driving off the Atābek and preventing the achievement of his aims' (Gibb 1932:259). The first fruit of this alliance was the capture of Banyas which, lying between Damascus and northern Galilee, was of great strategic importance to both allies. He was equally active in the south, blockading Ascalon with fortresses, and encouraging the building and rebuilding of castles to the east and south-east. During the 1130s the Hospitallers took on military functions and Fulk's appreciation of the value of such orders was shown by his grant of the castle of Bait-Jabrin, near Ascalon, to them in 1136. Thereafter, the military orders accepted an increasing responsibility for the guarding and upkeep of the major fortresses of the Crusader States.

Baldwin II's arrangements for the succession had been particularly concerned with the protection of his dynasty's rights: to this end he had determined not only the joint rule of Fulk and Melisende, but also the future succession of their elder son, Baldwin. In 1143, when Fulk died in a hunting accident, Baldwin III was only 13 years old and Melisende, as queen-regnant, took over rule, but during the 1140s Baldwin's growing discontent with his mother's domination eventually manifested itself in armed conflict. In 1152 he forced her to retire to her dower at Nablus, leaving him as sole ruler. The next year he led the siege of Ascalon, which finally brought down the last of the coastal cities which had resisted the Franks. However, within eight months of this success the full consequences of the failure of the Second Crusade became evident, for Nur-ad-Din was received into Damascus, making him a far more direct threat than the Fatimids had ever been. Only the Byzantine presence, although often more pervasive than the rulers of Antioch would have liked, kept the balance.

With stalemate in the north, the focus of crusader activity shifted to the south, stimulated by the possibilities opened up by the fall of Ascalon. Baldwin III died in 1163 without direct heirs and, after some hedging by the ecclesiastical leaders, was succeeded by his brother, Amalric. During the 1160s he became increasingly interested in the prospect of gaining control of Egypt, a country whose government he rightly perceived to be of little real substance, and to this end he led five expeditions there. In 1167 he actually managed to place forces in Alexandria and Cairo. But he lacked sufficient men and money to create a really solid occupation and sufficient patience fully to co-ordinate his attacks with those of the Byzantines, whose alliance he had gained following his marriage to Maria Comnena, great-niece of Emperor Manuel, in 1167. Moreover, he faced a formidable rival in Shirkuh, a Kurdish general sent by Nur-ad-Din to counter Frankish expansion. According to Baha'-ad-Din, Saladin's biographer, Shirkuh was deeply preoccupied with the project, 'laying his plans and thinking how to return to Egypt, dreaming of this and preparing the basis for this with al-'Adīl Nūr al-Dīn until the year 562 [1166–7]' (Richards 2001:42). Shirkuh took Cairo in 1169 and, although he did not live long enough to enjoy his success, he was succeeded by his nephew Saladin, who in 1171 proclaimed the return of the country to Sunnite orthodoxy. There was apparently no resistance and the last Fatimid Caliph died without knowing what had happened. Amalric has often been criticised for the diversion of Christian resources to Egypt, not the least by his own court chronicler, William of Tyre, who ascribed the policy to 'blind cupidity' (Babcock and Krey 1941:2:357–8), but Baldwin II's failure to impose Christian rule on Aleppo left expansion to the south as the more tempting prospect. Moreover, if Egypt had been opened up, it is possible that further western immigration would have been encouraged, thus increasing the numerical presence of the Franks in the east. By this time the nature of the manpower problem had changed considerably from that of the early twelfth century, for settlers had arrived in sufficient numbers to make the acquisition of estates within the relatively small kingdom quite difficult for newcomers (Harper and Pringle 2000:11). Although the failure of the Second Crusade led to a temporary fall in immigrants, by the 1160s more men were needed to fulfil the military objectives of the kings of Jerusalem than there was land available to enfeoff them. The alternative was a policy which was essentially conservative and defensive, a role which, as future events proved, was ultimately unsustainable. More pertinent, perhaps, is the view that Amalric's desire to seize Egyptian resources led him to neglect the Syrian defences without which the possession of Jerusalem was not strategically viable.

Nevertheless, whatever his mistakes, when Amalric died in 1174 it cannot realistically be argued that the downfall of the Crusader States seemed an immediate prospect. The resources of the Jerusalem monarchy, although drawn more from port revenues than traditional demesne income, remained substantial, while despite the losses of Antiochene territory, the Byzantine presence seemed to be an effective deterrent to over-ambitious Muslim leaders in Syria. Moreover, Latin defences had steadily become more formidable: the military orders could probably field three hundred knights each in the Kingdom of Jerusalem and perhaps as many again in the northern states, figures which could be matched by the lay fiefs. Great fortresses like the Hospitaller castles of Belvoir in northern Galilee and Krak des Chevaliers, east of Tortosa and Tripoli, dominated the surrounding countryside. Belvoir, built in a rectangle with a double line of huge walls, shows the Franks at their most confident, for it was as well-suited to garrison an effective field army as it was for more passive defence. It had originally been established by King Fulk in the late 1130s and then rebuilt by the Hospitallers after 1168. No attacker could enter the Jordan Valley south of the Sea of Galilee with impunity.

Yet the fundamental precariousness of the Crusader States is starkly evident during the late 1170s and early 1180s, for Saladin was able to undertake their systematic encirclement. Mutual suspicion prevented much co-operation between Saladin and Nur-ad-Din, but the latter died in 1174. When, in 1182, Andronicus I, Comnenus, seized power in Constantinople on the back of a wave anti-Latin popularism, the opportunity to close in on the Franks was evident. By February 1183 the Franks had become so concerned that they agreed upon the levy of an extraordinary tax on income and property, for which everyone was liable, although in practice a disproportionate burden fell upon the non-Christian population (Mayer 1978:177–80). These fears were soon justified, for in June Saladin acquired Aleppo, the crucial significance of which the Franks had long recognised. By 1185, through a mixture of shrewd alliances and threats, he had practically isolated the Latins. William of Tyre, even though he died well before the battle of Hattin, was fully aware of the power of Saladin.

> In spite of all our efforts, however, all attempts to restrain him have been in vain and, today, with tearful eyes, we see that our apprehensions have been realized. For so powerfully has he risen against us by land and sea that if the Dayspring from on high had not mercifully visited us, we should have no hope of resisting.
> (Babcock and Krey 1941:2:405)

William cannot have been alone among contemporaries in perceiving the danger, yet the Latins themselves made a substantial contribution to their own downfall, for the forces which faced Saladin on the Horns of Hattin in July 1187 were the product of a deeply divided society, uncontrolled by the hand of a strong king. Under Baldwin I and Baldwin II these divisions had not been very evident. Once the threat of theocratic rule had been overcome there were no other vested interests strong enough to make a serious challenge to the Jerusalem monarchy. However, by the 1130s some of the insignificant noble houses which had established themselves in Outremer began to consolidate their lines and to increase the scope of their dynastic ambitions, while at the same time the military orders and the Italian communes, upon which the Crusader States were becoming increasingly dependent for defence, began to make their influence felt. While the monarchy did not lack able exponents, these developments did make unified government more difficult than it had been during the first generation of settlement.

Historians of the Latin Kingdom of Jerusalem have, therefore, in recent years been particularly interested in these problems, pointing to evidence of possible noble revolt in the last years of Baldwin II's reign between 1129 and 1131 and, more seriously, in 1134 under King Fulk. In that year, Fulk's position was apparently threatened by a party among the nobles which both opposed his attempts to exclude Melisende from government and resented his policy of filling crown offices and royal castellanies with his 'new men', some of whom had Angevin connections, at the expense of older-established families, especially those with Norman associations (Mayer 1989). Although Fulk was ostensibly successful in dealing with this discontent in that its leader, Hugh, Count of Jaffa, was banished from the kingdom, he was nevertheless forced to concede his wife a much greater political role than she had had hitherto. Melisende was also the key figure in the slide towards civil war which occurred between 1149 and 1152, when her reluctance to share power with Baldwin III created two opposing parties among the barons of the kingdom. Even under Amalric, seemingly a powerful personality, restrictions were imposed on the monarchy, for he was forced to renounce his wife, Agnes of Courtenay, before he could succeed. Furthermore, at some time during the 1160s his issue of the assise on liege homage by which rear-vassals were empowered to appeal to the High Court in cases where they believed they had been denied justice from their immediate overlord, has been interpreted as a means of formalising baronial powers over matters which previously had been largely subject to royal will, untrammelled by the need for baronial consideration (Prawer 1968). Moreover, the growth of the military orders can be seen as a mixed blessing, for their awareness of their own importance to the defence of the east combined with their extensive juridical immunities made them difficult to control. If William of Tyre is to be believed (and on this matter he was by no means a disinterested observer), Amalric became incensed with the conduct of the Templars who, in 1173, killed an envoy from the dissident Muslim sect of the Assassins with whom the king had been negotiating and then refused to hand over the guilty brother to royal justice. Had he lived, says William, he had intended to take up the matter of the immunities of the military orders with the other leaders of Christendom (Babcock and Krey 1941:2:392–4).

Taken together, these incidents do suggest the existence of fissures within the Kingdom of Jerusalem and, indeed, both Tripoli and Antioch were equally subject to such struggles. They do, nevertheless, need to be kept in proportion. A comparison with England might serve to do this: the conflict between Baldwin III and Melisende was a minor affair in relation to the civil war between Stephen and Matilda; the assize on liege homage however interpreted (and there is still no consensus on its meaning) (Riley-Smith 1987:75–6) was no Magna Carta; the spat with the Templars produced no Thomas Becket. Yet the English political system remained stable, dynastic continuity was maintained, and monarchical prerogatives continued to be extensive. Indeed, conflicts between king and the other vested interests in Jerusalem were relatively mild in comparison with most contemporary European monarchies.

In fact, the really crucial period for the Latins in the east followed Amalric's death in 1174, for he was succeeded by his young son, Baldwin IV, who was both a minor and, as soon became evident, was suffering from leprosy. Minorities almost always encourage faction and in this case the need for a regency was prolonged by the royal illness, causing intermittent incapacity. Had the king been able to preside effectively, then the divisions among the Latins would not have been so dangerous to the crusaders as they were to become. Baldwin's personal courage is clear, but his inability to control the government for any sustained period meant that by the time of his death at the age of 24 in 1185, the leaders of the Latin Kingdom had largely crystallised around two opposing parties. These parties have often been portrayed as on the one hand representatives of the older, established families of Outremer, prominent among whom were Raymond III, Count of Tripoli and descendant of Raymond of Toulouse, and the Ibelins, obscure in origin but easily the most influential family in the east from this time on, and on the other, the so-called 'newcomers', as exemplified by the Lusignan brothers, one of whom, Guy, had married Sibyl, elder daughter of Amalric, and Gerard of Ridefort, Grand Master of the Temple, men despised by the baronage as outsiders. Raymond's party supposedly cultivated a cautious, defensive policy towards the Muslims, whereas the Lusignan faction favoured attack, often at the expense of common sense. In fact, this characterisation oversimplifies in several ways (Edbury 1993). The Lusignans were actually closely allied to the royal family which included not only Sibyl, but also her mother, Agnes of Courtenay, and uncle, Joscelin, titular Count of Edessa. Prominent barons like Reginald of Châtillon, who had been in the east since the time of the Second Crusade, were also supporters of what more accurately could be called the Courtenay party. In so far as distinct elements can be discerned in what, in many ways, remained a fluid situation, the chief struggle seems to have been between the paternal and maternal kin of Baldwin IV (Hamilton 2000:158). In the end, though, the Courtenays appear to have won. Baldwin V, son of Sibyl by an earlier marriage, succeeded the leper king in 1185 but, aged only 7, was incapable of ruling. His early death in September 1186 left the opportunity for Guy and Sibyl to seize the throne, bringing the kingdom to the edge of civil war just when the threat of Saladin was at its greatest.

In July 1187 this political division translated itself into the realities of the battlefield. Saladin was able to inflict a crushing defeat upon the crusader army because its leaders were more influenced by their own personal rivalries than by sound tactics. Count Raymond's advice to King Guy to maintained a static defensive position based on the springs at Saffuriyah was contradicted by Gerard of Ridefort, who persuaded Guy to march to the relief of Tiberias, under siege by Saladin. The army never made it, for it was cut down by the Muslim forces after nearly two days struggling towards its objective, leaving most of Jerusalem and Tripoli at the mercy of Saladin. By the end of 1188, he had taken massive advantage of his victory, for the only substantial base left to the Christians in the south was the city of Tyre, rescued by the timely arrival of the crusading forces of Conrad of Montferrat.

Saladin failed to wipe out the Christian presence completely, partly because of the arrival of reinforcements from the west, first those of Conrad of Montferrat and then, from 1190, the much greater armies of the Third Crusade, and partly because, like previous Muslim rulers, he was leader, not of a unified, homogeneous force, but of a coalition which he could hold together only for a limited period. By 1192 these circumstances led him to settle for a three-year truce. The partial reconquest achieved by the Third Crusade left the Latins with the important coastal cities, including Tyre, Acre, Haifa, Caesarea, Arsuf and Jaffa in the south (but without the city of Jerusalem itself), together with Tripoli and a rather truncated principality of Antioch in the north. Saladin did not live to see the expiration of the truce; he died in March 1193. His removal lifted the pressure on the rump of Crusader States that had survived his onslaught, for the divisive tendencies which had characterised the Muslim world during the first generation of crusader settlement, now reasserted themselves within the Aiyubid Empire. Not until the battle of La Forbie, near Gaza, in 1244, did the Franks suffer a defeat comparable to the catastrophe at Hattin. Equally, however, after Hattin no single strong figure emerged among the Latins who could reimpose monarchical control. Hattin not only gutted the kingdom but also ruined the monarchy. From now on, powerful vested interests – the upper baronage, the military orders, the Italian maritime cities – dominated this world. Only with the arrival of major leaders from the west, such as the Emperor Frederick II between 1228 and 1229 and King Louis IX between 1248 and 1254, was this dominance seriously challenged.

By the late twelfth century crusader society had developed distinct characteristics. The Latin settlers had quickly adapted to living in the many cities and towns of the Levant. Urban centres formed the basis of both secular lordships and ecclesiastical divisions and profits from the trade which passed through them made up the major part of their income. Some Franks did live in the countryside, as archaeological evidence of manor houses and 'planted' villages has increasingly shown, but for the great majority the towns were the centres of social and political life. Seigneurs with rural fiefs drew income from the land, but generally did not live there, preferring to leave the local economic structure intact. This environment had a strong influence on lifestyle. Muslim houses, clothing, food and medicine were all utilised by the settlers, and consequently they often presented an unfamiliar and, to some crusaders and pilgrims from the west, shocking spectacle. During the thirteenth century, when crusading seemed to absorb resources without limit yet brought almost no concrete successes, it was easy to lay the blame on effete settlers, supposedly addicted to an eastern way of life and lacking an appetite for sharp conflict with their Muslim neighbours (Riley-Smith 1978; Schein 1986).

The ambivalence in the relations between this society and western Christians was brought into even sharper relief by the social trends of the thirteenth century. After Hattin there was an intensification of the process already evident in which an upper caste of nobles, closely related to each other and particularly centred upon the key family of the Ibelins, was coming to see itself as an elite within the Crusader States, clearly superior to the lesser knights and burgesses on the one hand and largely independent of the monarchy on the other. These lordships have been described as 'palatinates', their holders granting out fiefs without reference to higher authority, minting their own coins, and administering high justice (Riley-Smith 1973b:26). They justified their position by reference to their conception of the origins of the Kingdom of Jerusalem, a conception which bore little relation to the *ad hoc* arrangements of reality, but a great deal to their own self-image as guardians of the supposed contract between king and 'people' made by Godfrey of Bouillon. They believed that the basis for this was contained in a compilation of laws known as the *Letres dou Sepulchre*, lost at the time of Hattin, although modern commentators now maintain that these were simply a collection of legal documents of relevance to the government of Jerusalem but with no systematic rationale or ideology. Not surprisingly, these nobles had a highly developed sense of legalism. Their leading thinkers were jurists: John of Beirut, Ralph of Tiberias and Balian of Sidon in the first half of the thirteenth century; John of Jaffa and Philip of Novara in the later years. Some time in the middle years of the century, John of Jaffa codified what he regarded as the laws of the kingdom in a compilation known as the *Assises de Jérusalem*.

It was therefore difficult for the king to assert himself, unless he could bring to bear overwhelming resources and prestige drawn from outside the kingdom. King Guy's position had been far from secure even before Hattin; after the disaster he could try only to develop a better reputation for himself through his deeds, an attitude which resulted in his apparently half-baked attempt to recapture Acre in 1189. His position was not helped when Sibyl died in 1190, severing his connection with the royal family in a land which, as the succession of Baldwin IV and Baldwin V had shown, set great store by hereditary links. In the end, his chief advantage lay in the patronage of Richard I who, after failing to effect a successful transfer of his new conquest of Cyprus to the Templars, allowed Guy to purchase it instead.

The addition of Cyprus to the Crusader States might seem a more than adequate compensation for the loss of Edessa, for the island was both more prosperous and more secure, but the acquisition was double-edged. It was an ideal base for crusaders from the west and indeed was pivotal in Louis IX's planning in 1248; moreover, it was a considerable potential source of supply in men and money to the hard-pressed front-line states on the mainland. However, in practice it did not always fulfil these roles, for its very advantages often acted as a strong attraction to colonisers and merchants who might otherwise have settled on the mainland, while its geographical position meant that it was much less involved in direct conflict with the Muslims than the mainland states, a situation reflected in the lack of development of its fortifications in the thirteenth century (Molin 2001:89–94). Moreover, Guy of Lusignan, anxious to reconstruct a viable economy after the damage done by the asset-stripping of Richard I and the Templars, was over-generous in his allocation of fiefs in the hope of recreating stable conditions. His successor in 1194, his brother Aimery, therefore found it necessary to rebuild royal income, a policy which led him to refuse to employ Cypriot revenues on the mainland when he accepted the crown of Jerusalem in 1197. While this afforded the island some measure of economic protection, Aimery mortgaged the island's political future by seeking investiture as king from a representative of the Hohenstaufen emperor, Henry VI, an initiative designed to deter possible Byzantine attempts to regain Cyprus. The long-term effect was to entangle Cyprus in the imperial wars of the early 1230s which followed Frederick II's crusade of 1228–9. It was not until 1247 that Innocent IV broke the link with the Hohenstaufen by releasing the reigning king, Henry I, from this allegiance.

With King Guy forced out and Sibyl's death in 1190, the key member of the ruling house of Jerusalem was now Sibyl's half-sister, Isabella, and until 1205 the kingdom was ruled by her successive husbands, Conrad of Montferrat (d. 1192), Henry of Champagne (d. 1197) and Aimery of Lusignan (d. 1205), only the last of whom was actually crowned. Only Aimery lived long enough to undertake the role with any conviction. After his coronation in 1197 he did not return to Cyprus and there are signs that he attempted to exercise monarchical power in a manner analogous to the kings in the period before 1174. Some time during this reign the laws of the kingdom were set down in a compilation known as the *Livre au Roi*, and in 1198 he was involved in a confrontation with Ralph of Tiberias, a noble whose outlook epitomised the legalism of the baronial class. But he had no effective successor, nor did he have available a central administration at all comparable with those developed by the Angevins or the Capetians, a defect which again emphasises the extent to which past rulers had been preoccupied with defence. While Philip II was reorganising his finances in a manner which enabled him to launch his successful attack on Normandy, the Latin kingdom was fighting for its very survival. Isabella died shortly after Aimery, leaving only a female and a minor to succeed in the person of Maria, her daughter by Conrad of Montferrat, emphasising yet again how unusual it was for a dynasty consistently to produce capable male heirs in the manner of the Capetians. The kingship must have seemed a very undesirable prize by this time, for it was not until 1210 that a husband could be found for Maria, even though she came of age in 1208, and then only in the person of a relatively obscure knight from Champagne, John of Brienne. When Maria died in 1212, John ruled as regent for their daughter, Isabella II, although retaining the title of king until 1225. But in that year there was a dramatic change, for in August Isabella became the wife of the greatest ruler in Christendom, the Emperor Frederick II.

Frederick's marriage to Isabella began a connection which was to last until 1268, first through Frederick himself, who held the title of king between 1225 and 1228, and thereafter through his son, Conrad (d. 1254) and grandson, Conradin (d. 1268). Neither of these even visited Outremer, however; it was Frederick who took a personal interest both as king and as regent for Conrad. Frederick had promised to go on crusade in 1215, but successive delays, for what seemed to Frederick to be good political reasons, had increasingly exasperated the papacy. When he did eventually reach Cyprus in July 1228 his relations with Pope Gregory IX had become so fraught that he was an excommunicate. This fact, together with his high-handed approach to what the baronage and, in particular, the Ibelins, regarded as their inalienable rights, ensured that his stay in Cyprus and Palestine was to be highly contentious.

Although Frederick's negotiations with al-Kamil, the Aiyubid sultan, accomplished the return of Jerusalem in February 1229, it was not an achievement greeted with great joy by the local Franks. They had a point, for it could be argued that he had not gained sufficient territorial concessions to ensure the long-term viability of the city in Christian hands, a problem which had led to the rejection of a similar offer during the Fifth Crusade. Nevertheless, not all the opposition had such an objective basis as this, for the upper clergy, the baronage and the military orders, by now accustomed to governing the crusader lands in their own way, did not find imperial lordship at all palatable. Frederick had particularly offended the Ibelins at the time of his arrival in Cyprus by demanding that John of Beirut, *bailli* during the minority of the Lusignan king of Cyprus, Henry I, hand over his fief in Beirut, together with all the Cypriot revenues accumulated since the death of the last king. Such an attempt at dispossession by royal fiat was, of course, quite contrary to the baronial conception of government, which regarded such an action as possible only through the judgment of the High Court. The reaction of the Franks was inevitably vehement. In a letter to the faithful, written in 1229, Patriarch Gerald of Lausanne, said that the emperor's activities in the east had been 'to the grave prejudice of the affair of Jesus Christ and in contempt of the Christian faith' (Luard 1880:3:179), while the pro-Ibelin chronicler, Philip of Novara, claimed that Frederick was so hated that when he left Acre in May 1229 the butchers, next to whose street he embarked, 'pelted him with tripe and bits of meat most scurrilously' (Hubert and La Monte 1936:91).

Although unable to continue his crusade in person, for papal troops had invaded the Kingdom of Sicily, Frederick nevertheless determined to make his authority felt, despite the legalism of the barons. In 1231 his marshal, Richard Filangieri, arrived as imperial *bailli*, established himself at Tyre, and thus inaugurated over a decade of war between the imperial forces and the baronage, who promptly formed themselves into a sworn association or commune to provide mutual support in their opposition to him. Intermittent fighting took place both in Palestine and Cyprus until, in 1243, Conrad, Frederick's heir, came of age. The baronage, following legal precedent, recognised him as king, while at the same time making a determined and successful attempt to drive Filangieri, whom they regarded as now having no vestige of authority left, out of Tyre.

While this has been seen as a victory of class interest over imperial centralisation (Mayer 1988:255), it is unlikely that either provided a long-term solution to the problems of survival faced by the Crusader States. Major expeditions continued to be mounted; some, like the crusades of Theobald, Count of Champagne, in 1239–40, and Richard of Cornwall in 1240–1, regained important territory, including Beaufort, Safad and Ascalon, and the former Christian territories on the west bank of the Jordan. But the events of 1244 demonstrate once again the fragility of the Frankish hold on Outremer. Most of the period since Saladin's death had seen little threat from the Aiyubids; indeed, it has been calculated that between 1192 and 1242 only eight years were not covered by a truce (Smail 1973:25). However, with Filangieri defeated, the disunity of the Aiyubids tempted the Franks once more to try their strength against Egypt, reinforcing their position by reverting to the old alliance with Damascus. As-Salih, the Egyptian sultan, had, however, gained an even more formidable ally in the Khorezmian Turks, a nomadic tribe driven west by the Mongol invasions. In July 1244 they seized Jerusalem and sacked it, and then moved south to join as-Salih. As at Hattin, the Franks had the option of avoiding battle and taking up a defensive position; as at Hattin they chose to risk confrontation. On 17 October 1244 at La Forbie, near Gaza, they suffered their worst defeat since 1187. After this, Frankish territory extended no further east than a line roughly between Beaufort and Safad and, perhaps even more importantly, their losses in manpower were devastating. There is no agreement in the sources about the exact figures, but in a letter written by the Templar, William of Rochefort, together with other survivors, it is claimed that among the military orders only thirty-three Templars, twenty-six Hospitallers and three Teutonic Knights had escaped (Luard 1880:4:342).

The losses at La Forbie accelerated a trend already evident before the battle. Although the baronage of Outremer have often been criticised for their apparently excessive concern with their caste and status, they had, nevertheless, struggled to defend the crusader territories. In the second half of the thirteenth century it became increasingly evident that they no longer had the economic strength to do this; only those with resources in manpower and money outside the Crusader States, such as the military orders and the Italian communes, had the means to recover from 1244. The last decades of the Latin settlement down to the loss of the Palestinian and Syrian mainland in 1291 were dominated by these powers; by that date only four fiefs in the former Kingdom of Jerusalem remained in lay hands (Riley-Smith 1973b:30). Indeed, the famous castles of the thirteenth century are those of the military orders: Athlit and Safad held by the Templars, Krak des Chevaliers by the Hospitallers, and Montfort by the Teutonic Knights.

These circumstances did nothing to ease the chronic tendency towards factional conflict. St Louis had imposed his strong will on government in Outremer between 1250 and 1254, following his unsuccessful crusade to Egypt during the previous two years, but soon after his departure, the War of St Sabas, a vicious civil conflict which lasted from 1256 to 1258, again undermined the Christians from within. The original dispute had arisen between the Venetians and the Genoese over the possession of the hill overlooking Acre on which stood the monastery of St Sabas. While legal proceedings were still in train, the Genoese suddenly seized the monastery, an action which quickly led to serious fighting with the Venetians. Behind the conflict lay long-standing commercial rivalry, yet crusader society had become so factionalised that other parties to whom this was of no direct concern were drawn in. The Templars, the Teutonic Knights, the Pisans and the Provençals supported the Venetians, while the Hospitallers and the Catalans were behind the Genoese. The baronage were equally split: Philip of Montfort, lord of Tyre, took his opportunity to expel the Venetians from Tyre, where they had been established since their great grant of privileges of 1123–4, while the Ibelin clan lent its weight to the Venetian cause. The war at sea in particular became quite large-scale, for the chief combatants could bring their Mediterranean fleets to bear; in so far as the war was 'won', the Venetian victory at sea in 1258 seems to have been the most decisive action.

Not surprisingly, the role of the crown was greatly devalued in comparison with the period before 1174. With the death of Conradin in 1268, the Hohenstaufen connection was ended and, instead, the High Court at Acre recognised the line of the kings of Cyprus which at this time meant Hugh III (I of Jerusalem). However, his right was disputed by Maria of Antioch, who had a claim in strict genealogical terms, but was turned down by the High Court. This would probably have been of little consequence had she not sold this claim to Charles of Anjou in 1277, thus adding a new partisan interest to the warring factions of Outremer. Charles himself was never able to visit Jerusalem, but until his power was undermined by the rising of the Vespers in 1282, he maintained a close interest in its affairs, supplying food, clothing and armaments, and sending his own *bailli* to represent his interests in the east.

Even had the Vespers not destroyed Charles's plans for a Mediterranean empire, it is unlikely that he could have saved the crusader lands for, from 1259, a new and ruthless regime established itself in Cairo, that of the Mamluks. They had formed a key element in the Egyptian armies since Saladin's time, as the following description by William of Tyre shows.

> It is the custom of Turkish satraps and of the great chiefs, who in the Arabic tongue are called amirs, to rear with great care certain young men, some of whom are slaves captured in war, others are bought or perhaps born of slave mothers. These youths are instructed in military science, and when they have reached manhood are given wages or even large possessions, according to the merit of each. These men are called in their own language mamluks. To them is entrusted the duty of protecting the person of their lord in the vicissitudes of battle, and upon them in no slight degree depends the hope of obtaining the victory.
>
> (Babcock and Krey 1941:2:431)

During the 1250s the Mamluks clawed their way to direct power through a series of violent assassinations, and in 1260 sealed their rise with an outstanding victory over the Mongols at the battle of 'Ain Jalut, near Nazareth. The clash between these two powers had placed the Franks in a dilemma, for the Mongol advance had been accompanied by horrific massacres, yet the brunt had been borne by Islam, culminating in the sack of Baghdad and the execution of the 'Abbasid Caliph in 1258. In the end the Franks refused to support the Mamluks, but they did allow the Mamluk Sultan, Kutuz, to pass through their lands in order to meet the Mongol threat. The resulting victory freed the Mamluks from immediate Mongol pressure and left Palestine and Syria open to Mamluk attack. Soon after 'Ain Jalut a leading general, Baybars, murdered Kutuz and took the sultanate for himself. Baybars reigned until 1277 and under his regime resources were more effectively harnessed than in the past enabling him to increase the size of the field army and to improve siege weaponry. Thus, in four major campaigns between 1265 and 1271 he conquered Caesarea, Haifa, Toron, Arsuf, Safad and Jaffa as well as most of Galilee. In 1268 Antioch itself fell. He was only temporarily checked by the arrival of the crusade of Edward of England in 1271. By 1277 the Franks were confined to a coastal strip extending only from Athlit in the south to Latakia in the north. Plans for co-operation with the Mongols, frustrated by mutual incomprehension and logistical failures, never came to fruition. In a letter to Edward, now King of England, written at the end of May 1281, the treasurer of the Hospital, Joseph of Cancy, said that he could never remember the Holy Land to have been in a worse condition than it was at this time, suffering from drought, disease and Muslim attack, so that it had not been possible to sow the fields. Cyprus and Armenia were in no better state. The situation was exacerbated by an embargo on supplies to Syria from the Kingdom of Sicily, previously a major source of support, because of the war between Charles of Anjou and the Byzantines (Sanders 1896:13).

The Holy Land, Cyprus and Armenia were not the only crusader lands struggling for survival in the second half of the thirteenth century. The crusader states set up in the years following the capture of Constantinople by the Fourth Crusade in 1204 were in a similarly dire condition. Although the Latins never succeeded in breaking Byzantine power, for three major dynasties in exile set themselves up at Nicaea,

Trebizond and Epirus, nevertheless they were able to use Constantinople as the foundation upon which they built a considerable network of states several times greater in size than the settlements in Palestine and Syria (see Map 11). In May 1204 Baldwin IX of Flanders was elected emperor at Constantinople to preside over what was to become known as the Empire of Romania, which extended on both sides of the Bosporus, beyond Nicomedia in Asia Minor to the east, and north of Adrianople to the borders of the Bulgar lands on the European side (Wolff 1969). Boniface of Montferrat, the official leader of the crusade, disappointed at his failure to become emperor, nevertheless struck out to the south and west, and within a few months had begun to carve out a kingdom based on Thessalonica, which he took in September 1204. Further south, two leading crusader knights, William of Champlitte and Geoffrey of Villehardouin, had conquered the Morea by the late summer of 1205. William, and after his death in 1208, Geoffrey, took the title of Princes of Achaea. The Venetians, leaders of the diversion of the crusade in the first place, showed particular interest in the control of key points in their commercial network, including Modon and Coron on the west coast of the Morea and the island of Crete, all of which they held by 1207. The long narrow strip of Negroponte (Euboea) and the island of Naxos in the southern Aegean, although not conquered by the Venetians, depended upon their support (Longnon 1969).

Although the city of Thessalonica was lost to Theodore of Epirus as early as 1224, the Latin presence remained substantial. Achaea, for instance, which emerged as the most powerful of these states, could raise as many as six hundred knights, roughly equivalent to the twelfth-century Kingdom of Jerusalem. Nevertheless, in the long term, the Frankish states in Romania and Greece suffered from the same problems of internal weakness and external pressure as their counterparts in Syria and Palestine; indeed, in one sense their position was even less tenable, for Constantinople and Athens lacked the emotive attraction to potential crusaders contained in the call to aid Jerusalem. Papal propaganda about the delights of settlement in Frankish Greece soon gave way to increasingly desperate attempts to persuade western Christendom that these lands were an essential part of the structure which supported the Holy Land itself, and as such the concession of equivalent indulgences for crusading there and even the diversion of funds meant for the Holy Land, were quite justified (Setton 1976:1–105). The papacy did not succeed. Even William II of Achaea was forced to concede most of his power to Charles of Anjou in order to survive, while Constantinople, bankrupt and almost bereft of defenders, fell to the strongest of the Byzantine states, that of Nicaea, under Michael VIII Palaeologus, in July 1261. Pope Urban IV claimed that news of this event had pierced the innermost parts of his heart as if with spears, while the Venetians, more practical although equally concerned, offered to transport crusaders who would try to recover it, free of charge, making an interesting contrast with their insistence on the commercial price for participants in the Fourth Crusade. Neither appeal evoked sufficient response to trouble the new Byzantine emperor, who rightly perceived the Mediterranean ambitions of Charles of Anjou to be a much greater threat.

The end for the Latins in Palestine and Syria came in May 1291, when Acre fell to al-Ashraf, the Mamluk sultan of Egypt. Those who could fled to Cyprus. Even the Templars saw no good purpose in fighting on and evacuated their great fortress at Athlit. The fall of Acre, however, did not signal the end of the crusades. Cyprus remain an independent kingdom until 1489 and it was from here that the military orders in particular tried to continue the war, launching attacks on the Egyptian coast and, in one

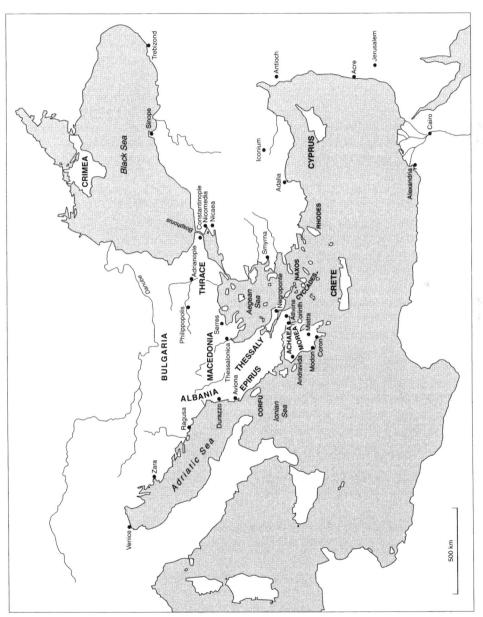

Map 11 The Crusader States in Romania and Greece

Templar initiative in 1302, briefly re-establishing themselves on the island of Ruad, off the coast at Tortosa. In 1309 the Hospitallers took Rhodes from the Byzantines, thus creating another Latin naval base in the eastern Mediterranean which lasted until 1522. Moreover, although Constantinople had fallen in 1261, the Byzantines did not regain all their former lands in Greece and the islands: Achaea survived until 1432, the Duchy of Athens to 1456, and the Venetian Duchy of Naxos until 1566. The ambiguity of the relationship between the crusader settlements and the west remains an abiding theme. No new crusade was launched as an immediate reaction to either 1261 or 1291 as had happened in response to the disasters of the past, yet the laments were loud, and crusading remained a major interest of western Christians for at least another two centuries.

Part IV

Perceptions of the world

16

The medieval world view

Plato (d. 347 BC) is the main western source for what Arthur Lovejoy calls 'otherworldliness' in western philosophy and religion (1942:35), that is the belief that human beings should strive to divest themselves of the visible, material world, in order to attain the invisible, eternal world. Their striving was directed towards their source, the Supreme Being (or the Idea of Good), which was perfection. The Supreme Being completed its perfection by its production of other beings, so that every conceivable being was realised. If it had not engendered other beings, 'it would lack a positive element in its perfection'. While Plato's pupil, Aristotle (d. 322 BC), did not find it necessary to postulate a theory of creation based upon the fecundity of God, he did nevertheless provide a hierarchical classification of beings, a graded scale rising from minerals eventually to humans, with each level containing both the elements of those that were below it and a distinctive feature of its own. In the medieval view, although human beings had only a pale semblance of the intelligence possessed by the angels, they were distinguished by their faculty of reason; equally they were connected to the animals beneath them in the hierarchy by their possession of senses. If the connecting link with rationality were to be in some way interrupted, then a possible consequence might be insanity, which was sometimes seen as the explanation of seemingly irrational acts like murder or suicide (Babcock and Krey 1941:2:386; Scott 2001:5:1343).

In the middle ages these ideas were organised into the scheme taken up by the Neo-Platonists of the late Roman Empire, who were originally centred upon Alexandria in the third century AD. Among them Plotinus (205–70) was the most important influence on the medieval world view. The scheme was passed on by both Church Fathers like St Augustine (d. 430) and pagan Roman philosophers such as Macrobius, his contemporary. Macrobius expressed it most strikingly in his commentary on *The Dream of Scipio* (*Somnium Scipionis*), which was originally the sixth book of Cicero's *De Re Publica*, itself an imitation of a section of Plato's *Republic*. In a now famous passage he explained:

> Mind emanates from the Supreme God and Soul from Mind, and Mind, indeed, forms and suffuses all below with life, and since this is the one splendor lighting up everything and visible in all, like a countenance reflected in many mirrors

arranged in a row, and since all follow on in continuous succession, degenerating step by step in their downwards course, the close observer will find that from the Supreme God even to the bottommost dregs of the universe there is one tie, binding at every link and never broken.

(Stahl 1952:145)

The links in this chain of ideas were consolidated by an anonymous late-fifth-century writer who has come to be known as the Pseudo-Areopagite. His importance in medieval eyes was exaggerated because he implied that he was a follower and contemporary of St Paul, which in turn led later medieval authors to identify him with Dionysius the Areopagite, an Athenian who had indeed been a follower of Paul. In the later eighth century this first incorrect identification had been compounded by a second, when it was claimed that the author was the same person as St Denis (d. 250), Apostle of the Gauls and founder of the famous abbey. The Pseudo-Areopagite wrote four books, of which the *Celestial Hierarchies* was the most important in influencing the medieval model, in particular through the translation and interpretation made by the Irishman, John Scotus Erigena (d. 877), who had lived at the court of the Carolingian, Charles the Bald. For the Pseudo-Areopagite 'the one tie' of Macrobius is light for, according to the Gospel of John, 1:1–9, God is Light.

> In the beginning was the Word, and the Word was with God, and the Word was God. The same was in the beginning with God. All things were made by him; and without him was not anything made that was made. In him was life; and the life was the light of men. And the light shineth in darkness; and the darkness comprehended it not. There was a man sent from God, whose name was John. The same came for a witness, to bear witness of the Light, that all men through him might believe. He was not that Light, but was sent to bear witness of that Light. That was the true Light, which lighteth every man that cometh into the world.

Light was strongest at the highest levels of the hierarchy, but nevertheless penetrated to all creation so that even the lowest and most material shared in it, as could be seen in the polished surfaces of material objects. This 'mirroring' of the light returned it to its source, binding the many into the unity which is the Christian faith (see Plate 14). For the Pseudo-Areopagite it was not possible to perceive God directly; the world offered a series of images through which the desire to contemplate the Divine Light was evoked. This theme can be seen most vividly in visual form in the mosaic programmes of the three great royal foundations of Norman Sicily, the cathedral at Cefalù (founded 1131), the Cappella Palatina in Palermo (founded 1140) and the great Cluniac monastic church and cathedral at Monreale (founded 1174). In each of them the image of the Pantocrator, the omnipotent Christ, presides over the buildings from the apse conch at the east end. Each displays an open book inscribed with the text from John, 8:12, in Greek and Latin, 'I am the light of the world; he that followeth me shall not walk in darkness, but shall have the light of life.' At Monreale the bronze doors of the west end are linked to this image through the inscription *Ego sum lux* at the top of the right-hand door showing the Ascension of Christ (Borsook 1990: 9, 26, 33–8, 56, 58, 63). It followed that evil elements avoided the light; that is, as Plotinus had defined it, they lacked good. Heretics, for instance, were often accused of holding obscene rites in

Plate 14 This painting from the central apse of the church of San Climent de Taüll in Catalonia shows Christ seated in Majesty on the arc of Heaven with the Earth beneath his feet. Around him is the Tetramorph, the symbols of the four Evangelists (Ezekiel 1:10). The book on his left contains the words, *Ego sum lux mundi* (I am the Light of the World) (John 8:12), and on either side of him are Alpha and Omega, the first and last letters of the Greek alphabet, showing him presiding over time. The work was paid for by the Erill family, lords of the Boí valley, probably from profits gained from the campaigns against the Moors led by Alfonso I of Aragon. © Museu Nacional d'Art de Catalunya (Barcelona).

secret, dark places, because, in the words of Philip the Fair's minister, William of Plaisians, during the trial of the Templars in 1308, 'he who acts evilly hates the light' (Lizerand 1964:122). The fact that the Templars sometimes held chapter meetings and receptions of new brothers in secret and at night was in itself regarded as cause for suspicion against them. Those who avoided the light, both in the transcendental and in the actual, physical sense, were opponents of the faith.

Positive proof of this ordering of the universe had already been provided by Pythagoras (d. *c*.580 BC), whose discovery of set mathematical relationships between musical tones showed that the natural world had been created as a unity. In the *Timaeus*, Plato later conceived of the universe as held together in a series of fixed geometrical proportions, established when the Supreme Being created order out of chaos. The idea is repeated in St Augustine's *De Musica* in which he describes the laws of music based on fixed arithmetical ratios, the intervals of the 'perfect consonances'. Bible illustration and church decoration sometimes show God in the act of creation, using a compass such as a contemporary mason might have used, or seated upon the elements, hand outstretched towards the light enfolding the angelic host (see Plate 15). This was a model used by the great philosophers of the age from Peter Abelard to Thomas Aquinas, and which provided Dante with his cosmology.

The hierarchy of being encompassed both invisible and visible elements. The *Celestial Hierarchies*, drawing on various biblical references provided a structure for the invisible, which in turn suggested to people on earth how the ideal society should be organised. Otto of Freising, all the more convinced because he supposed that the information had come from St Paul, described it in this way:

> Dionysius, that chief of theologians, posits three hierarchies (that is holy sovereignties) of angels and then, dividing each hierarchy into three orders, to complete nine orders of angels establishes three sets of three. In the first he places Seraphim, Cherubim, Thrones; in the second Dominions, Powers, Virtues; in the third Principalities, Archangels, Angels. He asserts moreover that the first hierarchy immediately surrounds the Trinity and is illuminated by it alone, but that the second, being midway between the first and the last, is both illumined by the preceding hierarchy and in turn illumines the succeeding.
>
> (Mierow 1966:500)

One of the roles of the angels was to mediate between God and humans, sometimes in the form of messengers. However, Lucifer, swollen with pride, and using the free will with which he had been endowed by God, had led a revolt which, according to Revelation, Chapter 12, had been defeated by the Archangel Michael. Thereafter, Lucifer (Satan) and his fellow conspirators among the angels (the demons) had waged their battle with God, enmeshing humans in the conflict whenever and however they were able (J.B. Russell 1984:159–207) (see Plate 16). Those who succumbed would be damned eternally (see Plate 17). 'For if it was merely to terrify the wicked that He said the punishments are eternal,' said Otto of Freising,

> we must believe also that it was merely to please that He said that the glory of the good is eternal. That such a view can by no means be maintained no one who recognises Him as the truth and the life can doubt.
>
> (Mierow 1966:486)

Plate 15 God's creation of the Firmament is one of 42 scenes in mosaic in the Genesis cycle in the nave of the cathedral at Monreale in the Kingdom of Sicily, which King William II began in 1174. (Photograph reproduced by permisson of Scala.)

In other words, after the Fall, Hell was the inevitable concomitant of Heaven.

From the late twelfth century onwards, what Jacques Le Goff has called 'the geography of the other world' (1984:2) gained a new and important region, that of Purgatory. The idea that there was an alternative to Heaven and Hell in which certain souls might be placed between death and the Last Judgement had been considered likely by the Church Fathers, but it was not until after 1170 that it acquired the specific characteristics of a place of trial for those who had committed venial sins, where the

Plate 16 The Archangel Michael led souls to God, protected Christians in battle and provided aid against the Devil. In Revelations 12:7–9, he is portrayed as overcoming the dragon (the Devil), as shown on the top right-hand side of the panel. Below left he is weighing souls, while on the right a hunter who tried to kill the ox, his symbol, is punished when the arrow rebounds into his eye. On the top left Raphael and Gabriel carry souls to Heaven. Michael's cult began in Phrygia, but in the West was associated with Monte Gargano after a vision of the late fifth century; Catalonia, *c.* 1120–50. © Museu National d'Art de Catalunya (Barcelona).

sentence of the inmates could be mitigated by the prayers of those left on earth. Less prominent in the contemporary mental picture, but emerging as a distinct entity at about the same time was a fourth region, the Limbo in which unbaptised children were placed. Lack of baptism meant exclusion from Heaven, but children seemed a special case, since they had not committed any sins of their own, despite bearing the unavoidable burden of original sin. During the twelfth century various views were held, including the idea that they were actually baptised by angels on God's command, but by the late thirteenth century the opinion of Thomas Aquinas that they went to Limbo, where they could love God and did not suffer pain, seems to have prevailed.

While the scholastics constructed a complicated theological scaffold around these concepts, medieval art produced many dramatic images of Heaven and Hell, of winged creatures representing angels, and of grotesque beings portraying demons, which could be understood in the most literal terms. For many people, the naked figure of the Devil, often with horns, tail and bat's wings, was much more 'real' then any theological debate on evil as a privation of good. Otto of Freising was well aware of the problems this created for many people. In the following passage he describes the representation of Heaven:

Plate 17 The Last Judgement dominated the west front of many cathedrals, as here at Amiens (completed 1236). The neat division into registers has sometimes been seen as a parallel to the homologous structure of contemporary scholastic writing. (Photo Regnaut.)

Now we must inquire what the blessedness of that country is. For we must not suppose that souls, after they have been stripped from the body, or after they have taken up spiritual bodies and are not inferior to the angelic spirits in purity and in rank, find delight in external things as men do in this life. Accordingly, whenever Holy Scripture says that their spirits are refreshed and affected by flowering and verdant meadows, by pleasant places, by the singing of birds, by fragrant things (such as cinnamon and balsam), such expressions should, it is clear, be interpreted spiritually rather than carnally. And yet, for the sake of the simple – who must be nourished on milk, not on solid food, whose understanding is not yet exercised and who cannot as yet comprehend spiritual delights – these things are frequently set down by certain teachers that the simple may thus be directed through the visible to the understanding and discovery of the invisible.

(Mierow 1966:508)

Explanation of those parts of the universe which were visible derived almost entirely from past authorities, in particular the second-century Alexandrian, Ptolemy, whose astronomical work, the *Almagest*, was translated into Latin from Arabic at Toledo in 1175. Ptolemy's work had in turn been based both on respect for Aristotelian physics and upon the astronomical observations made at the great academy at Alexandria, which had existed since the third century BC. With the Arab capture of Alexandria in 641, the intellectual heritage of the academy fell to the Muslims and it was by this path that it re-entered the west. The use of authorities was characteristic, but their structure was accepted for almost two thousand years until the Copernican revolution of the mid-sixteenth century because their assertions accorded with what medieval people observed. This was no mean feat, for they scanned the sky constantly and relentlessly recorded what they saw, often using an astrolabe to help them in their computations, and sometimes drawing up complex tables from the data obtained.

The Ptolemaic universe, as it has become known, was geocentric, that is, centred upon the earth, although it did not postulate that the whole structure existed in relation to humankind. The earth was a stationary sphere, around which was a series of transparent spheres. In each of the first seven rotated 'planets' in the following order: the Moon, Mercury, Venus, the Sun, Mars, Jupiter and Saturn. The Greeks thought that these moved around the earth in circles, but observation of irregularities led to the inclusion in the Ptolemaic model of epicycles, in which the planets either circled the Sun or simply a point in space, as well as following a path around the earth. Beyond these was the *Stellatum*, which contained the so-called fixed stars, although observations at Alexandria determined that these fixed stars did in fact move around the heavens, taking about thirty-six thousand years to make a complete circuit. It was inferred that there was a further sphere, not visible, called the *Primum Mobile* which, moved by God, provided the impetus for the rotation of all the rest. Finally, beyond the spatial comprehension of humans, lay the vault of Heaven itself. This universe was light, warm, and filled with music. The sense of gradation was equally strong in considering the elements which made up the universe, for the purest rose to the top in the form of aether, which existed just above the sphere of the Moon, while below, the recognisable elements of fire, air, water, and finally earth, made up the ever-varying environment of humankind. No human creature could alter this scheme. In Dante's words,

> No vicariate whether human or divine, can be equivalent to the authority from which it originates – as is easily seen. To take one example, we know that Peter's successor does not enjoy divine authority in regard to the workings of nature; for he could not make the earth rise or fire descend by virtue of the office entrusted to him.
>
> (Nicholl and Hardie 1954:74)

In keeping with the concept of an integrated universe, the movements of the heavens had direct effects upon the sublunary world. Just as the influences of the Sun and the Moon were evident, so too could the planets and stars affect events on earth. In Ambrogio Lorenzetti's great fresco in the Palazzo Pubblico in Siena, planets seen as having a benign influence (Venus, Mercury, the Moon) are shown in medallions linked to the scenes of good government, while those of malign aspect (Mars, Saturn, Jupiter) are connected to the scenes of tyranny (Larner 1971:84–5). The Church, however, was wary of any interpretation which suggested that events or individuals were in any way locked into an astrological prison, since this evidently contradicted the concept of free will, as well as opening the way for charlatans who could prey upon the superstitious. Nevertheless, astrology was deeply embedded in medieval culture. The early medieval world had inherited the idea that the pagan gods had once been mortal and Christian writers like the seventh-century encyclopaedist Isidore of Seville were therefore able to fit them into historical time. Moreover, although pagan belief in the divinity of the planets was unacceptable, it was impossible to eradicate the associations of their names.

Table 19 Astrological signs by Antiochus of Athens

Signs of the Zodiac	Seasons	Ages of Life	Elements	Winds	Qualities	Conditions	Humours	Temperaments	Colours
ARIES TAURUS GEMINI	Spring	Childhood	Air	South	hot-moist	liquid	blood	sanguine	red
CANCER LEO VIRGO	Summer	Youth	Fire	East	hot-dry	gaseous	yellow bile	choleric	yellow
LIBRA SCORPIO SAGITTARIUS	Autumn	Maturity	Earth	North	cold-dry	dense	black bile	melancholic	black
CAPRICORNUS AQUARIUS PISCES	Winter	Old Age	Water	West	cold-moist	solid	phlegm	phlegmatic	white

Source: J. Seznec (1953), *The Survival of the Pagan Gods*, tr. B.F. Sessions (New York: Pantheon), p. 47. (Reproduced by permission of Princeton University Press)

Belief that astral influence over human beings affected character, health and fortune, actually strengthened during the high middle ages, for systematic tables of correspondences (such as that constructed by Antiochus of Athens in the second century AD: see Table 19), had an especial appeal to the scholastic mind, while the acquisition of additional astrological information via Arab transmission of writers like Ptolemy in the thirteenth century added further depth and complication to the information already held (Seznec 1953:3–147).

Since it was believed that humankind was 'a little world composed of four elements', as the monk, Honorius of Autun (d. *c*.1130) put it (Migne 1895:1116), the linkage of the zodiac and the planets to important political, military or medical decisions (among others) seemed only logical. In the thirteenth century it became fashionable to employ court astrologers who could make the appropriate calculations from various combinations of data. Some of these astrologers held positions of great influence in the entourage of rulers like Frederick II. It is therefore not surprising that ecclesiastical disapproval could not eradicate popular belief in such a seductive subject as astrological prediction. The extent to which this was part of popular culture can be seen in an example taken from a century before Frederick II's birth. In the *Gesta Francorum*, the author describes a scene which he imagines to have taken place before the battle of Antioch in 1098, in which the Muslim Atabeg of Mosul, Kerbogha, was defeated by the crusading forces. In it Kerbogha's mother foretells her son's ruin.

> Therefore I, wretched woman that I am, have followed you from Aleppo, the fairest of cities, where by my observations and careful calculations I have looked into the stars of the sky, and studied the planets and the twelve signs of the Zodiac and all kinds of omens. In all of them I found prognostications that the Christian people is fated to defeat us utterly.
>
> (R. Hill 1962:55)

The appearance of occasional phenomena like shooting stars, comets or eclipses, or even unusual weather conditions, was often seen as significant. The anonymous author of the account of the conquest of Lisbon in 1147 believed that he saw the Christian victory foretold in the sky as a series of great white clouds drove back a bank of threatening black ones, just as if they had been drawn up in battle-lines (David 1976:88–91). Confidence in the meaning of such signs must have been common, for the Winchester chronicler, Richard of Devizes, uses an eclipse of the sun which occurred in June 1191 as a means of dismissing such interpretations as the province of the ignorant.

> Those who do not understand the causes of things marvelled greatly that, although the sun was not darkened by any clouds, in the middle of the day it shone with less than ordinary brightness. Those who study the working of the world, however, say that certain defects of the sun and moon do not signify anything.
>
> (Appleby 1963:35)

Simon of Montfort, the leader of the Albigensian Crusade, was equally contemptuous of the common belief in dreams as a vehicle for warnings and predictions. According to Peter of Les Vaux-de-Cernay, on the night of 9 September 1213, three days before he overcame the combined forces of Peter of Aragon and Raymond of Toulouse at the battle of Muret, his wife had a terrifying dream in which blood flowed freely from both her arms. When she told her husband, he dismissed her as a foolish woman. 'Do you think I am going to rely on dreams and auguries like a Spaniard?' He would not, he said, have been deterred even had he dreamt that he was about to be killed in the battle to come (Sibly and Sibly 1998:205).

Observers of the natural world, like Fulcher of Chartres, were nevertheless intensely interested in the activities of the heavens, though they were too sophisticated to fall into the trap of making precise prophecies. The following passage shows both Fulcher's acute power of observation and his implicit belief in the links between the movement of heavenly bodies and events on earth.

> In the year 1106 a comet appearing in the sky frightened us because we were suspicious of it. It was in the direction in which the winter sun is wont to set. It produced a brilliant white streak like a warp of linen thread of wondrous length. This portentous sign began to redden in the month of February on the day of the new moon. But not presuming to prophesy from it we committed to God the whole problem of what it signified. For fifty or more days that comet was seen every evening over the entire world. It is remarkable that from the beginning of its appearance the comet itself as well as its beautiful white streak faded a little every day until in the last days it lost the strength of its light and then ceased entirely to appear.
>
> (Ryan 1969:189–90)

The ancient world provided a geographical structure for the earth, as well as descriptions of animals, plants and minerals within it. The earth, they realised, was spherical and it had been deduced that there must be zones in the southern hemisphere which matched those of the north, that is temperate and arctic regions. The equatorial zone was largely covered by water which had two branches each in the east and west, dividing the world's land mass into four. Most accepted that the southern regions were inaccessible because the intervening equatorial zone was too hot for human survival. Indeed, St Augustine argued that the descent of all humankind from Adam and Eve and thence from the three sons of Noah meant that it was logically impossible for humans to have crossed the torrid zone in the first place. Thus to claim, as some did, that the Antipodes were inhabited by some monstrous race, was to deny both the origins of humanity and, by implication, to exclude any deviation from the perceived norm from partaking in that humanity (Flint 1984). There were, however, dissenters, especially writers with knowledge of Arabic work, who argued that the equatorial zone was indeed inhabited; others continued to be intrigued by the possibility of people living in the southern hemisphere, despite being told that such a belief was heretical, since Christ came to save the entire human race, not simply those who were accessible (J.K. Wright 1925:156–65).

Respect for authority remained the predominant influence so that, for instance, medieval bestiaries and encyclopaedias included a fair number of creatures described by the ancients, but which nobody had ever seen; but the picture was supplemented by personal experience. Sometimes it was a struggle to reconcile authority and observation, especially when the authority was biblical. Fulcher of Chartres, for instance, perhaps influenced by the intellectuals of his home-town cathedral school, was by no means uncritically deferential. He confessed himself baffled by the rivers of Eden, described in Genesis, Chapter 2.

> I can admire but never explain how and in what way this River Gihon, which
> we read comes out of Paradise with three others, seems to have found a second
> source since it has to the east the Red Sea and to the west our sea [the
> Mediterranean], into which it flows. For it has between itself and the east the
> Red Sea, and yet we read that Paradise is in the east. Therefore I greatly wonder
> how it resumes its course on this side of the Red Sea and how it crosses that sea,
> or whether it does cross it.

He found the same problem with the Euphrates, which seemed to have a double source,
but could find no one to explain it to him.

> I leave the explanation to Him who miraculously causes the water to be in the
> clouds, the streams to arise in the mountains, hills and valleys and to run swiftly
> through the crevices of hidden channels and, at last, wonderful to tell, to find
> the sea and be swallowed up in it.
>
> (Ryan 1969:217)

Fulcher and his contemporaries like the brothers Bernard and Thierry who remained
at Chartres can perhaps be seen as precursors of a more critical approach to
geography, represented in the thirteenth century by men like Roger Bacon and
Robert Grosseteste, and demonstrated in the most practical way by Marco Polo,
whose book contained such an astonishing quantity of new knowledge that many
doubted his veracity (Larner 1999:96–7, 108). The change was in keeping with the
thinking which first sought natural explanations of events before turning to the
miraculous (Ward 1982:4–6).

The areas about which Fulcher speculated were in fact on the edge of a world
which, in his own time, were largely inaccessible to westerners and therefore one
upon which they could project their fantasies. This world was the region of the
Indian Ocean, which they believed was an enclosed sea like the Mediterranean, and
on the borders of which, as Fulcher implies, they located the earthly Paradise. Within
it lay great riches, exotic and monstrous creatures, both human and animal, and
communities for whom the restrictions of Christian morality and western social
taboos did not exist (Le Goff 1980:189–200). The *Natural History* of Pliny the Elder,
who died in AD 79, was the chief medieval source for these monstrous races; he
recorded forty such peoples, although the number tended to grow over the medieval
centuries (Friedman 1981:5–25). Such a picture was typical of medieval utopian
visions, which were essentially based upon relief from material deprivations and
governmental oppression, set either in a land far away or in some past 'golden age'.
Nobody thought of constructing a future ideal society, since original sin could not
be eliminated, nor the Last Judgement prevented (Graus 1967). For some the fantasy
remained at this level, both beguiling and frightening, but this did not prevent some
clerics from drawing it into the Christian structure. The Apostles had supposedly
reached these places and converted the various parts of India so that, for example,
these races could be shown within a great sculptural programme such as that on the
tympanum at Vézelay (*c*.1120–32) (see Plate 18). Here the Apostles are given their
mission to spread Christianity and among the many peoples who line the lintel and
archivolt are the Panotii, a race with huge ears who, according to Pliny, lived in India
(Katzenellenbogen 1944). Half a century later, the continuing importance of this issue

Plate 18 The complex iconography of the tympanum of the narthex at Vézelay incorporates the connected themes of the Ascension of Christ and the Mission of the Apostles (Acts 1:4–9). The rich detail provides one of the fullest visual expositions of the medieval conception of the world, 1120s. (Photograph reproduced by permission of Scala.)

in a society still deeply concerned about the continuing success of Islam, is demonstrated by the capitals which had been destined for the shrine-grotto inside the Church of the Annunciation at Nazareth, which were carved with scenes from the lives of Saints Peter, James, Thomas and Matthew, the themes of which are all concerned with the mission of these apostles in the east (see Plate 19). Ironically, the capitals were never put in place because of the Christian disasters in the face of Saladin's attacks in 1187–9 (Folda 1986).

In the twelfth century India seemed, too, a likely location for the great Christian king in the east, known as Prester John. In 1122 a man claiming to be an archbishop from the Malabar coast had visited the papal court and described the existence of a powerful and rich Christian ruler in the east. To a society already well acquainted with Indian exotica and aware of the many Nestorian Christians in lands east of Jerusalem, this story seemed perfectly credible. This eastern ruler was given further substance in 1145 by Otto of Freising. He had been told by Hugh, Bishop of Jabala, that 'a certain John, a king and priest who dwells beyond Persia and Armenia in the uttermost East', had overcome the Persians in a three-day battle and would have come to the aid of Jerusalem had not his army been blocked by the River Tigris.

> It is said that he is a lineal descendant of the Magi, of whom mention is made in the Gospel, and that, ruling over the same peoples which they governed, he enjoys such great glory and wealth that he uses no scepter save one of emerald. Influenced by the example of his fathers who came to adore Christ in his manger, he had planned to go to Jerusalem.

> (Mierow 1966:443–4)

Plate 19 One of a series of five capitals intended for the shrine-grotto inside the Church of the Annunciation, Nazareth, but never placed in position. They show scenes from the lives of the Apostles, among which is this romanesque carving of the apocryphal story of the mission of St Matthew to the Ethiopians, 1180s. (Photograph reproduced by permission of Pantheon, Florence.)

Although it has been shown to have been forged in Germany as part of an imperial propaganda campaign, a further letter of *c.*1164, purporting to have been sent by Prester John to the Byzantine Emperor Manuel Comnenus, added many choice details to the legend, describing a land of almost perfect harmony and abundant material comforts. The pope's reply in 1177 was probably part of the same propaganda battle, but this did not prevent it from adding further gloss to the tale (Hamilton 1985). It was still current at the time of the Fifth Crusade, for in 1221 the papal legate, Pelagius, apparently believed that Prester John or a descendant of his was about to come to the aid of the Christians, having confused his army with that of the Mongols under Chingis Khan. The Mongol Empire in fact enabled the Christians to seek him out, but they did not find him. Nevertheless, the legend was so powerful that it continued to be part of the medieval world picture in the later middle ages, although by this time Prester John had been transferred to Ethiopia (believed to be joined to India by the enclosed Indian Ocean).

Medieval maps sometimes attempted to convey this received picture of world geography, even if only in a diagrammatic form. The so-called T-O maps showed a circle divided into three continents, the largest of which, Asia, occupied the upper semi-circle. However, such maps were not necessarily created for practical purposes; religious, philosophical or historical beliefs dominated the thinking of their makers (Edson 1997). Thus the desire to show the symbolic importance of Jerusalem placed Christ as ruler of the world and Jerusalem as its centre, a position which bears no relation to the concept of a sphere divided into northern and southern hemispheres, each with balanced climatic zones (see Plate 20). Jerusalem offered contemporaries a very potent image, especially after its capture in 1099. Pilgrims and crusaders often included a description of the holy places in their accounts of their journeys. The author of the *Gesta Francorum*, for instance, describes Golgotha, the place of the Crucifixion. He then continues:

> From thence, a stone's throw to the west, is the place where Joseph of Arimathea buried the holy Body of the Lord Jesus, and on this site there is a church, beautifully built by Constantine the king. From Mount Calvary the navel of the world lies thirteen feet to the west.
>
> (R. Hill 1962:98)

The special place of the city in the medieval world picture was reinforced by the glittering city described in Revelation which 'had the radiance of some priceless jewel'. Confusion between the heavenly and earthly city was therefore common, as Otto of Freising shows:

> John, therefore, to overthrow all these mistaken views, first strove to narrate the condemnation of the wicked city and its descent into the final fire; and afterwards when heaven and earth had been made new, he added – speaking of the glory of the heavenly, not the earthly Jerusalem – 'And I saw the holy city, new Jerusalem, coming down out of heaven'. How could he call that city holy which he had previously called Babylon, which slew the prophets and stoned those who had been sent to her? How could he call that city new which still continues under the old law? How, finally, could he claim that the city which was ever of the earth, earthy, descends out of heaven?
>
> (Mierow 1966:491–2)

Otto's distinction between the heavenly and the earthly cities was intended to make clear the difference between the unchanging eternal world of Heaven and the transient world below where, since human beings carried the burden of original sin, society faced the possibility of descent into chaos. Because of the chaotic power of sin, St Augustine allowed that secular rulers were necessary for the purpose of curbing it, a concept very clearly set out in the Proemium of the *Liber Augustalis*, the law collection promulgated by Emperor Frederick II in 1231.

> Because of the blemish of transgression implanted in them by their parents [i.e. Adam and Eve], they [men] conceived hatred among themselves for one another. They divided up the common ownership of property by natural law. Thus man, whom God created virtuous and simple, did not hesitate to involve himself in disputes. Therefore, by this compelling necessity of things and not less by the inspiration of Divine Providence, princes of nations were created

Plate 20 The fundamental importance of Jerusalem, in both the literal and the symbolic sense, is demonstrated by this map showing the city as the centre of the world. English Psalter, *c*.1265. (Photograph reproduced by permission of the British Library, MS. Add. 28681, f. 9.)

through whom the license of crimes might be corrected. And these judges of life and death for mankind might decide, as executors in some way of Divine Providence, how each man should have fortune, estate, and status.

(Powell 1971:3–5)

Human beings, nevertheless, occupied a key position in the hierarchy. According to Otto of Freising:

Every man is capable of reason, to the end that he may acknowledge God as his creator, and not overlook his own deeds because his heart is blind or fail to hear because his ears are deaf. In brief, the very form of man's body, not inclined towards the ground as the bodies of other animals are, but upright that he may give heed to the heavens, proves that man was created for this end. Besides, the inner man, made after the likeness of his Creator, receives the means of investigating the truth not only in relation to other beautiful and great creatures outside himself but also in relation to himself, because he has 'the light of the Lord's countenance set upon him as a seal'.

(Mierow 1966:402)

It followed that people should use their faculties to try to create an ordered society and, of course, the hierarchy of the universe presented a model which humankind could strive to imitate on earth.

In the twelfth century, however, the secular ruler whose position most closely corresponded with the model was the emperor. This fact, once the papacy had asserted its claim to the headship of the Christian commonwealth, inevitably led to prolonged debate over their respective roles. Just as in the sixth century, Justinian had expended all his resources in an effort to re-establish the Roman Empire so that once again human political and social organisation might form a unity imitating the heavenly prototype, so too did the German emperors see themselves as heirs to the Roman and Carolingian polity. In the words of Otto of Freising, 'the story of all realms or peoples returns to the condition of the Roman empire as to its source' (Mierow 1955:27), and over seventy years later, Frederick II's constitutions asserted that the head of the hierarchy on earth was the emperor, 'whom he elevated beyond hope of man to the pinnacle of the Roman empire and to the sole distinction of the other kingdoms at the right hand of divine power' (Powell 1971:4).

In the early fourteenth century, the concept still retained a grip on the imagination. Dante supported Henry VII's fruitless invasion of Italy for this reason and in *De Monarchia* (probably written between 1309 and 1313) again put forward the idea of the universal monarch:

The temporal monarchy that is called the Empire is a single Command exercised over all persons in time, or at least in those matters which are subject to time. Doubts about temporal monarchy give rise to three principal questions. The first is the question whether it is necessary for the well-being of the world. The second is whether it was by right that the Roman people took upon itself the office of the Monarch. And thirdly, there is the question whether the Monarch's authority is derived directly from God or from some vicar or minister of God.

(Nicholl and Hardie 1954:4)

To the first two questions he gave an affirmative answer, and to the third replied that such authority was indeed received directly from God, although he did finally concede that the emperor was subject to the pope in certain matters, since there was a connection between the earthly and the eternal life. Dante was influenced by both his intellectual background and his civil experience: a universal ruler was necessary in order to imitate the single ruler of heaven and was the only power capable of providing a solution to the problems of internecine strife, problems which hindered human beings from achieving the potentialities with which God had endowed them (Reeves 1965:86–92).

Dante's vision of the ideal political order was intellectually satisfying and in certain circles the idea of Empire continued to exercise a strong attraction. But it had never been acceptable to everybody. Despite providing a more complete analysis of the integrated body politic than anybody else had hitherto, John of Salisbury had still been highly indignant at the idea that it was encompassed within the imperial 'family'. In a letter commenting on the predetermined election of the anti-pope Victor IV at the Council of Pavia in 1160, he expressed his fear that the emperor 'should by his guile outwit and undermine the serenity of our prince' (Henry II), and went on to declaim, 'Who has appointed the Germans to be judges of the nations? Who has given authority to brutal and headstrong men that they should set up a prince of their own choosing over the heads of the sons of men?' He thought that he knew well what to expect, since he had been in Rome at the time of Frederick Barbarossa's accession and had seen 'his intolerable pride' (Millor and Butler 1986:206).

During the thirteenth century competing theories of political and social organisation gained in strength. The most decisive moment was the arrival in the west of Aristotle's *Politics*, translated by William of Moerbeke in 1260, for this offered a view of a political structure not derived from the reflection of the unified heavenly hierarchy, but one which flowed naturally from the coalescence of the various communities that made up human society. Thomas Aquinas accepted this formulation, arguing that 'it is natural for man, more than for any other animal, to be a social and political animal, to live in a group' (Phelan 1949:4). By the early fourteenth century such views had become an integral part of the continuing debate about the proper religious and political order, providing a theoretical justification for the independent state and sparking off discussion about the best form of direction for such a state. This was not only a consequence of the reappearance of the *Politics*; social and political attitudes had already been changing in a way which made it easier to accommodate (Post 1964). Although the notion of an imperial structure was compatible with Augustine's view of secular power, he had not actually prescribed this as the only proper earthly political order; it was equally possible that a variety of states could exist. Moreover, John of Salisbury had also seen the state as a natural organism, even though his concept of hierarchy was essentially static. By the thirteenth century this idea meshed with the increasing interest in 'natural man' which can be seen in both philosophy and art. The way, therefore, had already been prepared for a justification for monarchical or city-states as forces for positive good rather than simply regrettable necessities, a changing concept of the earthly world which contrasts with the more static view of the Ptolemaic universe beyond.

It was natural that human beings should strive to interpret historical changes, for they knew that they had occurred in the past, that they themselves were experiencing them in the present, and that therefore they would occur in the future, and so they sought for them a convincing framework (see Plate 14). They had two well-tried models which they could use, depending upon their ultimate purpose in writing. For histories of political events and descriptions of the fate of individuals, rulers and dynasties, the 'Boethian' approach was the most convenient, but when authors reached out towards a universalist scheme encompassing human history from the Creation to the Last Judgement, they needed to turn to the 'Augustinian' structure (Pickering 1965:2). The most ambitious historians, like Otto of Freising, sought to combine the two into a complete historical scheme.

Boethius (480–524) was a Roman consul who had served Theodoric the Ostrogoth, but who was imprisoned (and eventually executed) for alleged treason. While in prison he wrote *The Consolation of Philosophy* in which Philosophia tells him that he should not rely on Fortune which is, by definition, changeable. If he continues to do so, then he must be prepared to accept the consequences of adherence to 'the changing faces of the random goddess' (Watts 1969:55). From Boethius medieval commentators derived the striking image of the Wheel of Fortune, an image which they especially applied to the vicissitudes of political power. Fulcher of Chartres, for example, observing the uneven military career of King Baldwin I of Jerusalem and particularly sensitive to sudden change because of the dangers of living in a frontier society, refers explicitly to this source.

> Boethius on this point says, 'Although you see your hopes fall short of accomplishment, still there is a just order of things, and a perverse order is a matter of confusion in your mind. But the foolish man expects a turn of fortune, not what is deserved'.
>
> (Ryan 1969:174)

For Otto of Freising it was

> a sport most pitiable, a sport described by philosophers as the sport of fortune, that after the manner of a wheel makes the highest lowest and the lowest highest, but in real fact a state of things made uncertain in accordance with the nod of a God who exchanges kingdoms.

Otto suggests that instead of being subject to such vagaries, human beings might be challenged instead 'to forsake worldly misery and to seek the true life' (Mierow 1966:370). This point was well taken by the anonymous English crusader who seems to have written the first book of the *Itinerarium*, which Richard of the Temple attached to his account of the Third Crusade. For him this was the only way to explain the rise of Saladin.

> It was the caprice of Fortune that wished for these rapid changes. She raises up a rich man from a pauper, the lofty from the humble, a ruler from a slave. If we measured the value of things by rational judgement and not by general opinion, we would reckon the power that comes from worldly success as worthless, since too often it is the most evil and unworthy people who obtain it.
>
> (Nicholson 1997: 28)

The popularity of the Wheel in the twelfth and thirteenth centuries was no coincidence, for economic change promoted a much greater social fluidity than had been evident in the early middle ages, so that the image of fortunes ever rising and falling seemed particularly pertinent (A. Murray 1978:98–101). Medieval artists soon began to illustrate the idea; by the 1230s it had become a sufficiently common part of their repertoire for the Picard, Villard of Honnecourt, to include a sketch of how it should be drawn in his notebook of interesting architectural and artistic features. In the *Liber ad honorem Augusti*, by the Swabian court poet and chronicler, Peter of Eboli (d. *c*.1220), dating from the 1190s, the Wheel has turned so that Tancred of Lecce, the opponent of the Emperor Henry VI, lies abased at the bottom (see Plate 11).

The illustration is combined with a related theme, that of the Virtues and Vices. Above, Henry receives the symbols of his authority from the Virtues, the weapons representing Fortitude and the book of laws representing Justice. Henry is shown protected by the Virtues from Fortune, who looks up vainly in an attempt to involve him. She fails because Henry refuses to allow himself to be tempted by the Vices. According to Boethius, 'whatever moves any distance from the primary intelligence becomes enmeshed in ever stronger chains of Fate' (Watts 1969:136). In contemporary imperial propaganda, such as *The Play of AntiChrist*, the emperor is portrayed as the repository of all the Virtues, and here he has apparently overcome the inner battle with Vice which, according to the Christian view of the world, was the true condition of humankind. A strong influence on the depiction of the Virtues and Vices was the *Psychomachia* (or Inner Struggle) by the late-fourth-century poet and hymn-writer, Prudentius. His poem describes a great battle between the Virtues and Vices in which they face each other in single combat. After a massive struggle the Virtues eventually win (Male 1961:98–105, 364; Katzenellenbogen 1977:22–250). The moral was clear: human beings' earthly activity was useless unless it related to higher spiritual goals. Early illustrations showed either a symbolic representation of Virtues or versions of the great battle described by Prudentius, but during the twelfth century the influence of the idea of hierarchy provided a means of involving man directly. He was shown climbing Jacob's Ladder (as described in Genesis, Chapter 28), being assailed by the Vices and often falling in the face of assault.

These concepts were familiar at various levels across the whole intellectual and social spectrum, ranging from Peter Abelard, who ascribed the calamities of his life to Lust (for Heloise) and Pride (in his *Treatise on the Unity and Trinity of God*, burnt at Soissons in 1121) (McLaughlin 1967), to the Picard knight, Robert of Clari, who saw God as taking vengeance on the leaders of the Fourth Crusade because of their pride (McNeal 1936:125–6). The seven deadly sins had been established as the opposites of the Virtues by Pope Gregory the Great (d. 604); Pride was the worst because it actually led to the other vices, just as Humility was 'guardian of all the virtues', as William of Tyre expressed it (Babcock and Krey 1941:1:526). The anonymous priest who preached to the soldiers outside Lisbon in 1147 must have been confident that these themes would be familiar to his audience.

> At this point enters pride, the beginning of all sin; and 'the beginning of man's pride is to apostatize from God'. And to the pride of the Devil was added most spiteful envy, in order that he might tempt man to that through which he perceived himself to have been damned. Wherefore it has happened that corrective rather than destructive punishment has been so allotted to man that to whomsoever the Devil has offered himself for the imitation of his pride, the Lord has offered himself for the imitation of his humility.
>
> (David 1976:151)

One interesting effect, however, of the material growth of the twelfth and thirteenth centuries was a slow shift in this perception. Whereas in a world dominated by the Benedictines, whose founder saw their own most important characteristic as humility, pride was quite naturally seen as 'the beginning of all sin', the advent of eremitical groups, reformed monastic orders and, most importantly, the Franciscans, to whom poverty was the central tenet, persuaded many people that Avarice or Cupidity was the worst of all the sins (Little 1971) (see Plate 6). The content of polemical literature, taking sides in the contemporary controversies over the various new forms of religious life, reflects this shift. The anonymous author of the mid-twelfth-century treatise, *Libellus de diversis ordinibus*, speaks tartly about a species of ascetic competitiveness which had grown up.

> Indeed I have heard someone, and (except that it is shameful to say so) several people swollen with empty bombast, slandering the customs of another church and saying: 'What kind of rule is that, where there is so much eating and so little fasting, so little silence and so many courses are always being eaten?'... First they are led to the mountain and, as I might say, to the very peak of pride, and this pride soars so high that it cannot be seen, and since it is not perceived as pride it is believed to be humility; then Christ is despised, in that their neighbour is despised.
>
> (Constable and Smith 1972:36–9)

The Boethian approach was attractive to the ecclesiastical author since it provided many satisfying opportunities to draw out the moral and to dwell on the transitory nature of life on earth, but it lacked the macrocosmic historical scheme which incorporated visions of Creation, Antichrist and the Last Judgement. For this it was necessary to turn to St Augustine. Augustine set down the stages in the process of human salvation in relation to the six days of Creation which, in turn, could be seen in the six ages of man who travelled from infancy to senility. Each of these ages was subdivided like the parts of the day. For Augustine, the period between the Incarnation and the Second Coming which, since the latter had not yet occurred, encompassed the high middle ages, was the sixth and last stage before the Last Judgement; indeed, the evening of the last day had already been reached. Finally, 'after this present age God will rest, as it were, on the seventh day, and he will cause us, who are the seventh day, to find our rest in him' (Bettenson 1984:1091). Translated into contemporary terms, this meant the passage of four great empires which, according to Chapter 7 of the Book of Daniel, would rise and fall until the world's end. Otto of Freising expressed this in the following way:

> We are compelled even against our will to ponder upon the judgements of God and the instability of the world. For behold!... we see earthly pomp and power departing with time, even as the heavens revolve from east to west.... It was in this way that, clearly enough, earthly power passed from Babylon to the Medes, from them to the Persians, afterwards to the Greeks, finally to the Romans, and under the Roman name was transferred to the Franks....
>
> So when the Franks, who were most proficient in warfare, had greatly extended the bounds of their kingdom and had brought Rome, the capital of the world, under their sway... at that time becoming divided against one another... they foreshadowed the final outcome – that the earthly power which, fleeing so

to speak from the east to the west, had at last, so men fancied, found stability and peace, must in accordance with the saying of the Evangelist, be brought to desolation.

(Mierow 1966:357–8)

The universalist scheme necessarily involved the future as well as the past and present. The placing of the history of humankind in the future context was not some cheap form of fortune-telling, but the necessary culmination. In the Preface to his eighth and last book Otto writes:

> The Lord also in the beginning 'creating the heaven and the earth' produced matter that at first was invisible and without form, and afterwards reduced it to order and brought it into the light. We do not think therefore that we are doing amiss if, after enumerating the miseries of this present life, we attempt (in so far as God permits) to treat of the eternal rest of the saints as of light after darkness.
>
> (Mierow 1966:456)

But consideration of the future necessarily affected the present; it needed careful interpretation in relation to the contemporary world. In the 'wrong' hands, after all, it could (and occasionally did) become an agent of social and political instability. Not surprisingly, therefore, most of the reflections on the End are the work of intellectuals within the Church, whose aim was to strengthen the sense of continuity by placing contemporary events within the Christian structure, rather than of revolutionaries seeking to overturn the existing order by exploiting or reflecting popular millennial belief. The way that contemporary events were incorporated varied with the background and allegiances of the author. In the early middle ages interest had centred upon the Empire, but after the eleventh century reform speculation incorporated the papacy as well as or instead of the emperor, while the crusading effort against Islam also helped to stimulate a search for signs of Antichrist. Joachim of Fiore, who more than anyone else laboured to find coherent patterns in the past, present and future, saw some of these signs in his own time, one of which was the revival of Islam under Saladin (McGinn 1979:1–36, 94–143).

One particularly interesting attempt to fit contemporary events into this structure in a way which suited the author's allegiances can be seen in the *Play of AntiChrist*, dating from *c.*1160 and probably performed at the Hohenstaufen court. It is blatant imperial propaganda, but presented within an apocalyptic structure in the Augustinian mould. The story is that of the Emperor of the Romans who is intending to restore the world to imperial rule (the rightful order of things), despite the slackness of some of his predecessors. He therefore sends messengers to each king, beginning with the Franks, saying:

> The writings of historians tell us
> That once the whole world was a Roman fief.
> The strength of early men accomplished this,
> But the neglect of their successors squandered it.
> Though under them the imperial power fell,
> The majesty of our might shall win it back.

The imperial ambassadors then sing before the King of the Franks:

> The Emperor of the Romans sends his greetings
> To his renowned ally, the Frankish King.
> We trust, your grace, that you already know
> You are obliged to bow to Roman law
> Whence the decision of supreme empire,
> Forever binding and forever feared
> Now seeks you out. Therefore we summon you
> Into the Emperor's service, and we demand
> That you come quickly under his command.

The imperial goal is achieved with very little opposition except from the King of the Franks and the Heathen, both of whom he defeats. The emperor then goes to Jerusalem and gives up his crown to God, but now Antichrist appears and with the help of his servants, the Hypocrites, convinces the kings of the world that he is divine, even the King of the Teutons, who is more circumspect than the others. The prophets Elijah and Enoch, however, now appear and show the truth, at which Antichrist, overcome by rage, has them executed, but he cannot triumph because, as he summons all to worship him, God strikes him down with a thunderbolt and the play is finished (J. Wright 1967:71).

Although the Augustinian structure retained its hold on people's perceptions throughout the centuries under consideration, Jacques Le Goff has suggested there were nevertheless signs of its disintegration, significant for the future. Once again the challenge came from the effects of economic change, for time as seen by the merchant involved day-to-day calculations so that he could manipulate situations to favour himself. In Le Goff's words, 'time was pliable, and it was in this pliability that profit and loss resided'. There are distinct indications of this in Italian painting of the early fourteenth century, for the use of perspective and spatial relationships between individuals, as well as the appearance of portraits of individuals, contrasts with a world conceived in terms of the flat and eternal hierarchies of earlier art. As Le Goff sees it, the development of the practice of confession in the thirteenth century represents an attempt by the Church to encompass mercantile activity within its own biblical structure of time, but he argues that by the late Middle Ages, the ecclesiastical guardians of 'the traditional concept of time in Christian theology' could no longer hold their ground (Le Goff 1980:29–42).

As has been seen, medieval people were very respectful towards past authorities. The patterns of thought of the Greeks and the Romans and the authority of the Bible were fundamental in the framework within which they viewed the world. Nevertheless, the Chartrian scholar, William of Conches (d. 1154), maintained that it was necessary to seek a reason for everything and that recourse to supernatural intervention was needed only when events manifestly contradicted natural laws. The structure of received knowledge and faith was not therefore incompatible with observation. His contemporary, Adelard of Bath (d. *c.*1150) (who himself influenced William) was more adventurous, travelling extensively in Syria, Sicily and Spain in his efforts to gather scientific and mathematical knowledge from the Islamic world. In his *Natural Questions* (*Quaestiones naturales*), probably written in the mid-1130s, he presents himself as a reluctant expositor of what he had learned. This reluctance was not because he lacked confidence in his knowledge and approach but, he claimed, because of contemporary attitudes.

> The present generation has this ingrained weakness, that it thinks that nothing discovered by the moderns is worthy to be received – the result of this is that if I wanted to publish anything of my own invention I should attribute it to someone else, and say, 'Someone else said this, not I.'

For Adelard 'authorities' were comparable to a yoke, used to lead animals. In the treatise, written in the form of a dialogue between himself and his nephew, he accuses certain people of 'arrogating to themselves the title of authorities', thus enabling them 'to insinuate into men of low intellect the false instead of the true' (Gollancz 1920:91–2, 98–9).

Nevertheless, it is evident from the writing of Otto of Freising among others that these phenomena were not necessarily always perceived in the same way or at the same level by everyone. If, for instance, as William Durand, Bishop of Mende (d. 1296), following Gregory the Great, wrote, 'Pictures and ornaments in churches are the lessons and the scriptures of the laity', they were so only in so far as these laymen had the capacity to understand their meaning (E.G. Holt 1957:121). Beyond their literal appearance, it would have been necessary to explain their deeper meanings, where possible, so that a moral might be drawn or, with more difficulty, an allegorical or anagogical interpretation extracted. The common representation of the Four Evangelists, for example, as the four living creatures of the man (Matthew), the lion (Mark), the ox (Luke) and the eagle (John) surrounding a mandorla in the centre of which God is set, was open to interpretation in several different ways and is among the range of such subjects treated in depth by Durand (Male 1961:36–7) (see Plate 14).

In the end, no society can be entirely consistent – the Cistercian monks at Bordesley Abbey who made and sold arrow heads show that (Astill 1993:178) – but the outstanding characteristic of society between the mid-eleventh and the early fourteenth centuries was the determined attempt by Christians to create from their faith, their past inheritance and their own observation, a comprehensible, comprehensive and ordered picture of the cosmos.

17

Intellectual life

Peter Abelard was born at Le Pallet, near Nantes, the eldest son of a minor Breton noble, in about 1079. According to his own witness he was provided with a good education by a father who, although a soldier, had a passion for learning, 'until I was so carried away by my love of learning that I renounced the glory of a soldier's life … and withdrew from the court of Mars in order to kneel at the feet of Minerva'. His parallel of the lives of the soldier and the scholar is a just one, for he goes on to describe his choice in martial language. 'I preferred the weapons of dialectic to all the other teachings of philosophy, and armed with these I chose the conflicts of disputation instead of the trophies of war.' Again, just like the noble 'youth', who set out in search of adventure and material gain or, even more, on crusade, he left home accoutred for intellectual battle (Duby 1977:176–7). 'I began to travel about in several provinces disputing, like a true peripatetic philosopher, wherever I had heard there was a keen interest in the art of dialectic' (Radice 1974:58). By the age of 16 he had already begun these travels, having made his way to Loches where he studied under the nominalist philosopher, John Roscelin.

Loches, however, was a relatively minor city, and within the next five years Abelard reached Paris, which was already showing signs of emerging as an important educational centre. Here he joined the cathedral school at Notre-Dame, attracted by the reputation of William of Champeaux, the most famous realist philosopher of his day. The relationship was not a happy one.

> I stayed in his school for a time, but though he welcomed me at first he soon took a violent dislike to me because I set out to refute some of his arguments and frequently reasoned against him. On several occasions I proved myself his superior in debate.
>
> (Radice 1974:58)

The result was that Abelard set up his own schools, first at Melun and then at Corbeil, but the work involved seems to have led to a temporary nervous breakdown so that he returned to Brittany for a while. However, by 1108 he was back in Paris where, having quarrelled once more with William of Champeaux, he created another school at Mont Sainte-Geneviève. By his late twenties he had become well known as a teacher and philosopher, able to attract students to himself through his reputation.

His chief study was logic or dialectic, one of the seven liberal arts inherited by the twelfth century from the Roman world. The basic Roman syllabus of the trivium (grammar, rhetoric and dialectic) and the quadrivium (arithmetic, geometry, astronomy and music) was becoming the means by which medieval students would approach the two key subjects of the period, theology and law. While rhetoric had been crucial to the sophisticated Roman, called upon to perform in the Senate and the law courts, dialectic exercised a powerful attraction for men like Abelard, whose logical and organised minds sought to clarify and systematise the mass of often contradictory material inherited from Rome and the Christian Fathers and imperfectly transmitted through the disintegrating culture of the late Roman period. It is not surprising to find therefore that Abelard was attracted by the idea of using the skills that he had learned in the study of issues fundamental to contemporary society, the nature of God and the interpretation of Christian revelation, for the answers to such questions had direct application to the conduct of daily life. In short, he set out to become a theologian. To achieve this, in 1113 he went to the cathedral school at Laon, to the north-east of Paris, headed by the master, Anselm of Laon. But he was no more impressed than he had been by William of Champeaux.

> I therefore approached this old man, who owed his reputation more to long practice than to intelligence or memory. Anyone who knocked at his door to seek an answer to some question went away more uncertain than he came.... He had a remarkable command of words but their meaning was worthless and devoid of all sense. The fire he kindled filled his house with smoke but did not light it up.
>
> (Radice 1974:62)

Despite, or perhaps because of, his low opinion of contemporary teaching standards, Abelard now felt confident that he could earn his living as a teacher of philosophy and theology in Paris. From this time, too, he began to write; in *c*.1114 he produced an early version of his *Introduction to Theology*. However, it is noticeable from his account how important oral transmission had been. Abelard had learned his skills by debates, disputations, lectures; indeed, it has been argued that at this period, 'both text and image are secondary representations', essentially referring back to speech (Camille 1985:32), so that Abelard's writings should be seen in the context of a culture in which reading was not primarily a silent and internalised process, but one in which the material concerned was proclaimed aloud for discussion, explanation and questioning. Essentially Abelard remained the public jouster, as contentious and competitive as his secular and knightly contemporaries.

Moreover, also like contemporary seculars, Abelard was driven not only by ambition and aggression, but he found, rather to his surprise, by sexual desire as well.

> But success always puffs up fools with pride, and worldly security weakens the spirit's resolution and easily destroys it through carnal temptations. I began to think myself the only philosopher in the world, with nothing to fear from anyone, and so I yielded to the lusts of the flesh.
>
> (Radice 1974: 65)

This is a reference to his relationship with Heloise, the 17-year-old niece of Fulbert, a canon of Notre-Dame. In *c*.1117 he took lodgings at Fulbert's house, supposedly as

Heloise's teacher. He seduced her, Fulbert found out and drove him out, but Abelard continued to see her and she became pregnant. A child was born in secret in Brittany. Abelard then offered marriage, but it was agreed with Fulbert that this should be kept secret, presumably not to prejudice Abelard's career, for he could have looked for no advancement in the Church (and therefore in his intellectual pursuits) as a non-celibate. In fact Fulbert was 'anxious to seek satisfaction for the dishonour done to him' and spread the news, becoming abusive and violent when Heloise tried to stop him. Abelard had her taken to a nunnery at Argenteuil for protection, but Fulbert appears to have interpreted this as a device for putting her aside and took vengeance when, one night, members of his family bribed their way into Abelard's lodgings and castrated him. These dramatic events led to Abelard becoming a monk at St Denis, while Heloise, much against her will, was persuaded to take vows at Argenteuil.

Abelard then continued his intellectual career, apparently oblivious of Heloise's feelings. He did not subside into a peaceful and contemplative monastic existence; indeed, the whole tenor of his life had been that of active participation in the schools which were urban and cathedral-centred rather than rural and monastic. However, his *Treatise on the Unity and Trinity of God* turned the personal rivalries of his youth into official Church condemnation at the Council of Soissons in 1121, for the impetus for the action against him seems to have come from associates of Anselm of Laon. The council ordered the book to be burned. In the treatise Abelard tackles the problem of the nature of universals, which had provoked contemporary debate between the Realist and Nominalist schools, to both of whose teachings he had been exposed at Laon and Loches. The Realists ultimately derived their position from the limited corpus of Platonic writings then available; Aristotle was the intellectual progenitor of the Nominalists. Plato had declared that the only true realities were ideal 'forms', whereas Aristotle had believed that only individual things were fully real. Abelard found problems with both positions, since the Realist view manifestly failed to take account of the difference between individuals, whereas the Nominalist position threatened the very concept of the Trinity, seeming to deny its unity and bringing it close to tritheism. Abelard argued that individual phenomena existed, reconciling the individual with the Idea through the notion of the concept, which incorporates the features common to individuals within a group. A modern parallel might be the use of the term 'set' in mathematics, meaning a collection of (individual) numbers which can be treated as an entity. In the final analysis, however, these concepts were expressed in words simply because it was convenient to do so, and neither had any reality beyond this, nor were capable of describing the nature of God. Not surprisingly, the Realists, who believed that the Ideas existing in the mind of God were the foundations of Creation, seized on these views as a means of having their former tormentor condemned. On the face of it, such disputes were divorced from everyday life, but since the solution chosen determined fundamental perceptions of the Deity and of the material world in the twelfth century, their importance transcended what to the modern mind might appear to be merely a kind of philosophical game. In fact, the modern historian faces a similar problem, as he ponders the relationship between a term like 'feudalism' and the thousands of individuals who held land and jurisdictional rights and owed military service. For the 'nominalist' historian 'feudalism' possesses no external reality whatsoever, and since it often misleads, its value as a 'term of convenience' might also be regarded as highly doubtful.

After Soissons Abelard pressed on with the dialectical approach – it was after all a respectable method, already applied in the less sensitive area of canon law – but he did take care to explain his purposes. In his famous *Sic et Non*, the earliest version of which probably appeared in 1122, but was constantly reworked afterwards, he set down 158 questions on theological problems, each with the authorities pro and con, and invited the student to seek the truth by the application of the dialectical method. In his preface, however, he was meticulous in explaining that the exercise concerned 'the various dicta of the holy fathers', which no less a person than Augustine had warned could be erroneous or contradictory, and not the Old and New Testaments. 'The fathers make a very careful distinction between the Scriptures and later works. They advocate a discriminating, not to say suspicious, use of the writings of their own contemporaries' (Herlihy 1968:205–7).

In personal matters, however, Abelard continued to display his ability to attract trouble. His questioning mind exposed to the community of St Denis the fact that their patron saint had been wrongly identified with past figures, a piece of research for which he received no thanks from his fellow monks. He therefore obtained permission to set up a hermitage to the east of Paris at Nogent-sur-Seine, where he established a small house known as the Paraclete, a word used in the Bible to mean Holy Ghost. 'It had been founded and dedicated in the name of the Holy Trinity, but because I had come there as a fugitive and in the depths of my despair had been granted some comfort by the grace of God, I named it the Paraclete, in memory of this gift' (Radice 1974:90–1). Despite these consolations and despite his continuing attraction for students, he could not overcome feelings of persecution and, apparently to escape his enemies, in 1126 he accepted the abbacy of St Gildas, a monastery on a remote part of the Breton coast. This only exacerbated his misery, for the monks were so hostile to his attempts at reform that, he claimed, they even tried to murder him. His *Historia Calamitatum*, written in 1132 in the form of a letter of consolation to a friend, seems to have been an attempt to gain dispensation to leave St Gildas.

Certainly by 1135 Abelard was back teaching in Paris and there followed a very productive period both in the writing of new work like the *Ethics* and the expanding and rewriting of his *Christian Theology* (originally c.1123–4), *Introduction to Theology* and *Sic et Non*. In the late 1130s, however, he was again in conflict with authority. This time St Bernard was alerted by a complaint from his friend, William of St Thierry, who laid aside his own work of biblical commentary in order to combat the threat. William set out various errors which he alleged Abelard had made; Bernard tried to persuade Abelard to retract. On the contrary, this time Abelard determined to have it out with Bernard in open disputation. This was to take place at the Council of Sens in 1140, but Bernard, aware that he was no match for Abelard as a dialectician, convinced members of the council of Abelard's theological errors the day before. Abelard was probably aware of this and instead of defending himself appealed to Rome. His works were condemned and he was excommunicated. Abelard actually set out for Rome, but en route he stayed at Cluny where Peter the Venerable persuaded him to settle. He spent the last years of his life as a Cluniac monk, the sharpness of his mind undiminished as can be seen in his *Dialogue between a Philosopher, a Jew and a Christian*. He died in c.1142.

When Abelard died, twenty-two years had passed since he and Heloise had entered monastic life. But in 1129 Heloise and her fellow-nuns had been pushed out of their house at Argenteuil by Suger, Abbot of St Denis, as part of his drive to enforce his abbey's rights, and during the next two years Abelard had helped her establish a community at the Paraclete instead. There appears to have been little personal content in their meetings at this period, but the writing of Abelard's letter of consolation in *c.*1132 provoked an explosion which transformed this. Abelard's letter was written not to Heloise, but to a monastic 'friend', and belongs to a distinct genre in which the writer is required to stress his calamities so that the recipient may take comfort from the knowledge that another is worse off than he (Southern 1970:86–104).

The letter, moreover, was not simply a private communication; Abelard intended it for wider circulation and this is probably why Heloise saw it. Although there has been a long (and unfinished) controversy over the authenticity of the exchange of letters that appear to have followed, most modern authorities now accept that Abelard and Heloise were the authors (Brooke 1989:93–102). The correspondence expanded to eight letters in all. In the course of these, Heloise tells Abelard that he has neglected her and that he ought to be sending some consolation to her and the nuns of the Paraclete, since Abelard's letter has 'greatly increased our own feeling of desolation'. Abelard's rather complacent response that his failure to provide comfort or advice 'must not be attributed to indifference on my part but to your own good sense, in which I have always had such confidence that I did not think anything was needed', was quickly upset by her reply in which she presents him with her inner tensions in a manner which he could not ignore. Outwardly, she was pious, but inwardly she was still tormented by the past, by a sexual frustration which produced fantasies even while she was praying (Radice 1974:110–11, 119, 132–4). Thereafter Abelard took time and trouble to provide consolation in the form of letters of instruction concerning the role of the Paraclete and the role of women in monastic life, as well as writing a large number of hymns and sermons for her. Heloise, for her part, never referred to her own inner tensions again, but the letters convey the strong sense that the intellectual and emotional concerns of the individual, male or female, were becoming matters of serious and central concern in the twelfth-century mind.

Abelard's career is worth close study not only because of his evident greatness as a philosopher and logician, but also because it epitomises the profound changes taking place in the medieval intellectual landscape of the twelfth century. Although some of Abelard's work is abstract, and not all of it had long-term influence, nevertheless his life was bound up with the day-to-day realities of human relationships, both in his study and teaching and in his personal ties with Heloise. These relationships in turn reflect the wider changes taking place in the development of education, in the application of logic to the advanced subjects of law and theology, and in the appearance of humanism in the sense of a growing interest in human beings, their relationship to God, each other, and their own motives and emotions.

During Abelard's lifetime there was an educational revolution. It laid the basis for the huge increase in works of learning, literature and art that took place in the twelfth and thirteenth centuries, affecting every fact of life from governmental record-keeping to private religious devotion. When Abelard was born the main educational provision was in the monastic schools, where limited numbers of pupils drawn from the privileged classes, together with oblates sometimes coming from humbler backgrounds, pored over their Latin primers and the basic curriculum of the liberal arts. These schools still provided social and political leaders in Abelard's time, but the monasteries were beginning to lose their monopoly, for the provision of schools was an integral part of the reformation of cathedral chapters in the late eleventh century. Abelard's jousts took place in the cathedral schools and his students moved quite easily from place to place, unfettered by monastic restrictions. The extent to which monastic education had been marginalised by the mid-century can be seen in Otto of Freising's description of St Bernard's attempts to cope with Abelard and the theologian, Gilbert de la Porrée, Bishop of Poitiers.

> Now the aforesaid abbot was both zealous in his devotion to the Christian religion and somewhat credulous in consequence of a habitual mildness, so that he had an abhorrence of teachers who put their trust in worldly wisdom and clung too much to human argument. If anything at variance with the Christian faith were told him concerning anybody, he would readily give ear.
>
> (Mierow 1955:82)

Abelard himself made a significant contribution to the fame of Paris which began to attract ever larger numbers of students anxious to learn about the new logical methods and their relevance to theology. The openness of these schools could not of course escape the influence of their economic environment any more than the monasteries could. The masters quickly became dissatisfied with a system in which the right of granting the *licentia docendi*, the licence to teach, rested with the head of the cathedral chapter, and began to demand full powers to examine and grant licences. Education was expanding like trade, and like trade offered the possibility of profit to those able to cater for the new tastes. The following decree, issued by Alexander III at the Third Lateran Council in 1179, reflects both this increasing demand and what were coming to be seen as abuses which accompanied it.

> Since the church of God as a kindly mother is held to provide for those needs which pertain to physical welfare and those which contribute to the progress of souls, lest the opportunity of reading and education be denied poor children who cannot be aided by the resources of their parents, let some sufficient benefice be set aside in every cathedral church for a master who shall teach the clergy of the same church and poor scholars gratis, whereby the need for a teacher shall be met and the way to knowledge opened to learners.... And for the permission to teach [the *licentia docendi*] let no one demand any fee whatever, or ask anything from teachers under the cover of some custom, or forbid any fit person to teach if he seeks permission.
>
> (Thorndike 1944:21)

The intellectual and artistic impetus of the twelfth century was not confined to one region. Paris became central to the study of theology, but in southern Europe other cities became famous for law and medicine. Bologna, ideally situated on the trade routes of northern and central Italy, became a bustling commercial centre, very much in tune with contemporary needs and trends. The great conflict of empire and papacy had immediate impact in such a city, which responded by the expansion of the study of canon and Roman law, vital tools in the struggle. There was no single centre of learning within the city, since Gratian, whose canon law textbook, the *Decretum*, appeared in *c*.1140, lived at the monastery of San Felice to the west, while Irnerius, the pioneer of the study of Justinian's law codes, probably began the revival of Roman law at the church of San Stefano, on the other side of the city. The Mediterranean region was particularly sensitive to influences from past and contemporary civilisations. At Salerno in southern Italy and Montpellier in Provence this receptiveness stimulated existing studies of medicine. At Salerno there was a continuous tradition and a past literature of Greek medicine which received new impetus in the later eleventh century from Arabic works or Greek works with Arabic glosses. The translations of the monk Constantinus Africanus, himself of Arab descent, were slowly incorporated into the curriculum at Salerno, so that by the late twelfth century the standard texts included not only the Greeks, Hippocrates and Galen, but also works such as those of Isaac Judaeus. Salerno was well known for its practical demonstrations of anatomy and it remained an important centre for treatment. Nevertheless, the absorption of the texts was accompanied by an interest in the dialectical method, a trend which encouraged an increased concentration on theory in the higher study of medicine. Montpellier was equally open to outside influences, especially from the rich culture of Spain with its three religions. In particular, Jewish scholars forced out of the peninsula by the Almohade invasions brought access to Arabic medical and scientific literature.

Both the method and the content of Abelard's work exemplify contemporary trends, for the twelfth century saw a developing relationship between spoken and written communication. This underlines how a division between 'academic' and 'practical' concerns can sometimes be misleading. The most common form of teaching was by lecture and by formal disputation, both because of the fundamental importance of oral culture and of memory and because of the high cost of books and manuscripts. Even when written or illustrated versions of texts were produced they reflected this oral culture; it has been shown, for instance, that charters became generally acceptable only because for a long period they retained clear signs of their origins as spoken word (Clanchy 1979:226). Even though Abelard and his students were *litterati*, that is communicators in Latin, the spoken word remained important to them. Moreover, the labour of producing books was so great that their cost was bound to be very high (Cipolla 1967:58–62). Nevertheless, so powerful were the forces that demanded what the drafter of one charter called 'the making of lasting writing' in order to overcome 'the unreliability and transience of memory' (Duchesne 1631:237), that neither cultural habit nor economic pressure could stem the flood of written materials which the educational revolution of the twelfth century made possible. Henry I of England, a king with an acute awareness of the changes taking place, took a personal interest in the school at Laon, as well as encouraging the expansion of cathedral schools in England (Chibnall 1986:127–8). Abelard's contempt for the intellectual capacities of Anselm of Laon did not deter a stream of students from travelling to the school which he ran with his brother Ralph. Among these were members of the English Exchequer, sent to learn mathematics from Ralph, who had written a treatise on the use of the abacus (Cochrane 1994:24). From his lofty eminence at the head of the imperial family, Frederick Barbarossa may have looked down on the lesser rules of France, but it is clear that, in the twelfth century, it was to France that German clerics went to be educated, just as the sons of the nobility did in order to imbibe the ethos of knighthood (Leyser 1994a:117–18). By 1200 no ruler, even the most old-fashioned, could afford to be without trained officials and written records, while failure to keep in touch with the methods and content of contemporary academic concerns could seriously undermine the effectiveness of government.

Just as the changing educational environment determined where Abelard was able to pursue his intellectual aspirations, so too were his actual studies in logic and theology shaped by contemporary preoccupations. As with the schools, the beginnings of the revival can be found in the monasteries, most importantly with St Anselm at Bec in

Normandy. Anselm was born in 1033 at Aosta in northern Italy, but had left home after a family quarrel. In 1059 he became a monk at Bec, where he spent most of the rest of his life, apart from the last turbulent years as Archbishop of Canterbury. Anselm's importance arises from his attempts to elucidate the faith by applying the faculty of reason to fundamental questions concerning the nature of God and man's relationship to him. Nobody had tackled such issues in this way since the Church Fathers of the later Roman Empire, and in this sense his work represents a key turning-point in the intellectual revival of the high middle ages. The summit of his achievement was the two works which he called the *Monologion* and the *Proslogion*, completed between 1076 and 1078, shortly before he became abbot (Hopkins and Richardson 1974). Although the *Monologion* was rooted in the *De Trinitate* of St Augustine, nevertheless both books were remarkable for the absence of the conventional references to authorities and, as such, they represent Anselm's own original contribution to the question of the qualities and existence of God, most famously expressed in the ontological argument of the *Proslogion*. Their method and structure reflect Anselm's monastic environment; reason was used to reach conclusions at which Anselm had already arrived through extensive 'argument with himself', as his biographer, Eadmer, put it. Behind this lay his desire to tackle the questions which arose from his teaching in the monastic school. Although therefore Anselm pioneered the application of reason to the faith in the high middle ages, his approach naturally differed from the public confrontations which became familiar in Abelard's world of the schools (Southern 1990:113–37).

Anselm built on what had been salvaged from the past. The seven liberal arts had, like the medieval cosmology, ultimately been dependent for their content upon the learning of the ancient world, deriving from Plato and Aristotle. This learning reached the eleventh and twelfth centuries in partial form via the Church Fathers, especially St Augustine, and two scholars of the late Roman Empire, Boethius (d. 524) and Cassiodorus (d. 583). Further material had been recovered and put together in the seventh century by Isidore, Bishop of Seville (d. 636), who compiled, with the help of other scholars, a great encyclopaedia on a wide range of subjects, the contents of which were heavily plundered by twelfth-century reference hunters. A century after Isidore, the Northumbrian monk, Bede (d. 735) exploited the extensive library at Jarrow to produce a series of biblical commentaries which provided the basis of the quadripartite interpretation, through which the text could be understood and appreciated at different levels: literal, moral, allegorical, and anagogical (or mystical). It was upon these uneven foundations that twelfth-century scholars set about building the intellectual edifice of the high middle ages, although the emphases necessarily changed as the material available grew under the pressure of intellectual inquiry. Plato was particularly influential in the first half of the twelfth century, knowledge of his works being derived from the Neo-Platonists of the later Roman period and through a translation of his work known as the *Timaeus* (a contemporary of Plato after whom the book was named) in which Plato sets out his philosophy of Forms or Ideas in the form of a dialogue. As contact with Muslim civilisation increased, the available Aristotelian corpus was enlarged and, gradually, in the second half of the twelfth century, the attractions of his method of categorising became evident to the systematic minds of the schoolmen. This was not regarded as an end in itself; the aim was to prepare the student for the study of the Vulgate text of the Bible, derived from St Jerome's translation in the fifth century. A standard text had been achieved by the late twelfth century. Through such study there developed the subject of theology, in which knowledge was presented in order to serve the faith and the comprehension of God.

In Abelard's time approaches to theology were not uniform, although the dialectical method adopted first by Anselm had become standard by mid-century, when Peter Lombard (d. 1164), one of Abelard's pupils, used this method for his *Sentences*, although (unlike his teacher) he attempted to find a harmonious answer to the contradictions of the authorities he displayed. Other schools tackled the problems from a different angle. This was particularly true of the scholars from Chartres, whose importance was promoted by its Chancellor, Bernard of Chartres (1119–26). At Chartres there was particular emphasis on Plato: exponents like William of Conches (d. 1154) and Gilbert de la Porrée (d. 1154) attempted to construct a cosmology using the parts of Plato's works which they possessed, and the Bible. On the left bank of the Seine stood the Augustinian Abbey of St Victor (sometimes called the Victorine school, after its most important figure, Hugh of St Victor, d. 1141), where a third approach is discernible. For Hugh all natural knowledge contributed to an understanding of the Scriptures; material creation was valuable because it enabled the student to adopt an allegorical approach to biblical interpretation. From this there developed a whole world of symbolism, particularly evident in medieval art.

Among all these men, however, Abelard remains the most striking figure. This is so for two reasons. First, because in the *Historia Calamitatum* he set down an account of his life more fully than anyone else had done since St Augustine, and second because at an impersonal level, in his *Ethics*, he grappled with the problem of the relationship between human motivation and sin in a comprehensive examination of the moral problems which face every individual. In these senses the *Historia Calamitatum* and the *Ethics* are closely related, demonstrating from different viewpoint the growing emphasis on the importance of the individual and his or her relationship to God and the world around them. They are linked in another way too, for the catharsis provided by the *Historia Calamitatum* was itself a prelude to Abelard's very productive later years, years which included the writing of the *Ethics*. In the *Ethics* Abelard argues against the Augustinian view of original sin transmitted to all humans by Adam and, therefore against the doctrine of penance by which human beings atoned for their sinful acts. Instead, he stressed the importance of motive in determining guilt; people had the power of reason by which they could decide on the validity of an act and could therefore commit or refrain from sin. In its starkest form this could mean that, since they did not realise what they were doing, the crucifiers of Christ could not be said to have properly sinned, since ignorance affected motive (Luscombe 1971:62–3). Despite opposition to this extreme logical postulate – not least from St Bernard – Abelard's general argument can be seen to have had long-term influence in Thomas Aquinas's great compendium, the *Summa Theologica*. Here Thomas makes the distinction between a mortal or grave sin, committed with full knowledge, and a venial or light sin, in which there was some degree of inadvertency.

This stress on Abelard as an individual and on the centrality of internal motivation in his work is not accidental, for it reflects a fundamental change from an earlier age in which little confidence had been invested in the potential of human beings, locked as they were into an environment ruled over by a dominant and vengeful God. While it is true that the structure of the *Historia Calamitatum* is very formal, with each of the seven sections intended to point to a general moral, nevertheless within the restrictions of the genre Abelard provides information about his life, motives and emotions which is 'easily identified as his own' (Bagge 1993b:344). Thus in the first half of the twelfth century men as different as Bernard of Clairvaux, Guibert of Nogent and Guigo of La Grande Chartreuse, all became preoccupied with the problems of the inner self. St Bernard deplored what he believed to be Abelard's arrogant pursuit of a rational explanation of the nature of God, but he was just as convinced as Abelard of the importance of motivation in judging the nature of an external act. Murder occurred when one person struck down another through pride, malice or avarice; but the disinterested killing of the infidel for the Christian faith was a title to glory (Greenia 2000:33–43). For Guigo du Pin, Abbot of La Grande Chartreuse, writing in about 1129, the very idea of an attack upon the infidel was both futile and wrong if the individual concerned was not engaged in his own personal spiritual battle.

> It is pointless to wage war against external enemies without first overcoming internal ones. If we are unable first to subject our own bodies to our wills, then it is extremely shameful and unworthy to wish to put under our control any sort of military force. Who could tolerate our desire to extend our domination abroad over vast tracts of land while we put up with the most ignominious servitude to vices in those minute lumps of earth that are our bodies? O most beloved, let us therefore first to all conquer ourselves so that we may then go forth in safety to combat external enemies; let us rid our minds of vices before we rid lands of pagans.
>
> (Barber and Bate 2002:213)

By the mid-twelfth century 'humanism', in the sense of a stress on the role of people within an ordered universe which stemmed from a God who took human flesh and was crucified for human beings' redemption had become the loom which held together the diverse strands of intellectual, literary and artistic creativity of the period. After *c*.1150 increased access to Greek philosophical and scientific works meant that it was even more important to study the problems arising from this new knowledge in the context of Christian teaching; in short, it offered a creative 'friction' in which scholarship flourished (Southern 1970:47). Moreover, given the development of a system of thought which aspired to encompass the universal order and humankind's place in it, this view was not confined to Christian intellectuals grappling with theoretical theological and moral problems; it was equally pervasive in politics and commerce. During the thirteenth century, for instance, it prepared the way for the view of 'the state' as a natural formation deriving from the community rather than simply as an inadequate remedy for a humankind sunk in sin, just as in commercial transactions growing confidence in a monetary and credit system replaced the literal and cumbersome exchange procedures of the earlier middle ages. Both politics and commerce increasingly relied upon the human instruments of documentation for such systems to succeed. John of Salisbury best represents this broad humanism. He was educated in the Parisian schools, yet had had much practical experience of ecclesiastical and governmental affairs, and travelled widely to the most important intellectual and political centres of the west. A master of Latin style and more deeply imbued with the classics than any of his contemporaries, his works reflect the many facets of his world, for they include a treatise on logic (the *Metalogicon*), on government (the *Policraticus*) and on the papal court (the *Historia Pontificalis*), as well as a great letter collection written at a level not achieved since the first century AD.

During the thirteenth century the rapid development of the schools, the sharpening of logical method and the enlargement of the scope of the higher subjects, underwent a process of refinement. The increasingly formal award of the *licentia docendi* was accompanied by a process of institutional consolidation which began to turn the leading *studia*, like Paris and Bologna, into universities. The scholars of Bologna had received Frederick Barbarossa's protection as early as 1158, for the emperor thought it appropriate to defend against all injuries those 'by whose knowledge the world is illuminated in obedience to God and to us, his ministers, [and] the life of the subjects is shaped' (Weiland 1893:1:249). He meant, of course, that the study of Roman law provided him with an ideological basis for his imperialism which he could use to counter papal claims to superiority. In 1200 Philip II conceded full clerical privileges to the masters and students of Paris; in 1215 Innocent III granted them the right to elect their own officials, a concession which largely freed them from local clerical control. The authorities saw the academics as a nascent corporation whose trade was learning, and were prepared to find a place for them within the structure like other urban corporations. Indeed, in 1231, Gregory IX referred to the Paris *studium* as 'wisdom's special workshop' (Le Goff 1980:136–40). Nevertheless, the structure was still sufficiently impermanent for the suspension of lectures and a boycott of Paris by the masters in 1229 to be an effective means of bringing pressure. Their return to Paris in 1231 was preceded by the bull *Parens scientiarum*, conceded by Gregory IX, in which the rights of the masters and the legal protection which should be enjoyed by the scholars were explicitly recognised. By this time settled modes of learning and distinctive academic dress had been adopted by the masters of arts and the faculties of theology and law. Even so, they were not entirely free of threats to their position: for most of the thirteenth century the chancellor (representing the cathedral chapter) retained a measure of control over the masters, while from 1229 the presence of the friars, who refused to act in concert with the other masters, was a regular source of friction (Thorndike 1944:35–9).

Although Paris provides the northern archetype for medieval university development, not all cathedral schools expanded into universities, even when they were as important as Chartres, while not all universities emerged from cathedral schools, for several thirteenth-century foundations were created by ecclesiastical and secular authorities, well aware of their value. Toulouse, Rome and Avignon were set up by the papacy; Naples by Frederick II. In other cases the tactic of secession turned into permanent departure, as in the growth of Cambridge from a group of masters who had left Oxford. There was an equal variety of constitutional constructions, whereas in Paris the pace was made by the masters of arts, in Bologna, where many of the scholars were of mature age, the dominant element was the students, who banded together to protect their position from encroachment by the commune.

The willingness of the secular and ecclesiastical authorities not only to support existing *studia*, but also to establish institutions of their own, underlines the value of the thirteenth-century university to the authorities. One of the provisions of the Treaty of Paris of April 1229, imposed on Raymond VII of Toulouse by the French Crown after the Albigensian Crusades, was the establishment of a university at Toulouse, for which the count was obliged to provide 4,000 marks to support fourteen masters for ten years. The hierarchy of subjects, as set down in the salary scales, reflects the intellectual and administrative developments of the previous century: 50 marks per annum for the masters of theology, 30 for canon law, 20 for liberal arts and 10 for grammar (Devic and Vaissète 1973:883–94). Governments needed ever-increasing numbers of trained officials. Hubert Walter's university may have been the Exchequer and a century later, Enguerrand of Marigny, who served Philip the Fair, had risen through a similar practical financial background, but a growing proportion of such officials were university trained. Enguerrand was in fact quite unusual in the midst of a government of lawyers. Indeed, so great was the need for skilled officials and so strong the lure of a successful and possibly lucrative career, that pressures grew even in the twelfth century for the truncation of academic studies to enable careerists to get a foot on the ladder as quickly as possible. It is likely that more students turned away from the study of the pagan classics because they did not see any relevance in them to their own ambitions than ever shunned them because of their Christian scruples (H.O. Taylor 1914:2:159). Despite such attitudes the links between academic study and governmental needs remained strong, for the universities served as repositories of knowledge to which rulers could turn for advice on the central questions of the day. In October 1307 some of the Templars arrested by Philip IV's officials were brought before the masters of Paris who witnessed their confession, while in 1308 and again in 1310 the masters were asked for their opinions on matters of faith and jurisdiction, as the king attempted to find a way to circumvent the prevarication of Pope Clement V (Barber and Bate 2002: 258–63; Lizerand 1964:56–83).

The transformation of the schools into structured institutions was parallelled by the successful integration of the methods and materials of twelfth-century learning into an ordered scholasticism. In the second half of the twelfth century Aristotle's logical writings, known as the *Novum Organon*, had become available. This, together with the commentaries of the Muslim philosophers on the texts – most importantly Ibn Roshd, known as Averroës (d. 1198) – provided Christian intellectuals with the tools for a systematic and comprehensive investigation of the natural world and the position of humankind within it. None of the scholars of the thirteenth century could remain untouched by these changes, but necessarily the extent to which the application of Aristotelian logic and philosophy could legitimately be applied to matters of faith produced some sharply differing reactions. These ranged from the position perhaps best represented by the Franciscans, Alexander of Hales (d. 1245) and St Bonaventura, prepared to use Aristotelian constructions essentially as an adjunct to the faith, to men like Siger of Brabant (d. 1284), who was condemned in 1277 for what was alleged to be the pursuit of Aristotelian philosophy to the detriment of Christian teaching.

Dominican intellectuals led by Albert the Great (d. 1280) and his pupil Thomas Aquinas offered a middle way, although three years after his death even some of Aquinas's propositions were condemned. Nevertheless, with Aquinas the building of a logically ordered hierarchy of knowledge within a Christian framework reached its most sophisticated form, in which the various individual branches of study formed the foundation for a natural philosophy, attainable through human reason and the senses, itself in turn subordinate to divine revelation, surpassing the human capacity for reason. Within such a scheme the fundamental philosophical questions could be subjected to searching analysis. Aquinas was a professor of theology at Paris. He died in 1274 before he could complete his massive scheme to provide a systematic exposition of theology. The following extract from his *Summa Theologica* conveys better than any description the refinement of logical method achieved, while at the same time showing how an ethical issue which was as central to Aristotle and the early Church Fathers as it was to contemporaries – that of the legitimate use of property could be resolved (see Plate 8).

Whether Almsgiving is a matter of precept?

We proceed thus to the Fifth Article:

Objection 1. It would seem that almsgiving is not a matter of precept. For the counsels are distinct from the precepts. Now almsgiving is a matter of counsel, according to Dan. iv, 24: *Let my counsel be acceptable to the King*; (Vulg., *to thee, and*) *redeem thou thy sins with alms*. Therefore almsgiving is not a matter of precept.

Objection 2. Further, it is lawful for everyone to use and to keep what is his own. Yet by keeping it he will not give alms. Therefore it is lawful not to give alms: and consequently almsgiving is not a matter of precept.

Objection 3. Further, whatever is a matter of precept binds the transgressor at some time or other under pain of mortal sin, because positive precepts are binding for some fixed time. Therefore, if almsgiving were a matter of precept, it would be possible to point to some fixed time when a man would commit a mortal sin unless he gave an alms. But it does not appear how this can be so, because it can always be deemed probable that the person in need can be relieved in some other way, and that what we would spend in almsgiving might be needful to ourselves either now or in some future time. Therefore it seems that almsgiving is not a matter of precept.

Objection 4. Further, Every commandment is reducible to the precepts of the Decalogue. But these precepts contain no reference to almsgiving. Therefore almsgiving is not a matter of precept.

On the contrary, No man is punished eternally for omitting to do what is not a matter of precept. But some are punished eternally for omitting to give alms, as is clear from Matth. xxv, 41–43. Therefore almsgiving is a matter of precept.

I answer that, As love of our neighbour is a matter of precept, whatever is a necessary condition to the love of our neighbour is a matter of precept also. Now the love of our neighbour requires that not only should we be our neighbour's well-wishers, but also his well-doers, according to 1 John iii, 18: *Let us not love in word, nor in tongue, but in deed, and in truth*. And in order to be a person's well-wisher and well-doer, we ought to succour his needs: this is done by almsgiving. Therefore almsgiving is a matter of precept.

Since, however, precepts are about acts of virtue, it follows that all almsgiving must be a matter of precept, in so far as it is necessary to virtue, namely, in so far as it is demanded by right reason. Now right reason demands that we should take into consideration something on the part of the giver, and something on the part of the recipient. On the part of the giver, it must be noted that he should give of his surplus, according to Luke xi, 41: *That which remaineth, give alms*. This surplus is to be taken in reference not only to himself, so as to denote what is unnecessary to the individual, but also in reference to those of whom he has charge (in which case we have the expression *necessary to the person* taking the word *person* as expressive of dignity). Because each one must first of all look after himself and then after those over whom he has charge, and afterwards with what remains relieve the needs of others. Thus nature first, by its nutritive power, takes what it requires for the upkeep of one's own body, and afterwards yields the residue for the formation of another by the power of generation.

On the part of the recipient it is requisite that he should be in need, else there would be no reason for giving him alms: yet since it is not possible for one individual to relieve the needs of all, we are not bound to relieve all who are in need, but only those who could not be succoured if we did not succour them. For in such cases the words of Ambrose apply, *Feed him that dies of hunger: if thou hast not fed him, thou hast slain him.* Accordingly we are bound to give alms of our surplus, as also to give alms to one whose need is extreme: otherwise almsgiving, like any other greater good, is a matter of counsel.

Reply Objection 1. Daniel spoke to a king who was not subject to God's Law, wherefore such things as were prescribed by the Law which he did not profess, had to be counselled to him. Or he may have been speaking in reference to a case in which almsgiving was not a matter of precept.

Reply Objection 2. The temporal goods which God grants us, are ours as to the ownership, but as to the use of them, they belong not to us alone but also to such others as we are able to succour out of what we have over and above our needs. Hence Basil says: *If you acknowledge them, viz., your temporal goods, as coming from God, is He unjust because He apportions them unequally? Why are you rich while another is poor, unless it be that you may have the merit of a good stewardship, and he the reward of patience? It is the hungry man's bread that you withhold, the naked man's cloak that you have stored away, the shoe of the barefoot that you have left to rot, the money of the needy that you have buried underground: and so you injure as many as you might help.* Ambrose expresses himself in the same way.

Reply Objection 3. There is a time when we sin mortally if we omit to give alms; on the part of the recipient when we see that his need is evident and urgent, and that he is not likely to be succoured otherwise – on the part of the giver, when he has superfluous goods, which he does not need for the time being, as far as he can judge with probability. Nor need he consider every case that may possibly occur in the future, for this would be to think about the morrow, which Our Lord forbade us to do (Matth. vi, 34), but he should judge what is superfluous and what necessary, according as things probably and generally occur.

Reply Objection 4. All succour given to our neighbour is reduced to the precept about honouring our parents. For thus does the Apostle interpret it (1 Tim. iv, 8) where he says: *Dutifulness is profitable to all things, having promise of the life that now is, and of that which is to come,* and he says this because the precept about honouring our parents contains the promise, *that thou mayest be longlived upon the land* (Exod. xx, 12): and dutifulness comprises all kinds of almsgiving.

(Fathers of the English Dominican Province 1916:9:416–19)

Latin was the vehicle for the flowering of these disciplines, but the renaissance of Latin did not, indeed perhaps could not, have appeared in isolation. In a culture so strongly influenced by oral communication, vernacular languages were certain to retain their importance, even if, as in the case of English, political circumstances pushed some of them into temporary subordination. Because Latin already had an established grammar and vocabulary from the Roman past and because it was used by the clerical and literate class, it was employed for writing earlier and more extensively than the vernaculars, where regional variation and deep-rooted oral tradition remained particularly influential. Nevertheless, especially during the twelfth century, the volume of vernacular literature began to grow, providing a channel through which the laity absorbed epic poetry, chivalric romance and historical works. Moreover, even the most 'literate' in the clerical sense possessed their own vernaculars, and indeed sometimes wrote in that form or at least were influenced by both literary streams in their thoughts and forms of expression. Therefore, although the intellectual concerns of the period have often been seen in class terms – a clergy distinct from the laity by its Latin education – the divisions were not as acute as they might appear, because in so many ways these literatures shared a common background.

Epic stories of male bravery and loyalty, deceit and cowardice, particularly lent themselves to a poetic and oral rendering, and held great appeal to the western European nobility throughout the period, despite competition from the newer forms of romance from the mid-twelfth century onwards. Such action stories are found particularly in Norse, Germanic and Celtic languages, in the Castilian epic of the Cid (Hamilton and Perry 1984), and in the French *chansons de geste*, which gained a strong following because of their preoccupation with conflicts against the Muslims. The most famous of these is the *Song of Roland* (Burgess 1990), a tale which penetrated sufficiently deeply into twelfth-century society for it to be illustrated in such varied media as stained glass, sculpture and manuscript illumination, while the popularity of the name Rolando among the Italian nobility in the thirteenth century shows that the values which it projects had not been entirely superseded by the more fashionable romances, nor were they exclusive to France (Larner 1980:101). It tells the story of an attack on the rear-guard of Charlemagne's army in the pass of Roncesvalles in the Pyrenees, an attack resulting from a treacherous alliance between Ganelon, Roland's stepfather, and the Muslims. Roland is killed and Charlemagne avenges his death. In keeping with contemporary preoccupations, the motivations of the principal participants are essential elements, although necessarily lacking the painstaking dissection of the schoolmen. Roland is the brave and dashing hero, Oliver, a companion of common sense and shrewdness, Turpin, a fighting archbishop who nevertheless conscientiously fulfils his clerical duties, and central to all, Charlemagne, the sagacious and dignified leader, taking decisions in counsel with his baronage in the correct twelfth-century fashion.

The world portrayed in Roland and the Cid is masculine and brutal, but the romance literature of the twelfth and thirteenth centuries reflected changes both in the self-perception of the lay upper classes and in their living standards. The Church had prepared the way for the new self-image by trying to inculcate what it believed to be a superior scale of values, while material changes can be seen in long and elaborate descriptions of the new consumer society of the aristocracy. Idealistic motivation was demonstrated in the courtly love stories of devotion to a lady, which may have found their origins in Provence, and in the reworking of the Celtic legends of Arthur and his knights and various stories from Greek and Roman mythology and history. The Arthurian legend gained a particularly strong hold, especially after the version of English history conjured out of the imagination of Geoffrey of Monmouth in the mid-twelfth century became well known (L. Thorpe 1980). The round table was added by the French poet Wace (Mason 1928), and the scope of the stories was greatly extended by following the exploits of individual knights, the quest for the Grail providing the unifying element. Again, the best exponents of the genre, such as Chrétien of Troyes

(d. 1180), attempted to penetrate beneath the surface by analysing the springs of action through their portrayal of human relationships (Staines 1990). However, the essential unity of this renaissance can perhaps best be illustrated by a work of German romance, *Parzival*, written c.1200, by the knight Wolfram of Eschenbach (d. 1220). Here the structure of the knightly quest provides an effective vehicle for the ultimate fulfilment of religious faith (Hatto 1980).

A civilisation which built so much upon the past inevitably took the recording of its history very seriously. Although in the classical world history was not included among the seven liberal arts, nevertheless, in the words of the Byzantine historian John Kinnamos, 'The task of historical writing was not deemed dishonourable to those of old who were wise. Many of them became highly esteemed thereby' (Brand 1976:13). The twelfth-century Latin west shared this view, which was heavily reinforced by an urgent desire to show the striking changes of the age and to present them within a planned explanatory structure in contrast to the mere listing of the annalists. Otto of Freising was the most ambitious in his scheme and the most reflective in his analysis, but many other able men, less all-embracing in their approach, were attracted by the urge to explain events, draw moral lessons, justify actions by themselves and others, provide material for preaching or entertainment, or simply to keep a record of what had happened so that it would not be forgotten. 'In the dark haze of this world everything would be hidden if the light of letters failed,' said Helmold of Bosau (Tschan 1935:43).

In shedding this light they showed a greatly increased awareness of the problems of historical form, which parallels the methodical approaches being adopted in the treatment of theology, law and medicine. According to Odo of Deuil,

> It is necessary to go back and forth – to progress and turn back in my story – for although many things present themselves for description, the account should not be confused by the wealth of subjects. Many events happen at the same time, but in discourse one must observe a sequence.
>
> (Berry 1948:33)

William of Tyre, with sixteen years' training in the schools of France and Italy behind him, was even more overtly influenced by contemporary preoccupations, warning that 'the lofty dignity of historical events many suffer loss through feeble presentation and lack of eloquence' (Babcock and Krey 1941:1:54).William, above all, set himself high standards, showing himself especially sensitive to the pressures of patronage.

> In the words of our Cicero, 'Truth is troublesome, since verily from it springs hatred which is poisonous to friendship; but compliance is even more disastrous, for, by dealing leniently with a friend, it permits him to rush headlong to ruin' – a sentiment which seems to reflect on the man who, in defiance of the obligations of duty, suppresses the real facts for the sake of being obliging.
>
> (Babcock and Krey 1941:1:53–4)

Appearances, of course, can be deceptive. In practice, few chroniclers intended to provide a reliable, eye-witness narrative of events, since neither their aims, nor their mental outlook, shaped by their belief in supernatural intervention and the value of past authorities, led them to regard this as a necessarily important objective. The pitfalls of interpreting accounts of the recording of heresy provide as good a case study as any to demonstrate this point (Moore 1975:107). Not many felt constrained to justify lifting material from elsewhere by quoting classical authority for the practice, as did Jocelin of Brakelond, who claimed that 'according to Seneca it is not presumptuous to adopt something that has been well told by someone else' (Greenway and Sayers 1989:61). John of Salisbury perhaps sums up best of all the objectives of the twelfth-century historian, at the same time neatly incorporating references to the Bible and to a classical author.

> My aim, like that of other chroniclers before me, shall be to profit my contemporaries and future generations. For all these chroniclers have a single purpose: to relate noteworthy matters, so that the invisible things of God may be clearly seen by the things that are done [Romans, i. 20], and men may by examples of reward or punishment be made more zealous in the fear of God and pursuit of justice. Yes indeed, anyone ignorant of these things who claims knowledge of holy writ or worldly wisdom, may be said to make himself a laughing-stock. For, as the pagan says, 'The lives of others are our teachers' [Cato]; and whoever knows nothing of the past hastens blindly into the future. Besides, the records of the chronicles are valuable for establishing or abolishing customs, for strengthening or destroying privileges; and nothing, after knowledge of the grace and law of God, teaches the living more surely and soundly than knowledge of the deeds of the departed.
>
> (Chibnall 1956:3)

It has been pointed out that the 'literary history' of men like William of Tyre and John of Salisbury was no longer attractive to the leading intellectuals of the thirteenth century, nor was there any historian who took up the challenge to write in the light of the prophetic structure of Joachim of Fiore, which was so influential otherwise (Smalley 1974:180–1). Nevertheless, although the writing of history broke no new ground thereafter, a wide variety of works was produced, including vernacular narratives like Geoffrey of Villehardouin's account of (and justification for) the Fourth Crusade, the Icelander Snorri Sturluson's great saga of the Norwegian world from the earliest kings to 1162, illustrated histories of which Matthew Paris, artist and chronicler combined, is the most versatile example and, in keeping with contemporary scholasticism, the encyclopaedic approach, epitomised by the Dominican, Vincent of Beauvais, whose *Speculum historiale* made up a major part of his *Speculum universale*. At times the line between historical romance and historical authenticity could be a fine one, especially in vernacular pieces designed to appeal to audience. The so-called Minstrel of Reims, writing in 1260, managed to combine the two, for while he can be a useful source of information of the events of his own lifetime, his portrayals of the activities of previous generations bore little or no relation to reality, despite being about real people and settings (Stone 1939). More obviously intellectual, but equally fictional, was the creation of 'national' histories, purporting to show the extensive lineage of contemporary peoples. French and English chroniclers had taken the lead in this field, but a striking later example was *The Deeds of the Hungarians*, written between 1282 and 1285 by Simon of Kéza, a cleric and diplomat at the court of King Ladislas IV. Simon's research was extensive, even though his assertion that it was from the Huns that the Hungarians took their origins was a completely bogus device designed to justify the Magyar conquest of Pannonia, previously occupied by their Hunnish 'ancestors' (Veszprémy and Schaer 1999). Perhaps, however, the best indication of contemporary interest in history can be seen in the extent to which it was pursued in more modest ways at local monastic houses, where it had long been believed that that labouring in the scriptorium was equivalent to the manual work prescribed by the Rule of St Benedict. Here, historical writing ranged from the recopying of an earlier work or the life of a saint to the creation of a continuous house chronicle, kept going by successive hands (B. Dodwell 1979; Chibnall 1984:113).

If the best historians of the twelfth century showed themselves in touch with the increasingly rigorous approach of the theologians and the lawyers, they also responded to the growing interest in the role of the individual, becoming less concerned with 'the invisible things of God', as John of Salisbury put it, or with stylised modes for portraying kings and other leaders borrowed from authors like Suetonius. A measure of the extent to which these ideas had been absorbed can be gained not from looking at the most advanced, the Italian communes, where mercantile manipulation of daily changes encouraged observation, but at the most conservative, the monastic houses. Jocelin of Brakelond's famous portrait of Abbot Samson conveys a vivid idea of the man and owes nothing to stylisation.

> Abbot Samson was of medium height and almost completely bald. His face was neither round nor long, and he had a prominent nose and thick lips. His eyes were crystal clear, with a penetrating gaze, and he had extremely sharp hearing. His eyebrows were bushy and were frequently trimmed. As soon as he caught a slight cold he became hoarse. On the day of his election [28 February 1182] he was 47 years of age, and had been a monk for seventeen years. There were then only a few grey hairs in his red beard and very few indeed in his hair, which was black and wavy, but within fourteen years of his election he had turned as white as snow. He was a very serious-minded man and was never idle. His health was excellent, and he liked to travel on horseback or on foot, until he was prevented by old age.
>
> (Greenway and Sayers 1989:36)

Any survey of the intellectual renaissance of the high middle ages must concentrate upon those who extended the frontiers of knowledge and methodology, but it is equally important to realise that these changes depended on a widening base of literacy and an increasing knowledge and use of documents. Jocelin of Brakelond gives a revealing insight into the way that this diffusion of learning had begun to impinge upon monastic society by the early thirteenth century. In 1202 the Abbey of Bury St Edmunds chose as its new prior, Herbert, the abbot's chaplain. But Herbert said that he was not fit for the office since he was not learned enough to preach a sermon appropriate to such a position.

> The abbot, however, to comfort him, and speaking as if to belittle men of learning, replied lengthily that he could quite well memorize and re-use other people's sermons, as was not unusual. And he went on to condemn colourful rhetoric and flowery words and exquisite prose in sermons, maintaining that in many churches the sermon is given to the convent in French, or more appropriately in English, so as to be edifying rather than showily learned.

These remarks were quickly seized upon by those whom Jocelin calls 'uneducated brothers', who clearly harboured resentment against the Latinists in their midst.

> They said to one another, 'Now let our philosophers understand the consequences of their philosophizing! Now it is clear what comes of their philosophy! Our good clerks have done so much declining in the cloister that they have all been declined!'
>
> (Greenway and Sayers 1989:113–15)

Their resentment arose from a growing sense of inferiority consequent upon the increased importance of learning in the early thirteenth century. Jocelin's 'uneducated brothers' felt themselves excluded from the growth of what Brian Stock has aptly designated 'textual communities', that is the identification of groups with a specific body of written texts, rather than with the more traditional ties like family, place or institution (Stock 1983: 88–92). In fact, by this time some, perhaps many, ordinary knights, had enough Latin to understand the documents which affected their lives, even though they could by no stretch of imagination be described as philosophers, while by the later years of the century in England even smallholders and serfs used documents, although the task of drawing them up remained the province of specialists. It has been estimated that in thirteenth-century England there must have been about 8 million charters produced for these classes alone (Clanchy 1979:1, 33–5).

These changes can be seen from a different angle in fourteenth-century Florence. Giovanni Villani estimated that of a population of 90,000 in 1338, about 10,000 children were being educated at least to the level at which they could read (Villani 1969:3:324). Modern research shows that 'when the level of three formal teachers per 1,000 population is reached, rates of adult illiteracy are low.... Further additions of teachers will then affect the level of general culture rather than the mere skills of reading and writing' (Cipolla 1969:26). For Villani's Florence to reach such a point would mean the existence of 270 teachers, a figure which is quite likely if there were 10,000 children at school, giving a ratio of 1 to 37. Florence, therefore, had reached, perhaps passed, the point of cultural 'take-off'.

18

Art and society

One of the most famous documents of the early Cistercian era is St Bernard's *Apologia* to his friend, William, Abbot of St Thierry in the diocese of Reims, written in 1125. William was very much in sympathy with Cistercian ideals, so the contents were not aimed at him, but rather at existing Benedictine orders, in particular the Cluniacs. However, contrary to received opinion, the Cluniacs were not the exclusive target; St Bernard appears to be condemning the use of 'luxurious and excessive' art and architecture within the monastic movement as a whole, including some previous examples in his own order (Rudolph 1990: 159–91). After expressing his astonishment that 'monks could be so lacking in moderation in matters of food and drink, and with respect to clothing and bedding, carriages and buildings', he turns the full power of his invective upon each of them, culminating in a great attack upon the superfluities of monastic decoration.

> I shall say nothing about the soaring heights and extravagant lengths and unnecessary widths of the churches, nothing about their expensive decorations and their novel images, which catch the attention of those who go in to pray, and dry up their devotion. To me they seem like something out of the Old Testament; but let them be, since it is all to the glory of God. However, as one monk to another, may I ask the question which a heathen poet put to his fellows. 'Tell me, O priests,' he said, 'why is there gold in the holy place?' I shall put the question slightly differently, I am more interested in the sense of the text than in its precise words. 'Tell me, O poor men,' this is my question, 'tell me, O poor men – if you are really poor men – why is there gold in the holy place?'
> (Casey 1970:52, 63–4)

By the 1120s St Bernard did indeed have many targets for an attack upon monastic extravagance in building and decoration. Along pilgrimage routes like those through France and Spain to Santiago de Compostela stood a string of heavily decorated abbey churches at Vézelay, Conques, Moissac and Toulouse among others, while Cluny itself had become a massive edifice with eleven nave bays and four aisles, double transepts, and a ring of radiating chapels around the choir. The building was 609 feet long with vaults 97 feet high. St Bernard was prepared to concede that there was a distinction between the monks and the laity on this issue.

Bishops have a duty toward both wise and foolish. They have to make use of material ornamentation to rouse devotion in carnal people, incapable of spiritual things.

Monks, however, had no such excuse.

> For the sake of Christ we have abandoned all the world holds valuable and attractive. All that is beautiful in sight and sound and scent we have left behind, all that is pleasant to taste and touch. To win Christ we have reckoned bodily enjoyments as dung. Therefore, I ask you, can it be our own devotion we are trying to excite with such display, or is the purpose of it to win the admiration of fools and the offerings of simple folk? Living among gentiles, as we do, it seems that we now follow their example, and do service to their idols.

Motivation therefore must be base: either a failure to renounce the world in accordance with their vows, or a desire for vainglory or admiration, or a crafty way of attracting donations or, perhaps worst of all, adherence to the cult of images, to idol-worship.

> Let me speak plainly. Cupidity, which is a form of idolatry, is the cause of all this. It is for no useful purpose that we do it, but to attract gifts. You want to know how? Listen to the marvels of it all. It is possible to spend money in such a way that it increases; it is an investment which grows, and pouring it out only brings in more. The very sight of such sumptuous and exquisite baubles is sufficient to inspire men to make offerings, though not to say their prayers. In this way, riches attract riches, and money produces more money. For some unknown reason, the richer a place appears, the more freely do offerings pour in. Gold-cased relics catch the gaze and open the purses. If you show someone a beautiful picture of a saint, he comes to the conclusion that the saint is as holy as the picture is brightly colored. When people rush up to kiss them, they are asked to donate. Beauty they admire, but they do no reverence to holiness. This is the reason that churches are decked out, not merely with a jewelled crown, but with a huge jewelled wheel, where circles of lamps compete in radiance with precious stones. Instead of candle-sticks we see tree-like structures, made of much metal and with exquisite workmanship, where candles and gems sparkle equally.
>
> (Casey 1970:64–5)

Drawing on a long tradition deriving from the Church Fathers, he makes a powerful social point, especially pertinent in the context of contemporary economic expansion (Rudolph 1990:84–97).

> The walls of the church are aglow, but the poor of the Church go hungry. The stones of the church are covered with gold, while its children are left naked. The food of the poor is taken to feed the eyes of the rich, and amusement is provided for the curious, while the needy have not even the necessities of life.
>
> (Casey 1970:65–6)

Even so, he was prepared to accept that these decorations 'do harm only to greedy and shallow people, not to those who are simple and god-fearing'. What he cannot take is the existence of such lavishness in the monastery itself, an aversion which provoked a great rhetorical denunciation of Romanesque sculpture, in particular those elements which portrayed hybrid creatures 'against nature' (Rudolph 1990:120–2).

> What excuse can there be for these ridiculous monstrosities in the cloisters where the monks do their reading, extraordinary things at once beautiful and ugly? Here we find filthy monkeys and fierce lions, fearful centaurs, harpies, and striped tigers, soldiers at war, and hunters blowing their horns. Here is one head with many bodies, there is one body with many heads. Over there is a beast with a serpent for its tail, a fish with an animal's head, and a creature that is horse in front and goat behind, and a second beast with horns and the rear of a horse. All round there is such an amazing variety of shapes that one could easily prefer to take one's reading from the walls instead of from a book. One could spend the whole day gazing fascinated at these things, one by one, instead of meditating on the law of God. Good Lord, even if the foolishness of it all occasion no shame, at least one might balk at the expense.
>
> (Casey 1970:66)

The *Apologia* contains of course a considerable element of caricature and in places the language is as extravagant as the sculpture and architecture he is denouncing. Nevertheless, neither the deliberate exaggeration nor the existence of many literary antecedents for such outbursts should be allowed to obscure the fundamental strength of feeling. St Bernard's denunciation grew quite naturally from the nature of the Cistercian Order; over-elaboration in building both symbolised the material decadence of contemporary society and contributed to its intensification. St Bernard was, indeed, only the most famous of such ascetics. In the eleventh century Peter Damian wrote of the fate of one abbot who, as punishment for his obsession with costly and elaborate building schemes in life, was obliged to erect scaffolding in Hell for ever (Migne 1853:144:465). Guibert of Nogent, although neither Cistercian nor hermit, nevertheless, in a reference to the contemporary fashion for elaborate shrines, felt constrained to demand who was worthy to be enclosed in gold and silver when the Son of God was walled up in the most vile rock (Migne 1880:626). Later in the twelfth century, Peter Cantor, rector of the cathedral school at Paris and, in his last years, a Cistercian (d. 1197), made an even more explicit link between social injustice and architectural splendour, claiming that money spent on costly buildings meant that there was now less charity and almsgiving for the sustenance of the poor. Monastic and ecclesiastical buildings constructed from the usury of avaricious men would come to ruin (Migne 1855b:256–7; Baldwin 1970:1:66–72).

The consequence of such attitudes was that the Cistercian Order became the only one of the reformed communities to develop a distinctive architectural style of its own, largely transcending regional styles. The use of sites free from the encumbrances of existing buildings combined with the high degree of central control exercised through the annual convention of abbots meeting in the General Chapter meant that the Cistercian style and layout became as familiar in Fountains and Fossanova as it had in Burgundy. The best existing example is the Abbey of Fontenay, built between 1139 and 1147. The church is very plain with no capitals or clerestory and, most characteristic, a squared off sanctuary, for circular apses clearly seem to be associated in Cistercian minds with Cluniac extravagance. The west front once had a narthex similarly unadorned, a feature which was exported to countries like England where otherwise the narthex was almost unknown. The nave is spanned by a pointed barrel-vault, founded on heavy piers, while the aisle-vaults are placed at right-angles to the nave to eliminate lateral thrust, leaving the main source of light as the high aisle windows above cloister level. The cloister itself is to the south of the church, again containing very simple capitals which contrast with the historiated carvings of Romanesque abbeys like Moissac. The refectory is at right-angles to the cloister unlike traditional Benedictine houses where it runs along it. Fontenay also contains many of the auxiliary buildings necessary for subsistence, including a pigeon house, a bakery, a forge, a guesthouse and a gatehouse, and its setting in a quiet and well-watered valley, even today still preserves some sense of the original Cistercian solitude. The same attitude prevailed towards manuscript illumination, for chapter regulations forbade all illuminated initials or the use of colour in manuscripts, on the grounds that they undermined serious meditation.

But the Cistercian style had only a relatively short lifespan; the ideals were already faltering even during St Bernard's time. By 1213 the General Chapter found it necessary to forbid future use of pictures and sculptures, except for the image of the Saviour, as well as varied pavements and superfluous buildings (Canivez 1933:1:404). Yet, the Cistercian abbey of Royaumont (north of Paris), founded in 1228 in memory of King Louis VIII and dedicated with lavish ceremonial in 1236, attracted just such elaboration because of its association with the crown. As a royal necropolis it tended to accumulate precious objects: in 1263 the General Chapter told the abbot to take away 'the pictures, effigies and sculptures, hangings, [and] columns with angels recently placed around the greater altar' so that the former humility and simplicity of the Order be restored (Canivez 1935:3:11). The changes were, as can be seen, against the wishes of the General Chapter, but as the early Cistercians had known, association with the secular world meant that its pressures would be almost impossible to resist.

Pressure from royal patrons, however, was only part of the reason for the absorption of Cistercian architecture into the European mainstream. The fact was that by the late twelfth century the Cistercians too had been gripped by the fashion for building in the emerging new style, a style later pejoratively designated 'Gothic' by renaissance men infected with the fever of classicism. The key figure in the development of Gothic has usually been seen as Suger of St Denis, a personality of quite different cut from St Bernard, although the actual nature of Suger's role in this change has been the subject of considerable reinterpretation (Kidson 1987). From the late 1130s Suger began extensive rebuilding and refurbishing of the ancient and venerated church of the abbey, and between 1144 and 1149 he wrote two books justifying this: the *Libellus Alter de Consecratione Ecclesiae Sancti Dionysii* and *Liber de Rebus in Administratione Sua Gestis*. Both books reflect Suger's desire to demonstrate to future generations his central role in the abbey and, indeed, in the Kingdom of France.

In Chapters 6 and 7 of the *De Consecratione*, Suger brings the work to an appropriate climax with a lovingly detailed description of the great ceremony of consecration of the rebuilt choir of the abbey church which took place on 11 June 1144. King Louis VII and Queen Eleanor headed those present, who included seventeen archbishops and bishops, all carefully named by Suger, so that it is known that men as important as Samson of Reims and Theobald of Canterbury attended. In addition, 'of the diverse counts and nobles from many regions and dominions, of the ordinary troops of knights and soldiers there is no count'. After the consecration of the vessel they proceeded to the translation of the sacred relics, contained in shrines which Suger believed to have been executed at the time of King Dagobert I (d. 638). All prostrated themselves, chanting and weeping.

> For these are the holy men who gave over their bodies as a testimony to God; who for our salvation, burning with the fire of charity, left their land and kin; who with apostolic authority taught the faith of Jesus Christ to all Gaul; who fought for Him like men; who, naked, conquered scourges and, fettered, [conquered] wild and famished beasts; who sustained, unscathed, extension on the rack and the fire of the furnace, and finally blissful decapitation by blunted axes.

This was followed by a procession led by the king holding the silver reliquary of St Denis which took the assembly through the cloisters and back into the church. The relics were then replaced on the altars, which were in turn themselves consecrated. Finally, the culmination was the solemn celebration of masses performed 'so festively, so solemnly, so different and yet so concordantly, so close [to one another] and so joyfully that their song, delightful by its consonance and unified harmony, was deemed a symphony angelic rather than human' (Panofsky 1979:113, 117, 119–21). It was this choir of which Suger was so proud, which has generally been seen as fusing together for the first time those elements which have come to be regarded as Gothic.

The rebuilding of the abbey church was probably projected after the abortive invasion of France by the Emperor Henry V. The greatly increased prestige which the abbey acquired after its focal role in overcoming this threat brought many more visitors and pilgrims, especially to the abbey's two annual fairs. Here religious feeling, political prestige and economic advantage were closely intertwined, for crowds had initially been attracted by the abbey's relics which in turn stimulated the fairs. On the face of it, at least, therefore, Suger's justification for rebuilding was based upon the inadequate size of the existing basilica. Only one thing was lacking in Dagobert's church, said Suger, 'that he did not allow the size that was necessary'. His account of the consequences lacks nothing in drama.

> At times you could see, a marvel to behold, that the crowded multitude offered so much resistance to those who strove to flock in to worship and kiss the holy relics, the Nail and Crown of the Lord, that no one among the countless thousands of people because of their very density could move a foot; that no one, because of their very congestion, could [do] anything but stand like a marble statue, stay benumbed or, as a last resort, scream.

He has special mention of the pious women caught in the mêlée, 'for the narrowness of the place forced the women to run toward the altar upon the heads of the men as upon a pavement with much anguish and noisy confusion'.

Suger takes pains to stress, however, that he had only acted in consultation with his brethren, in complying with their 'devoted and reasonable requests'. Manifest signs of God's approval had been shown during the course of building, especially in the revelation of appropriate building materials when none seemed at hand, such as the quarry at Pontoise and the great trees needed for beams found in the valley of the

Chevreuse. Moreover, when there had been a great storm during the course of construction and the vaults had been exposed to the elements, they had held despite the fact that other buildings in the vicinity had been destroyed. Final evidence of divine sanction was to be found in the speedy completion of the choir in the symbolically significant time of three years and three months (Panofsky 1979:86–9, 40–1, 92–7, 42–5, 48–51).

Having made the decision to rebuild, Suger set aside 200 *livres* per annum for the project, on the expectation that 150 *livres* would be derived from pilgrims' contributions. The remainder was presumably drawn from the abbey's own resources which he had thoroughly reorganised soon after becoming abbot in 1122. Under Suger the previously dilapidated estates of St Denis were transformed: direct cultivation was resumed and lay advocates removed; the peasantry were forced to substitute a proportion of the harvest for the fixed rents which they had been accustomed to pay; new land was colonised and brought into cultivation; and the abbey's records combed to enable him to enforce all potential rights and claims (Constable 1988:X; Duby 1974:218–19). Although it is clear that Suger unduly minimised the contribution of his predecessor, Abbot Adam, nevertheless, through a combination of his own formidable administrative skills and the good fortune to be operating within an expanding economy, he did have an immense impact upon the abbey's revenues, thus enabling him to undertake an extensive programme of construction which included not only the church, but the other monastic buildings as well (Grant 1998:208–37).

It is unlikely that at this stage he had an overall plan for rebuilding, for in 1130 he spent large sums of money repairing the nave and having the walls painted with murals. Then, in 1137, he began the construction of a new façade, further west than the old one, incorporating a triple porch and two great towers, all with a crenellated top. Behind the new façade, the nave was reached by the insertion of a narthex of two storeys, both of which displayed ribbed vaulting. This was largely finished by 1140, and at this point Suger turned to the choir, the rebuilding of which was of crucial importance for his planned presentation of the relics of the abbey's saints. The choir (or, strictly speaking, the retrochoir) was built between 1140 and 1144, using the existing crypt as a foundation, although its height was increased. It consisted of an ambulatory with nine shallow chapels, built in such a manner as virtually to remove the divisions between the chapels. This, combined with the insertion of two tall windows in each chapel, left relatively little wall area and allowed the entrance of a great deal of light filtered by the stained-glass windows. The choir, ambulatories and chapels were vaulted in the same way as the narthex (see Figure 4). Plans had, too, apparently been prepared for the nave, for some work was done on it in 1149, but nothing substantial had been accomplished by Suger's death in 1151.

As well as the actual rebuilding Suger spent huge sums on decoration and embellishment: bronze-gilded doors and a great sculptural programme on the façade, stained-glass windows in the choir, gold and precious stones adorning the altar-panels and, in the heart of the church a great cross, 21 feet in height, behind the main altar. Appropriate inscriptions explained, appealed and exhorted. In a conspicuous gesture, Suger, showing that talent for effective publicity which is his trademark, took off his own ring so that it could be placed in the golden altar frontal, thus encouraging other leading figures to do the same (Panofsky 1979:54–7).

Suger was able to build in this way because he had at his disposal an architect of outstanding ability, whose solutions to the technical problems encountered in rebuilding the choir in particular were to have lasting influence, even in buildings where the overall aims of the patrons bore little relation to those of Suger. Although in his writings he suggests that he had certain models in mind, in particular Hagia Sophia at Constantinople and the building which the Latins believed to be the Temple of Solomon at Jerusalem, it is evident that the practical influences on the architect came from nearer home. There was relatively little in the Ile-de-France except perhaps for the Merovingian cathedral in Paris, but the main constructional elements which were to be fused into the Gothic style were already available in adjacent regions. Anglo-Norman models provided the ribbed vault: Durham Cathedral choir, completed in 1104, is the first example of a combination of rib and groin, although it seems unlikely to have been a direct influence on the St Denis architect. In Normandy itself there were several examples of ribbed vaults, although they were supported by much thicker walls than was usual in the Paris area at this time. If the vaulting could be found in Normandy, pointed arches, the second conspicuous feature of early Gothic, were a feature of Burgundian buildings. The arch 'broken' in the middle offered much greater flexibility than the great round barrel vaults traditionally found in Romanesque churches, for, by setting the arches at different angles, consistency of height could be achieved and a web could be formed directing the thrust of the vault along chosen lines. By relieving pressure in this way, walls could be thinner and apertures for glass much more frequent.

Nevertheless, Suger's importance can be exaggerated. The first actual complete Gothic church was that of Sens, whose archbishop, Henry Sanglier (1122–42), has some claim to be counted among the founders of the new style, for he may have been thinking about his new cathedral as early as 1130, although the choir was not consecrated until 1164 and the nave not completed until at least 1175. Moreover, the constructional features which Suger used already existed and had contributed to many impressive buildings in other regions, while his own approach to the rebuilding of the abbey seems to have lacked an overall plan which could have made it into a unified whole. Indeed, while the choir was of fundamental importance for the future, the west front was very much in the Norman tradition, following a pattern already seen at the abbey church of Jumièges and at St Etienne at Caen. As well as using elements from existing buildings in neighbouring regions, he was also evidently influenced by the more remote past, particularly by the churches of the early Christian era he had seen on his visits to Rome, most notably during his extended stay in 1123 (Grant 1998:255–8). Above all, as the *De Consecratione* shows, the central concern for Suger was the creation of an appropriate vessel to enclose the abbey's precious relics, an attitude very much in keeping with the eleventh-century interest in saints and their relics which had led to the rebuilding of many of the great Romanesque abbey churches along the pilgrimage routes. In this, however, Suger took his interest further than in the past, for he allocated one of the doorways of the façade to the local saints, thus initiating a practice which was to be extensively imitated in the twelfth and thirteenth centuries. The consistent thread, therefore, in Suger's life was not a self-conscious promotion of a new architectural style, but rather his absorption in his abbey and its patron, St Denis.

Suger's aspirations, achievements and methods contrast with those of his direct contemporary Bernard of Clairvaux on almost every count and doubtless Bernard must have felt the same about the rebuilding of St Denis as he had about Cluny and other contemporary Benedictine houses two decades earlier. One story, told by Suger with evident satisfaction, encapsulates the difference. He cannot pass over what he calls 'a

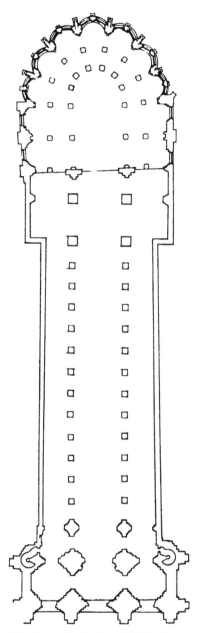

Source: S. M. Crosby, J. Hayward, C. T. Little and W. D. Wixom (1981), *The Royal Abbey of Saint-Denis in the time of Abbot Suger* (1122–1151) (New York: Metropolitan Museum), p. 20.

Figure 4 Plan of Suger's additions at St Denis

merry but notable miracle which the Lord granted us', when monks from Cîteaux and Fontevrault offered him a large quantity of gems which they had been given in alms. 'We, however, freed from the worry of searching for gems, thanked God and gave four hundred pounds for the lot though they were worth much more' (Panofsky 1979:58–9). Yet a direct confrontation between Suger and St Bernard never materialised. Suger's role as Capetian adviser gave him a political leverage which was useful to St Bernard in promoting the cause of Church reform, while Suger's political instincts persuaded him that it was sensible to avoid a clash with such a charismatic figure. By 1127, therefore, Bernard was writing to Suger congratulating him on the changes he had brought about in the hitherto worldly community of St Denis, claiming that 'shame for the past encourages the austerity of this new way of life' (B.S. James 1998:113). For his part, Suger occasionally strikes a defensive note, explaining that he did not embark upon his building project 'with any desire for empty glory nor with any claim to the reward of human praise and transitory compensation' (Panofsky 1979:40–1).

In fact, it was not a simple polarisation, for St Bernard was by no means indifferent to artistic beauty and, indeed, he was prepared to accept that the laity needed aids of this kind. In a letter to the people of Rome after disturbances in the city, probably in 1146, he wrote lamenting the damage which had been caused to the city's churches.

> Consider for what reason, for what purpose, by whom and for whose benefit you have only lately squandered all the revenues and ornaments of your churches. Whatever gold or silver could be found in the vessels of the altar, on the sacred images themselves, has been torn off and carried away by impious hands. How much of all this have you still got in your purses now? But the beauty of the Lord's house has been irretrievably lost.
>
> (B.S. James 1998:392–3)

St Bernard died in 1153, but he could not have stemmed the tide. After 1150, episcopal civic pride, frequent disasters to existing buildings, especially fire, developing technical expertise, and economic growth combined to produce an unprecedented number of building projects in the Ile-de-France and neighbouring regions, particularly concentrated in the four or five decades on either side of the year 1200. Taking that year as a fulcrum, architectural historians have generally made a broad division into early Gothic, from the 1130s to *c*.1190, high Gothic, from the beginning of the building of Chartres (1194) and Bourges (1195) until the 1230s, and the Rayonnant style, from the 1230s and extending into most of the fourteenth century (Stoddard 1972:167–71, 279–88). These broad and rather arbitrary divisions are based, first, upon an early period in which exteriors retain the mural appearance of Romanesque, but in which too there are many experiments in structure, especially in the use of ribbed vaults and the greater proportion of the wall given over to glass. Sens, with its choir and nave completed by the late 1170s, and Laon, built between the 1150s and 1215, are characteristic. Notre-Dame at Paris (early 1160s to 1200), too, can be counted as falling within this phase, although built on a far more grandiose scale than any of its predecessors. With Chartres and Bourges greater overall unity was achieved, partly as a consequence of the more widespread diffusion of the flying buttress from the 1170s, which helped architects find solutions to the structural problems of the past, and partly because of a better understanding of theoretical geometry, perhaps itself a consequence of the translation of Euclid's *Elements* by Adelard of Bath and others. By the 1230s most of the technical problems had been mastered and from this time there is much greater emphasis upon decoration, especially in the form of ornate window tracery and delicate rose windows. The Sainte-Chapelle in Paris, built during the 1240s to house the Crown of Thorns purchased by Louis IX, is the most famous example of royal patronage, influencing in turn other small chapels like St Germer de Fly (Branner 1965). New churches such as St Urban at Troyes (begun 1262) also fall into this category, as do alterations made to existing buildings, most notably the rebuilding of St Denis, which, begun in 1231, is one of the earliest examples of the development of the Rayonnant style (Bruzelius 1985).

The association of the spread of Gothic with the expansion of Capetian power both in the Ile-de-France and beyond into Normandy and Languedoc, is striking, but the waves travelled further than this. England, a country closely connected with France, both politically and in ways of thought, was particularly influenced, as can be seen in the great cathedrals of Canterbury, Salisbury, Lincoln, Ely and Wells, among others, although as in other countries the 'French style' was subject to distinct regional variations. The style was taken up too in southern France in such churches as Clermont-Ferrand, Rodez and Carcassonne, and in Spain, including Burgos, Toledo, León and, in the early fifteenth century, Seville. German cathedrals include Magdeburg and Cologne, while in both Germany and Italy the style was particularly utilised in town churches under civic patronage.

A measure of the growing confidence of French architects in handling the new style can be taken from the increasing height of the cathedrals, from the nave at Sens at 81 feet to the choir vaults at Beauvais, almost twice the height at just over 157 feet. Paris at 108 feet was the first of the really large-scale cathedrals. With footings 30 feet deep it was evidently planned in this way from the beginning. The verticality of the interiors was emphasised by the relative diminution of the width of the nave. This had its effects even in the more modest early Gothic cathedrals; Laon is actually 2 feet lower than Sens, but looks much taller because the nave is 14 feet narrower. Once the full structural possibilities of flying buttresses were exploited, as they were at Chartres and Soissons, the clerestory could be lengthened below the spring of the vault, helping to give the nave a unity which it had previously lacked. At Chartres too, a more satisfying aesthetic effect is achieved by bringing the columns in a continuous run to the floor. The most integrated Gothic cathedral was perhaps achieved by the builders of Amiens, which was begun in 1220. The three storeys of the nave are immaculately linked to the vaults, while the central mullion of the clerestory is continued into the triforium, thus joining the parts into one. The crown of the vaults is 137 feet compared to a nave width of only 45 feet, which is the same as Reims (begun 1211), but 14 feet higher. Balance is achieved by the horizontal bands of foliage carving (see Plates 21 and 22).

Exteriors became equally distinctive, for this mode of construction enabled deep portals to be created which in turn offered greater potential for the realisation of much more extensive sculptural programmes than the relatively flat fronts of Romanesque. Whereas Romanesque sculpture was very much part of the wall surface, in the mature Gothic cathedrals the trend towards the production of more fully rounded and balanced figures was accelerated by the possibilities contained in the new buildings. The central portal at Senlis, dating from *c.*1170–5, offers an early example of an integrated programme which emanates directly from contemporary social and religious attitudes. The main theme is the Coronation of the Virgin and the portal illustrates her death, ascension and coronation, as well as the Tree of Jesse showing the human ancestry of

Plate 21 The fortress-like nature of many romanesque churches with their thick walls and small windows, as here at Chapaize (Saône-et-Loire), contrasts with the new possibilities opened up by the technical advances of the twelfth century, which produced the style which came to be known as Gothic.

Christ. The jamb statues, which are typological Old Testament figures, link with this in representing the sacrificial death of Christ. This is probably the first portal given over completely to this theme, but it was later to become common, reflecting the growing popularity of the cult among the people, as well as the intellectual effort expended by theologians like St Bernard in interpreting the Virgin as Bride of Christ which in turn was identified with the Church.

Plate 22 The vaulting of the choir at Amiens cathedral (completed 1269) shows the masterly degree of integration achieved by the architects of thirteenth-century Gothic. (Photograph reproduced by permission of Scala.)

This increased interest in the human Christ and his mother was matched by sculptors who strove to render them in appropriate form. In France, at least, this trend was partly a consequence of the growth of pilgrimage and crusade to Jerusalem. Those who risked their lives to tread where Christ had trod and who wept at the sight of the holy places were attracted by such an art. Moreover, churchmen, worried about the threat of heretics like the Cathars who denied the existence of a human Christ, were anxious to combat what they saw as pernicious teaching. The sculpture at Chartres conveniently encapsulates the changes, for the west front, dating from *c*.1150, escaped the great fire of 1194, whereas the northern and southern façades, constructed in the first and second decades of the thirteenth century respectively, reflect the new stylistic developments. Although the heads show some signs of differing types, the figures on the west façade remain integral to the architecture, retaining the characteristic elongated shape of French Romanesque. The sculptures on the northern and southern portals, on the other hand, incorporate credible centres of gravity which, combined with more individual faces and draperies appear to enfold genuine human figures.

The aim was to incorporate all this within a well-proportioned and balanced façade reflecting the geometrical consonance of God's ordered creation. This was most successfully achieved at Paris. The lower part of the façade is a square 142 feet per side, but with towers added it becomes a square and a half or, if a line is taken from the gallery of kings, two overlapping squares. The squares can therefore be divided into a series of rectangles in a ratio of two to three. In a famous and influential book Erwin Panofsky (1973) argued that there was a close connection between the methods of scholastic thought and the Gothic structural scheme. By the thirteenth century the application of the new logical methods to the study of theology had become standardised and this led to the production of formally structured works, carefully divided and sub-divided, most famously in Aquinas's *Summa Theologica*. In Panofsky's view, just like the *Summa*, the cathedral too aims at a totality, with the sculptures and stained glass embodying the range of Christian knowledge, theological, moral, natural and historical. The whole structure is arranged into what Panofsky calls homologous parts, that is the parts are interrelated, but at the same time preserve their separate identity. An example of how this is expressed within the overall framework can be seen in a High Gothic portal such as that showing the Last Judgement on the west front at Amiens (*c*.1225). Here the careful division into registers represents just such an approach (see Plate 17), contrasting with the treatment of the same subject in a Romanesque cathedral such as that at Autun, dating from the 1120s.

Panofsky's arguments are seductive, but they have not been universally accepted, for there is in fact little concrete proof of the direct influence of scholasticism upon Gothic buildings. Robert Branner (1979:143) pointed out that symbolic interpretations were written after the event and may not therefore be good evidence of the intentions of the original patrons and architects, while Roberto Salvini argues that the *Summae* reached their full flowering only in the late thirteenth century, thus giving Gothic art 'a clear priority'. In short, art is a primary means of expression and not a surrogate of other activities (Salvini 1969:35). Salvini's warning is timely. Modern research has increasingly emphasised the importance of oral and visual communication as well as the written culture (Clanchy 1979:202–30; Camille 1985). Nevertheless, it may be legitimate to draw parallels rather than to assert the dominance of one medium over another. For example, the same trends can be seen in the more complex page layouts of late-twelfth- and thirteenth-century books, where the text is often broken up into sections which can be glossed and referenced. The text can be said to be set out in an almost architectural manner, a tendency which ultimately expresses itself in the building of an encyclopaedic mansion, epitomised by Vincent of Beauvais' *Speculum Majus*, which appeared in the mid-thirteenth century. The perception of the earthly society as an ordered structure reflecting the greater harmonies of the universe was, as has been seen, a basic pillar supporting the thirteenth-century world view.

Just as the driving force behind Clairvaux and St Denis came from the respective leaders of these communities, so too did the secular clergy promote the construction of their new cathedrals. Henry Sanglier had, in fact, been a close friend of St Bernard since 1126, having inspired him to write a treatise on the proper mode of episcopal life, and it has been thought that the restraint of both scale and decoration seen at Sens emanates from this association. Others were less modest. Maurice of Sully, Bishop of Paris between 1160 and 1196, inaugurated an entirely new scale of cathedral building in the Ile-de-France, with the erection of Notre-Dame. At Bourges, 140 miles to the south, his brother, Archbishop Henry of Sully, topped even Paris with a nave rising to 123 feet. The similarities in plan to Paris reflect both the family connection and the fact that Bourges had been part of the royal demesne since about 1100, but the treatment of its shape with its series of three graded levels around the entire vessel and the omission of transepts makes it a very distinctive building in itself.

Men like these drew heavily on the Church's own resources. The evidence for Paris in the thirteenth century shows that the need to finance building campaigns led to fundamental changes in the social and economic relationship between the chapter and its dependent peasants, a pattern repeated in the vicinity of most other large cathedral towns (M. Bloch 1964). Even so, such resources were often insufficient in themselves. Royal and noble patronage was therefore of substantial importance: at Chartres, Blanche of Castile paid for the north façade windows, Peter of Dreux, Count of Brittany, the south windows and portal statuary, while their representation in the windows shows that the local noble houses of Courtenay, Montfort, Beaumont and Montmorency were also active participants. There was, too, often a close connection between the chapter and the local mercantile community; at St Denis and Chartres, for instance, the regular cycle of fairs had grown up under the protection of the Church. At Chartres twenty-five different trades or crafts are illustrated in the windows, ranging from clothiers to wine-merchants, while in the clerestory windows in the choir the occupations of contemporary Chartrains are associated with Old Testament images, such as the link between the carpenters and Noah building the ark in the north aisle. At Amiens there was a much greater dependence upon one commodity, the production of woad, grown in the surrounding fields to be processed into blue dye. Although they no longer survive, it is known that eleven of the twelve windows donated by the burghers were associated with woad production, that one of the three rose windows came from the same source, and that burgher donations provided for seven of the apsidal chapels (Kraus 1978:41–9). In this sense the Gothic cathedrals developed within the urban milieu, but this is not the same as saying that they are 'bourgeois art' (Hauser 1951:181–2). The substantial influences were ecclesiastical and royal rather than bourgeois, while co-operation between the chapter and burghers was by no means invariable, as the violent dispute between them at Reims in the years 1233 to 1236 demonstrates.

The relationship with the wider community could be equally ambiguous. On the one hand, both peasantry and town dwellers were exploited to pay for these great building works; in that sense, the cathedrals creamed off a substantial proportion of the increased income generated by economic growth. Indeed, it has been argued that the famous trade windows at Chartres can more realistically be interpreted as the chapter's presentation of an ideal Christian society, its hierarchy established to support the directive role of the Church, rather than a series of willing donations by a pious populace (Williams 1993:20–30, 139–45). On the other hand, there was a deep well of genuine popular enthusiasm, seen in the willingness to make donations, especially under the inspiration of precious and revered relics. One of the most potent was the Virgin's tunic at Chartres. When the old cathedral burnt down on 10 June 1194, the tunic had fortunately been preserved in the crypt. The local people, however, believed that it had been lost and with it both its miraculous protection and its ability to generate income from pilgrims. Its reappearance was brilliantly stage-managed. According to an anonymous treatise of c.1210, known as *The Miracles accomplished by the Blessed Virgin Mary in the Church of Chartres*, on a certain feast day the clergy assembled the entire populace of the city at the place where the church had been and, with great ceremony, brought out from the crypt the chest in which the Virgin's tunic had been preserved (Thomas 1881:510). With typical ecclesiastical taste for seeking consonances, the author of the *Miracles* compared the survival of the tunic with the miraculous 'escapes' of the Old Testament, like Jonah and the Whale and Daniel in the Lions' Den. The city could once again be confident of the Virgin's protection and of her desire for the cathedral to be rebuilt. However, the author was well aware that this could not be done without a sustained effort, explaining that the gifts of laypeople would not have been adequate without the granting of three years' revenues by the bishop and canons. When that ran out in 1197 the relics were sent on a fund-raising tour, which drew a ready response in an environment already attuned to the cult of the Virgin.

Gothic found its origins in a hitherto insignificant region of western Christendom, but its rise was paralleled by the equally striking development of the political power of the Capetian kings, the growth of whose authority and territory matched – and indeed promoted – the spread of the new style. In turn the region provided the intellectual and economic foundations which made both these phenomena possible. By 1250 French culture was dominant in the west and Paris was the leading city in northern Europe. The building of the Sainte-Chapelle on the Ile-de-la-Cité, adjacent to the royal palace, encapsulates this achievement. The architect was probably Thomas of Cormont, brought in from Amiens, where he had been working in the 1230s. The fabric seems to have been completed in 1246 and it was consecrated in 1248. It was connected to the palace at two levels, but the outstanding feature is the incorporation into the upper chapel of tall, thin stained-glass windows which occupy three-quarters of the total height. The unity of the chapel is achieved by placing the figures of the apostles which line the walls half over the dado, beneath the windows, and half over the windows, and by repeating the pattern of the blind arches of the arcade in the window tracery. Branner (1965:57–8) has compared it to a huge reliquary casket in which the decoration has been turned inside and, indeed, the influence of metalwork designs on small caskets is clear. But it was also a reliquary casket in the literal sense in that it was built to hold prized relics from Constantinople which Louis IX had obtained at great expense and difficulty from Venice, pawnbroker to the bankrupt Latin emperor, Baldwin II. The most important of these was the Crown of Thorns, but the collection also included part of the True Cross, the Holy Lance, and a sponge and a nail from the Passion. The image of France as God's kingdom shone out from this chapel, for had not Christ chosen France above all others to be the guardian of his most precious relics?

It is impossible to encompass the whole range of architectural and artistic development in western Christendom in a single chapter, but some sense of its diversity and richness can be gained from examining the relationship between artistic and social change in the Italian peninsula, a region which in many ways contrasted with France. Whereas the Capetian kings had consolidated their hold on the country and a recognisable French entity had begun to emerge, repeated attempts by the emperor to impose an overall authority in Italy had clearly failed. The rise of Italian artistic influence in the second half of the thirteenth century took place in an environment of political fragmentation in which a plethora of patrons – the papacy, the Angevins, the Italian city-states – competed in their expenditure on artistic and architectural projects which promoted their political role and catered for their religious and social needs.

The first important steps were in sculpture and they were taken in Pisa in the outstanding workshop of the era, that of Nicolà Pisano. While Pisa itself was in relative decline by the mid-thirteenth century, it remained prosperous and populous, proud of its history and position in the world. Indeed, the economic criterion for cultural advance seems to be, not active expansion, but the previous achievement of sustainable surpluses. This is the setting for the sudden appearance of one of the most striking works of art of the thirteenth century, the carved pulpit in the baptistery at Pisa, dated 1260. Nicolà was born in the early 1220s and may possibly have come from Apulia, but by 1250 he was already resident in Pisa. To be commissioned to carve the pulpit he must already have been responsible for some important works which are now lost. The baptistery was of central importance to the commune, for it was here that public acts of fundamental religious and social importance took place: the admission of infants into the Christian membership, the great rituals of Easter, the reconciliation of disputes, the reincorporation of exiles (Becker 1981:143–4). The comprehensiveness of the themes carved on the pulpit reflect this importance, encompassing an encyclopaedic sweep comparable to the portals of French cathedrals. The pulpit is hexagonal in shape and supported by seven columns, moving from the beasts and the wild men at the bottom to the Virtues at the top, together with patriarchs and kings in the spandrels. Finally, the five top panels illustrate the life of Christ from the Nativity to the Last Judgement (White 1987:74–83). Nicolà benefited from working in an environment with so many outside influences: the contact with Lombardy and France by means of the Via Francigena to the north, the Hohenstaufen court to the south, and the Levantine trading links which brought a Byzantine connection. The most obvious inspiration, however, was to be found in Pisa itself, where there were many antique works available, especially from the late Roman period, as well as a number of Greek sculptors, themselves brought up in the Byzantine tradition. His great skill was the adaptation of these classical models to contemporary needs. He worked in a milieu which valued an active civic life more than the isolation of monastic contemplation and which, like France, but for somewhat different reasons, related directly to the humanity of Christ and the Virgin rather than to a remote and avenging Jehovah. For such a society the humanising of previously iconic figures became essential and ultimately pervaded all areas of artistic endeavour.

The carving of the Pisan baptistery pulpit inspired the competitive spirit in nearby Siena; civic pride in these relatively compact but wealthy political units provided no small part of the impetus for artistic and architectural production. In 1265 Nicolà's shop was contracted to provide Siena with a similar pulpit, but decidedly grander in scope. Siena's pulpit had seven panels to Pisa's five, incorporating the Massacre of the Innocents, as well as two panels for the Last Judgement, showing the saved on one side and the damned on the other. At the front of the pulpit the Liberal Arts replaced the wild men, perhaps reflecting French influence. The Pisano shop can next be identified in another work of urban sculpture where once more the commune intended to show its public face, the water fountain at Perugia, dated 1278. The Fontana Maggiore has three tiers in which the water is intended to cascade from the bronze group in the centre down to the middle tier of twelve sides and finally by means of animal heads into the lowest basin, which has twenty-five sides. Such a structure left plenty of space for the kind of encyclopaedic programme for which the shop had become famous and which had become fashionable in the all-embracing world of the commune. The panels show the Labours of the Months, the Liberal Arts, Old Testament events, scenes of Roman antiquity, examples of Aesop's fables, saints, kings and prophets. At the same time, however, the Perugian authorities meant the fountain, which was prominently placed between the cathedral and the Palazzo dei Priori, to convey a more overt political message: that Perugia was the protective mother of its citizens, providing them with all their needs, intellectual, spiritual and material. Therefore, here too are legendary figures from the city's past, Heulixtes, its supposed founder, Bishop Herculanus, its defender against the Visigoths, and St Laurence, its patron saint. Symbolic figures of classical mien in the recognisable style of the Pisano shop emphasise the point: Ecclesia Perusina, the Perugian Church, Augusta Perusia, with a cornucopia, Domina Chiusi, representing the region from which the city drew most of its grain, and Domina Laci, referring to the source of fish in Lake Trasimeno. Finally, there are individuals of strictly contemporary relevance, Ermanno da Sassoferato, Captain of the People, and Matteo da Corregio, the podestà (Wieruszowski 1944:20, 26–7; White 1987:88–91).

Two important members of the Pisano shop made their mark as individual artists, Arnolfo di Cambio and Nicolà's son, Giovanni. While Arnolfo continued to work in a discernibly classical style, Giovanni's often emotional and dramatic approach shows more evident Gothic influence, a difference which belies the idea that the workshop system imposed a stifling conformity. Both, however, were formed by the environment created by their patron. Arnolfo's first known independent work demonstrates this. This is the tomb of Cardinal de Bray, Archdeacon of Reims, *c.*1282, in the church of San Domenico, Orvieto. The cardinal lies between curtains held back momentarily by acolytes, while above Saints Mark and Dominic intercede with Christ and the Virgin. His face has some standard workshop features, but its shape and expression are specific to the cardinal (see Plate 23). The tomb is only one of a series commissioned by great figures of the Church, their naturalistic elements reflecting the same desire for recognisable contemporary figures that can be seen in communal works (White 1987:93–100; Gardner 1992:97–102).

Like his father, Giovanni found ready employment in the communes, although some of his inscriptions seem to imply frustration at the lack of proper recognition of his genius, a feeling perhaps made more acute by the fame of his contemporary, Giotto. From 1285 Giovanni sculpted the figures on the façade of Siena cathedral, where they were originally spaced out across its full extent so that again the emphasis on separate figures demanded skill in presenting their individuality. At Pistoia (1300–1) and in the cathedral at Pisa (1302–10), Giovanni developed further the programmes on carved pulpits for which his father had become famous. The Pisan pulpit in particular combines the depth of the medieval intellectual and religious system with explicit communal symbolism. Here are shown the Life of Christ and of John the Baptist, the figures of the Evangelists, the Virtues and the Liberal Arts, the personification of Ecclesia, and the Sibyls, inspired women of ancient Greece gifted with prophecy. Among the figures at the base is that of Charity, depicted as a woman breast-feeding her two children, this figure in turn founded upon an eagle, the symbol of Imperial Pisa (Wieruszowski 1944:26; White 1987:133–9).

Plate 23 Arnolfo di Cambio's tomb of Cardinal William of Bray, Archdeacon of Reims, who died in 1282, reflects both his classical training and the more representational approach demanded by the nature of Italian civic life in the later thirteenth century. (Photograph reproduced by permission of Alinari.)

The work of the Pisano shop accurately reflected communal needs, which demanded a very public art. By means of the pulpit, the fountain, the tomb and the façade, they provided the setting for the great events of the city-state, while at the same time creating a permanent environment seen constantly by the inhabitants. Indeed, John White's comparison of the tomb of Cardinal de Bray to a stage complete with curtains about to fall can be applied more broadly. The pattern of the figures on the façade of Siena cathedral, for example, is much more suggestive of the great back wall of a Roman theatre with its niches for individual statues than the tightly organised programmes around deep portals so typical of the façades of northern France.

The use of art and architecture as a vehicle for communal propaganda reaches its apotheosis in Siena. Indeed, in one sense the city itself fulfilled this function, in that the setting for its most important secular building, the Palazzo Pubblico, was closely controlled by the *Noveschi* through the issue of detailed planning regulations. From 1297 the buildings around the Campo had to conform to a certain pattern which insisted on the use of columns, but precluded balconies. Moreover, the all-pervading influence of the governing body equally affected the city gates and the covered water supplies or fountains like the Fonte Nuova, begun in 1298. Gate façades, in fact, were particularly effective places for conveying political messages (White 1987:160). The Palazzo Pubblico itself contained the most overtly political art in communal Italy, culminating in Lorenzetti's fresco containing the Allegories of Justice, the Common Good and Tyranny, in the Sala della Pace. But the Sala della Pace was the room set aside for the meetings of the inner ruling body, the *Noveschi*, and therefore less public than the adjoining council chamber, the Sala del Mappamondo. Here the room was dominated by two large frescoes at either end, painted by Simone Martini, significantly designated official painter to the commune. On the east wall, painted in 1315, is a great *Maestà*, still very striking, but now only a pale reflection of the original, which was heavily decorated with gold. The Madonna is surrounded by a 'court' of angels and saints, including the four patron saints of the city at her feet. Above her head hangs a canopy or baldachin and around the borders are the black and white colours of Siena. The courtly and hieratic setting centred on the Virgin serves to emphasise her role as Queen of Heaven, while at the same time she is linked directly to the city itself over which she presides as its protector both against external enemies and, emphasised by exhortatory inscriptions, against anyone who within the city 'despises me and deceives my land' (Larner 1971:80–1). Thirteen years later, balancing this spiritual guardianship, Martini painted the equestrian portrait of Guidoriccio da Fogliano, who held the communal post of captain general of war. He is shown riding through the *contado*, having captured a castle (possibly Montemassi) and now en route to take the small town of Sassoforte, as yet unhung with the black and white of Siena. The evident likeness in the portly, rather complacent figure has been stamped upon a stylised landscape, empty of people and vegetation, symbolising the imposition of Sienese power.

Although the need to establish a political identity combined with the wealth to pay for it made the communes eager to invest in art and architecture, they were not the exclusive patrons of the era. Both papacy and monarchy remained, as they always had been, concerned to promote appropriately favourable images, and were well aware that art and building were effective means of so doing. Until the pontificate of Clement V, papal patronage in Rome played an important part in the artistic development of the late thirteenth century and, indeed, after 1309, as it became evident that residence at Avignon was semi-permanent, the popes re-emerged as major patrons. Two popes in particular stand out, each for their own reasons concerned to reassert papal supremacy by elevating the importance of Rome as the see of St Peter. Nicholas III (1277–80) was especially concerned to protect the interests of his own family, the Orsini, while at the same time attempting to reduce the growing influence of Charles of Anjou who, as has been seen, was beginning to outstrip his promoter. Nicholas IV (1288–92), although not from the Roman nobility, was the first Franciscan pope, and was closely associated with the interests of the Colonna family, which had extensive connections in the order. Their patronage therefore took the form of the lavish redecoration and repair of important Roman churches linked to their families and allies. Nicholas III began a programme of fresco decoration of Old St Peter's, San Lorenzo and San Paolo fuori le Mura, most of which has since been lost, but there are important works surviving from the 1290s. Pietro Cavallini's mosaics of the Life of the Virgin in Santa Maria in Trastevere and frescoes of the Last Judgement on the west wall of Santa Cecilia in Trastevere, are among the works that Nicholas set in train. Nicholas IV was particularly interested in the Colonna church of Santa Maria Maggiore, where he added an apse and transept in which a new programme was set in mosaic by Jacopo Torriti. It was largely paid for by indulgences and by fines such as the 1,000 gold ounces extracted from the Chiarenti banking house of Pistoia for usurious practices (Gardner 1973:1–41). The main subject is the Coronation of the Virgin, a choice which shows the direct influence of the Franciscans who popularised the cult in Italy, but below the central mandorla can also be seen the two kneeling figures of the donors, Nicholas IV and the Cardinal Giacomo Colonna, small in scale but highly coloured in order to stand out. The use of the techniques of mosaic and fresco, the attention paid to examples of the antique which were readily available, and the effort taken to remodel late Roman churches, all served to emphasise the continuity of the papacy as an institution and the primacy of the see of Rome itself.

Angevin artistic patronage was equally politically motivated, most strikingly in the panel by Simone Martini showing St Louis of Toulouse crowning Robert of Anjou, painted in 1317 or soon after (see Plate 24). Louis had been heir to the Angevin throne, but in 1296 he renounced it in favour of his brother Robert, before taking the Franciscan habit. The next year he was made Bishop of Toulouse by Boniface VIII, but he died before taking up the appointment. His father, Charles II, originally opposed to his son's wishes, now tried to exploit the situation, pressing the *curia* for canonisation as his Capetian cousin had achieved for Louis IX in 1297. Robert was equally interested in the cause when he succeeded to the throne ten years later, but he had the additional motivation that he wished to demonstrate his legitimate right to the crown, given both the circumstances of his inheritance and a potential rival claim from the Hungarian branch of the family. The panel is therefore a direct reflection of Robert's political interest with the saint seated in traditional frontal monarchical fashion, while Robert kneels in the pose of the donor. The king then receives his crown from a saint who, dressed in Franciscan habit and rich dalmatic, is both humble and authoritative at the same time. It is believed that a further panel, now lost, was originally in place above this scene, and showed Christ presiding over the crowning (Gardner 1975:16–29). The message closely matches the growing attention being paid to royal burials in which elaborate funeral ceremonies came to symbolise the transfer of the kingship (Hallam 1982a:366–7).

The successful invasion of the Angevins had ensured that there would be no such imperial continuity. Frederick II, deeply committed to the idea of an empire founded

Plate 24 Simone Martini's panel shows the crowning of Robert of Anjou at Naples by his brother, St Louis of Toulouse, a striking piece of visual propaganda intended to emphasise Robert's right to the throne, following Louis' renunciation in order to join the Franciscans in 1296. Painted not before 1317. (Photograph reproduced by permission of Scala.)

in Rome, had consistently attempted to cast the image of his regime in these terms. The portal of his hunting lodge at Castel del Monte, near Andria in Apulia, for example, which was finished in 1246, has an evidently classical inspiration. Fluted pilasters with Corinthian capitals lead to a triangular tympanum which, it is thought, once contained reliefs of Frederick and his son Manfred. However, while this may have had significance for future generations, it cannot have had much contemporary propaganda value in such a remote place. It is not even clear whether Frederick himself ever lived in it. More pertinent was the portal at Capua, built in 1234, which formed a vast wall in which were set niches containing figures, again not dissimilar to the backdrop of a Roman theatre. Originally one contained a statue of Frederick himself, pointing imperiously, and denouncing those who might attempt to disrupt his protectorate (Van Cleve 1972:332–40). But the determination of the papacy to eliminate the Hohenstaufen blocked any future development of Frederick's Romanism. Not until March 1312, with the arrival of the Emperor Henry VII in Pisa, having made an alliance with the city eighteen months before, was there again a serious attempt at pro-imperial political art. Giovanni Pisano was employed to sculpt groups around the Porta di San Ranieri of the cathedral. On the one side, a Virgin and Child with a kneeling figure representing Pisa, was accompanied by the words, 'I am Pisa, handmaid of the Virgin, tranquil under her protection'. On the other was Henry himself, 'There rules Henry known as a friend to Christ' (Pope-Hennessy 1972:11–12).

However, the artistic flowering of the Italian peninsula cannot be seen only in terms of the political aspirations and self-images of the governing elites. There was, too, a deep need for forms of religious expression which satisfied the contemporary perception of God as the suffering Christ on the Cross who had lived as a man in the midst of human society. This was especially true of the commercially orientated societies of the city-states, where guilt and contrition for activities such as usury, found outlets in support for movements advocating a rejection of materialism. Until well into the seventh century the Church had been deeply concerned to combat Arianism, whose adherents refused to accept that the elements of the Trinity were co-eternal, and therefore the ecclesiastical authorities had seen an especial need to stress God's divinity in all its fullness. But as the economy became more sophisticated and Arianism disappeared, there seemed less need for such a view. Greater reliance was placed on monetary and judicial systems which worked only because society had confidence in them. Such attitudes affected the relationship with God, increasingly seen in personal terms rather than as a capricious punitive force (Becker 1981:4–17). While the rise of the Franciscans was the most overt indicator of these changes and this is strongly reflected in art and building, the Italian cities and towns showed a remarkable enthusiasm for a wide range of religious movements, including all the orders of friars, lay religious fraternities and heretical groups like the Waldensians and the Cathars.

The first illustrations inspired by the Franciscans concentrated upon the life of the saint himself, using source material provided by the accounts of Thomas of Celano and references of those who had witnessed him preaching or knew of special events such as his meeting with the Sultan of Egypt. The oldest surviving example of a developing cult is a large icon-like representation of St Francis on an altarpiece at Pescia (near Lucca), by Bonaventura Berlinghieri, dated 1235. Six scenes set along the sides record famous incidents, including the Stigmatisation and the Preaching to the Birds. A little later and a good deal cruder artistically are some early panels by Margaritone (Margarito d'Arezzo, 1216–93) or his shop, in which the stigmata are prominently displayed. Later works are more often based on the official life of St Bonaventura, which reflects the Conventual position within the order. These include a much more extensive account of his life in twenty scenes on an altarpiece at Santa Croce in Florence by an anonymous artist, probably from the late 1260s, and the famous fresco cycle in the upper church at Assisi, dating from the 1290s, which may be by Giotto. In a context of growing discontent among the Spirituals, the submission of St Francis and his followers to the papacy is carefully emphasised (see Plate 9).

The Franciscan cult found a second major form of expression in devotion to the Virgin Mary, already well established in France and illustrated in stained glass and stone. In Italy, however, it was particularly associated with St Francis. According to Thomas of Celano,

> Toward the Mother of Jesus he was filled with an inexpressible love, because it was she who made the Lord of Majesty our brother. He sang special *Praises* to her, poured out prayers to her, offered her his affections, so many and so great that the tongue of man cannot recount them. But what delights us most, he made her the advocate of the order and placed under her wings the sons he was about to leave that she might cherish them and protect them to the end.
>
> (Habig 1980:521)

One striking example of this devotion in art can be seen in the small panel known as the Madonna of the Franciscans, painted by Duccio in the 1290s, probably as one wing of a triptych. Here, three Franciscans kneel at her feet in various degrees of obeisance, while the child reaches out to them (Cole 1980:31–4).

Just as Francis's devotion to the Virgin encouraged the spread of her Cult, so too did his whole life, culminating in the stigmata of 1224, invite comparison with that of the suffering Christ. Portrayals of Francis move from the iconic or the glove-puppet to more realistic representations of the man himself set within his familiar town and countryside. Sometimes, as in the Crucifixion by Giunta Pisano in San Francesco at Arezzo, *c.*1240, Francis is shown at the feet of the crucified figure. More often the influence is less direct but equally potent, in that Italian artists increasingly painted Christ with sunken head, pale features and tortured body as they developed the techniques to accommodate contemporary interests. In Florence, this change was accomplished with considerable rapidity, first by Coppo di Marcovaldo and then, more effectively, by Cimabue who, in turn, influenced and perhaps taught Giotto. The figure portrayed in Cimabue's Crucifixion for Santa Croce, *c.*1285, shows this change from the formality of the past (see Plate 25).

Dominican influence was especially powerful through the order's direct patronage, particularly after 1300. A spectacular example is Simone Martini's large polyptych for the altar of the house of Santa Caterina at Pisa completed in 1320 in time for the holding of the order's general chapter there. In the centre is the Virgin and Child with God the Father above; saints and prophets are set into the other panels. The scale is ambitious, for it includes forty-four pictures, but they are not stereotyped clones; indeed the individuality of the saints, together with clear inscriptions, answered contemporary needs. It is perhaps a little ironic that one such portrayal – that of the plump features of Thomas Aquinas – itself became a prototype for later depictions of him (Cannon 1982). Apart from the two great mendicant orders, lay religious fraternities, although much smaller, could also sometimes muster surprising resources when they wanted to acquire an appropriate image for their cult. One such group was that of the Laudesi, a

Plate 25 The change in the concept of God from the avenging Lord of the Old Testament to the human, suffering Christ of the New Testament is movingly depicted here by the Florentine master Cimabue. Church of Santa Croce. *c.*1285. (Photograph reproduced by permission of Scala.)

Florentine fraternity whose members were largely drawn from the artisan class. They spent most of their income on singing masses for the deceased, but the Virgin was the centre of their ritual and to this end they used 150 *lire* on a painting of her by the great Sienese master, Duccio. The finished work, known now as the Rucellai Madonna, uses perspective and colour to striking effect (White 1979:32–42). The artisans must have thought their money well spent.

The commissioning of paintings and sculptures was accompanied by a similar increase in the number of churches and municipal buildings which provide their setting, but in neither case was there such a striking development of style as had been experienced in northern France. In Italy, however, indigenous styles were strong and, despite the vicissitudes of the barbarian invasions, the structure of urban life had been maintained more successfully than anywhere else in the west. The techniques of mosaic and fresco therefore continued to be used as they had been in the past and both demanded large areas of wall space rather than the glass cages of the Gothic world. More than anywhere else, too, Roman remains were available, exercising a pervasive influence on artists, sculptors and architects, and convincing the rulers of great cities like Perugia and Siena that it was prestigious to connect their origins with those of Rome. Indeed, the attraction of the antique was not confined to Italy. Major twelfth-century patrons, like Suger and Henry of Blois, Bishop of Winchester, looked to Rome for inspiration and, in Henry's case, for the acquisition of classical statues as well.

Three types of buildings stand out from this period: the cathedrals of Tuscany, the aisleless churches of the friars, and the town halls of the municipalities. The cathedrals had been promoted by communal rivalry begun by the rebuilding of Orvieto in the 1290s and ended by Siena's spectacular failure to outdo all the others when the cathedral extension was abandoned in the 1340s. The mendicant churches were designed for preaching unimpeded by physical obstacles in the nave, but their relative simplicity also accorded with the professed objectives of the orders which built them. The same partial acceptance of Gothic can also be discerned in the town halls and the palazzi of the captains and podestà which sprang up in most urban centres in Lombardy, Tuscany and Umbria during the thirteenth century. Large rooms with Gothic vaulting are contained within an overall design which, often with an open loggia below and a hall on the first floor, owed more to the imperial palaces of the past than to north French styles. As in France, the connection between function and design is strong, for the placing and nature of these palazzi reflect the growing dominance of the secular oligarchy. Therefore, early examples, especially in the north, like that of Bergamo (begun 1199) show a close connection with the overriding concerns of commerce and religion, with the market square on one side and the cathedral on the other. But later examples in Tuscany and Umbria in particular emphasise the independence of the oligarchy by removing the town halls from these proximities. Instead, they are designed as part of an integrated layout which includes a large open piazza where the ceremonials of the commune could be performed and the authority of the consuls affirmed.

While the best known figure in the rise of Gothic is that of a patron, Suger of St Denis, it is significant that it is a painter, Giotto di Bondone, whose name dominates the artistic world of Italy in the late thirteenth and early fourteenth centuries. Although Suger wrote two books on the rebuilding of St Denis, he does not mention his architect by name, whereas in 1334, when Giotto was made capomaestro of building in Florence, the appointment seems to have been partly motivated by the fear that, unless he were sufficiently honoured and rewarded, he might be tempted to take up residence elsewhere (Larner 1971:275). Indeed, it is even argued that Giotto was such a valuable property that he was employed by the ruling Guelph party in Florence as a type of communal representative, to be sent to paint for other powers which the commune wished to cultivate (R. Smith 1978). Certainly, he is known to have worked in a very large number of places in Italy, including Naples, Rome and Milan, as well as small towns in Tuscany, Umbria and the Romagna, although examples of his work have not survived in all these places.

Giotto was from a peasant background, born in a village near Florence in *c*.1267. He was probably apprenticed in Florence by 1280, and when this was completed he seems to have set out to use his talent to develop a position as a small businessman. Although the main source of his income must have come from his workshop, he is also known to have leased houses, acted as guarantor for loans, bought and sold property on a modest scale, and rented out looms. By 1320 he had become a member of a professional association, the Arte di Medici e Speziali. He did not become rich, but he did achieve a wealth and status far beyond anything which would have been possible in the peasant society from which he had come. In this sense his life represents that of many thousands of others, drawn into the towns by the greater opportunities offered there.

His work equally reflects the influences upon contemporary Italian art perhaps better than any other single individual. The Scrovegni Chapel at Padua, which he probably painted between 1303 and 1306, not only encompasses the political attitudes of the city-states in the anti-imperial propaganda in the depiction of Justice and Injustice, but also is itself a product of the city's economic environment. Enrico Scrovegni's father had been a usurer so notorious even in the Italian commercial world that he was assigned a place in Dante's Hell. It seems likely that Enrico's patronage of the chapel, containing the whole narrative of Christ's salvation of the world culminating in the Last Judgement, was an attempt at expiation both for himself and his father. Although Enrico himself is shown kneeling on the side of the saved, Giotto did not otherwise spare his patron, for usurers hang by the strings of their money-bags in the section of the Last Judgement given over to Hell. But Padua was not the greatest commercial centre in Italy. Much more prominent was Giotto's base, Florence, and here he worked for clients whose financial network dwarfed that of Scrovegni. The Bardi and the Peruzzi were among the chief banking families of Florence and their connections were international in scope. Yet they too attempted to clean off the taint of money by commissioning Giotto to decorate their chapel at Santa Croce with narratives of two archetypal ascetic figures, St Francis and St John the Baptist. In the Bardi chapel, for example, there are six scenes from the life of St Francis, including his conversion to poverty. Three other Franciscan figures, famous for their renunciations, are also shown: St Louis of Toulouse, St Clare and St Elizabeth of Hungary.

Most of all, Giotto's work demonstrates the religious tastes of his place and time. The faith in the Virgin Mary as an approachable intercessor needed to be matched by portrayals of her which brought the onlooker into contact. In the Madonna and Child with Angels from the church of San Giorgio in Florence, probably late 1290s, Giotto created just such a figure, a sympathetic mother who looks at and not through the seeker after her aid. This view of the Virgin naturally reinforced the public appetite for details of her life on earth. In the Scrovegni Chapel the walls are divided into horizontal narrative bands, beginning at the top of the south wall and ending at the bottom of the north wall. Within these bands Giotto not only developed very fully the fragmentary and apocryphal sources of the Virgin's life, but also incorporated the lives of her parents Joachim and Anna. The natural culmination of these events is the life of Christ, which completes the narratives. Within each individual scene the expressive faces, the solid bodies, the strong sense of movement, and the realistic spatial relationships communicated directly with the laity of the Italian communes. But the more diligent the observers, the more they will be rewarded, for the layout enables the panels to be 'read' in several ways. Indeed, ultimately the choice of the scenes to be included was to some extent subordinated to this scheme. A vertical reading of the south wall, for example, reveals the 'Adoration of the Magi' above 'Christ washing the feet of the Disciples' and, a little further on, the 'Flight into Egypt' above 'Christ brought to judgement before Caiaphas'. The same principle is followed through to the dividing band, within which are quatrefoils containing further scenes. One such scene shows Jonah disappearing into the whale, from which he was released after three days, placed

Plate 26 The emphasis on the consonances of the Old and New Testaments could be shown in painting as well as in biblical commentary. In the Scrovegni chapel in Padua, Giotto, following Christ's own reference in Matthew 12:39–41, placed the story of Jonah and the Whale (Jonah 1:15–17), seen as prefiguring the Resurrection, next to the scene of the Lamentation. (Photograph reproduced by permission of Scala.)

next to the major narrative scene of the Lamentation before the Resurrection (see Plate 26). In the Scrovegni chapel Giotto adopts the method of correspondences so fundamental to the medieval approach to the Old and New Testaments for his own purposes, so that the onlooker is presented with a series of complex but still accessible interrelationships in Christ's life from which he might draw moral lessons and gain spiritual edification (Alpatoff 1947).

19

Western Christendom and the wider world

Byzantium and Islam dominated the Mediterranean world in the early middle ages. The Byzantines had survived the barbarian invasions of the fourth and fifth centuries and, under Justinian between the 530s and the 560s, had even tried to regain control of north Africa, Italy and Spain. Although after Justinian the attempt to recreate the Roman Empire could not be sustained, the conviction that the world could be properly reconstructed and ordered only under Byzantine aegis remained fundamental to rulers of Constantinople. Byzantine survival in the face of the determined threats of first the Persians, who were overcome by Heraclius during the 620s, and then the new power of Islam, which began to expand outside the Arabian Peninsula after the death of the Prophet in 632, did much to justify and deepen this conviction. The rise of Islam was spectacular and permanent; during the 630s the Persian Empire was engulfed and the Byzantines so decisively beaten in battle that they lost Palestine, most of Syria and Egypt. During the remainder of the seventh century Islam, despite schisms within itself, spread across north Africa, and in 711 crossed to the northern shore and began a conquest which was to encompass most of Iberia. Although this effort could not be consolidated outside the peninsula, Islamic power was able to make its presence felt in the Frankish lands, in the islands of the western Mediterranean and along the Italian coast, until the early years of the eleventh century. It was a measure of Byzantine resilience and depth that despite two prolonged and determined attempts to capture Constantinople – between 668 and 676 and 717 and 718 – Islam was unable to complete its Mediterranean expansion by toppling Byzantium. In the early eleventh century the Byzantines could, with justice, still see themselves as the true heirs of the Christian Roman Empire.

But with the death of Basil II, the last great Macedonian emperor, in 1025, the empire began to decline for, although he had once again extended Byzantine power into Armenia in the east and Bulgaria in the west, ruthlessly crushing all opposition, both external and internal, he had neglected to provide an effective heir. None of his successors, first the husbands of his nieces and then members of aristocratic families who were able to seize power, could maintain his conquests. Between 1025 and 1081, when Alexius I Comnenus began to re-establish imperial stability, there were thirteen emperors and empresses, a turnover which in itself is an illuminating comment on the state of Byzantine government which was so dependent upon the personality and qualities of the emperor himself. Weakness at the centre opened the way to internal conflict between the great aristocratic families of the provinces, whose domination of the land and the army made them essential to imperial defence, and the civil aristocracy who held the key to central power in Constantinople. Incompetent emperors and internal disintegration meant that the empire found itself unable to ward off a number of eager and persistent predators. From the middle of the eleventh century they began to perceive that Byzantium's external show had little solid backing and the Normans, the Patzinaks and the Kumans, and the Seljuk Turks, began to encroach upon Byzantine territory from the west, the north and the east respectively. The crushing defeat of the Byzantine army by the Seljuks at Manzikert in eastern Asia Minor in 1071 demonstrated to the world in the most dramatic fashion the imperial inability to defend the frontiers, while at the same time opening up Asia Minor to a disorganised but damaging invasion of Seljuk ghazi leaders, which quickly swallowed up most of the peninsula, including the great city of Nicaea itself. Equally significant was the Norman seizure of the Adriatic port of Bari in the same year, removing Byzantine presence on the Italian mainland for the first time since the era of Justinian.

The Byzantine crisis of the eleventh century coincided with the revival of the west, bringing more frequent contact between the two parts of Christendom and culminating in the great joint venture of the crusades. The reformed papacy created the context for this, for the reunification of the Christian Church under papal headship was, from the beginning of the reform movement, an article of faith. But the relationship between Constantinople and Rome had never been easy, especially when Byzantine inability to provide effective protection for the papacy in the eighth century had led to a papal alliance with the Franks, rapidly followed by the erection of a rival emperor in the west when Pope Leo III had crowned Charlemagne in 800. Moreover, the issue of ultimate authority in the Church had been given an additional edge by the development of differences of custom and rite during the long separation, most noticeably the western incorporation of the words *filioque* in the Creed, an addition which meant that the western Church had become accustomed to chanting that the Holy Ghost proceeded from the Father and the Son. This contradiction of Byzantine usage had led to the pope's omission from the diptychs of the patriarchal churches of Constantinople in 1009, an omission which implied that the pope was no longer regarded as sound in the faith. For papal headship to be acknowledged relations needed to be re-established and to this end Leo IX sent Cardinal Humbert of Silva Candida to Constantinople in 1054. Leo IX's death and the personality clash between Humbert and the Patriarch Michael Cerularius destroyed these initial papal plans, but the 'schism' of 1054 was not terminal, for the struggling Byzantine emperors could not afford further multiplication of their enemies, while papal ambitions were not to be diverted by the ill-temper of undiplomatic individuals. Michael VII negotiated with both the Normans and the papacy in the years immediately after Manzikert, contacts which led Gregory VII to formulate his abortive plan for a holy war in the east, while Alexius I was shrewd enough to see the opportunities opened up by the election of the ecumenically minded Urban II in 1088. The consequence was the Byzantine delegation to Piacenza in 1095 and the pope's appeal to the Council of Clermont in November of that year.

The crusades brought westerners of all social classes into direct contact with the Byzantines and, through the reports of these crusaders, both verbal and written, conveyed an image to a wider public. In one sense, they were deeply impressed. None of them had ever seen a city like Constantinople before, nor had even the most sophisticated experienced anything like the elaborate ceremonial of Byzantine court life. Indeed, the Byzantine political structure was designed to convey an image which was a reflection on earth of the Heavenly Kingdom; an indispensable element in this was the creation of awe in the minds of barbarian outsiders. Despite the fact that his record of the Second Crusade was written partly to place the blame for its failure upon the Byzantines, even Odo of Deuil did not try to disguise the impact Constantinople had upon him.

> Before the city stood a spacious and impressive ring of walls enclosing various kinds of game and including canals and ponds. Also, inside were certain hollows and caves which, in lieu of forests, furnished lairs for the animals. In that lovely place certain palaces which the emperors had built as their springtime resort are conspicuous for their splendor.
>
> (Berry 1948:49)

It is not difficult to understand that such a place was capable of fermenting a potent mixture of wonder and avarice in the minds of some crusaders. Indeed, despite its political vicissitudes, the Rabbi Benjamin of Tudela, who visited the city in 1167–8, was still able to assert that wealth like that of Constantinople was not to be found in the whole world (Adler 1907:13).

Thoughtful commentators could see the advantages of co-operation with such a power, even if some of its gloss had worn off after the disasters of the eleventh century. In the view of Fulcher of Chartres,

> it was essential that all establish friendship with the emperor since without his aid and counsel we could not easily make the journey, nor could those who were to follow us by the same route. To them [the princes] indeed the emperor himself offered as many *numisma* and garments of silk as pleased them, and the horses and money which they needed for making the journey.
>
> (Ryan 1969:80)

Even Odo of Deuil praised the arrangements made by the Emperor Manuel to receive the army of Louis VII as it crossed the Balkans, blaming troubles upon the conflicts engendered by the Germans who had preceded them (Berry 1948:45).

The crusaders, however, had been led to believe that the cause of Christianity was at stake and that death in this cause would be regarded by God as martyrdom, granting to the recipient everlasting glory. Yet, despite the magnificence of the palaces of Constantinople and the care taken to receive the crusading leaders, it soon became evident that their co-religionists did not see the world in the same way as they did. In particular, the circumstances which led to the surrender of Nicaea in June 1097 seem to have gone down in western lore as the archetypal example of what was wrong with the Greeks. According to the author of the *Gesta Francorum*, the Turks eventually decided that their position was hopeless and offered the city to Alexius in return for their freedom. To the author's evident incredulity the emperor agreed.

The emperor, who was a fool as well as a knave, told them to go away unhurt and without fear; he had them brought to him at Constantinople under safe-conduct, and kept them carefully so that he could have them ready to injure the Franks and obstruct their crusade.

(R. Hill 1962:17)

The fact was that the Byzantines were not fighting a holy war, but trying to recover lost territory in Asia Minor. Their aims seem to have been quite limited and specific, for they concentrated upon controlling the coasts and the important river valleys rather than reincorporating the difficult interior (Hendy 1970). Moreover, St Augustine's views on the just war were not read in the east, nor would they have been appreciated. John Kinnamos, one of Manuel I's secretaries, described strategy as an art, in which it was necessary to know when it was appropriate to flee as well as when to press home one's advantage. 'Since many and various matters lead to one end, victory, it is a matter of indifference which one one uses to reach it' (Brand 1976:129–30). Many western crusaders saw this attitude as treachery, an opinion greatly strengthened by their personal experiences in struggling to cross the interior of Asia Minor, which was not only difficult terrain, but also extremely dangerous because of the apparent indifference of the Byzantines to its security. No twelfth-century crusader army passed through central Asia Minor unscathed; most foundered there and failed to reach Palestine as an effective fighting force. Moreover, no crusading army travelling overland could carry sufficient supplies to feed itself without foraging; since the major part of the journey lay in Byzantine territory there was certain to be friction.

Such differences in outlook, methods and objectives sometimes led the crusaders to forget any logistical help which they had received and, instead, to convince themselves that the Byzantines were positively hostile. The idea that Alexius was trying to obstruct the First Crusade might be dismissed as pro-Norman bias, except for the fact that it was widely believed in the army as a whole. Raymond of Aguilers, for instance, chose to describe the massacre of the People's Crusade as a Byzantine betrayal, brought about because the emperor had forced the peasants, 'unfamiliar with both the locale and the art of war', to cross the Straits, where they became easy victims for the Turks (H. Hill and L.L. Hill 1968:27). This view persisted and indeed gained in virulence during the twelfth century. In his account of Richard I's capture of Cyprus from the 'emperor' Isaac Comnenus in May 1191, Ambroise calls him a tyrant who lived in vice and corruption and compares his treason to the two worst examples he can think of, Judas and Ganelon. The friendship between him and Saladin, he asserted, had been sealed by the drinking of one another's blood (Ailes and Barber 2003:2:50–1). For Odo of Deuil, the Turks were actually better than the Greeks (Berry 1948:141), while Robert of Clari, in the early thirteenth century, claimed that the Byzantines were worse than the Jews (McNeal 1936:94).

Even those with more ready access to the councils of the leaders were quite prepared to express similar views. William of Tyre, although favourable towards the idea of an alliance between the Kingdom of Jerusalem and the Byzantine Empire during his own time in the 1160s and 1170s, nevertheless condemned Alexius I out of hand as a perjurer because of his failure to come to the aid of the crusaders at Antioch. Indeed, William's dislike of Alexius is so strong that his objectivity largely deserts him when he comes to this subject.

Thus, more and more, day by day, the trickery of the Greeks and the treachery of the emperor were revealed. There was now no one of the chiefs to whom it was not plain, in fact clearer than the sun at midday, that Alexius was pursuing our people with intense hatred and that he detested the whole Latin race.

(Babcock and Krey 1941:1:146)

Otto of Freising, who suffered directly from the disasters of the German expedition during the Second Crusade in 1148, was apparently prepared to believe that Alexius was in collusion with the Turks and fishes up the old story of the surrender of Nicaea to prove his point (Mierow 1966:416).

Such obvious evil could stem only from innate defects. Here twelfth-century writers could draw upon a tradition of extravagant abuse which was as old as the empire itself, becoming particularly pertinent with the growth of rivalry between the eastern and western parts of the empire in the late fourth century. Thus, according to Odo of Deuil, 'whoever has known the Greeks will, if asked, say that when they are afraid they become despicable in their excessive debasement and when they have the upper hand they are arrogant in their severe violence to them' (Berry 1948:57–9). The Cistercian chronicler of the Fourth Crusade, Gunther of Pairis, used this view to justify the pillage of relics which, he maintained, the Greeks were unworthy to hold.

Greece, the scum of scum – a people impious to Greek kings,
Whom it was wont to butcher or blind.
An evil city, full of deceit and unworthy of the sun's light.
Constantinople: A hardworking folk – but only for flim-flam;
A people ignorant of government, happily subject to no law;
Citizens of sacrilege, a people impious to its own king;
An idle, cowardly rabble, an unfaithful burden to its kings;
A people in whom evil deceit has found a comfortable home.

(Andrea 1997:90)

Even William of Tyre, whose admiration for the Emperors John and Manuel is quite open, more than once resorts to the cliché that one should beware Greeks bearing gifts, implying that they were flatterers who could not be trusted.

Lethargic, effete and untrustworthy, they could not compare with, for example, the fighting qualities of the sturdy and masculine Germans. According to the Byzantine historian Niketas Choniates, who was probably present in his capacity as Grand Logothete, in 1196 ambassadors from Henry VI came to Constantinople to threaten the empire, and were amazed to see the court of Emperor Alexius III dressed in the most dazzling attire, supposedly to impress them. Niketas believed that this had exactly the opposite effect, quoting the Germans as saying that if the negotiations failed, the Byzantines 'would have to stand in battle against men who are not adorned by precious stones like meadows in bloom, and who do not swell in pride like beads of pearls shimmering in the moonlight'. Among the German warriors 'clotted beads of sweat from their day-long toil outshine the pearls in the beauty of their adornment' (Magoulias 1984:262). Indeed, the rivalry between the two imperial claimants in east and west gave extra bite to German dislike of Byzantium, a feeling which, as William of Tyre suggests, was evidently reciprocated.

> For it is well known that the Greeks have always looked with distrust on all
> increase of power by the western nations (as they still do), especially by that of
> the Teutonic nation, as rivals of the empire. They take it ill that the king of the
> Teutons calls himself emperor of the Romans. For thereby he seems to detract
> too much from the prestige of their own emperor, whom they themselves call
> monarch, that is, one who rules supreme over all and therefore is the one and
> only emperor of the Romans.
>
> (Babcock and Krey 1941:2:170)

It is noticeable that John Kinnamos, while generally favourable to Louis VII of France,
took particular satisfaction from the defeat of the Germans in Asia Minor during the
Second Crusade. 'Then it was possible to observe those who were formerly rash
braggarts, who attacked in the fashion of irresistible brutes, cowardly and ignoble and
incapable of either doing or planning anything' (Brand 1976:68). As this passage
implies, western accusations were not entirely without foundation. According to
Niketas Choniates, the Germans did indeed suffer from ambushes laid by the Greeks
as well as from food profiteering and fraud (Magoulias 1984:38–9).

Lack of military co-operation and political rivalry impinged heavily on the crusaders
and these problems in turn had damaging effects upon the papal aim of repairing the
religious divergences which had developed during the early middle ages. Differences in
ritual, liturgy and language were exaggerated by the conflicts which arose from the
crusades until Odo of Deuil, abandoning all restraint, abused the Greeks as heretics,
whose deaths were as a consequence quite justified (Berry 1948:55–7). While the papacy
always took care to distinguish between schism and heresy, the populace on both sides
took little notice of this distinction. In April 1182 a cousin of the late Manuel I,
Andronicus Comnenus, achieved a *coup d'état* in Constantinople, in the course of
which he gathered support by exploiting the deep-seated hatred of the populace for the
Latins who were mostly settled in the colony along the Golden Horn. William of Tyre's
description of the terrible massacre which followed shows his profound disillusionment
with the policy of unity in which he had once believed, and emphasises the depth of
religious animosity which now existed.

> Regardless of treaties and the many services which our people had rendered to
> the empire, the Greeks seized all those who appeared capable of resistance, set
> fire to their houses, and speedily reduced the entire quarter to ashes. Women
> and children, the aged and the sick, all alike perished in the flames. To vent their
> rage upon secular buildings alone, however, was far from satisfying their unholy
> wickedness; they also set fire to churches and venerated places of every
> description and burned, together with sacred edifices, those who had fled
> thither for refuge. No distinction was made between clergy and laymen, except
> that greater fury was displayed toward those who wore the honourable habits
> of high office or religion. Monks and priests were the especial victims of their
> madness and were put to death under excruciating torture.
>
> (Babcock and Krey 1941:2:464–5)

The massacre reveals the dark side of this splendid city, an aspect of which Odo of
Deuil had been well aware despite his admiration for the palaces, parks and water
system. As in the Tuscan cities of the thirteenth and fourteenth centuries, beneath the

splendours of the property owned by the wealthy, there was a warren of squalid alleyways in which crime flourished (Berry 1948:65), a breeding-ground for the xenophobia of 1182.

The ferocity of the attack of 1182 demonstrates the degree to which relations had deteriorated. It was not exclusive to one side. In 1185 the forces of King William II of Sicily, reviving the long-standing Norman rivalry with the empire, devastated Thessalonica, Byzantium's second city. According to the account of the Greek archbishop, Eustathius, the barbarians, as he calls them, cut down anybody that they could find, often piling up the bodies in obscene positions in derision. Even the city's dogs were killed, he claims.

> Chaste women were contaminated in the sanctuaries by the lust of the enemy, and offenses against their purity were carried out against married women, and against virgins not required to lead a chaste life and against the spouses of God [nuns] who are witnesses against the guilty. If this had happened to only one of them, the evil would of course have been less, but it became so common among these women, one might say like a urinal used by all, that one cannot lament them enough.
>
> (Geanakoplos 1984:367)

Therefore, although a series of quite specific events led to the sack of Constantinople by the men of the Fourth Crusade, it is clear that the ability of the Venetians to manipulate the army between 1202 and 1204 was greatly helped by the predisposition of many crusaders to believe ill of the Greeks. By 1204 a stereotyped Greek – violent, perfidious, effeminate and a religious deviant – was firmly implanted in the western mind. Moreover, the empire in which he lived was possessed of fabulous wealth and prize relics, neither of which it had any moral right to hold. Yet, although the crusades had helped create a public opinion which was bitterly hostile to Byzantium, once Constantinople had actually been taken by the Latins and large principalities and fiefs had been carved out in Greece and the islands, they were unable to turn these experiences into a positive commitment to defend the new states.

Western attitudes towards the empire of Romania and Frankish Greece in the thirteenth century suggest that, except for special interests like those of the Venetians, hostility to Byzantium was more a consequence of the empire's alleged obstruction of the crusade to the Holy Land, than of a desire to see the demise of Byzantium as such. Certainly, after 1204, the papacy found it difficult to stimulate much enthusiasm for either settlement or crusade among the general public in the west. When Michael Palaeologus regained Constantinople for the Byzantines in 1261 it was lamented that the whole city was desolate, for Latin slavery had brought it into ruin. Because so little had been done towards its upkeep, the Byzantines seem to have believed that the Latins had lost all confidence that they could retain Constantinople indefinitely (Migne 1865:219). Neither Innocent III's glowing picture of a land full of material delights, nor the indulgences offered by Honorius III in an attempt to garner support for the crusade of William IV of Montferrat between 1217 and 1225, had much effect, and by the 1230s and 1240s the Latin emperor was forced to tour the west trying to stimulate interest and support. The fall of Constantinople in 1261 brought forth a tragic outpouring from Urban IV, but the reaction of most westerners was to complain about papal demands for taxation to pay for an expedition to recover it. Only the Venetians, whose trading interests were at stake and, from the 1260s, Charles of Anjou, who dreamt of a Mediterranean empire, were prepared to provide practical help. Indeed, in 1262 Urban IV found it necessary to tell Franciscan preachers to relay the Venetian offer of free passage for crusaders to Constantinople, while an indulgence of between forty and one hundred days could be granted even to those who merely turned up to listen to the preaching (Guiraud 1901:46–8).

Once the immediate shock of 1261 had passed, even the popes moderated their stance, for Michael Palaeologus hoped to deflect Angevin threats by reviving papal hopes that Church union could still be achieved, even though the Latins had lost political control of Constantinople. Under Gregory X (1271–6) the matter was brought to a head, for he was not prepared to tolerate Michael's manoeuvrings any longer. At the Council of Lyon in July 1274 Byzantine representatives actually conceded papal primacy and the insertion of *filioque* into the Creed. The victory was apparently rubbed in at a mass in the cathedral of St John at Lyon on 28 July in which Greek-speaking Dominicans and Franciscans 'solemnly chanted, in a very loud voice, the creed; and when they came to the article "Which proceeds from the Father and the Son", they chanted [it] solemnly and devotedly three times' (Geanakoplos 1984:218). Although it was backed by the Patriarch of Constantinople and ruthlessly imposed by Michael VIII, the agreement commanded little support among the Byzantines, while in the west Gregory X's successors lacked the tact to make its assimilation any easier. Not surprisingly the union of 1274 was short-lived; in 1307 Clement V excommunicated Michael's successor, Andronicus II, for persistently refusing to implement it.

At the same time western attitudes towards the crusade were changing. While many people still believed in the need for military expeditions, many also now saw these as a means of opening up a country to missionary work. Some friars actively sought martyrdom in Islamic territories, although, as the Franciscans who tried to bring the Christian message to Seville in 1219 found, even the most provocative behaviour did not always bring the desired results (C.C. Smith 1989:2:26–31). More practical proponents accepted the need to establish political and military control first, so that by the late thirteenth century crusade and mission were seen, not as alternatives, but as complementary (Kedar 1984:133–5). This point was not lost on the Byzantines, who distrusted all western projects on the grounds that, in one way or another, they were a means of imposing Latin culture. The proposals made by the Norman lawyer, Peter Dubois, in *c*.1307, are a case in point. Dubois, obsessed with a dream of French hegemony in the whole of the Mediterranean, advocated the establishment of schools in which boys and girls could be taught oriental languages, including Greek, thus enabling them to take on the Byzantines on their own ground. Once the system was in operation, there would then be loyal Franks available to begin the task of conversion and assimilation. Moreover, those girls sufficiently attractive 'in face and figure' and educated by this system, should be married off to Greek clerics, since the Greeks refused to accept the western tradition of clerical celibacy in any case.

> Wives with such education, who held the articles of faith and the sacraments according to Roman usage, would teach their children and husbands to adhere to the Roman faith and to believe and sacrifice in accordance with it. They would employ arguments and opportunities far more effective than those which by the wiles of his wives led Solomon, the wisest of men, into idolatry. Such women, through love of their native land, would arrange to have many girls

from these schools married to their sons and other leading men of the land, especially to clerics who eventually are to be elevated to prelacies. They would have chaplains celebrating [Mass] and chanting according to the Roman ritual, and would gradually by this means draw the inhabitants of those districts to the Roman ritual.

But Greek suspicion was more than justified, for this Latinisation was not to be achieved by peaceful persuasion; the essential preliminary was first the conquest of the Holy Land and, on the return journey, the installation of Charles of Valois, brother of Philip IV and husband of Catherine of Courtenay, heiress to the Latin claims to Constantinople, as emperor (Brandt 1936:176–7, 119, 156).

It is difficult to know whether ideas such as those of Dubois were widespread for, considered overall, his plans were largely impractical and he never achieved the position of influence at the French court which he seems to have coveted. Hostile attitudes to Byzantium were widespread in the twelfth century because crusading ventures were dependent upon Greek help at least for their initial survival in the Balkans and, in particular, in central Asia Minor. With the fall of Constantinople in 1204 and the huge increase in Mediterranean shipping capacity in the thirteenth century, there was less reason for the Byzantines to impinge upon the public consciousness and the issue lost much of its urgency.

Views of the Muslim world were similarly moulded by contemporary events. There seems to have been considerable though scattered information on the nature of Islam available to westerners in the early middle ages, yet it was not until the crusading era that anyone felt impelled to collate this material and fashion it into a definable image. Signs of this change can be demonstrated by examining the differing reactions of the Castilians and the French to the capture of Toledo in 1085. Alfonso VI of Castile, long used to dealing with the Muslim taifa states, agreed that the inhabitants should keep their lives and property, as well as a mosque, but the newly elected Archbishop of Toledo, Bernard of Sédirac, clearly found this attitude incomprehensible. According to Rodrigo Ximénez de Rada (d. 1247), one of his successors in the see, while the king was away he 'entered the chief mosque of Toledo, and having purged it of the filth of Muhammad, set up an altar of the Christian faith, and placed bells in the main tower so that the Christians could be called to worship' (C.C. Smith 1988:1:88–91). During the crusading period it was necessary for clerical propagandists to show that Muslims were responsible not only for an illegal conquest of God's patrimony, but also for atrocities committed against Christians in the Holy Land and elsewhere, atrocities which were the inevitable result of distorted religious belief and foul social practices. A direct concomitant of the Holy War, therefore, was the creation of a 'Saracen' stereotype, just as the emergence of the Greek stereotype was one of its by-products.

One of the most popular accounts of Urban II's Clermont speech was that written by Robert the Monk some time before 1107. Robert had been present at Clermont, but neither he nor the pope whom he claimed to be quoting based their views of the Muslims on any objective evidence. For Robert the circumstances of the crusade were part of a divine plan in which Muslim cruelty was part of the structure. According to Robert, the Turkish invasion had devastated the Christian east, destroying churches and enslaving their congregations.

> And it pleases them to torment their victims with a foul death, for they pierce them in the navel, drag out the head of the intestines, which they tie to the trunk of a tree and, in this way, flog them round it until, the viscera having been extracted, they fall prostrate to the ground. They fire arrows at those tied to trees; they strike at their extended necks with a naked sword and see whether they can decapitate them with one blow. What shall I say about the execrable debauching of the women, about which it is worse to speak than to remain silent.
>
> (Robert the Monk 1866:727–8)

As a participant in the crusade, Raymond of Aguilers was able to add greater verisimilitude, for he claims that his information came from actual victims, the Maronite Christians of the Lebanese Mountains.

> But if some because of God's grace defied the pagans, they were forced to hand over their beautiful children to be circumcised and trained in the Koran. Furthermore, fathers were murdered, while mothers were abused and their children snatched from their arms. The flaming evil passions of this race of men incited them to tear down churches of God and the saints, break to pieces images, gouge out the eyes of the more indestructible and use the statues as targets for their arrows. They tumbled altars and made mosques of the great churches. But if some poor tormented Christian soul wanted an image of God or a saint in his home, he had to pay for it month after month, year after year, or else see it trampled and crushed in filth. What I am about to relate is really too disagreeable. They placed youths in brothels and exchanged their sisters for wine for more lewdness.
>
> (H. Hill and L.L. Hill 1968:109)

The idea that the Turks had desecrated Christian images was perpetuated by William of Tyre, who had studied the contemporary accounts of the First Crusade for his own history. According to William, the Turks had 'spent their rage as if on living persons' (Babcock and Krey 1941:1:296).

In the Christian view these actions were intimately related to the corrupt nature of the Islamic faith, although it is not to be expected that the writers would produce an entirely consistent picture. The author of the *Gesta*, who had a penchant for placing imaginary speeches in the mouths of Muslims, has an Egyptian emir, defeated by the Christian army near Ascalon, in August 1099, crying out to the spirit of the gods, and swearing 'by Mohammed and by the glory of all the gods' never to raise another army, thus depicting Islam as polytheistic and Mohammed as a deity (R. Hill 1962:96). Over ninety years later, at the time of the Third Crusade, Ambroise even claimed that they carried a banner into battle on which Mohammed was depicted (Ailes and Barber 2003:2:80).

Among many the image of Muslims as polytheistic and idolatrous persisted, but during the twelfth and thirteenth centuries some clerical writers in particular came to accept that Islam was a monotheistic religion. This was not, of course, to its credit. According to the anonymous priest who described the conquest of Lisbon in 1147 they used this simply as a means of abusing the cult of the Virgin and the concept of the Trinity, declaring it unworthy of us that we should venerate the son of a poor woman with as much reverence as if he were God himself, and should call him both God and the Son of God, although it is well known that there is one God only.

To emphasise this opinion the defenders of Lisbon spat, urinated and defecated upon the cross, before finally throwing it at the Christians (David 1976:130–3). In the mid-thirteenth century Matthew Paris accepted that they believed in one God and abominated idolatry but still repeated the twelfth-century stories that the reason for this was that Mohammed mixed some good doctrines with the bad in order to seduce the unwary more easily. Not surprisingly, a fraud such as Mohammed met an appropriately vile death, falling into a dungheap as a consequence of his epilepsy and drunkenness and choking on his own vomit. While lying there he was smothered by an ugly sow and 'for this reason the Saracens to the present time hate and abominate pigs more than any other animals' (Luard 1880:3:360).

Muslim society was appropriately and consequently perverted. Descriptions of sexual practices had the double advantage of illustrating the point and keeping the reader's attention. Raymond of Aguilers manages to use this as a means of denigrating the Egyptians and complimenting the Franks at the same time. The intention of the sultan, he said, was to capture all Frankish males under the age of 20, together with Frankish women, and then mate them with his own people and 'thereby breed a warrior race from Frankish stock' (H. Hill and L.L. Hill 1968:32). The anonymous priest at Lisbon declared that the city was notorious for attracting anyone with debased sexual tastes (David 1976:95), while Matthew Paris claimed that one of the attractions of Islam was a free and easy attitude towards sex which contrasted with the strictness of Christianity. This helped to explain how Islam had gained so many adherents, for Mohammed had encouraged sexual activity to increase the numbers of his sect (Luard 1880:3:352, 356).

Such views have strong affinities with the *chansons de geste*, especially in ideas expressed by writers such as the author of the *Gesta* and Ambroise, and it seems likely that they drew on a common tradition (M. Bennett 1986). Indeed, Ambroise's account was written in verse with the intention of being read aloud. Epic songs did much to spread views of the Islamic religion among the nobility with whom they were a popular entertainment. Collation of these songs has produced a picture of Muslims who spent their time abusing Christianity and destroying churches. The Muslims themselves were often presented as physically ugly (a characteristic emphasised by Ambroise as well) and addicted to practices like polygamy and buying and selling their women. They frequently ate their prisoners. According to C.M. Jones (1942), these songs are at base the story of a stereotyped duel between true and false gods and, inevitably, the Saracens are betrayed by the inability of their supposed deities to combat the power of Christ. Sculptural reliefs, such as those to be seen on the facades of Romanesque churches along the pilgrimage routes to Compostela in western and southern France and northern Spain, conveyed the same message through a different medium. Equestrian figures ride in triumph against Islam, a triumph partly justified by the sinfulness of the Muslims, sunk in vices which the virtuous Christian soldiers must avoid (Seidel 1976).

Yet the hostility shown by westerners towards the cultures of Byzantium and Islam, while undoubtedly very real, can be exaggerated. The rhetoric of an Odo of Deuil or a Robert the Monk catches the eye, but it can create an unbalanced picture. Odo's extremist view of the Greeks, derived from the experiences of Louis VII's army during the Second Crusade, was not apparently shared by the king himself. Although in a letter to his regent, Abbot Suger, in 1148 he writes of 'the fraud of the Emperor', he nevertheless also explains that Manuel had received them well on their arrival at Constantinople and attributes the problems of their journey across Asia Minor to Turkish attacks, food shortages and the terrain, rather than to Byzantine treachery (Delisle 1878:495–6). Similarly, Conrad III does not blame Manuel for the disasters which befell the German army but instead emphasises that he had been received at Constantinople with more honour than had been shown to any of his predecessors (Hausmann 1969:354–5). The good relations established led, in October 1148, to an alliance between Manuel and Conrad against their common enemy, Roger of Sicily. William of Tyre, too, while his disillusion with Byzantium after the massacre of 1182 is very evident, nevertheless wrote favourably of the Emperor John and enjoyed a good relationship with the Emperor Manuel, whom he visited in 1167 as an envoy of King Amalric. This visit in turn was part of growing links between the Byzantines and the Latins of the east which resulted in the marriage of the king to Maria Comnena in 1167 and culminated in a joint land and sea operation in Egypt in 1169 (Babcock and Krey 1941:2:348–9).

Nor were all views of the Muslims denigratory, for, in the eyes of the Latin nobility who fought them, the Turks (if not the Egyptians) were soon perceived to possess the heroic fighting virtues so valued by their class. As far as the author of the *Gesta Francorum* was concerned the Turks were superior to the Greeks; he had Kerbogha, the Turkish Atabeg of Mosul, proclaim that they would not give up lands to the crusaders which they had seized from 'an effeminate people'. The Turks, alleged the *Gesta*, were of common stock with the Franks, and if only they had maintained Christian belief 'you could not find stronger or braver or more skilful soldiers' (R. Hill 1962:67, 21). This view foreshadows the developing chivalric culture of the twelfth-century nobility, a culture which found a place for the chivalrous Saracen and the beautiful Muslim princess who is converted to Christianity. Saladin provided a model for the former. A typical example is the story told by the Minstrel of Reims in 1260 about Eleanor of Aquitaine and Saladin at the time of the Second Crusade.

> And when Queen Eleanor perceived how the king [Louis VII] had failed her, and when she had heard tell of the goodness and the prowess and the understanding and the bounty of Saladin, she was desperately enamoured of him in her heart. And she sent greeting to him by one of her dragomans, and bade him know of a surety that if he would contrive to carry her away she would take him to be her lord and would forswear her own religion.

Saladin therefore sent a galley for her and she was discovered only at the last moment, just as she was about to board ship, taking with her two coffers of gold and silver (Stone 1939:258–9). The story is of course as fictional as that of the hysterical Saracen of the *chansons de geste*, cursing his 'gods' in fury after his defeat, and it says more about the sexual fantasies of contemporary western nobles than it does about the realities of Christian–Muslim relationships. Nevertheless, as early as 1191, Richard I was able to use the idea of a dynastic link with Saladin's family as a negotiating ploy, despite the bitterness of the wars between them, so such stories might well reflect a certain climate of opinion despite their romantic flavour (Gillingham 1999:184–5).

To a limited extent the emerging chivalric values of the twelfth century had some direct influences on attitudes towards the Muslims, especially among the Latins in the east who daily came into contact with the Islamic world. The famous descriptions of Frankish society by Usamah Ibn-Munqidh, Emir of Shaizar, give some indication of this. On one occasion, Usamah records how King Fulk told him that he had been made very happy.

> I replied, 'May Allah always make the king rejoice! What made thee rejoice?' He said, 'I was told that thou wert a great knight, but I did not believe previous to that that thou wert a knight.' 'O my lord,' I replied, 'I am a knight according to the manner of my race and my people.'

The recognition by the military classes of these two cultures that they had something in common created a degree of mutual tolerance which could sometimes produce embarrassing incidents when newcomers from the west, unversed in this freemasonry, stepped into a society they did not understand. Usamah had grown sufficiently friendly with some of the Templars at Jerusalem for them to put at his disposal a small oratory in which he could pray. One day when he was at prayer a Frank entered, grabbed him from behind, and turned him towards the east, telling him 'This is the way thou shouldst pray!' Twice the Templars intervened to restrain the man, explaining to Usamah that he had arrived only recently in the kingdom and 'has never before seen anyone praying except eastward' (Hitti 1987:94, 163–4). The testimony of Ibn Jubayr, the Spanish Muslim who visited the Crusader States in 1184, suggests that this was not an isolated incident, for he saw two churches in Acre which had been converted from mosques, but in which Muslims were allowed to worship on one side of the building (Broadhurst 1952:318–19). Even Frankish visitors to the east, however, could sometimes adapt quite quickly. One such visitor actually proposed to Usamah that he send his 14-year-old son back to the west with him to learn 'wisdom and chivalry' (Hitti 1987:161).

Even after periods of concentrated warfare the enemy could still be seen as a recognisable human being and not just as a stereotype. Oliver of Paderborn, the chronicler of the Fifth Crusade, was clearly affected by the mercy shown to the crusaders in 1221 after their surrender.

> When these agreements had been firmly settled through hostages and oaths, the Sultan was moved by such compassion toward us that for many days he freely revived and refreshed our whole multitude. Finally when our affair had been disposed and settled, he procured ships and provisions for a just price, along with safe conduct. Who could doubt that such kindness, mildness, and mercy proceeded from God? Those whose parents, sons, and daughters, brothers and sisters we killed with various tortures, whose property we scattered or whom we cast naked from their dwellings, refreshed us with their own food as we were dying of hunger, although we were in their dominion and power.
>
> (Gavigan 1971:139)

At the beginning of the twelfth century Guibert of Nogent had presented Islam as a heresy in the Arian tradition (Levine 1997:32–3); later contacts with Islam persuaded some Christians that attempts should be made to evangelise as well as conquer. This attitude was strengthened by the growing popularity of public preaching in the west in the thirteenth century. James of Vitry, Bishop of Acre between 1216 and 1228, and

Francis of Assisi, both believed in this approach, although in Francis's case there was an evident willingness to suffer martyrdom which James did not share. There were, however, limits to the concept of mission. Neither saw this as an alternative to the crusade; indeed, it was quickly recognised that preaching (as opposed to martyrdom) stood little chance of gaining its ends if it were not preceded by Christian rule. St Francis's famous meeting with the Sultan al-Kamil near Damietta in 1219 came nearest to the methods of earlier missionaries like St Augustine of Canterbury, who had sought to convert peoples through their leaders, but neither Francis nor the later mendicants enjoyed any success. Even the English Franciscan, Roger Bacon, who thought that crusades were hardly conducive to conversion because they provoked rather than reconciled the Muslims, conceded the need to attack those who remained obstinate. The official view, as expressed by Pope Innocent IV, was that conquest must precede the drive towards conversion (Kedar 1984:97–203). However, the experience of the Crusader States suggests that it is unlikely that this approach would have yielded very much. Crusader chroniclers might praise the bravery of the Turks, but they showed almost no interest in the Muslim subject population of the Kingdom of Jerusalem, who were given no rights in the conquered lands. Some Muslims were baptised and intermarried with the Franks, but no systematic effort was ever made at widespread conversion (Mayer 1978:175–87).

Although popular stereotypes of the Saracen remained current throughout the period, the twelfth and thirteenth centuries did see the emergence of a much wider variety of views about the Muslims. There was a divergence between the intellectual and the popular view. Peter the Venerable's researches into the nature of Islamic belief and his commissioning of a translation of the Koran and other Muslim writings by the school at Toledo in the mid-twelfth century epitomise the spirit of inquiry and disputation which had infused western thought since the late eleventh century, even though Peter's interest was to gather material for a tract against Islam. Otto of Freising was concerned to correct what he saw as popular misconceptions about Islamic belief, as his rewriting of the early-twelfth-century accounts of the martyrdom of Tiemo, Archbishop of Salzburg, during the crusade of 1101, shows.

> That he suffered for his faith in Christ a most reliable tradition affirms, but that he demolished idols is difficult to believe because, as is well known, the Saracens universally are worshippers of one God; they accept the Books of the Law and also the custom of circumcision and do not even reject Christ and the Apostles and the apostolic men; they are cut off from salvation by one thing alone, the fact that they deny that Jesus Christ, who brings salvation to the human race, is God or the Son of God, and hold in reverence and worship as a great prophet of the supreme God, Mahomet, a deceiver of whom mention was made above.
>
> (Mierow 1966:411–12)

A less exalted intellectual than Otto, for all his belief that Lisbon under the Muslims was a sink of iniquity, the anonymous author of the *Conquest of Lisbon* makes an appeal to God that the defeated Muslims should be brought to see the truth of Christianity rather than be punished for their ignorance (David 1976:182–5).

In the thirteenth century a new and awe-inspiring force intruded into this world, that of the Mongols. The nomads of the Asiatic steppe had always in part relied for their survival on predatory attacks on neighbouring, more settled peoples. At various times mobile tribes like the Huns and the Turks had extended their range to the Middle East and the Mediterranean, but none managed to create such a massive land empire as the Mongols achieved in the course of the thirteenth century. The expansion had begun with Chingis Khan, who seized power in 1206. He invaded China, taking Peking in 1215, but the first effects were felt further west in 1218 when some Mongol envoys were murdered by the Khorezmian Turks in eastern Iran and Chingis moved in to take revenge. Thereafter Islam experienced the full force of the Mongols, who ruthlessly cut down any opposition, massacring thousands in a systematic reign of terror intended to discourage resistance. By the 1220s the peoples around the Caspian Sea had been attacked and the chronicler of Novgorod reported the appearance of unknown tribes, whose origins, faith and language were a complete mystery. 'God alone knows who they are,' he wrote in 1224 (Michell and Forbes 1914:64). Although Chingis died in 1227, his third son, Ögödai, continued the conquests, reaching as far west as Poland and Hungary before his death in 1241. Succession disputes interrupted their progress but Mongol power in the western steppe lands was consolidated under another son, Batu, who established himself on the Lower Volga. After the short reign of Kuyuk (d. 1248), the new Khan, Möngke, turned against the symbols of Muslim power in the Middle East, destroying the Assassins in 1256 and smashing Baghdad in 1258. Only the new succession disputes following Möngke's death in 1259 prevented the third main Islamic power, Egypt, from becoming the next victim, for it was a weakened Mongol force that the Mamluks defeated at 'Ain Jalut in 1260. The power struggle among the Mongols was settled in 1262 when Kubilai (Möngke's younger brother) defeated his rivals, but he showed less interest in the western conquests than his predecessors and the real significance of his reign is for Chinese rather than Islamic or Christian history. From this time the Mongols in the Middle East formed a number of separate political units rather than contributing towards the greater empire.

The appearance of the Mongols forced both Islam and Christendom to reappraise their views of the world. Matthew Paris, his interest aroused by the many rumours which were picked up at St Albans, recounts some of the stories current in the west. In 1238 he learned that representatives of the Assassins had come to ask for the alliance of England and France against them. According to them the Mongols had disproportionately large heads and lived off raw meat, including human flesh, although these lurid tales did not apparently affect the complacent, even frivolous, reception accorded the Muslim envoys. Two years later Matthew had had news of the ferocity of the Mongol onslaught and, in 1241, heard tales of conspiracies between them and both Frederick II and later, through trickery, the Jews. According to a letter received by the Archbishop of Bordeaux and copied by Matthew in 1243, female victims of the Mongols were divided into 'the old and the ugly', who were consumed as food, and 'the beautiful', who suffered multiple rape until they died (Luard 1880:3:488–9; 4:76–8, 119–20, 131–2, 273). Some saw the Mongols as having a set of stereotyped characteristics which had typified western views of Islam during the first phase of contact. Others, although equally struck with horror, were stimulated to place them in an apocalyptic context. For them, the Mongols were to be identified with the tribes of Gog and Magog which, it was prophesied, would devastate the world before the coming of Antichrist and the Last Days (McGinn 1979:149–57).

It fell, however, to the papacy to act upon the frightening news that had been received. In 1245 Innocent IV sent John of Plano Carpini, an elderly Franciscan, together with a companion, another Franciscan, Benedict the Pole, on a mission to the Mongols with the double objective of complaining about the massacres and attempting to persuade them that their best hope was to receive Christian baptism. John travelled to Batu's camp in southern Russia, where it was decided that he should be taken to witness the *kuriltai*, the great assembly which met to choose the new Khan. Transported by relays of horses, he reached Karakorum in time for the election in August 1246, and in his account leaves a vivid description of his experiences. However, Kuyuk's reply to the papal message shows that the cultural barrier was almost total.

> You have also said that supplication and prayer have been offered by you, that I might find a good entry into baptism. This prayer of thine I have not understood. Other words which thou hast sent me: 'I am surprised that thou hast seized all the lands of the Magyar and the Christians. Tell us what their fault is.' These words of thine I have also not understood. The eternal God has slain and annihilated these lands and peoples, because they have neither adhered to Chingis Khan, nor to the Khagan [i.e. the supreme ruler], both of whom have been sent to make known God's command.

He rejected the opportunity to become what he described as 'a trembling Nestorian Christian', for 'from the rising of the sun to its setting, all the lands have been made subject to me.' His message to the pope was:

> Now you should say with a sincere heart: 'I will submit and serve you.' Thou thyself, at the head of all the Princes, come at once to serve and wait upon us!' At that time I should recognise your submission.
>
> (Dawson 1980:85–6)

For the Mongols all universal powers, whether represented by pope or caliph, were opponents of their own divinely appointed mission to conquer the world.

Despite the disappointment and, indeed, menace, which emanated from the papal mission, rumours, fed partly by the presence of Nestorian Christians in the Mongol ranks, continued to spread that the Mongols were intending to convert to Christianity. Some saw their hostility to Islam more as a consequence of religious belief than as a matter of geography. Even so, well-informed Christians like Louis IX, who had contacts with the Mongols during his crusade between 1248 and 1254, harboured few illusions about either military or religious co-operation. According to Joinville, looking back on these affairs, the king bitterly regretted that he had ever sent envoys to the Mongols (Shaw 1963:288). He may well have come to this conclusion after receiving the account of the mission of William of Rubruck, which set out from Louis's court at Acre in 1253. He went not as an envoy, but as a priest, in the hope of spreading the faith, but his detailed narrative underlines the frustration of dealing with the Mongols. Following one interview with Möngke, he wrote, 'If I had had the power of working miracles like Moses, he might have humbled himself' (Dawson 1980:197). Within a decade of William's visit Kubilai had come to power and the break-up of the western parts of the empire began, leaving individual Mongol leaders the task of maintaining their positions as best they could. For most of them this meant acquiring the support of populations which were largely Muslim. Although in the east Kubilai remained amenable to visits by westerners, including the Polos and the mendicants, any slim hope that a Mongol–Christian alliance could revive the sinking fortunes of the Crusader States largely vanished by the 1260s, despite sporadic attempts at reviving it. Religious missions did continue – most notably that of the Franciscan, John of Monte Corvino, sent by Nicholas IV in 1289 – but their most important consequences were the creation of Christian outposts in China rather than the conversion of the Mongol leadership.

Although the papal missions to the Mongols were essentially unproductive, the appearance of this new and important pagan people did serve to clarify papal thinking about the proper relationship between Christians and non-Christians. At the time of the First Crusade the papacy had not progressed much beyond the idea that the Islamic occupation of the holy places was an aggressive attack upon Christian lands, which Christians were quite justified in repelling. But the transformation of the eastern drive against the Slavs into a crusade in the mid-twelfth century, and the incursions of the Mongols during the thirteenth century, convinced the papacy that the problem was more complicated, and that the papal position needed to be defined with greater precision. In keeping with the self-image of the reformed papacy, Innocent IV claimed jurisdiction over all peoples, whether Christian or not, on the basis of papal responsibility for all humankind's salvation, but he was equally anxious to show that he was acting on a legal basis. This meant that intervention could be justified only if pagan or infidel rulers were not providing justice (and such injustice included the encouragement or toleration of 'perverted' religious practices) or if missionaries sent by the papacy were not properly received. Some canonists, like Hostiensis, believed that Innocent's view was too restrictive, arguing that infidels possessed no rights in any case because of their beliefs, although it is doubtful if this made much difference in practice, since it seems unlikely that any non-Christian ruler would meet Innocent's conditions unless forced to do so. Innocent's thinking was to lead to the compilation of a list of eighteen peoples to whom missionaries should be sent, ranging from the Bulgarians to the Nubians, apart from those defined as pagans or Saracens (Muldoon 1979:3). It seemed that the world of the late thirteenth century was a much bigger place than it had been in 1095.

Chronology

The following list is intended for rapid reference, but it should not be invested with any more importance than that, since chronologies are no more objective than any other form of historical writing. In particular, they have a bias towards events which can be specifically dated, like battles, as opposed to long-term developments which are less easy to pinpoint, such as the spread of Catharism, thus falsely suggesting a value judgement as to the relative importance of these matters. For additional information see R.L. Storey (1973), *Chronology of the Medieval World 800 to 1491* (London: Barrie and Jenkins).

1048	Election of Pope Leo IX
1053	Defeat of papal forces by the Normans at Civitate
1054	Schism between the western and eastern Churches
1059	Reform of papal electoral process
1061	Death of Cardinal Humbert of Silva Candida
1066	Battle of Hastings
1071	Fall of Bari
1071	Battle of Manzikert
1072	Death of Cardinal Peter Damian
1075	*Dictatus Papae*
1077	Reconciliation of Henry IV to the Church at Canossa
1084	Foundation of Chartreuse
*c.*1084	Consecration of the third church of San Marco, Venice
1085	Capture of Toledo by Alfonso VI of Castile
1086	Domesday Book
1086	Invasion of Spain by the Almoravides
1088	Beginning of the building of the third church at Cluny
1091	Completion of the Norman Conquest of Sicily
1095–9	First Crusade
1098	Foundation of Cîteaux
1106	Battle of Tinchebrai

1109	Death of St Anselm
1111	Paschal II concedes regalia to secular rulers
1113	Hospitallers recognised as an independent order
1119	Foundation of the Templars
1120	Foundation of the Premonstratensians
1120	Wreck of the White Ship
1121	Condemnation of Abelard at the Council of Soissons
1122	Concordat of Worms
1123	First Lateran Council
1130	Roger II crowned King of Sicily at Palermo
1137–51	Rebuilding of the Abbey-Church of Saint-Denis
1137	Union of Aragon and Catalonia under Ramón Berenguer IV
1139	Second Lateran Council
1139	Treaty of Mignano
1139	Arrival of Matilda in England
*c.*1140	Gratian's *Decretum*
1140	Condemnation of Abelard at Sens
*c.*1141	Death of Orderic Vitalis
1142	Death of Peter Abelard
1144	Capture of Edessa by Zengi
1147	Invasion of Spain by the Almohades
1147	Capture of Libson by Afonso I of Portugal
1147–8	Second Crusade
1151	Death of Suger of St Denis
1152	Marriage of Henry of Anjou to Eleanor of Aquitaine
1153	Death of St Bernard
1155	Execution of Arnold of Brescia
1156	Creation of the Duchy of Austria
1156	Death of Peter the Venerable, Abbot of Cluny
1158	Death of Otto of Freising
1158	Decrees of Roncaglia
1164	Death of Peter Lombard
1164	Death of Heloise
1167	Formation of the Lombard League
1170	Murder of Thomas Becket
1176	Battle of Legnano
1176	Battle of Myriokephalon
1177	Peace of Venice
1179	Third Lateran Council
1180	Death of John of Salisbury
1183	Peace of Constance

*c.*1186	Death of William, Archbishop of Tyre
1187	Battle of Hattin
1189–92	Third Crusade
1190	Foundation of the Teutonic Knights
1193	Death of Saladin
1194	Beginning of the rebuilding of Chartres Cathedral
1194	Conquest of Sicily by Henry VI
1196	Battle of Alarcos
1200	Grant of charter to the University of Paris by Philip II
1201–4	Fourth Crusade
1202	Death of Joachim of Fiore
1202–4	Conquest of Normandy by Philip II
1204	Capture of Thessalonica by Boniface of Montferrat
1205	Conquest of the Morea by William of Champlitte
1206–27	Conquests of Chingis Khan
1209–26	Albigensian Crusades
1212	Battle of Las Navas de Tolosa
1214	Battle of Bouvines
1215	Magna Carta
1215	Fourth Lateran Council
1218–21	Fifth Crusade
1221	Death of St Dominic
1222	Golden Bull of Hungary
1226	Death of St Francis
1226	Teutonic Knights invited into Prussia
1228–9	Crusade of Frederick 11
1229	Treaty of Paris
1230	Union of Castile and León under Ferdinand III
1231	*Liber Augustalis*
1236	Capture of Córdoba by Ferdinand III
1237	Battle of Cortenuova
1241	Mongol invasion of Hungary and Poland
1242	Defeat of the Teutonic Knights by Alexander Nevsky
1244	Loss of Jerusalem by Christians
1245	Deposition of Frederick II at the Council of Lyon
1245–6	Mission of John of Plano Carpini to the Mongols
1247	Coronation of Haakon IV of Norway
1248	Capture of Seville by Ferdinand III
1248–54	First Crusade of St Louis
1249–50	Swedish expedition to Finland
1252	Florence and Genoa strike gold florins
1258	Treaty of Corbeil

1259	Death of Matthew Paris
1259	Treaty of Paris
1260	Carving of Pisan baptistery pulpit by Nicolà Pisano
1260	Battle of 'Ain Jalut
1260	Battle of Montaperti
c.1260	Polos begin travels in Mongol Empire
c.1260	Beginning of paper manufacture at Fabriano
Early 1260s	Compilation of *Siete Partidas*
1261	Recapture of Constantinople by Michael Palaeologus
1266	Battle of Benevento
1266	Greenland accepts Norwegian king
1267	Iceland accepts Norwegian king
1268	Battle of Tagliacozzo
1269	Battle of Colle di Val d'Elsa
1270	Crusade of St Louis to Tunis
1274	Death of Thomas Aquinas
1274	Second Council of Lyon
1274	Death of St Bonaventura
1278	Defeat of Otakar of Bohemia
1280	Death of Albertus Magnus
1282	Sicilian Vespers
1282–3	Conquest of Wales by Edward I
1283	Teutonic Knights complete conquest of Prussia
1290	Expulsion of the Jews from England
1291	Fall of Acre
1291	Vivaldi brothers attempt to find sea route to India
1297	Reform of Venetian election procedures to Great Council
1300	Papal Jubilee
1302	Battle of Courtrai
1302	Peace of Caltabellotta
1302	Bull, *Unam Sanctam*
1303	Attack on Boniface VIII at Anagni
c.1303–6	Painting of Scrovegni Chapel by Giotto
1306	Expulsion of the Jews from France
1307–14	Trial of the Templars
1309	Clement V takes up residence in Avignon
1311	Completion of Duccio's *Maestà*
1311–12	Council of Vienne
1315–17	Severe famine in northern Europe
1319	Dynastic Union of Norway and Sweden
1321	Death of Dante Alighieri
1337	Death of Giotto

Bibliography

This bibliography provides basic information on the themes surveyed in the book, although many of the works recommended probe their subjects much more deeply than this. Where possible, a selection of sources in English translation is provided at the end of each section. It is followed by the References, an alphabetical list of all the works referred to in the text. This bibliography aims both to facilitate rapid cross-reference and to suggest works which enable more detailed study of specific issues to be undertaken, particularly through the collections of source material and the periodical literature.

Reference

Basic definitions, biographical details, and chronological and geographical information can be acquired from some of the excellent reference books available. Three of the most comprehensive are J. Strayer (ed.) (1982–9), *Dictionary of the Middle Ages*, 12 vols (New York: Charles Scribner's Sons), F.L. Cross and E.A. Livingstone (eds) (1997), *The Oxford Dictionary of the Christian Church*, 3rd edn (Oxford: Oxford University Press) and J.B. Friedman and K.M. Figg (eds) (2000), *Trade, Travel and Exploration in the Middle Ages. An Encyclopedia* (New York and London: Garland). Invaluable concise guides include C.R. Cheney (ed.) (2000), *Handbook of Dates for Students of English History* (London: Royal Historical Society) (originally 1945), J. Hall (1992), *Dictionary of Signs and Symbols in Art* (London: John Murray) (originally 1974) and D.H. Farmer (2003), *The Oxford Dictionary of Saints*, 5th edn (Oxford: Clarendon) (originally 1978).

General

Preconceptions about the way to present a synthesis of the history of a wide geographical area over a period of two centuries or more are challenged by the following books, published over half a century by seven historians of very different background and temperament: R.W. Southern (1953), *The Making of the Middle Ages* (London: Hutchinson), F. Heer (1962), *The Medieval World. Europe 1100–1350*, tr. J. Sondheimer (London: Weidenfeld and Nicolson), J. Le Goff (1988), *Medieval Civilization, 400–1500*, tr. J. Barrow (Oxford: Blackwell) (originally 1964), R.I. Moore (2000), *The First European Revolution, c.970–1215* (Oxford: Blackwell), W.C. Jordan (2001), *Europe in the High Middle Ages* (London: Allen Lane) and C.W. Hollister and J.M. Bennett (2002), *Medieval Europe. A Short History*, 9th edn (Boston, Mass. and London: McGraw-Hill) (originally 1964).

Part I The social and economic structure

1 The physical environment

An atlas is essential. J. Engel (ed.) (1970), *Grosser Historischer Weltatlas*, vol. 2, *Mittelalter* (Munich: Bayerischer Schulbuch-Verlag) covers the period from *c*.600 to *c*.1500 and encompasses the known world in those centuries. Moreover, human society is not presented only in terms of the distribution of political power, for the movements of nomads, the establishment of monastic networks and the growth of towns are among the subjects illustrated. It can usefully be employed in conjunction with D. Matthew (1983), *Atlas of Medieval History* (London: Facts on File), which supplements the maps with sharp comment and additional illustrations, and A. MacKay and D. Ditchburn (1997), *Atlas of Medieval Europe* (London: Routledge). The relationship of human beings to their environment is covered from three different but equally important angles in C.T. Smith (1978), *An Historical Geography of Western Europe before 1800* (London: Longman), W.H. McNeill (1977), *Plagues and Peoples* (Oxford: Blackwell) and W.C. Jordan (1996), *The Great Famine: Northern Europe in the Early Fourteenth Century* (Princeton, NJ: Princeton University Press). Jordan's work has valuable insights into the impact of environmental factors upon the economy and society of the high middle ages as a whole, as well as an important synthesisation of developments in this field. The controversial question of climatic fluctuations is placed in a convincing context by E. Le Roy Ladurie (1972), *Times of Feast, Times of Famine. A History of Climate since the Year 1000*, tr. B. Bray (London: Allen and Unwin) (originally 1967). R. Bartlett (1993), *The Making of Europe. Conquest, Colonization and Cultural Change 950–1350* (London: Allen Lane) is a penetrative analysis of the forces which shaped European expansion, making particularly imaginative use of maps, diagrams and graphs. There is much here relevant to other subjects in this book, especially to Chapters 2 and 3.

2 Social structure

The obvious starting-point is medieval religious belief. B. Hamilton (2003), *Religion in the Medieval West*, 2nd edn (London: Hodder Arnold) explains the basic issues so often ignored or assumed in other books. The activities and mental outlook of the nobility are analysed in M. Keen (1984), *Chivalry* (New Haven, Conn. and London: Yale University Press), in the essays by G. Duby (1977), *The Chivalrous Society*, tr. C. Postan (London: Edward Arnold) and in P. Contamine (1984), *War in the Middle Ages*, tr. M. Jones (London: Blackwell) (originally 1980). The realities of the interaction between the two are effectively demonstrated by M. Strickland (1996), *War and Chivalry. The Conduct and Perception of War in England and Normandy, 1066–1217* (Cambridge: Cambridge University Press). For some of the new perspectives emerging from recent research on the role of noble women, see the essays in T. Evergates (ed.) (1999), *Aristocratic Women in Medieval France* (Philadelphia, Pa: University of Pennsylvania Press). A good basis for the study of the peasantry can be gained from two complementary works, those of R. Fossier (1988), *Peasant Life in the Medieval West*, tr. J. Vale (Oxford: Blackwell) (originally 1984) and W. Rösener (1992), *Peasants in the Middle Ages*, tr. A. Stützer (Oxford: Polity Press) (originally 1985). Both make use of recent work in archaeology and anthropology. However, their geographical focus is different in that Fossier draws particularly on the many fine regional studies in France, while Rösener concentrates upon the German and Slavic regions. Between them they offer a more nuanced picture than has often been the case, especially in their discussion of peasant relationships and of material culture. M. Mollat (1986), *The Poor in the Middle Ages. An Essay in Social History*, tr. A. Goldhammer (New Haven, Conn. and London: Yale University Press) (originally 1978) discusses the lives of both rural and urban poor, attitudes towards them and reactions by them to their circumstances. Overviews of urban life are E. Ennen (1979), *The Medieval Town*, tr. N. Fryde (Amsterdam: North-Holland) and D. Nicholas (1997), *The Growth of the Medieval City. From Late Antiquity to the Early Fourteenth Century* (London: Longman). The latter includes fourteen city plans which, used in combination with the text, are valuable in showing the stages in the growth of representative cities across Latin Christendom. Two increasingly important subjects are introduced by S. Shahar (1983), *The Fourth Estate. A History of Women in the Middle Ages*, tr. C. Galai (London: Methuen) and (1989), *Childhood in the Middle Ages* (London: Routledge). N. Orme (2001), *Medieval Children* (New Haven, Conn. and London: Yale University Press) is a fine illustrated study which concentrates mainly on England. See, too, S. Reynolds (1984), *Kingdoms and Communities in Western Europe, 900–1300* (Oxford: Clarendon), which through an examination of lay collective activity, challenges many of the conventional wisdoms on the period. A good overall picture of social attitudes in a specific region can be gained from the three rather different approaches of L. Paterson (1993), *The World of the Troubadours. Medieval Occitan Society, c.1100–c.1300* (Cambridge: Cambridge University Press), M.G. Pegg (2001), *The Corruption of Angels. The Great Inquisition of 1245–1246* (Princeton, NJ: Princeton University Press) and E. Le Roy Ladurie (1978), *Montaillou. Cathars and Catholics in a French Village 1294–1324*, tr. B. Bray (London: Scolar Press). Finally, D. Stenton (1962), *English Society in the Early Middle Ages (1066–1307)* (Harmondsworth: Penguin) remains a model of how a general survey can be created from the sensitive use of specific documentary examples.

Sources are necessarily diffuse. On the French nobility, for example, there is a good selection of documents by T. Evergates (tr.) (1993), *Feudal Society in Medieval France. Documents from the County of Champagne* (Philadelphia, Pa: University of Pennsylvania Press). Two chroniclers with their own very distinct agendas are Guibert of Nogent and Lambert of Ardres, J.F. Benton (1970), *Self and Society in Medieval France. The Memoirs of Abbot Guibert of Nogent* (New York: Harper and Row) and L. Shopkow (tr.) (2001), *The History of the Counts of Guines and the Lords of Ardres* (Philadelphia, Pa: University of Pennsylvania Press). For the other end of the spectrum, see M. Goodich (ed.) (1998), *The Other Middle Ages: Witnesses at the Margins of Medieval Society* (Philadephia, Pa: University of Pennsylvania Press).

3 Economic development

Among the most useful general surveys are R-H. Bautier (1971), *The Economic Development of Medieval Europe*, tr. H. Karolyi (London: Thames and Hudson), which is particularly strong on the Mediterranean, R.S. Lopez (1971), *The Commercial Revolution of the Middle Ages, 950–1350* (Englewood Cliffs, NJ: Prentice-Hall) and N.J.G. Pounds (1994), *An Economic History of Medieval Europe*, 2nd edn (London: Longman). The main focus of Peter Spufford's (2002) *Power and Profit. The Merchant in Medieval Europe* (London: Thames and Hudson) is on the late middle ages. Nevertheless it contains much valuable information on the thirteenth century, as well as many pertinent illustrations, carefully tied into the text. The sections on the development of communications in Chapter 4 are especially relevant, as are the clear descriptions of operations such as the manufacture of cloth in Chapter 5 and on mining in Chapter 7. The French historian, Georges Duby, has been deeply influential since the early 1960s. Two of his works of synthesis are (1968), *Rural Economy and Country Life in the Medieval West*, tr. C. Postan (London: Edward Arnold) (originally 1962) and the slighter but more immediately accessible (1974), *The Early Growth of the European Economy. Warriors and Peasants from the Seventh to the Twelfth Century*, tr. H.B. Clarke (London: Weidenfeld and Nicolson). The papers gathered in G. Astill and J. Langdon (eds) (1997), *Medieval Farming and Technology. The Impact of Agricultural Change in Northwest Europe* (Leiden: Brill) give a very coherent view of how new ideas were applied to agriculture, especially in Flanders, one of the most advanced regions of medieval Europe. Again, it is worth tackling a specific region as well, as in D. Abulafia (1977), *The Two Italies. Economic Relations between the Norman Kingdom of Sicily and the Northern Communes* (Cambridge: Cambridge University Press).

The collection of documents in R.S. Lopez and I.W. Raymond (trs) (1998), *Medieval Trade in the Mediterranean World* (New York: Columbia University Press) (originally 1955) remains the best of its kind, illustrating, among other things, the immense range of different types of contracts created by medieval merchants.

Part II The Church

4 The papacy

There are concise introductions by J.H. Lynch (1992), *The Medieval Church. A Brief History* (London: Longman) and F.D. Logan (2002), *A History of the Church in the Middle Ages* (London: Routledge). W. Ullmann (1972), *A Short History of the Papacy in the Middle Ages*

(London: Methuen), reflects the author's especial interest in ideological influences. More comprehensive are the three balanced surveys by F. Kempf (1980), *The Church in the Age of Feudalism* (*History of the Church*, vol. 3, ed. H. Jedin and J. Dolan), tr. A. Biggs (London: Burns and Oates), C. Morris (1989), *The Papal Monarchy. The Western Church 1050–1250* (Oxford: Clarendon) and I.S. Robinson (1990), *The Papacy, 1073–1198* (Cambridge: Cambridge University Press). Another way of examining the changing nature of the papacy over this period is to look at key pontificates: H.E.J. Cowdrey (1998), *Gregory VII* (Oxford: Clarendon), H. Tillmann (1980), *Pope Innocent III*, tr. W. Sax (Amsterdam: North-Holland) (originally 1954), J. Sayers (1994), *Innocent III. Leader of Europe, 1198–1216* (London: Longman), J.C. Moore (2003), *Pope Innocent III (1160/61–1216). To Root Up and to Plant* (Leiden: Brill) and S. Menache (1998), *Clement V* (Cambridge: Cambridge University Press). Tillmann is not only a good study of a pivotal pontificate, but also, by means of its thematic arrangement, a useful guide to the general preoccupations of the thirteenth-century papacy. It should, however, be read in conjunction with Moore's chronological approach, which conveys a good sense of how Innocent coped with his many problems as they occurred. R.W. Southern (1970), *Western Society and the Church in the Middle Ages* (Harmondsworth: Penguin) is of great value for all four chapters in this part, especially in demonstrating how the apposite example can be used to illuminate a general theme. It will, however, be appreciated more if the reader is forearmed with a little previous knowledge.

The best place to begin on the sources is B. Tierney (1990), *The Crisis of Church and State, 1050–1300* (Englewood Cliffs, NJ: Prentice Hall) (originally 1964), which presents the vital documents of the period, together with a series of neat introductions.

5 The crusades

During the 1970s and 1980s this became one of the most popular subjects of study in this period, attracting international interest. J. Riley-Smith (ed.) (1991), *The Atlas of the Crusades* (London: Times Books) contains some striking maps and reconstructions, together with short introductions to the major themes. H.E. Mayer (1988), *The Crusades*, tr. J. Gillingham (Oxford: Oxford University Press) (originally 1965) and J. Riley-Smith (1987), *The Crusades. A Short History* (London: Athlone Press) are the best one-volume syntheses. Mayer is particularly strong on critical biographical information, while Riley-Smith gives the subject much wider geographical and chronological scope than has been usual in the past. The most comprehensive coverage is the collaborative work edited by K. Setton (1969–90), *A History of the Crusades*, 6 vols (Madison, Wis. and London: University of Wisconsin Press). Like most collective works it is uneven in quality and it has taken so long to publish that parts of it are out-of-date (the original edition of the first volume appeared in 1955). Nevertheless, its wide scope and its detailed biographical and geographical information make it an essential tool. Among many excellent studies of specific crusades are J. France (1994), *Victory in the East. A Military History of the First Crusade* (Cambridge: Cambridge University Press), D.E. Queller and T.F. Madden (1997), *The Fourth Crusade. The Conquest of Constantinople, 1201–4*, 2nd edn (Philadelphia, Pa: University of Pennsylvania Press) and J. Powell (1986), *Anatomy of a Crusade, 1213–1221* (Philadelphia, Pa: University of Pennsylvania Press). Queller and Madden, for example, make a balanced assessment of the many elements involved in this complex expedition, which clarifies the issues without taking sides.

There is an exceptionally wide range of translated sources available, since contemporary chroniclers and poets found the subject difficult to resist, and there was a constant stream of letters from crusaders, popes, legates, the military orders and the Frankish settlers in Outremer. Collections of sources, which illustrate this variety, can be found in L. Riley-Smith and J. Riley-Smith (trs) (1981), *The Crusades. Idea and Reality 1095–1274* (Documents of Medieval History, 4) (London: Edward Arnold), E. Peters (ed.) (1998), *The Chronicle of Fulcher of Chartres and Other Source Materials*, 2nd edn (Philadelphia, Pa: University of Pennsylvania) and A.J. Andrea (with B.R. Whalen) (tr.) (2000), *Contemporary Sources for the Fourth Crusade* (Leiden: Brill).

6 Monasticism and the friars

The most useful general introductions are by C.H. Lawrence (1989), *Medieval Monasticism. Forms of Religious Life in Western Europe in the Middle Ages*, 2nd edn (London: Longman) and (1994), *The Friars* (London: Longman). G. Constable (1996), *The Reformation of the Twelfth Century* (Cambridge: Cambridge University Press) covers a shorter chronological span, but provides depth on a crucial period of monastic change. His introductory chapter offers an important series of definitions, particularly of what he calls 'the vocabulary of religious life'. In the substantive chapters which follow there is a wealth of concrete illustrations. The most important orders are covered by L.K. Lekai (1977), *The Cistercians: Ideals and Reality* (Kent, Ohio: Kent State University Press), A.J. Forey (1992), *The Military Orders. From the Twelfth to the Fourteenth Centuries* (London: Macmillan), J. Moorman (1968), *A History of the Franciscan Order* (Oxford: Clarendon), and W.A. Hinnebusch (1965, 1973), *The History of the Dominican Order*, 2 vols (New York: Alba). P.D. Johnson (1991), *Equal in Monastic Profession. Religious Women in Medieval France* (Chicago: University of Chicago Press) examines why women entered the religious life, their lives as nuns, and the changing role of nunneries within the wider community. Although mainly based on evidence derived from northern France, the conclusions drawn are of general validity. A stimulating context is provided by the first half of L.K. Little (1978), *Religious Poverty and the Profit Economy in Medieval Europe* (London: Elek).

However, recent interest in the monastic orders has generated a renaissance of studies in this field. For example, since the early 1990s, there have been great changes in the perception of the Cistercians and their relationship to the contemporary world. Three of the works which have made substantial contributions to that changing perception are C. Berman (2000), *The Cistercian Evolution. The Invention of a Religious Order in Twelfth-Century Europe* (Philadelphia, Pa: University of Pennsylvania Press), who argues (controversially) that many of the early Cistercian documents, which purport to describe the original ideals, do not date from the period of the first two generations of the Order and, by implication, must therefore be seen as later propaganda. Constable (above) shows that 'the desert' was more a part of 'the rhetoric of reform' and need not be taken too literally, for many Cistercian houses were not far from centres of population or well-frequented routes, and C. Bouchard (1991), *Holy Entrepreneurs. Cistercians, Knights, and Economic Exchange in Twelfth-Century Burgundy* (Ithaca, NY and London: Cornell University Press), using charter evidence from Burgundy, shows that the economic ideals of the Order relate more to the views of a specific group of abbots led by St Bernard, meeting in 1134, than they do to the usual practice of the Order. A rigid structure of rise and decline therefore must be abandoned in favour of a more nuanced picture of Cistercian history in the twelfth and early thirteenth centuries.

Our image of the monks and the friars of the high middle ages is particularly derived from the lives of two saints of the Church, Bernard of Clairvaux and Francis of Assisi, and there are copious sources on both of them. Some impression of St Bernard's dynamic role can be gained from his letters, B.S. James (tr.) (1998), *The Letters of St Bernard of Clairvaux*, introd. B.M. Kienzle (Stroud: Sutton Publishing) (originally 1953). A comprehensive assembly of sources on St Francis has been published by the Franciscan Institute of St Bonaventure University, New York (1999), *Francis of Assisi. The Saint, The Founder, The Prophet*, 3 vols (New York: New City Press), which includes his own writings.

7 Popular religion and heresy

A strong sense of popular attitudes can be gained from R. Finucane (1977), *Miracles and Pilgrims. Popular Beliefs in Medieval England* (London: Dent) and J-C. Schmitt, *Ghosts in the Middle Ages. The Living and the Dead in Medieval Society*, tr. T.L. Fagan (Chicago and London: University of Chicago Press). The latter includes an important chapter on Hellequin's Hunt. Susan Reynolds (1991), 'Social Mentalities and the Case of Medieval Scepticism', *Transactions of the Royal Historical Society*, 6th series, vol. 1, 121–41, challenges modern assumptions that belief in one form or another was universal. A very clear and comprehensive coverage of heresy is M.D. Lambert (2002), *Medieval Heresy. Popular Movements from the Gregorian Reform to the Reformation*, 3rd edn (Oxford: Blackwell). More limited in chronological scope but very effective in analysing the problems of interpretation presented by the evidence is R.I. Moore (1985), *The Origins of European Dissent* (Oxford: Blackwell) (originally 1977). The most comprehensive coverage of the Waldensians and Cathars are E. Cameron (2000), *The Waldenses. Rejections of Holy Church in Medieval Europe* (Oxford: Blackwell) and M.D. Lambert (1998), *The Cathars* (Oxford: Blackwell). The methods used to try to repress the Cathars are described in W.L. Wakefield (1974), *Heresy, Crusade and Inquisition in Southern France, 1100–1250* (London: Allen and Unwin). B. Hamilton (1981), *The Medieval Inquisition* (London: Edward Arnold) provides a concise description of an emotive subject. More wide-ranging is E. Peters (1986), *Inquisition* (New York and London: Free Press, Macmillan). There are many fine studies of specific aspects of the position of the Jews in medieval Christendom, but for an overall view see K.R. Stow (1992), *Alienated Minority. The Jews of Medieval Latin Europe* (Cambridge, Mass. and London: Harvard University Press), which provides an account of both medieval Christian attitudes towards the Jews and a history of the Jewish communities themselves. Given the frequent movement of the Jews in the medieval period, both voluntary and forced, H. Beinart (1992), *Atlas of Jewish History* (New York: Simon and Schuster) is a useful aid.

Source collections include J.R. Shinners (ed.) (1997), *Medieval Popular Religion, 1000–1500. A Reader* (Peterborough, On.: Broadview Press), R.I. Moore (tr.) (1975), *The Birth of Popular Heresy* (Documents of Medieval History, 1) (London: Edward Arnold), E. Peters (ed.) (1980), *Heresy and Authority in Medieval Europe* (Philadelphia, Pa: University of Pennsylvania Press) and J.R. Marcus (1965), *The Jew in the Medieval World* (New York: Atheneum). These all cover a range of materials, but see M. Bull (1999), *The Miracles of Rocamadour. Analysis and Translation* (Woodbridge, Suffolk: Boydell Press), for a particular genre of sources, that of twelfth-century miracle stories.

Part III Political change

8 The Empire

Translations of the work of prominent German historians mean that the English reader is much better served than in the past. These include K. Hampe (1973), *Germany under the Salians and the Hohenstaufen*, tr. R. Bennett (Oxford: Blackwell) (originally 1968), A. Havercamp (1988), *Medieval Germany*, tr. H. Braun and R. Mortimer (Oxford: Oxford University Press) (originally 1984) and H. Fuhrmann (1986), *Germany in the High Middle Ages c.1050–1200*, tr. T. Reuter (Cambridge: Cambridge University Press). There are, too, studies of individual rulers: I.S. Robinson (1999) *Henry IV of Germany, 1056–1106* (Cambridge: Cambridge University Press), P. Munz (1969), *Frederick Barbarossa. A Study in Medieval Politics* (London: Eyre and Spottiswoode), K. Jordan (1986), *Henry the Lion. A Biography*, tr. P.S. Falla (Oxford: Clarendon Press) (originally 1979) and D. Abulafia (1987), *Frederick II. A Medieval Emperor* (London: Allen Lane). A perceptive pamphlet by J. Gillingham (1971), *The Kingdom of Germany in the High Middle Ages* (London: Historical Association) should alert the reader to some of the less credible assumptions of German historiography. It is important too to grasp the realities of regional power as shown in B. Arnold (1991), *Princes and Territories in Medieval Germany* (Cambridge: Cambridge University Press). Care should be taken not to see the Empire simply in relation to Germany however, and here the value of R. Folz (1969), *The Concept of Empire in Western Europe from the Fifth to the Fourteenth Century*, tr. S.A. Ogilvie (London: Edward Arnold) (originally 1953) becomes evident.

A rich source for the crucial period of change in the eleventh century is T.E. Mommsen and K.F. Morrison (eds) (1962), *Imperial Lives and Letters of the Eleventh Century* (New York: Columbia University Press). In the absence of any surviving court chronicle for Frederick II, the account of Frederick Barbarossa's reign by Otto of Freising and his continuator Rahewin,

C.C. Mierow (tr.) (1955), *The Deeds of Frederick Barbarossa* (New York: Columbia University Press), is a quite pivotal narrative. However, the views of their contemporary, Helmold of Bosau, a less elevated practitioner of chronicle writing than Otto, provide a quite different perspective, especially in seeing the Empire from a provincial perspective, F.J. Tschan (1935), Helmold, Priest of Bosau, *The Chronicle of the Slavs* (New York: Columbia University Press).

9 The Kingdom of Sicily

There is almost complete chronological coverage in G.A. Loud (2000), *The Age of Robert Guiscard. Southern Italy and the Norman Conquest* (London: Longman), H. Houben (2002), *Roger II of Sicily. A Ruler between East and West* (Cambridge: Cambridge University Press), D. Matthew (1992), *The Norman Kingdom of Sicily* (Cambridge: Cambridge University Press) and J. Dunbabin (1998), *Charles I of Anjou. Power, Kingship and State-Making in Thirteenth-Century Europe* (London: Longman). D.C. Douglas provides the essential outlines of the century between 1050 and 1150 in his two works, (1969), *The Norman Achievement, 1050–1100* (London: Eyre and Spottiswoode) and (1976), *The Norman Fate, 1100–1154* (London: Eyre Methuen), although not everybody would agree with the overall interpretation he offers. On the actual workings of government, Evelyn Jamison's work remains fundamental. It is still accessible in the 1987 reprint of her *Norman Administration of Apulia and Capua*, ed. D. Clementi and T. Kolzer (Darmstadt: Scientia Verlag Aalen) (originally 1913). Even so, research in this field has moved on, as can be seen in H. Takayama (1993), *The Administration of the Norman Kingdom of Sicily* (Leiden: Brill). He stresses the importance of placing changes within a firm chronological structure, as all the offices in the records are not contemporaneous. The nemesis of Charles of Anjou is described by S. Runciman (1958), *The Sicilian Vespers* (Harmondsworth: Penguin). However, while the *Vespers* demonstrates Runciman's great narrative skill, it has little to say about the political, social and economic structures of the Kingdom. For the relationship between Sicily and the other states of the region in this period, see D. Abulafia (1997), *The Western Mediterranean Kingdoms, 1200–1500. The Struggle for Dominion* (London: Longman).

Translated sources are not so abundant as they are for the crusades, but the three important narratives of the so-called Hugo Falcandus, Archbishop Romauld II of Salerno and the letter to Peter, Treasurer of the church of Palermo, are collected together in G.A. Loud and T.E.J. Wiedemann (trs) (1998), *The History of the Tyrants of Sicily by 'Hugo Falcandus', 1153–69* (Manchester: Manchester University Press). For the earlier years, see E. van Houts (tr.) (2000), *The Normans in Europe* (Manchester: Manchester University Press), section V.

10 The Italian city-states

There are good introductions by D.P. Waley (1988), *The Italian City-Republics*, 3rd edn (London: Longman) (originally 1969), and J.K. Hyde (1973), *Society and Politics in Medieval Italy. The Evolution of the Civil Life, 1000–1350* (London: Macmillan), while J. Larner (1980), *Italy in the Age of Dante and Petrarch 1216–1380* (London: Longman) surveys the many complicated aspects of the period with clarity and precision. For greater depth and more recent historiography, see P. Jones (1997), *The Italian City-State. From Commune to Signoria* (Oxford: Clarendon). Waley has also written an attractive study of Siena, the best preserved of the late medieval Italian cities, (1991), *Siena and the Sienese in the Thirteenth Century* (Cambridge: Cambridge University Press). The author's research in the Sienese archives teases out some remarkable detail about the lives of the Sienese in the period between 1250 and 1310. The interpretative work of M. Becker (1981), *Medieval Italy. Constraints and Creativity* (Bloomington, Ind.: Indiana University Press) is rewarding, but best read after gaining a basic grip on the period. Although the Hohenstaufen necessarily feature very strongly in the history of medieval Italy, the relationship of the city-states with the Empire is most effectively brought out in the less obvious period of the early fourteenth century in W.M. Bowsky (1960), *Henry VII in Italy. The Conflict of Empire and City-State, 1310–13* (Lincoln, Nebr.: University of Nebraska Press).

The upheavals of mid-thirteenth-century Italy are colourfully described by the Franciscan, Salimbene, who was an eye-witness of many of the events, J.L. Baird, G. Baglivi and J.R. Kane (trs) (1986), *The Chronicle of Salimbene de Adam* (Binghamton, NY: Center for Medieval and Early Renaissance Studies, Binghamton). There are extracts from Giovanni Villani's description of Florence in the early fourteenth century, as well as his opinionated views of the wider European scene in R.E. Selfe and P.H.Wicksteed (trs) (1896), *Selections from the First Nine Books of the Croniche Fiorentine of Giovanni Villani* (London: Archibald Constable).

11 The Capetian monarchy

The essential introduction here is E.M. Hallam and J. Everard (2001), *Capetian France 987–1328*, 2nd edn (London: Longman). Note the effective use of maps and diagrams. Although primarily concerned with earlier centuries, see too J. Dunbabin (1985), *France in the Making 843–1180* (Oxford: Oxford University Press) and M. Bull (ed.) (2002), *France in the Central Middle Ages, 900–1200* (Oxford: Oxford University Press). Basic to the understanding of the rise of the Capetians is their relationship with the English kings, for which there is an excellent concise overview by J. Gillingham (2001), *The Angevin Empire*, 2nd edn (London: Arnold). A rounded picture of the most successful of the Capetians in this conflict is J. Bradbury (1998), *Philip Augustus. King of France, 1180–1223* (London: Longman). A wide-ranging study of Louis IX is provided by J. Richard (1992), *Saint Louis: Crusader King of France*, ed. and abridged by S. Lloyd, tr. J. Birrell (Cambridge: Cambridge University Press) (originally 1983). American historians are especially prominent in this field. A sample of the work of three of the most important can be seen in the journal *Viator*, vol. 19 (1988), 193–246. Here, papers on Philip II, Louis IX and Philip IV by J. Baldwin, W.C. Jordan and E.A.R. Brown respectively have been brought together in '*Persona et Gesta*: the Image and Deeds of the Thirteenth-Century Capetians'. In turn, much of the inspiration for their work stems from J. Strayer, whose (1980), *The Reign of Philip the Fair* (Princeton, NJ: Princeton University Press) is the product of a lifetime's study. Again, focus on key regions is helpful. D. Nicholas (1992), *Medieval Flanders* (London: Longman) examines a county of crucial importance not only to the Capetians, but also to the emperors and the kings of England as well.

There are fascinating chronicle accounts of aspects of some reigns, all written from rather different viewpoints. These include R.C. Cusimano and J. Moorhead (trs) (1992), Suger, *The Deeds of Louis the Fat* (Washington, DC: Catholic University of America Press) and V.G. Berry (tr.) (1948), Odo of Deuil, *The Journey of Louis VII to the East* (New York: Norton). One of the reasons for the fame of St Louis is the accessible and personal account of his life by his friend, John of Joinville, Seneschal of Champagne, which is available in a convenient (although unannotated) form in M.R.B. Shaw (1963), Joinville and Villehardouin, *Chronicles of the Crusades* (Harmondsworth: Penguin).

12 The Kingdom of England

Both H.R. Loyn (1982), *The Norman Conquest*, 3rd edn (London: Hutchinson) (originally 1965) and D. Matthew (1966), *The Norman Conquest* (London: Batsford) make good starting-points, and the essays of J. Le Patourel (1976), *The Norman Empire* (Oxford: Clarendon) extend the chronological scope. The exceptionally wide-ranging volume in the New Oxford History of England by R. Bartlett (2000), *England under the Norman and Angevin Kings, 1075–1225* (Oxford: Clarendon), is, as the title suggests, much more than an account of political events. R. Frame (1990), *The Political Development of the British Isles, 1100–1400* (Oxford: Oxford University Press) and R.R. Davies (1990), *Domination and Conquest: The Experience of Ireland, Scotland and Wales, 1100–1300* (Cambridge: Cambridge University Press) are excellent analyses of the fraught relationships between the English Crown and these countries. There are authoritative studies of all the English kings during this period, but it is instructive to look at the varied approaches of M.T. Clanchy (1983), *England and her Rulers 1066–1272* (London: Fontana), W.L. Warren (1973), *Henry II* (London: Eyre Methuen), D.A. Carpenter (1996), *The Reign of Henry III* (London: Hambledon Press) and M. Prestwich (1997), *Edward I* (New Haven, Conn. and London: Yale University Press) (originally 1988). J.C. Holt (1992), *Magna Carta*, 2nd edn (Cambridge: Cambridge University Press) offers many insights into the realities of power in the early thirteenth century.

English Historical Documents (Oxford: Oxford University Press) is a series unmatched for other countries. Volumes 2 and 3 covering 1042–1189 and 1189–1327 respectively are by D.C. Douglas and G.W. Greenaway (eds) (1981) (originally 1953), and H. Rothwell (ed.) (1975).

13 The Iberian kingdoms

There are three good introductions, none of which substantially duplicates the others despite covering similar periods. J.F. O'Callaghan (1975), *A History of Medieval Spain* (Ithaca, NY and London: Cornell University Press) is best for a basic factual outline, which is especially important given the complications of a world in which the emergence of the 'five kingdoms', is considered a simplification. A. MacKay (1977), *Spain in the Middle Ages. From Frontier to Empire 1000–1500* (London: Macmillan) provides a convincing interpretative context, and D. Lomax (1978), *The Reconquest of Spain* (London: Longman) uses this central theme as the backbone around which a wider structure is built. Although these books begin to make medieval Iberia more familiar to English readers, there is still a need for treatments of individual kingdoms and rulers and important themes, such as T.N. Bisson (1986), *The Medieval Crown of Aragon* (Oxford: Clarendon) and R. Fletcher (1989), *The Quest for El Cid* (London: Hutchinson). For most of this period a substantial part of the peninsula was controlled by Muslim rulers, whose world is described by H. Kennedy (1996), *Muslim Spain and Portugal. A Political History of al-Andalus* (London: Longman).

There are three excellent source collections, C.C. Smith (tr.) (1988, 1989), *Christians and Moors in Spain*, 2 vols (Warminster: Aris and Phillips), O.R. Constable (ed.) (1997), *Medieval Iberia. Readings from Christian, Muslim, and Jewish Sources* (Philadelphia, Pa: University of Pennsylvania Press) and S. Barton and R. Fletcher (trs) (2000), *The World of El Cid. Chronicles of the Spanish Reconquest* (Manchester: Manchester University Press).

14 The states of eastern and northern Europe

For Poland, the earlier chapters of N. Davies (1981), *God's Playground: A History of Poland*, vol. 1, *The Origins to 1795* (Oxford: Clarendon) and A. Gieysztor (1968), 'Medieval Poland', in *History of Poland*, edn A. Gieysztor, S. Kieniewicz, E. Rostworowski, J. Tazbir and H. Wereszycki (Warsaw: Polish Scientific Publishers) are useful. An already complicated situation was excerbated by crusaders and, from the thirteenth century, by the Teutonic Knights, for which see E. Christiansen, *The Northern Crusades*, 2nd edn (Harmondsworth: Penguin, 1997). For Hungary, P. Engel (2001), *The Realm of St Stephen. A History of Medieval Hungary, 895–1526*, tr. T. Palosfalvi. English edn edited by A. Ayton (London: I.B. Tauris) and K.J. Kosztolnyik (1987), *From Coloman the Learned to Béla III (1095–1196)* (East European Monographs, 120) (New York: Columbia University Press) provide basic chronological treatments. N. Berend (2001), *At the Gate of Christendom. Jews, Muslims and 'Pagans' in Medieval Hungary, c.1000–c.1300* (Cambridge: Cambridge University Press) examines the unique position of Hungary as the only country in Latin Christendom in which non-Christians were incorporated voluntarily rather than by conquest. This is particularly enlightening on the postion of the Kumans, hardly tackled elsewhere.

Scandinavia exercises great fascination for British historians in the Viking period, but thereafter interest diminishes until the sudden re-emergence of Sweden as a great power in the seventeenth century. However, there is, now, B. Sawyer and P. Sawyer (1993), *Medieval Scandinavia. From Conversion to the Reformation, c.800–1500* (Minneapolis, Minn. and London: University of Minnesota Press), which adopts a thematic approach. This complements but does not replace L. Musset (1951), *Les Peuples scandinaves au moyen âge* (Paris: Presses Universitaires de France), which remains the only other general work in a non-Scandinavian language. Two works on the fascinating subject of northern colonisation are G. Karlsson (2000), *Iceland's 1100 Years. The History of a Marginal Society* (London: Hurst) and K.A. Seaver (1996), *The Frozen Echo. Greenland and the Exploration of North America, c.1000–c.1500* (Stanford, Ca: Stanford University Press).

15 The Crusader States

The two most influential crusader historians of their generation, Jean Richard and Joshua Prawer, have both written important books entitled *The Latin Kingdom of Jerusalem* in 1953 (tr. J. Shirley 1979, Amsterdam: North-Holland) and 1972 (London: Weidenfeld and Nicolson) respectively, although they are now beginning to look dated. An excellent study of a key period in the history of the kingdom is B. Hamilton (2000), *The Leper King and his Heirs. Baldwin IV and the Crusader Kingdom of Jerusalem* (Cambridge: Cambridge University Press). The conquest of Cyprus by Richard I in 1191 ultimately added a new state, which is afforded concise and clear coverage in P. Edbury (1991), *The Kingdom of Cyprus and the Crusades, 1191–1374* (Cambridge: Cambridge University Press). The other Crusader States are less well served in terms of good sytheses, although the first generation of Latins at Antioch is described in as much detail as the sources allow by T. Asbridge (2000), *The Creation of the Principality of Antioch, 1098- 1130* (Woodbridge, Suffolk: The Boydell Press). This book is also valuable in explaining the geographical and cultural issues which continued to be fundamental in the history of the region throughout the Latin period. A good sense of the problems created by the need to support the Latins in the east can be gained from J. Phillips (1996), *Defenders of the Holy Land. Relations between the Latin East and West, 1119–1187* (Oxford: Clarendon). K.M. Setton (1976), *The Papacy and the Levant*, vol. 1 (Philadelphia, Pa: American Philosophical Society) is a very sound account of relations with the Latin Empire and Greece, while P. Lock (1995), *The Franks in the Aegean 1204–1500* (London: Longman) surveys the Latin occupation.

Two chroniclers dominate the history of the twelfth century, both written by clerics resident in the east for a considerable proportion of their lives: Fulcher of Chartres (1970), *A History of the Expedition to Jerusalem, 1095–1127*, tr. F.R. Ryan (Knoxville, Tenn.: University of Tennessee Press) and William of Tyre (1943), *A History of Deeds done beyond the Sea*, tr. E.A. Babcock and A.C. Krey, 2 vols (New York: Columbia University Press). For Antioch, see T. Asbridge and S.B. Edgington (trs) (1999), *Walter the Chancellor's The Antiochene Wars* (Aldershot: Ashgate). A good selection of sources, including an important version of the Old French Continuation of William of Tyre and several very informative letters, is P.W. Edbury (tr.) (1996), *The Conquest of Jerusalem and the Third Crusade* (Aldershot: Scolar Press). The durability of F. Gabrieli (tr.) (1984), *Arab Historians of the Crusades*, tr. E.J. Costello (London: Routledge) (originally 1969), testifies to its value as a means of understanding something of the Muslim point of view.

Part IV Perceptions of the world

16 The medieval world view

The emphasis among French medieval historians upon *mentalité*, that is the study of the medieval mental outlook, has reawakened historians to the value of this approach. In the past more attention was paid to this subject by literary specialists like C.S. Lewis than by historians.

R. Cook and R.B. Herzman (2003), *The Medieval World View. An Introduction*, 2nd edn (New York: Oxford University Press) (originally 1983) and C. Erickson (1976), *The Medieval Vision. Essays in History and Perception* (New York: Oxford University Press), tackle different aspects of this, although neither would claim to be comprehensive. The thought-processes behind the making of what are now called maps are analysed by E. Edson (1997), *Mapping Time and Space. How Medieval Mapmakers Viewed their World* (London: The British Library). John Larner's (2001) *Marco Polo and the Discovery of the World* (New Haven, Conn. and London: Yale University Press) dispels misconceptions about the creation, aims and content of Marco's book. This can usefully be used in combination with John Friedman, *The Monstrous Races in Medieval Art and Thought* (Cambridge, Mass. and London: Harvard University Press). Together these books show how medieval men conceived of the world and its peoples in those regions which were beyond their usual geographical range. An idea of the French approach, which might be described as empathy disciplined by the texts, can be seen in the essays of J. Le Goff (1980), *Time, Work and Culture in the Middle Ages*, tr. A. Goldhammer (Chicago and London: University of Chicago Press). Notable for its combination of common sense and sympathetic treatment of medieval attitudes is B. Ward (1982), *Miracles and the Medieval Mind. Theory, Record and Event 1000–1215* (London: Scolar Press).

17 Intellectual life

Like Bernard Hamilton, John Baldwin has a good appreciation of what newcomers to the subject need to know before they can tackle medieval intellectual history. His (1997), *The Scholastic Culture of the Middle Ages, 1000–1300* (Prospect Heights, Ill: Waveland Press) (originally 1971) is therefore a good place to begin. Baldwin's introduction can usefully be followed by R.N. Swanson (1999), *The Twelfth-Century Renaissance* (Manchester: Manchester University Press) and C. Morris (1972), *The Discovery of the Individual, 1050–1200* (London: SPCK). R.W. Southern's deep understanding of this world is nicely demonstrated in two of his works, one a biography, the other a wide-ranging synthesis: (1990), *Saint Anselm. A Portrait in a Landscape* Cambridge: Cambridge University Press) and (1995, 2001), *Scholastic Humanism and the Unification of Europe*, 2 vols (Oxford: Blackwell). The bold ideas of men like Adelard of Bath, William of Conches and Thierry of Chartres are examined with great clarity by Tina Stiefel in (1985), *The Intellectual Revolution in Twelfth-Century Europe* (London and Sydney: Croom Helm). As she sees them, these men invented the discipline of natural science in their efforts 'to break out of the mould of traditional thought'. The mass of writing on Abelard is overwhelming, so the provision of a concise and authoritative introduction is vital; D.E. Luscombe (1979), *Peter Abelard* (London: Historical Association) provides just such a starting-point. M. Clanchy (1997), *Abelard. A Medieval Life* (Oxford: Blackwell) is an exceptional study of an exceptional man. While the brilliance of Abelard catches the eye, the apparently more mundane work of the lawyers was equally facing up to the great challenges which the changes of the twelfth century presented. J.A. Brundage (1995), *Medieval Canon Law* (London: Longman) is not only a good introduction to the subject, but also shows how the conclusions of the canon lawyers touched the lives of almost everyone. The actual workings of the universities are well described in A.B. Cobban (1975), *The Medieval Universities. Their Development and Organisation* (London: Methuen).

In an age when individual achievement and influence increasingly shaped perceptions, the best sources are often the writings of those individuals. A few examples of the many different genres are B. Radice (tr.) (1974), *The Letters of Abelard and Heloise* (Harmondsworth: Penguin), G. Nederman (tr.) (1990), John of Salisbury, *Policraticus. Of the Frivolties of Courtiers and the Footprints of Philosophers* (Cambridge: Cambridge University Press) and D. Staines (tr.) (1990), *The Complete Romances of Chrétien of Troyes* (Bloomington, Ind.: Indiana University Press). The standard collection of documents on the universities, which includes a wide variety of types of sources, remains L. Thorndike (ed.) (1944), *University Records and Life in the Middle Ages* (New York: Columbia University Press).

18 Art and society

Art historians tend to live in one world, historians in another, and it is often left to the reader to bring the two aspects together. Nevertheless, there are a number of books which show greater interdisciplinary awareness than most. R. Branner (1979), *Gothic Architecture* (New York: Braziller) (originally 1961) is a concise introduction, and W.S. Stoddard (1972), *Art and Architecture in Medieval France* (New York: Harper and Row) offers a clear survey of all the important buildings. However, the subject is changing fast, as can be seen in the important and wide-ranging book by C. Wilson (1990), *The Gothic Cathedral* (London: Thames and Hudson). To locate Suger in his own milieu, see L. Grant (1998), *Abbot Suger of St-Denis. Church and State in Early Twelfth-Century France* (London: Longman). A fine explanation of the development of a specific cathedral within its setting is N. Orme (1986), *Exeter Cathedral as it was, 1050–1550* (Exeter: Devon Books). On the men who turned the patrons' wishes into solid reality see the excellent short guide by N. Coldstream (1991), *Medieval Craftsmen. Masons and Sculptors* (London: British Museum Press). The formative period of Italian art is covered by A. Smart (1978), *The Dawn of Italian Painting 1250–1400* (Oxford: Phaidon), while J. Larner (1971), *Culture and Society in Italy, 1290–1420* (London: Batsford) is an excellent demonstration of how to place art in its proper historical context, as is D. Norman (ed.) (1995) *Siena, Florence and Padua. Art, Society and Religion, 1280–1400*, 2 vols (New Haven, Conn. and London: Yale Univerity Press), a series of interlinked, illustrated essays, originally prepared for The Open University. J. White (1987), *Art and Architecture in Italy, 1250–1400* (Harmondsworth: Penguin) (originally 1966) is an authoritative survey of all the major works and an indispensable point of reference. R. Salvini (1969), *Medieval Sculpture*, tr. P. Murray and L. Murray (London: Michael Joseph) contains a large corpus of annotated illustrations and is a great stimulus to the proper observation of visual evidence. Finally, E. Male (1961), *The Gothic Image. Religious Art in France in the Thirteenth Century*, tr. D. Nussey (New York: Harper and Row) (originally 1913) is a fundamental handbook for the interpretation of medieval painting and sculpture.

The two most famous individual influences on our view of the role of art and architecture in the twelfth century are by Suger and St Bernard, for which see E. Panofsky (tr. and ed.) (1979), *Abbot Suger on the Abbey Church of St Denis and its Art Treasures*, 2nd edn, ed. G. Panofsky-Soergel (Princeton, NJ: Princeton University Press) (originally 1946) and C. Rudolph (1990), *The 'Things of Greater Importance'. Bernard of Clairvaux's 'Apologia' and the Medieval Attitude toward Art* (Philadelphia, Pa: University of Pennsylvania Press). Both editors provide their own very definite interpretative structures for the texts. In about 1260 the Dominican, James of Voragine (d. 1298), completed his compilation of stories of the saints known as *The Golden Legend*. It achieved wide circulation, apparently as a manual for preachers but, for the modern historian, it is an invaluable handbook for interpreting sculpture, stained glass and painting, as well as offering insight into contemporary perceptions of the nature of sanctity and the importance of miracles; there is an English translation by W.G. Ryan (1992), *The Golden Legend. Readings on the Saints*, 2 vols (Princeton, NJ: Princeton University Press). Two useful collections, which include material relating to the changing position of the artists and architects, some of which can be seen in the nature of their contracts, are C. Davis-Weyer (ed.) (1986), *Early Medieval Art, 300–1150. Sources and Documents* (Toronto: University of Toronto Press) and T.G. Frisch (ed.) (1987), *Gothic Art, 1140–c.1450. Sources and Documents* (Toronto: University of Toronto Press). The actual techniques of the early twelfth century are described in J.G. Hawthorne and C.S. Smith (trs) (1979), Theophilus, *On Divers Arts* (New York: Dover) (originally 1963).

19 Western Christendom and the wider world

The best means of establishing the context is to read J.R.S. Phillips (1998), *The Medieval Expansion of Europe*, 2nd edn (Oxford: Clarendon). The scope of this book takes it well beyond the themes of this chapter, however, and there is much here which is very relevant to other key matters (see especially Chapters 3 and 16). Three books which examine the societies covered in this chapter in their own right rather than simply in relation to the west are M. Angold (1997), *The Byzantine Empire 1025–1204. A Political History*, 2nd edn (London: Longman), P.M. Holt (1986), *The Age of the Crusades. The Near East from the Eleventh Century to 1517* (London: Longman) and D.O. Morgan (1986), *The Mongols* (Oxford: Blackwell). Indicative of the interesting material available are N. Daniel (1960), *Islam and the West. The Making of an Image* (Edinburgh: Edinburgh University Press), B.Z. Kedar (1984), *Crusade and Mission. European Approaches to the Muslims* (Princeton, NJ: Princeton University Press), and C. Hillenbrand (1999), *The Crusades. Islamic Perspectives* (Edinburgh: Edinburgh University Press).

There are highly individual perceptions of the Latins in the twelfth century by Anna Comnena, daughter of the Byzantine emperor, Alexius I, and Usamah Ibn Munqidh, Emir of Shaizar: E.A.R. Sewter (1969), *The Alexiad of Anna Comnena* (Harmondsworth: Penguin) and P.K. Hitti (tr.) (1987), *An Arab-Syrian Gentlemen in the Period of the Crusades. Memoirs of Usamah Ibn-Munqidh* (London: I.B. Taurus) (originally 1929). The fascinating accounts of those sent to meet the Mongols are in C. Dawson (ed.) (1980), *The Mission to Asia* (London: Sheed and Ward) (originally 1955).

References

Abulafia, D. (1977), 'Kantorowicz and Frederick II', *History*, vol. 62, 193–210.

Abulafia, D. (1981), 'Southern Italy and the Florentine Economy, 1265–1370', *Economic History Review*, vol. 33, 377–88.

Abulafia, D. (1983), 'The Crown and the Economy under Roger II and his Successors', *Dumbarton Oaks Papers*, vol. 37, 1–14.

Abulafia, D. (1985), 'The Norman Kingdom of Africa and the Norman Expeditions to Majorca and the Muslim Mediterranean', in *Anglo-Norman Studies*, vol. 7: *Proceedings of the Battle Conference, 1984*, ed. R.A. Brown (Woodbridge, Suffolk: Boydell Press), 26–49.

Adler, M.N. (tr.) (1907), Benjamin of Tudela, *Itinerary* (London: Henry Frawde).

Ailes, A. (1982), *The Origins of the Royal Arms of England. Their Development to 1199* (Reading: Graduate Centre for Medieval Studies).

Ailes, M. and M. Barber (trs) (2003), *The History of the Holy War. Ambroise's Estoire de la Guerre Sainte*, vol. 2 (Woodbridge, Suffolk: Boydell Press).

Albon, G.A.M. d' (ed.) (1913), *Cartulaire général de l'Ordre du Temple 1119?–1150* (Paris: Champion).

Alpatoff, M. (1947), 'The Parallelism of Giotto's Paduan Frescoes', *Art Bulletin*, vol. 29, 149–54.

Andrea, A.J. (ed. and tr.) (1997), *The 'Hystoria Constantinopolitana' of Gunther of Pairis* (Philadelphia, Pa: University of Pennsylvania Press).

Appelt, H. (ed.) (1975–90), *Die Urkunden Friedrichs I*, in *Monumenta Germaniae Historica. Diplomata Regum et Imperatorum Germaniae*, vol. 10, parts 1–4 (Hanover: Hahnsche).

Appleby, J.T. (tr.) (1963), *The Chronicle of Richard of Devizes of the Time of King Richard the First* (London: Thomas Nelson).

Appleby, J.T. (1965), *England without Richard 1189–99* (London: G. Bell).

Arbois de Jubainville, H. de (1961), *Histoire des Ducs et des Comtes de Champagne*, vol. 3 (Paris and Troyes: Durand).

Arnold, B. (1985), *German Knighthood 1050–1300* (Oxford: Clarendon).

Arnold, B. (1997), *Medieval Germany, 500–1300* (London: Macmillan).

Asbridge, T.S. and S.B. Edgington (trs) (1999), *Walter the Chancellor's The Antiochene Wars* (Crusade Texts in Translation, 4) (Aldershot: Ashgate).

Astill, G.G. (1993), *A Medieval Industrial Complex and its Landscape: The Metalworking Watermills and Workshops of Bordesley Abbey* (CBA Research Report 92) (York: Council for British Archaeology).

Avril, J. (ed.) (1995), *Les Statuts Synodaux Français du XIIIe Siècle*, vol. 4, *Les Statuts Synodaux de l'Ancienne Province de Reims* (Collection de Documents Inédits sur l'Histoire de France, 23) (Paris: Editions du Comité des Travaux historiques et scientifiques).

Babcock, E.A. and A.C. Krey (trs) (1941), William of Tyre, *A History of Deeds done beyond the Sea*, 2 vols (New York: Columbia University Press).

Bagge, S. (1993a), 'The Norwegian Monarchy in the Thirteenth Century', in *Kings and Kingship in Medieval Europe*, ed. A.J. Duggan (London: Centre for Late Antique and Medieval Studies, King's College London), 159–77.

Bagge, S. (1993b), 'The Autobiography of Abelard and Medieval Individualism', *Journal of Medieval History*, vol. 19, 327–50.

Baldwin, J.W. (1970), *Masters, Princes and Merchants. The Social Views of Peter the Chanter and his Circle*, 2 vols (Princeton, NJ: Princeton University Press).

Baldwin, J.W. (1986), *The Government of Philip Augustus. Foundations of French Royal Power in the Middle Ages* (Berkeley, Calif.: University of California Press).

Banks, S.E. and J.W. Binns (eds and trs) (2002), Gervase of Tilbury, *Otia Imperialia. Recreation for an Emperor* (Oxford: Clarendon).

Barber, M. (1981), 'Lepers, Jews and Moslems: The Plot to Overthrow Christendom in 1321', *History*, vol. 66, 1–17.

Barber, M. and K. Bate (trs) (2002), *The Templars* (Manchester: Manchester University Press).

Barlow, F. (1980), 'The King's Evil', *English Historical Review*, vol. 95, 3–27.

Barlow, F. (1999), *The Feudal Kingdom of England 1042–1216*, 5th edn (London: Longman).

Barton, S. and R. Fletcher (trs) (2000), *The World of El Cid. Chronicles of the Spanish Reconquest* (Manchester: Manchester University Press).

Bautier, R-H. (1978), 'Diplomatique et histoire politique: ce que la critique diplomatique nous apprend sur la personnalité de Philippe le Bel', *Revue Historique*, vol. 259, 3–27.

Beach, A. (2004), *Women as Scribes. Book Production and Monastic Reform in the Twelfth Century* (Cambridge: Cambridge University Press).

Becker, M. (1981), *Medieval Italy. Constraints and Creativity* (Bloomington, Ind.: Indiana University Press).

Beech, G. (1964), *A Rural Society in Medieval France: The Gâtine of Poitou in the Eleventh and Twelfth Centuries* (Baltimore, Md: Johns Hopkins University Press).

Bennett, M. (1986), 'First Crusaders' Images of the Muslims: The Influence of Vernacular Poetry?', *Forum for Modern Language Studies*, vol. 22, 101–22.

Bennett, M.K. (1954), *The World's Food. A Study of the Interrelations of World Populations, National Diets, and Food Potentials* (New York: Harper).

Benton, J.F. (1967), 'The Revenue of Louis VII', *Speculum*, vol. 42, 84–91.

Benton, J.F. (tr.) (1970), *Self and Society in Medieval France. The Memoirs of Abbot Guibert of Nogent (1064?–c.1125)* (New York: Harper and Row).

Berend, N. (2001), *At the Gate of Christendom. Jews, Muslims and 'Pagans' in Medieval Hungary, c.1000–c.1300* (Cambridge: Cambridge University Press).

Berman, C. (2000), *The Cistercian Evolution. The Invention of a Religious Order in Twelfth-Century Europe* (Philadelphia, Pa: University of Pennsylvania Press).

Berry, V.G. (tr.) (1948), Odo of Deuil, *The Journey of Louis VII to the East* (New York: Norton).

Bettenson, H. (tr.) (1984), Augustine, *Concerning the City of God against the Pagans* (Harmondsworth: Penguin).

Biller, P. (1996), 'The Preaching of the Waldensian Sisters', *Heresis*, vol. 30, 137–68.

Biller, P. (1999a), 'Northern Cathars and Higher Learning', in *The Medieval Church: Universities, Heresy, and Religious Life. Essays in Honour of Gordon Leff*, ed. P. Biller and B. Dobson (Woodbridge, Suffolk: Boydell Press), 25–53.

Biller, P. (1999b), 'William of Newburgh and the Cathar Mission to England', in *Life and Thought in the Northern Church c.1100–c.1700. Essays in Honour of Claire Cross*, ed. D. Wood (Woodbridge, Suffolk: The Boydell Press), 11–30.

Bisson, T.N. (1978), 'The Problem of Feudal Monarchy: Aragon, Catalonia, and France', *Speculum*, vol. 53, 460–78.

Blake, E.O. and C. Morris (1985), 'A Hermit Goes to War: Peter and the Origins of the First Crusade', *Studies in Church History*, vol. 22, 79–108.

Bloch, J-R. (1934), *L'Anoblissement en France au temps de François Ier* (Paris: Librairie Félix Alcan).

Bloch, M. (1964), 'From the Royal Court to the Court of Rome: The Suit of the Serfs of Rosny-Sous-Bois', in *Change in Medieval Society. Europe North of the Alps, 1050–1500*, ed. S.L. Thrupp (New York: Appleton-Century-Crofts), 1–13 (originally 1939).

Bloch, M. (1973), *The Royal Touch. Sacred Monarchy and Scrofula in England and France*, tr. J. E. Anderson (London: Routledge and Kegan Paul) (originally 1924).

Boas, A.J. (1999), *Crusader Archaeology. The Material Culture of the Latin East* (London: Routledge).

Boase, T.S.R. (1933), *Boniface VIII* (London: Constable).

Bolton, B. (1972), 'Innocent III's Treatment of the Humiliati', *Studies in Church History*, vol. 8, 73–82.

Bornstein, D.E. (tr.) (1986), Dino Compagni's *Chronicle of Florence* (Philadelphia, Pa: University of Pennsylvania Press).

Borsook, E. (1990), *Messages in Mosaic. The Royal Programmes of Norman Sicily 1130–1187* (Woodbridge, Suffolk: The Boydell Press).

Bouchard, C. (1991), *Holy Entrepreneurs. Cistercians, Knights, and Economic Exchange in Twelfth-Century Burgundy* (Ithaca, NY and London: Cornell University Press).

Boussard, J. (1976), *Nouvelle Histoire de Paris. De la fin du siège de 885–886 à la mort de Philippe Auguste* (Paris: Hachette).

Bowsky, W.M. (1960), *Henry VII in Italy. The Conflict of Empire and City-State, 1310–13* (Lincoln, Nebr.: University of Nebraska Press).

Bowsky, W.M. (1981), *A Medieval Italian Commune. Siena under the Nine, 1287–1355* (Berkeley, Calif.: University of California Press).

Boyer, M.N. (1951), 'A Day's Journey in Medieval France', *Speculum*, vol. 26, 597–608.

Brand, C.M. (tr.) (1976), John Kinnamos, *The Deeds of John and Manuel Comnenus* (New York: Columbia University Press).

Brandt, W. (tr.) (1936), Pierre Dubois, *The Recovery of the Holy Land* (New York: Columbia University Press).

Branner, R. (1965), *St Louis and the Court Style in Gothic Architecture* (London: Zwemmer).

Branner, R. (1979), *Gothic Architecture* (New York: George Braziller).

Braudel, F. (1973), *Capitalism and Material Life 1400–1800*, tr. M. Kochan (London: Weidenfeld and Nicolson).

Broadhurst, R.J.C. (tr.) (1952), *The Travels of Ibn Jubayr* (London: Jonathan Cape).

Brooke, C.N.L. (1989), *The Medieval Idea of Marriage* (Oxford: Oxford University Press).

Brown, E.A.R. (1974), 'The Tyranny of a Construct: Feudalism and the Historians of Medieval Europe', *American Historical Review*, vol. 79, 1063–88.

Brown, E.A.R. (1976), 'Royal Salvation and the Needs of the State in Late Capetian France', in *Order and Innovation in the Middle Ages. Essays in Honor of Joseph R. Strayer*, ed. W.C. Jordan, B. McNab and T.F. Ruiz (Princeton, NJ: Princeton University Press), 365–83.

Brown, E.A.R. (1987), 'The Prince is Father of the King: The Childhood Character of Philip the Fair of France', *Medieval Studies*, vol. 49, 282–334.

Brown, S. (tr.) (1964), *The Register of Eudes of Rouen* (New York: Columbia University Press).

Brundage, J.A. (1967a), 'The Crusader's Wife: A Canonistic Quandary', *Studia Gratiana*, vol. 12, 425–41.

Brundage, J.A. (1967b), 'The Crusader's Wife Revisited', *Studia Gratiana*, vol. 14, 241–51.

Brundage, J.A. (1969), *Medieval Canon Law and the Crusader* (Madison, Wis. and London: University of Wisconsin Press).

Bruzelius, C.A. (1985), *The Thirteenth-Century Church at Saint-Denis* (New Haven, Conn.: Yale University Press).

Bull, M. (1993a), 'The Roots of Lay Enthusiasm for the First Crusade', *History*, vol. 78, 353–72.

Bull, M. (1993b), *Knightly Piety and the Lay Response to the First Crusade in the Limousin and Gascony, c.970–c.1130* (Oxford: Clarendon).

Bullough, V. and C. Campbell (1980), 'Female Longevity and Diet in the Middle Ages', *Speculum*, vol. 55, 317–25.

Burgess, G. (tr.) (1990), *The Song of Roland* (Harmondsworth: Penguin).

Bynum, C.W. (1987), *Holy Feast and Holy Fast. The Religious Significance of Food to Medieval Women* (Berkeley, Calif.: University of California Press).

Camille, C. (1985), 'Seeing and Reading: Some Visual Implications of Medieval Literacy and Illiteracy', *Art History*, vol. 8, 26–49.

Campbell, B.M.S. (1997), 'Economic Rent and the Intensification of English Agriculture, 1086–1350', in *Medieval Farming and Technology. The Impact of Agricultural Change in Northwest Europe*, ed. G. Astill and J. Langdon (Leiden: Brill), 225–49.

Canivez, N.J.M. (1933–5), *Statuta Capitulorum Generalium Ordinis Cisterciensis ab anno 1116 ad annum 1786*, vols 1–3 (Louvain: Bibliothèque de la Revue d'Histoire Ecclésiastique).

Cannon, J. (1982), 'Simone Martini, the Dominicans and the Early Sienese Polyptych', *Journal of the Warburg and Courtauld Institutes*, vol. 45, 69–93.

Carpenter, D.A. (1985), 'King, Magnates and Society: The Personal Rule of King Henry III, 1234–58', *Speculum*, vol. 60, 39–70.

Carus-Wilson, E.M. (1954), 'An Industrial Revolution of the Thirteenth Century', in *Essays in Economic History*, ed. E.M. Carus-Wilson (London: Edward Arnold), 41–60.

Casey, M. (tr.) (1970), 'Cistercians and Cluniacs: St Bernard's Apologia to Abbot William', in *The Works of St Bernard*, vol. 1, *Treatises*, 1 (Shannon, Ireland: Cistercian Publications).

Celli-Fraentzel, A. (1932), 'Contemporary Reports on the Medieval Roman Climate', *Speculum*, vol. 7, 96–106.

Chibnall, M. (ed. and tr.) (1956), John of Salisbury, *Historia Pontificalis* (Oxford: Clarendon).

Chibnall, M. (ed. and tr.) (1969–80), *The Ecclesiastical History of Orderic Vitalis*, 6 vols (Oxford: Clarendon).

Chibnall, M. (1984), *The World of Orderic Vitalis* (Oxford: Clarendon Press).

Chibnall, M. (1986), *Anglo-Norman England 1066–1166* (Oxford: Blackwell).

Cipolla, C.M. (1967), *Money, Prices and Civilisation in the Mediterranean World, Fifth to Seventeenth Centuries* (New York: Gordian Press) (originally 1956).

Cipolla, C.M. (1969), *Literacy and Development in the West* (Harmondsworth: Penguin).

Clanchy, M.T. (1968), 'Did Henry III have a Policy?', *History*, vol. 53, 207–19.

Clanchy, M.T. (1979), *From Memory to Written Record. England 1066–1307* (London: Edward Arnold).

Clément, P.A. (1984), *Les Chemins à travers les âges en Cevennes et Bas Languedoc* (Montpellier: Les Presses du Languedoc).

Clementi, D.R. (1953–4), 'Some Unnoticed Aspects of the Emperor Henry VI's Conquest of the Norman Kingdom of Sicily', *Bulletin of the John Rylands Library*, vol. 36, 328–59.

Cochrane, L. (1994), *Adelard of Bath. The First English Scientist* (London: British Museum Press).

Cole, B. (1980), *Sienese Painting. From its Origins to the Fifteenth Century* (London and New York: Harper and Row).

Comet, G. (1997), 'Technology and Agricultural Expansion in the Middle Ages: The Example of France North of the Loire', in *Medieval Farming and Technology. The Impact of Agricultural Change in Northwest Europe*, ed. G. Astill and J. Langdon (Leiden: Brill), 11–39.

Constable, G. (1982), 'The Financing of the Crusades in the Twelfth Century', in *Outremer. Studies in the History of the Crusading Kingdom of Jerusalem presented to Joshua Prawer*, ed. B.Z. Kedar, H.E. Mayer and R.C. Smail (Jerusalem: Yad Izhak Ben-Zvi Institute), 64–88.

Constable, G. (1988), 'Suger's Monastic Administration', in *Monks, Hermits and Crusaders in Medieval Europe* (London: Variorum).

Constable, G. (1996), *The Reformation of the Twelfth Century* (Cambridge: Cambridge University Press).

Constable, G. and B. Smith (trs) (1972), *Libellus de diversis ordinibus et professionibus qui sunt in Aecclesia* (Oxford: Clarendon).

Cowdrey, H.E.J. (1968), 'The Papacy, the Patarines, and the Church of Milan', *Transactions of the Royal Historical Society*, vol. 18, 25–48.

Cowdrey, H.E.J. (1970), *The Cluniacs and Gregorian Reform* (Oxford: Clarendon).

Crane, T.F. (ed.) (1890), *The Exempla or Illustrative Stories from the Sermones Vulgares of Jacques de Vitry* (London: Folk-Lore Society).

Critchlow, F.L. (tr.) (1928, 1934), Bernat Desclot, *Chronicle of the Reign of King Pedro III of Aragon*, 2 vols (Princeton, NJ: Princeton University Press).

Cronne, H.A. (1970), *The Reign of Stephen 1135–54. Anarchy in England* (London: Weidenfeld and Nicolson).

Curzon, H. de (ed.) (1886), *La Règle du Temple* (Paris: Société de l'Histoire de France).

Cusimano, R. and J. Moorhead (trs) (1992), Suger, *The Deeds of Louis the Fat* (Washington, DC: Catholic University of America Press).

Daunou, P.C.F. and Naudet, J. (eds) (1840), *Vie de Saint Louis par Le Confesseur de la Reine Marguerite*, in *Recueil des Historiens des Gaules et de la France,* vol. 20 (Paris: Imprimerie Royale).

David, C.W. (tr.) (1976), *De Expugnatione Lyxbonensi* (New York: Octagon) (originally 1936).

Davies, N. (1981), *God's Playground: A History of Poland*, vol. 1 (Oxford: Clarendon).

Davis, R.H.C. (1967), *King Stephen* (London: Longman).

Dawson, C. (ed.) (1980), *The Mission to Asia* (London: Sheed and Ward).

Delaborde, H.F. (ed.) (1882, 1885), *Oeuvres de Rigord et de Guillaume Le Breton. Historiens de Philippe-Auguste*, 2 vols (Paris: Société de l'Histoire de France).

Delisle, L. (ed.) (1878), *Epistola Ludovici Francorum Regis ad Sugerium*, in *Recueil des Historiens des Gaules et de la France*, vol. 15 (Paris: Victor Palmé).

Demus, O. (1988), *The Mosaic Decoration of San Marco, Venice* (Chicago: University of Chicago Press).

Devic, C. and J. Vaissète (eds) (1973), *Histoire générale de Languedoc*, ed. A. Molinier, vol. 8 (Toulouse: Privat) (originally 1879).

Dickson, G. (1989), 'The Flagellants of 1260 and the Crusades', *Journal of Medieval History*, vol. 15, 227–67.

Dickson, G. (2000), 'The Genesis of the Children's Crusade (1212)', in *Religious Enthusiasm in the Medieval West* (Aldershot: Ashgate), 1–52.

Dodwell, B. (1979), 'History and the Monks of Norwich Cathedral Priory', *Reading Medieval Studies*, vol. 5, 38–56.

Dodwell, C.R. (tr.) (1961), Theophilus, *The Various Arts* (London: Thomas Nelson).

Donkin, R.A. (1978), *The Cistercians: Studies in the Geography of Medieval England and Wales* (Toronto: Pontifical Institute of Medieval Studies).

Douglas, D.C. (1976), *The Norman Fate, 1100–1154* (London: Eyre Methuen).

Douglas, D.C. and G.W. Greenaway (eds) (1981), *English Historical Documents*, vol. 2, *1042–1189* (London: Eyre Methuen).

Duby, G. (1966), 'Les Pauvres des campagnes dans l'Occident médiéval jusqu'au XIIIe siècle', *Revue d'Histoire de l'Eglise de France*, vol. 52, 25–32.

Duby, G. (1968a), *Rural Economy and Country Life in the Medieval West*, tr. C. Postan (London: Edward Arnold).

Duby, G. (1968b), 'Northwestern France: The "Youth" in Twelfth-Century Aristocratic Society', in *Lordship and Community in Medieval Europe. Selected Readings*, ed. F.L. Cheyette (New York: Holt, Rinehart and Winston), 198–209.

Duby, G. (1974), *The Early Growth of the European Economy. Warriors and Peasants from the Seventh to the Twelfth Century*, tr. H.B. Clarke (London: Weidenfeld and Nicolson).

Duby, G. (1977), *The Chivalrous Society*, tr. C. Postan (London: Edward Arnold).

Duby, G. (1980), *The Three Orders. Feudal Society Imagined*, tr. A. Goldhammer (Chicago: University of Chicago Press).

Duby, G. (1990), *The Legend of Bouvines*, tr. C. Tihanyi (Cambridge: Polity Press) (originally 1973).

Duchesne, A. (1631), *Histoire généalogique de la Maison Royale de Dreux, et quelques autres familles* (Paris: S. Cramoisy).

Dugdale, W. (ed.) (1846), *Monasticon Anglicanum*, vol. 1 (London: Bohn).

Dunbabin, J. (1988), 'From Clerk to Knight: Changing Orders', in *The Ideals and Practice of Medieval Knighthood*, vol. 2, *Papers from the Third Strawberry Hill Conference 1986*, ed. C. Harper-Bill and R. Harvey (Woodbridge, Suffolk: Boydell and Brewer).

Dunbabin, J. (1998), *Charles I of Anjou. Power, Kingship and State-Making in Thirteenth-Century Europe* (London: Longman).

Duvernoy, J. (1965), *Le Registre d'inquisition de Jacques Fournier 1318–25*, vol. 2 (Toulouse: Privat).

Duvernoy, J. (1976), *Le Catharisme*, vol. 1, *La Religion des Cathares* (Toulouse: Privat).

Dyer, C. (1997), 'Medieval Farming and Technology: Conclusion', in *Medieval Farming and Technology. The Impact of Agricultural Change in Northwest Europe*, ed. G. Astill and J. Langdon (Leiden: Brill), 293–312.

Edbury, P.W. (1993), 'Propaganda and Faction in the Kingdom of Jerusalem: The Background to Hattin', in *Crusaders and Muslims in Twelfth-Century Syria*, ed. M. Shatzmiller (Leiden: Brill), pp. 173–89.

Edgington, S. (ed. and tr.) (2004) Albert of Aachen, *Historia Hierosolymitana* (Oxford: Oxford University Press).

Edson, E. (1997), *Mapping Time and Space. How Medieval Mapmakers Viewed their World* (London: The British Library).

Edwards, J.G. (1946), 'Edward I's Castle-Building in Wales', *Proceedings of the British Academy*, vol. 32, 15–81.

Eidelberg, S. (tr.) (1977), *The Chronicle of Solomon bar Simson*, in *The Jews and the Crusaders. The Hebrew Chronicles of the First and Second Crusades* (Madison, Wis.: University of Wisconsin Press).

Ekdahl, S. (2002), 'The Strategic Organization of the Commanderies of the Teutonic Order in Prussia and Livonia', in *La Commanderie. Institution des ordres militaires dans l'Occident médiéval*, ed. A. Luttrell and L. Pressouyre (Paris: Comité des Travaux historiques et scientifiques), 219–42.

Ekkehard of Aura (1895), *Hierosolymita*, in *Recueil des Historiens des Croisades, Historiens Occidentaux*, vol. 5 (Paris: Imprimerie Nationale).

Ellenblum, R. (1998), *Frankish Rural Settlement in the Latin Kingdom of Jerusalem* (Cambridge: Cambridge University Press).

Emerton, E. (ed.) (1966), *The Correspondence of Gregory VII* (New York: Octagon).

Emery, R.W. (1941), *Heresy and Inquisition in Narbonne* (New York: Columbia University Press).

Emery, R.W. (1959), *The Jews of Perpignan in the Thirteenth Century* (New York: Columbia University Press).

Engel, P. (2001), *The Realm of St. Stephen. A History of Medieval Hungary, 895–1526*, tr. T. Palosfalvi. English edition ed. by A. Ayton (London: I.B. Tauris).

Farmer, S. (1998), 'Down and Out and Female in Thirteenth-Century Paris', *American Historical Review*, vol. 103, 345–72.

Fathers of the English Dominican Province (trs) (1916), *The Summa Theologica of St Thomas Aquinas*, vol. 9 (London: Burns, Oates and Washbourne).

Fawtier, R. (1965), *The Capetian Kings of France. Monarchy and Nation 987–1328*, tr. L. Butler and R.W. Adam (London: Macmillan).

Ferreiro, A. (1983), 'The Siege of Barbastro 1064–5: A Reassessment', *Journal of Medieval History*, vol. 9, 129–44.

Fletcher, R. (1989), *The Quest for El Cid* (London: Hutchinson).

Flint, V. (1984), 'Monsters and the Antipodes in the Early Middle Ages and the Enlightenment', *Viator*, vol. 15, 65–80.

Flori, J. (1975), 'La Notion de Chevalerie dans les Chansons de Geste du XIIe siècle. Etude historique de vocabulaire', *Le Moyen Age*, vol. 81, 211–44, 407–45.

Folda, J. (1986), *The Nazareth Capitals and the Crusader Shrine of the Annunciation* (Philadelphia, Pa: Pennsylvania State University Press).

Foreville, R. (tr.) (1952), Guillaume de Poitiers, *Histoire de Guillaume Le Conquerant* (Les Classiques de l'Histoire de France au Moyen Age) (Paris: Société d'Edition 'Les Belles Lettres').

Foreville, R. (1965), *Latran I, II, III, et Latran IV* (Paris: Editions de L'Otrante).

France, J. (1994), *Victory in the East. A Military History of the First Crusade* (Cambridge: Cambridge University Press).

Fraser, C.M. (1957), *A History of Antony Bek, Bishop of Durham 1283–1311* (Oxford: Clarendon).

Friedman, J.B. (1981), *The Monstrous Races in Medieval Art and Thought* (Cambridge, Mass., and London: Harvard University Press).

Fügedi, E. (1986), *Castle and Society in Medieval Hungary 1000–1437* (Budapest: Akademiai Kiado Hungary).

Fügedi, E. (1998), *The Elefánthy. The Hungarian Noblemen and his Kindred* (Budapest: Central European University Press).

Gardner, J. (1973), 'Pope Nicholas IV and the Decoration of Santa Maria Maggiore', *Zeitschrift für Kunstgeschichte*, vol. 36, 1–41.

Gardner, J. (1975), 'Simone Martini's St Louis of Toulouse', *Reading Medieval Studies*, vol. 1, 16–29.

Gardner, J. (1992), *The Tomb and the Tiara. Curial Tomb Sculpture in Rome and Avignon in the Later Middle Ages* (Oxford: Clarendon).

Gasiorowski, A. (1977), 'Rex Ambulans', *Quaestiones Medii Aevi*, vol. 1, 139–62.

Gathorne-Hardy, G.M. (1956), *A Royal Imposter. King Sverre of Norway* (London: Oxford University Press).

Gavigan, J.J. (tr.) (1971), Oliver of Paderborn, *Historia Damiatana*, in *Christian Society and the Crusades*, ed. E. Peters (Philadelphia, Pa: University of Pennsylvania Press), 49–139.

Geanakoplos, D.J. (1984), *Byzantium. Church, Society and Civilization Seen Through Contemporary Eyes* (Chicago: University of Chicago Press).

Gibb, H.A.R. (tr.) (1932), *The Damascus Chronicle of the Crusades Extracted and Translated from the Chronicle of Ibn al-Qalanisi* (London: Luzac).

Gieysztor, A. (1959), 'La porte de bronze à Gniezno. Document de l'histoire de Pologne au XIIe siècle', in *Conferenze pubblicate a cura dell'Accademia Polacca di Scienze e Lettere Biblioteca di Roma* (Rome: Angelo Signorelli), fasc. 4, 1–24.

Gillingham, J. (1971), *The Kingdom of Germany in the High Middle Ages* (London: Historical Association).

Gillingham, J. (1976), 'The Emperor Frederick II by T.C. Van Cleve', *English Historical Review*, vol. 91, 358–63.

Gillingham, J. (1999), *Richard I* (New Haven, Conn. and London: Yale University Press).

Gillingham, J. (2001), *The Angevin Empire*, 2nd edn (London: Arnold).

Gimpel, J. (1976), *The Medieval Machine* (London: Gollancz).

Goldin, S. (1997), 'The Socialisation for *Kiddush ha-Shem* among Medieval Jews', *Journal of Medieval History*, vol. 23, 117–38.

Gollancz, H. (ed. and tr.) (1920), Adelard of Bath, *Dodi Ve-Nechdi* (London: Oxford University Press).

Górecki, P. (1992), *Economy, Society and Lordship in Medieval Poland, 1100–1250* (New York: Holmes and Meier).

Grabois, A. (1985), 'The Crusade of King Louis VII: A Reconsideration', in *Crusade and Settlement*, ed. P.W. Edbury (Cardiff: University College Cardiff Press), 94–104.

Grant, L. (1998), *Abbot Suger of St-Denis. Church and State in Early Twelfth-Century France* (London: Longman).

Graus, F. (1967), 'Social Utopias in the Middle Ages', *Past and Present*, vol. 38, 3–19.

Greenia, C. (tr.) (2000), Bernard of Clairvaux, *In Praise of the New Knighthood* (Cistercian Fathers Series, 19B) (Kalamazoo, Mich.: Cistercian Publications).

Greenway, D. (2002), Henry of Huntingdon, *The History of the English People 1000–1154* (Oxford: Oxford University Press).

Greenway, D. and J. Sayers (trs) (1989), Jocelin of Brakelond, *Chronicle of the Abbey of Bury St. Edmunds* (Oxford: Oxford University Press).

Grudzinski, T. (1974), 'The Beginnings of the Feudal Disintegration in Poland', *Acta Poloniae Historica*, vol. 30, 5–31.

Guiraud, J. (ed.) (1901), *Les Registres d'Urbain IV (1261–64)*, vol. 2 (Paris: Bibliothèque des Ecoles Françaises d'Athènes et de Rome).

Habig, M. (tr.) (1980), *St. Francis of Assisi. Omnibus of Sources* (London: SPCK).

Hallam, E. (1982a), 'Royal Burial and the Cult of Kingship in France and England, 1060–1330', *Journal of Medieval History*, vol. 8, 359–80.

Hallam, E. (1982b), 'Philip the Fair and the Cult of St. Louis', *Studies in Church History*, vol. 18, 201–14.

Hamilton, B. (1978), 'The Cathar Council of Saint-Félix Reconsidered', *Archivum Fratrum Praedicatorum*, vol. 48, 23–53.

Hamilton, B. (1985), 'Prester John and the Three Kings of Cologne', in *Studies in Medieval History presented to R.H.C. Davis*, ed. H. Mayr-Harting and R.I. Moore (London: Hambledon Press), 177–91.

Hamilton, B. (1994), 'Wisdom from the East', in *Heresy and Literacy, 1000–1530*, ed. P. Biller and A. Hudson (Cambridge: Cambridge University Press), 38–60.

Hamilton, B. (1995), 'Ideals of Holiness: Crusaders, Contemplatives, and Mendicants', *International History Review*, vol. 17, 693–712.

Hamilton, B. (1999), 'The Cathars and Christian Perfection', in *The Medieval Church: Universities, Heresy and the Religious Life. Essays in Honour of Gordon Leff*, Studies in Church History: Subsidia 11 (Woodbridge, Suffolk: Boydell Press), 5–23.

Hamilton, B. (2000), *The Leper King and his Heirs. Baldwin IV and the Crusader Kingdom of Jerusalem* (Cambridge: Cambridge University Press).

Hamilton, R. and J. Perry (eds and trs) (1984), with introduction and notes by I. Michael, *The Poem of the Cid* (Harmondsworth: Penguin) (originally 1975).

Harper, R.P. and D. Pringle (2000), *Belmont Castle. The Excavation of a Crusader Stronghold in the Kingdom of Jerusalem* (British Academy Monographs in Archaeology, 10) (Oxford: Oxford University Press).

Harvey, B. (1993), *Living and Dying in England, 1100–1540. The Monastic Experience* (Oxford: Clarendon).

Harvey, P. (1973), 'The English Inflation of 1180–1220', *Past and Present*, vol. 61, 3–30.

Hatto, A.T. (tr.) (1960), Gottfried von Strassburg, *Tristan* (Harmondsworth: Penguin).

Hatto, A.T. (tr.) (1980), Wolfram von Eschenbach, *Parzival* (Harmondsworth: Penguin).

Hauser, A. (1951), *The Social History of Art*, vol. 1 (London: Routledge and Kegan Paul).

Hausmann, F. (ed.) (1969), *Die Urkunden Konrads III.*, in *Monumenta Germaniae Historica. Diplomata Regum et Imperatorum Germaniae*, vol. 9 (Vienna: Hermann Bohlaus Nachf.).

Hendy, M.F. (1970), 'Byzantium 1081–1204: An Economic Reappraisal', *Transactions of the Royal Historical Society*, vol. 20, 31–52.

Herlihy, D. (1968), *Medieval Culture and Society* (New York: Harper and Row).

Herlihy, D. (1975), 'Life Expectancies for Women in Medieval Society', in *The Role of Women in the Middle Ages*, ed. R.T. Morewedge (Albany, NY: State University of New York), 1–22.

Heslop, T.A. (1990), 'Romanesque Painting and Social Distinction: The Magi and the Shepherds', in *England in the Twelfth Century. Proceedings of the 1988 Harlaxton Symposium*, ed. D. Williams (Woodbridge, Suffolk: Boydell Press), 137–52.

Hill, B.H. (ed.) (1972), *Medieval Monarchy in Action. The German Empire from Henry I to Henry IV* (London: Allen and Unwin).

Hill, H. and L.L. Hill (trs) (1968), Raymond of Aguilers, *The History of the Frankish Conquerors of Jerusalem* (Philadelphia, Pa: American Philosophical Society).

Hill, R. (tr.) (1962), *The Deeds of the Franks* (London: Thomas Nelson).

Hill, R. (1979), 'Crusading Warfare 1097–1130: A Camp Follower's View', in *Proceedings of the Battle Conference on Anglo-Norman Studies*, vol. 1, 1978, ed. R.A. Brown (Ipswich: Boydell Press), 75–83.

Hilton, R.H. (1962), 'Rent and Capital Formation in Feudal Society', in *Second International Conference of Economic History* (Aix-en-Provence), vol. 2, 33–68.

Hinnebusch, W.A. (1965), *The History of the Dominican Order*, vol. 1 (New York: Alba).

Hitti, P.K. (tr.) (1987), *An Arab-Syrian Gentleman and Warrior in the Period of the Crusades. Memoirs of Usamah Ibn-Munqidh* (London: I.B. Tauris) (originally 1929).

Hollister, C.W. (1985), 'Henry I and the Invisible Transformation of Medieval England', in *Studies in Medieval History presented to R.H.C. Davis*, ed. H. Mayr-Harting and R.I. Moore (London: Hambledon Press), 119–31.

Hollister, C.W. and J.W. Baldwin (1978), 'The Rise of Administrative Kingship: Henry I and Philip Augustus', *American Historical Review*, vol. 83, 867–905.

Holmes, U.T. and F.R. Weedon (1962), 'Peter of Blois as a Physician', *Speculum*, vol. 37, 252–6.

Holt, E.G. (ed.) (1957), *A Documentary History of Art*, vol. 1 (New York: Doubleday).

Holt, J.C. (1972), 'Politics and Property in Early Medieval England', *Past and Present*, vol. 57, 3–52.

Holt, J.C. (1981), 'The Prehistory of Parliament', in *The English Parliament in the Middle Ages*, ed. R.G. Davies and J.H. Denton (Manchester: Manchester University Press), 1–28.

Holt, J.C. (1984), 'The Loss of Normandy and Royal Finance', in *War and Government in the Middle Ages*, ed. J. Gillingham and J.C. Holt (Woodbridge, Suffolk: Boydell and Brewer), 92–105.

Holt, J.C. (1992), *Magna Carta*, 2nd edn (Cambridge: Cambridge University Press).

Hook, J. (1979), *Siena. A City and its History* (London: Hamish Hamilton).

Hopkins, J. and H. Richardson (eds and trs) (1974), Anselm of Canterbury, vol. 1, *Monologion, Proslogion, Debate with Gaunilo, and Meditation on Human Redemption* (London: SCM Press).

Hoppenbrouwers, P. (1997), 'Agricultural Production and Technology in the Netherlands *c.*1000–1500', in *Medieval Farming and Technology. The Impact of Agricultural Change in Northwest Europe*, ed. G. Astill and J. Langdon (Leiden: Brill), 89–114.

Houben, H. (2002), *Roger II of Sicily. A Ruler between East and West* (Cambridge: Cambridge University Press).

Housley, N. (1982), *The Italian Crusades. The Papal–Angevin Alliance and the Crusades against Christian Lay Powers, 1254–1343* (Oxford: Clarendon).

Housley, N. (1986), *The Avignon Papacy and the Crusades 1305–78* (Oxford: Clarendon).

Howlett, R. (ed.) (1884), William of Newburgh, *Historia Rerum Anglicarum*, in *Chronicles of the Reigns of Stephen, Henry II and Richard I*, vol. 1 (Rolls Series, 82) (London: Longman).

Howlett, R. (ed.) (1889), *The Chronicle of Robert of Torigny*, in *Chronicles of the Reigns of Stephen, Henry II and Richard I*, vol. 4 (Rolls Series, 82) (London: Eyre and Spottiswoode).

Hubert, M.J. and J.L. La Monte (trs) (1936), Philip of Novara, *The Wars of Frederick II against the Ibelins in Syria and Cyprus* (New York: Columbia University Press).

Huillard-Bréholles, J.L.A. (ed.) (1852), *Historia Diplomatica Friderici Secunda*, vol. 1(ii) (Paris: Plon).

Huygens, R.B.C. (1981), *De constructione castri Saphet. Construction et fonctions d'un château fort franc en Terre Sainte* (Amsterdam: North-Holland).

Hyde, J.K. (1966), *Padua in the Age of Dante* (Manchester: Manchester University Press).

Hyde, J.K. (1972), 'Contemporary Views of Faction and Civil Strife in Thirteenth- and Fourteenth-Century Italy', in *Violence and Disorder in Italian Cities, 1200–1500*, ed. L. Martinès (Berkeley, Calif.: University of California Press), 273–307.

Hyde, J.K. (1973), *Society and Politics in Medieval Italy. The Evolution of the Civil Life, 1000–1350* (London: Macmillan).

James, B.S. (tr.) (1998), *The Letters of St. Bernard of Clairvaux*, introd. B.M. Kienzle (Stroud: Sutton) (originally 1953).

James, J. (1982), *Chartres. The Masons who Built a Legend* (London: Routledge and Kegan Paul).

James, M.R. (tr.) (1983), Walter Map, *De Nugis Curialium*, revised C.N.L. Brooke and R.A.B. Mynors (Oxford: Clarendon).

Jamison, E. (1938), 'The Sicilian Norman Kingdom in the Mind of Anglo-Norman Contemporaries', *Proceedings of the British Academy*, vol. 24, 237–85.

Jamison, E. (1987), *The Norman Administration of Apulia and Capua*, ed. D. Clementi and T. Közler (Darmstadt: Scientia Verlag Aalen) (originally 1913).

Jedin, H., K.S. Latourette and J. Martin (eds) (1970), *Atlas zur Kirchengeschichte* (Freiburg: Herder).

Jessopp, A. and M.R. James (trs) (1896), *The Life and Miracles of St William of Norwich by Thomas of Monmouth* (Cambridge: Cambridge University Press).

Johnson, P.D. (1991), *Equal in the Monastic Profession. Religious Women in Medieval France* (Chicago: University of Chicago Press).

Johns, J. (2002), *Arabic Administration in Norman Sicily. The Royal Diwan* (Cambridge: Cambridge University Press).

Johnstone, H. (tr.) (1951), *Annales Gandenses* (London: Thomas Nelson).

Jones, C.M. (1942), 'The Conventional Saracen of the Songs of Geste', *Speculum*, vol. 17, 201–25.

Jones, P. (1997), *The Italian City-State. From Commune to Signoria* (Oxford: Clarendon).

Jordan, K. (1986), *Henry the Lion. A Biography* (Oxford: Clarendon).

Jordan, W.C. (1979), *Louis IX and the Challenge of the Crusade* (Princeton, NJ: Princeton University Press).

Jordan, W.C. (1986), *From Servitude to Freedom. Manumission in the Senonais in the Thirteenth Century* (Philadelphia, Pa: University of Pennsylvania Press).

Jordan, W.C. (1989), *The French Monarchy and the Jews. From Philip Augustus to the Last Capetians* (Philadelphia, Pa: University of Pennsylvania Press).

Jordan, W.C. (1996), *The Great Famine. Northern Europe in the Early Fourteenth Century* (Princeton, NJ: Princeton University Press).

Jotischky, A. (1995), *The Perfection of Solitude. Hermits and Monks in the Crusader States* (University Park, Pa: Pennsylvania State University Press).

Kantorowicz, E. (1957a), *The Emperor Frederick the Second, 1191–1250*, tr. E.O. Lorimer (London: Constable) (originally 1927).

Kantorowicz, E. (1957b), *The King's Two Bodies. A Study in Medieval Political Theology* (Princeton, NJ: Princeton University Press).

Kantorowicz, E. (1958), *Laudes Regiae. A Study in Liturgical Acclamations and Medieval Ruler Worship* (Berkeley, Calif.: University of California Press) (originally 1946).

Katzenellenbogen, A. (1944), 'The Central Tympanum at Vézelay: Its Encyclopedic Meaning and its Relation to the First Crusade', *Art Bulletin*, vol. 2, 141–51.

Katzenellenbogen, A. (1959), *The Sculptural Programs of Chartres Cathedral* (Baltimore, Md: Johns Hopkins University Press).

Katzenellenbogen, A. (1977), *Allegories of the Virtues and Vices in Medieval Art* (New York: Kraus) (originally 1939).

Kedar, B.Z. (1972), 'The Passenger List of a Crusader Ship, 1250: Towards the History of the Popular Element in the Seventh Crusade', *Studi Medievali*, vol. 13, 267–79.

Kedar, B.Z. (1983), 'Gerard of Nazareth, a Neglected Twelfth-Century Writer of the Latin East: A Contribution to the Intellectual History of the Crusader States', *Dumbarton Oaks Papers*, vol. 37, 55–77.

Kedar, B.Z. (1984), *Crusade and Mission. European Approaches towards the Muslims* (Princeton, NJ: Princeton University Press).

Kemp, B.R. (ed.) (1986), *Reading Abbey Cartularies*, vol. 1 (Camden Fourth Series, 31) (London: Royal Historical Society).

Kern, F. (1948), *Kingship and Law in the Middle Ages*, tr. S.B. Chrimes (Oxford: Blackwell).

Kidson, P. (1987), 'Panofsky, Suger and St Denis', *Journal of the Warburg and Courtauld Institutes*, vol. 50, 1–17.

Kitzinger, E. (1976), *The Art of Byzantium and the Medieval West. Selected Studies*, ed. W.E. Kleinbauer (Bloomington, Ind.: Indiana University Press).

Knowles, D. (1934), 'The Diet of the Black Monks', *Downside Review*, vol. 52, 275–90.

Knowles, D. (1963), 'Cistercians and Cluniacs: The Controversy between St Bernard and Peter the Venerable', in *The Historian and Character and Other Essays* (Cambridge: Cambridge University Press), 50–75.

Kosztolnyik, K.J. (1981), *Five Eleventh-Century Hungarian Kings. Their Politics and Relations with Rome* (New York: Columbia University Press).

Kötzschke, R. (ed.) (1912), *Quellen zur Geschichte der Ostdeutschen Kolonisation im 12. bis 14. Jahrhundert* (Berlin: Teubner).

Kraus, H. (1978), *Gold was the Mortar. The Economics of Cathedral Building* (London: Routledge and Kegan Paul).

Krautheimer, R. (1980), *Rome. Profile of a City, 312–1308* (Princeton, NJ: Princeton University Press).

Krey, A.C. (ed.) (1921), *The First Crusade. Accounts of Eye-Witnesses and Participants* (Gloucester, Mass.: Peter Smith)

Krieger, K-F. (1996), 'Obligatory Military Service and the Use of Mercenaries in Imperial Military Campaigns under the Hohenstaufen Emperors', in *England and Germany in the High Middle Ages. Challenge and Change*, ed. A. Haverkamp and H. Vollrath (Oxford: Oxford University Press), 151–68.

Lacarra, J.M. (1947–8), 'Documentos para el Estudio de la Reconquista y Repoblación del Valle del Ebro', in *Estudios de Edad Media de la Corona de Aragón*, vol. 3 (Zaragoza: 'Heraldo de Aragón').

Lambert, M.D. (1998), *Franciscan Poverty. The Doctrine of Absolute Poverty of Christ and the Apostles in the Franciscan Order, 1210–1323*, rev. and expanded edn (New York: Franciscan Institute).

Lambert, M.D. (2002), *Medieval Heresy. Popular Movements from Bogomil to Hus*, 3rd edn (Oxford: Blackwell).

Lane, F.C. (1973), *Venice. A Maritime Republic* (Baltimore, Md: Johns Hopkins University Press).

Langlois, C. (1901), *Saint Louis. Philippe le Bel. Les derniers Capétiens directs (1226–1328)* (vol. 3 (ii), *Histoire de France*, ed. E. Lavisse) (Paris: Hachette).

Larner, J. (1971), *Culture and Society in Italy, 1290–1420* (London: Batsford).

Larner, J. (1980), *Italy in the Age of Dante and Petrarch 1216–1380* (London: Longman).

Larner, J. (1999), *Marco Polo and the Discovery of the World* (New Haven, Conn. and London: Yale University Press).

Larson, H.M. (1929–30), 'A Medieval Swedish Mining Company', *Journal of Economic and Business History*, vol. 2, 545–59.

Larson, L.M. (1908), 'The Household of the Norwegian Kings in the Thirteenth Century', *American Historical Review*, vol. 13, 459–79.

Larson, L.M. (tr.) (1917), *The King's Mirror* (Scandinavian Monographs, 3) (New York: Oxford University Press).

Leclercq, J. (1979), *Monks and Love in Twelfth-Century France. Psycho-Historical Essays* (Oxford: Clarendon).

Lecoy de la Marche, A. (ed.) (1867), *Oeuvres complètes de Suger* (Paris: Société l'Histoire de France).

Le Goff, J. (1980), *Time, Work and Culture in the Middle Ages*, tr. A. Goldhammer (Chicago and London: University of Chicago Press).

Le Goff, J. (1984), *The Birth of Purgatory*, tr. A. Goldhammer (London: Scolar Press).

Le Grand, L. (ed.) (1901), *Statuts d'Hôtels-Dieu et de Léproseries* (Paris: Picard).

Lekai, L.K. (1977), *The Cistercians. Ideals and Reality* (Kent, Ohio: Kent State University Press).

Le Patourel, J.H. (1979), 'The Norman Conquest – 1066, 1106, 1154?', in *Proceedings of the Battle Conference on Anglo-Norman Studies*, vol. 1, ed. R.A. Brown (Ipswich: Boydell Press), 103–20.

Le Roy Ladurie, E. (1972), *Times of Feast, Times of Famine. A History of Climate since the Year 1000*, tr. B. Bray (London: Allen and Unwin).

Le Roy Ladurie, E. (1978), *Montaillou. Cathars and Catholics in a French Village 1294–1324*, tr. B. Bray (London: Scolar Press).

Levine, R. (tr.) (1997), Guibert of Nogent, *The Deeds of God through the Franks* (Woodbridge, Suffolk: Boydell Press).

Lewis, A.W. (1976), 'The Capetian Apanages and the Nature of the French Kingdom', *Journal of Medieval History*, vol. 2, 119–34.

Lewis, A.W. (1982), *Royal Succession in Capetian France* (Cambridge, Mass.: Harvard University Press).

Leyser, K.J. (1982), *Medieval Germany and its Neighbours, 900–1250* (London: Hambledon Press).

Leyser, K.J. (1994a) 'Frederick Barbarossa and the Hohenstaufen Polity', in *Communications and Power in Medieval Europe. The Gregorian Revolution and Beyond*, ed. T. Reuter (London: Hambledon Press), 115–42.

Leyser, K.J. (1994b), 'The Anglo-Norman Succession, 1120–25', in *Communications and Power in Medieval Europe. The Gregorian Revolution and Beyond*, ed. T. Reuter (London: Hambledon Press), 97–114.

Little, L.K. (1971), 'Pride Goes before Avarice: Social Change and the Vices in Latin Christendom', *American Historical Review*, vol. 76, 16–49.

Little, L.K. (1978), *Religious Poverty and the Profit Economy in Medieval Europe* (London: Elek).

Lizerand, G. (ed.) (1964), *Le Dossier de l'Affaire des Templiers* (Les Classiques de l'Histoire de France au Moyen Age) (Paris: Société d'Edition 'Les Belles Lettres').

Lomax, D. (1978), *The Reconquest of Spain* (London: Longman).

Longnon, J. (1969), 'The Frankish States in Greece, 1204–1311', in *A History of the Crusades*, vol. 2, ed. K.M. Setton (Madison, Wis. and London: University of Wisconsin Press), 234–74.

Lopez, R.S. (1943), 'European Merchants in the Medieval Indies: The Evidence of Commercial Documents', *Journal of Economic History*, vol. 3, 164–84.

Lopez, R.S. (1971), *The Commercial Revolution of the Middle Ages, 950–1350* (Englewood Cliffs, NJ: Prentice-Hall).

Lopez, R.S. and I.W. Raymond (trs) (1998), *Medieval Trade in the Mediterranean World* (New York: Columbia University Press) (originally 1955).

Lot, F. and R. Fawtier (1958), *Histoire des Institutions Françaises au Moyen Age*, vol. 2 (Paris: Presses Universitaires de France).

Loud, G.A. (1982), 'Royal Control of the Church in the Twelfth-Century Kingdom of Sicily', *Studies in Church History*, vol. 18, 147–59.

Loud, G.A. (1983), 'The Church, Warfare and Military Obligations in Norman Italy', *Studies in Church History*, vol. 20, 31–45.

Loud, G.A. and T.E.J. Wiedemann (trs) (1998), *The History of the Tyrants of Sicily by 'Hugo Falcandus', 1153–69* (Manchester: Manchester University Press).

Lourie, E. (1975), 'The Will of Alfonso I', *Speculum*, vol. 50, 635–51.

Lovejoy, A.O. (1942), *The Great Chain of Being. A Study of the History of an Idea* (Cambridge, Mass.: Harvard University Press).

Loyn, H.R. and J. Percival (eds) (1975), *The Reign of Charlemagne* (Documents of Medieval History, 2) (London: Edward Arnold).

Luard, H.R. (ed.) (1865), *Annales Monasterii de Waverleia*, in *Annales Monastici*, vol. 2 (Rolls Series, 36) (London: Longman, Green).

Luard, H.R. (ed.) (1880), Matthew Paris, *Chronica Majora*, vols 3, 4, 5 (Rolls Series, 57) (London: Longman).

Luchaire, A. (1901), *Louis VII. Philippe-Auguste. Louis VIII (1137–1226)* (vol. 3(i), *Histoire de France*, ed. E. Lavisse) (Paris: Hachette).

Luchaire, A. (1908), *Innocent III. Les Royautés Vassales du Saint-Siège* (Paris: Hachette).

Lunt, W.E. (1934), *Papal Revenues in the Middle Ages*, 2 vols (New York: Columbia University Press).

Luscombe, D.E. (tr.) (1971), Peter Abelard, *Ethics* (Oxford: Clarendon).

Luttrell, A. (1989), 'The Latins and the Smaller Aegean Islands, 1204–1453', in *Latins and Greeks in the Eastern Mediterranean after 1204*, ed. B. Arbel, B. Hamilton and D. Jacoby (London: Frank Cass), 146–57.

Lyon, B. (1963), 'Encore le problème de la Chronologie des Corvées', *Le Moyen Age*, vol. 69, 615–30.

McGinn, B. (ed.) (1979), *Visions of the End. Apocalyptic Traditions in the Middle Ages* (New York: Columbia University Press).

MacKay, A. (1977), *Spain in the Middle Ages. From Frontier to Empire 1000–1500* (London: Macmillan).

MacKay, A. and G. McKendrick (1979), 'Confession in the *Cantigás de Santa María*', *Reading Medieval Studies*, vol. 5, 71–88.

McLaughlin, M.M. (1967), 'Abelard as Autobiographer: The Motives and Meaning of his "Story of my Calamities"', *Speculum*, vol. 42, 463–88.

McNeal, E.H. (tr.) (1936), Robert of Clari, *The Conquest of Constantinople* (New York: Octagon).

McNeal, E.H. and R.L. Wolff (1969), 'The Fourth Crusade', in *A History of the Crusades*, vol. 2, ed. K. Setton (Madison, Wis. and London: University of Wisconsin Press), 152–85.

McNeill, W.H. (1977), *Plagues and Peoples* (Oxford: Blackwell).

McNulty, P.A. (ed.) (1959), St Peter Damian, *Selected Writings on the Spiritual Life* (London: Faber and Faber).

Magnou-Nortier, E. and A.M. Magnou (eds) (1996), *Recueil des Chartes de l'Abbaye de la Grasse*, vol. 1, *779–1119* (Collection de Documents Inédits sur l'Histoire de France, 24) (Paris: Editions du Comité des Travaux historiques et scientifiques).

Magoulias, H.J. (tr.) (1984), *O City of Byzantium. Annals of Niketas Choniates* (Detroit, Mich.: Wayne State University Press).

Maitland, F.W. (ed.) (1889), *Select Pleas in Manorial and other Seignorial Courts* (London: Selden Society).

Male, E. (1961), *The Gothic Image. Religious Art in France in the Thirteenth Century*, tr. D. Nussey (New York: Harper and Row) (originally 1913).

Marczali, H. (ed.) (1901), *Enchiridion Fontium Historiae Hungarorum* (Budapest: Athenaeum).

Marongiù, A. (1963–4), 'A Model State in the Middle Ages: The Norman and Swabian Kingdom of Sicily', *Comparative Studies in Society and History*, vol. 6, 307–20.

Martinès, L. (1972), 'Political Violence in the Thirteenth Century', in *Violence and Disorder in Italian Cities 1200–1500*, ed. L. Martinès (Berkeley, Calif.: University of California Press), 331–53.

Martinès, L. (1980), *Power and Imagination. City-States in Renaissance Italy* (New York: Knopf).

Mason, E. (tr.) (1928), *Arthurian Chronicles represented by Wace and Layamon* (London: Dent) (originally 1912).

Matthew, D. (1966), *The Norman Conquest* (London: Batsford).

Mayer, H.E. (1978), 'Latins, Muslims and Greeks in the Latin Kingdom', *History*, vol. 63, 175–92.

Mayer, H.E. (1988), *The Crusades*, tr. J. Gillingham, 2nd edn (Oxford: Oxford University Press).

Mayer, H.E. (1989), 'Angevins *versus* Normans: The New Men of King Fulk of Jerusalem', *Proceedings of the American Philosophical Society*, vol. 133, 1–25.

Mayr-Harting, H. (1972), *The Coming of Christianity to Anglo-Saxon England* (London: Batsford).

Menache, S. (1980), 'Les Hébreux du XIVe siècle: La Formation des stéréotypes nationaux en France et en Angleterre', *Ethno-Psychologie. Revue de Psychologie des peuples*, vol. 35, 55–65.

Ménager, L-R. (1959), 'L'Institution monarchique dans les Etats normands d'Italie', *Cahiers de civilisation médiévale*, vol. 2, 303–31, 445–68.

Menendez Pidal, R. (1955), *Primera Crónica General de España que mando componer Alfonso el Sabio* (Madrid: Nueva Biblioteca de Autores Españoles).

Michell, R. and N. Forbes (eds) (1914), *The Chronicle of Novgorod 1016–1471* (London: Camden Society).

Mierow, C.C. (tr.) (1955), Otto of Freising and Rahewin, *The Deeds of Frederick Barbarossa* (New York: Columbia University Press).

Mierow C.C. (tr.) (1966), Otto of Freising, *The Two Cities. A Chronicle of Universal History to the Year 1146 AD* (New York: Octagon) (originally 1928).

Migne, J.P. (ed.) (1853), Peter Damian, *Epistolae*, in *Patrologia Latina*, vol. 144 (Paris: Garnier).

Migne, J.P. (ed.) (1855a), Eckbert of Schonau, *Sermones contra Catharos*, in *Patrologia Latina*, vol. 195 (Paris: Garnier).

Migne, J.P. (ed.) (1855b), Peter Cantor, *Verbum Abbreviatum*, in *Patrologia Latina*, vol. 205 (Paris: Garnier).

Migne, J.P. (ed.) (1855c), Peter of Blois, *Epistolae*, in *Patrologia Latina*, vol. 207 (Paris: Garnier).

Migne, J.P. (ed.) (1865), Nicephorus Gregoras, *Byzantina Historia*, in *Patrologia Graeca*, vol. 148 (Paris: Garnier).

Migne, J.P. (ed.) (1880), Guibert of Nogent, *De Pignoribus Sanctorum*, in *Patrologia Latina*, vol. 156 (Paris: Garnier).

Migne, J.P. (ed.) (1891), *Innocentii III P.P. Regestorum Lib. X*, in *Patrologia Latina*, vol. 215 (Paris: Garnier).

Migne, J.P. (ed.) (1895), Honorius of Autun, *Elucidarium*, in *Patrologia Latina*, vol. 172 (Paris: Garnier).

Milis, L.J.R. (1992), *Angelic Monks and Earthly Men. Monasticism and its Meaning to Medieval Society* (Woodbridge, Suffolk: The Boydell Press).

Millor, W.J. and H.E. Butler (eds) (1986), *The Letters of John of Salisbury*, rev. ed. C.N.L. Brooke, vol. 1 (Oxford: Clarendon).

Mitteis, H. (1975), *The State in the Middle Ages*, tr. H.F. Orton (Amsterdam: North-Holland).

Molin, K. (2001), *Unknown Crusader Castles* (London: Hambledon and London).

Mommsen, T.E. and K.F. Morrison (eds) (1962), *Imperial Lives and Letters of the Eleventh Century* (New York: Columbia University Press).

Monk of Lido (1895), *Historia de Translatione Sanctorum Magni Nicolai*, in *Recueil des Historiens des Croisades. Historiens Occidentaux*, vol. 5 (Paris: Imprimerie Nationale).

Moore, R.I. (ed.) (1975), *The Birth of Popular Heresy* (Documents of Medieval History, 1) (London: Edward Arnold).

Moore, R.I. (1977), *The Origins of European Dissent* (London: Allen Lane).

Moorman, J. (1968), *A History of the Franciscan Order* (Oxford: Clarendon).

Morris, C. (1972), *The Discovery of the Individual, 1050–1200* (London: SPCK).

Morris, C. (1993), 'The *Gesta Francorum* as Narrative History', *Reading Medieval Studies*, vol. 19, 55–71.

Morrison, K.F. (1962), 'Canossa, a revision', *Traditio*, vol. 18, 121–48.

Morrison, K.F. (1980), 'Otto of Freising's Quest for the Hermeneutic Circle', *Speculum*, vol. 55, 207–36.

Mortet, V. and P. Deschamps (eds) (1995), *Recueil de textes relatifs à l'histoire de l'architecture et à la condition des architectes en France au moyen âge XIe–XIIIe siècles*, 2 vols in one (Paris: Editions du Comité des Travaux historiques et scientifiques) (originally 1911–29).

Muldoon, J. (1979), *Popes, Lawyers and Infidels. The Church and the Non-Christian World 1250–1550* (Philadelphia, Pa: University of Pennsylvania Press).

Murray, A. (1972), 'Piety and Impiety in Thirteenth-Century Italy', *Studies in Church History*, vol. 8, 83–106.

Murray, A. (1978), *Reason and Society in the Middle Ages* (Oxford: Clarendon).

Murray, A.V. (1989), 'The Origins of the Frankish Nobility in the Kingdom of Jerusalem, 1100–1118', *Mediterranean Historical Review*, vol. 4, 281–300.

Murray, A.V. (1992), 'Dynastic Continuity or Dynastic Change? The Accession of Baldwin II and the Nobility of the Kingdom of Jerusalem', *Medieval Prosopography*, vol. 13, 1–28.

Musset, L. (1951), *Les Peuples scandinaves au moyen âge* (Paris: Presses Universitaires de France).

Nederman, C.J. (eds and trs) (1990), John of Salisbury, *Policraticus. Of the Frivolities of Courtiers and the Footprints of Philosophers* (Cambridge: Cambridge University Press).

Nelson, J. (1972), 'Society, Theodicy and the Origins of Heresy', *Studies in Church History*, vol. 9, 65–77.

Nicholl, D. and C. Hardie (trs) (1954), Dante, *Monarchy and Three Political Letters* (London: Weidenfeld and Nicolson).

Nicholson, H.J. (tr.) (1997), *Chronicle of the Third Crusade. A Translation of the Itinerarium Peregrinorum et Gesta Regis Ricardi* (Crusade Texts in Translation, 3) (Aldershot: Ashgate).

Noble, P. (1973), 'Attitudes to Social Class as Revealed by some of the Older Chansons de Geste', *Romania*, vol. 94, 359–85.

O'Callaghan, J.F. (1975), *A History of Medieval Spain* (Ithaca, NY and London: Cornell University Press).

Oschinsky D. (ed.) (1971), *Walter of Henley and Other Treatises on Estate Management and Accounting* (Oxford: Clarendon).

Otis, L.L. (1985), *Prostitution in Medieval Society. The History of an Urban Institution in Languedoc* (Chicago: University of Chicago Press).

Panofsky, E. (1973), *Gothic Architecture and Scholasticism* (New York: Meridian) (originally 1951).

Panofsky, E. (eds and trs) (1979), *Abbot Suger on the Abbey Church of St Denis and its Art Treasures*, ed. G. Panofsky-Soergel (Princeton, NJ: Princeton University Press) (originally 1946).

Partner, P. (1972), *The Lands of St. Peter* (London: Eyre Methuen).

Peal, A. (1986), 'Olivier de Termes and the Occitan Nobility in the Thirteenth Century', *Reading Medieval Studies*, vol. 12, 109–30.

Pegues, F.J. (1962), *The Lawyers of the Last Capetians* (Princeton, NJ: Princenton University Press).

Perroy, E. (1962), 'Social Mobility among the French *Noblesse* in the Later Middle Ages', *Past and Present*, vol. 21, 25–38.

Phelan, G.B. (tr.) (1949), Thomas Aquinas, *On Kingship to the King of Cyprus*, intro. I.T. Eschmann (Toronto: Pontifical Institute of Medieval Studies).

Phillips, J. (1996), *Defenders of the Holy Land. Relations between the Latin East and the West, 1119–1187* (Oxford: Clarendon).

Phillips, J.R.S. (1998), *The Medieval Expansion of Europe*, 2nd edn (Oxford: Clarendon).

Pickering, F.P. (1965), 'Notes on Fate and Fortune', in *Medieval German Studies presented to Frederick Norman* (London: Institute of Germanic Studies), 1–15.

Plesner, J. (1934), *L'Emigration de la campagne à la ville libre de Florence au XIIIe siècle*, tr. F. Gleizal (Copenhagen: Gyldendal).

Pope-Hennessy, J. (1972), *Italian Gothic Sculpture* (London: Phaidon).

Post, G. (1964), 'The Naturalness of Society and the State', in *Studies in Medieval Legal Thought. Public Law and the State, 1100–1322* (Princeton, NJ: Princeton University Press), 494–561.

Potter, K. (tr.) (1955), William of Malmesbury, *Historia Novella* (London: Nelson).

Potter, K. (tr.) (1976), *Gesta Stephani* (Oxford: Clarendon).

Poulsen, B. (1997), 'Agricultural Technology in Medieval Denmark', in *Medieval Farming and Technology. The Impact of Agricultural Change in Northwest Europe*, ed. G. Astill and J. Langdon (Leiden: Brill), 115–45.

Powell, J.M. (1962), 'Medieval Monarchy and Trade. The Economic Policy of Frederick II in the Kingdom of Sicily', *Studi Medievali*, vol. 3, 420–524.

Powell, J.M. (tr.) (1971), *The Liber Augustalis or Constitutions of Melfi promulgated by the Emperor Frederick II for the Kingdom of Sicily in 1231* (Syracuse, NY: Syracuse University Press).

Powell, J.M. (1986), *Anatomy of a Crusade, 1213–1221* (Philadelphia, Pa: University of Pennsylvania Press).

Powicke, F.M. (1961), *The Loss of Normandy, 1198–1204* (Manchester: Manchester University Press).

Prawer, J. (1952), 'The Settlement of the Latins in Jerusalem', *Speculum*, vol. 27, 490–503.

Prawer, J. (1968), 'The Nobility and the Feudal Regime in the Latin Kingdom of Jerusalem', in *Lordship and Community in Medieval Europe*, ed. F.C. Cheyette (New York: Holt, Rinehart and Winston), 156–79.

Prawer, J. (1988), *The History of the Jews in the Latin Kingdom of Jerusalem* (Oxford: Clarendon).

Pryor, J.R. (1982), 'Transportation of Horses by Sea during the Era of the Crusades', *Mariner's Mirror*, vol. 68, 9–27, 103–25.

Pryor, J.R. (1988), *Geography, Technology and War: Studies in the Maritime History of the Mediterranean* (Cambridge: Cambridge University Press).

Queller, D.E. and T.F. Madden (1997), *The Fourth Crusade. The Conquest of Constantinople 1201–4*, 2nd edn (Philadelphia, Pa: University of Pennsylvania Press).

Radice, B. (tr.) (1974), *The Letters of Abelard and Heloise* (Harmondsworth: Penguin).

Rady, M. (2000), *Nobility, Land and Service in Medieval Hungary* (London: Palgrave).

Raepsaet, G. (1997), 'The Development of Farming Implements between the Seine and the Rhine from the Second to Twelfth Century', in *Medieval Farming and Technology. The Impact of Agricultural Change in Northwest Europe*, ed. G. Astill and J. Langdon (Leiden: Brill), 41–68.

Raine, J. (ed.) (1839), Robert of Graystanes, *Historia de statu ecclesiae Dunelmensis* (London: Surtees Society).

Reeves, M. (1965), 'Marsiglio of Padua and Dante Alighieri', in *Trends in Medieval Political Thought*, ed. B. Smalley (Oxford: Blackwell), 86–104.

Renn, D.F. (1973), *Norman Castles in Britain* (London: John Baker).

Renouard, Y. (1949), *Les Hommes d'Affaires du Moyen Age* (Paris: Librarie Armand Colin).

Renouard, Y. (1963), 'Les Voies de communication entre la France et le Piémont au Moyen Age', *Bollettino storico-bibliografico subalpino*, vol. 61, 233–56.

Reynolds, R.L. (1930), 'Merchants of Arras and the Overland Trade with Genoa', *Revue Belge de Philologie et d'Histoire*, vol. 9, 495–533.

Reynolds, R.L. (1952), 'Origins of Modern Business Enterprise', *Journal of Economic History*, vol. 12, 350–65.

Richard, J. (1992), *Saint Louis. Crusader King of France*, ed. S. Lloyd, tr. J. Birrell (Cambridge: Cambridge University Press) (originally 1983).

Richard, J. (1999), *The Crusades, c.1071–c.1291*, tr. J. Birrell (Cambridge: Cambridge University Press).

Richards, D.S. (2001), *The Rare and Excellent History of Saladin by Baha al-Din Ibn Shaddad* (Crusade Texts in Translation, 7) (Aldershot: Ashgate).

Riley, H.T. (tr.) (1861), *Liber Albus. The White Book of the City of London, Compiled AD 1419 by John Carpenter, Common Clerk, and Richard Whitington, Mayor* (London: Griffin).

Riley-Smith, J. (1973a), 'Government in Latin Syria and the Commercial Privileges of Foreign Merchants', in *Relations between East and West in the Middle Ages*, ed. D. Baker (Edinburgh: Edinburgh University Press), 109–32.

Riley-Smith, J. (1973b), *The Feudal Nobility and the Kingdom of Jerusalem 1174–1277* (London: Macmillan).

Riley-Smith, J. (1978), 'Peace Never Established: The Case of the Kingdom of Jerusalem', *Transactions of the Royal Historical Society*, vol. 28, 87–102.

Riley-Smith, J. (1980), 'An Approach to Crusading Ethics', *Reading Medieval Studies*, vol. 6, 3–19.

Riley-Smith, J. (1983), 'The Motives of the Earliest Crusaders and the Settlement of Latin Palestine, 1095–1100', *English Historical Review*, vol. 98, 721–36.

Riley-Smith, J. (1986), *The First Crusade and the Idea of Crusading* (London: Athlone Press).

Riley-Smith, J. (1987), *The Crusades. A Short History* (London: Athlone Press).

Riley-Smith, L. and J. Riley-Smith (trs) (1981), *The Crusades. Idea and Reality 1095–1274* (Documents of Medieval History, 4) (London: Edward Arnold).

Riquet, M. (1976), 'Saint Louis Roi de France et les Juifs', in *Septième Centenaire de la Mort de Saint Louis. Actes des Colloques de Royaumont et de Paris (21–27 mai 1970)* (Paris: Société d'Edition 'Les Belles Lettres'), 345–50.

Robert the Monk (1866), *Historia Iherosolimitana*, in *Recueil des Historiens des Croisades. Historiens Occidentaux*, vol. 3 (Paris: Imprimerie Imperiale).

Robinson, I.S. (1978), *Authority and Reason in the Investiture Contest. The Polemical Literature of the Investiture Contest* (Manchester: Manchester University Press).

Robinson, I.S. (1990), *The Papacy, 1073–1198. Continuity and Innovation* (Cambridge: Cambridge University Press).

Robinson, I.S. (1999), *Henry IV of Germany, 1056–1106* (Cambridge: Cambridge University Press).

Romanin, S. (ed.) (1853), *Storia Documentata di Venezia* (Venice: P. Naratovich).

Roquebert, M. (1985), 'Le Catharisme comme tradition dans la "familia" languedocienne', *Cahiers de Fanjeaux*, vol. 20, 221–41.

Ross, J.B. (tr.) (1982), Galbert of Bruges, *The Murder of Charles the Good* (Toronto: University of Toronto Press) (originally 1959).

Rossiaud, J. (1988), *Medieval Prostitution*, tr. L.G. Cochrane (Oxford: Blackwell).

Rothwell, H. (ed.) (1975), *English Historical Documents*, vol. 3, *1189–1327* (London: Eyre and Spottiswoode).

Rudolph, C. (1990), *The 'Things of Greater Importance'. Bernard of Clairvaux's 'Apologia' and the Medieval Attitude toward Art* (Philadelphia, Pa.: University of Pennsylvania Press).

Russell, F.H. (1975), *The Just War in the Middle Ages* (Cambridge: Cambridge University Press).

Russell, J.B. (1984), *Lucifer. The Devil in the Middle Ages* (Ithaca, NY and London: Cornell University Press).

Russell, J.C. (1972), *Medieval Regions and their Cities* (Newton Abbot: David and Charles).

Ryan, F.R. (tr.) (1969), Fulcher of Chartres, *A History of the Expedition to Jerusalem 1095–1127* (Knoxville, Tenn.: University of Tennessee Press).

Salvini, R. (1969), *Medieval Sculpture*, tr. P. Murray and L. Murray (London: Michael Joseph).

Salzman, L.F. (1968), *Edward I* (London: Constable).

Sanders, W.B. (tr.) (1896), *A Crusader's Letter from the Holy Land*, vol. 5 (London: Palestine Pilgrims' Text Society).

Sawyer, B. and P. Sawyer (1993), *Medieval Scandinavia, c.800–1500* (Minneapolis, Minn. and London: University of Minnesota Press).

Scalia, G. (ed.) (1966), Salimbene de Adam, *Cronica* (Bari: Guis, Laterza).

Schein, S. (1986), 'The Image of the Crusader Kingdom of Jerusalem in the Thirteenth Century', *Revue belge de Philologie et d'Histoire*, vol. 64, 704–17.

Scott, S.P. (tr.) (2001), *Las Siete Partidas*, ed. R.I. Burns, vols 1, 2, 5 (Philadelphia, Pa: University of Pennsylvania Press).

Seaver, K.A. (1996), *The Frozen Echo. Greenland and the Exploration of North America, c.AD 1000–1500* (Stanford, Calif.: Stanford University Press).

Seidel, L.V. (1976), 'Holy Warriors: The Romanesque Rider and the Fight against Islam', in *The Holy War*, ed. T.P. Murphy (Columbus, Ohio: Ohio State University Press), 33–77.

Sephton, J. (tr.) (1899), *Sverrissaga. The Saga of King Sverri of Norway* (London: David Nutt).

Setton, K.M. (1976), *The Papacy and the Levant*, vol. 1 (Philadelphia, Pa: American Philosophical Society).

Seznec, J. (1953), *The Survival of the Pagan Gods*, tr. B.F. Sessions (New York: Pantheon) (originally 1940).

Shaw, M. (tr.) (1963), Joinville and Villehardouin, *Chronicles of the Crusades* (Harmondsworth: Penguin).

Shirley, J. (1996), *The Song of the Cathar Wars. A History of the Albigensian Crusade* (Aldershot: Scolar Press).

Sibly, W.A. and M.D. Sibly (1998), Peter of les Vaux-de-Cernay, *The History of the Albigensian Crusade* (Woodbridge: The Boydell Press).

Smail, R.C. (1969), 'Latin Syria and the West 1149–87', *Transactions of the Royal Historical Society*, vol. 19, 1–20.

Smail, R.C. (1973), *The Crusaders* (London: Thames and Hudson).

Smalley, B. (1974), *Historians of the Middle Ages* (London: Thames and Hudson).

Smith, C.C. (tr.) (1988, 1989), *Christians and Moors in Spain*, vol. 1, *711–1150*, vol. 2, *1195–1614* (Warminster: Aris and Phillips).

Smith, D. and H. Buffery (trs) (2003), *The Book of the Deeds of James I of Aragon. A Translation of the Medieval Catalan Llibre dels Fets* (Crusade Texts in Translation, 10) (Aldershot: Ashgate).

Smith, R. (1978), 'Giotto: Artistic Realism, Political Realism', *Journal of Medieval History*, vol. 4, 267–84.

Southern, R.W. (1963), *Saint Anselm and his Biographer* (Cambridge: Cambridge University Press).

Southern, R.W. (1970), *Medieval Humanism and Other Studies* (Oxford: Blackwell).

Southern, R.W. (1990), *Saint Anselm. A Portrait in a Landscape* (Cambridge: Cambridge University Press).

Spiegel, G.M. (1975), 'The Cult of St Denis and Capetian Kingship', *Journal of Medieval History*, vol. 1, 43–70.

Spufford, P. (2002), *Power and Profit. The Merchant in Medieval Europe* (London: Thames and Hudson).

Stahl, W.H (tr.) (1952), Macrobius, *Commentary on the Dream of Scipio* (New York: Columbia University Press).

Staines, D. (1990), *The Complete Romances of Chrétien de Troyes* (Bloomington, Ind.: Indiana University Press).

Stevenson, J. (ed.) (1875), Ralph of Coggeshall, *Chronicon Anglicanum* (Rolls Series, 66) (London: Longman).

Stock, B. (1983), *The Implications of Literacy. Written Language and Models of Interpretation in the Eleventh and Twelfth Centuries* (Princeton, NJ: Princeton University Press).

Stoddard, W.S. (1972), *Art and Architecture in Medieval France* (New York: Harper and Row).

Stone, E.N. (tr.) (1939), *The Chronicle of Reims (La Chronique de Rains). Written by an unknown Minstrel of Reims in the year 1260*, in *Three Old French Chronicles of the Crusades* (Seattle, Wash.: University of Washington).

Strayer, J.R. (1939), *Studies in Early French Taxation* (Cambridge, Mass.: Harvard University Press).

Strayer, J.R. (1969), 'Normandy and Languedoc', *Speculum*, vol. 44, 1–12.

Strayer, J.R. (1971), 'France: The Holy Land, the Chosen People, and the Most Christian King', in *Medieval Statecraft and the Perspectives of History. Essays by Joseph R. Strayer*, ed. J.F. Benton and T.N. Bisson (Princeton, NJ: Princeton University Press), 300–14.

Strayer, J.R. (1980), *The Reign of Philip the Fair* (Princeton, NJ: Princeton University Press).

Stubbs, W. (ed.) (1864), *Itinerarium Peregrinorum et Gesta Regis Ricardi* (Chronicles and Memorials of the Reign of Richard I), vol. 1 (Rolls Series, 36) (London: Longman, Green).

Stubbs, W. (ed.) (1870), Roger of Howden, *Chronica* (Rolls Series, 51) (London: Longman).

Stubbs, W. (ed.) (1889), William of Malmesbury, *Gesta Regum Anglorum*, vol. 2 (Rolls Series, 90) (London: Eyre and Spottiswoode).

Takayama, H. (1993), *The Administration of the Norman Kingdom of Sicily* (London: Brill).

Taylor, C. (2000), 'The Letter of Héribert of Périgord as a Source for Dualist heresy in the Society of Early Eleventh-century Aquitaine', *Journal of Medieval History*, vol. 26, 313–49.

Taylor, H.O. (1914), *The Medieval Mind. A History of the Development of Thought and Emotion in the Middle Ages*, 2 vols (London: Macmillan).

Tellenbach, G. (1940), *Church, State and Christian Society at the Time of the Investiture Contest*, tr. R.F. Bennett (Oxford: Blackwell).

Thoen, E. (1997), 'The Birth of "The Flemish Husbandry": Agricultural Technology in Medieval Flanders', in *Medieval Farming and Technology. The Impact of Agricultural Change in Northwest Europe*, ed. G. Astill and J. Langdon (Leiden: Brill), 69–88.

Thomas, A. (ed.) (1881), 'Les Miracles de Notre-Dame de Chartres. Texte Latin Inédit', *Bibliothèque de l'Ecole des Chartes*, vol. 42, 505–50.

Thorndike, L. (ed.) (1944), *University Records and Life in the Middle Ages* (New York: Columbia University Press).

Thorpe, B. (ed.) (1849), Florence of Worcester, *Chronicon*, vol. 2 (London: English Historical Society).

Thorpe, L. (tr.) (1980), Geoffrey of Monmouth, *The History of the Kings of Britain* (Harmondsworth: Penguin) (originally 1966).

Thrupp, S. (1941), 'Social Control in the Medieval Town', *Journal of Economic History*, vol. 1, Supplement, 39–52.

Tierney, B. (1964), *The Crisis of Church and State 1050–1300* (Englewood Cliffs, NJ: Prentice Hall).

Tierney, B. (1965), 'The Continuity of Papal Political Theory in the Thirteenth Century: Some Methodological Considerations', *Medieval Studies*, vol. 27, 227–45.

Treharne, R.F. and I. Sanders (eds) (1973), *Documents of the Baronial Movement of Reform and Rebellion, 1258–67* (London: Clarendon).

Tschan, F.J. (tr.) (1935), Helmold, Priest of Bosau, *The Chronicle of the Slavs* (New York: Columbia University Press).

Tschan, F.J. (tr.) (1959), Adam of Bremen, *History of the Archbishops of Hamburg-Bremen* (New York: Columbia University Press).

Unger, R.W. (1980), *The Ship in the Medieval Economy, 600–1600* (London: Croom Helm).

Van Cleve, T.C. (1972), *The Emperor Frederick II of Hohenstaufen* (Oxford: Clarendon).

Veszprémy, L. and F. Schaer (1999), Simon of Kéza, *The Deeds of the Hungarians* (Budapest and New York: Central European University Press).

Vicaire, M. (1964), *St Dominic. His Life and Times*, tr. K. Pond (London: Darton, Longman and Todd).

Villani, Giovanni (1969), *Chronica*, notes by I. Moutier and F.G. Dragomanni, vols 1–3 (Frankfurt: Minerva GMBH).

Vollrath, H. (1996), 'Ideal and Reality in Twelfth-Century Germany', in *England and Germany in the High Middle Ages. Challenge and Change*, ed. A. Haverkamp and H. Vollrath (Oxford: Oxford University Press), 93–104.

Wakefield, W.L. and A.P. Evans (eds) (1969), *Heresies of the High Middle Ages* (New York: Columbia University Press).

Waley, D. (1978), *The Italian City-Republics*, 2nd edn (London: Longman).

Ward, B. (1982), *Miracles and the Medieval Mind. Theory, Record and Event 1000–1215* (London: Scolar Press).

Warner, G.F. (ed.) (1891), Gerald of Wales, *De Principis Instructione Liber*, in *Giraldi Cambrensis Opera*, vol. 8 (Rolls Series, 21) (London: Eyre and Spottiswoode).

Warnkoenig, L.A. (1835), *Histoire de la Flandre et des Institutions Civiles et Politiques jusqu'à l'année 1305*, vol. 1 (Brussels: Hayez).

Warren, W.L. (1984), 'The Myth of Norman Administrative Efficiency', *Transactions of the Royal Historical Society*, vol. 34, 113–32.

Warren, W.L. (1987), *The Governance of Norman and Angevin England 1086–1272* (London: Edward Arnold).

Watt, J. (1965), *The Theory of Papal Monarchy in the Thirteenth Century. The Contribution of the Canonists* (London: Burns and Gates).

Watt, J. (tr.) (1971), John of Paris, *On Royal and Papal Power* (Toronto: Pontifical Institute of Medieval Studies).

Watts, V.E. (tr.) (1969), Boethius, *The Consolation of Philosophy* (Harmondsworth: Penguin).

Weaver, J.R.H. (ed.) (1908), *The Chronicle of John of Worcester 1118–40* (Anecdote Oxoniensia. Medieval and Modern Studies, 13) (Oxford: Clarendon).

Weiland, L. (ed.) (1893, 1896), *Constitutiones et Acta Publica Imperatorum et Regum*, vol. 1, *911–1197*, vol. 2, *1198–1272*, in *Monumenta Germaniae Historica. Leges Sectio IV* (Hanover: Hahnsche).

White, J. (1979), *Duccio, Tuscan Art and the Medieval Workshop* (London: Thames and Hudson).

White, J. (1987), *Art and Architecture in Italy, 1250–1400* (Harmondsworth: Penguin).

Wieruszowski, H. (1944), 'Art and the Commune in the Time of Dante', *Speculum*, vol. 19, 14–33.

Wieruszowski, H. (1963), 'Roger II of Sicily, *Rex Tyrannus*, in Twelfth-Century Political Thought', *Speculum*, vol. 38, 46–78.

Wieruszowski, H. (1966), *The Medieval University* (New York: Van Nostrand).

Wilkinson, B. (1963), *Constitutional History of England 1216–1399, with Select Documents*, vol. 1 (London: Longman).

Wilkinson, J., with J. Hill and W.F. Ryan (1988), *Jerusalem Pilgrimage 1099–1185* (London: Hakluyt Society).

Williams, J.W. (1993), *Bread, Wine and Money. The Windows of Chartres Cathedral* (Chicago: University of Chicago Press).

Wilson, A.E. (ed.) (1961), *Custumals of the Manors of Loughton, Willingdon and Goring* (Lewes: Sussex Record Society, 60).

Wilson, C. (1990), *The Gothic Cathedral* (London: Thames and Hudson).

Wolff, R.L. (1969), 'The Latin Empire of Constantinople, 1204–61', in *History of the Crusades*, vol. 2, ed. K. Setton (Madison, Wis. and London: University of Wisconsin Press), 186–233.

Wright, J. (tr.) (1967), *The Play of AntiChrist* (Toronto: Pontifical Institute of Medieval Studies).

Wright, J.K. (1925), *Geographical Lore at the Time of the Crusades* (New York: American Geographical Society).

Zema, D.B. (1947), 'Economic Reorganisation of the Roman See during Gregorian Reform', *Studi Gregoriani*, vol. 1, 137–68.

Index of persons

Index of places

Subject index

Printed in the USA/Agawam, MA
February 21, 2012